Helen Bevington

❀

When Found,
Make a Verse Of

❀

Simon and Schuster
New York, 1961

First Printing

Library of Congress Catalog Card Number: 61–12853
Manufactured in the United States of America
By Geo. McKibbin & Son, Inc., New York

The following poems, by myself and others, have appeared in print before. I should like to thank the original publishers for their kind permission to print them again.

"r-p-o-p-h-e-s-s-a-g-r" by E. E. Cummings, from *Poems 1923–1954,* copyright 1935 by E. E. Cummings (Harcourt, Brace & World, Inc.).

"Sunday Morning" from *The Collected Poems of Wallace Stevens,* copyright 1931, 1954 by Wallace Stevens (Alfred A. Knopf, Inc.).

"A Windowful of London," "Midsummer Night," "The Elizabethan Maid," and "The Teacher," by Helen Bevington, from *The New Yorker.*

"The Company of Scholars" and "The Reading Room, British Museum," by Helen Bevington, from *The Times Literary Supplement.*

"The World Is a Book" by Helen Bevington, from *The New York Times Book Review.*

"Turner's Sunrise" by Helen Bevington, from *The Carolina Quarterly.*

"Oceans of Dr. Johnson," "Do What You Love," "Herrick's Julia," "Sweet Land of Pantisocracy," "January Jasmine," and "Inspiration of Lady Mendl" from *Dr. Johnson's Waterfall* by Helen Bevington (Houghton Mifflin Company).

"Journal Intime," "Academic Moon," "Dear Prue," "Mr. Fitzherbert," "The Pink Shelf," "A Few More Oddities," and "Holly" from *Nineteen Million Elephants* by Helen Bevington (Houghton Mifflin Company).

"Samuel Pepys Slept Here," "At Hyères, on the Mediterranean," "A Walk with Bertrand Russell," "Timothy," "Mr. Eliot's Profile," "Talk With a Poet," "The Suitable Day," and "The Verity of Lies," from *A Change of Sky* by Helen Bevington (Houghton Mifflin Company).

To B.

CONTENTS

❄

Foreword • 15

I. OF DIARIES AND JOURNALS

II. OF MODERN POETRY

7

III. Of Light Verse

IV. Of Poetry Itself

V. OF THE ODDITIES OF AUTHORS

VI. OF THE ART OF LETTER WRITING

VII. OF WAYS TO LIVE AND WAYS TO DIE

VIII. OF A CHANGE OF SKY

IX. OF PEOPLE

X. Of the Countryside

XI. Of the Education of Myself

✤

FOREWORD

✤

One day some years ago while reading Dombey and Son *I came to Chapter 15, where, in the midst of the story, there were six words of exhortation and command: "When found, make a note of." I reached for my notebook and made a note of Dickens's note to make a note of what I had just found. Thereafter, as this book shows, I tried not only to follow his good advice but even, occasionally, to improve upon it. When found, I also made a verse of.*

❀

OF NOT KEEPING A DIARY

❀

Surely I can never keep a diary. It is clear that I would not write a truthful one. I would place my life too much in a shining light. I would try to end by saying, like Hazlitt, that I have had a happy life, and I would leave out, day by day, the grievances and the discomforts. The diarists I have read, from Pepys to Amiel to André Gide, deal honestly and tenderly with these. They turn easily to passionate and painful inquiry about themselves, though I remember that Montaigne had no use for the moaners, people who "talked discomforts," which he found the dullest talk of all. Emerson, too, in *The Conduct of Life,* tells us to be quiet on this subject:

"There is one topic peremptorily forbidden to all well-bred, to all rational mortals, namely, their distempers. If you have not slept, or if you have slept, or if you have headache, or sciatica, or leprosy, or thunderstroke, I beseech you, by all angels, to hold your peace."

*   *   *

Yet two entries in Sir Walter Scott's diary show how desperately hard it is at times to hold your peace:

December 18, 1826: "I shall tire of my Journal if it is to contain nothing but biles and plasters and unguents."

January 2, 1827: "I had resolved to mark down no more griefs and groans, but I must needs briefly state that [with pain] I am nailed to my chair...."

❀

THE JOURNAL OF MR. WHITE

OF SELBORNE

❀

I would gladly keep a journal (the kind of diary that looks out rather than in); that is, if I had a talent for experience like Thoreau or Mr. White of Selborne.

"It is in vain to write on the seasons," said Thoreau, "unless you have the seasons in you."

At one time in my life I read the fourteen volumes of Thoreau's journals and believed that he and I inhabited the same natural world. Now I read, more often, Mr. White of Selborne, knowing better how elusive any world is. I read him for his terseness. He provides glimpses of wonderfully compact events, like this: "The air is soft. Violets blow. Snow lies under hedges. Men plow." A word or two, like "Here and there a lamb," records at once the nature of a day.

*　　　*　　　*

The brevities of Mr. White were native, I think, to his mind, but they also resulted in part from a lack of room on the page. He kept a "Naturalist's Journal," so-called, with each week represented by one page ruled into narrow columns, where he entered daily records of the wind and the weather. Only the right-hand column, headed "Miscellaneous Observations and Memorandums," allowed him to make brief notes on the cultivation of his garden ("Turnip-greens come in"); the news in Selborne ("Black cap sings." "Men wash their sheep"); the growing number of his nephews and nieces ("The 42nd nephew and niece, now living"); or his social life ("Mr. Littleton Etty called. Long-tailed titmouse").

These are a few entries, each in its entirety, from Gilbert White's *Journal*:

JANUARY 3, 1768 [the first entry]:

Horses are still falling with their general disorder. It freezes under people's beds.

JUNE 10, 1768:

The nightingale, having young, leaves off singing, and makes a plaintive and a jarring noise.

MARCH 21, 1769:

Goose sits; while the gander with vast assiduity keeps guard; and takes the fiercest sow by the ear and leads her away crying.

AUGUST 20, 1769:

Bulls begin to make their shrill autumnal note.

DECEMBER 4, 1770:

Most owls seem to hoot exactly in B flat according to several pitch-pipes used in tuning of harpsichords, and sold as strictly at concert pitch.

JUNE 9, 1773:

Swifts sit hard.

AUGUST 6, 1773:

The male and female ants of the little dusky sort come forth by myriads, and course about with great agility.

JULY 1, 1774:

Farmer Canning plows with two teams of asses, one in the morning and one in the afternoon: at night these asses are folded on the fallows; and in the winter they are kept in a straw-yard where they make dung.

APRIL 24, 1777:

The cock green-finch begins to toy, and hang about on the wing in a very peculiar manner. These gestures proceed from amorous propensities.

AUGUST 14, 1790:

Young hirundines cluster on the trees. Harvest-bugs bite the ladies.

JANUARY 29, 1791:

Three gallons of brandy from London.

MARCH 10, 1792:

Brother Benjamin, and wife, and Rebecca dined with us. White water-wagtail.

*   *   *

"All pleasantries," said Voltaire, "ought to be short, and, for that matter, gravities too."

✳

JOURNAL INTIME

✳

"On this day my Niece Brown was delivered of her 4th child, a girl, which makes the 41st of my nephews and nieces now living. Boiled up some apricots with sugar to preserve them."
—GILBERT WHITE, *Journal*, August 20, 1784

I must begin my Journal, say, mañana,
When I find diligence, serve God, and mend,
And sift my days and number my increases,
And the apricots are ripe at summer's end;

When I have learned, like Mr. White of Selborne,
The keep of small dominions, and I am
Like him fair-spoken: for July, the swallows,
Or, for December, "Here and there a lamb";

Meticulous to note, it being April,
The amorous finches (so is spring unfurled),
To count the first hepatica and towhee,
"A green woodpecker laughs at all the world";

And pleased to turn, like Mr. White reposeful,
With open mind to the advanced affairs
Of June: "Swifts sit hard," "Goose resorts to gander,"
"Ants, big with egg, come out from under the stairs."

It will be time to item my possessions
As they grow seasonable: for August, say,
The waxwings—or a plenitude of nieces;
When the apricots bear witness and it's May.

❁

JOHN RUSKIN'S DIARY

❁

John Ruskin wrote in his diary on March 31, 1840 (when he was only twenty-one): "I have determined to keep one part of a diary for intellect and another for feeling."

This was to provide the Classic and the Romantic approach to Ruskin. One part would politely entertain the mind and not the senses; it would be rational and wise, full of idea, exuding good taste and common sense, avoiding all excess. The other part would reveal the inner world of feeling; it would be passionate and intense, preoccupied with self, given to flights of anguish and delight, moved possibly to tears.

Poor young man, his head was never to know what happened in the heart.

PEPYS AT THE GEORGE INN

Samuel Pepys brought his diary along when he visited the cathedral town of Salisbury in June, 1668. He stayed at an inn called The George, already three hundred years old. On June 10, a Wednesday, he says in the *Diary*: "Come to the George Inn, where lay in a silk bed; and very good diet. To supper; then to bed." Next day, after a sight-seeing trip on horseback to Stonehenge, where he found the stones prodigious ("God knows what their use was"), Pepys returned to the inn, had dinner, and paid the reckoning for food and lodging, an amount so exorbitant "that I was mad . . . and come away in that humour."

Nearly three hundred years later, The George is now The Old George. On the top floor, up two flights, is the large room where for those two nights in June Pepys slept. This year in England, it is the room where for one night I too slept. Of course, Pepys was there with his wife and I with my husband, on occasions approximately 100,000 nights apart. But as it turned out, two people, Pepys and I, were as many as I could account for in one bed in one small poem.

※

SAMUEL PEPYS SLEPT HERE

※

Mr. Pepys slept where I sleep
Tonight in Salisbury at an inn,
And kept the same account I keep
(Now in the room that Pepys slept in),

And so the matter is twice-said:
That up two flights and through this door
Pepys came to sleep in a silken bed
(A hundred thousand nights before).

Here, in the flesh, he found repose
(The bed is hospitable and large),
Wearied at last, his diary shows,
Of fretting at an overcharge,

And dreamed, perhaps—but not of me
In some dark century ahead
Who would so love his company
And share so decorously his bed.

Nothing of this, the night before,
Concerned him. He departed then
Next day for Bristol, by this door.
It seems he did not come again.

VIRGINIA WOOLF'S DIARY

In the beautifully readable diary of Virginia Woolf, published, though still in small part, more than a dozen years after her death, I find only one flaw—that she took herself too seriously as a writer. She pinned the label to her breast and proudly wore it there. "I am a writer," it said, as if to be one was more real than to be a person. Yet to claim that role is like having the odd courage to say, "I am a poet," or "I am an artist," or "I am a philosopher." I don't know how or when one reaches that certainty. These are occupations. For only a few can they become titles, even then hardly self-bestowed.

"All writers are unhappy," says Virginia Woolf in an entry for September 5, 1940. "The wordless are the happy." And I am foolish enough to ask, then why write? She would answer me coldly, for she dedicated herself to the imaginary life, a writer withdrawn from reality yet elected to interpret it for others. Surely the profession of doctor, lawyer, even college professor, tends to affect the ego less centrally.

Virginia Woolf loved Montaigne. As she recognized with deep insight in writing of him, he "succeeded in the hazardous enterprise of living," and achieved a miraculous adjustment. It was Montaigne, however, who said he wished to be a man first, a writer afterwards. To be a man was to him the greatest concern of all. "Good God," he cried, "how I would hate to be thought a pretty fellow with my pen, but an ass at everything else!"

❋

SNAKES IN EMERSON'S JOURNAL

❋

I saw two small copperhead snakes today, in March, down by the path to the woods. When they saw me nearby, they glided away together, along the path in the sun, and soon disappeared into the pine trees. I went slowly back to the house, marveling that everything that happens to me has the same result: it reminds me of something I've read. "Not to eat, not for love," I said aloud.

But what was the rest of it? The words made no sense all morning until I found the passage, in Emerson's *Journal* for April 11, 1834:

"Went yesterday to Cambridge and spent most of the day at Mount Auburn; got my luncheon at Fresh Pond and went back again to the woods . . . seeing many things, four snakes gliding up and down a hollow for no purpose that I could see—not to eat, not for love, but only gliding."

*   *   *

By September 5, 1854, twenty years older and wiser, Emerson was looking not at snakes but at turtles. Considering the working of their intellects, he came to this conclusion: "All the thoughts of a turtle are turtle."

TURTLE THOUGHTS

Turtle thoughts are turtle. All are confined,
Like Emerson's, to what is on his mind:
Which is in part tranquillity, and in part
Only a simple quaking of the heart.

When the high, turtle-lashing winds prevail,
He draws his neck in, hustles in his tail,
And thinks, with reason, from his dwelling place
That rain is falling on his carapace.

Or when, by chance, these very tempests hurtle,
Toss, fling him upside down, and turn him turtle,
Flat on his plastron he perceives this new
Idea, having nothing else to do.

But when, in sunshine, fluttering and reeling,
His mind is free and heightened now with feeling,
He harbors lighter thoughts (a human habit)
Like love, or running races with a rabbit.

From which it seems, as Emerson wisely said,
A turtlebrain is turtle. In his head
Are many musings and, such as they are,
Like mine they rarely get him very far.

IDEAS IN A COLLEGE COURSE

※

It was noon on the eighteenth of September, the beginning of the college term. The first meeting of English 134, my class in modern poetry, had just come to an end. Forty students had listened to me for fifty minutes and had filed out. Only one stayed behind to say a word.

"I'm a history major," he said. "To tell the truth, I've never liked modern poetry or any other poetry. Do you want to know why I'm taking your course?"

I smiled and prepared to leave the classroom. "To win a bet?" I said.

"For an idea," he said. "I'm graduating and going into the army in June. I decided to give your course a try before it's too late. I thought it might have an idea."

"An idea," I said.

"That's all," he said.

I walked down the long deserted corridor, cursing my luck. Damn the boy, I thought. Now I'll have him on my mind all year. I'll look at him each day and wonder, meeting perhaps his stony glance. An idea! Why should my course have anything so tremendous as an idea to give him?

I stood still. I could hear the boy's footsteps receding at the other end of the hall. Should I shout and run after him? It had finally occurred to me to ask if the course had an idea

30

for me. It had ideas all right, earth-shaking ideas. You had only to be in need of them.

I breathed deep in relief. There was nothing I ought to tell the needy student; let him find out for himself. By the time I reached the outside door, I was without anxiety.

❀

IDEAS IN MODERN POETRY

❀

Ideas, I said to myself, are what poetry is about—ideas stated with passionate intensity. The first three poets that came to mind proved me easily right.

In Gerard Manley Hopkins is the idea of looking. He looked to find the inscape of a thing, its inner nature, the very essence by which it expresses itself. The dazzling sense he had of that inscape he called instress, and these are his two great experiences: a way of looking and a way of feeling when he looked. Hopkins saw the *self* in everything. It flashed out in the fire of the kingfisher, the flame of the dragonfly, the buckling of the windhover in the morning sun.

> Each mortal thing does one thing and the same:
> Deals out that being indoors each one dwells;
> Selves—goes itself; *myself* it speaks and spells,
> Crying *What I do is me: for that I came.*

* * *

In Dylan Thomas is the idea of the lost world of child-hood. It is a world where joy once endlessly existed, where even though we have forgotten, gladness began over again with each day. For the child life deals in ecstasy, with sun-light and wonder:

> In the sun born over and over,
> I ran my heedless ways

But, as Wordsworth also knew, the child in us dies. Time holds us green and dying and we grow up one day to a "childless land."

*   *   *

In Wallace Stevens is the idea of pattern, of a necessary order, revealed in the world before our eyes. Here on earth is our paradise, our only one, where man has a divinity within himself and creates his own gods. Stevens is pleased with life the way it is. Accept it, he says, the beauty of this reality. He offers us perishable bliss, this particular Eden on earth instead of a heaven to come:

> We live in an old chaos of the sun,
> Or old dependency of day and night,
> Or island solitude, unsponsored, free,
> Of that wide water, inescapable.
> Deer walk upon our mountains, and the quail
> Whistle about us their spontaneous cries;
> Sweet berries ripen in the wilderness;
> And, in the isolation of the sky,
> At evening, casual flocks of pigeons make
> Ambiguous undulations as they sink,
> Downward to darkness, on extended wings.

*　　*　　*

Poetry *is* idea. For good measure, I said to myself, let me not forget Yeats. The best idea of all, perhaps, is in his statement of tragic joy. We begin to live, he says, only when we conceive of life as tragedy and understand it to be truly and persistently tragic. The fortunate ones are those who recognize with a strange joy the terror of existence. With a "gaiety transfiguring all that dread," they learn to love life because it is life. They accept it for what it is, terrifying, brutal, unjust, and they rejoice to be alive, rejecting negation and despair.

In the poem "Lapis Lazuli," Yeats studies two ancient Chinese figures carved on a blue stone, a piece of lapis lazuli. He sees the two gay old men slowly climbing a high mountain and surveying the tragic scene everywhere around them. They are followed by a serving man carrying a musical instrument, while over them flies a long-legged bird, a symbol of longevity:

> There, on the mountain and the sky,
> On all the tragic scene they stare.
> One asks for mournful melodies;
> Accomplished fingers begin to play.
> Their eyes mid many wrinkles, their eyes,
> Their ancient, glittering eyes, are gay.

❁

THE STARS WITH HOPKINS

❁

It seems an odd idea to my students that poetry, like all art, leads us away from itself, back to the world in which we live. It furnishes the vision. It shows with a sudden intense clarity what is already there. Wallace Stevens called poetry the necessary angel of earth, "Since, in my sight, you see the earth again."

You see the stars with Hopkins. Years ago I noticed that I was no longer looking at the night sky by myself; I was trying to see what he saw. Astronomers, of course, observe the constellations, but these are never visible to me. The poet Hopkins stands at my elbow, pointing over the sky, crying "Look, look!" (unlike the poet Auden, who looks too, but is discouraged by the view up there:

> Looking up at the stars, I know quite well
> That, for all they care, I can go to hell).

I can hardly expect to find all the shining things that Hopkins found. The fireflies. The lights of a city. The phosphorescence deep in a wood. The beady eyes of forest creatures. Dew on the grass at sunrise. White poplar leaves in a wind. Doves starting up from a barnyard. The May hawthorn blossom. The March willow bloom. And, because

he saw Christ in everything, the stable itself of the Nativity.
I never see them all, but I stare anyway, up at the stars. "Look,
look!" he cries.

❁

THE STARLIGHT NIGHT

❁

Look at the Stars! look, look up at the skies!
  O look at all the fire-folk sitting in the air!
  The bright boroughs, the circle-citadels there!
Down in dim woods the diamond delves! the elves'-eyes!
The grey lawns cold where gold, where quickgold lies!
  Wind-beat whitebeam! airy abeles set on a flare!
  Flake-doves sent floating forth at a farmyard scare!—
Ah well! it is all a purchase, all is a prize.

Buy then! bid then!—What?—Prayer, patience, alms, vows.
Look, look: a May-mess, like on orchard boughs!
  Look! March-bloom, like on mealed-with-yellow sallows!
These are indeed the barn; withindoors house
The shocks. This piece-bright paling shuts the spouse
  Christ home, Christ and his mother and all his hallows.

CUMMINGS' GRASSHOPPER

Mr. Cummings says, "Look, a grasshopper!" As I walk through a summer field, I stop to watch a live one because he tells me how it behaves, like a bumbling clown. As we look, he says, the r-p-o-p-h-e-s-s-a-g-r starts backward in some disarray, gathers itself up to full size, to a powerful PPEGORHRASS, and leaps! arriving lopsidedly on a bending blade of grass. With some effort to regain its balance, it rearranges itself, becoming what it is supposed to be: a grasshopper. All this happens in the poem before one's eyes, and the semicolon at the end suggests there is a leap or two still to come. More than a notation, it is a portrait in action, a real grasshopper portrait:

                              r-p-o-p-h-e-s-s-a-g-r

                        who

           a)s w(e loo)k
           upnowgath
                        PPEGORHRASS

                                        eringint(o-

           aThe):l
                 eA
                    !p:
           S   a

                        (r

```
rIvInG              .gRrEaPsPhOs)
                                    to
rea(be)rran(com)gi(e)ngly
,grasshopper;
```

❋

THE GRASSHOPPER COURSE

❋

One of my students took a volume of E. E. Cummings home with her at Christmas time to introduce the poet to her parents. On the first evening, she turned to her favorite, the grasshopper poem, meaning to impress them and promptly created a crisis in the home. The very look of it exploding on the page appalled them. Her father and mother were nonplused, but more than that they were indignant and mightily offended. "Is this what I send you to college for?" shouted her father. "Do they really *teach* you this nonsense?"

My student seemed pleased, on the whole, with the way Cummings shook up her family. Now in that household my course is known as the grasshopper course.

TALK WITH MR. CUMMINGS

This spring Mr. Cummings himself came to the University one evening to read a group of his poems. He had a beguiling voice that seemed in love with the words he said—a pleasant voice for words like "When the world is puddle-wonderful," not so good, I thought, for something as strong as "puke" or "pink vomit."

At the Dean's house afterward, I asked him a question long on my mind, if he had ever found a way to read aloud the grasshopper poem, to pronounce "r-p-o-p-h-e-s-s-a-g-r," and so on. He looked rather startled. "There are some poems that can't be read aloud," he said. "Mine and other people's."

Then "No!" he added, quickly. "Have you?"

Mr. Cummings was so mild and amiable all evening that I felt, for the first time with any poet, an odd kind of embarrassment in talking with him. There he was in the flesh, a character I had been lecturing about for the last ten years. I was aware of the liberties I had taken, freely praising, damning, defining him and his poems, sometimes calling him names, like oddity, funnyman, or clown.

Yet when he left the gathering that night, he innocently kissed my hand and asked me to let him know the next time I came to New York.

POEMS AS NOTATIONS

❀

Some poems bother me, the ones that are only a bare jotting from the poet's notebook. I want the poet to try, at least, to turn his notes into a poem. A little picture, a scene or moment set down without particular meaning, is not necessarily a poem. Dorothy Wordsworth's *Journal* proves this fact only too well, bursting as it is with poetic material that her brother later used. He made immortal sense of it.

William Carlos Williams has jotted down a great many agreeable memoranda in his time. There is a note about plums in the icebox that begins

> I have eaten
> the plums
> that were in
> the icebox

It goes on to say they were delicious and were probably being saved for breakfast. No more. There is one about a cat stepping into a flowerpot, about the pink pompoms on his wife's bedroom slippers, about green parsley in a glass. A notation called "Stop: Go—" was recently quoted in an admiring critical essay by his friend Marianne Moore:

                a green truck
                dragging a concrete mixer
                passes
                in the street—
                the clatter and true sound
                of verse

I don't know why a clattering truck has the true sound of verse, and I don't know why verse should clatter anyway, but Miss Moore says in praise of this poem that Mr. Williams "dislikes the tawdriness of unnecessary explanation." Perhaps she is teasing him. Worse still, perhaps she is teasing me.

❁

W. H. DAVIES' "SHEEP"

❁

A poem of our time that I think about in the middle of the night is "Sheep" by W. H. Davies. In twenty lines (five quatrains), the poet tells a tale of fearsome adventure that began one day in Baltimore. A man came up to him and asked him to sail to Glasgow the next Tuesday in the company of 1800 sheep.

Davies went. I don't wonder that he wrote about such a voyage, though I marvel that he tried to crowd the whole story into a little verse where he had to take the first twelve lines merely to set up the plot. By line twelve, Davies has been paid fifty shillings for the job, has cleared the harbor's mouth, and is "in the salt sea deep" apparently alone for a couple of weeks with his 1800 sheep.

He has eight lines left, and eight can say miracles. That is the length of the octave of a Petrarchan sonnet; it is the whole of the ottava rima at the end of "Lycidas." Still, for eight lines that is also a depressing lot of sheep.

> The first night we were out at sea
>   Those sheep were quiet in their mind;
> The second night they cried with fear—
>   They smelt no pastures in the wind.
>
> They sniffed, poor things, for their green fields,
>   They cried so loud I could not sleep;
> For fifty thousand shillings down
>   I would not sail again with sheep.

It has become quite a sober poem, filled with sleeplessness and lonely, bleating cries. Yet I can't help thinking what a really great opportunity Davies had and missed. There he was in the middle of the Atlantic, tired and wakeful in the midst of his tremendous cargo. The rest of us, unable to get to sleep at night, begin to count over our imaginary sheep. Davies, until he dozed off, could have counted up to 1800 real live ones. Then when he came to write the poem, he needn't have ended it so flatly, sick to death of his subject and much in need of a good night's rest.

THE MEANING OF

"A COOKING EGG"

If I were Mr. Eliot, I should want to do something in the public interest about "A Cooking Egg," either to clarify or to disclaim the poem. For a starter, I should identify Pipit, since she cannot be everyone at once that the critics call her: a child of five, an aged spinster, the poet's former mistress or his present one. Pipit may be someone he knew when he was a child, his playmate now grown up—or of course she may not. The poem may deal with the ravages of time and with unfulfilled love, or it may not, depending all the while on the age and qualifications of Pipit. "I shall not want Pipit in Heaven," the poet says, not very revealingly, and chooses Lucretia Borgia for his bride instead.

> But where is the penny world I bought
>   To eat with Pipit behind the screen?
> The red-eyed scavengers are creeping
>   From Kentish Town and Golder's Green;

It is late and he is growing old, it seems, a cooking egg who is no longer strictly fresh.

In a recent symposium in England, seven critics tried in vain to agree about Pipit and the meaning of "A Cooking

Egg." C. S. Lewis in an essay (*De Descriptione Temporum*) writes about this alarming predicament, a new and final kind of obscurity that poetry has achieved in our time:

"To say that all new poetry was once as difficult as ours is false; to say that any was is an equivocation. Some earlier poetry was difficult, but not in the same way. Alexandrian poetry was difficult because it presupposed a learned reader; as you became learned you found the answers to the puzzles. Skaldic poetry was unintelligible if you did not know the *kenningar,* but intelligible if you did. And—this is the real point—all Alexandrian men of letters and all skalds would have agreed about the answers. I believe the same to be true of the dark conceits in Donne; there was one correct interpretation of each and Donne could have told it to you. Of course you might misunderstand what Wordsworth was 'up to' in *Lyrical Ballads;* but everyone understood what he said. I do not see in any of these the slightest parallel to the state of affairs disclosed by a recent symposium on Mr. Eliot's *Cooking Egg.* Here we find seven adults (two of them Cambridge men) whose lives have been specially devoted to the study of poetry discussing a very short poem which has been before the world for thirty-odd years; and there is not the slightest agreement among them as to what, in any sense of the word, it means."

*   *   *

FLUELLEN: "Aunchient Pistol, I do partly understand your meaning."

PISTOL: "Why then, rejoice therefore."

—*Henry V*

❀

THREE RUBBER STAMPS

FOR POETRY

❀

Voltaire once wrote: "Let us place at the end of every chapter of metaphysics the two letters used by Roman judges when they did not understand a plea:

> *N.L., non liquet,* not clear."

I need a rubber stamp *N.L.* to keep beside me for daily use when I read a volume of modern poetry, Wallace Stevens, say, or the latest collection of Pound's inscrutable *Cantos.*

A second rubber stamp might well contain the three words for the three qualities that Anatole France said all good writing must possess:

> Clarity
> Clarity
> Clarity

A third rubber stamp, the neatest, ought to quote these perfectly reasonable words from Saki, "The Square Egg,"

> In baiting a mousetrap with cheese,
> always leave room for the mouse.

MR. ELIOT'S ROSE GARDEN

❀

> Any nose
> May ravage with impunity a rose. (*Sordello*)

I begin the class meeting and my lecture, which is to be this morning on timelessness, with the memory of the rose garden in *Burnt Norton*. I take a deep breath, stare fixedly at the clock on the wall opposite, and state the opening idea of the poem, "The time is always now." My voice is heavy with conviction, but my heart quails. I stare at the clock with a time-ridden mind, anxious, filled with strain and tension; and it becomes the figure of the Wheel (with spokes) on which we are whirling and revolving wildly in this time-world of flux and change, around and around and around the still center, the garden itself where timelessness is. We are on the outer rim this morning, moving fast.

I am, then, a fraud as teacher, a mere slave of time in a world of mortality, circling to decay? I am. "The time is always *now*," I repeat less certainly, gripping the desk, trying hard to overhear myself. But the time only races madly on to 10:10 when the class hour will be over and Mr. Eliot's eternal stillness will have to wait for illumination until next week. "Go, go, go," says the bird, and the irony in his voice is loud and clear.

45

❀

AUDEN AND MacNEICE

ON THE MODERN POET

❀

On his arrival in 1939 from England, the country he had fled, I heard W. H. Auden speak in New York on the subject of "The Poet in a Topsy-turvy World." He was clear indeed as to the role of the poet in a disordered world like ours: the poet is a misfit—as in Freud's view the artist must always be—in conflict with his environment and his fellow man. As the inheritor of the Waste Land, he is in permanent exile there. Let him be content to be not like other men, but misunderstood, neglected, unread, alone, at odds with an unpoetic world. Let him accept his isolation as an artist and remain aloof, shunning the usual hostages to fortune like women and children. And so on.

Now I read a statement by Louis MacNeice, once a poet of the so-called School of Auden. Is this the voice of mid-century? I ask myself. With no nonsense about it, Mr. MacNeice stoutly declares, twenty years later, "I would have the poet able-bodied, fond of talking, a reader of news-papers, capable of pity and laughter, informed in economics, appreciative of women, involved in personal relationships, actively interested in politics, susceptible to physical impressions."

The poet begins to sound like an ordinary man again.

꙰

SYMBOLISM IN YEATS

꙰

Attached to Yeats's poem, "The Cap and Bells," written in 1893, is a comical note. It reveals, in an artless way, the mystifying nature of the symbolic poem, where the poet himself cannot remember, later on, what in the world his highly charged symbols were supposed to be symbolic of.

The poem tells of a jester who, after sending the young queen first his soul and then his heart, which she coldly rejected, offered her his cap and bells. These she approved of and passionately took:

> She laid them upon her bosom,
> Under a cloud of her hair,
> And her red lips sang them a love-song
> Till stars grew out of the air.

"The poem has always meant a great deal to me," Yeats reflected, scratching his head in perplexity over the poem six years later, "though, as is the way with symbolic poems, it has not always meant the same thing." I think he was forgetting how young and twilit a poet he had lately been, young and decidedly misty.

A STORY FOR ROBERT FROST

❀

To read Robert Frost is to meet an explicit poet, simple and, whatever the complexity of his idea, clear. His is not the poetry of obscure symbol, but of the real countryside, described with fidelity, the real experience. One need not worry much about the private vision, the spirit of the place, the overtones, the symbol, the mystery.

Mr. Frost must appreciate, if he happens to know it, a story told about Constable. Once when the poet William Blake looked at a collection of Constable's drawings and greatly admired them, he exclaimed, "Why, this is not drawing but inspiration!"

"I meant it for drawing," Constable quietly answered him.

❀

MOONPOEMS

❀

A solacing thought, if one worries about the survival of poetry, is that even yet it is brimful of talk about the moon. Wallace Stevens defines his role of poet as a writer of moonlight:

The book of moonlight is not written yet
Nor half begun, but, when it is, leave room
For Crispin.

As for the Imagists, though modern and experimental in technique, they were from the first great moon watchers. Richard Aldington claimed to see a pregnant woman up there:

At night, the moon, a pregnant woman,
Walks cautiously over the slippery heavens.

Or he leered over the kitchen sink at her, "an awkward Venus,"

The moon
With a rag of gauze about the loins.

F. S. Flint observed a moon made of sour cream, unpleasantly dead:

On black bare trees a stale cream moon
hangs dead, and sours the unborn buds.

Walter de la Mare in his Georgian days wrote some of the loveliest moonpoems of our time. "How strange that moonlight should move one so much," he reflected, and looked again at the silver lady of the night:

Slowly, silently, now the moon
Walks the night in her silver shoon

T. S. Eliot was able to see her, on the contrary, as a tired old whore:

The moon has lost her memory.
A washed-out smallpox cracks her face,
Her hand twists a paper rose,
That smells of dust and eau de Cologne

E. E. Cummings watched a round and bouncy ball in the sky:

mOOn Over tOwns mOOn

or he asked:

who knows if the moon's
a balloon, coming out of a keen city
in the sky—filled with pretty people?

Even in this week's *New Yorker,* I notice without surprise that a younger poet, Theodore Roethke, is moonstruck:

The moon's my mother—how I love the moon!

＊　　　＊　　　＊

Edmund Gosse's housemaid, however, one night set down the truly immortal poem of this century about the moon. It is quoted by E. F. Benson in his *As We Were:*

Oh moon, lovely moon, with thy beautiful face,
Careering throughout the boundáries of space,
Whenever I see thee, I think in my mind,
Shall I ever, oh ever, behold thy behind.

❁

SCIENTISTS LOOK AT THE MOON

❁

Not long ago, I heard that a group of scientists at Woods Hole had sallied out one night to have a look at the moon. They bent down together to peer at it with their heads between their legs, and found it to be somewhat smaller than usual from that angle. The moon just rising over the horizon appeared to their inverted eyes about as big as a moon riding high and full in the sky. Viewed upside down, it had noticeably shrunk to a littler sphere.

On the first bright evening thereafter, accompanied by a professor, I made a moon test of my own in North Carolina, famous in song for its large and luminous moons ("Carolina moon, keep shining . . ."). Like the real poets, I write what verse I can about moonlight, since (besides the other eternal themes of love and death) it is always there to look at. In serious poetry, however, the moon is generally normal in size and right side up.

❀

ACADEMIC MOON

❀

I have been walking under the sky in the moonlight
With a professor. And am pleased to say
The moon was luminous and high and profitable.
Moonlit was the professor. Clear as day.

He had read, of late, how extraordinary moons are
Upside down. Aloft in the night sky
One drifted upright, in the usual fashion.
But the professor, glad to verify

Hypothesis or truth, when he is able—
Even, it seems, to set the moon askew—
Proposed that we reverse our own perspective.
And, on the whole, it *was* a lovelier view

Of white circumference—smaller now, he fancied,
A tidier sphere. This last I could not tell
From so oblique an angle. I only remember
Enjoying the occasion very well.

❋

A PROFESSOR EXPLAINS

❋

Shortly after this verse, "Academic Moon," appeared in *The New Yorker,* I was happy to read in that magazine a letter to the editors from a professor at Cornell. Professor M. E. Bitterman, in a friendly way, wished to clarify my verse with a little scholarly annotation. He began by saying:

"Miss Bevington and the professor are walking in the moonlight, you remember. The professor . . . proposes an informal experiment, and soon the two are lying on the grass for the purpose of observing the satellite in radically altered perspective."

Professor Bitterman then turned to the subject of "lunar phenomenology," or what is known as the "moon illusion," and quoted Dr. Edwin G. Boring of Harvard on the proper technique of observation:

"When the moon is big upon the horizon, lie down on your back with your head toward the moon, hanging the head over a log or stone or the edge of a table. The moon, huge but a moment before, is now quite small, small enough to make you exclaim. *Or stoop over and view the horizon moon between your legs.* [italics mine] Again it shrinks."

What pleased me most in all this was Professor Bitterman's fresh interpretation of the poem. He conjured up an academic love scene and freely arranged the two (un-married) people in it side by side, flat on the grass. I am only sorry that this sensible idea had never before occurred to me. It proves, of course, that you can't fool around in verse with anything so romantic as a moon. You only end with a love scene on your hands.

❁

SWANPOEMS

❁

The moon is one thing, hard to ignore, but I am astonished that there should be so many modern poems about swans. They seem to have usurped the place of the English night-ingale in poetry, beginning with Mallarmé's famous swan caught in the ice of the lake, and Yeats's "Wild Swans at Coole,"

> Upon the brimming water among the stones
> Are nine-and-fifty swans.

I wonder about these contemporary birds, why, in a realistic age like ours, they are forever drifting on the still water, conventional and traditional in style, instead of, say, waddling out of the lake and climbing up to amble on the shore. A swan doesn't live its whole life afloat, anyway, except in poetry. It moves absurdly about, a very clumsy bird on dry land, as Chaucer noticed six hundred years ago when he spoke, in the Summoner's Tale, of foolish friars as "Fat as a whale, and walkynge as a swan."

Rilke has an exquisite poem "The Swan," but it is really a picture of man himself and his two experiences of life and death. In the touching analogy, man is shown to be like a swan as he walks heavily on this earth with his unsteady gait. Dying, he moves at last down to the waters that softly receive him; and there like a king swan, "Ever more kingly, more mature," he silently, serenely floats away.

❀

THE SWAN

❀

Like a wild swan at Coole,
He drifts on the still water,
Mysterious, beautiful,

To the classic pose withdrawn,
Like swans more legendary,
Or a literary swan,

Till at last he is moved to take
With quick majestic motion
Sudden leave of the lake

And waddle to the shore,
Oh! revealing his short bowlegs
And his posterior,

The tottery walk, the roll
From one black leg to the other,
He, the incomparable.

And I am wonderstruck
At him now, emerged from the water—
This beautiful white duck.

❁

MISTAKES ABOUT

THE NIGHTINGALE

AND THE SWAN

❁

Poetry makes its mistakes about both nightingales and swans. Though everyone (except a poet) knows about the nightingale that only the cock bird sings, yet in song her name is Philomel, who as a maiden was raped by the cruel Tereus, the king of Thrace. She leans her breast upon a thorn and sings on in grief her plaintive, mournful note. And still she cries, "Tereu, tereu," she who was so rudely forced, Eliot says. She sings her "pity-pleading strains," Coleridge tells us. She cries, "Eternal passion! Eternal pain!" Matthew Arnold so closely observes.

With swans, too, as with nightingales, the error results from a persistent myth. There is the classic picture of Leda and the swan to blind the poet's eyes ("A sudden blow: the great wings beating still / Above the staggering girl").

In *Oxford Life,* Dacre Balsdon writes of the true mating of these birds from actual observation:

"And you may see at this season, a stupendous sight, the mating of two swans. Side by side they wriggle their necks excitedly under the water, as if in an ecstasy of fishing. Then the lord-swan mounts his bride who, during the nuptial act, is all-submerged. The ecstasy ended, they face one another, breast to breast and, it seems, they stand on the surface of the water as they stretch their necks taut into the upper air, rubbing their heads together, no longer swans but, both of them, a great extension of neck. Necking, in fact. Then, suddenly, it is over. They are floating side by side, a dull married couple.

"It is a thrilling act that you have witnessed. Was it, perhaps, Zeus himself, you wonder, and Leda? But no. There is the silence of an Oxford evening, disturbed only by the bells. There is no thunder from Olympus.

"Your companion, an undergraduate, says, 'How odd. That was not a bit like Yeats's poem on the subject.' "

*   *   *

Swan is another name for a poet. Virgil was "the Mantuan swan," Fenelon *le cygne de Cambrai,* Shakespeare the Swan of Avon, Anna Seward the female Swan of Lichfield, and so on. This usage is based upon still another time-honored myth, for of course swans do not sing, not even when they are about to die. Poetry is full of this charming misconception. Chaucer says, in the *Parlement of Foules,* "The jalous swan, ayens his deth that singeth." Shakespeare, in *Othello,* has Emilia say, "I will play the swan/ And die in music." Byron cries, in *Don Juan,* "There, swan-like, let me sing and die." And Coleridge makes a witty epigram:

57

Swans sing before they die—'twere no bad thing
Did certain persons die before they sing.

*   *   *

"Were I a nightingale, I would act the part of a nightingale," wrote Epictetus; "were I a swan, the part of a swan."

❀

A MEETING WITH DYLAN THOMAS

❀

In 1953, the year that he died, Dylan Thomas came to read his poems to a crowded and hushed auditorium at the University. He could easily have filled the outdoor stadium, and the same silence would have prevailed to catch the pure gold magic of his voice. Afterwards, sweating profusely in the heat of the May night, he shook his head in impatient anger and told me how much he hated to read his own poems aloud. A word or a line on the page would speak out to him sorrowfully, he said, calling him a fool. "Fool," it would cry in reproach, "why don't you go back to work?"

So long as anyone would keep talking that night, Dylan Thomas talked, drank beer, chain-smoked, and refused to go to bed, though he had to be in New York next morning for a rehearsal of *Under Milk Wood*. Sometime after midnight I remember telling him that I knew his poem "In Country Sleep" by heart and proceeding, with absurd temerity, to explain to him what it was about. It concerned,

I said, a young child who is told at bedtime never to fear the fairytale witch or redridinghood wolf, for she lives in safe and holy country. The poet, her father, sits beside her bed and comforts her ("my dear, my dear") with the doubtful solace that she need fear nothing at all, only the Thief—

My dear this night he comes and night without end my dear
Since you were born:

He comes slyly in the night like the fox and the wind, her father says, as he has come to her every night of her life. The child does not realize her danger. She yearns for him to come, because she cannot yet know, so young, of what to be afraid. Time is the Thief, I said, who steals from her each night a little of her life and leaves her naked and forsaken.

Dylan Thomas listened raptly, as if to some remarkable, breath-taking tale that he had never heard before. When I had finished, he sat for a while frowning in thought. He seemed reluctant to speak, and I began to wonder if perhaps I had offended him by unraveling his lovely poem. At last he spoke. "No," he said, gently, "it isn't like that at all."

"In Country Sleep" is not about a child at bedtime with her father, he said. It is a love poem, one he had written to his wife, addressed to someone who is much loved, extremely dear. The lover is in the bed beside his beloved, whispering the passionate words of solace and warning to her in the long night. He tells her of the Thief, who is the destroyer of love:

He comes to leave her in the lawless sun awaking
Naked and forsaken to grieve he will not come.

59

The Thief is the jealousy that steals and changes and destroys the purity of love.

"Something like that," Dylan Thomas said, with an apologetic shrug of his shoulders. And we both laughed.

This will teach me, I hope, not to ask a poet what his poem means, especially not to interpret it for him to his face. My own solution still seems to me very good. In the end, though, I must modestly admit that the Thief is his Thief, not mine.

❄

TALK WITH A POET

❄

A thing Dylan Thomas once said
About poetry haunts me most—
Still echoed derisively
By his sweating, chainsmoking ghost,
Told me in anger first
By the public poet who read
His verse on platforms aloud:
"Fool," the poems said,
"Why don't you go back to work?"

Spoken in mocking rage
Of words, words he did not write,
All the shining handiwork
Half-wrought in that good night,

All the images of the dream
Too quickly forfeited—
I hear his dark voice again:
*"Fool!" the poems said,
Scornfully.* But he is dead.

❀

WOMEN POETS

❀

The writing of poetry, even in our time, has an odd effect
on women. Or it may only be that odd women become poets.
Whatever the reason, the eccentricity has been there more or
less since the time of Sappho, the strange lady of Lesbos.
There are the spinsters, sometimes the recluses, like Emily
Brontë, Emily Dickinson, Christina Rossetti. Or there is
Mrs. Browning, about whom I heard Mrs. Cecil Woodham-
Smith speak in a radio broadcast in London as a poet who
wrote "the best poetry that any woman has yet written in the
English language." It is a frightening thought.

The literary historian Van Wyck Brooks has his hands
full in furnishing statistics about Amy Lowell. She weighed
over 200. Her bed had 18 pillows. She owned 10,000 black
cigars and kept 7 sheep dogs. She published some 700 poems
and left behind that bold but inaccurate criticism of her own
worth: "I'm the only member of my family," said Amy
Lowell, "who is worth a damn."

Edith Sitwell's eccentricities are her stock in trade: she

is an eccentric. Perhaps one example will suffice: up to the time she was made a Dame of the British Empire, she refused to be called anything but Dr. Sitwell in recognition of her honorary degrees. Then the multiple honors given her began to pile up and create a problem, which she has solved in her own fashion by signing herself, "Dame Edith Sitwell, D.B.E., D.Litt., D.Litt., D.Litt."

Marianne Moore wears a three-cornered hat, roots for the Dodgers, and keeps, at least in her poems, a private zoo. She has written a whole bestiary by now, full of tropical lizards, mollusks, pelicans, mongooses, cobras, monkeys, porcupines, and armadillos. She is understandably fond of the panda and the jerboa—but she has not written about human love. Her elephant is fog-colored, her lion has a chrysanthemum head—but what she says about poetry is not true of her own, that it ought to "steady the soul."

❀

THE WORLD OF JOHN BETJEMAN

❀

In London in 1949, I heard John Betjeman read his poems at a Book Exhibition in Grosvenor House. Before he began, he said with a wry smile, "I give myself two more years before I'm found out." That was twelve years ago. Taking longer than he predicted, the public has found the man out to be not a fraud but a poet.

Good heavens, what kind? He is a topographical poet,

landscape poet, poet of ecclesiastical architecture, poet of the provinces, and poet of the suburbs. He exhibits strong feeling, amounting to a hard-breathing passion, for places. Landscape haunts his mind wherever he goes. "I love suburbs," says John Betjeman, "and gaslights and Pont Street and Gothic Revival churches and mineral railways, provincial towns and garden cities." For thirty years he has had a love affair with England, with what is most English about it. A large part of his fervor is kept for the Church of England: the structure and architectural design, the bells, the ritual and service in Anglican cathedrals and parish churches. Then his poems carry such rapt titles as: "Church of England thoughts occasioned by hearing the bells of Magdalen Tower from the Botanic Garden, Oxford, on St. Mary Magdalen's Day," or simply, "St. Saviour's, Aberdeen Park, Highbury, London, N."

To be sure, he is a comic poet as well, wonderfully carried away, though I understand that he resents, now that he is writing his autobiography in blank verse, being taken lightly as a funnyman. He seems to me funny. The amatory poems sing of his passion for various powerfully limbed, athletic girls whom he pursues, usually on a tennis court. Pam is one of the large women tennis players who fill him with an awed weakness:

Pam, I adore you, Pam, you great big mountainous sports girl,
Whizzing them over the net, full of the strength of five. . . .

My favorite is the unnamed strong girl who casts her blazing eyes on him and leaves him overpowered, "winded, wilting, weak," in a poem called "The Licorice Fields at Pontefract":

Red hair she had and golden skin,
Her sulky lips were shaped for sin,
Her sturdy legs were flannel-slack'd,
The strongest legs in Pontefract.

Yet in his variety John Betjeman is bewildering. There are sudden and unnerving shifts in mood that remind me of the afternoon in 1949 when he read aloud. At one moment he was making us laugh by reciting a dizzy and outrageous verse in galloping anapests; at the next he was revealing in a dark, morbid poem his terror of death, especially of dying in anguish and despair alone in a hospital. In "Cottage Hospital," he asks himself fearfully (still in anapests) how horrible that last gasping moment of life will be:

And say shall I groan in dying,
    as I twist the sweaty sheet?
Or gasp for breath uncrying,
    as I feel my senses drown'd
While the air is swimming with insects
    and children play in the street?

He is contradictory, but it may be only as a naturally gay man, a lightwit, is who carries around with him a sense of doom. I think his eye for looking at the world is as sharp and piercing as Aunt Mary Emerson's, noted by her nephew in his *Journal:* "My aunt had an eye that went through and through you like a needle. 'She was endowed,' she said, 'with a fatal gift of penetration.' "

Aunt Mary alarmed everybody by seeing too much.

KARL SHAPIRO

AND MY UNCLE TOBY

❄

Both Karl Shapiro and my Uncle Toby are tormented by flies. And how differently each in his own way and century, in the literary fashion of his time, addresses the miserable insect.

"I'll not hurt thee," says my Uncle Toby, rising from his chair and going across the room with the fly in his hand,—"I'll not hurt a hair of thy head." "Go," says he, lifting up the sash and opening his hand as he spoke to let it escape; "Go, poor devil, get thee gone, why should I hurt thee?—This world surely is wide enough to hold both thee and me."

Karl Shapiro, in his poem "The Fly," hurls out his heavy anger and violent disgust, crying, "O hideous little bat, the size of snot." The hateful, stinking fly maddens him as his worst enemy:

> Shod in disease you dare to kiss my hand
> Which sweeps against you like an angry flail.

Shapiro, a grown man, seeks the fly's death, swats it with his hate, crushes it, mangles it, smears its blood, tears its body, exposes its white and pasty guts, and beats it furiously as one beats a rat.

Somehow I find my Uncle Toby, sentimental to the end, a far more restful man with a fly, and I prefer to sit around relaxed with him in the hot weather. He is modest and innocent, given over to the wisdom of love. My Uncle Toby can't hate anything. Especially he could never work himself up to a towering passion to hate a fly.

❊

HOW TO EAT AN ORANGE

❊

A breath-taking poem in the London *Times Literary Supplement* (December 18, 1959) is called "How to Eat an Orange." It has the fourteen rhymed lines of a Shakespearean sonnet, and it gets right to work on the unpeeled fruit:

> First you must roll it in your hands
> To loosen the firm outer skin.
> Peel this all off.

The directions are clear. Next you halve the orange with clean fingers and pared nails. You eat it with a whetted appetite and your joints wet with juice. In the last climactic line you spit out the pips.

It reminds me strongly of another recent poem called "Paring an Apple." It also reminds me of the topics we used to assign for the first themes in Freshman English, such as "How to Wash Dishes," or "How to Make a Meat Loaf."

My students, however, never wrote this kind of thing in verse.

This is a sample, undoubtedly, of the work of "The Movement" in England by the new conservative poets who write about hard facts, in the plain style. Kingsley Amis says, "Nobody wants any more poems on the grander themes for a few years." To avoid such themes, they write vividly about how to run a vacuum cleaner, or what it feels like to step suddenly on a beetle.

❀

THE REAL TOADS

❀

Marianne Moore defines poetry as "imaginary gardens with real toads in them." Nowadays one finds plenty of real toads to worry about, but what are missing are the necessary gardens. Worse still, they are very often dead toads.

Richard Wilbur's poem is called "Death of the Toad." It tells of the poor thing caught horribly in a power mower, which has chewed and clipped its legs. Dying, the toad pours its "rare original heartsblood" back into the earth.

Richard Eberhart has a whole assortment of dead animals, including a putrid lamb, whose "guts were out for the crows to eat," that smells to high heaven among the daisies (all right, a daisy garden); and a groundhog, whose decaying and miserable corpse seething with maggots the poet thoughtfully pokes with a stick.

There are the recent poems of Ted Hughes, in England, about a dead otter and two dead fish. He also offers a view in nine stanzas of a dead pig, beginning "The pig lay on a barrow dead." He says it looked to him like a sack of wheat, which he thumped without remorse. Live pigs, he reflects, are more fun; they eat cinders and dead cats (something I did not know). And he ends, with a final dismal stare:

> They were going to scald it.
> Scald it and scrub it like a doorstep.

These real toads ought anyhow to be alive. I think they ought as well, ugly as they are, to wear at least a tiny jewel of poetry shining in their heads.

HORACE DEFINES VERSE

In the *Ars Poetica,* Horace tells clearly enough the way to write verse. I am not sure that his method applies to poetry, for Horace speaks of deftness rather than intensity; of order and arrangement, not passion. But for the verse writer, he is persuasive. His answer is noble and enough:

"I shall aim a poem so deftly fashioned out of familiar material that anybody might hope to emulate the feat, yet for all his efforts sweat and labor in vain. Such is the power of order and arrangement, such the charm that waits upon common things."

❀

MORRIS BISHOP DEFINES VERSE

❀

In his preface to a light collection, *A Bowl of Bishop,* Morris Bishop writes more learnedly than Horace about the nature of verse. The first principle, he says, is strictness of

form, the second incongruity, the third logic. Well. I turn
the page quickly and read a sample of his own light verse:

Many a man has read my rhymes and did not like a word of 'em;
And very many more there be who never even heard of 'em.
I do not mind if you should find these poems misbegotten;
"It's all a matter of taste," I'd say, "and your taste is rotten."

Whatever the form, incongruity, logic, the sense of these
words is wonderful. They remind me of a couplet in a much
earlier piece of verse, Bramston's eighteenth-century "Man
of Taste," where the principles are no doubt the same, but
the idea is far less amiably put:

> This is true taste, and whoso likes it not,
> Is blockhead, coxcomb, puppy, fool and sot.

❀

IDEAS FOR LIGHT VERSE

❀

Now and then when I am asked to talk to a student forum
or a women's club, I choose the subject "Ideas for Light
Verse." Once a lady brought pencil and paper under the impression that we were going to compose ballads or limericks
together.

I say that I believe Yeats was right about it when he said,
"People do not invent. They remember." Ideas, light as
goose feathers, are everywhere, requiring only good eyesight

and good hearing to detect them. The only difficulty is that one is, most of the time, forgetful or asleep. What I wish for most, I think, is a talent for experience and a long memory. I grieve for the light and shining events that all my life I must have overlooked and forgotten.

A verse is usually the result of a couple of ideas joining together, like two separate raindrops merging on a windowpane, Robert Frost says. One day lately, for example, I was reading Spenser's *Shepheardes Calender,* which contains the lovely song of the shepherd boy Thomalin who scorned love till at length he was himself wounded by the arrow:

> Of hony and of gaule in love there is store:
> The honye is much, but the gaule is more.

It was a midsummer day and the grasshoppers were lively in the meadow below my house. As I read, I remembered an old story about a grasshopper: how once in ancient Delphi a Greek singer broke a string of his lyre, and there was silence till a passing grasshopper kindly took the minstrel's place and filled in the missing notes of the refrain. (The Greeks kept grasshoppers and cicadas around as pets for their chirping.) Spenser's couplet seemed to me the kind of love song that the grasshopper might have tried obligingly to sing. That was the way the verse began.

HONEY AND GALL

Then the poet broke the G string
Of his lyre. And there was no song,
Till a grasshopper happened by

That came and perched on the lyre
And fiddled away on its wing
To restore the sweet lost tune,

To chirp of love and desire
The whole long shrill afternoon.
And the grasshopper sang of all

That love is, the bitter and sweet,
The mixture of honey and gall,
Like a sigh returned to the air

From a lyre played once before:
The honey, it softly sang,
Is much, but the gall is more.

Then at last the daylight went
And the grasshopper, wearied of
Rehearsing all afternoon

The same old complaint of love,
Forgot, and grew indolent,
And fiddled but half the tune.

The honey is much, it sang,
And again with a lingering touch
It sang, *but the honey is much.*

❀

TALK WITH MOLLY

❀

I had a mild argument with Molly, who is English, about Ogden Nash, whether or not he is good at rhymes. "How can you doubt it?" I cried, amazed that she should question his skill. The old master. His rhymes are outrageous but highly professional, I said. He knows exactly what he is doing.

Triumphantly, Molly recited the two lines:

I think it clever of the turtle
In such a fix to be so fertile.

"Isn't that terrible?" she demanded. Since her pronunciation was British: *turtle* and *fertile,* I had to agree it fell heavily on the ear.

*   *   *

Molly and I had another literary argument, about sloe gin. The question was one of enjoyment and how you would put it into words. On a hot summer afternoon we sat on my porch drinking sloe gin, and Molly's memory was deeply stirred as she looked into her glass at the cool purple-pink color. It reminded her, she said, of the heavy purple sloes that grow and ripen in the Cotswolds on the blackthorn tree. In her childhood she had loved to fill her mouth with them. Like Hopkins:

> How a lush-kept plush-capped sloe
> Will, mouthed to flesh-burst,
> Gush!—flush the man, the being with it, sour or sweet,
> Brim, in a flash, full!

Sloe gin reminded me, I said, of concubines and strumpets. It was purple with passion, pink with sin, like the pink ladies in the pictures by Toulouse-Lautrec. It belonged in a red-plush fancy house in Paris, where surely none of the pretty inmates ever drank anything else. All of this clearly showed, I reflected,

> A sentimental strain in Molly.
> I like to think it tastes of folly.

※

RHYMES

※

Dryden confessed that a rhyme often helped him to a thought. I am in favor of rhymes, intentional ones as aid or ornament to verse, and love them for their own sake, much in the fashion that my children did. Both of them rhymed young. Philip at four or five began a book called "Poems for Helen the Mother," which dealt heavily in rhymes like "Helen is nice and so is rice." Three-year-old David composed in his bath. One day he announced dreamily, "I can say a poem."

"You can?" I said. "Whose poem?"

"Mine."

"Say it, then."

"Sourpuss,
   Picklepuss."

RICHARD ARMOUR'S IDEA

Richard Armour had a gracious idea concerning him and me. He thought we might write a book of verse together about professors and the academic scene, since we both are professors who have written light verse about that comic spectacle.

"I am mindful of Wordsworth and Coleridge's *Lyrical Ballads,*" he wrote me, "though which of us would be Wordsworth and which of us Coleridge I am not prepared to say."

I took this remark as a promising sample of Richard Armour's lighthearted wit, and though we had not met and were teaching at colleges three thousand miles apart, I was pleased to be invited. Surely professors look the same on either coast.

A final sentence in his letter discouraged me. "This academic grove is overdue for a trimming," he said; and faced with these probably true words, I knew I was not one fit for the work. My verses about professors belong to a careless past before I began to teach, when as a faculty wife looking on at the academic swirl I could marvel at the ludicrous types on campus. I easily saw then, with Horace Walpole, "the gigantic littleness of a schoolmaster."

These days professors seem to me, on the whole, wise and enlightened human beings. I overhear them sometimes in the classroom shouting away about beauty, truth, and the struggle of men's souls. Only one of them really sounds funny to me any more: myself.

❀

A CLOSE READING OF THE TEXT

❀

The professor speaks of love until the bell rings,
Love, the concern of English poetry,
That once seemed not beyond the understanding,

But now ambiguous, it has to be
Studied in classrooms and elucidated,
If possible by an authority.

One speaks. From lecture notes, all passion spent,
He annotates the poem, so to prove
By exegesis, gloss, and emendation,

That it was he John Donne was thinking of
And once implored, as poet to professor,
For God's sake hold your tongue, and let me love!

❊

A HEADSHAKING

OVER DOROTHY PARKER

❊

Now Dorothy Parker, in her sixties, has grown sober and turned grimly against her own wonderful light verse of thirty years ago. It grieves me, it makes me wince, to read in a recent interview her harsh words: "My verses are no damn good. Let's face it, honey, my verse is terribly dated— as anything once fashionable is dreadful now."

Fashionable? Her verse was about her young and witty and passionate self. How could anything become dated that

had to do immortally with love?

> Whose love is given over-well
> Shall look on Helen's face in hell,
> Whilst they whose love is thin and wise
> May view John Knox in paradise.

O lady, come back, come back, and try to save this world again by love.

POETESS

❀

No matter what kind of verse a woman writes, nobody alive or dead deserves to be called a poetess. Dr. Johnson in his *Dictionary* scornfully defined a poetess for all eternity as a "she poet." Yet *The New York Times* still employs the word, as if there were actually a female way of writing poems, and I see that *Time* magazine has gone further than usual in its passing condescension. In a piece about Poetess Edna St. Vincent Millay, it refers to Elinor Wylie remarkably enough as a *fellow* poetess.

I like better the word poetaster that *Time* hurled at me once ("One of the pleasantest poetasters around"). Though it's a word to throw at a dog, I had rather be scorned as a dabbler, a rimester, a paltry would-be poet, than referred to, in the next paragraph, by the absurd title of Poetess Bevington.

OBSCURITY AT HOME

❀

A well-disposed lady in London once told me she liked my verse because, she said, it taught her a great deal about the birds, trees, and flowers in America (about the sex life, did she mean, of the birds and bees?).

"The cardinal," she went on, appreciatively. "You write so often about it. Of course I have not seen one, never having been in America, and I had always thought the cardinal was a flower. But you have made it perfectly real, even vivid, before my eyes. It must be a very attractive tree!"

Oh, I thought, blushing. What verse of mine is as clouded as all that? The Carolina cardinal may look like a tree to her, but if so it is a bright red tree and, by God, it always sings. "Cardinals were singing in this wood," a verse begins, not very subtly. Another says:

> Now mindful of his own red wings,
> The cardinal there preens and sings.

A third ends, "He sings. I hear the cardinal."

WHAT IS POETRY?

BOSWELL: "Then, Sir, what is poetry?"
DR. JOHNSON: "Why, Sir, it is much easier to say what it is not."

Boswell must have chosen an off day to ask the question. The answers are always plentiful. Everybody knows what poetry is, and says so, especially in our time:

R. P. BLACKMUR: "Poetry is life framed and identified."
JOHN HALL WHEELOCK: "A poem is a way of knowing."
RICHARD WILBUR: "The poem is an effort to make or discover some pattern in the world. . . . It is a conflict with disorder."
PAUL ENGLE: "Poetry is ordinary language raised to the Nth power."
RAINER MARIA RILKE: "Verses are not, as people imagine, simply feelings. They are experiences."
CARL SANDBURG: "Poetry is hyacinths and biscuits."
T. S. ELIOT: "We must learn what poetry is—if we ever learn —from reading it."
WALLACE STEVENS: "Poetry is the supreme fiction, madame."
MARIANNE MOORE: ". . . imaginary gardens with real toads in them."
DYLAN THOMAS: "Poetry is what in a poem makes you laugh, cry, twist your toes, twinkle, prickle, be silent, know you are alone and not alone in an unknown world."

84

❀

MENCKEN'S BELLYACHES

❀

Henry L. Mencken did no harm to poetry when he damned poems as "pretty little bellyaches." It is, come to think of it, really useful language. Those who despise poetry and deplore its existence now have these scornful words to hurl. Nobody else minds in the least.

The difference in point of view is too great for hurt feelings or for argument. Some reject it, like Mencken. Others have an attitude like that expressed by the English poet and critic John Wain: "But poetry is not read only for pleasure; it is read because it is so important that we dare not neglect it."

*   *   *

"Yet as a person with a raging tooth runs her eyes in a chemist shop over green bottles with gilt scrolls on them lest one of them may contain a cure, she considered: Keats and Shelley; Yeats and Donne...."

—VIRGINIA WOOLF, *Between the Acts*

THE ART OF DISARMING

It takes a lot of disarming talk, however, not to frighten people away from poetry. Marianne Moore tries to placate the reader by saying, in her poem called "Poetry," "I, too, dislike it: there are things that are important beyond all this fiddle." Fiddle, of course, is what she has spent her whole life about. Wallace Stevens described poetry as "Such tank and tank and tunk-a-tunk-tunk." It was the supreme fiction, he admitted, and he was Crispin, the comedian as the letter *C;* the serious jester, for whom poetry made an endless study of existence; a clown, perhaps, but an aspiring clown.

*　　*　　*

Both David Hume and Nietzsche called poets liars. Hume described them as "liars by profession." Nietzsche cried out, "The poets? The poets lie too much."

*　　*　　*

> Sir, I admit your general rule,
> That every poet is a fool:
> But you yourself may serve to show it,
> That every fool is not a poet.
> —MATTHEW PRIOR

* * *

"A man may play the fool everywhere else," said Montaigne, "but not in poetry."

❀

THE NEED TO BE A POET

❀

On an otherwise blank page at the beginning of Lytton Strachey's biography *Elizabeth and Essex* are these arresting words, reasonable and true even if used by him to introduce a book of prose:

"It is almost always disastrous not to be a poet."

Strachey had said this thing earlier in writing an essay about Francis Bacon. "His intellect swayed him too completely," Strachey reflected. Bacon had the dangerous fault in him of too little poetry.

* * *

Or had he? John Aubrey shows us a hardly prosaic Bacon choosing to ride one day in the rain in an open coach because it was April and springtime. Bacon observed that the rain was very wholesome—because, he said, of the nitre in the air and the *Universal Spirit of the World.*

HOW DO POETS WRITE POEMS?

❀

It's a fair question unless you require an answer: how *do* poets write poems? I have been reading a book by Phyllis Bartlett, *Poems in Process,* that tries to say. She has looked into the working habits of poets since the time of Milton to find out what happens. Her book deals with the three stages in the making of a poem: the inspiration that began it, the act of composition itself, and the final step of rewriting and polish.

Inspiration proves hard to assess. Poets will describe the mood in which they wrote, or the time of day, but how can they account for the need to write at all? In the past they were more given to the fine frenzy of the dedicated poet, though Stephen Spender today readily admits to a "gift for inspiration." Wordsworth said the mind of a poet must be in a state of enjoyment, calling himself "one of the happiest of men." Coleridge believed in the deep power of joy, and in 1794 wrote to Southey, "When a man is unhappy he writes damned bad poetry, I find."

The seasonal urge is strong in poets. Milton wrote chiefly in winter. Keats looked for spring to wake him up (as it did in the miraculous months of April and May, 1819). Burns chose the autumn. Longfellow liked the month of September. Shelley flourished in the hot months. Some poets, like Wordsworth, have gone outdoors to work. Others, like

Auden, keep to the curtained room. Schiller needed the smell of rotten apples about him to make a poem. Tennyson and Walter de la Mare had to smoke. Auden drinks lots of tea, Spender coffee; Hart Crane drank alcohol. Pope, Byron, and William Morris were creative late at night. And so it goes. In the end the greatest single incentive to poetry is always love, the impetus of love, lust, longing, and desire. And, of course, men have their dreams, sometimes their visions of other worlds, like Coleridge and Blake and AE.

A look at the second stage, the actual writing of the words, shows even more distractingly how broad the poetic experience is. Any method is good that produces a good poem. Some poets habitually write with ease and speed, as in Keats's view they ought ("If poetry comes not as naturally as the leaves of a tree it had better not come at all"). Byron dashed off the cantos of *Don Juan;* Browning wrote *Strafford* in ten days. Still, the hard way appears to be the common way. Early drafts of poems, work sheets, notebooks that show an arduous preparation for poetry, all these betray the endless labor and headache of writing. By far the most revealing sections of Miss Bartlett's book are these two that deal with the making of a poem on through its painful revision. There the struggle speaks for itself. Since poets can hardly know how they write a poem, we need not badger them to find out. The poems tell far more than the poets do.

If finally there is no formula for the writing of a poem, who expected to find one? Miss Bartlett says her aim is the enlightenment of young writers who may be taught the ways of successful poets. I can't guess what the young will gain except perhaps solace, the chance to look at ordeal and say, "I am not the first." The brave new poet may learn one of two things: to be daunted by the tortured example of others, or, if he prefers, to remain undaunted.

❀

THE POET AS SINGER

❀

We complain today that the poets no longer sing. They talk to themselves in low conversational tones, expecting to be overheard (Marchbanks says, in *Candida,* "That is what all poets do: they talk to themselves out loud; and the world overhears them"). Sir Herbert Read even urges poets not to be audible, but to keep private and remain unheard: "Never lift your voice—modern poetry has an inaudible wavelength."

Yet in a golden age, Pindar and Sappho sang. The Elizabethans were lyric poets in the true sense: "to be sung to the lyre." Campion's lyre was a real one; it was a lute. I have no idea whether he wrote the poems first and afterward set them to music, or whether he added the words to existing songs. It may have made no difference to him which came first. His words and notes, he said, were coupled "lovingly together."

Unlike our modern poets, Campion remembered that, if a song is to be heard, he must trust the rest of us to become singers, too:

> All these songs are mine, if you express them well.
> Otherwise they are your own. Farewell.

THE ELIZABETHAN MAID

Why was she sung and played,
In one long serenade,
Elizabethan airs
Throughout her love affairs?
Were they with cither players
And lutanists, poor maid?

Never a quiet minute
But a man wooed her in it
With Morley melodies,
Dowland in two-part glees,
Byrd tunes and harmonies
For harpsichord and spinet.

There must have been easier
Ways to make love to her
Than to sing madrigals
With her at intervals
To viol and virginals,
Lute, harp, and dulcimer!

POETRY OF SUNSET AND SUNRISE

❀

Someone said to me at a cocktail party, at what you might call the sunset hour, that there isn't much poetry in existence about sunsets. The party itself reminded me of Emily Dickinson's "Bring me the sunset in a cup." But for some reason, perhaps because the word suggests a cliché, like the "sunset of life" or Tennyson's "Sunset and evening star," most of the praise in poetry is given to the sunrise. An alba is a lament of lovers having to part at dawn. An aubade is a lyric piece to recite in honor of the rising sun. As in *Hudibras:*

> And like a lobster boiled, the Morn
> From black to red began to turn.

I think there isn't even a sunset goddess. Aurora or Eos is a splendid goddess of the dawn, who gave Tennyson the brilliant power to visualize her: "And thee returning on thy silver wheels." She rides down in a rosy chariot drawn by white-winged horses. She opens the eastern gates of morning, carrying light and shedding tears like dew to make the flowers grow. She is a lady rich in many lovers, by one of whom, a Titan, she became the mother of the winds and all the stars.

But then, as Shakespeare says in *Timon of Athens,* "Men shut their doors against a setting sun."

PLANE AT DAWN

The crescendo of the jet
Wakes me, and out of the east
It comes roaring, shaking my bed,
Like Ben Hur's race overhead,
A skyrocket in July,

And it's dawn. And I open one eye
To squint through the pale goldmist
At this chariot of sunrise,
By the white-winged horses still drawn
Careering across the sky's

Pink clouds, rose, gold, amethyst.
All hell breaking loose in the air
This morning, I realize,
Is only Aurora up there,
The mother of winds and stars.

❀

POETIC WORDS IN POETRY

❀

Words I dislike in poetry are the over-poetic ones, like *spindrift* for the spray of the sea, or a *bosky* wood to describe a thicket. Like *oriel* when one means a large bay window. Like *crepuscular* for twilight, *shard* for a fragment, *bole* for the trunk of a tree.

Dr. Johnson said, "Words too familiar, or too remote, defeat the purpose of the poet." I have only to read Richard Aldington's poem about the moon, which ends,

> And here am I looking wantonly at her
> Over the kitchen sink

to believe that a kitchen sink is as jarring as a bosky wood. Between these two is the language of poetry, to which the extremes of language never fit.

*　　　*　　　*

> It was only in a word, but still a word
> Stays in the mind and has its children too.
> —CHRISTOPHER FRY, *The Dark Is Light Enough*

DOWSABELL

Michael Drayton had a queer taste in names. There is the chilly, unreal lady of his sonnets called Idea. There is the fair maiden of his ballad with the odd name of Dowsabell. She used to make me laugh when I read the poem:

> Quoth he, so had I done full well
> Had I not seen fair Dowsabell
> Come forth to gather May.

I think better of the name now, since I came across it in the dictionary, *dowsabell,* a common noun though obsolete. In the sixteenth century it was a word for sweetheart, especially a country girl. Drayton meant to imply that his Dowsabell was a maiden *douce et belle,* a pretty little pastoral love, a gentle, rustic little dowsabell.

❋

GENTILLESSE

❋

The one word that I love best in the language is a lost word, no longer in poetry or in the minds or on the tongues of men: Chaucer's word *gentillesse*. It has an unspeakable eloquence. It means all that a word can mean: the possession of all virtue ("Vertu to sewe, and vyces for to flee"), a true nobility, a true humility, a true charity, and, heaven help us, good breeding besides. Gentillesse is not a matter of birth or riches. It comes not from our ancestors, says Chaucer, but only from God. Of him "we clayme oure gentillesse."

❋

THE WORD LOVER

❋

"I'm a word man."—E. B. WHITE
"Words, words, words."—SHAKESPEARE

A word man,
Like a man in love

(*And this word "love," which greybeards call divine*),
Speaks with the passion he would prove,
Familiar in his mouth as bread or wine.

A word man says—
Unpack my heart with words—
Them all, but with the lust to tell
True words from untrue, if he can,
And 'tis a kind of good deed to say well.

Yet such a man
To make the weeper laugh, the laugher weep,
Still is no man
To say which word is true, or even half-,
If with his tongue he cannot win a woman.

❀

ON POETRY

❀

I talked tonight at the University, and my subject was "Poetry." The student who invited me to speak chose the title himself. It seemed to me, on the whole, a hopeless one, without beginning and without end, limitless and inexhaustible, but I didn't say so. "For a full half-hour?" I asked.

"Right," he said. "But feel entirely free to keep on talking. Take thirty-five minutes, if you need to."

I took thirty and told them, as Matthew Arnold once said, that the future of poetry is immense.

DR. JOHNSON'S CUPS OF TEA

Macaulay speaks of that inextinguishable thirst.

Sir Joshua Reynolds reminded Dr. Johnson on one occasion that he had just drunk eleven cups. Replying, "Sir, I did not count your glasses of wine, why should you number up my cups of tea?" Johnson calmly asked for a twelfth.

A Mrs. John Scott used to tell that she herself had helped him one evening to fifteen cups of tea. Once at Dunvegan Lady Macleod poured out sixteen cups for him and then asked if a small basin would not save him trouble and be more agreeable. "I wonder, Madam," he answered, "why all the ladies ask me such impertinent questions. It is to save yourselves trouble, Madame, and not me." At this, the story goes, Lady Macleod was silent and resumed her task. Later she put the quantity that she had poured out for him at "twenty-two dishes."

Dr. Johnson described himself as "a hardened and shameless tea-drinker . . . whose kettle has scarcely time to cool; who with tea amuses the evening, with tea solaces the midnight, and with tea welcomes the morning."

So far as I know, Robert Louis Stevenson gives the largest actual count of the cupfuls of Dr. Johnson, though what the source is of this remarkable number I have not been able to discover. In "Aes Triplex," Stevenson says: ". . . his heart, bound with triple brass, did not recoil before twenty-seven individual cups of tea." Stevenson was by nature an exaggerator. And so am I.

❀

THE OCEANS OF DR. JOHNSON

❀

I never take a cup of tea
But I consider pleasurably
That, poured a twenty-seventh cup,
Dr. Johnson drank it up.

Before that mighty thirst was quenched,
Pot by pot, his hostess blenched
And, marveling, took fearful count
To be exact in the amount.

Perhaps his dryness had diminished,
Say, when the twenty-first was finished,
Yet being in a social mood
He drank to thrust out solitude,

Extending the complacent hour,
The festive rite, by staying power.
And twenty-seven cups would be
His limit, his capacity.

HOW FAT WAS GIBBON?

A thing I am curious about is how fat Edward Gibbon really was. I have found an illuminating account of him, written in the eighteenth century by Edmond Malone, who knew the historian well. The story that he tells shows Gibbon to be, for all his pride in his person, a decidedly plump and billowing man:

"When he was introduced to a blind French lady, the servant happening to stretch out her mistress's hand to lay hold of the historian's cheek, she thought upon feeling its rounded contour that some trick was being played upon her with the *sitting* part of a child, and exclaimed, '*Fi donc!*' "

❀

JOHN AUBREY'S STORY

OF SIR THOMAS MORE

❀

John Aubrey's finest touch, I think, was in his writing about Sir Thomas More, the best and most valiant life of the *Brief Lives*. More was a witty man. His discourse, says Aubrey, was "extraordinary facetious." In the following tale told by Aubrey, More doesn't actually speak aloud, but he sounds mighty facetious all the same.

"In his *Utopia* his lawe is that the young people are to see each other stark-naked before marriage. Sir William Roper, of Eltham, in Kent, came one morning, pretty early, to my Lord, with a proposall to marry one of his daughters. My Lord's daughters were then both together abed in a truckle-bed in their father's chamber asleep. He carries Sir William into the chamber and takes the Sheete by the corner and suddenly whippes it off. They lay on their Backs, and their smocks up as high as their arme-pitts. This awakened them, and immediately they turned on their bellies. Quoth Roper, I have seen both sides, and so gave a patt on the buttock, he made choice of, sayeing, Thou art mine. Here was all the trouble of the wooeing."

✽

OPENING WORDS

IN SHAKESPEARE'S PLAYS

✽

When Shakespeare begins a play with a line of sheer poetry, I wonder how he dared to waste its eloquence by saying it too soon. No audience is ever quiet and alert enough to listen to the opening words. Yet Richard III cries,

> Now is the winter of our discontent
> Made glorious summer by this sun of York.

King Ferdinand, in *Love's Labour's Lost,* movingly begins,

> Let fame, that all hunt after in their lives,
> Live registered upon our brazen tombs
> And then grace us in the disgrace of death.

In *Henry IV, Part I,* the King speaks with sorrowful emphasis,

> So shaken as we are, so wan with care,
> Find we a time for frightened peace to pant,
> And breathe short-winded accents to new broils
> To be commenced in strands afar remote.

Thus the brooding of a king, or it may be a lover's sigh, will start the play. Antonio confesses, in *The Merchant of Venice,*

> In sooth, I know not why I am so sad:
> It wearies me, you say it wearies you,

And lovesick Orsino cries, in *Twelfth Night,*

> If music be the food of love, play on;
> Give me excess of it, that, surfeiting,
> The appetite may sicken, and so die.

I feel more easy when the play begins less vividly, with a loud, confused noise, like the brawling of the servants in *Romeo and Juliet,* or a tempestuous crash of thunder and the sound of shipwreck in *The Tempest.* Or with a determined shout, like "Hence!" in *Julius Caesar,* or "Who's there?" in *Hamlet.* During these outcries, we gather our wits to listen.

Most sensible of all is the opening speech in *Timon of Athens,* when a mere Poet happens along and says, "Good day, sir."

KEATS'S THREE TREES

※

One warm night in May 1819, Joseph Severn went with a party of friends to the Spaniards Inn in Hampstead. During the gay evening he missed John Keats from the company and stepped outside to look for him. He found him at last lying beneath a pine tree, listening entranced to the song of a nightingale overhead. A day or two later, at his home in Wentworth Place, Keats wrote the "Ode to a Nightingale."

This is the story told on a placard over the fireplace in the Spaniards Inn. Its impressive charm for me lies in the fact that here is the *third* kind of tree under which Keats is said to have been lurking when he heard the nightingale. I can only believe it was a very restless and lively bird. His friend Charles Brown, with whom he lived in Wentworth Place, gave this account:

"In the spring of 1819 a nightingale had built her nest near my house. Keats felt a tranquil and continual joy in her song; and one morning he took his chair from the breakfast table to the grass-plot under a plum tree, where he sat for two or three hours. When he came into the house, I perceived he had some scraps of paper in his hand ... and this was his *Ode to a Nightingale,* a poem which has been the delight of every one."

Charles Brown, who ought to have known, clearly identified it as a plum tree with Keats underneath. Yet the very tree (so they tell you now at Wentworth Place) still survives beside the house, and strangely enough it is a mulberry. I know, because I have eaten big red mulberries off it.

❀

WORDSWORTH AND THE BIRDS

❀

It seems extraordinary to me that Wordsworth couldn't tell one bird from another.

In his poem "The Tables Turned," he invites friend Matthew to quit his books and

> Come, hear the woodland linnet,
> How sweet his music! on my life,
> There's more of wisdom in it.

Mary Moorman, in her delightful biography of Wordsworth, recognizes this proof of his ignorance, but she minds not in the least. You never find linnets in a wood, Mrs. Moorman admits in a footnote. Therefore, he must have meant, she says, "all the smaller singers who inhabit trees and bushes." This is really too Wordsworthian of her! I find it odd of a nature poet to call any little passing bird a linnet.

*   *   *

However, Dorothy Wordsworth reveals a fact of far more importance about her brother than his scant knowledge of birds. As she sat one day watching him, she noted in her *Journal:*

"William tired himself seeking an epithet for the cuckoo."

And again, in a later entry, she wrote:

"William kindled, and began to write the poem."

❀

WAKEFUL WITH BEN JONSON

❀

Tormented by sleeplessness, I was reading Ben Jonson's *Discoveries* in bed (a book full of talk about poetry in which he sounds still alive today, disturbed by the present fallen state of verse: ". . . now letters only make men vile . . . [a man] is upbraidingly called a Poet, as if it were a most contemptible nickname").

I found Ben Jonson unable to sleep himself, consuming a whole miserable night staring at his big toe. Ranged round it as on a battlefield, in menacing formations on the coverlet, were great companies of foot soldiers, who fought furiously and slaughtered each other in his imagination.

I turned off the light and looked at my own moonlit toe. It made me wakeful as the hoot owl outside in the summer woods.

THE INSOMNIAC

❀

Ben Jonson, wakeful as an owl one night,
Studied his big toe in the pale moonlight,
While round it Turks and Romans fought and bled,
Tartars slew Carthaginians in his bed—
And still, however restful was the sight,
He couldn't sleep a wink, Ben Jonson said.

❀

THE WALK OF GRAY AND WALPOLE

❀

Recently I read a description by David Cecil of the poet
Thomas Gray, "a short plumpish figure with a tottery walk."
The word *tottery* reminded me how companionable he and
Horace Walpole must have looked wandering over Europe
in 1739–40 on the grand tour together. Walpole, who was
tall as a beanpole and slender to excess, had a prim gait
that he himself called "the march of a dabchick." While
the dabchick minced elegantly along, the poet tottered. A
lady of Walpole's acquaintance, the daughter of Sir John

Hawkins, remembered how he always entered a room, "in that style of affected delicacy, which fashion had then made almost natural, knees bent and feet on tiptoe, as if afraid of a wet floor."

❀

WALPOLE AND

MADAME DU DEFFAND

❀

One lady at least, Madame du Deffand, adored Horace Walpole with a really enduring passion. It is true that she never saw his walk or indeed his face, since she was totally blind when they first met. I am pained to think that the fastidious and disdainful Walpole once wrote of her, twenty years his senior, as "an old blind debauchée of wit." That she deserved more kindness of him her ardent letters make clear, over a period of fifteen years until her death in 1780. "Let us love each other," wrote Madame du Deffand to Walpole. "I do not think we could do better."

*   *   *

As for the lady's wit, it was she who made the neat reply to the story of St. Denis's miraculous walk (after he was beheaded at Paris in the year 272), a walk of six miles with his head in his hands. She said,

"Il n'ya que le premier pas qui coûte."

❄

WRITERS AGREE

❄

SYDNEY SMITH: "A man is the happier for life for having once made an agreeable tour."

WILLIAM COWPER:

> "How much a dunce that has been sent to roam
> Excells a dunce that has been kept at home!"

*   *   *

G. K. CHESTERTON: "The lights of London must be a wonderful sight if you can't read."

LOGAN PEARSALL SMITH: "What could be more enchanting than the voices of young people when you can't hear what they say?"

*   *   *

ANTHONY TROLLOPE: "In truth I do not care for the stars. I care, I think, only for men and women."

DR. JOHNSON TO MRS. THRALE: "A blade of grass is only a blade of grass. Men and women are *my* subjects of inquiry."

❋

WRITERS DISAGREE

❋

Wordsworth kindled when he wrote a poem. Coleridge heated diapers on his knee by thinking of poetry.

But Colette, drained of all bodily heat, grew cold and needed blankets while she was writing.

*   *   *

JOHN DONNE: "No man is an island."

MATTHEW ARNOLD: "Yes! in the sea of life enisled,
                  With echoing straits between us thrown,
                  Dotting the shoreless watery wild,
                  We mortal millions live *alone*."

*   *   *

The poet Thomas Gray wrote that he had found a sense of divinity in his journey up to the Grande Chartreuse.

Matthew Arnold, taking the same path, discovered doubt.

*   *   *

"Every day and every hour, every minute, walk around yourself and watch yourself, and see that your image is a seemly one."
                    —FATHER ZOSSIMA in *Brothers Karamazov*
"I long ago looked at myself from all angles."
                    —ANDRÉ GIDE, *Journal*, 1944.

✳

WRITERS REPEAT

✳

I innocently note in my reading how often there is the repetition of an idea. It is well enough for André Gide to observe (as others doubtless have observed before him): *"Toutes choses sont dites déjà, mais comme personne n'écoute il faut toujours recommencer."* Yet I always wonder if a writer trusts that what he is saying will seem original and brand new.

In John Bright's *Diary*, the entry for December 30, 1868, contains a pleasant account of a dinner party at Osborne with Queen Victoria. The talk became informal and even jolly. "I quoted a saying of my brother Thomas," writes John Bright, "who 'wondered, considering how beautiful the children are, where all the queer-looking old fellows come from.' This caused some merriment in which the Queen joined quite heartily."

A generation or so later, G. K. Chesterton discovered the same paradox. He wrote about it like this: "There must be something radically wrong with education since there are so many extraordinary children in the world and all grownups are such duds."

Virginia Woolf, considering the idea in her sensitive and delicate fashion, gazed about her one day from her seat in the compartment of a train and wrote: "If they begin originally like that, one muses, looking at a child of three, what is the process that turns them into that? And here one looks at a heavy old man with a dispatch box; or at an overdressed red-faced woman."

They must all have been reading Wordsworth's great ode to childhood, and thinking with him of the years that bring "the inevitable yoke."

THE FLOWERS OF LITERATURE

Among other immortal literary matters are everywhere the flowers of literature. Disraeli, for instance, wore a yellow primrose. Oscar Wilde held a lily in his hand. Tennyson plucked the flower in the crannied wall, Whitman saw lilacs blooming in the dooryard, and Herrick had a bed of tulips. Dickens's favorite flower was the geranium. Burns's love was like a red, red rose, Wordsworth's like a violet by a mossy stone. T. S. Eliot had a hyacinth girl.

And outflowering them all was Henry Adams, who likened himself to a wilted begonia.

※

CHEKHOV AND THE EGO

※

Chekhov claimed that he had the painful disease of autobiographophobia. To read any details about himself, he once said in a letter, or still more actually to write them down, was a torture. This is one of the better chronic ills to acquire, I think, one that counteracts somewhat the malady of self-love. It reduces the swelling ego and halts a little the spread of self-esteem.

※

A FEW MORE ODDITIES

※

Chekhov was never rich. Yet had he been,
He would have kept a harem of serene
Fat wives, all with their buttocks painted green.

* * *

Poor Lamb. A stammer when he spoke
Improved his gentle little joke,
Which had a point—but one that went
Best with an impediment.

Mr. Thoreau, so odd and frank,
Found *Leaves of Grass* a little rank,
But wondered, when it came to this,
Whose thoughts he blushed at. Walt's, or his?

*   *   *

Anthony Trollope ignored the stars,
Galaxies, planets, Andromeda, Mars.
Once, calmly, beneath a sky lit all up,
"I do not care for the stars," said Trollope.

*   *   *

Ben Jonson drank canary,
A gracious wine like sherry,
Which made him high
As a kite.—And I
Am the beneficiary.

*   *   *

Henry Adams once debated
Whether or not he was educated.
It took 500 pages to give
The answer in the negative.

*   *   *

Fanny Burney told her son,
"Never, my child, call anyone
A fool."—The boy replied the more
Amazed, "Then, what's the word made for?"

*   *   *

"Marriage is a great improver,"
Wrote Miss Jane Austen, who was moved
By the connubial bliss about her
To stay forever unimproved.

*   *   *

A line or two of poetry
Helped Coleridge warm his infant son.
He'd heat a diaper on his knee
While writing an immortal one.

*   *   *

John Donne was driven to the street
By wailing cries and toddling feet,
Being a poet and, alas,
With 12, a paterfamilias.

*   *   *

Wordsworth had a natural daughter
Far away from Derwentwater.
His nature poems he could make
Better at an English Lake.

*   *   *

"You have but two topics, yourself and me,"
Said Johnson to Boswell, wearily.
"I am sick of both." What both could tell
Was who made him sicker than Samuel.

MY DEAREST CASSANDRA

The friendly letters I should like to receive are those Jane Austen wrote to her sister Cassandra. "I always loved Cassandra," she said, "for her dark eyes and sweet temper." Because the love was deeply returned, Jane Austen ran on in her letters in the easy, intimate way one adopts with someone who smiles at the words. They undoubtedly talked in this fashion, with a good deal of laughter. When Cassandra was briefly from home, Jane gave her the store of news of neighbors and small excursions: a call on Mrs. Lance, a visit from Mrs. Digweed, the ball the night before. "I am still a cat if I see a mouse," Jane reminded her.

"We found only Mrs. Lance at home, and whether she boasts any offspring besides a grand pianoforte did not appear."

"Mrs. H. Digweed looks forward with great satisfaction to our being her neighbors. I would have her enjoy the idea to the utmost, as I suspect there will not be much in the reality."

"I cannot anyhow continue to find people agreeable; I respect Mrs. Chamberlayne for doing her hair well, but cannot feel a more tender sentiment." (At a later date:) "The friendship between Mrs. Chamberlayne and me which you predicted has already taken place, for we shake hands whenever we meet."

"Miss Langley is like any other short girl, with a broad nose and wide mouth, fashionable dress and exposed bosom."

"I do not think I was very much in request. People were rather apt not to ask me [to dance] till they could not help it; one's consequence, you know, varies so much at times without any particular reason."

❊

CASSANDRA

❊

The prettier Miss Austen of the two,
Cassandra was—the older one. A few,
Like Jane herself, believed her the more wise
And talented sister. But it's hard to tell
About someone no longer visible.
"I always loved Cassandra for her dark eyes,"

Jane wrote of her (a word or two of Jane's,
And there she is:) a pretty girl with brains,
The quiet one—but now forever quiet—
The one who never trifled with her pen
Or told her heart and scribbled it again,
Having no wish, perhaps, to clarify it.

Yet how alike they were. They seemed to share
A life (almost), inseparable as a pair,
Who laughed and talked and dearly loved a ball—

Lord Portsmouth's ball, in fact—or paid the three
Miss Biggs of Manydown Park, or formally
Were paid (as Jane wrote afterward), a "call":

"They came and they sat and they went." And so the days
Passed in routine with household tasks, with ways
To boil a chicken tender, endless talk
Of velvet bonnets or a muslin gown,
Or Mrs. Lance, or gossip of the town,
The pleasures of a book, a country walk—

Cassandra. Jane. Except, once in a while,
Jane, sewing by the fire, would suddenly smile,
Jump up and run across the room, and write
Words at her desk. Then, quietly as before,
She would return to work a little more
Beside Cassandra, sewing by lamplight.

It was the only difference: a small
Habit of Jane's, not impolite at all,
Of scribbling things, something imagined, heard.
And the real way of telling them apart
Was only this: Jane spoke and revealed her heart.
Cassandra listened, saying not a word.

POPE ON NOTHING

❀

Alexander Pope, in a letter to Henry Cromwell, April 27, 1708:

"I have nothing to say to you in this letter; but I was resolved to write to tell you so. Why should not I content myself with so many great examples of deep divines, profound casuists, grave philosophers, who have written, not letters only, but whole tomes and voluminous treatises about nothing? Why should a fellow like me, who all his life does nothing, be ashamed to write nothing; and that to one who has nothing to do but to read it? But perhaps you will say, the whole world has something to do, something to talk of, something to wish for, something to be employed about: but pray, sir, cast up the account, put all these somethings together, and what is the sum total but just nothing? I have no more to say, but to desire to give you my service (that is nothing) to your friends, and to believe that I am nothing more than your, etc., etc."

* * *

Horace Walpole, writing in July 19, 1789, to his dear friend Mary Berry, tells of a French lady who complained in a letter to her husband:

"*Je vous écris, parceque je n'ai rien à faire; et je finis, parceque je n'ai rien à vous dire.*"

123

*   *   *

"Peace, peace, Mercutio, peace! Thou talk'st of nothing."
—*Romeo and Juliet*

❁

HORACE WALPOLE ON HIMSELF

❁

The young Walpole, aged 25, August 20, 1743, in a letter to John Chute. Subject: his own fastidious self.

"I am so far from growing used to mankind by living amongst them, that my natural ferocity and wildness does but every day grow worse. They tire me, they fatigue me; I don't know what to do with them; I don't know what to say to them; I fling open the windows, and fancy I want air; and when I get by myself, I undress myself, and seem to have had people in my pockets, in my plaits, and on my shoulders!"

❀

EPISTLE TO HORACE

❀

"My great ambition is not to grow cross."
—From a letter of Horace Walpole

Horace, allow me to inquire
How far ambition got you? Not to grow
Cross is, you might say, anyone's desire
(Even the man who is already so).
Yet as I read your letter, I'm regretful
Never to know, milord, with certainty
Whether it was more mellow or more fretful
You finally turned out to be.
  There was the gout, for one thing. Ah!
How did you learn with ripeness on your mind
To live with pain and leave a formula
For amiability behind?
There were the times, the strife, the day's disaster,
Which nature never wholly fitted you
To meet with patience like a saint in plaster.
There was the scorn, the ennui—then, too,
A chance remark of yours, not undismaying,
That blights and east winds follow the April spring.
I read it as another way of saying
With summer is no mellowing.
  Yet once determined, led by that ambition

To live serene, by living to fourscore
You proved tenacious, Horace. In addition,
Of course, you died a bachelor,
And the heart's yearning hardly overwrought you
As it perturbed the lady. In one letter,
"O, let us love each other," she besought you.
"I do not think we could do better."

   Two passions that you did avow (not many)
Sound fairly cheerful, if a little pale:
A love for lilacs, affable as any,
A feeling for the nightingale.
And these—with wealth besides and leisure—
Tend to persuade me you grew less a scold
Than imperturbable at last, in measure.
But since you left the end of it untold,
And since men are ambitious, I've no doubt
The only thing to do is toss
A coin to say how mellow you turned out.
I hope not cross, Horace. Not very cross.

❀

VOLTAIRE ON THE SOUL

❀

Voltaire, in a letter to James Boswell, February 11, 1765.
Subject: Soul.

"You seem sollicitous about that pretty thing call'd Soul. I
do protest you, I know nothing of it: nor wether it is, nor what it

is, nor what it shall be. Young scolars, and priests, know all that perfectly. For my part, I am but a very ignorant fellow.

"Let it be what it will, I assure you my soul has a great regard for your own."

❀

SYDNEY SMITH

ON HOW TO AVOID LOW SPIRITS

❀

Sydney Smith, in a letter to Lady Georgiana Morpeth:

Foston, Feb. 16th, 1820

Dear Lady Georgiana,

... Nobody has suffered more from low spirits than I have done—so I feel for you.

1. Live as well as you dare.

2. Go into the shower-bath with a small quantity of water at a temperature low enough to give you a slight sensation of cold, 75° or 80°.

3. Amusing books.

4. Short view of human life—not further than dinner or tea.

5. Be as busy as you can.

6. See as much as you can of those friends who respect and like you.

7. And of those acquaintances who amuse you.

8. Make no secret of low spirits to your friends, but talk

of them freely—they are always worse for dignified concealment.

9. Attend to the effects tea and coffee produce upon you.

10. Compare your lot with that of other people.

11. Don't expect too much from human life—a sorry business at the best.

12. Avoid poetry, dramatic representations (except comedy), music, serious novels, melancholy sentimental people, and everything likely to excite feeling or emotion not ending in active benevolence.

13. *Do good,* and endeavour to please everybody of every degree.

14. Be as much as you can in the open air without fatigue.

15. Make the room where you commonly sit, gay and pleasant.

16. Struggle by little and little against idleness.

17. Don't be too severe upon yourself, or underrate yourself, but do yourself justice.

18. Keep good blazing fires.

19. Be firm and constant in the exercise of rational religion.

20. Believe me, dear Lady Georgiana. . . .

❀

RICHARD STEELE TO HIS WIFE

❀

My choice of impassioned love letters is any letter to Prue
from Richard Steele. Their charm is brevity. Prue, busy at
home, would have time to enjoy a note like this—the
sweetest protestation a lady may receive:

March 28th 1713

Dear Prue
   I will do every thing you desire your own way.

Yrs Ever
Richard Steele

❀

DEAR PRUE

❀

(From her obliged, obedient servant,
Richard Steele)

At noon he wrote her to remind
A lady to be lovingkind,

Alert, by afternoon, for him,
Expectant in the interim
Of evening, hopeful of the night.
He wrote at intervals, contrite,
Impassioned, when it would occur
To him, so languishing for her,
From Button's Coffee House, from town,
To set a protestation down.
The more convivial he grew
The oftener he sighed, "Dear Prue,"
And in forlorn dispatches said
He pined to be with her abed,
Would fly, within a pint of wine—
Another and another line
Of desperation, words that were
Rhapsodic of return to her,
Enough to fill a modest tome.
Instead of simply going home,
The mail brought Richard Steele. (Dear Prue,
I wonder which he meant to do.)

❀

MARGARET PASTON

TO HER HUSBAND

❀

Margaret Paston, in the fifteenth century, was a loving
and obedient wife who yearned to please, as in this letter of
March, 1454, "to be delivered in haste."

Right worshipful husband,

I recommend me to you, beseeching you that you be not displeased with me, though my simpleness caused you for to be displeased with me; by my truth it is not my will neither to do nor say that should cause you for to be displeased, and if I have done, I am sorry thereof, and will amend it; wherefore I beseech you to forgive me, and that ye bear none heaviness in your heart against me, for your displeasure should be too heavy to me to endure with.

THE NEW LETTER WRITER

"Complete automation comes to letter writing.
Now you can write, address, and sign as many as
3,000 letters per hour."—From an advertisement

The trouble is, I hardly know,
Intimately, 3,000 people.
At most I've counted 6 or 8,
Which seems a lot, a gracious number,
To whom in letters I might owe
I might with love communicate.

And yet it being in my power
To send at random now epistles
To 30,000? by the day,
To everybody, by the hour,

Vowing my love by automation—
Sweet automatic words to say—

I need but learn the gentle art
Of meaning, 50 times per minute,
The same love letter from my heart
With the same protestation in it
That I am yours, collectively.
So far, the thought depresses me.

BRANDEIS AND THE COMIC SPIRIT

In June I was invited to Brandeis University to take part in a panel discussion of the Comic Spirit. The invitation alarmed rather than tempted me, but the idea of such a theme for sober discussion gave me a lifting pleasure for days. Perhaps the best thing to do in an age of anxiety is to stop and investigate the Comic Spirit. I don't know exactly what it is, unless it is perpetual gaiety of heart, vitality, gusto, something like that, the opposite of the tragic view of life. I know only certainly that it exists and I'm for it.

George Meredith wrote a rather flat essay on its uses, not as one of the possessors. Chaucer had it in abundance, Aristophanes, Horace, Rabelais, Cervantes, Molière. Falstaff fairly exuded it, and my Uncle Toby, the Wife of Bath, Parson Adams, Mr. Micawber. These were the life enhancers, the rejoicers. Who in this angry world has it now? I should have gone to find out.

ON GUSTO

The essay of Hazlitt's I turn to most often is the little piece "On Gusto." I reread it because I like gusto, in people and in books, and think of it as a necessity of life. Unhappy as Hazlitt was, he knew its virtue and was willing to settle for gusto in the end.

The great artists always possess gusto. Hazlitt notes its effect in Titian: "Not only do his heads seems to think—his bodies seem to feel." There is life in his pictures: the flesh is real flesh and the blood circulates.

Michelangelo had gusto, of course, or vitality, or relish, or whatever it is. They all had it, of necessity. "Whenever we look at the hands of Correggio's women or of Raphael's," says Hazlitt, "we always wish to touch them."

So it is with the poets: they make the flesh come alive. They convey their own appetite for life. Chaucer's unrepentant Wife, with her bold red face and loud prattling, her colt's tooth, is no mere invention; she is turbulent with living and she means to the heart what she cries so lustily, "Blessed be God that I have wedded fyve!"

With perfect gusto, the Nurse tells and retells a charming story of Juliet, how the child tumbled on her head one day when she was only learning to walk:

"...she broke her brow;
And then my husband—God be with his soul!
A' was a merry man—took up the child:
'Yea,' quoth he, 'dost thou fall upon thy face?
Thou wilt fall backward when thou hast more wit;
Wilt thou not, Jule?' and, by my holidame,
The pretty wretch left crying and said 'Ay.'
To see, now, how a jest shall come about!
I warrant, an I should live a thousand years,
I never should forget it: 'Wilt thou not, Jule?' quoth he;
And, pretty fool, it stinted and said 'Ay.' "

    LADY CAPULET. "Enough of this: I pray thee, hold thy peace."

    NURSE. "Yes, madam: yet I cannot choose but laugh,
To think it should leave crying and say 'Ay.'
And yet, I warrant, it had upon its brow
A bump as big as a young cockerel's stone;
A parlous knock; and it cried bitterly:
'Yea,' quoth my husband, 'fall'st upon thy face?
Thou wilt fall backward when thou comest to age;
Wilt thou not, Jule?' it stinted and said 'Ay.' "

❀

THE BIRD IN HAND

❀

I was happy for no reason.
There was no reason.
Much that I saw distinctly was never so at all.
The sun itself was nearer pearl than topaz,
Yet it entangled me
In its blinding reality.

Topaz or gold,
Someday or the day after,
Is high noon of the sort I might have waited for.
Yet if the heavens served, unreasonably,
What was the use to wait
Till the time was appropriate?

❊

THE FURIES

❊

Three in number.
Three against one,
After me in unison.
Dames of wrath whose ire converges,
Faith, Hope, Charity with scourges,
The "compassionate" ones, who hasten
To lash and bloody me and chasten—

Save me! from Furies kind as these,
The terrible Eumenides,
Implacable to him who errs,
Of vengeance the deliverers,
Whose rage is righteous rage.
SAVE ME!
A sinner, from their clemency.

✿

THE WISDOM OF WILLIAM MORRIS

✿

When I look at my own house, I think wistfully of the good sense that William Morris would teach me. He once said (in a lecture on "The Beauty of Life"),

"... if you want a golden rule that will fit everybody, this is it: *Have nothing in your houses that you do not know to be useful or believe to be beautiful.*"

I choose to believe that the advice rules out most gadgets. It meets Thoreau halfway in the matter of simplicity. It echoes the Greeks, whose possessions had both utility and grace. It mixes, as Horace said, the *utile* with the *dulce*.

Where, then, is the time and skill for the acquiring of beautiful saucepans, or of stirring spoons that stir the soul?

❀

THOREAU'S SIMPLICITY

❀

It was Henry S. Canby, in his biography *Thoreau,* who made me understand Thoreau's kind of simplicity.

"The dominant idea of *Walden,*" Mr. Canby says, "which is simple, has been abundantly misunderstood. Thoreau's problem is the poor student's (or artist's or scientist's) who wishes to study, investigate, create, in a society which will not pay him enough for the proceeds of his labor, and is not interested in his brand of happiness. His solution is self-reliance, simplification of living, willingness to labor with the hands if necessary, resignation of everything not essential to his particular temperament, and a shrewd study of how he can provide for his sustenance with the least waste of time. This solution is worthless, however, unless it brings with it an expansion of every taste, interest, vocation, and avocation which is possible to the experimenter, wished for by him, and practicable in a life of disciplined simplicity. Walden calls for more life, not less....

"If you wish to get married, if you love good wine, if you must live in a library, or go to Europe, or belong to a country club—these are merely the terms of your problem. The principle is the same—simplify in what is not necessary for your content."

*　　　*　　　*

"You must get your living by loving," Thoreau said.
"Do what you love," he said. "Pursue your life."

❈

DO WHAT YOU LOVE

❈

"Do what you love," he said. "Pursue your life."
And having no mind for trifles, or a wife,
He borrowed a narrow axe and built his hut
To live alone in, loving aloneness. But,
Aware of preferences like yours and mine,
"Do what you love," he said, and cut white pine
And shaped his own world, one within his means,
Then in a smaller clearing planted beans.

Even for love, he schemed and raised more fuss
Than would occur offhand to most of us,
Desiring more: The time for sitting still.
Companion of the loon and whippoorwill.
A margin to his days. The woods. The pond.
Room to pursue and circle, look beyond,
Look to his life. For Thoreau would improve
The nick of time, he said, and in it move.

And screaming jays, each bullfrog, came to be
Part of this beautiful economy.

GREEK SIMPLICITY

Yet simplicity itself, one may easily recognize, is far from simple.

J. A. K. Thomson (in his book *Irony*) describes the Ironical simplicity of a Greek writer like Herodotus. He calls it a profound simplicity which is neither naïve and childlike in its experience, nor false, but artistic and more than a little touched with irony. He says: "We hear much of Greek plainness and Greek simplicity. Let us not forget that these virtues would never produce the effect they do if the simplicity were only simple and the plainness merely plain."

*   *   *

". . . and the jealousy of God is manifest in this," wrote Herodotus (with Ironical simplicity), "that he has let us taste the sweetness of life."

MARCUS AURELIUS ON SIMPLICITY

It is hard to say whether the simplicity recommended by Marcus Aurelius is nearer to that of Herodotus or of Thoreau. It agrees with both:

"Some seek for themselves private retiring places, as country villages, sea-shores, mountains. . . . But this (thou must know) proceeds from an extravagant simplicity. For at what time soever thou wilt, it is in thy power to retire into thyself, dwelling within the walls of a city as on a sheepfold in the hills. And the true man is he who, mixing with his fellows, gently maintains the independence of his soul."

And again: "Let no man have it in his power to say of you with truth, that you lack simplicity or goodness; make it a lie for anyone to think this of you. It is within your power: for who can hinder you from being good and simple?"

"Be content with what you have—find there your principles of life."

THE UTTER SIMPLICITY OF DIOGENES

It was Diogenes
Who asked the inestimable boon
That no shadow fall between
Him and the shining sun,

Who at even a conqueror's
Shadow drew the line,
Requiring of Alexander
"Stand out of my sunshine"—

The same Diogenes
Who looked for an honest man
In shadows, with a lantern
That lighted him in vain,

And having in darkness proven
Nowhere an honest one,
Rested with no man's shadow
Between him and the sun.

✽

A SIMPLE MAN OF ATHENS

✽

I hear your voice in my ear
(My mind's ear, O Hippoclides)
Saying, "Remember me."

I remember Hippoclides
Who was young and in love, a suitor
For the hand of Agariste.

Heartheavy was his desire
To take for his own this well-wooed
Daughter of Clisthenes,

And hot was his resolve
To outrival all the others
Whose fever it was to win her.

Alas. In Hippoclides
Burned the competitive spirit
Fiercer than in most men,

So fierce a blaze at the feasting
Given by Clisthenes
For the lovers of Agariste—

Where the victor would be chosen—
That Hippoclides, aspiring
To stun and astonish, did so.

First ordering flutes, he danced madly,
Atwirl, like a nimble flea.
Then seeing the guests confounded

And old Clisthenes apoplectic,
He stood on his head on the table.
He waved both legs in the air.

"O son of Pisander," down-thundered
The voice of the loved one's father,
"You have danced away your marriage!"

I remember Hippoclides,
How in love he was and how shaken
At the loss of Agariste,

How enlightened of having made
A fool of himself in vain.
But, more and more, I remember

That cool and splendid loser
Who, legs in air, simply answered,
"Hippoclides doesn't care."

*   *   *

The fine tale of the wooing of Agariste is told by Herodotus. Hippoclides, he says, was the favorite picked to win
the girl, excelling as he did all the other suitors in beauty
and wealth, until at the banquet he tried too hard and outdid himself. Agariste then married a man named Megacles.

THE MOTTOES OF ISAK DINESEN

❁

I see by *The New York Times* that Isak Dinesen on a visit to America spoke to the Institute of Arts and Letters in New York. I especially admire the title of her lecture, "Mottoes in My Life." That is a likely subject, full of inspiration. One of her wisest mottoes in a long life, she says, was "*Pourquoi pas?*" Another (along with the rest of us) was "This too will pass."

I have stayed awake tonight trying to remember mottoes of my own. There have been dozens, but a favorite few have lasted longer than the rest as maxims or rules of conduct. For some reason they are often in French.

There is Montaigne's "*Je ne fais rien sans gayété.*" And "*La vie est un songe.*"

There is Thoreau's "Do what you love."

There is one B. taught me when I first knew him. He wrote it into my notebook one day as we sat together in an English class at Columbia. Now when I finally stop to ask him the source of this elegant motto, he says he found it in *The Cloister and the Hearth: "Courage, mon camarade, le diable est mort."*

Perhaps the best one, the most useful of all, is a lovely line from the Old English poem "Deor's Lament." Deor was a minstrel who lost his place to another minstrel and consoled himself in his misery by thinking of the trials and misfortunes of others; and by saying, "That he surmounted. So this may I."

❃

THE BETTER PROVERB

❃

Better a feather in the hand
Than birds of plumage in the sky.

Better a puddleful of moon
Than heaven if a cloud pass by.

Better a sleeping wood than owls,
Better no worse a world than this.

Better a snotty child than his
Nose wiped off. As the saying is,

Better than the antithesis.

WHAT IS A MAN?

"What a piece of work is a man!" reflects Hamlet. ". . . the beauty of the world! the paragon of animals!"

"A poor forked animal," cries King Lear.

"A monkey shaved," observes W. S. Gilbert.

"The glory, jest, and riddle of the world!" exclaims Pope.

*   *   *

Plato defined a man: a two-legged animal without feathers. But Diogenes plucked a cock and brought it into the Academy and said, "This is Plato's man." For this reason, an addition had to be made to the definition: "with broad flat nails."

—DIOGENES LAËRTIUS

※

MONTAIGNE AND MOI-MÊME

※

Montaigne's writings reflect everywhere his long look at himself as a man. It was the great study of *moi-même,* and about himself he said he was the most learned man alive. "We must try," wrote Montaigne, "to cultivate our own authenticity."

*　　　*　　　*

"I judge of my condition," he said, "only by what I actually feel and not by my fears and reasoning. Would you like to know how much I gain? Look at those who behave otherwise."

"I speak truth, not my bellyful but as much as I dare: and I dare a little the more as I grow older."

"I pay little attention to the particular stone I stumble over, but I learn to suspect my gait throughout, and try to steady myself."

"I try to become as agreeable as I see others offensive, as constant as others are fickle, as gentle as others are gruff, and as decent as others are unspeakable. But I have set myself an impossible goal."

"When I dance, I dance; when I sleep, I sleep. When I stroll in an orchard, sometimes my thoughts wander to other things, but again they return to my walk, the orchard, the sweetness of solitude, and to myself."

"I have never seen a greater monster or miracle in the world than myself."

"My métier and my art is to live."

✻

MYSELF

✻

(After worrying over a piece of dialogue in *Tristram Shandy*)

And who are you? said he.
Don't puzzle me, said I.
Montaigne, for one, has given a soberer reply.

Montaigne knew who he was
All right. He was "*Moi-même,*"
Which any man might argue was also true of him,

Save that becoming oneself
Is uphill work to be,
Like Montaigne to speak out one's authenticity,

Like Thoreau to offer
A strong dose of oneself.
With individualists, like these, on the shelf,

Whose reality was real,
Who always, beyond doubt,
Had an identity and nothing to worry about—

Why am I left still baffled, echoing with a sigh,
And who are you? said he.
Don't puzzle me, said I.

*   *   *

Anything that Laurence Sterne said, I suppose, ought to be taken with a grain of salt.

Once Miss Monckton, a friend of Dr. Johnson's, had the rare courage to speak to him in praise of the writings of Sterne. "I am sure they have affected *me*," she said.

"Why, that is because, dearest, you're a dunce," said Dr. Johnson.

❀

ON GROWING RIPE

❀

"Men must endure
Their going hence, even as their coming hither:
Ripeness is all."

Ripeness is all. There is the tragic view of life, as Edgar recognized it and spoke in anguish, crying out the bitter truth in *King Lear*. At the end of life, ripeness is all there

In the same world, the comic view exists as well, wholly different but perhaps in its way as useful and as real. It says: Ripeness is enough. It is the view that Chaucer's old Reeve takes as he defines the way to become, in time's own fullness, a ripe man:

"To have an hoor heed and a grene tayl,
As hath a leek."

❃

LIGHT AND AIRY

❃

"I fancy that I grow light and airy. A man that does not begin to grow light and airy at seventy is certainly losing time if he intends ever to be light and airy."

—Dr. Johnson in a letter to Mrs. Thrale, 1779

To sweeten life a little
He feigned, oh, not Ariel's
Nimbleness in the air.
But, to be plausible,

Inventing a light heart,
He wrote to Mrs. Hester
Airy as an old bird
Or as a dancing master.

So to belie the years
By playful commonplaces,
As if unscathed by time
He harped on airs and graces,

With tidings that, of him,
Surely astonished her—

Poor Dr. Johnson become,
Of all things, airier.

And yet she must have known
How an old man pretends
To frolic in the wild gales,
In the fierce and terrible winds.

❁

OF WAYS TO DIE

❁

Even in finding a way to die, a man may be very resource-
ful. Aeschylus, for example, was killed when a turtle fell on
his bald head from the claws of an eagle in the air. Henry
I died of a surfeit of lampreys. Anacreon choked to death on
a grape. Rilke died of the scratch of a rose. Montaigne came
to die, as he said he would, not of the stone but of having
been alive.

Now I read of Mr. Fox (Charles James Fox), who in his
own original fashion died of a languor. The London *Observer* of September 14, 1806, reported the event:

"Yesterday evening, at seven o'clock, an express arrived from
Chiswick, announcing the decease of this eminent character. It
appears that the languor with which he was afflicted on Friday,
continued to increase, till vitality became extinct."

*　　　*　　　*

The *Observer* failed to quote the supposed last words of Mr. Fox, which sound more than languorous; they sound really tired. To his wife he said at the end, "It don't signify, my dearest, dearest Liz."

* * *

Surely the longest title of a poem in existence has to do with Mr. Fox's death. It is Wordsworth's "Lines composed at Grasmere, during a walk one Evening, after a stormy day, the Author having just read in a Newspaper that the dissolution of Mr. Fox was hourly expected."

Mr. Fox was dying in Chiswick and Wordsworth was walking in Grasmere. He reflected thus:

> But when the great and good depart
> What is it more than this—
>
> That Man, who is from God sent forth,
> Doth yet again to God return?
> Such ebb and flow must ever be,
> Then wherefore should we mourn?

❀

THE DYING OF HENRY FIELDING

❀

On Wednesday, June 26, 1754, Henry Fielding took leave of his three small children and went to Lisbon to die. "On this day," he wrote, "the most melancholy sun I had ever beheld arose and found me awake at my house at Fordhook." Having by this time no use of his limbs, he had to be conveyed as a helpless invalid to the *Queen of Portugal* where he was hoisted aboard in a chair lifted with pulleys. That day Fielding was more than ever aware of the heartless ways of his fellow men. Once again he noted, though quite impersonally, the fact of their inhumanity. He heard their jeers and laughter as he was swung aboard the ship. In this fashion, aged forty-seven, a haggard man of frightful appearance, wasted with gout and dropsy, he began his last voyage:

"I think, upon my entrance into the boat, I presented a spectacle of the highest horror. The total loss of limbs was apparent to all who saw me, and my face contained marks of a most diseased state, if not of death itself. Indeed, so ghastly was my countenance, that timorous women with child had abstained from my house, for fear of the ill consequences of looking at me. In this condition I ran the gauntlope (so I think I may justly call it) through rows of sailors and watermen, few of whom failed of paying their compliments to me by all manner of insults and jests on my misery. No man who knew me will think I conceived any personal resentment at this behaviour; but it was a lively picture of that cruelty and inhumanity in the nature of men which I have often contemplated with concern, and which leads the mind into a train of very uncomfortable and melancholy thoughts."

*　　*　　*

Anaxagoras said to a man who was grieving that he was dying in a foreign land, "The descent to Hell is the same from every place."

—DIOGENES LAËRTIUS

✤

OF DEATH

✤

Jeremy Taylor, of death:

"It is the same harmless thing that a poor shepherd suffered yesterday, or a maid-servant today; and at the same time in which you die, in that very night a thousand creatures die with you, some wise men, and many fools. And the wisdom of the first will not quit him, and the folly of the last does not make him unable to die."

*   *   *

"*Dieu me pardonnera,*" said the dying Heine. "*C'est son métier.*" But whether he meant that to forgive is merely God's profession and His business, or that with so wide an experience it is the thing God does best of all, His peculiar talent, I cannot say.

*   *   *

John Aubrey, in *Brief Lives,* wrote this of Isaac Barrow:

"As he laye unravelling in the agonie of death, the standers-by could hear him say softly, *I have seen the glories of the world.*"

157

✿

THE JOURNEY IS EVERYTHING

✿

Now as B. and I set out in September for Europe for the fifth time, I wonder if I have learned anything at all about travel. One thing I know and rather regret is that I always have to take myself along. When I walk, say, the streets of Seville, the person there is I, a fact more uneasy and far more bothersome in Spain than at home where I am used to it. There I prefer to become a new self who speaks Spanish perfectly, looks at the world with dark smoldering eyes, and wears a mantilla.

I know also, because Montaigne has taught me, that it is not the arrival anywhere, nor is it the eventual return, that matters: the journey itself is the idea. One need not be concerned, he says, about where one is to spend the night (a lesson I have learned imperfectly so far), for when a wise man travels it is his destination that concerns him least of all.

"The journey," says Montaigne, "is everything."

❁

RETURN TO LONDON

❁

On the first day of my return to London, I have seen the most splendid and extraordinary sights:

A little Anglia with the number plate JOY 940.

A long queue at Trafalgar Square beside a street sign that warns, in large letters, "No Waiting."

The royal banner flying over Buckingham Palace to say the Queen is at home.

Two green hotwater bottles and a two-foot refuse container for tea leaves, labeled "Tea Leaves," in the bathroom.

Ye Olde Curiosity Snack Bar.

The pub called "The Windsor Castle," near Victoria Station, made modern and stylish by an additional entrance, "The Windsor Castle Dive."

A book advertisement in the London *Times* for *Fifty Years of Birdwatching, Its Successes and Failures.*

A defense in the Manchester *Guardian* of the right of citizens to compose whatever epitaphs they please for their own tombstones.

A FIRST DAY IN LONDON

❀

The sights I saw! There was a little Anglia
Wearing the number plate JOY 940.

A bespoke tailor shop. A pelican
Walking as I was in St. James's Park.

I found three letters in the London *Times*
Ending, "I am, Sir, your obedient servant,"

And seagulls' eggs, for lunch at the Savoy,
Elegantly served hardboiled with finger bowl,

Then wandered to the Thames and the Embankment
To look at gulls in guilty recollection.

Chrysanthemums were in bloom in window boxes,
The trees were full of starlings by the river.

A Mrs. Dingle on the bench beside me
Showed me the bridges and the Lambeth Palace.

I drank tea at the Dorchester, I dined
On roast beef on the Strand with English mustard,

Stayed for the final feature at the Odeon:
"God Save the Queen" (11:24),

And took to bed a green hotwater bottle
At midnight, in the chill of my hotel room.

❁

THE BIRD WATCHER

❁

Birdwatchers are a passionate and devoted lot. One of them lives at the Hotel Sandringham where we are staying. He is a retired naval commander, a bachelor of the gentlest mien, and that odd type of Englishman who appears to care almost exclusively about birds. Hampstead Heath, just around the corner from us, is this watcher's watching place; or, for nightingales, Epping Forest or Virginia Water. But he likes, too, simply to sit at the window of his room and watch for any kind of little bird to hop upon his sill.

This morning at breakfast, as I looked up to see him arrive in the dining room, his air was so gratified that I thought, "What can he have seen now, a cuckoo?" Greeting me with a delighted "Good morning," he leaned across his small table to speak softly to me at mine. "My dear," he said in his benign way, "may I—if you have finished your breakfast, of course—may I invite you to come up with me to my room? I have a treat for you. I think I can show you a perfectly splendid tit."

✻

A BOOK WITH MY NAME

✻

In the British Museum Reading Room, I have found a book that bowls me over. The title is *Helen Bevington. A True Story.* It was written by an unidentified E. E. and published in London in 1868. After discovering it by accident in the catalogue, I enjoyed startling the desk attendant by signing the call slip with my name in two places: the title of the book wanted and the reader who wanted it. Unless there are other Helen Bevingtons now alive, and they are literate, I am probably the only person on the planet who covets this book, a fearsomely sentimental novel of unparalleled dullness. Yet finding it is like finding oneself as a small and dusty exhibit in a great museum.

✻

JULES RENARD

✻

I met Jules Renard in the British Museum today in a book. It was a quick friendship. I came across his *Histoires Naturelles* (in translation) and saw on every page what a highly amiable man he was. Jules Renard, who died in 1910, was an amused observer, one who at night counted over his images like coins before going to sleep.

Of the sparrow hawk he said, "One would think he hung from the sky by a thread. Suddenly the thread snaps, the hawk falls . . ."

The pigeon: "All their lives they remain rather stupid. They will believe that children are got by billing and coo-ing."

The elephant: "He is almost lost in baggy trousers that have been hitched too high, and a little bit of string hangs down behind."

The goat: "His odor goes on in front. After it has arrived one still doesn't see him."

The adder: "What belly has dropped this ache?"

The ant: "Every one of them is like the figure 3. And there are so many of them . . . so very many . . . 33333 33333333 . . . to infinity."

*   *   *

Maurice Ravel set a group of these delightful animal portraits to music, one of them *Le Cygne:* "He glides on the pond like a white sleigh, from cloud to cloud." André Gide observed fretfully of Jules Renard that he used the *mot juste,* but always in pizzicato.

�֎

THE READING ROOM,

BRITISH MUSEUM

✤

I was warned of thieves. When I became a Reader,
Or ticket holder, of the Reading Room
(Which seats 393 such holders
Of season passes, any one of whom
Could be a rogue or scholar, we may assume),

They cautioned me. Such articles of value
As I possessed—the ornaments of my mind?
My little fund of knowledge?—must be guarded,
For thieves, they said, take any wealth they find.
And yet, what kind of thief was this? What kind

Would pick my brain for gold and not my pocket?
Lightfingered of ideas, would he come
To pilfer one as poor as he, a Reader,
Who never had ideas too burdensome,
Or knew where her next thought was coming from?

Or was the loot he wanted not mine, either?
But lying upon my desk, unguarded, free—
The shiny precious stuff, the coin, the treasure,
The beauty and truth a thief would weep to see,
And yet could come by only honestly.

✿

TURNERS IN THE TATE

✿

Today B. and I walked among the Turners in the Tate Gallery, particularly to view his gold explosive sunrises. Somebody has said that they look exactly like a fried egg on a plate.

They dazzle. I have the impression of Turner fearlessly lifting his morning face at dawn to stare straight into the sun. As it begins to rise higher and higher in yellow brilliance, he blinds himself to try to catch the glory of it. The tears come to his eyes, his vision blurs like his canvas, and he hurries to paint what is altogether too bright for a man to dare to contemplate, the sun itself.

✿

TURNER'S SUNRISE

✿

I miss the sun. Especially this winter
In London is a famine of the sun.
One reads the *Times* for glitter in Majorca,
For news of Naples being shone upon,
Sunlight in Tunis, and is no contenter.

167

Or one looks twice at emeralds and sapphires
In Bond Street windows, in the London mists;
Or wanders through the Tate, where sun exists
In retrospect—as liquid fire to Turner,
And as a god to the Impressionists.

There one is like the visitor who stood
With Turner once before a gold sunrise,
Questioning its verisimilitude.
It was no sun that he could recognize.
"But," answered Turner, "don't you wish you could?"

❀

KARL MARX AT HIGHGATE

❀

It's hard to believe that Karl Marx lived for thirty-five
years in London, more than half his life. After being tried
in Prussia for high treason, acquitted but exiled in 1849, he
first sought refuge in Paris. The French, reluctant to let him
stay, said he could remain only if he lived in some small provincial town. But England was both generous and indifferent. She took Karl Marx in and forgot him. He lived in
London in poverty, worked daily in the British Museum, and
when he died was buried in utter obscurity beside an outer
wall in the Highgate Cemetery.

Last Saturday at Highgate, in a bleak November mist,
B. and I found the new grave of Karl Marx, where he has

been moved recently to a place more befitting the fame of the most splendid resident there. The late afternoon was drizzling and lonely. The look of it was a desolate gray, even to the few pale seagulls in the deepening sky. How handsome the new grave was, covered with bright wreaths, flanked by imposing tombstones! Karl Marx now lay in state, across the narrow path from the ashes of Herbert Spencer.

❀

THE COLD IN LONDON

❀

This afternoon is the first time I have felt glacial all winter in London. It was at the sight of my own breath in the Murrays' icy living room. There was a blazing fire and plenty of hot tea. The curtains were drawn, the doors were shut for warmth, and in the English fashion one window was thrown wide open to keep us alert and healthy.

My breath in that chill temperature embarrassed me by emerging in large puffs, as if my thoughts were steamy. The puff increased to a spout when I spoke, like the balloons in comic strips, and I was sorry I had nothing comical to say. Since Mrs. Murray's remarks were very misty, too, our talk together became a visible and fascinating performance. Words hung between us and mingled before they finally dissolved into nothingness. Only people with their heads in the clouds have a right to speak in this nebulous way.

LONDON FOG

I always wanted to see a real London fog, the kind that Dickens called a London Particular. In the end, after two winters spent here, I have had enough of that chilling, shadowy, terrible vapor that comes right into the house to live with you and stays chokingly in the throat, tasting of soft coal. For days the newspaper stories of a fog are spectacular, how a man spent the night in a telephone box on his own street, unable to grope his way home, and so on. If you dare to venture out, there are ghosts wearing nose masks who loom up frighteningly, and it is courting death to cross the street. There is no escape; you are enveloped, blinded, lost like a damned soul forever in a thick, dense, vaporous hell.

The only thing to do, if it can be reached, is to go to the nearest pub. The Coach and Horses, our local, is the pleasantest place I know in which to be fogbound. It is like being in a small lifeboat with no rescue in sight but with plenty of good company, warm beer, a blazing coal fire, jars of cut red roses, and the inextinguishable Mrs. Ellen Totten herself as barmaid.

A stranger stopped me in the High Street lately after one of these Particulars, bowed, and said, "I beg your pardon, but aren't you the American lady who likes our fogs?"

A WINDOWFUL OF LONDON

There are the spires of chimney pots
To say it's London—and St. Paul's
Gray dome to prove it on clear days.

More often, in the fogs and haze,
What's clear is the absurdity
Of all my windowful of view

And nothing visible to see,
Except a pigeon, one or two,
Except sometimes the wheel of gulls

That dive and vanish in the waves
Of mist, from Highgate to St. Paul's.
Only if I look down, below,

Is there the clarity of walls
And Brussels sprouts (a small green row)
In one back garden, which becomes

A guide to London, and a view.
Because my vistas hitherto
Have been like this, not grand or many—

A pear tree like the pear below,
An old man spearing leaves—it seems
As good a windowful as any.

❄

GORKY'S FILM

❄

Last night in London I saw a Russian film called "My Universities," taken from the last volume of Maxim Gorky's trilogy of autobiography. There was a particular word in the picture that enlightened and taught me. At a grievous period of Gorky's young manhood, during his bitter education in poverty, man's inhumanity, man's ignorance, man's hopelessness, he became so lost in despair that he tried to end his life. Afterwards, he lay many months in hospital with a bullet wound in his chest, so long that slowly he had time to recover a belief in life and in himself. It was then he made up his mind to live, as he later wrote, "a long and stubborn life."

The word *stubborn* was the revelation.

THE WORD "JOLLY"

❀

Britons use the word *jolly* so often as a counter word to describe anything that it becomes ludicrous. Yesterday at the rental library of Boots the Chemist, an elderly book borrower launched upon a long, anguished account to the librarian of the recent illness and death of his elderly dog. The man was distracted by grief, and the tears that stood in his eyes moved his listener to a very real sympathy.

"That's jolly sad," she murmured.

❀

FREE BOOKS AT HARDING'S

❀

Harding's bookshop on Great Russell Street in London deserves a brass plaque for its heroic efforts to tempt people to read books. Outside their front door this winter, on a shelf of books much reduced in price, there is one sizable collection bearing the inviting sign: "These books are free. Take one."

Among them is an almost complete set of George Meredith, the volumes battered but readable. Though I pass the shop daily on my way to the British Museum, I have never yet seen a passer-by step up and carry a book off under his arm. Nor have I done so myself. I like Meredith, but as a foreigner from a capitalist country I feel reluctant to benefit from England's socialized schemes, her free medical care and free books. I think I ought to pay at least sixpence for a copy of *The Ordeal of Richard Feverel.* In the end I have put off rereading it a while longer.

❀

THE LONDON TIMES, 1798

❀

Better than history books, I like to read old copies of newspapers. This morning I read today's London *Times* and the *Times* for October 3, 1798, which a friend lent me. To-day's news is stuffy by comparison.

On page one of the *Times* of 160 years ago, a live male elephant, about three years old, is offered for sale at twelve o'clock noon tomorrow in London, together with 1095 elephant's teeth.

A reward of two hundred pounds will be given for information leading to the capture of a young highwayman who robbed a postboy near Farnborough. The rogue dashed up on a horse with a white face, presented a horse-pistol, and rode off with the mail.

Last night an affray occurred opposite the Admiralty, and

the large surly mob to prove its power demanded that every man of genteel appearance take off his hat.

Major General Trench is in Ireland putting down a rebellion.

Mr. Pitt was seen walking in the park yesterday in perfect good health.

The King, Queen, and Princesses have been staying at Maiden Castle, watching the sports of the country people on a recent afternoon, such as:

A pound of tobacco to be grinned for.

A Michaelmasday goose to be dived for.

A pig, prize to whoever catches him by the tail.

On page two is the news of Admiral Nelson's glorious victory over the French Fleet off the mouth of the Nile. All this for sixpence.

❀

THE MOMENT

❀

We walked up Christchurch Hill
And the lupins were in flower,
All of three years ago.
I remember Christ Church bell
Ringing the quarter hour

And the moment reminding you
Of a painting by Matisse,
"*Luxe, calme et volupté.*"

175

You said he must have meant
This calm, this luxury,

And we laughed, remembering
Matisse's two lovers well—
Their starknakedness. I said
Then our portrait ought to say,
"*Luxe, calme et felicité.*"

❀

THE STATUE OF SHAKESPEARE

❀

Leicester Square is the once quiet, once handsome square, the fashionable address of Fanny Burney and of Sir Joshua Reynolds, who lived there in comfortable elegance in the eighteenth century. When I see it, I can think only of the words of the popular song, "Goodbye, Picadilly, Farewell, Leicester Square." It is noisy and turbulent now, heavy with traffic, laid out around a small dusty park of no visible charm, except that in the center of it there is a modest statue of Shakespeare. He stands leaning one arm upon the several volumes of his writings, while he looks with a quizzical eye toward the large, gaudy, neon-lighted movie houses, featuring Alec Guinness and Frank Sinatra, that surround him: the Empire, Odeon, Warner, and Leicester Square Theater.

They say that this is the only statue of Shakespeare in all London.

THE BARD IN LEICESTER SQUARE

❀

Isn't it odd, his statue being there
Among the picture palaces? And yet
You might expect a bard in Leicester Square

With *Richard III* now showing in VistaVision
(The neon sign skyrocketing in mid-air)
And Technicolor for the film revision.

Nearby, *The Ladykillers* (Odeon) brings
Vast London crowds—but nothing like his play
Of lust and murder and the death of kings,

A bloody entertainment fit for all,
Passed by the censors who have shut their eyes
To what is fearsome but historical,

Yet certify *The Tender Trap* "adult,"
In CinemaScope (the Empire), its appeal
Mature, perhaps, and moral difficult.

He ought to feel at home in Leicester Square,
Surrounded by the cinemas. Here the plot
Is spun by passion and no worse for wear,

The sweet and bitter fancy never stale.
Here all the people are familiar people,
Diverted by the sameness of the tale.

And here—a pigeon roosting on his brow—
Is still the Bard, who leans upon his works
And overlooks the scene before him now

As if to say, with musing emphasis,
The words of his dark film across the Square:
"All-seeing heaven, what a world is this!"

❀

THE MEETING OF
THE JOHNSON SOCIETY

❀

The Johnson Society of London met yesterday in, of all
places, the Lecture Gallery of the Alpine Club. Professor
James Clifford of Columbia University, the Johnson scholar
and a beloved member of this group, had secured an invitation for us. The doorman showed us the way. "You'll want
the Johnsonians," he said, not mistaking us for climbers just
back from scaling the Alps. We were the last to enter the
chilly little room before the meeting began.

Some forty people had come for Dr. Johnson's sake. There
was the elderly vicar in gaiters. Alone in the front row sat
a white-haired, red-faced old gentleman already asleep. I

counted three hearing aids. More than half the group consisted of elderly ladies in hats, scarves, gloves, fur coats, and overshoes. On the platform the chairman rose unsteadily to his feet and murmured a few words that provided no clue as to the subject of the lecture or the credentials of the lecturer. The speaker himself, who had a stammer, wore a disconcerting half-smile that came and went with little reference to what he had to say. During his reading of a paper on Dr. Johnson's dislike of the poet Thomas Gray (whom Johnson never met but whose Odes he found "dull upon stilts") the audience waited like a Greek chorus for its turn to speak. Or like Gilbert and Sullivan fans, they were ready with passages learned by heart. At the description of Johnson and Boswell as "a mountebank and his zany," they picked up the first word and sang out the phrase "and his zany" as if at a rally.

This was my first impression, and it was altogether wrong. I should know by this time not to trust to appearances in an English audience, no matter how fey. Here was a company of devotees, gathered to share admiration for (and knowledge of) a great man. There were distinguished scholars among them. The lecture was given by an eminent biographer of Gray. The meeting was chaired by the Master of a college at Cambridge. Once, at tea afterwards, when I ventured to mention a letter of Fanny Burney's (which I had been reading only the day before) about an accidental meeting with Boswell, a courtly gentlemen beside me said indulgently, "Yes, yes, charming piece. They met on a Sunday outside St. George's Chapel, as you remember."

DR. JOHNSON'S LESSON IN LOGIC

❀

Who drives fat oxen should himself be fat.
And who is fat himself should drive fat oxen.
Like Dr. Johnson, if I argue that
"Who drives fat oxen should himself be fat,"
Conversely, what is there to quibble at
Or, vice versa, seek a paradox in?
Who drives fat oxen should himself be fat,
And who is fat himself should drive fat oxen.

❀

THE DOORMAN AT THE ALPINE CLUB

❀

The kindly doorman of the Alpine Club evidently feared that, after two hours with the Johnsonians, I might forever confuse their learned Society with the Club itself, a far more rugged association of explorers and mountaineers. As I waited for B. to find his coat, the doorman beckoned me to follow him. He led me mysteriously down a passage into an inner library and with a flourish brought me up to the fireplace.

"There we are!" he cried proudly. "You may touch it, if you like, and make a wish."

He pointed to the mantelshelf where a tiny piece of rock was supported on, and almost overwhelmed by, a gleaming silver pedestal. The rock was a souvenir from the very summit of Mount Everest, a fragment that Richard Hillary had brought down in his pocket and presented to the Alpine Club. I touched it reverently.

❊

ADVENTURE AT THE ALPINE CLUB

❊

He pointed to the tiny piece of rock
Supported on a silver pedestal.
"Touch it," the stranger said, "and make a wish."

So I came closer to the mantelshelf
And, wishing, touched the relic lightly lest
It wear away from too much reverence.

It was, before my eyes, Mount Everest
(As even a saint's fingerbone is he),
The height, brought down by Hillary himself,

The conquered peak, now visible to me.
It was the quest but on a pedestal . . .
I could remember holding in my hand

Another relic a friend brought me once
Inside a matchbox. "Make a wish," he said,
And it, too, was a tiny piece of rock,

A bit of glassy radioactive sand,
Fused by the blast that he had helped set off
In the red desert of Los Alamos.

To touch and wish upon it, I suppose,
Was natural with either monument—
If one believes that wishing helps at all.

❀

A WALK ALONG THE CAM

❀

During the February evenings in Cambridge, we used to walk along the Cam. Whether the nights were misty and black, or, occasionally, moonlit and misty, the narrow path glistened as brilliantly as the water. It seemed that we followed a stream beside a stream, both winding into the darkness. There was nothing but the glitter at one's feet and, ahead, the tall poplars against the sky.

It reminded me of Pascal, "Rivers are roads which move." Soon after, when B. bought me a copy of *The Prelude* in London, I found Wordsworth's poetry about the same thing:

> the road's
> Watery surface glittered in the moon
> And seemed before my eyes another stream.

It troubles me to think that I might have tried to make that image, imperfectly, in a verse of my own. This is a solemn chance that one takes.

❃

A WALK TO GRANTCHESTER

❃

The village of Grantchester is only a few miles, three or four, across the Grantchester meadows in fen country, and through the turnstiles from Cambridge. B. and I walked there one February afternoon shortly after lunch. We delayed along the way to watch the hundreds of jackdaws in the pale-green meadows, but eventually we came up to the tiny village and to the churchyard in the center of it. There stood the large clock in the tower of Grantchester church. There stood the clock at *ten to three*. B. and I laughed. We stared and laughed again, pleased to think that a town would so admire its poet that it would stop the clock in his honor and memory.

> Stands the church clock at ten to three?
> And is there honey still for tea?

How long, we wondered, had it been stopped—since the poet's death in 1915? What would he himself have said to this piece of sentiment? There was no one about to tell us, and so we went on into the small Anglican church. A little later, thinking of our own tea at the end of the walk back to Cambridge, we stepped out into the churchyard and glanced again, rather absently, at the clock. Suddenly we knew that the ghost of Rupert Brooke had offered us greeting. The hands of the Grantchester clock had moved steadily on. They stood now at three-fifteen.

❀

A SITTING ROOM IN TRURO

❀

"I do not believe in ghosts," said Madame de Staël, "but I am afraid of them."

The two wispy old ladies, possibly mother and daughter, occupied the hotel sitting room in Truro. They had finished their tea and, ignoring our intrusion, continued to read loudly to each other as to someone quite deaf. The elder would choose a faded letter from the large mahogany box on the sofa between them. She would read with painstaking care, clearly and deliberately, shouting out each separate word with a stern emphasis: "I shall not be coming down to Cornwall in August. Your devoted nephew, Oliver."

After studying the signature, she would drop her head and slowly tear the letter once across, then, nodding to her companion, lay the two pieces on the tea tray. Immediately the other took her turn, speaking more tenderly but as succinctly, weighing the ghostly words as if every particle of the meaning must be got by heart: "It was so good to have tea with you on Thursday. Violet."

I saw how tiny the sheets were, like the tiny restrained messages. They tore easily, like old letters.

HOTEL SIGNS

A little hotel, or inn, where we have stayed for a week in England—the White Hart at Blechingley, in Surrey—states on the inn sign that it possesses and offers to its patrons "the amenities." This we have found to be altogether true. The White Hart has every amenity on hand that we need, or can recognize: it is pleasant and agreeable, it is comfortable, it has excellent manners, it is full of civility.

I remember that at home in Richmond, Virginia—a city whose billboards I know well from driving often between the North and the South—the Thomas Jefferson Hotel offers its guests "prestige." What new kind of amenity is this, I wonder? Nearby, the Hotel Raleigh promises "no conventions," which I certainly hope doesn't mean a lack of the social conventions, especially the fine old convention of morality. Perhaps this is only another way, after all, of observing the amenities.

SHEEP IN DUBLIN

❈

On our way this morning to St. Patrick's Cathedral in Dublin (the Anglican cathedral where Swift preached for some thirty-two years and Stella sat before him in the congregation), we stopped to read a street sign, printed in Gaelic and English in bold, admonitory letters. It said:

"Parents are requested not to allow their children to follow and beat sheep being driven through the streets."

The words called up a lovely pastoral image of the city, and thereafter I kept looking for sheep along the curb and roadside. Yet this may be a piece of Irish wit, or a sign left over from Swift's own day, for in all Dublin I have not seen so much as a stray lamb.

❀

A WALK ALONG THE LIFFEY

❀

B. and I have walked this whole day long beside the River Liffey, out Lucan way from Dublin, beside the lovely Anna Livia Plurabelle herself. Though B. did see some washing on a line, we didn't catch a glimpse of Joyce's two gossipy washerwomen on the opposite banks who tell her story, unless it may be that by now one was changed into a stone and the other into an elm tree.

"The chittering waters of," I kept thinking, "all them liffeying waters of. . . . I feel as old as yonder elm. . . . I feel as heavy as yonder stone. . . . Tell me, tell me, tell me, elm! . . . Beside the rivering waters of, hitherandthithering waters of."

*　　　*　　　*

Now I know the reason for this deep, incredible green, the color of shamrocks, and for the haunting sense one has that in Ireland the very *idea* of green first existed. In the early spring countryside, the brightest emerald moss runs up and down the trees. Everywhere, everything, from earth to sky, is a green blur.

❀

A LADY OF DUBLIN

❀

At the Standard Hotel, I met an aged lady,
An Irish Lady Somebody, jeweled and lonely.
What a proud old dame she was! One not to be crossed,
Not by Americans, certainly not by me.
I remember in the hotel lounge that evening
How, boasting of her knowledge of my country,
She swore Virginia was south of North Carolina;
And though I live in North Carolina myself,
I half agreed, in the face of such conviction.
There wasn't a map. So we left it south of, her way.
A map, or tears, would hardly have made a difference.

❀

THE HYACINTH FIELDS OF HAARLEM

❀

This is a day in April drowned in hyacinths. We drove for
miles beside the hyacinth fields near Haarlem, between
Haarlem and The Hague, past hundreds of acres filled with
masses of white, blue, lavender, pink flowering hyacinths.

Once we stopped, almost swooning with the perfume, and a gardener beckoned to us and filled our arms brimming full of them. We put them in the car, where they covered the whole back seat with great spikes of blossom, and we drove on till evening with this musky, heady fragrance accompanying us. It was hyacinth air that we breathed. We had hyacinth thoughts. They filled my nose and my mind so overpoweringly that, like Catherine Morland in *Northanger Abbey,* I might have said, "I have just learnt to love a hyacinth."

The Dutch housewives, too, must love these brilliant flowers, apparently without sickening of them. In every house beside the great hyacinth fields we saw bowls of bloom in the windows and on the doorstep, scenting up the lives of the farmer and his family. How is it that a man can work all day in the fields and then bear to come home to such sweetly odorous nights?

In the evening we delighted the hotel keeper at Dordrecht by presenting him with our carload of the still fresh hyacinths. Soon on our small table at dinner appeared an enormous bowl filled with them, at nose level, so that first the soup, then the fish, then the cheese had the distinct flavor of hyacinth. When we went to bed—oh no!—there they were, large masses of flowers in a jar under the window, perfuming the very moonlight in our room.

✺

TO-DO IN VENICE

✺

I learned the phrase in Paris for the noise of the motor cars, but it applies equally well to this uproar in Venice: *un tohu-bohu inimaginable.* The time is five in the afternoon, the Saturday before Easter, in the Piazza of St. Mark's. The municipal band plays, at the top of its brasses, music from *Parsifal.* The square overflows with flying pigeons and laughing people, nearly everyone a vivacious Italian in holiday mood. In and out of the glittering church of San Marco stream the devout, and the sun shines heavily down on them and on the gilded bronzes over the portal. All is movement and immense hurly-burly, broken suddenly, as the music crashes to a stop, by the loud, piercing chimes far above our heads of the great pealing bells of the Campanile. It is earsplitting. It is too much!

Then like the grand finale of the musical comedy, out from the harbor and down the square marches a brisk group of American sailors in their dazzling Navy whites. Behind them, just over their shoulders, looms the American cruiser the *Newport News,* a bright and sunlit flag flying triumphantly from its stern.

❋

A LADY OF SIENA

❋

They have so many old palaces in Siena
That we stayed in one ourselves: the Palazzo Rizzio,
Now only a bit decayed, like the old Marchesa.
You heard her muttering, "*Sì, sì, sì, sì, sì,*"
In a quick descending scale, all hours, to tourists,
Who tired of so much veal and no hot water.
And if at last you spoke, too, the Marchesa
Would shrug and answer, "*Sì, sì, sì, sì, SI!*"

❋

THE LEANING TOWER OF PISA

❋

To climb the Leaning Tower in the footsteps of Galileo, I
left the perpendicular at Pisa. It proved to be a poor idea to
deviate in this fashion, staggering about on the diagonal inside a round marble tower nearly eight hundred years old
that leans, so they tell in Pisa, sixteen feet off center these
dark days, more than in Galileo's golden time. Because the
tower was built in three sections, each in a different epoch,

the leaning is not even uniform. The thing slants from gallery to gallery—eight arcaded galleries in all up to the turret of the seven bells.

I was uniformly oblique, reeling all the way. Yet the summit, as in all sharp climbs, was worth the ascent. There, at last, was the spot from which the heavy bodies may well have plummeted. There was the Arno far below, and beyond the level plain of Tuscany rose the high-sloped Apennines. In the distance lay the blue Leghorn harbor and the sea. Up there, too, listing beside me, was an extremely pregnant Italian woman who, for some odd reason, with her own center of gravity upset, had chosen a leaning tower for a spring day's outing. Her beaming face was drowned in sweat and she panted hard from the awful struggle. Like the tower she leaned alarmingly, but *backwards,* in the opposite direction, and the sight completed the havoc in my head. It was dizzying beyond belief. Yet we nodded and smiled at each other, like two explorers who had scaled the heights and chanced to meet at the top of Mt. Everest.

"*Torre pendente,*" she whispered, with an expressive sigh.
"*Sì,*" I replied.

❀

A WOMAN IN ROME

❀

At the great door of St. Peter's, the woman paused
And, shifting the baby to her left arm, spread
A yellow handkerchief on its dark head.

192

Then murmuring to the child, its bobbing crown
Devoutly golden, its small bottom bare,
She hurried down the aisle to where the Saint
Rose in the vast cathedral—Peter there,
His foot worn smooth by kisses. Worshipfully,
The woman put the child's mouth to the stone,
Then knelt and added a hot kiss of her own.

❊

THE YOUNG AT HEART

❊

In the Musée d'Art Moderne in Paris, the upper floor is given over to the work of *Les Jeunes.* It made an enormous impression on me. Up there are the wonderful young, they who have everybody's style but their own, they who imitate the masters with impudent courage and bright, carefree exaggeration. Matisse is improved upon, and Picasso emerges with a strong touch of Chagall. Braque, Rouault, Miró, Paul Klee—all are copied but with splash and fling, at the same time overstated and outdone. The pictures are splendid and blinding, but embarrassingly alike. With so many of them together, they seem loud and a little vulgar. It is group art, of course, by *Les Jeunes,* where no man dominates the scene and no artist is an individual who has so far declared himself.

I see the same charming likeness when I read the young modern poets. Those whom we call the mid-century group are, even yet, the young at heart, *Les Jeunes.*

❀

THUS TO REVISIT

❀

I have learned this strange thing, too, about travel: one may return to a place and, quite unexpectedly, meet oneself still lingering there from the last time. This is especially true of visits to cathedrals. Inside the door, on the first flag-stone at the head of the center aisle, suddenly right at one's feet are one's own footsteps. With a shiver one steps gingerly into them. Twenty years ago a former, younger, more eager self stood (is it possible?) in the exact spot, trying to make permanent the memory of an overwhelming pleasure. The heart was beating a little fast then, remember? One was in love with a place, and with a number of other things as well.

For a moment or two the glimpse is disturbingly real. One stares around at the unchanging cathedral and thinks, "Oh, how young and how happy I was that day!"

A TOWN ON THE MEDITERRANEAN

We have traveled to the town of Hyères on the Côte d'Azur for the reason that Robert Louis Stevenson wrote some haunting words about it: "I was happy only once, and that was at Hyères." This seems to me sufficient reason for going anywhere—especially to such a place beside the blueness of La Mer, in a semicircle of hills under a brilliant gold sky. The almond trees are in blossom. It is a place of palms, especially, and cork trees, cypress, eucalyptus, fig, raisin, olive, mimosa. In the grass are grape hyacinths and *boutons d'or,* a kind of buttercup. The mistral is *modéré à assez fort.* At the restaurant "Chez Marius," the *omelette aux fines herbes* is a masterpiece. The people are fashionable, for Hyères is a small resort town beside the sea.

This week there has been a Carnival des Fleurs, with a procession of monstrous yet wildly happy faces on the huge painted figures bobbing along the Avenue des Iles d'Or. Sailors from Toulon laughed and threw confetti, stuffing it into the mouths of pretty girls as they passed.

But the pink stucco villas and the Romanesque churches, even on the Rue Paradis, are deeply pockmarked from machine-gun fire. On the *plage* is terrible proof still of the folly of the world, for more than four hundred villas were destroyed there when the invasion of France by the Franco-American army began on August 15, 1944. It was launched from two small islands, Port-Cros and Levant, just off the coast of Hyères. We have come a little too late for pure delight.

Can one be happy at Hyères? I keep asking myself the question, knowing when I look at the fearful scars that it is foolish even to ask.

❀

AT HYÈRES

❀

"I was happy only once, and that was at Hyères."
—ROBERT LOUIS STEVENSON

It suffered a little in the war.
Yet nothing hurt the turquoise sea
Or flawed the gold Provençal sky.
The mistral moves unceasingly.

One almost chooses to ignore
All but felicity, at Hyères
May still say, *"Le soleil est Dieu,"*
And mean the sunstruck hillsides there,

The olive trees new-leafed in silver
(Nearly unspoiled), vines partly green,
Or walk the Avenue Gambetta
Casually, be almost serene

Under the palms, where *boutons d'or*
And hyacinths spring in the grass,
Gay sailors from Toulon, a nun
Riding a bicycle, will pass;

Where the pink stucco villas, flecked
By gunfire, or a church will show
Merely a hint of ravage—where
One may be almost happy so,

And more felicity than flaw
Remains. Only one must avoid
The *plage,* where the bombardment was,
Choosing the mountains, undestroyed,

The untouched sea. One must forget
The stricken beach, ignore it there,
Preferring the eucalyptus trees
And palms, survivors at Hyères.

Otherwise even a gold sky
Is blemished, the perpetual blue
Leaves one uncomforted. (Perhaps
Turning the eyes away will do.)

❀

WHAT NAME FOR MY HOUSE?

❀

In Cassis-sur-mer, near Marseille, there is a pale brown, locust-colored villa perched high over the shimmering Mediterranean with the name *La Cigale Chantant.* It seems about to take off into azure space. I love to look at it, at the way it is poised momently for flight.

Then I remember my own house at home that has no name at all, but that deserves of me some carefree and lighthearted and winging title like this one. Mine, however, is a white brick house in the Carolinas, perched solidly on a low hill set about with triangular cedars and tall loblolly pines. Mine is built on a concrete slab, earthbound, with radiant heat in the floors and air conditioning in the air. It would be pretty silly to call it a singing cicada.

*   *   *

I think of my house sometimes as *Casa Dolorosa,* because of the two large weeping willows, the weeping plum tree, and the weeping cherry, all growing dolorously together in the dooryard. The tearful effect is achieved by the lovely pendent branches that seem to droop and mourn in a graceful, causeless melancholy. Such a name, too, is inaccurate and misleading, I suppose; it has nothing at all to do with lament or tears within.

THE NAME OF SHANTIH

Last night I met a man from India, one of whose given names is Shantih. I wanted to cry three times over when I spoke to him, "Shantih, shantih, shantih," the hopeful last words of *The Waste Land,* the calm ending to an Upanishad. It seemed wonderful to me that a father had called his child Shantih, the peace which passeth understanding; and that the child was now become a man who talked ardently, with a bitter impassioned face, of early war between India and Pakistan over Kashmir.

VISIT TO ARLES

The wonder of Arles is that it looks everywhere like a Van Gogh. The likeness is incredible. "I want to paint a Provençal orchard of astounding gaiety," he wrote once to his brother, and there it is before the eyes in April. There are the same plane trees, the drawbridge, the vineyards in the sun, and the Arlésiens. Outside of Arles, we stopped the car beside a shining buttercup meadow, golden in the sun, beyond which lifted the little town of orange roofs to an overly azure sky. Van Gogh must have been painting it when he wrote in a letter to Theo, "How lovely yellow is!"

I believe in the advice of J. B. Priestley, in his book of pleasures called *Delight,* not to look from things to pictures that depict them (for the photographic likeness), but always from pictures to things. We need not check our vision with the artist's, says Priestley. "His vision should shape and color ours."

❋

TRANSATLANTIC FLIGHT

❋

This time, to cross is wider sky. This time,
To fly is over a forever sea.
I was not planetary till this time.

Below lies London, yet a breath or two,
Or better say, below is Samarkand,
Whose world so quickly I'm a stranger to

As we turn upward to the long way home
Into the headwinds—climb and climb by way
Of heaven and the Arctic Circle. *Home?*

Is nearly three miles up? And northerly?
It lies due west and closer to the earth,
Or there I had remembered it to be!

Yet if we are to prove that west is north,
Deny the compass, fly without a star
(Three miles below, the flittering lights are gone),

If this is to be homebound, then we are.

*   *   *

Forget the sea mist. Downhill is the sea
And this a plunging ship, but in mid-air.
Forget that there is nothing anywhere

Over the North Atlantic but the night
Skywide around us. O, forget how well
We have departed from the reasonable!

Unlearn the terror now, the nothingness
Beyond this wing tip, the devouring seas!
Be merry, gentle. Strangle such thoughts as these.

*   *   *

I know, I know. The walls of other rooms
Have circled me before, kept out the night.
This is the same encompassing a while.

It is the sleeping child across the aisle,
Who bears a charmed life in this warmth and light.
It is the man beside me, and so near

(*I have no other but a woman's reason*)
Let me believe to face the dark, but here,
Is one way to outface it. Or to lessen.

*   *   *

What name is this, *The Rainbow,* for a plane
That spans the tumult without rain or sun?
The arc of this queer spectrum was begun

Midnight in London. Now, at midnight still,
It drops to earth in Iceland (New York time),
And so, what time is it? No time at all?

A time to spare, unchronological?
Whatever it's o'clock, the windswept hour
Is long enough, the sleet, the glassy cold,

Beside an airstrip and a beacon tower.
Have we touched Iceland only to behold
This loneliness—and we so punctual?

*   *   *

On the first edge of light it lies, a world
No one has ever seen but from the sky.
Yet such a witness of that world am I

This morning over a new continent
Half-lost in cloud and barren like the moon,
So ice-bare, empty, an unpeopled place,

It seems to me the bottom side of space,
And I can only wish it different,
Or I unmoved by such topography.

*   *   *

But these are mountains, the Laurentian range,
Where green grows under us, where everything
Is far, at last, from seawinds and sea-change,

Where flight, at last, is south and favoring.
Were I to count to ten and shut my eyes
And then look straight down, *down,* I might discover—

There *is* a tiny road! not flourishing,
Not such a length to be excited over,
But man-made. And for that incredible.

*   *   *

Circling from out the sky we ribbon down,
As if in us were no anxiety,
At the lag end, to hurry the descent,

But rather a more lingering desire
To view the earth, the air, impartially,
As if we thrived in either element.

And yet I am one transatlantic flier
Who looks with love on Idlewild below
And with hot longing on each beckoning strip,

Aflame to further the relationship.
I have been overnight how quick to learn
This desperate love, taught dearly in the sky,

This lusting for the world of roofs and trees,
Which we are skimming now, but casually,
To which, but at a snail's pace, we *return.*

IX

Of People

✿

MR. WHITE, TRAVELER

✿

Mr. White of Selborne was one of the great travelers, and he stayed at home. Like Thoreau, who said he had traveled a good deal in Concord, Mr. White walked the wide world of Selborne, a tireless sight-seer with a taste for the spectacular:

"This morning I saw the golden-crowned wren, whose crown glitters like burnished gold."

"A quack at this village ate a toad to make the country people stare."

In his wanderings, no word ever escaped him of discomfort or dismay. He followed the path of the field cricket and observed the habits of worms. He watched bats drink on the wing, like swallows, taking a quick sip as they skimmed over a pool or river. (Like Virgil's bees, he said, they drank flying.) He learned the secrets of the harvest mouse and the stone curlew; he saw how the tail of a wagtail wags, up and down, "like that of a jaded horse"; he listened enraptured to the song of the yellow willow wren.

LESSONS FROM TWO ARTISTS

❀

I have learned two lessons lately from two artists. The first was from Clare Leighton. One afternoon while she was living in Durham we talked of her woodcuts, and she brought out her recent work, spreading it widely over the floor of the living room. It was but a single woodcut, in many versions, of an old Carolina woman in a rocking chair. Clare arranged these prints in progression, dozens of them, all so nearly alike that no one but her could have guessed the proper order. Yet between the first and the last was a beautiful and telling difference. With each revision she had changed perhaps a single line in the wooden block, seeking always the right tone and texture. Thus the impressions of light and shade became more delicate, the old woman gained slowly in character. That, I realized, was the way to create: to seek clarity over and over and over again.

*   *   *

One evening in New York at the home of my friend Gerard Hordyk, a Dutch painter, Gerard brought out a Victorian costume he had recently acquired and asked me to try it on. He was so enchanted with the dress, its color, its severity and quaintness, that he wanted to paint it, necessarily with someone inside. It had belonged to a fairly small lady, whoever that proper Victorian was, but since I wore it comfortably Gerard asked me to come as model the next morning to his studio.

There, by late afternoon, after painting silently through the long day, he had finished the experimental first draft, in oils on a square yard of canvas. It was a picture of a dress, the exact look, the painstaking reproduction. Here was a prim and stiff, voluminous brown dress, trimmed with rickrack, buttoned high at the neck, upright and unyielding. The lady out of Godey's Lady's Book stood with one hand firm upon a straight Victorian chair. I recognized her, but I did not like her. She had no character at all.

The next day was a tiring repetition of the first, except that the canvas was larger and Gerard was even more taciturn. Once he snatched away my support, the chair, and when I tottered put in my hand a small fan. Once when I gasped in fatigue he sent for a cup of black coffee. Again in the late afternoon, there was a picture, not of course complete but well under way. I stared at it for a long time in unbelief. The lady seemed to have my figure, but she came lightly out of the eighteenth century, in a blue and silver mist. Her pale blue gown was soft and full but pliant; she was walking, one might say, in a French garden. I liked her very much, though I could not say who she was. She was a being out of Gerard's imagination. This was his own true vision of a stupid brown dress. This time he had looked through his own eyes.

Gerard has sold the picture to a lady from Ithaca, New York. One day I hope to knock at her door and ask to see it again. The wearer of the dress turned out unexpectedly well, and sometimes I miss her company. More than that, I want to see again exactly what it was that Gerard did, for he worked not as a copier, after all, but as a creator. This is the lesson that he quietly taught me.

*   *   *

Gerard reminds me of Utrillo, who used to copy at night picture postcards of French cathedrals. Yet it is said in his praise that it is always Sunday in his paintings. No picture postcard ever gave him that *air de dimanche,* the look he himself achieved of piety and utter quiet.

❁

LYTTON STRACHEY'S SISTERS

❁

I sat in a large armchair under a water color of Lytton Strachey. During tea Miss Pernel, the sister who was for years the head of Newnham College in Cambridge and known affectionately there as "The Streak," told us of the bombings in Bloomsbury during World War II. Of that large family at 51 Gordon Square, only Miss Philippa had stayed out of the worst of it. (Here Miss Philippa interrupted to say that in general she preferred to live or die exactly where she was.) Yet when more and more houses were being demolished in the immediate neighborhood, the police called one day and requested her to leave. She agreed willingly enough to go. After a few days, the same two bobbies returned, knocked at the door of the Strachey house, and found her still there.

"When do you expect to be off, Miss Strachey?" they asked her.

"Whenever you are ready to remove me," she said. "Do you want to take me now?"

"How do you mean?"

"I mean bodily."

Nobody tried to carry her out. She lived on alone throughout the blitz, at home in Bloomsbury.

*   *   *

Miss Philippa was once Secretary of the London and National Society for Women's Suffrage. She has been for many years, like her mother before her, President of the Feminist Society in England. She has published a "Memorandum on the Position of English Women in Relation to that of English Men," and she is one of the old-line feminists. To meet her is, in these times, like running into a Buchmanite or a Fabian Socialist. You are amazed to find the person and the cause still alive.

Miss Philippa, surviving well, a sturdy figure with bristling iron-gray hair, is even yet happily embattled for the cause of women's rights. On a second afternoon at tea in Gordon Square, she lectured me vigorously for an hour on the subject, unaware that her fiery words were largely wasted on one who would make a poor convert, being at heart more like that little woman in Keats's sonnet:

> God! she is like a milk-white lamb that bleats
> For man's protection.

MISS STRACHEY

I had tea with Miss Strachey. And over the teacups
That winter afternoon in Gordon Square,
She announced at once, "I am a Feminist,
One of the old indomitable order."
So we talked, of course, of women and rights for women,
Endorsing a strict equality of the sexes.
I recall she spoke in praise of women pirates
While I replied by quoting Margaret Fuller:
"And let them be sea captains, if they will!"
We passed the hour delightfully embattled,
In sweet accord, till as I rose to go
Miss Strachey changed the subject and asked politely
If I had any children. "I have two sons,"
I answered her. . . . And visibly moved, amazed,
She turned and looked dumfounded in my eyes.
Then, stiffening, she delivered the reproof.
"*Why*," asked Miss Strachey hotly, "aren't they daughters?"

MISS STEPHEN ON DRUIDS

I overheard Miss Dorothea Stephen telling B. about a friend of hers who is a Druid. I leaned forward to listen. We had come to call on Miss Stephen, who lives alone these days in Winchester. Her father was the eminent Victorian Fitzjames Stephen, brother of Leslie Stephen, and she is the last survivor of seven children of that talented and remarkably intellectual family. Miss Dorothea makes one dare to want to be eighty-five. Her mind is so vigorous that her thoughts seem to fill her mouth and actually puff out her cheeks before she can express them. She will sit with cheeks full, mouth tightly shut, her face growing redder and redder until at last the words simply explode.

"A Druid?" I said, interrupting. I longed to ask if the lady traveled up to Stonehenge for her religious rites. "Are there really Druids in England now?"

"There are," said Miss Stephen. "And very spineless they've become, my dear. Very secular." She thought hard, puffing out her cheeks. "Druids!" she cried, explosively. "I hardly know how to explain them to you. They don't *do* anything these days. They don't even believe in blood sacrifice."

❀

PROFILE OF

MRS. CECIL WOODHAM-SMITH

❀

I didn't like the compliment paid in a Profile in the London *Sunday Times* to Mrs. Cecil Woodham-Smith, the admirable biographer of Florence Nightingale and historian of the Charge of the Light Brigade. Meaning to define and praise this very keen lady in a gracious word, the sketch called her "A woman with an edge."

The idea embarrassed me, for it argues a tart temper and a sharp tongue, and thus provides Mrs. Woodham-Smith with the profile of a witch. I naturally believe that a woman should be praised for her curves, not angles. One likes to be told about her soft answers and rounded replies, not, heaven forbid, about her *edge,* the thin cutting side of the blade.

*   *   *

It reminds me of another peculiar compliment, one of the unkindest I have ever read. It was paid in his lifetime to Erasmus Darwin, doctor, poet, and member of a small literary circle at Lichfield in the eighteenth century: "He was everybody's second-best friend."

*   *   *

The funniest, I think, is Paul Claudel's compliment to André Gide as a writer, in praise of his great and lasting contribution to literature: "I particularly admired your use of the pluperfect subjunctive."

❀

A CALL ON JEREMY BENTHAM

❀

At University College, London, where we politely inquired for Jeremy Bentham, we had only a brief wait before he was wheeled out and we were left alone with him. He sat in a large cabinet on wheels, a lovable old gentleman leaning on his favorite stick (which he had called Dapple, as he named his teapot Dick). His waxen face was gently benevolent under a large beaver hat, and the neat black habit fitted snugly over his quiet skeleton. Though Jeremy Bentham died in 1832, at the age of 84, here he was on earth, not ghost but mortal, a sprightly man looking very much alive. (At the time of his death, in accordance with the directions of his will, his skeleton was preserved and suitably clothed, topped with a head of wax, and given as a bequest to University College.) I found disconcerting only the sight of his mummified head lying at his feet. Otherwise it was a genuine and rare pleasure to meet him.

I greatly admire Jeremy Bentham for this attachment to the world, as well as for his simple outlook. As a philosopher he believed, like me, in the pursuit of happiness. He then proposed an answer to all our ills, "the greatest happiness of the greatest number," and even listed 14 simple pleasures for us to seek and enjoy (such as wealth, good name, piety, benevolence) and 12 simple pains to avoid (like desire, disappointment, and regret).

> For pain he had a plan,
> The kind old gentleman.

Being a consistent thinker, Bentham was genuinely fond of pleasure himself. If poetry, which he disliked, was not one to him, neither is it listed as a pain. He especially liked to eat and talk and tame mice. He enjoyed flowers and lived with them; he delighted in music and kept a piano in each room of his house. Most of all, he liked to make people happy. That, I told myself, staring happily at the benign figure of Jeremy Bentham, was the main thing.

❀

THREE WISE MEN

❀

In my lifetime, I have been lucky to see in the flesh three of the century's wise men, the philosophers. What they had in common was a rational view. Each one in an informal and unguarded moment behaved like a reflective man, you might almost say like Emerson's Man Thinking.

Einstein was merely trying to open a window. On a morning in the 1930s, he was up on the nineteenth floor of the tower of the Riverside Church in New York, having been invited to a ceremony in the church where his face is carved among the faces over the portal. He was wandering about alone and, for some reason, trying to open a window, perhaps because it was there, a problem to solve. In the office where I was a secretary, he stopped in front of a tricky casement window that required several manipulations before you cranked it open, looked timidly at it with arms behind his back, and blinked his eyes. After a long minute, he put both hands out, opened the window without effort as far as it would go, and wound it shut. Then he blinked again, smiled at me gently, and walked away.

*   *   *

John Dewey sat outside a drab little café in Montmartre, listening to bawdy French songs. B. and I sat at a table near him. Though as students at Columbia University, where he was a professor, we knew him slightly and had even talked with him that morning in the Louvre, we did not try this evening to catch his eye or speak. The singer, who was only mildly bawdy, lounged at the door of the café and sang of love, underscoring the words now and then with a suggestive wink or shrug at which there were a few snickers. John Dewey was the picture of a benevolent man taking an apéritif. The unchanging expression on his face was charitable; he looked neither bored nor inattentive, only peaceful and a little sleepy. Whatever he heard that August night he had no objection to. But then it is possible his French was no better than mine.

*   *   *

Bertrand Russell refused to eat his salad. He was having dinner with B. and me at our house before giving a lecture at Duke University one evening in 1951, and he ate like a hungry man. He ate with relish, except for the salad which he rather impatiently refused.

Then he told of an evening some years before, in New York, when he had sat at dinner beside Norman Thomas who, with Bertrand Russell, was to speak that night at a large public meeting. He noticed that Mr. Thomas was eating very little, only pecking at a tiny salad in front of him.

"What's the matter, Thomas?" he asked. "Have you lost your appetite?"

Mr. Thomas explained that he never ate more than a green salad before speaking at a lecture. A few leaves of lettuce were enough to sustain him.

"What?" roared Bertrand Russell in shocked astonishment. "Do you really expect, Thomas, to win America to Socialism on a *salad?*"

❊

A DAY WITH BERTRAND RUSSELL

❊

At 8:30 that morning, the little maid at the Hotel Sandringham knocked timidly. She opened the door of our room and, of all things, dropped a curtsy. "Lord Russell is on the telephone," she said.

On a September morning in London in 1952, Bertrand Russell was calling to invite B. and me to spend the day with him at his home in Richmond. He had written a few weeks earlier, in a letter to us in America, "I shall never forget the pleasure of the evening when I first met you. . . . I hope you will come to England again before long, and give me a somewhat longer taste of your delightful assemblage of things

217

to be noted and remembered." Then he reminded me of the particular thing noted and remembered from that evening. "But for you," he said, "I should never have known of Julia's double chin."

I was thinking, as we crossed the river by train to Richmond, of the talk about Herrick's Julia. Before dinner on the evening that Bertrand Russell spent with us in North Carolina, he had strolled around the living room, comfortably talking, smoking his pipe, sipping a cocktail, and looking over the books and pictures there. When he came across a volume of my verse in the bookcase, he picked it up and sat down with it, turning almost at once to a poem about Julia and Herrick's dither over a girl who had a double chin. Bertrand Russell was astonished at this revelation and delighted to hear it. To prove it really true, I hunted up the passage in Herrick's poem "Upon His Julia" and showed him the lines:

> Black and rolling is her eye,
> Double chinned, and forehead high.

In 1952, when we visited him, he was living in a large Victorian house at 41 Queen's Road, Richmond, where he occupied the whole third floor by himself while his son John, Viscount Amberley, his son's wife and their children, lived in the rest of it, and the small children were encouraged to make as much racket as they pleased so long as they left their grandfather alone. The house faced Richmond Park, the whole green expanse, but the street itself was a modest suburban one. Bertrand Russell's rooms were modest, sparely furnished with more books than furniture and a severe portrait of an ancestor, one of the Dukes of Bedford.

The first thing he did on our arrival at 11:00 was to produce my volume of verse and read aloud the same poem about Julia and her double chin. This led to two hours of talk and laughter about books and people. Part of that time he read aloud a story, "Mr. Bowdler's Nightmare," from the collection of stories he was in the midst of inventing to be called *Nightmares of Eminent Persons,* and when his voice tired he handed over the manuscript to B. to continue the reading. It was a frightful nightmare that Mr. Bowdler had, in which poor Mrs. Bowdler discovered behind locked doors and duly read a copy of the unexpurgated Shakespeare, after which she had to be taken to an asylum, "shouting Shakespearian obscenities to the whole street as she was borne away." No one enjoyed this racy tale more than the author himself, who stopped it several times to bark out his quick, sharp laugh and look hard into each of our faces to make sure we were amused.

He talked of people with that astounding memory of his, never fumbling for a date or faltering for a word. Of Titus Oakes, for example: a terrible scoundrel, he said, about whose villainy we are too unconcerned, one of the really evil men of history. Of Bernard Shaw, a man without conscience, he said, though that was a common enough failing, but the only man he had ever known without a heart. Of T. S. Eliot, who forsook philosophy for the church and so lost Bertrand Russell's respect and regard. Of David Lloyd George ("I spent years of my life trying to hate Lloyd George, but without success. He was too lovable, much like Churchill: political scoundrels both, but you could not really dislike them"). Of Winston Churchill ("The first time I saw him I was having my hair cut. The barber pointed to a pink, round-faced Harrow schoolboy in the next chair. 'Do you know who that is?' he asked me. 'That's Randolph Churchill's young cub' ").

The cook thrust her head in at the door to announce lunch. As we drank our sherry, she spread a cloth on the table beside us. And the three of us went on talking over Dover sole and wine while B. and I tried, in vain, to match the light and perfectly relaxed mood of our host. He told us that he had learned to relax and to drink whisky after he was well past forty, when he had finally seen the virtue of both habits and had taken them up together at once.

That afternoon we walked in Richmond Park. It was a cold, windy September day, and Bertrand Russell wore his coat collar turned up around his reddened face and ears. It seemed at first that we were merely taking a brisk stroll through the vast, almost deserted park. He began to talk about Henry VIII, who had once stood in that place watching for the signal from the Tower of London to tell him that Anne Boleyn was dead; and who reminded Bertrand Russell of a fine theory he has about royalty. It is that the English reigns have always alternated between rulers who were sinful and rulers who were good. He started with the sinful Henry to illustrate the unfailing event (which I now see on reflection has been far from dependable); but I remember best his account from Victoria's reign forward. Since Victoria herself was overly virtuous and Edward VII the eternal playboy, since George V was kindly and dull and Edward VIII too rebellious to stay a king, since George VI was undoubtedly good—it follows that the present ruler, Elizabeth, is supposed, even obliged, by tradition to take the downward path. He said that he enjoys sitting back, waiting to see.

We walked on and on. Suddenly Bertrand Russell turned and led us down a path toward the great handsome house in the park where he had lived as a child. He was taking us to Pembroke Lodge, the home of his Victorian grandfather, Lord John Russell, and his grandmother, who had had the care of him from the time he was four years old after his parents died. He liked to reflect, he said smiling, that she

brought him into touch with the Romantic poets, for she
was actually born in the same year as the poet Shelley.

❊

A WALK WITH BERTRAND RUSSELL

❊

We walked in Richmond Park. And, though only Septem-
    ber,
The late afternoon was chill and leadengray
And the park deserted, or nearly, I remember.
Few Londoners about. In the ending day,
A hurrying man, his dog on leash, might pass us,
Or a child stand raptly watching the fallow deer.
Yet it seemed like a vast estate, two thousand acres
Spread before us, and we the possessors here.
    Perhaps it was the trees that gave the illusion
Of privilege and domain—in the interlace
Of English elms, in the landed wealth of beeches—
That kept the look of a proud and different place.
Perhaps it was the extent, the lordly distance,
Where kings had walked (like us) through deepening green,
That now, in a public park, was the imposture.

    Or perhaps the more deceptive may have been
Another, a private, view of unreality
In these more disparate days. We came at last,
But casually, as if returned from strolling,

To Pembroke Lodge—where, rising out of the past,
Encircled by its lawns and formal gardens,
A great reposeful house of timeless air,
It stood as if unchanged, in stateliness;
As if its master, not yet departed there,
Now waited still, expecting us (but oddly),
As if he bid us welcome at his door.
Yet the door was locked and barred! Like passing strangers—
Was that the meaning of the visit?—or
Like trespassers, we peered into the windows,
And within we saw the barren dark rooms, oh,
Not empty, with their rows of stout tea tables
Where the drawing rooms had been a world ago.
And where before was Bertrand Russell's schoolroom
Stood now the tea urns and white crockery
That served the thirsty customer, in season.
At Pembroke Lodge we had come too late for tea.

And it was now. And the gray afternoon was fading
In Richmond Park. Were it an earlier time,
We should have known by the child within that doorway,
Or descending from the oak he used to climb.
Or we might have heard the coach and the master's greeting
On his return from London and Parliament,
Or discovered the Lady Frances in the garden,
Now where her roses grew to ornament
This stately teahouse.
                              (I remember asking,
Bemused, "Are you a sentimental man?"—
"Quite sentimental," he said lightly, smiling
At so absurd a question.)
                              And rather than
Prolong the matter now—it being September,

Too late and chill for lingering, nearly dark—
We turned away quite briskly, I remember.
We walked through the shadowed trees out of the park.

❀

HERRICK'S JULIA

❀

I

(A catalogue of her charms, from his various poems)

To Julia: How rich and pleasing thou my Julia art
             In each thy dainty and peculiar part!

Her lips: Sweet are my Julia's lips and clean
             As if o'erwashed in Hippocrene.

Her breath: Breathe, Julia, breathe, and I'll protest,
               Nay more, I'll deeply swear
             That all the spices of the East
               Are circumfused there.

Her voice: So smooth, so sweet, so silvery is thy voice
             As, could they hear, the damned would make
               no noise.

Her face: Black and rolling is her eye,
             Double chinned, and forehead high.

Her nose:	And a nose that is the grace And proscenium of her face.
Her teeth:	White as Zenobia's teeth, the which the girls Of Rome did wear for their most precious pearls.
Her skin:	Would I see lawn, clear as the Heaven, and then? It should be only in my Julia's skin.
Her sweat:	Would ye oil of blossoms get? Take it from my Julia's sweat.
Her tears:	She wept upon her cheeks, and weeping so, She seemed to quench love's fires that there did glow.
Her breasts:	Display thy breasts, my Julia, there let me Behold that circummortal purity.
Her nipples:	Have ye beheld (with much delight) A red rose peeping through a white? . . . Or ever marked the pretty beam A strawberry shows half drowned in cream?
Her legs:	Fain would I kiss my Julia's dainty leg, Which is as white and hairless as an egg.
Her belt:	As shows the air, when with a rainbow graced, So smiles that riband 'bout my Julia's waist, Or like—nay 'tis that zonulet of love Wherein all pleasures of the world are wove.

Her petticoat: Thy azure robe I did behold,
As airy as the leaves of gold,
Which erring here and wandering there
Pleased with transgression everywhere.

Her dress: When as in silks my Julia goes,
Then, then (methinks) how sweetly flows
That liquefaction of her clothes.

Her perfume: How can I choose but love and follow her
Whose shadow smells like milder pomander!

❧

HERRICK'S JULIA

❧

II

(My own catalogue)

Her perfume: Whenas in perfume Julia went,
Then, then how sweet was the intent
Of that inexorable scent.

Her very shadow walked in myrrh
And smelled (itself) of pomander,
And Herrick could but covet her.

Her legs: The sight of Julia's dainty limb
Recalled a smooth white egg to him.

225

| | And when he saw a smooth white egg, |
| | I guess he thought of Julia's leg. |

Her double chin:	All that was fair, all that was neat
	Did Herrick love: her silvery feet,
	Her golden head, her double chin.
	(Conceive the dither he was in.)

Her dress:	There was the riband at her throat,
	Her silken air, her petticoat,
	The soft pretension of her dress
	To kindle in him lovingness.

The rest of her:	They took his homage and his heart.
	So too did every other part:
	Her breasts, her eager lips, her hair.
	I think she pleased him everywhere.

| The whole: | Then for his subjugation, ah, |
| | There was the total Julia. |

❀

MADAME PANDIT

❀

I saw Madame Pandit (in November, 1955) being given an honorary degree by the Queen Mother Elizabeth, who had herself become the Chancellor of the University of London in a ceremony at the Royal Festival Hall. It was a spectacle of two rare women. The Queen Mother, in a black cap and robe somewhat royally bedecked with gold, looked wholly feminine as she walked in procession and sat in a great chair in the center of a stage crowded with distinguished professors and scholars (B. among them) from all over the world. Once seated, she gave a quick tug at the skirt of her blue gown to be sure that it was covering her knees and lightly touched her pearls.

When her turn came, Madame Pandit stood with head uncovered to hear the commendation read by Ifor Evans, Provost of University College. It was a witty piece that referred among other fine praises to her cookery, and it made her smile. Her bearing was much like the Queen Mother's. Each was a charming woman who looked well in academic robes but adorned them in a way quite different from the usual scholar.

Madame Pandit knelt on a stool, and the Queen Mother rose to place the doctor's hood over her bowed head. The next gesture was delightful. The Queen Mother stooped and with hovering arms seemed about to embrace the lady before her. What she did with tender care was to place and then pat down the hood all around Madame Pandit's neck and shoulders, adjusting it with a critical eye and smoothing out the wrinkles to be sure that it was as neatly fitting as the neckline of a new dress.

The following evening, at a reception at St. James's Palace, while we waited in a long, elegant queue that formed up the great staircase and through the rooms leading to the small chamber where the Queen Mother received, two by two, the hundreds of guests, we found Madame Pandit the next in line ahead of us. Beside her stood a gorgeous Indian lady in a scarlet and gold sari, wearing a caste mark on her forehead and glittering diamonds fastened in her hair and, splendidly, in her nose. Madame Pandit wore a pale-blue gown and no jewels. With her dark eyes and calm smile, she was without doubt the most beautiful woman in the procession.

❀

HOMAGE TO MADAME PANDIT

❀

The strict advantage is, in being a woman,
That it is wisdom to be more than wise:
Always a sequent lady, listened to

And looked at, rational but beautiful,
Who must be learned by heart or head, but twice,
Who is two selves and never less than two.

In London where I saw Her Excellency,
The High Commissioner of India,
She was her double, and so equally

There seemed to me no difference in kind
Whether I chose her beauty or her mind.
She was all beauty. Or all blindness I.

※

MR. ELIOT AT

"THE FAMILY REUNION"

※

It was good fortune to see in London, twenty years later, a production of his early play, *The Family Reunion.* To see it past Mr. Eliot's famous profile as we sat in the theater directly behind him was better still. The profile, I soon realized, wouldn't tell me much, but I have long been resigned to the fact that Mr. Eliot does not give himself away. As one who never explains what a poem means, so this evening while the Furies attacked Harry, Lord Monchensey, he did not smile or weep. "We must learn to suffer," the play says, and Mr. Eliot faced the stage stoically like any playgoer, enduring to the end.

I had therefore to watch the action for myself, as it was presented by the Cambridge Players during the second of three evening performances they gave in London. Since this was neither the opening nor the closing night, Mr. Eliot had apparently modestly chosen to attend the play on the middle evening, unless of course he saw it for three nights running. However it was, two of his countrymen were alone of all the audience in taking any notice of the celebrated poet in the stalls.

Near the close of the final scene, as Harry finds out his need for expiation and begins his quest, "We must all go," he says, "each in his own direction." Then the curtain comes down. We rose and followed Mr. Eliot up the aisle, only to discover shortly that he had lost his own direction out of the theater and had no idea where to find an exit. It was well worth the price of admission to B. that night to be able to point out to Mr. Eliot the way that he must go.

❀

MR. ELIOT'S PROFILE

❀

There,
At a performance of *The Family Reunion,*
Was surely Mr. Eliot. How distracting
In the dark stalls to recognize his profile!
It is true it interfered somewhat with the acting.

Bleakly outlined before one, it seemed immobile,
Like any playgoer's in London, lifting a little
From time to time but not in tears or rejoicing.
The look, I thought, was thoroughly noncommittal.

Whether his rueful drama pleased Mr. Eliot,
Or what the words said to him in tragic confession,
Was not revealed. At the shadowy final curtain,
He rose from his seat without a change of expression.

I might have leaned forward to ask, then, his opinion
Of what the play meant. But he might have answered,
    "Whatever

It means to you"—and that, I must have admitted,
Is the thing I never know. Or hardly ever.

❀

FRANCIS HACKETT AT DINNER

❀

At the small dinner party, Francis Hackett talked the most. He told of his life as editor, biographer, and Irishman. We took delight in his wit—except that towards the end of the dinner, when he had somehow got a large blob of whipped cream on his nose and seemed unaware of the fact, we found it hard to watch at all soberly and listen. The danger was that we would laugh harder and oftener than he expected us to. Every time we looked, there it was! Finally his wife, who was sitting opposite him, could bear no more. With uplifted hand, she silenced his words.

"I have been casting about for some time," she said, "to find a way of conveying a message to you. It is this: you have whipped cream on the end of your nose."

Mr. Hackett picked up his napkin and calmly wiped his face. "My dear," he murmured, "you have found the perfect way."

❀

THE COMPANY OF SCHOLARS

❀

(In the Scholars' Room, Harvard University)

In the still room, a scholar frowns in thought,
Glasses in hand. One with a balding head,
Conscious of doing neatly what he ought,
Thrusts little notes in little pigeonholes.
Two sit on cushions, as if scholarship
Had tired their bottoms as it tried their souls.

A place of refuge is a ridded place,
A world apart, a planet not so far
From any moon as from the marketplace.
That scholar has removed his hearing aid
To turn off all the silence. Several are
Hidden by works as by a barricade.

Contentedly a few sit gathering dust
Amid the motes and particles of learning.
Others have baffled faces, as they must.
There is the furrowed brow, the daunted look,
The hopeful gleam, the clarity—the turning,
Turning, turning of pages in a book!

A company of "Whims and Humourists"
One of their number calls them, scholars leading

A gay life, golden as an alchemist's.
And while a rather bookish thing to quote,
Pleased with the thought the scholar clears his throat,
Puts on his glasses, and resumes his reading.

❊

COLETTE

❊

Today Colette is dead. She has given me hours of pleasure in my life, not all of it of her own making. I always happened to read her books in delightful places, as on shipboard. She belonged on the *Ile de France,* with wine for lunch and a nap afterwards in her singular company. Perhaps she owed me a debt for being so relaxed and accommodating a reader, but she repaid it by her own good nature. I remember reading *Cheri* one night in the oldest hotel in Charleston, South Carolina, on a trip to the camellia gardens. Even now the plot of her novel seems bedecked with flowers.

I like the charming story of how Colette came to write *Pour un Herbier,* a collection of pieces about flowers. Once or twice a week for a year or so during the 1940s, a publisher sent her a large, gorgeous bouquet. He asked her in return whenever she felt like it to write a portrait of the lily, the rose, the hyacinth, the tulip, the poppy, whatever took her fancy, saying anything that came into her head when she looked at his gift of flowers. "And then," wrote the publisher with the kind heart, "we will make a little volume of them." Characteristically, however, these flower studies pretty as they are tell more about men than about hyacinths. A man, says Colette, finding himself betwixt the devil and the deep blue sea, does not fail to choose the worse alternative—which is to say at least that a man is not a flower.

B. does not like Colette. He thinks she told too freely everything she knew, especially about love.

*　　*　　*

There is a story that, shortly before she died, Colette saw a film based on her own multi-colored career. She exclaimed, "What an interesting life I had. And how I wish I had realized it sooner!"

❀

PRAISEGOD BAREBONES

❀

I know very little about the seventeenth-century preacher Praisegod Barebones, but I am glad to have heard the ring of his mighty name. He must have been a lean and fanatical old Anabaptist. By day he sold leather in London's Fleet Street. By night he became a fierce defender of the Lord and held forth, in his own house, to large zealous groups that squeezed in to listen to his terrifying hellfire sermons. I can see his eyes burning red from here.

Horace Walpole once said he loved anything that marked a character strongly. Praisegod Barebones—there was a name to mark a man! By the same measure, how much is one to say for a modern-day evangelist who calls himself "Billy" Graham?

✿

A NOTE ON LORD CHESTERFIELD

✿

To explain the character of Lord Chesterfield, and something of his failure as a father, F. L. Lucas (in *The Search for Good Sense*) tells a strange and moving story from Poland about love—the love for one's child that the glacial Chesterfield, with all his paternal advice and solicitude in 400 letters to his son, was without the natural affection ever to understand.

The tale is of a fool of a man whose cruel mistress demanded of him, as the price of her love, his aged mother's heart. Mr. Lucas writes, "The fool rushed off and hacked it out; but, as he tore back with it to his trollop, he tripped on a stone and fell. And he heard the heart murmur—

" 'My son, are you hurt?' "

THE DEATH OF MR. FITZHERBERT

"Poor Mr. Fitzherbert hanged himself on Wednesday."
So writes Horace Walpole in a letter of January 5, 1772. The
bare facts are that Mr. Fitzherbert went to his stable that
afternoon and hanged himself with a bridle.

Five years later, on the evening of September 15, 1777,
Boswell tells of Dr. Johnson holding forth about this man,
and painting a strange, contradictory portrait of him, the
late Mr. Fitzherbert of Derbyshire.

"There was (said he) no sparkle, no brilliancy in Fitzherbert; but I never knew a man who was so generally ac-
ceptable. He made everybody quite easy, overpowered nobody by the superiority of his talents, made no man think
worse of himself by being his rival, seemed always to listen,
did not oblige you to hear much from him, and did not oppose what you said. Everybody liked him: but he had no
friend, as I understand the word."

"I remember a man," writes Mrs. Piozzi many years later,
recording a conversation on the same subject with Dr. Johnson—"I remember a man much delighted in by the upper
ranks of society, who upon a trifling embarrassment in his
affairs hanged himself behind the stable door, to the astonishment of all who knew him as the liveliest companion and
most agreeable converser breathing. 'What upon earth,' said
one at our house, 'could have made Fitzherbert hang him-

self?' 'Why, just his having a multitude of acquaintance,' replied Dr. Johnson, 'and n'er a friend.' "

❃

MR. FITZHERBERT

❃

At least the words they left of Mr. Fitzherbert
Are final. Dr. Johnson had his say,
And who will quiz him now? Or ask Mrs. Piozzi?
Who now recalls the gentleman, anyway?

Still I regret, in coming upon his likeness,
That they should leave *two* portraits of him—
Here the one and, neatly canceling it, the other
Mr. Fitzherbert, late of Derbyshire.

The first is full-length: of a man of honor,
Estate, wealth, grace, felicity. Much is made
Between them of the pleasant host, the great squire,
His genial ways, the courtesy he displayed,

And how the whole world liked him. This is unquestioned,
Since Dr. Johnson never praised beyond
A man's deserts. The words of Mrs. Piozzi
Seem puzzled and regretful, even fond—

Unless it may have been the *second* portrait
Of him she meant. Whatever there of pride

They saw too late, it was a Mr. Fitzherbert
No one had cared to fathom until he died,

When, overlooked till now, the truth was plainer,
Though everybody liked him. To the end,
Said Dr. Johnson, he had a real felicity
But, *as I understand the word,* no friend.

They may have been mistaken. Or this dark portrait
Is not yet, certainly, the one they meant?—
Not Mr. Fitzherbert who hanged himself on Wednesday,
But something kinder, a little different.

*   *   *

Wednesday is a day, at least, on which to die. When Falstaff asks himself about the word honour: "What is honour? a word. What is in that word honour? What is that honour? air. . . . Who hath it?" his answer to the last question is "he that died o' Wednesday."

❀

SYDNEY SMITH IN THE COUNTRY

❀

The Rev. Sydney Smith had extraordinary balance and good sense. He went off to a living in Yorkshire in 1809, in his middle years, as Herrick went reluctantly to Devon, and learned to be a country parson although the charm of the simple life had never existed for him. "Whenever I enter a village, straightway I find an ass," he once remarked.

He scarcely knew a turnip from a carrot. There was no literate neighbor within seven miles, and, as he made rueful note, he was actually twelve miles from a lemon. Yet he had a farm of three hundred acres to manage alone, and he stayed on in Yorkshire for twenty years, in high spirits. Being an incurably cheerful man, quick to learn how to live rather than to bear with life, Sydney Smith was soon writing to Lady Holland:

"I hear you laugh at me for being happy in the country, and upon this I have a few words to say. In the first place, whether one lives or dies I hold, and always have held, to be of infinitely less moment than is commonly supposed. But if life is the choice, then it is common sense to amuse yourself with the best you can find where you happen to be placed. . . . In short, if my lot be to crawl, I will crawl contentedly; if to fly, I will fly with alacrity. But, as long as I can possibly avoid it, I will never be unhappy. . . ."

❀

I LIVE HERE

❀

B. and I were always discovering places to which we intended to return eventually and spend the rest of our lives. Once it was Innsbruck in the Austrian Alps. Once it was an island in Loch Lomond where the white heather was thick as a bear rug, heavily in bloom. Once B. made up his mind we would retire, in good time, to Montpellier, where Rabelais studied and the Provençal sun is yellow gold. The University would provide us with books and the South of France with the wine to read them by. Rabelais would provide us with *le rire immense*.

I became aware of the hollowness of these dreams lately when an English friend came to visit us. Cliff, whom we knew well for nearly a year in London, had flown down to North Carolina on a brief trip to this country and was, at the moment I speak of, sitting on our porch with a highball in his hand. The October countryside was without doubt beautiful. Below us lay the still-green meadow with the grazing Hereford cattle moving over it. The woods beyond were red gold with beech and sweet gum except for the green of the loblolly pines. I turned to see whether Cliff was properly awed by the spectacle, so fine that I felt immodest to be the possessor of it. He was staring off at the yellow sunlit hill in the distance.

"Helen," he said, thoughtfully, "I've wondered about this. Didn't you find it rather an awful wrench to come back?"

"Come back?" I repeated.

"From London," Cliff said. "You always seemed to love being there. I wonder if you minded very much having to return."

I looked into my glass. "Well, Cliff," I finally said. "I live here."

❁

A STREET IN NORTH CAROLINA

❁

My street goes nowhere. A longwinded street,
It takes a while to verify the view
That nowhere really is worth going to

(I live about halfway). You pass my door
On the ride out and back from having been
To what is bona fide, genuine

Nowhere. And it's a pine tree in the sun
That bears a notice, weatherstained but neat:
"Speed is checked by radar." Yet my street

Is leisurely enough for tired cats,
Field mice and possums cross it, sleepy-eyed,
Where it relaxes into countryside,

A scattered house or two, the cedar trees,
A clearing, a green river, a stand of pine.
(The white house in the conifers is mine.)

❀

SWINE ON THE DOORSTEP

❀

Last Sunday evening I thought I heard visitors at the front door. I went to discover five large black hogs in a solid row on the doorstep. They stood quietly like expected guests, arriving at the appointed hour. My first impulse was to ask them right in, but instead I hastily brought out some refreshment (a green salad) while B. went for help. I had to urge the biggest one, who weighed about 200 pounds, not to step on the azaleas. Otherwise they were well-bred and sociable and we spent an agreeable half hour together, though I felt more and more like Circe, as Odysseus says of her, "... Circe went out from the house wand in hand, opened the doors of the piggery and let out what seemed a drove of nine-year-old fat hogs."

We have lots of guests in the country: the quail in the yard, an occasional possum, the cottontails, a stray blue heron. The shy meadowlarks venture up from the meadow in a gang of twenty or so to walk under the trees. Two guinea hens in June came and circled the house for days, round and round, making a noise like a rusty wheel squeaking as it turns. Once a mother beagle and five puppies arrived yelping out of nowhere and stayed with us for a week.

My neighbor who owns the five hogs says we are to have a large ham soon for our delicate sense of hospitality.

In Gilbert White's *Natural History of Selborne,* there is a story of a sow whom I would be proud to welcome on my doorstep. She was a fine turbulent animal with a long history of fruitfulness at which Mr. White marveled and rejoiced.

For some ten years this prolific sow, belonging to a neighbor of his, produced two litters a year with ten and once twenty to a litter. So notably lusty was she that she would disappear at intervals, traveling by herself and opening all the intervening gates to get to a distant farm where a boar was kept. Up to her seventeenth year she was so fertile that, when finally killed for bacon in the spring of 1775, she had given birth to 300 pigs. Mr. White points to this as "a prodigious instance of fecundity."

❀

TIMOTHY THE TORTOISE

❀

Timothy was Mrs. Snooke's tortoise. She kept him in her garden at Ringmer for nearly forty years and, dying in March 1780, left him to her dear nephew, Gilbert White of Selborne. Mrs. Snooke couldn't have found a more wildly suitable gift. After the funeral, Mr. White eagerly brought his tortoise home and buried him in *his* garden, from which Timothy now and then emerged, heaving up the earth. For the next thirteen years, until Mr. White's own death, he closely observed and made entries in the *Journal* as well as comments in the *Natural History of Selborne* of how Timothy came and went between the poppies and sowthistles, how he spent his dull days and achieved for his pains longevity. Heaven only knows when Timothy finally got around to dying. Mr. White says (quoting Pope), the old tortoise was "much too wise to walk into a well," and the chances are he suffered no accident but in the end simply died of being turtle. His placidity of nature was of great concern to Mr. White, as appears in these entries:

"When one reflects on the state of this strange being, it is a matter of wonder to find that Providence should bestow such a profusion of days, such a seeming waste of longevity, on a reptile that appears to relish it so little as to squander more than two-thirds of its existence in a joyless stupor, and be lost to all sensation for months together in the profoundest of slumbers."

"We put Timothy into a tub of water, and found that he sunk gradually, and walked on the bottom of the tub: he seemed quite out of his element, and was much dismayed."

"When we call loudly through the speaking trumpet to Timothy, he does not seem to regard the noise."

✻

TIMOTHY

✻

A turtle—not a turtledove—
Was Timothy. Or, by nomenclature,
I may mean tortoise (something of
That general nature).

At least within a shell, withdrawn,
He had his being (and was British),
A reptile timid as a fawn,
And far less skittish.

To Timothy the world was made
Of pink hepaticas, not bustle,
Of Mr. White of Selborne's shade
And cool leaf rustle,

Of torpor amid fleurs-de-lis
And summer poppies, bright and garish,
And life was but longevity
In Selborne parish.

When nightingales complained in grief,
When mourned the Hampshire lark or missel,
Timothy ate a poppy leaf
And one sowthistle,

And listened only to the years
(Wise Timothy) and found them quiet.
They put no strain upon his ears,
Or on his diet,

They gave him lilies and content,
They brought of time and tide a blending.
For all he knew they really meant
To be unending.

So the cacophony of bird,
Or Mr. White of Selborne's tootle,
To Timothy seemed as absurd
As it seemed futile.

For what had Mr. White to say,
More than a lark whose days were counted,
Of everlasting yea and nay?
Of time surmounted?

Or what had Timothy to hear
From shouts and tumult like his master's,
A speaking trumpet to his ear
Among the asters?

Timothy crept within his shell,
Serene mid hollyhock and myrtle.
For what has anyone to tell
(In fact) a turtle?

※

HESTER AND THE NUTHATCH

※

The pleasant thing about my neighbor Hester is that she loves life and is on close terms with it. She is the enjoyer of this countryside, more than the rest of us who are busy running to and fro. When I asked her recently what she had been doing all that day, she began, "Well, at 8:30 this morning I was looking at a nuthatch."

"What did you think of it?" I asked.

"I didn't think anything at all of it," Hester said stoutly, "except that it was a nuthatch."

There, I reflected, is the difference between us, to her everlasting credit. If I were able to recognize this same bird (which is unlikely), I would try to do something to change the experience into words, at least look up *nuthatch* in the encyclopedia, or see what Thoreau had to say about it or Edwin Way Teale. (The nuthatch used to be called a nuthack because of its habit of hacking nuts. It is a small, creeping bird of bold disposition, sharp beak, and short tail. It ascends a tree in zigzags, looking for nuts.)

Hester, on the other hand, sees no reason whatever for trying to sum up a nuthatch. She merely enjoys standing there, looking at a bird.

THE MOCKINGBIRD

❊

A mockingbird in the maple tree, now in May, sings straight through the moonlit night. Last evening my friend Lewis, a great bird watcher and bird listener, and I stood under the tree listening to him, while Lewis named the various birds that the mocker chose freely to mimic: the cardinal, the flicker, the thrush, and so on, improvising under the moon, changing melody, pouring forth at the top of his voice in a nonstop song flight his lovely borrowed song.

"Listen," said Lewis. "He is mimicking himself now as a young bird."

I believe, of course, anything in the bird line that Lewis cares to tell me. This, he said, is a dialogue between the mocker as a fledgling, making his loud insistent cries from the nest, and his worried parent answering him, chirping love and admonition in reply. It was like hearing an opera with the libretto in hand.

✻

THE ART OF GIVING

✻

My neighbor Howard is giving away his vegetables again, a talent of his. He stopped yesterday in the pouring rain with our share of a truckload of corn for all the countryside. To-day in rubber boots and more rain, he brought great red tomatoes to the door.

Some years ago he took a truckload of produce to Haiti, the colored section of town, and stood beside it on a street corner trying to give it away to passers-by. For a while he was ignored and completely unsuccessful. Then one Negro woman whom he approached stopped and asked him the price of his corn.

"There isn't any price to it," Howard said. "I just want to give you some."

"What's the matter with it?" asked the woman, suspiciously.

"Nothing's the matter with it," Howard said. "I've got more corn than I need, that's all. If you can use some, take it. It's free."

Before she accepted an armful, the woman looked hard into his face and asked one more question.

"What's the matter with you?" she said.

❈

NATURE NOTES

IN THE NEW YORK TIMES

❈

On Sunday morning I turn first of all to the editorial page of *The New York Times*. Its fourth leader is a piece on Nature, expertly written, full of things like sumac and bird cries, serene, hopeful, and informative. Though Thoreau once advised, "Read not the Times, Read the Eternities," he hadn't seen this particular item in Sunday's newspaper. It does what it can with eternal matters to offset the front-page news of the week.

It gives me news of the seasons and where we have arrived nationally—plunged into October, perhaps. Our own seasons in the Carolinas tend to be a little advanced or awry, so that Mayflies fly forth in April, and June bugs reel and bump into the face by the middle of May. In a mild year, the January jasmine blooms promptly in December. I sometimes think that only Venus herself is seasonal down here. She at least becomes an evening star on time.

*   *   *

> I've never been to Timbuktu,
> I've never been to China,
> But of all the places I've never been
> I prefer North Carolina.
>
> > —A newspaper verse in Richard Walser's
> > collection, *Nematodes in My Garden of Verse*

❃

POSTCARD FROM HERE

❃

Here winter is winterspring,
And the Mayfly mates in April.
The time of the singing of birds
Is nearly all the time.

In this green world, the hoot owls
Live to the age of fifty.
The same well-being marks
The doves and dragonflies.

A May night brings the June bug,
The moths do turns and handsprings,
A kind of thriving stirs
The sweet and lovely air,

So I'm taking breathing lessons,
Hoping to smell the rapture
Here early like the Mayfly,
And emulate the hoot owl.

✺

NATURE LOVERS

✺

Thoreau was a real nature lover. He dearly loved a swamp, for example, and nothing pleased him more than to wade and muck about in the stagnant water, sinking blissfully into the dense brown slime among the gnats and mosquitoes. Now and then in his *Journal* he would write a passionate love passage about a tree. "I love and could embrace the shrub-oak with its scaly garment of leaves rising above the snow. . . . I felt a positive yearning to one bush this afternoon." He unfortunately was like that: when he fell in love, it was with a shrub oak.

Emerson said of Thoreau that he knew the country like a fox or bird, as well he might, a man who willingly rejected the company of people in favor of small animals. But though Emerson himself was a nature lover, or at least friendly disposed, it was with a difference: his feelings were not so much involved. He looked at a tree but not with passion, never with much appetite.

"Let us be men," Emerson calmly remarked, "instead of woodchucks."

＊

THE TWELVE MONTHS IN THE
CAROLINAS

＊

I. JANUARY JASMINE

Jasmine flower,
Brief and wary,
On the breast
Of January,

Yellow in the sun
And little,
Tentative of bud
And petal,

Quicker than the quince
Or cherry,
Enterprising,
Solitary,

Quicker to be out
Than spring,
Doubtful of
A welcoming.

II. A WAY OF LOOKING

Some take back February
And with practiced eye
Give it a second try,

In charitable mood, as one
Who born believing ought
Harbors a second thought,

And finds it tolerably
Springlike, as hope should be
On closer scrutiny.

*   *   *

III. THE VERITY OF LIES

"And you were a liar, O blue March day."
—GERARD MANLEY HOPKINS

There were the unseen birds
And the delusion
Of green boughs. There was intermittent sun
To warm us (lightly) to a false conclusion.
It was a fraud,
But an inspiring one.

Like truth too bright-embroidered
Or like May
Imagined, like desire upon the mind—
Either you had forgotten yesterday

And offered skies
Of a deceptive kind,

Meaning to dupe us,
And you were a liar,
O blue March day, one hard to justify,
Or else you said,
An honest falsifier,
This lovely, loud, anticipatory lie.

*   *   *

IV.   PASS OVER LIGHTLY

Pass over lightly any doubt
Of love or April held too soon—

Before the silver trees were out,
Before the unacknowledged moon

Turned lately to a golden one—
And over my oblivion.

V. MAY IS A SUITABLE DAY

> "I am a lady who loves decorum."
> —From a letter of Mme. de Sévigné

Green is the willow, as green should be,
Seawater blue is the sky,
And I am a lady who loves decorum—
I wonder why.

A sensible passion stirs my heart,
A rational thought my head,
As everywhere *un petit air de dimanche,*
Like a golden thread,

Embroiders the morning, the still skyblue,
The green of the willow tree.
And I am a lady who loves the look
Of propriety.

*　　*　　*

VI. JUNEMOON IN THE RIVER

A porcelain moon lies in the glittery
River like a piece of china,
A small white glazed ceramic fluttery
Earthenware dish set in the watery
Stream to cool among the willows.
And what a night to study pottery!

VII.   MIDSUMMER NIGHT

You always see the same side of the moon.
You hear the crickets in the usual dark,

The same night-witted, customary tune.
Cicadas are afiddle in the trees,

Habitual above you is a star,
The tree frog is a bore in companies,

July repeats itself in whippoorwills,
Sounding as weary of them as you are—

If it's the owls you want to hear in Spain,
If you would count the cats in Zanzibar.

*   *   *

VIII.   AUGUST IN THE SUN

Lemon, saffron, topaz, gold—
Yellow cowslips in the sun
Gilded for comparison,
What is yellower than these?

Age is. With its spinet keys,
Parchment, mummy wrappings, old
Hands at benedicites.

IX. SEPTEMBER WINDS

The day began with water music
And plenty of woodwinds—such an air
As came, you'd say, from an *oboe d'amore,*
Light in tone for a love affair,
Or came from a wailing *flûte d'amour,*
Low in pitch for the overture.

But the sound increased with the river willows
Loudly scraping, weatherblown,
And the brasswinds rose to the squeal of trumpets
And howled with the horns and the deep trombone.
"LOVE!" they blared at the *oboe d'amore,*
The flute, so thin and so amatory.

*　　*　　*

X. GOLD OCTOBER

Again the veering days
Turn over a gold leaf
As if to mend their ways;
Creating the optical
Illusion that life and they
Are gold, perpetual;
Ashine with the pretense
That to be, in fact, undying
This year is the difference.

Yet not wholly concealed
Are the deceitful crows,

The yellow nibbled fields,
And over the graying woods
Hawks rising in the sky
Like winter platitudes.

So whatever the mild air
Of a gold leaf floating down
To leave the poplar bare,
Whatever the fine retards,
What will come of it will come.
Patience, and shuffle the cards.

*   *   *

XI.   NOVEMBER

Tailend of the year,
Time of the fall of the leaf,
Is, O my dear—

When clouds move like the sea,
Whitecaps that froth and foam
Over you and me—

Time to turn away
From squinting at this late sun
To the next, later one.

XII. HOLLY

It being late, I look again for holly,
Now that the woods are gray and lost and bare,
Now that I move so readily in silver.
Only the evergreen has tarried there—
Of all the world this trace of green remaining,
Scrub pine and cedar, left forgetfully
Beyond the summer leaf. It takes small cunning
In such a wood to find the holly tree
And, in December, little subtlety.

THE SUSQUEHANNA RIVER

❀

I have been reading a book about the Susquehanna River, by Carl Carmer, led to do so because of a striking comment in a book review. It said, "A good deal has taken place on the banks of the Susquehanna since Captain John Smith first sailed up the river." I was able to agree. One event that has taken place is my own birth. My name was Smith, too, but the Captain is not to be blamed.

A month or two after I was born on the banks of the Susquehanna, in the village of (flow gently, sweet) Afton, I left the town and the river forever. At least, I tell myself, I came a lot closer than the poet Coleridge, who only dreamed of life beside the lovely, winding Susquehanna. I was given it to drink.

SWEET LAND OF PANTISOCRACY

On the green banks of the river,
By the Susquehanna stream,
Robert Southey meant to labor,
S. T. Coleridge meant to dream.

Near the peewee's cry, the flicker
In the willows, where the loon
Would affright the sisters Fricker
Of a winter afternoon,

In Utopia eternal,
Robert Southey meant to dwell
On the principle fraternal.
S. T. Coleridge meant as well.

Fed on poetry and manna
From a large communal dish,
Sharing from the Susquehanna
What was edible in fish,

Fat on locusts there and honey
In the reedy wilderness,
Had they found the passage money
When the sisters murmured yes,

Poet Southey, the immortal
Coleridge then had wandered free,
Singing of the Susquehanna
And of Pantisocracy.

Yet the population thicker
Never grew along that shore
To include the sisters Fricker.
As Lake poets evermore

By a less fraternal water,
By a more narcotic stream,
Robert Southey went to labor,
S. T. Coleridge meant to dream.

❀

THE FIRST BOOK

❀

The first book I ever bought was from a traveling salesman. He came to the door when I was five with a volume called *Through Eye-Gate and Ear-Gate into the City of
Child's Soul.* I remember the title because my father, listening from the living room, objected loudly to it. "Dear God!"
cried my father in exasperation. "What kind of name for a
book is that?"

As if these were words to invite him in, the salesman entered the room and sat down in a rocking chair. He held the

book in his lap and rocked. I stood near the visitor and looked with mild interest at the volume that so annoyed my father. When the salesman handed it to me, I stared at the title, which I was able to read, but I made no attempt to leaf through the pages. At this tableau my father grew impatient. "Do you *want* the book?" he groaned, incredulously. I nodded my head.

"What are you taking for it?" he asked the salesman.

"One dollar," the man replied softly.

My father fished into his wallet for a dollar bill. This he handed over to me. "You'll have to buy it yourself," he said. "I haven't the heart."

❀

THE PRELUDES

❀

My mother always plays Chopin
In my dark memory. From halflight,
The Preludes turned the room to shadow.

And in the halfdark I was near her,
Beside her, leaning against the keys
So that she couldn't play them. Or

I pressed against her on my knees
Till she cried out, but in strict time,
Staccato, imploring me to move!

267

So I would crouch beside the pedals,
Drowned in the streaming notes above,
And wait in the dark, flooded cave

For her return. To touch her dress
Might mean I would be sent away
From her, for all my childishness.

And I would stare at her white arms
And throat, her dark eyes that looked straight
Into her loneliness. And wait.

❊

MISS THATCHER

AND THE PINK SHELF

❊

When I went back this summer to the town in New York
State where I lived more than thirty years ago, the only person who seemed to me still youthful and unchanged was
Miss Thatcher, the librarian. By keeping her nose in a book,
she had preserved her person and her sanity. As a young girl
I used to be a little afraid of Miss Thatcher, especially when
I took a volume from her "Pink Shelf" of erotic books hidden behind her office door and she grimly checked it out for
me, first staring hard at the title and then regarding me
with a long and steady look.

Later when I wrote a verse about that tempting pink shelf,
which had rested lightly on my conscience for years, I hoped

that Miss Thatcher (there given the name of Miss Green) would never see it. Of course she did; she reads everything. This summer she told me that when she had come upon the verse she had remembered me well and kindly as a child. I was, she said, a Reader. A Reader, Miss Thatcher said with the capital letter in her voice, was always welcome to his share of the pink books.

❀

THE PINK SHELF

❀

I was well pleased myself
With that particular shelf.
Each book of verse or story
Now banished there I think
Had proved over-amatory.
That is why they called it pink,
A blushing hidden lore
On a shelf behind a door.
It was there I loved to tarry
Among ardors so sublime
As patron of the library,
A young reader at the time.

Yet Miss Green seemed unaware
Of Ovid and Baudelaire
And me, with girls so shady
(Each pink seductive tome)

As *Manon* and *The Pretty Lady*.
I took *Water Babies* home,
Prudently, though my taste
Inclined to books either chaste
Or in Miss Green's collection
Of amours on that shelf.
I always liked her selection,
Being fond of pink myself.

❀

THE EDUCATION OF MYSELF

❀

The education of myself began one day in March at the University of Chicago. It happened suddenly during the spring term of my junior year. I was eighteen years old and I saw a blinding light. That day I went into the university bookstore and bought two notebooks, one of them to hold a list of books that was beginning to gather in my head. Yesterday a professor had murmured a lovely title, *The Golden Treasury,* which became my first entry, page 1. The second entry was Bernard Hart's *The Psychology of Insanity,* though I have forgotten now why I wanted to read it.

For the second notebook I had no clear plan except to put it to immediate use. When I returned to my room, I thought for a while and then wrote on the inside cover, "Chiefly about Life." The book, secret and indispensable, became a major part of my education. Thereafter, anything I read, in a book, magazine, or newspaper, was a possible source of material.

It might contain powerful and enlightened words that I could copy into my notebook.

Heaven pardon my taste, but at least it was catholic. From Carl Van Vechten's current popular novel *Peter Whiffle,* I wrote: "A man with a broad taste in food is inclined to be tolerant in regard to everything," and believing tolerance to be a good thing, I stopped disliking any food. Out of F. Scott Fitzgerald's silliest volume, *Flappers and Philosophers,* I took this: "All life is just a progression toward and then a regression from one phrase 'I love you.'" From Richard Hooker, *Of the Laws of Ecclesiastical Polity,* I noted and learned by heart what happiness is: "Happiness therefore is that estate whereby we attain, so far as possibly may be attained, the full possession of that which simply for itself is to be desired, and containeth in it, after an eminent sort, the contentation of our desires, the highest degree of all our perfection."

I set down Milton's prayer to the heavenly muse: "What in me is dark / Illumine," and wrote in large letters from *Peer Gynt,* "Troll, to thyself be enough." Occasionally, I even quoted my professors if, like Professor Percy Boynton, they were given to aphorisms: "I dissent from the rather fatuous dictum that all the world loves a lover. Most of us are bored and embarrassed by him."

It was the first of my notebooks, all chiefly about life. Since that spring I have always kept one to catch the powerful words, wherever they are. When found, I have made a note of. Sometimes lately I am aware that time has brought real changes to my mind and to the tone of my selections, which tend to lack their former earnestness and sobriety. Only yesterday I came across a useful quotation from Max Beerbohm, another definition of what happiness is. He called it "a four-post bed in a field of poppies and mandragora."

On bokes for to rede I me delyte,
And to hem yive I feyth and ful credence,
And in myn herte have hem in reverence.
  —Chaucer, *The Legend of Good Women*

AS IF

What John Skelton said
Maybe John Skelton knew,
And the devil is dead.—Is *dead?*

Maybe Max Beerbohm knew
What happiness is? when he said
That it's a four-post bed

In a field of poppies and
Mandragora. Some do
Give the answers, as if they knew.

Much virtue in *as if*.

THE NAMING OF FAVORITE WRITERS

❀

This morning a student rushed into my office to ask me the names of my favorite writers. Students often make sudden peremptory demands upon one when the idea occurs. The girl stood with pencil poised, too hurried even to sit, and obediently I began at random: Chaucer, Montaigne, Madame de Sévigné, Thoreau, Mr. White of Selborne, Horace, Campion, Donne, Herrick—"Wait," she said. I repeated more slowly, adding Marcus Aurelius. It seemed to me that she left disappointed: the list was not a success, it was not really what she wanted. Where, for one thing, were my contemporaries?

I remember a class at Columbia, when I was a student, taught by Carl Van Doren who recited to us one day the names of those he loved best. I recall clearly who they were: Euripides, Lucretius, Montaigne, Fielding, Heine, Shaw, Socrates, and Leonardo da Vinci. They so appealed to me that I am astonished to think I did not take over the whole company for myself. It appears that I have got a list of my own.

❀

PICTURE POEMS

❀

"The Teacher" is an emblem or picture poem, which with doubtful taste I twisted and shaped into a pattern of diminishing and expanding lines, from hexameter to monometer and back again. Before it was printed in *The New Yorker,* however, the editors requested that I change it back, arranging the lines sensibly to look like an ordinary stanza. They wanted no monkey business like a verse in the outline of a fan, and I bowed to their better judgment.

Samuel Butler (in one of his "Characters") tells about the small poet who outdid all others by forcing a poem into the picture of a frying pan. His words, as well, were made to sound like the loud hissing and sputtering and frying that goes on at the stove in this utensil. I should love to have seen that picture poem.

Butler laughed scornfully at such nonsense. The irony is that the epitaph on his monument in Westminster Abbey should say:

> The Poet's fate is here in emblem shown:
> He asked for Bread and he received a Stone.

❁

BOOKS AND PICTURES IN

MY LIBRARY

❁

With two stout new volumes, the poems of Wallace Stevens and the poems of E. E. Cummings, I have increased my private collection. Someday it is to become a whole library, whose virtue will lie in its poetic simplicity. The books will all be thick, compact, solid objects, with an air of fatness and finality to them. Each author will be represented by his works, but in one handy volume. Every book in the vast library will bear exactly the same title: *Collected Poems*.

* * *

I plan to build, as well, a special kind of art collection. It will consist of the many paintings since the Middle Ages of Adam and Eve, side by side in a snake-free garden, holding the shining red apple as yet uneaten in their hands. The moment is just *before* the temptation, while our general parents are still smiling and innocent, pure of heart and free of guile.

Though they are yet without sin, the fig leaves covering their nakedness are already carefully and guiltily in place.

THE POETRY OF BEAUFORT'S SCALE

❋

Nobody ever told me about Beaufort's scale. I found it for myself this morning, when I was trying to write a verse and needed to know the velocity of a zephyr, the strength of a passing breeze. I looked up *breeze* in the dictionary and was referred to *gale, Beaufort's scale,* a promising rhyme right at the start. Breezes turned out to be exact and various: light ones moving up to 7 miles per hour, gentle to 12, moderate to 18, fresh to 24, and strong to 38.

It was Sir Francis Beaufort, a British admiral, who in 1805 devised a scale to measure the strength and force of winds. He was clearly a poet, one who dealt in breezes and gales. These he numbered from 0 to 12 to indicate the calamitous change in tempo that accompanies the increase of the wild, wild winds. From a perfect calm (0), when smoke rises vertically, a man first begins to feel the wind in his face. The leaves rustle. In alarming progression, loose paper whirls about, trees sway, walking grows effortful, twigs break, chimney pots fall, trees are uprooted, structures fail—until, at last, panic and terror descend upon the world! At hurricane strength and beyond (12), the terrible tornadic winds take over, roaring down destruction on us at more and more miles per hour.

When that time comes, as Sir Francis observed, devastation occurs.

※

OLD LADY SPRING

※

"Spring travels northward seventeen miles a day."
—From an editorial, *The New York Times*

Spring travels northward seventeen miles a day—
A lady of retards, a dallier
Who loiters in green air, who fools away
Her time with hyacinths. A shillyshallyer

Surviving to the Age of Jet, she moves,
Poor antique lady, by reluctant stages
Up from Miami and its pleasure groves.
And haste is not, to her, the wisdom of the ages.

Even a passing breeze—that in one hour
Covers her mileage in the twenty-four—
Is not her style. She waits for things to flower
(With miles to go before she reaches Baltimore).

A horse-and-buggy type, a lady frail
To lag in gardens, letting time unravel,
Slower than any wind in Beaufort's scale,
Yet with a thousand miles and more to travel

Upward in six days, along Route 1
Slower than light or sound, but free from worry,
Through Jacksonville, Augusta, Richmond, Washington,
She comes at last, if not apace. O lady, hurry!

❀

BLEAKNESS AT NAG'S HEAD

❀

B. and I went for a weekend in late September to Nag's Head, a great stretch of seashore on the Outer Banks of North Carolina. When we returned, a friend inquired, "Why in the world would you go there now in the fall of the year? It's so *bleak!*" Remembering the wide ashen sky, the gray wind-whipped ocean, the miles and miles of solitary beach, I could only ask in return, "What is wrong with bleakness?"

I am aware these days of a growing fondness, even preference, for bleak and bitter things. I like a bitter taste in food, a dryness in wine, and now it turns out a bleakness in landscape. It is time to drink a little wormwood in the company of Mithridates and Cliff Klingenhagen.

*   *   *

C. S. Lewis offers a word in defense of such a choice. In the volume *Surprised by Joy,* he affirms his belief that if a scene is bleak then one ought to give oneself up completely to the experience of bleakness. He advises seeking out "the places of the most grim squalor in a squalid town" and "on a dismal day the most dismal and dripping wood." A way to find joy, he says, is by accommodation, "on a windy day to seek the windiest ridge."

❀

THE EIGHTEEN-INCH MARGIN

❀

A way to find anything—even loneliness, perhaps—is by accommodation. The word loneliness itself is poignant, as in Chekhov's wistful notation in a notebook: "A field with a distant view, one tiny birch tree. The inscription under the picture: loneliness."

A few years ago, E. B. White took the trouble to measure his own loneliness. During the summer of 1948, alone in New York in a 90-degree heat, he measured with careful eye and hand as yardstick, using the greatest accuracy, and found the plight he was in to be exactly eighteen inches in length.

Such a distance, Mr. White says (in *This Is New York*), is the "eighteen-inch margin" between people in a crowded city. It is the narrow extent, the little space, the gap, the loneliness that separates one everywhere from the next person. At a drugstore counter, at a bar, at the theater (how well I remember), the stranger is at one's side, standing at one's elbow within touching distance, only eighteen inches away. To find him there, remote and indifferent, is to be helplessly alone.

THE NEW FAUST

The story of the damnation of Faust is told again this week, perhaps for the thousandth time. The new version, in a cartoon in *The New Yorker,* seems to me to dispose of the legend altogether. After thinking it over, I believe I shan't worry any longer about the value to the devil of my own worldly and perfidious soul.

In the picture the devil arrives to tempt and win to eternal damnation a contemporary mortal. The man is obviously living very well, pursuing pleasure with a drink in his relaxed hand as he lolls on his expensive terrace. His condition is like Belial's, all sloth and ignoble ease. "What?" he cries to Satan in pleased astonishment. "Do you mean to say I haven't sold my soul already?"

*   *   *

"Why this is hell," says Marlowe's Mephistopheles, "nor am I out of it."

❁

WHEN TO USE A QUOTATION?

❁

B. told me the other night that he often yearns for the right moment in which to quote a line from Anatole France (*The Human Tragedy*): "And leaning on the Archangel's shoulder, the man wept bitterly."

The Archangel is Satan. No occasion ever arises to justify so grave a comment, B. says. It never fits naturally into any conversation, and for this fact he is sorry. He took me by surprise, for I thought guiltily of the page in my notebook where the same quotation, independently found and admired, is kept and often meets my eye. One day the excuse will come, all right, for bringing in the Archangel. Then, damn it, B. will get it said first.

* * *

On the same page in my notebook, I see, is another comment of arresting and eloquent charm. It is a Chinese adage, quoted by F. L. Lucas in *Literature and Psychology*. When, I wonder, will the perfect opening ever come to *say* it to somebody?—

> "It is useless to go to bed to save
> the light, if the result is twins."

※

AN "EXHAUSTIVE" BOOK

※

Today I gave B. a Concordance of the Bible, for the sole reason that, being a passionate collector of books of reference, he wanted it. Then it turned out that we now had a Concordance but no Bible in the house. The fact that it was called "Exhaustive" (the Rev. James Strong's *Exhaustive Concordance,* containing, for example, every single instance, every last occurrence in the Bible of the articles *a, and,* and *the*) pleased us both very much, seeming to justify the price and recommend the gift. B.'s own mind is somewhat thorough and exhaustive in itself, given to complete recall, testing all possibilities.

Right away he asked me to think of a word to look up. On a bright, cheerful day, the first one that came into my head was "darkly," which appears only once in the Bible, the way you see through a glass darkly. "Darkness," oh my, is everywhere, especially in the Book of Job ("I have made my bed in the darkness").

After that, we thought of lighter words, such as "belly" ("Thy belly is like a heap of wheat") and "the whore of Babylon." She appears to be the same attractive lady of Revelation as the "scarlet woman" ("arrayed in purple and scarlet colour upon a scarlet coloured beast, full of names of blasphemy, having seven heads and ten horns"). Hollywood should put her into a film.

❋

THE LESSON OF M. BUREAU

❋

When I met recently a professor from the University of Liége, a M. Bureau, I taught myself to remember his name by thinking of a chest of drawers. I wondered, though, why surnames almost never refer to a piece of furniture or to the possessions *within* a house. House itself is common enough, but you don't find people named Bed or Armchair, Sofa, Stove, Sink, Rug, or even Door or Doorknocker. Why isn't there a Mr. Bookshelf or a Mrs. John Teacup? I can think so far of only two exceptions: Pott and Kettle. Wall is familiar, but it may well be an outside wall.

This is a strange thing, since names are everywhere represented outside and beyond the house: Wood, Field, Garden, Gate, Bird, Brook, Pool, Pond, River, Hill, Mountain, Forest, Bush, Tree, Branch, Flower, Berry, Stone, Moss, Mudd, and so on. There was the poet John Greenleaf Whittier. And I once knew and admired a Miss Appletree.

❀

READING ALOUD IN BED

❀

B. likes to read aloud and I like to listen, particularly in bed. Our only problem is to keep me awake, since B. sees no virtue or advantage in reading aloud to himself. He employs various unfair means to discover my state of consciousness, like giving my name to one of the characters, if it is a novel, or without changing his tone of voice saying, "The quick brown fox jumped over the lazy dog," or "I love you, I love you, I love you."

We have had to rule out Macaulay, the most soporific of writers, at least for me. Much as I enjoyed listening to the *History of England,* Vol. I, during the winter, it was so sleep-inducing that I heard only one sentence a night. By the time we had sailed along the stream of Macaulay's dependent clauses, parenthetical expressions, and qualifying phrases to reach the first period, I was lulled and lost. Neither words of history nor words of love could wake me up.

＊

OF LOVE, A FEW NOTES TAKEN

＊

I. EIGHTEENTH-CENTURY LADY

"Ladies were frighted of everything but a man."
—WILLIAM IRVING, *John Gay's London*

Uneasy, unstrung, unnerved, upset, and aflutter,
Anxious, ashiver, atremble, a pigeonheart,

Of all the quakers and shakers I am no braver than,
She is the lady entirely my counterpart,

Frighted of everything in the Eighteenth Century
Except (undaunted as we are) a man.

II. THE SEVENTH HEAVEN

"The seventh heaven is formed of divine light beyond the power of tongue to describe."
—Brewer's *Dictionary of Phrase and Fable*

The first is silver, where the stars
Hang out like lamps on a golden chain.
The second is gold. The third is pearl.
Heaven Four outglows Aldebaran.
Five is crystal, Six is ruby,
Snow and fire in the ultimate sky,
But O, my love, of the seventh heaven
None will say, and they know why.

And so do I.

*　　*　　*

III. SUNDAY

"It [Sunday] should be different from another day
People may walk, but not throw stones at birds."
—Dr. Johnson

I'll walk on Sunday and in silk,
And throw to you a silken word
It wouldn't hurt a man to hear,
And couldn't hit a mockingbird.

288

No wood thrush will be safer, no
Field sparrow, or its family,
Than you will be of any stone
Or stonyheartedness from me.

*　　　*　　　*

IV. CATEGORIES

"*Category* should be used by no-one who is not prepared to
state (1) that he does not mean *class*, & (2) that he knows the
difference between the two words."—Fowler's *Modern English
Usage*

The mind is categorical. I could,
For instance, put into one pigeonhole
As Yeats did, *Flesh,* into another *Soul.*

I could count angels on a needle point
With half a mind, and save the other part
(A solitary chamber) for the heart,

Yet hold within my head the separate stars,
Remember verse, invent myself a story,
Keep bees in still another category.

Because the mind is its own place, I could,
With items of such breadth and magnitude,
Fill every pigeonhole—yet think of you.

I could. My love, how constantly I do.

V. NOW WITH MY LOVE

"Where to thy haunts two kindred spirits flee."
—KEATS, *To Solitude*

Now with my love I walk alone
And without any company—
Solitary on the earth
With him for sociability,

Where, individual, apart,
By myself yet by his side,
I walk alone with him as one,
Not separate but unified,

At once (together) less than two,
If singleness is so construed
As his and mine. And with my love
I walk alone in solitude.

LOVE SCENE, SUNSET LAKE

The lake is dark and silent. I am beholden
To you for your nearness and love and prayerfully glad
For your skill with boats, especially in pitchblack water.
I wish I were in my bed! I wish I had

More mettle, or else a less oddly consuming desire
To please a man when he chooses to beckon me
Onto a moonless lake, alone, at midnight.
I wish I could please you but not so heroically,

Not where we are, in this tangle of reeds together
Along the shore, a thicket of boughs overhead
Reaching for me with terrible clinging fingers.
"*Listen!*" you whisper. Isn't that what you said?

What else can I do *but* listen? but quail? but shiver?
To hear what you hear, my love, the one bullfrog
Hoarse in the dark beyond us. In jetblack darkness,
One edible bullfrog waits out there on a log.

*   *   *

Goodbye, goodbye, my love. And if forever, then—
Where am I now? In the damned lake, up to my chin!

Caught in these frightful grasses! ... But forward, forward,
I see him.... *My God, but what am I stepping in?*

Tomorrow (if it comes), you'll have his legs for breakfast
(Unless he eats me first). Quick! Shine the light,
Into his eyes! Suppose he should turn and find me
Creeping upon him, and leap! I'd die of fright....

Forgive me, this is it, relax, frog, I beg you,
And don't let me fail him now. Both hands, now, spring!
I've missed? Oh, no, no, I haven't! the fat, wet monster!
And what do I do next, oh! with this fearful thing?

I bear him off to the man in the boat. I extend this
Bullfrog to you, with my heart. With my compliments.
Here, TAKE HIM! BEFORE I DROWN! ... I really have
    pleased you?
Then it's one way, my love. (One that doesn't make much
    sense.)

❀

KARL ON MT. PARNASSUS

❀

Karl is the only man in the world I happen to know who
has climbed Mt. Parnassus, except for Byron, who rode a
mule up there. Last night Karl told of the rocky climb he
took up the sacred mountain last August in the congenial

company of a Greek guide and his mule, both of whom knew no English.

Unlike Chaucer's Franklin, who said apologetically (of his lack of eloquence), "I sleep never on the mount of Pernaso," Karl spent a whole night up there. At 8000 feet on a holy summit once consecrated to Apollo, he slept dreamlessly and returned next day to Delphi.

The hills of Parnassus, as one might expect in our time, are more than ever rock-strewn and barren, though asphodel grows on the lower slopes (which is as far up as most poets get). Instead of gods reciting or bacchantes dancing, there are only black goats feeding and a lot of loneliness. You still hear Parnassian song, however, Karl says. All about you is the steady song of crickets, and everywhere over Parnassus is the grieving, haunting melody of the goat bells.

❈

HOLY WATER FROM DELPHI

❈

Karl's wife Ann brought back a little water to me from the Castalian spring at the foot of Mt. Parnassus, the sacred spring of poetry. It comes from a deep clear pool (but in a trickle now) dedicated to Apollo and the Muses, and is supposed to inspire whoever drinks it with the true fire and passion of song. I haven't had the heart to drink any, though in the tiny glass bottle it looks potent, even pure. What are the odds, the perils? What would one hope or fear from holy water when the gods themselves are dead? Perhaps, as the oracle once told, the Castalia now drops only tears.

*   *   *

For more than a thousand years, men came to Castalia to consult the oracle. Agamemnon, Homer says, visited the spring before he set out for Troy. In that long ago, a priestess of the shrine sat on a three-legged stool over a fissure in the rock and in a frenzy cried out wild and incoherent words which a priest changed into verse, the poems of the golden god Apollo.

In 390 A.D. Theodosius closed the shrine forever. Ann copied down and gave me what is still kept as a bitter last oracle from Delphi:

Daphne does not have divination
Nor a home any more the god.
Nor within the rocks does the Pythia rave the interpretation.
Wan the light falls on the ferocious Phaidriades
And tears drip
Dumb, the Castalia drops tears.

In our time, Yeats has written an obscure and incoherent poem called "News for the Delphic Oracle," but I only believe after reading it that the god stopped inspiring poets long, long ago.

✻

SPEAKING OF SPRINGS

✻

To find the Fountain of Eternal Youth
(There being *three,* I hear, in Florida),
Or as immortally seek after truth
By drinking deep of the Pierian spring—
Each is a quest, an ancient enterprise,
I've often dreamed of as accomplishing,

Like you, perhaps. One, sacred to the Muses,
A spring, a source, a well of poetry,
Has even in this ailing world its uses.
The other, flowing nectar from the earth
To change men into gods forever young,
Has yet, among the thirsty of us, worth,

Or so I reasoned until now. But lately
Two travelers with cautionary tales
Of their own journeys, meant to educate me,
Have warned me these elixirs are *no more.*
They say the quest for poetry and youth
And immortality is over. For

The traveler to Florida, elated
To find his fountain, took a brimming cup,
And brought back word that it was chlorinated.

The traveler to Greece, who in one minute
Might slake what thirst? at the Pierian spring,
Said that there wasn't any water in it.

And, God knows, either is a dangerous thing.

❀

THE GIANT SEQUOIA

❀

A friend of mine, who is a biologist at Harvard, sent me a few seeds a while ago. "Here are your seeds. Love, Ned," he wrote on the small envelope, because last summer in Cambridge I begged for a few from the collection he had brought back with him from California. I then planted a half dozen of these narrow seeds, about ¼ inch long, in a flower pot with peat moss and lots of water. Now at last one thin, fragile green shoot has come up. It is remarkably tiny, very frail, but I trust it is the real thing: a giant sequoia.

I shall watch closely this potential giant that belongs in mist and cloud in the Sierra Nevadas at an altitude (like that of Parnassus) of 8000 feet. So far it looks like a green prickle, but if it stays alive and hardy it will make a fine inheritance for my children and their descendants for the next three or four thousand years. John Muir called it the Big Tree, one that should grow, I figure, to be as wide as my house and as high as the radio tower on the next hill. At the moment it is a giant sequoia all of two inches high. Give it time.

*   *   *

A professor of botany at Duke University, whose advice we asked as to how to care for the tender young sequoia over the winter, says it will probably be winter-killed if left outdoors and probably die in the house from too much dryness and heat. A nicely balanced dilemma. I have decided to keep it inside, where the fact that it may not prove immortal makes it no different from the other occupants. On the other hand, if it persists it will teach us a long lesson in survival and the will to live.

*   *   *

The sequoia reminds me of a great oak said to be nine hundred years old that I saw in the Middleton gardens, famous for its live oaks, in Charleston. ("Three hundred years to grow, three hundred years to live, and three hundred years to die," said the oak about itself in T. H. White's *The Sword in the Stone*.) Because of its long life span, I stopped to embrace the tree and thus reach back for a moment to the eleventh century and the Norman Conquest. I have often touched old ruins for the same reason, but they feel vastly different from old trees. To the flesh this oak had vitality—the spectacular quality of being, as no doubt it was on a day in 1066, alive.

THE CACTUS PLANT

A cactus plant has its own peculiar use in the home. At the cocktail party, I stood crowded against a low table, listening to a group of my friends whose talk grew louder by the minute. I leaned forward to raise my voice in my turn. Suddenly a very sharp prick from behind stopped me short. It came like a cry of admonishment, clear as a bell, plain as if I had been spoken to. "Hold on!" it said, reproachfully. "Not so loud!"

A moment afterward with more foolish words on my tongue, I leaned forward again, only to be silenced and abashed by the same quick means. This time I looked behind me to discover the small horny cactus, all spines erect, perched and watchful at the edge of the table. "Thank you, I have the message," I said, and moved a little to the right to make room at that prickly spot for the next guest.

A DUFY WATERCOLOR

We have just mounted, framed, and hung a Dufy watercolor print called "The Open Window" in the dining room. Now we look freely out of the two windows, the real one of that room at our carlot, woodpile, daffodil garden, and dogwood tree; and Dufy's window—with its bowl of red flowers on the sill—at the bright green terraces of southern France, the steep vineyards, and the luminous orange trees.

I think the picture must be of St. Paul de Vence, where in 1950, in our room in the hotel, there was a window flung wide open with a view exactly like Dufy's. It is true that Dufy's blue and yellow window frame is drawn sadly askew and lopsided. His trees are so hastily sketched as not to be called trees at all but, rather, tiny green daubs; his hills are a mere curving stroke of brown paint; his gaudy colors are childish, louder than life. But obviously that is not the way to look through his open window. If I back away from it and narrow my eyes a little, I recognize the view perfectly and even my joy as an earlier observer, in brilliant reality in a Mediterranean sun.

❁

LADY AT THE WINDOW

❁

Donna della finestra
At the window of the mind—
Like a Venetian lady
Leaning upon the sill,
Like a fair Florentine
Half-hid by the windowblind,
Or Roman, or Veronese,
At her casement still;

Like a cinquecento lady,
Windowframed and waiting,
She is someone forever
Longing for someone—
Donna della finestra,
Like a portrait by the Old Masters,
Who knew well that a lady
In love is always one.

✿

STANDING ON ONE'S HEAD

✿

A friend sent me in the morning mail a newspaper clipping pasted on a postcard. It told of Prime Minister Nehru, now in his seventies, starting every day by standing on his head for three minutes. An aide explained to a reporter: "This is not yoga but just an elementary exercise to improve his blood circulation."

I have been standing on my head since I was about five years old. At first the performance was intermittent and largely for purposes of showing off. Then sometime in my twenties I read about Lady Mendl, who stood on her head daily in her advancing years to achieve longevity and prolong the sweet bloom of youth. Thereafter this was my single exercise, still faithfully adhered to. I am always confident upside down that it may be doing me some good.

In 1933 I saw a play in New York called *Spring in Autumn,* by Martinez Sierra, in which Blanche Yurka played an opera singer who stood on her head before the footlights in a tight black satin gown to sing an aria from—I've forgotten now, either *La Bohème* or *La Traviata.* My own choice is Wagner, to gasp out each morning all that I know of the "Liebestod" from *Tristan und Isolde.* If I ever fall and break my neck, the tune will make a good requiem.

※

INSPIRATION OF LADY MENDL

※

Youth and longevity,
Priceless to her and me,
She once attributed
To standing on her head.

Therefore upon my own
Skull, on my cranial bone—
Though a peculiar way
Of holding time at bay,

One hoisted foot in air
And one astray somewhere—
Like Lady Mendl I
Too the quick years defy

Doggedly on my crown,
Reflecting upside down
How sweet is youth to me!
How dear longevity!

❀

A BREATHING LESSON

❀

Because of a slight cough and a heaviness in the chest, B. has been given a breathing lesson by his doctor. The idea of tinkering with his intake of breath appeals to B. not at all. He assumes he already knows how to breathe. The trick is to blow out for thirty seconds at a time to rid the lungs of stale air and let fresh air rush in to take its place. This is rather tempestuous work, which heaves the breast.

I know the kind of breathing B. would like, but I will not remind him of the answer right there on his bookshelf. In 1780 Philip Thicknesse wrote *The Valetudinarian's Bath Guide, or The Means of Obtaining Long Life and Health,* and in it he recommended a wholesome method of taking in gulps of pure air: by breathing the breath of young virgins.

"Everybody has experienced the sweetness of the breath of cows," Philip Thicknesse argued. Young girls properly brought up have a sweet breath, too, the fragrancy of which "falls little short of that of cows." It is clear to Thicknesse that innocent girls are the answer.

The solution is fine, but the logic strikes me as odd, since he never explains why one should go to the trouble to ferret out the maidens, chaste maidens at that, instead of walking into a meadowful of cows and breathing in. Thicknesse does say that he got these hints on breathing from Hermippus, who he thinks was either a tutor or a director of a college of young virgins.

※

A POOR MEMORY

※

A poor memory (like mine) is not a poor thing to possess if one may have it in common with the literate and the wise. Madame de Sévigné once wrote in a letter to her daughter, "*C'est un plaisir, ma belle, que de n'avoir point de memoire.*"

Montaigne created a memory for himself on paper. He was obliged to write down his deepest thoughts if he wanted to have them still around by tomorrow. "*La vie est un songe,*" he said, but his dreams were only chimeras, more foolish than sorrowful, that did not stay with him till morning. He too had no memory at all.

*   *   *

In saying so, I have forgotten Montaigne's mustaches. They acted as a discreet aid to memory, often telling him where he had been and what he had been up to. When he was young they reminded him, he said, of the "close-smacking, sweetness-moving, love-alluring, and greedy-smirking kisses of youth," which stuck hauntingly to his mustaches, giving off fragrant memories to the air for a whole day afterward.

✿

MADAME DE SÉVIGNÉ

AND THE SPIRIT

✿

By now it seems she walks immortal,
Who in her own enlightened way
Of walking on the earth, in person,
So lightly took mortality.

Too little, yet, a soul or spirit
To do so lamentable a thing
As pose as one, she found the body
More natural and flattering

To move about in, firm of step,
Within the daylit world, a mortal,
Who for her perishable flesh
Is bodiless now and immortal.

THE HOLY CITY OF ALEXANDRIA

Yeats chose for his celestial city (the heaven of his mind) Byzantium. The holy city of my imagination is Alexandria, a place of poetry and books, learning and love. It was here that Alexander the Great, who founded it in 332 B.C. and meant to make it the capital of his world conquests, instead occupied his tomb.

A Poet of the third century B.C. described its academy as the "bird-coop of the Muses."

Euclid flourished here in 300 B.C. and said, "There is no royal road to geometry."

About 270 B.C. the words of the Septuagint came to exist.

Its two great libraries contained books of philosophy, physic, and the stars. When a foreigner visited the city, his books were seized to increase the splendid collection, and he was given copies instead.

Callimachus, a Greek poet, was a librarian at Alexandria about 250 B.C. He is credited with eight hundred works, which must have been admirably short works, for he once wisely said, "A big book is a big evil."

Caesar in his time dallied here with Cleopatra, and in 30 B.C. Antony and Cleopatra lost all for love.

In the second century A.D., Ptolemy of Alexandria invented a magnificently wrong cosmology, with this world the center of God's eye; and it became the Ptolemaic theory of an orderly, created universe, useful at least to Milton in writing of Heaven and Hell.

Finally, it was here that the Arabs, who burned Alexandria in 652, found a place still beautiful and wise, with books "sufficient to heat the 4,000 baths of the city for six months."

❀

TAKING STOCK WITH PEPYS

❀

At the year's end, when the mind quails before another twelvemonth, there is Pepys. Each December 31 he totted up his purse and took stock of self, wife, family, estate, and state of the nation, all with incredibly good grace and humble, thankful heart.

"Blessed be Almighty God," he wrote at the end of 1660, for the good health he had, at age 27, and about £300 clear in the world, "a most handsome and thriving condition."

Four Decembers later, he was still thriving (with more than a thousand pounds to his name), so much so that he was at a loss to lay his well-being to a hare's foot or to the taking every morning of a turpentine pill. He wrote, "I am in good esteem with everybody, I think," and kissed his wife a merry new year as the clock struck.

By the end of 1665 (now worth the sum of £4,400), Pepys viewed, but hardly with dismay, a world that was fast going to pieces. It was the fearful time of the onset of the plague, and his aunt Bell was already dead of it, yet he exclaimed to his *Diary,* "I have never lived so merrily." The future only filled him with the strange confidence that he would go right on doing so.

What followed was the terrifying year of doom, of plague and fire, 1666, almost spelling the finish for London and for Pepys. Of this close call, and his own near-ruin, he wrote: "Thus ends this year of publick wonder and mischief to this nation, and therefore generally wished by all people to have an end." "Yet, blessed be God!" he added, and having somehow survived destruction by the skin of his teeth, looked forward hopefully, with faith and thankfulness and few regrets.

XII

The World Is a Book

❋

THE WORLD IS A BOOK

❋

"Now welcom somer, with thy sonne softe"
—*Parlement of Foules*

Now welcome, summer. With thy *sonne softe*
Upon my head, the possibilities
Of pure escape again begin to haunt me—
Like June, say, in the higher Pyrenees.
I would depart for Zanzibar tomorrow,
Save for a qualm or two. There is, of course,
Always the thought that, if an ass goes traveling,
Proverbially he'll not come home a horse.
There is the man who journeyed to Beersheba
And cried out, " 'Tis all barren!" So when I
Notice the look of flowering around me
And feel this qualm about a change of sky,

Then I remember. There are other tourists,
More like Thoreau who laughed at Zanzibar
As somewhere full of cats, yet chose to travel
Farther to Walden where the cattails are.
Or like that global Mr. White of Selborne
Who wrote a guidebook, journeys out of June,
Full of such planetary shrine and wonder

As hoot owls hooting in B flat, in tune;
A swallow in the air; a flight of lapwings;
The hayricks of July; the August field
Where harvest bugs walk up and bite the ladies.
And there it is, the perfect trip revealed—

A tour of world affairs with summer in it,
Priced modestly, in my own dooryard. Oh,
Even the vision of the prophet Daniel,
Who dreamed that "Many shall run to and fro
And knowledge shall be increased" yields to my vision!
For what some find in Tanganyika some
Find in a book—and stay at home to read it,
Maintaining thus an equilibrium.
I plan to travel, therefore, in this region
Among the lilies, like a bibliophil,
Though neither book, nor swallow, makes a summer,
The poet says. No doubt a dozen will.

For one, the book of Marvell: in his garden
Are worlds to visit ripening and serene,
Where, in green shade, you think not only green thoughts
But (to your credit) of an amorous green.
For one, the book of Herrick: which is Devon
And quite another country, timeliest
For roses, roses, everywhere—though really
The place to find them is at Julia's breast
And look for Herrick, also. With the poets
Are ever Julias; so who wouldn't come
To do, instructed by poetic meters,
A bit of gardening there! (Te-tum, te-tum.)

No fairer worlds, if this is world enough,
Perhaps need mention. Yet I can't deny
Its landscape may look to the next beholder,
As Chaucer said, not worth a butterfly.
"In every country dogges bite," goes the warning;
And books are queer abiding places, where
Some may prefer to curl up with a Trollope,
Or some to travel with Montaigne the stair
Up to a thousand volumes in a tower—
While others have the summer in them. They
Oftener read, I think, the book of moonlight,
Or any text on meadowlarks, by day,

And wait to hear the grass grow—while the skeptics,
Like Dr. Johnson, call it only grass—
And even argue if a man goes traveling
In that domain he'll not come home an ass.
Whatever the topography, the world *is*
A book, it seems, although as Wordsworth said
The opposite is true: "And books, we know,
Are a substantial world." From all I've read,
I'd have it both ways and in either country
(As Wordsworth saw it, or St. Augustine),
Content to come and go by either journey
Now in the summer when the world is green—
Especially, I hope, an amorous green.

ABOUT THE AUTHOR

HELEN BEVINGTON *was born in New York State and educated at the University of Chicago and Columbia University. She is now an associate professor of English at Duke University in Durham, North Carolina, where her husband, Merle Bevington, is a professor. Her three published collections of poems are entitled* Doctor Johnson's Waterfall (*1946*), Nineteen Million Elephants (*1950*) *and* A Change of Sky (*1956*). *Many more of her poems have appeared in* The New Yorker *and* The Atlantic Monthly. *The* New York Sunday Times Book Review *has run a specially written poem of hers on the front page of several holiday issues in recent years.*

818
B

Bevington, Helen
When found, make a verse
of.

Wilmington Public Library
Wilmington, N. C.

RULES

1. Books marked 7 days may be kept one **week.**
Books marked 14 days, two weeks. The latter
may be renewed, if more than 6 months old.

2. A fine of two cents a day will be charged on
each book which is not returned according to the
above rule. No book will be issued to any person having a fine of 25 cents or over.

3. A charge of ten cents will be made for
mutilated plastic jackets. All injuries to books
beyond reasonable wear and all losses shall be
made good to the satisfaction of the Librarian.

4. Each borrower is held responsible for all
books drawn on his card and for all fines accruing on the same.

THE TEAM THAT WOULDN'T DIE

The Philadelphia Phillies
World Champions 1980

THE TEAM THAT WOULDN'T DIE

The Philadelphia Phillies
World Champions 1980

by
Hal Bodley

Foreword by Rich Ashburn

SERENDIPITY
PRESS

in association with
the Philadelphia National League Club

To PAT . . .

*for picking me up and encouraging me at
a very difficult time.*

THE TEAM THAT WOULDN'T DIE
Philadelphia Phillies World Champions 1980

Copyright © 1981 by Hal Bodley
Published by Serendipity Press, Building C, Suite 102
3801 Kennett Pike, Wilmington, Delaware 19807

The News-Journal Company, Wilmington, Delaware, has authorized the republication of its material appearing in this book.

Bill Conlin's column, as quoted, originally was printed in *The Philadelphia Daily News* on September 22, 1980.

The publisher acknowledges contributions by *The Sporting News* including several regular season, the league championship and World Series boxscores.

Library of Congress catalog card number 81-50806
ISBN 0-914988-06-9

Printed in the United States of America

Design by POCO Enterprises

Contents

Foreword

After slogging through 80 consecutive years of baseball without an ultimate victory.

After suffering 51 losing seasons, highlighted by one five year stretch when they lost over 100 games each season. After being humiliated in the league championship play of 1976, 1977 and 1978.

After losing badly in two previous, generations-apart World Series appearances (1915 and 1950). After losing 23 games in a row in 1961—a major league record. After blowing a 6½ game lead and a pennant in 1964 by losing 10 straight games in September.

After all this, it was inevitable that someone would write a book if the Phillies ever won a World Series.

No writer is better qualified than Hal Bodley. Hal is sports editor of the Wilmington, Delaware, News-Journal papers and columnist for the Gannett News Service. He was recently elected president of the Associated Press Sports Editors, an organization representing over 400 sports editors. As a sports writer and columnist, Hal has been covering the fortunes of the Phillies for the last 23 years.

The Team That Wouldn't Die is an appropriate title for Bodley's book. Almost everyone buried the Phillies when they lost a four game series to the Pirates in early August, dropping six games behind Pittsburgh. And twice in the league championship play offs against the Houston Astros the Phillies were six outs away from elimination. (In one of those games they trailed Nolan Ryan by four runs in the eighth inning.) Finally, of course, they had to come from behind to win three of the four games they took from Kansas City in the World Series. Hal does an outstanding job of capturing the mood of these moments in *The Team That Wouldn't Die*.

In fact, Bodley accurately covers the trials and tribulations of the 1980 Phillies from start to finish.

The Phillies had a lot of problems in spring training. They were a good team but they weren't good enough to win a division title, let alone a World Series, at least according to the experts. And they had a new manager, Dallas Green, who had alienated many of his key players.

The 1980 Phillies were a team that fought for most of the season. They fought the manager, they fought each other, they fought the press and they fought the fans. But with about six weeks of the season left to play, something happened—the Phillies started fighting the team they were playing against. After reading *The Team That Wouldn't Die*, you can draw your own conclusions as to how and why they turned their season around.

Bodley has not pulled any punches in his interviews with the players or the front office. You'll read some very candid, sometimes startling, sometimes controversial statements from players and management alike.

Owner Ruly Carpenter frankly talks about his strained relationship with the press and also gives us the inside story of the firing of Danny Ozark and the hiring of Dallas Green. Ruly reveals the story of his "intercession" in signing Garry Maddox to a long-term contract when it appeared Maddox would leave the Phillies.

Phillies Player Personnel Director Paul Owens discusses

the clubhouse meeting he called on the West Coast, a meeting in which he ripped into Maddox and Larry Bowa. After that meeting, by the way, there was a significant improvement in the quality of play by the Phillies.

Dallas Green is the only Phillies manager who can say he won a World Series for the Phillies. But he paid the price. He was and still is publicly maligned by his players. In *The Team That Wouldn't Die* Green explains many of the discipline problems he encountered after taking over for the easy-going, unflappable Danny Ozark. He tells of his knock-down, drag-out clubhouse meetings and of his near-miss fight with pitcher Ron Reed in the Pittsburgh Pirates' visiting dugout.

Bodley hits a grand slam home run in his interview with pitcher Steve Carlton—yes, the same Steve Carlton who hasn't been interviewed by a writer in years.

The "cool" Mike Schmidt articulately reveals his feelings about the 1980 season and why he, all of a sudden, started picking up the big hits. You'll also see a side of him that will surprise you.

Bake McBride reveals the inside story of his "feud" with Schmidt after Mike was awarded the Most Valuable Player honor in the World Series.

The sensitive Garry Maddox tells a poignant story of his childhood and of a frightening tour of duty in Vietnam. Maddox also goes into detail about his troubles that started from "day one" with Dallas Green.

The irrepressible Tug McGraw discusses his early days with the Phillies when "I was rejected by the players." And he tells a heart-warming story of his relationship with his wife, Phyllis.

You'll read how Pete Rose separates his not-so-personal, personal life from his play on the diamond. And he describes the incredible catch in the sixth game of the World Series when he grabbed the foul ball that bounced off Bob Boone's mitt.

Author's Remarks

It was a cold, March afternoon in 1958 when my mother dropped me off at the train station in Wilmington.

Armed with an old Crown Graphic camera and a battered Smith-Corona portable typewriter, I was off on an adventure that would be the beginning of my life's work.

I was going to Clearwater, Florida to cover the Philadelphia Phillies in spring training! I had worked summers as the sports editor of the Delaware State News in Dover while struggling through the University of Delaware, so when I suggested it would be nice for me to go to spring training, the little daily newspaper had no objections. I had to pay my own expenses, of course, but who cared?

It took the Silver Meteor 24 hours to make the trip; it seemed like an eternity.

I stayed at the Fort Harrison Hotel and it was there I met Allen Lewis of the Inquirer and Ray Kelly of the Bulletin and Byrum Saam, the announcer. For some reason—they've never told me why—these men took me under their arms and for two weeks I got a cram course in how to cover a major-league baseball team.

"The first thing is stop asking for Seven-and-Seven," growled Ray Kelly. "You're in the big leagues now. It's CC and ginger. And when we go on road trips, the rookie always pays the tolls. So get up the two bucks. Fast!"

For me, covering a baseball team had to be just about the most exciting thing a man could do, especially someone who was a frustrated athlete.

My dad, a Delaware banker, took me to my first major league game in 1950. It was the opening contest of the 1950 World Series at Shibe Park. Jim Konstanty was the starting pitcher for the Phillies against the Yankees and lost 1–0. From that day on, even though my father envisioned a career in law for me, I wanted to do something with baseball.

It has been fun.

I've lived and died with the Phillies for 30 years, 23 as a sports writer.

When the Phillies finally won their first world championship in 1980 I felt the need to do something more lasting than newspaper stories.

I mentioned my idea to J. Blan vanUrk, publisher at Serendipity Press, after the second game of the World Series and that's when the seed for *The Team That Wouldn't Die* was planted. Jack vanUrk accepted the idea and the four months it has taken to produce this volume have been the most educational, the most grueling and the most rewarding of my career. VanUrk, and his indefatigable vice president, Frederick H. "Hawk" Pollard, have been tremendous. Without their assistance, and constant screaming about missing deadlines, this project would never have been finished.

I also must recognize the patience of John Curley, president and publisher, and Sidney Hurlburt, executive editor, of the News-Journal papers. I know I neglected my duties as sports editor while writing this book, but they never said a word. Maybe it was because my assistant, Tom Lindley, covered for me so well.

And then there was Dick Kaegel, managing editor of The Sporting News. He encouraged me and never said anything when I was late with my weekly column for that publication.

I did over 75 interviews for the book and over 100 hours of audio tape was typed into readable transcript by Beth Miller of my sports staff. When she couldn't handle it my secretary, Theresa Taylor, did—with a giggle.

The Phillies' front office, especially Baron Larry Shenk and Bill Giles, went out of their way to help. So did Paul Owens and Ruly Carpenter.

As I neared the end I thought back to a day in 1953 when I was playing outfield for the Smyrna High School Eagles. I dropped a fly ball and was immediately taken out of the game. "Bodley," Coach Bob Everett said, "I think you better stick to sports writing if you want to make the big leagues. You're not going to make it as a player."

That was about the time my English teachers, Mr. and Mrs. Charles V. Williams, steered me to journalism.

"You'll write a book someday," Ruth Williams said. I laughed and didn't believe her. Know something? She was right, but it took a Phillies' world championship for it to happen.

Hal Bodley
March 1981

After 98 seasons . . .
the wait was worth it

For one brief moment the mass of humanity became scary quiet. Tug McGraw took a long, deep breath, obviously trying to reach back inside his tired body for something extra.

The pitch was a fastball. Down the middle.

Willie Wilson swung and missed and it was over. The Philadelphia Phillies were finally world champions! They had defeated the Kansas City Royals 4–1 to win the World Series and complete one of the most incredible seasons in baseball history.

The 65,838 fans who jammed Veterans Stadium for the sixth game of the autumn classic on the night of October 21, 1980 exploded as the zany McGraw, fists clenched high above his head, leaped off the mound. Teammates were all over the diamond jumping and celebrating, exorcising the frustrations of years gone by.

Hundreds of policemen kept the near-delirious fans back with dogs and guns and horses as a crescendo of fireworks brightened the sky above the South Philadelphia playground.

It had taken 98 years but the Phillies had finally reached the promised land.

While the long-suffering fans started their own celebration that would last into the winter and be remembered for

years to come, the beaten Royals slowly filed to their dressing room, the numbing shock just beginning to set in.

For the Phillies, the ghosts of 1915 and 1950 and 1964 and those three disappointing playoff years had finally been buried.

"We're world champions and nobody will ever forget that," third baseman Mike Schmidt kept shouting above the hysteria that swept the clubhouse that jubilant night. "We're world champions! World champions!"

Owner Ruly Carpenter and Manager Dallas Green and Player Personnel Director Paul Owens, the men who molded and pampered and encouraged the team, hugged each other and cried tears of joy.

"We had heart! We had character!" Green, drenched in champagne, yelled. "We're an unbelievable baseball team right now; we could beat anybody in the world. The city has wanted a championship for a long time and we've finally got our niche now."

Yes, the 1980 Philadelphia Phillies finally made it. They survived a gut-wrenching month of baseball that will go down as one of the most exciting our national pastime has known.

Too many times the doormat or the court jesters of the National League, the Phillies had waited a long time for a world championship.

The first game in National League history was played in Philadelphia in 1876 between Boston and the Philadelphia Athletics. The '76 team, however, didn't last the season leaving the city without a National League representative until 1883 when Alfred J. Reach purchased the Worcester, Mass., club and moved it to Philadelphia, adopting "Phillies" as the official team name.

In 1915, Pat Moran, who had taken over as manager after finishing his playing career, guided the Phils to a World Series date against the Boston Red Sox.

Hall-of-Fame pitcher Grover Cleveland Alexander and

right fielder Gavvy Cravath were the outstanding players on the 1915 team which won the pennant with a percentage of .592, lowest to win a National League title up to that point.

After winning 31 games, including 12 shutouts during the regular season, Alexander defeated Boston 3–1 in the Series opener with an eight-hitter. Among the Red Sox he retired on a groundout was Babe Ruth, then a young left-handed pitcher, who was used in that game as a pinch-hitter. That was Ruth's only appearance in the World Series, even though he was the American League leader in games won that season with 18.

The Red Sox then won four straight by one run—three in a row by 2–1 and the final 5–4.

Late in 1943 the Phils were sold to the late Robert R. M. Carpenter Sr. after baseball commissioner Judge Kenesaw Mountain Landis ordered lumberman Bill Cox to sell the franchise. Cox allegedly had been involved in gambling practices that Judge Landis felt were detrimental to baseball. There had been nine other owners between Reach and Carpenter.

To stimulate interest, a contest was conducted to find a nickname for the Phillies. For 1944 and 1945 the players were known as the Blue Jays, although the official title "Phillies" was maintained.

Carpenter, a Du Pont Company executive from Wilmington, Delaware, immediately turned the club over to his son, Robert R. M. Jr., and seven years later the Phillies, now known as the "Whiz Kids," rose to become National League champions again.

As in 1915 with Alexander and in 1980 with Steve Carlton a great pitcher helped get them there—Robin Roberts, now a Hall of Famer.

The 1950 Phils, managed by Eddie Sawyer, had a terrific battle down the stretch with the Brooklyn Dodgers, winning the pennant on the final day of the season on Dick Sisler's historic home run at old Ebbetts Field.

The New York Yankees, managed by Casey Stengel and

with a line-up that included Joe DiMaggio, swept the World Series in four games. They won each of the first three by one run and the fourth 5–2.

So, when the Phillies shocked Kansas City in the first game of the '80 Series, it was their first victory in a World Series since Grover Cleveland Alexander did it in 1915.

After the disappointment of 1950, the Phils began gradually to fall, eventually becoming the worst team in the league, if not the majors. They regrouped briefly in 1964 under Gene Mauch and appeared certain to return to the World Series. With 12 games to go they returned from a West Coast trip leading the National League by 6½ games. Red, white and blue banners were already being hung at Connie Mack Stadium.

What followed was the worst nightmare in the franchise's not-so-proud history.

The Phils lost their next 10 games and were on the sidelines watching St. Louis and the New York Yankees battle in the World Series when October arrived.

After 29 years as club president Bob Carpenter moved up to the position of chairman of the board on November 22, 1972, and turned over the presidency to his son, Robert R. M. (Ruly) Carpenter III.

Young Carpenter, who by this time had served his apprenticeship with grass-roots baseball veteran Paul Owens, began with the Pope's help to give the organization a new look. Together they began building a solid foundation for years to come, a blend of outstanding proven talent and youngsters from a revamped minor-league system.

In 1976, under Manager Danny Ozark, the Phils won the National League Eastern Division championship before losing three straight games to Cincinnati in the best-of-five playoffs.

The Phillies, still unable to shed their "chokers" tag, also won the East title in 1977 and 1978, but managed just one victory from the Los Angeles Dodgers in each of those years.

With celebrated free-agent Pete Rose signed to a four-year, $3.2 million contract, the Phillies were odds-on favorites not only to win their division in 1979, but also to go to the elusive World Series. Instead, crippling injuries to key players—almost the entire pitching staff at one point—plus other internal problems, turned 1979 into a haunting disaster.

When it became obvious the Phils were out of it and a change necessary, Carpenter and Owens replaced Ozark, who had piloted the club since 1973, on August 31, 1979 with "interim" Manager Dallas Green.

Green, the team's minor-league director, agreed to stay on only until the end of the season. His career goal was to replace Owens when the latter retired and he felt leaving the front office to become manager would be a detour. But Green did such an outstanding job the last month of the '79 season that Owens coaxed him into signing a one-year contract as manager for 1980.

Even though he admittedly had the talent to vault the Phillies back to the top, it was Green's approach to the job he never liked in the first place that in the end made the biggest difference.

As late as September 1, Green wasn't sure his methods were working, but he says he never gave in to the super-egos and sensitive feelings of a team that was to bring the franchise its first world championship.

To get there the Phillies survived a dramatic race to the wire with the Montreal Expos to win their fourth Eastern Division title in five years, then out-lasted Western Division champion Houston in the sometimes bizarre best-of-five League Championship Series.

To get past the gritty Astros the Phils had to rally in each of their victories, not to mention coming back from a two-games-to-one deficit with consecutive triumphs in the Astrodome. The last four playoff games went to extra innings with the Phillies coming from behind to take the clincher 8–7 in 10 innings.

The road to their first National League pennant since 1950 was so grueling, so excruciating the World Series seemed almost anti-climactic.

But the Phils, by now nicknamed "the Cardiac Kids," rallied from deficits in the first two games at Veterans Stadium and watched the Royals even the Series in Kansas City before taking the fifth and sixth games to win it all.

To become world champions, the Phillies had to pick up the pieces and rebuild a season that many times appeared to be falling apart.

Problems started in spring training when the Major League Players Association voted to strike on May 22 if a new basic agreement with the owners was not reached. These negotiations weighed heavily on catcher Bob Boone, the National League's player representative, and shortstop Larry Bowa, the Phils' player rep.

It was on April 1 the board of directors of the players association voted to cancel remaining spring-training exhibition games, a gesture intended to convince owners how serious the players were about striking in May.

As news of this decision was flashed across the country, the Phillies were en route by bus from Pompano Beach, Florida where they had played an exhibition game with the Texas Rangers, to Cocoa.

When Paul Owens heard the news he made a quick decision. He phoned Dallas Green, ordered the manager to continue on to Cocoa and keep the team overnight at a motel, then return to spring-training base Clearwater the following morning.

Days later, Owens' decision was regarded as a stroke of genius. While players from other teams quickly packed up and left their camps, the Phillies remained intact. When they returned to Jack Russell Stadium the next morning, they took a vote and agreed to remain in Florida for the remaining week of spring training and to work out under Dallas Green's supervision—though at their own expense.

While the threat of a strike still remained, the players showed a measure of unity by remaining and were probably more ready to open the season than many other teams.

The strike was avoided by the 11th-hour compromise between the players' association and owners on May 22, and the season, once in jeopardy, continued.

The Phillies, who struggled much of the first half even though they remained very close to the top of their division, were dealt a blow that could have been devastating on the morning of July 8.

With the national media assembled in Los Angeles for the All-Star Game, the Trenton (New Jersey) Times, in a copyrighted story, reported that members of the team, including Mike Schmidt, Pete Rose, Larry Bowa and Greg Luzinski, might be involved in the illegal acquisition of amphetamines.

Most area newspapers, picking-up on what few facts the Trenton story contained, turned the episode into a circus. Already strained relations between the Phillies and the media became much worse.

At the All-Star Game break the Phillies were in second place in National League East with a 41–35 record. They trailed Montreal (42–34) by a game with defending world champion Pittsburgh (42–37) in third place, a game and a half back.

In the beginning, the players did not accept Green's team concept.

They snickered when they arrived in Clearwater for the start of spring training and saw large signs in the clubhouse proclaiming the "We, Not I" theme.

"When are the pompon girls arriving?" blurted shortstop Larry Bowa, which just about summed up many of the players' reaction to Green's sometimes-sophomorish philosophies of managing.

Criticism didn't bother Green. He stuck by his guns. He hurt a few feelings, dented a few egos and returned the Phillies to the No. 1 perch in the East and an eventual world championship.

Was Dallas Green's way the right way?

"I think the end results speak for themselves," he said. "I think now there are more people in our locker room who understand what I tried to do than there were in March—or even July. I think there are a lot of guys who were tired of fighting me. I might get caught a few times, but I'm always going to get my licks in."

How did the Phillies, who were picked by very few to win their division, do it?

They did it with a marvelous blend of multi-talented veterans and hungry, eager youngsters.

They did it with Steve Carlton winning 24 of 33 decisions, posting a 2.34 earned run average and winning his third Cy Young Award as the National League's No. 1 pitcher.

Without the man they call Lefty the Phils would have gone nowhere, especially in the early weeks of the season when the pitching staff was the club's Achilles' heel.

Dick Ruthven, coming off 1979 elbow surgery, started slowly but ended with a 17–10 record and 3.55 ERA.

Injury-prone Larry Christenson was out much of the year, but gave the Phils three strong starts the last month of the season.

Aside from Carlton, the Phils' starting corps got a big boost from rookie right-handers Bob Walk and Marty Bystrom. Walk, with the team most of the year, was 11–7. Bystrom, who arrived with the September 1 call-ups, was 5–0 with an incredible 1.50 ERA. He was made eligible for the playoffs and World Series when Nino Espinosa was placed on the disabled list and Randy Lerch was dropped in favor of lefty reliever Kevin Saucier.

During the off-season Owens and Green searched high and low for bullpen help. They came close to landing Sparky Lyle from the Texas Rangers during the winter meetings, but the deal was snuffed because of a clause in Lyle's contract that guaranteed him a broadcasting job with the Rangers at $50,000 a year for 10 seasons after his retirement as a player.

There was much irony attached to that no-trade. First, two of the players mentioned on the Phillies' side of it had great years.

Veteran reliever Tug McGraw, who was to be the hero of the playoffs and World Series, gave the Phillies more relief than they ever expected.

After coming off the disabled list on July 17, McGraw worked 52 innings in 33 games, allowing just three earned runs. He was 5–1 during that span and picked up 13 of his 20 saves. During the Phils' surge to the top the last five weeks, Tug allowed just one earned run, that on September 2. From that time on he was in 15 games, had five saves and five victories.

Bake McBride, also mentioned in the original Lyle deal, was probably the most consistent offensive player. He hit .309 and drove in a career-high 87 runs on gimpy knees and aching feet.

Finally, there was Lyle himself. Owens managed to pry the left-handed reliever from Texas on September 13 for a player to be named later (Saucier). Although Lyle was not eligible for post-season play, he took some of the heat off the weary McGraw as the Phillies rumbled down the stretch.

And then there was Michael Jack Schmidt, unanimous choice for the coveted National League Most Valuable Player Award who was also named MVP for the World Series.

Schmidt's 48 home runs set a major league record for a third baseman. He also led the National League with 121 runs batted in, a slugging percentage of .624 and in total bases with 342. He was runner-up to the St. Louis Cardinals' Keith Hernandez in runs scored, 111–104.

"Winning the division title was the key to the year," said Schmidt, who led the Phils with 17 game-winning runs batted in. "There were times during the season when people gave up on us. Yet we came back and won it. We made believers out of a lot of people.

"Plus, we had to battle to win it. We had more problems. We had to have intensity throughout the year. We'd never really been in a tough pennant race before. We never had to play great baseball in September before. The other years when we won, all we had to do was just hold on."

The Phils ran up a 23–10 record from September 1 to October 4 when they clinched the division title on Schmidt's two-run homer for a 6–4, 11-inning victory over Montreal in the rain and cold at Olympic Stadium.

That victory was the Phils' sixth in a row and climaxed a week during which their backs were repeatedly against the wall because the Expos, who had been in first place most of the second half, were also winning. But the Phils won six of their last seven and 19 of 27, for a 51–36 record after the All-Star Game break.

Maybe just as important was the fact they won 21 of their final 28 road games to finish 42–39 in that department, their best since they were 48–33 away from Veterans Stadium in 1976.

After September 1 they were 12–4 in one-run games, an indication of the job the bullpen did. At the All-Star break they were 13–15.

Over the last five years (1976–80) the Phillies have won more games, 467, than any other National League team.

But all of this merely scratches the surface.

How *did* the Phillies do it?

You have to keep coming back to George Dallas Green.

On a dreary Friday afternoon in Clearwater, April 4 to be exact, Green dropped a bomb. Win or lose, the 1980 Phillies were going to fly his colors.

He announced that five rookies had made his team for the trip North. He also said he was cutting pitchers Rawly Eastwick and Doug Bird, infielder Buddy Harrelson and outfielder Mike Anderson.

Because of long-term, guaranteed contracts that move cost Ruly Carpenter an estimated $1 million, but as startled veterans looked around the clubhouse that day they got the message: This was going to be Dallas Green's baseball team and he was going to do it his way—at any cost.

The rookies who made the 25-player roster were pitcher Scott Munninghoff, catcher Keith Moreland, infielder Luis Aguayo and outfielders George Vukovich and Lonnie Smith.

Some thought Green's drastic action was merely a grandstand play to make up for all the years of frustration he had when Danny Ozark refused to give promising talent from the organization a chance.

"No, that's not it," Green insisted. "We feel the younger players we have decided to keep have earned the right. Their play in spring training here has told me that they want to be a part of this baseball team. That's what this game is all about. I think these guys have earned the right to go North with us. The guys we are keeping are well-schooled in fundamentals and are ready to accept the pressures of major-league baseball.

"I was determined all winter to do something bench-wise and bullpen-wise that would help the Phillies. We weren't able to do it through a trade, but I feel by changing faces and giving these kids an opportunity we're accomplishing what we set out to do."

"There is no way we can win the division with this team," a veteran player said. "You cannot go against Pittsburgh and Montreal with rookies. No way."

But the rookies did go to war for the Phillies and Dallas Green. Munninghoff and Aguayo were returned to Oklahoma City of the American Association early, but the other three, along with Walk, were outstanding.

The rookies had fun, but in the end Green probably enjoyed their success more than they did.

They would burst into the clubhouse after victories like silly high-school sophomores. There was laughing and horse-play and celebration.

In the beginning the crusty old veterans didn't know what to think of these young whippersnappers. Didn't they know that when you put on the Phillies' pinstripes you're supposed to be cool, unemotional? Don't get high after victories, low after defeats. Face the world the same everyday.

The Class of '80 refused to accept that. They let their emotions—and talents—flow.

"OK, it's old school to hope you can put some juice into a 162-game schedule," Green said. "But somewhere along the line emotion will help you and emotion will carry you through some rough times. The kids brought the freshness, they brought the 'I Don't Care About You, Veteran' type thing that we needed to crack that somber look in the dugout. We had to get some juice.

"We couldn't count on Tug McGraw slapping his leg and Pete Rose sliding on his belly to do it. That was about the only emotion this team had. Every now and then Larry Bowa got it going pretty good, but to some degree Bowa was part of that old clan, the group that had become very staid in its ways.

"There is no question in my mind that had we gone with the same people we had in 1979, we would not be champions. And that's not necessarily a knock on their talent. It's a knock on the way the thing had been built up. Danny Ozark had allowed this to become a very distinct 'Class Society.'"

Green chose his words carefully. "Eight starters. They were the starters. The bench was the bench. Period. Pitchers were the pitchers. Period. There was no team. It was a distinct class situation. Pitchers hated the players, the players hated the pitchers. The bench kept their mouths shut because they knew they couldn't help and weren't going to get an opportunity to help, so they kept their mouths shut.

"And, consequently, when we were one or two runs down

that's why—when everybody looked down the bench, including me—you saw nothing. You saw a row of statues sitting up against the wall with no hope whatsoever of winning the game. And I really wanted to change that."

The rookies played the major role in that but Green is not sure the old guard still believes there was a change.

"Those guys will tell you it was no big deal," he said. "But they climbed on the bandwagon and were saying no matter how many runs down we were, we weren't beaten. Hey, they were saying, 'We're the Cardiac Kids and we can come back—we don't play until we get a couple of runs down.' They're all the same guys who knew that was impossible in other years. The kids had to break that spell. I've never seen a bunch with more juice."

Smith, who played in 100 games as a replacement for Greg Luzinski in left and Bake McBride in right, batted .339. He broke Richie Ashburn's 1948 club record for stolen bases by a rookie with 33. When Lonnie was in the line-up, he led off, with Pete Rose batting second. His lightning speed gave the Phils a weapon they had lacked for years.

Moreland, who had seven game-winning RBI, batted .412 as a pinch hitter and ended his rookie year with a .314 average.

The first half of the season was more of a shakedown cruise than anything else for Green who preached a grind-it-out, hunt-and-peck brand of baseball that not all of his players subscribed to.

A svelte Greg Luzinski, who went from 238 pounds to 215, electrified the opening-night crowd of 48,460, the 10th opening in Veterans Stadium history, when he blasted a three-run homer in the first inning to lead the Phillies to a 6–3 conquest of Montreal.

The Phils were 6–9 in April, but 17–9 in May thanks to Carlton's 9–2, 1.84 start coupled with the consistent hitting of

Schmidt, McBride and Manny Trillo. And through May 20, Luzinski was hitting .261 with 10 homers and 21 RBI.

The defending-champion Pirates, in the past always slow starters, vaulted out to a 19–9 record by May 15, with the Phillies and Cubs tied for second place in the Eastern Division, five games back.

"We'd play well for a week or so, then fall back into our same old habits," Green said. "We just were not able to sustain anything. Had it not been for the job Steve Carlton did, we would not have been in the race by the All-Star Game."

On Memorial Day, in another of those no-love-lost grudge matches with the Pirates, Larry Bowa singled home the winning run off reliever Kent Tekulve in a two-run ninth inning that gave the Phils a 7–6 victory. The game had been marred by a bench-clearing free-for-all in the sixth inning which brought both the Phillies and the 45,394 paying customers to life on the sultry evening. By winning, the Phils took over first place in the division, moving .004 points ahead of the Pirates.

"Sure, the fight may have helped spark a comeback," said Bowa. "But fights can help spark the other team, too. I remember the Pirates were 11 games behind us one year and they really came after us."

The Phils were unable to hold onto first place for more than 24 hours at any one time and by the All-Star Game, won by the National League 4–2 over the American League, the would-be world champions were scuffling to stay close.

Green was once described as a Don Quixote jousting with a roomful of fragile, over-sized egos.

August 10 will go down as Black Sunday in Green's diary. That was the day the Phillies dropped a double-header in Pittsburgh to fall six games behind the Pirates and Expos with 55 to play. That was also the day Green blew his top between games, exploding in an emotional tirade.

Then, as the Phils lost the second game, Green and relief

pitcher Ron Reed had a shouting argument in the dugout in front of the team. Had players and coaches not jumped in, blows probably would have been landed.

"A lot of managers have yelled and shouted between games of a double-header," said Green, "but when I went jaw-to-jaw with Ronnie, I was kind of anxious to see how the guys would handle it. There was a chance it could have really hurt the ball club. But we came out of it and I gave the guys credit. They put the thing behind and went after the season."

The road home, though, was rough.

On August 31, the Phils lost the second straight game at San Diego. The following day Paul Owens held his first team meeting prior to the game with the Giants at Candlestick Park. He singled out Garry Maddox and Bowa for not playing up to their potential. He said he would take any player on if they wanted to fight him and, in the end, he asked the players to put their personal goals aside and play the last month of the year for Paul Owens and Ruly Carpenter.

"What the Pope's meeting did was back up everything I had said earlier," Green remembers. "What gave me an edge was the fact Paul and Ruly gave me the hammer. And every player knew that."

The Phillies took over first place again that day and although they once more failed to keep it in their grasp, they set the stage for the final month of the season and the most exciting baseball the franchise has ever known.

Route to the Playoffs
"It was a rough two weeks at the end."

On Friday morning, September 26, Dallas Green rolled out of bed at his West Grove, Pennsylvania home, brewed a cup of coffee and turned on the radio.

"The weather outlook is not too encouraging for the Phillies' weekend series with Montreal," the announcer crackled. "Twenty percent chance of rain tonight, 80 percent Saturday and Sunday, heavy at times."

Green's coffee didn't taste very good.

The Phillies' season had dwindled to just 10 days—a three-game series against the Expos at Veterans Stadium, four at home against the Chicago Cubs, followed by a certain-to-be-crucial three-gamer at Olympic Stadium the following weekend.

"A rainout! A damn rainout! That's one thing we don't need," Green remembers shouting. "This is no time for a double-header."

As recently as September 1, Green wasn't sure the Phillies were dedicated enough to his philosophies to come out on top during a tense stretch run. Or, as Pete Rose called it, racehorse baseball.

They had stayed in or near first place in National League East for several days early in the month, but Montreal and defending champion Pittsburgh were making the race a game of musical chairs.

On September 8, the Phils ripped the Pirates 6–2 at the Vet, snapping a 2–2 tie with four runs in the eighth.

The following night, brilliant relief pitching by Dickie Noles and Warren Brusstar carried them to an exciting 5–4 conquest over their cross-state nemesis, a jarring setback that dropped Pittsburgh 3½ games behind Montreal and lifted the Phils to within a half-game of the first-place Expos.

It seemed the Phillies were ready to make their move, but a double-header loss to St. Louis on September 12 left them two games behind the Expos and people were saying they were finished.

By the time the Phils took the field on September 25, the Expos had fallen to the Cubs at Chicago's Wrigley Field 5–4 and were already jetting to Philadelphia for the first of two showdowns.

Marty Bystrom, the rookie phenom, glanced at the scoreboard, swallowed hard and then pitched six brilliant innings, allowing only Hubie Brooks' leadoff double in the third. In the seventh, the Mets scored before Noles arrived to douse the fire. Sparky Lyle worked the eighth and ninth, sealed the 2–1 victory and the Phils were in first place by a half-game over the Expos.

As the mob of reporters filed into Green's stuffy office that night, the manager finally admitted the upcoming games were more important than any the Phils had played to date.

"I am finally willing to say the next three days are critical," said Green. "We're ready for them (Expos) and they're ready for us. If we get the pitching I expect, we'll win it."

Dick Ruthven, with a 16–10 record, was chosen to pitch the Friday night battle against Dave Palmer, 7–5.

"I think the Friday night game is a big, big game," said Rose. "I hate to say one game is the key, but if we can beat the Expos in the first one, they'll be two back in the loss col-

Pete Rose, as he has been doing for 18 seasons, crashes into Houston catcher Bruce Bochy in the 10th inning to score the winning run in the Phils' 5-3 victory over Houston which squared the National League playoffs at two games apiece.

umn and have to face Steve Carlton, the best pitcher in base-ball, on Saturday."

On the final day of the 1979 season, Carlton and the Phillies had stung the Expos 2–0, knocking them out of a chance to at least tie the Pirates for the Eastern Division flag. As a result, Montreal arrived at Veterans Stadium on the night of September 26 seeking revenge. They were in a position to determine their own fate, to end the Phils' hopes.

The two teams had not played since June 30 and were even after 12 games.

There was optimism in the Phils' camp. They had won seven of their last 11 games and 12 of 17. Of the 16 won in September, nine had been by one run. Even though they had been in first place only 11 days, including the first two of the season, they were now ready to make their move.

Green insisted, months before, the season would boil down to the final 10 days and his Phillies would be in the thick of it.

There was one important fact about those final 10 days that must be mentioned. After three games in Philadelphia, the Expos would return to Montreal for three with St. Louis, followed by an open date on October 2. While the Expos were resting that Thursday, the Phillies would be completing a four-game set with last-place Chicago.

"The fact we have one more game than they do before we go to Montreal can work two ways," said Green. "If we win, it can help us. If we lose, it won't help one bit."

A World Series atmosphere swept through Veterans Stadium on September 26 as 50,887 came for the opener against Montreal. But it wasn't pennant fever that gave the contest all the earmarks of a chess match in the early going. Actually, both teams left their bats in the clubhouse.

The Phils took a 1–0 lead in the second inning when Garry Maddox drilled Dave Palmer's hanging curve to the lower deck in left field. It was Maddox' 11th homer of the season but, ominously, it looked like the only run the Phils might manage on the cold night.

Montreal did not get a hit off right-hander Dick Ruthven until the fourth when Rowland Office singled with two out. In the sixth, however, the Expos began to apply the pressure. Jerry White laced a two-out gapper to left-center for a double. Rodney Scott followed with a grounder in the hole and although shortstop Larry Bowa got there, he did not get his glove down and the ball scooted under it to left as White scored.

Ruthven worked out of a jam in the seventh and Tug McGraw, who was riding an 0.63 earned run average since coming off the disabled list July 17, completely stymied the Expos in the eighth and ninth.

Bake McBride led off the ninth.

The ball started climbing into the cool night air, higher and higher, forming a majestic arch before it finally dropped in the Phillies' bullpen.

The roar from the frantic mob started as the ball shot off Bake's bat and vibrated around the Vet until the hero of the moment was summoned from the clubhouse celebration to take another bow.

Bake McBride tells people he is unemotional, but there were traces of tears in his eyes that night and his voice trembled as he spoke of the ninth-inning home run that gave the Phillies their dramatic 2–1 victory and a 1½-game lead over Montreal.

"I try not to get caught up in emotion," said McBride. "I came to the park tonight telling myself this was just another game and I tried to approach it that way. But when I hit it, I felt something inside of me. It was one of the most exciting moments I've ever had in professional baseball."

By the time McBride got to first base there was no doubt

he had won the tense struggle at the expense of Dave Palmer. As Bake started toward second, he shot his clenched fist in the air. Once, twice, three times.

"The adrenalin was flowing," said McBride. "When I hit it, I immediately went into my home-run trot, then it dawned on me the wind was blowing in, so I started running harder. When I saw it drop over the fence, I relaxed."

"I feel a lot better than I did yesterday," bubbled Green. "These guys want to win. I've told you that all along. I'm really happy they're enjoying all of this."

"You have to shift gears in a hurry after a game like this," McBride warned. "You have to think about tomorrow. Don't forget, we have five more games with Montreal and four with Chicago. This is a long way from over."

"We've bounced back many times this year," said Montreal Manager Dick Williams. "This loss shouldn't bother us at all. The Phillies have super pitching going tomorrow with Steve Carlton, but even if we lose, it won't wipe us out."

While Williams was talking, members of the Montreal media were complaining about how uncooperative McBride and other Phillies were after the victory. McBride remained in the trainer's room immediately after the game.

The Saturday and Sunday games were scheduled for mid-afternoon starts—to accommodate national television—at a time when the glare and shadows make playing in Veterans Stadium treacherous at best.

Carlton (23–8) pitched Saturday's game against the Expos' Scott Sanderson (15–10) and was not as sharp as he had been most of the year.

Montreal won 4–3, snuffing out a ninth-inning rally with the aging arm of left-handed reliever Woodie Fryman.

The Phillies actually led twice. They jumped in front on Mike Schmidt's 44th homer in the first inning, hit to celebrate his 31st birthday. They then went ahead again 2–1 on Manny

Trillo's leadoff blast in the second. Montreal had tied in the top of the second on Gary Carter's 27th home run.

The Phillies didn't score again until the ninth off Elias Sosa, but the Expos by then had taken a 4–2 lead, breathing new life into their pennant drive.

With the Expos leading 3–2, it appeared reliever Warren Brusstar was out of trouble in the eighth when he got Larry Parrish to hit a ball back to the mound. With one out and runners on first and second the ground ball should have started a rally-snuffing double play, but just as Brusstar went after it he was blinded by the sun. The ball squirted into center field and Andre Dawson scored.

"That sun was bright," said Brusstar. "I couldn't see anything. The ball got on top of me before I saw it. I just missed. I started grabbing like crazy but I couldn't get to it. It's ironic. Just what I wanted, a ground ball. I thought it would be a double play."

The Phils scored once in the ninth, but Fryman came in to fan Lonnie Smith for the final out.

"We had 'em on the ropes, but couldn't put the coup de grace on 'em," said Green. "We got two runs on homers Friday night and two of our runs on homers today. We've got to play better offense somehow."

"The Phillies have used the long ball on us," explained Williams, "but we've gotten some big two-out hits. I'll tell you one thing, I like our chances a lot better than I did at 11 p.m. yesterday."

"This wasn't one of Carlton's finest hours," moaned Green. "He struggled all day. He didn't have a real good slider and that's usually his bread-and-butter.

"We're right back where we started, a half-game on top. A win today would have been super, but Montreal had something to say about that."

On Sunday, with one out in the seventh inning a large

paper airplane rose from the huge audience, climbed to about 50 or 60 feet, then made a beautiful landing near second base.

Those remaining in the crowd of 40,305 enthusiastically applauded the touch-down. In fact, it was one of the loudest reactions during the warm, sultry autumn afternoon.

Before—and after—most of the customers sat in a daze. Maybe they could not believe what they were seeing as Montreal stoned the lethargic Phillies 8–3. Or maybe they believed what they were seeing because they had seen it so many times before from this group of enigmatic, multi-talented athletes.

Dallas Green had seen it before. Maybe that's why he quickly gulped down a post-game beer, then immediately ordered another—and another.

The third game in the first best-of-three showdown left the Phils only a half-game behind Montreal in National League East, but the way the Phils lost, the gap seemed much wider with only seven games to play.

"Considering how we played the last two days it does seem more than a half-game," admitted Green. "I don't think anybody in our clubhouse, if they can look in the mirror—or if they will look in the mirror—can really appreciate the way we have played. I don't think that's Philly baseball and it's proven not to be winning baseball. If I had the answer, I would have straightened it out by now."

Green, the strain showing on his leathery face, had to stomach the insanity of network television that forced the Phils to start at 3:05 p.m. The late-afternoon sun pierced the top of the stadium, making outfield play in late innings a horror show.

With the game still 2–1 and the Phils hopeful of getting to Montreal ace Steve Rogers, the Expos broke it open. With runners on first and second, Chris Speier hit a liner to center off reliever Dickie Noles, who had taken over for ineffective starter Bob Walk. Maddox, considered by many the best center fielder in the world, had made a zillion of those catches on the run. This time he lost the ball in the sun, two runs scored and Speier stopped at third where Rogers singled him home. Suddenly, a 2–1 struggle was a 5–1 Montreal laugher.

On the last day of August in San Diego, Garry Maddox missed two routine fly balls and it turned out he did not have his sunglasses on.

When Green was told by a reporter the five-time Gold Glove center fielder did not have his sunglasses flipped down when he went after Speier's ball, the manager stopped trying to defend him.

"I don't think having the glasses down would have made any difference," Maddox told reporters earlier. "The first thing you have to do is go for the ball, which I did. Glasses don't help you on a ball hit directly in the sun."

"Well, all I know is when I'm out in the sun I can see better with sunglasses," said Green. "Having them down certainly would not have made the catch more difficult. But that field is treacherous that time of the day. There's a glare and the sun is coming right in the outfielder's eyes. But the bottom line is Montreal played under the same conditions. They hit the ball, they fielded the ball and they won. We didn't."

"I can feel for Garry Maddox," said Montreal outfielder Andre Dawson. "The sun was a real pain all day. It's worse here than a lot of places because there's a space between the light supports and the rest of the stadium. That makes it hard to block out the sun. You never know where it's going to come out at. And playing late in the day was the worst part of all. The sun just hangs there, right in front of you. Sunglasses don't mean a whole lot."

Green had a lot to get off his chest as darkness crept over South Philadelphia.

He started with network television.

"The fact TV controls baseball bothers me," he said. "I know both teams have to play under the same conditions, but

I've seen us get hurt by it too much. I saw that 1977 playoff game in the rain against Los Angeles here that was totally ridiculous. This isn't football. Television people have no understanding about the sun, shadows and the glare—and really could care less."

An hour had gone by, several beers had been swilled and Green was still groping. The two losses, especially the second, were so typical of his 1980 Phillies. They won the important opener of the series, playing like champions. They opened up a 1½ game lead, then packed it in.

"But I feel better about our team now," he said, "I think we have proven this month we can win one-run games, and we can win clutch, tough games. I think we've proven we can win them by staying within ourselves and doing things we're capable of doing.

"But this team again goes back to the same old thing— that we need a constant reminder. I'm supposed to be that reminder, yet we get our feelings hurt when I remind.

"I said we were physically and mentally prepared for this weekend and I still think that. But so many little things seem to affect this team that they don't play over or that they don't go after. It gets me thinking again and it all goes back to character, whether or not they really want it.

"We've got to put aside every problem we've got in the world right now and concentrate on the one thing we have to do which is win."

Green seemed to swallow a whole can of beer with one, long flowing sip.

"We've got to do the things we have to do to win, regardless of personal problems, regardless of personal frustrations, regardless of personal wants, likes or dislikes. I think they're capable of doing that, but so far they haven't done it."

Green had a hard time getting to sleep that Sunday night. He tossed and turned, worrying about the team's lack of punch.

The nucleus of the attack was in a dreadful slump. Bob

Boone, Pete Rose, Greg Luzinski and Mike Schmidt were a collective 7-for-87. That's an .080 batting average. Boone was 0-for-19, Rose 3-for-31, Luzinski 2-for-21 and Schmidt 2-for-16.

By the time Green got to the Vet the following afternoon, he had just about made his mind up. He would make some startling changes in the line-up—changes that could blow up in his face or ignite the Phillies and carry them to the Eastern Division title.

Once the line-up was posted in the clubhouse it did not take long for news to travel all over the spacious stadium. Green was benching Greg Luzinski, Garry Maddox and Bob Boone, replacing them with Lonnie Smith, Del Unser and Keith Moreland.

The manager's bold decision sent shock waves through the clubhouse, creating an atmosphere so tense and testy that visitors found themselves tip-toeing around.

"We're a half-game back with seven to go," an outspoken player said, shaking his head. "So what does Dallas Green do? He benches three of the most important players on this team. I can't believe it. There's no way we're going to win this thing without them. No way. And by the time we get to Montreal, you can just about forget about the three guys he's sat down. He's lost them for the rest of the year; that's what he's done, lost 'em."

Jayson Stark of The Philadelphia Inquirer was one of the first reporters to arrive in the clubhouse. And one of the first players he spotted was Garry Maddox.

The center fielder asked the reporter to come into a room off the clubhouse where they talked behind a closed door for nearly 30 minutes.

"He thinks my story this morning was the reason Green has benched him," Stark told the large press-box contingent later. "All I did was write what happened on Sunday. Garry Maddox lost a ball in the sun. That's what I wrote."

By the time Larry Christenson, who was back from elbow

surgery, took on the Cubs' Rick Reuschel, an Associated Press report of the Maddox–Stark confrontation was already arriving at newspapers and radio stations all over the country.

"I intended my conversation with Jayson Stark to be private, between him and me," Garry Maddox would say much, much later. "I'm sorry he had to make such a big thing of it."

As fans and would-be historians look back on the Phillies' drive to their first world championship, they all agree the final 10 days of the regular season, the playoffs and the World Series gave America some of the most exciting, most bizarre baseball it has ever seen.

And no game was more important than the Phils' 6–5, 15-inning return-from-the-dead triumph over the Cubs on September 29.

Keep in mind the Expos, powered by two straight victories over the Phils in Veterans Stadium, were home to play the Cardinals three times, followed by that open date on October 2. The Phils would arrive for the three-game final, beginning October 3.

So, with Garry Maddox, Greg Luzinski and Bob Boone benched, the Phils opened their final homestand of the year.

In a sense, this historic day in Phillies' history started and ended with Garry Lee Maddox.

The sensitive outfielder put aside his sulking long enough to deliver one of the Phillies' most important hits of the season in the dramatic, "must" victory.

Moments after Maddox ripped his clutch, two-out single up the middle in the 15th inning, Manny Trillo laced a bases-loaded single to give the Phils their 6–5 decision.

Hours before, news of John Tamargo's three-run homer that vaulted Montreal to a 5–2 victory over St. Louis sent a murmur through the Veterans Stadium crowd of 21,127.

The Phils were locked in a 3–3 tie when the Expos finished their game, assured of nothing worse than a half-game lead in National League East.

In the top of the 15th the nothing-to-lose Cubs took advantage of shoddy relief pitching and equally shoddy defense to skip in front 5–3.

But the Cubs were not in last place by mistake. Relievers Doug Capilla and Dennis Lamp coughed up the lead and instead of the Phils being an alarming 1½ back, they remained a half-game behind Montreal after the 4-hour, 27-minute ordeal.

"I'll never forget that game," Green said many, many times later. "It wasn't a very good feeling after they scored those two runs in the 15th. Here we're looking up at a two-run deficit and Montreal has already beaten St. Louis. Yeah, I had a sick feeling in my stomach."

"This is the kind of game that can give you momentum," said Pete Rose, who drove in three of the Phils' runs. "People in town today acted like we were finished after losing two games to Montreal over the weekend. If I'm not mistaken, the newspaper says we're even in the loss column and only a half-game back. I really look for us to play well against the Expos up there next weekend. It should be a whale of a series.

"In a sense, I'm sorry we had to win this game this way because the relief pitching of Tug McGraw and Sparky Lyle was so outstanding that it is almost forgotten now. We just could not afford to lose this game tonight."

Those fans who remained did not give the Phillies much chance in the 15th.

Capilla, however, got in immediate trouble when he walked Lonnie Smith and Rose. With McBride batting the runners advanced on a wild pitch before Bake grounded out to score Smith. That brought up Mike Schmidt, with Rose on third. Lamp was summoned and got Schmidt to pop up to second.

Maddox stepped to the plate. He had entered the game in the 12th after Del Unser, who had doubled with one out in the 11th, was lifted for a pinch runner. Garry fouled Lamp's

first pitch off, then singled to bring Rose home. Keith Moreland singled to left and Larry Bowa, giving the Phils a tough
at-bat, walked to load the bases.

Trillo, who had singled twice earlier, then singled Maddox home and the exhausted Phillies wobbled off the field with
one of their most important victories of the year.

As Bowa trotted from second to the dugout, he threw his
arm up in an obscene gesture to the fans who had lustily booed
the Phils earlier in the game. As the fiesty shortstop entered
the clubhouse, he shouted that the fans were the worst in the
world. Those two incidents would come back to haunt Bowa
and at the same time spur him on to his best play of the year.

"Maddox was not benched because he lost the ball in the
sun on Sunday," Green told the large gathering of reporters
moments after the game. "He had been sporadic at the plate
and I thought since I was going with Moreland and Lonnie
Smith, I might as well give Unser a chance in center."

If Green's gamble of sitting down Maddox, Boone and
Luzinski was not enough, he chose that night, long after most
of the reporters were in the press box filing their stories, to
come down hard again on his players.

"I get the feeling," he said, "we're not all together in this
thing. I wouldn't be surprised if there aren't a few guys out in
that clubhouse who are rooting against us not to win this thing.

"The last two weeks I've been checking up on some
things. I've watched these guys very closely. I've watched how
they attend to their business and it's almost back to the same
old thing, the we're-gonna-do-it-our-way type thing. And
we've just missed some serious breakdowns."

When pushed, Green added: "It's all the little things they
continue to do, things they know tick me off. Hell, we're fighting for a pennant. This is a time when you have to put everything aside. I don't care if it's at home, if it's in the clubhouse,
if it's the manager. You just gotta put it all aside and say, 'It's
We, Not I.'

"I'm not talking about every guy on this team. I'm not making any blanket statements. I'd say 90 percent of these guys care, they want to win. The rest . . . well, they can look in the mirror. They know who they are."

Earlier, Larry Bowa had criticized Green on the short-stop's radio show. When Bowa's comments were repeated for Green, the manager got red in the face.

"I don't want to get into a battle with Larry Bowa," he said. "If I were ever to open up on Larry Bowa, he'd never play another inning of baseball in Philadelphia—and that's official.

"I feel, deep down, Larry really, sincerely, wants to win. But I think he tries to be more than what Larry Bowa can be. I feel he tries to handle more than Larry Bowa can handle."

Green got up, walked around.

"I could quit. That's what Danny Ozark did after seven years. He just quit. He threw the authority over to them. He said, 'Here, do it your way.' Now, I can see why.

"Well, these guys aren't going to give me any ulcers. They might give a weaker guy an ulcer, but they won't give me no bleeping ulcer. We've got six games left and I'm gonna battle like hell to win those six games.

"What people don't know about me is I sincerely want to win. I want to win for Paul Owens, I want to win for Ruly Carpenter. Sure, I want to win for Dallas Green a little bit but, most of all, I want to win for the organization.

"What these guys want . . . I don't know. I don't think it's just the fat contracts, either. I think it's a total rebellion against authority.

"And the only thing that will straighten the whole thing out is if we win the whole damn thing and then we (front office) are allowed to do what we want."

Whether Green was right or wrong, the next three nights at Veterans Stadium were total successes. Well, almost.

On September 30, Marty Bystrom flirted with a no-hitter

for more than four innings and wound up with a four-hitter for seven while his teammates exploded for a firestorm of 15 hits and a 14–2 breeze over the Cubs. The victory gave Bystrom a 5–0 record and an incredible 1.50 ERA.

The Expos remained a half-game up with a 5–2 conquest of St. Louis.

Maybe all the finger-pointing, snarling and internal bickering of the last three days was pushed aside by such an easy, determined victory. That thought, however, proved nothing more than that—an optimistic thought.

Green stayed with his same starting line-up that he had fielded the night before, with Boone, Maddox and Luzinski on the bench. The next day the skipper decided to put the regulars back in. After all, he reasoned, if this trio was to play against the Expos in the three-game showdown, it would need some work against the Cubs.

Garry Maddox was back in center, Luzinski in left and Boone behind the plate according to the line-up card that was posted by late afternoon on October 1. When the Phils took the field, though, Unser was the center fielder.

Only Maddox knows what went through his mind. In essence, he took himself out of the line-up on a night when his glove might have given Steve Carlton his first career no-hitter.

Carlton had to settle for a brilliant two-hitter and his 46th career shutout as the Phils whipped Chicago 5–0 to remain a half-game behind Montreal, an 8–0 winner over St. Louis.

Through seven innings Carlton allowed the Cubs just a second-inning walk. Mike Vail led off the eighth with a sinking liner to center that Del Unser was unable to reach. He made a valiant try, but the ball bounced a few feet in front of the 36-year-old outfielder.

Most of the 25,658 who were on hand on the crisp night vow Maddox would have caught the ball.

With two out in the ninth Bill Buckner lined a pitch off the tip of Manny Trillo's glove for the second Cubs' hit. Trillo probably should have caught the ball, but had Vail's liner not fallen in, Buckner, who was to win the National League batting title with a .324 average, would not have gotten to the plate in the ninth.

"When I got to the park I saw my name in the line-up," said Maddox when reporters surrounded him at his locker. "I told Bobby Wine that my finger was bothering me. We have been having trouble generating offense and because of the finger, I did not think I could swing the bat well. I wanted him to know that."

When the coach relayed the information to Green, the manager did not hesitate. He substituted Unser.

"If a player does not think he can play, he's not going to start," said Green, obviously masking his real sentiments. "I will never ask a player to go out there if he is hurt."

Maddox explained he had hurt his finger on September 17 in Pittsburgh and that it had continued to bother him, most recently in the September 28 loss to Montreal.

Weeks later Green revealed his true feelings over that incident.

"Garry Maddox was wrong in what he did and he knew it," Green said during an interview at his home. "When I put his name up on the board as playing that day, he told Bobby Wine he could not play. He told the press something different. And that's OK. I accepted that because I say if that's what Garry Maddox said, then that's what he said. I'm not going to get into a hissing contest about what he said. He knows what he said and Bobby Wine knows what he said. That's between those two guys, not between me and Garry Maddox.

"But at the same time, if his finger was too bad to play one day, how did it miraculously get better enough to play the next day? So, I sat him the next day without asking him. And he never came to me, but he went to the doctor. But he didn't go to the doctor for his finger. It was something else. It was his way of saying, 'Hey, I'm OK.' And I understand that. And

I started to play him after that, when I felt he could contribute."

While Montreal took the day off, the Phils made the most of their October 2 home finale against Chicago. Bob Walk, with relief help from Tug McGraw who gained his 19th save, defeated the Cubs 4–2 on Mike Schmidt's 46th homer and Keith Moreland's clutch RBI single.

A long rain delay helped tire the Phils even more, but when they boarded a United Airlines charter for the flight to Montreal they were dead even with the Expos, both with 89–70 records. The best-of-three weekend in Olympic Stadium was to decide the National League East champion.

Dinner was served soon after the post-midnight charter lifted off the runway at Philadelphia International airport.

Bobby Wine, a former player and Phillies' coach since 1972, sat in the front row of the first-class section with a reporter who had covered the team since 1958.

"I have a very good feeling about this weekend," said Wine as he sliced into his steak. "I've been around this team for a long, long time. I think you're going to be surprised how well they play in Montreal. There's a determination I have never seen before. They just don't think they are going to lose. That is good."

A gentle rain was falling when the jet touched down at Mirabelle, one of two Montreal airports. This one, located much farther from the city than Dorval, is used mostly for charters and international flights.

Normally, there is a lot of grousing by the players upon arrival in Montreal because of the inconveniences caused by clearing customs.

"I have good news for you," Traveling Secretary Eddie Ferenz announced over the plane's loud speaker. "Because it is so late, we are not going to have to go through customs. Agents are going to come aboard the team busses, so please be polite."

Actually, it was learned later, Ferenz had given the agents tickets to the sold-out series and they, in turn, did not require the Phils to have their personal luggage inspected.

The Expos had come a long way from the sad clowns who used to perform in Parc Jarry. After 11 seasons as also-rans, they were ready to win their first division title and the city was abuzz with baseball talk.

Scott Sanderson and Dick Ruthven, both right-handers, would oppose each other in the Friday night game. On Saturday, it would be Steve Rogers against Larry Christenson.

"While the Phillies were beating the Cubs, our guys were home recharging their batteries," said Montreal Manager Dick Williams. "I expect the club to be fully rested for the weekend."

"There's one thing about playing up here the final three games," said Green. "It's certainly better than having to look at the scoreboard. You're gonna know rather quickly what's going on."

So, it came down to the best-of-three. The Philadelphia Phillies vs. the Montreal Expos.

"We feel rather confident about what we have to do," said Green, whose team had won 19 of its last 25 games on the road. "We're not afraid of Olympic Stadium because we play better there than most teams. The Expos beat us in our park, so they know it can be done."

Mike Schmidt pulled himself out of bed on the morning of October 3, coughing and wheezing and suffering from the flu.

"I was afraid to take my temperature," he said. "I knew it was up there pretty good."

Schmidt, however, shrugged off the virus long enough to blast a home run and drive in another with a sacrifice fly as the Phillies stunned Montreal 2–1 in the opening round of the showdown.

Now, instead of having to win two out of three, the Phils

needed just one out of two. The dazed Expos needed a sweep in the two remaining games.

Schmidt's sacrifice fly in the first inning gave the Phils a 1–0 lead against loser Sanderson, while his sixth-inning homer made it 2–0 and enabled him to tie Eddie Mathews at 47 for the most ever hit by a National League third baseman.

The Expos, cheered on by a loud crowd of 57,121, turned the duel into a nail-biter when they closed the gap to 2–1 in their sixth. But brilliant relief pitching by Sparky Lyle and Tug McGraw stymied the Expos the rest of the cold, damp night.

Lyle snuffed Montreal's biggest threat moments after the Expos had scored their run, worked out of trouble in the seventh, then turned it over to the remarkable McGraw, who retired the last six Expos in a row, striking out five of them.

The air-tight relief enabled Ruthven to record his 17th victory in 27 decisions. He allowed just three hits before leaving with two out in the sixth.

"This might be the most gratifying 5⅔ innings I have ever pitched," said Ruthven.

"This weekend has started off very much like last weekend," said McGraw. "I tried to contain myself because I want to pitch tomorrow. I don't want last weekend to repeat itself."

"We had the opportunities, but were unable to cash in," sighed Dick Williams. "How vital are the next two games? Well, we have to win both of them, that's how vital they are. But we did it last weekend.

"Somebody said they have good pitching going for them now. Well, we have good pitching going for us, too. Our ace, Steve Rogers, is going Saturday. Tonight, it boiled down to pitching and defense. We had both and they had both. They had a little more."

Schmidt, who said he refused to take antibiotics because he was fearful they might make him light-headed, also chipped in with a single and a walk. The homer was his third in as many days and his eighth in 14.

"Maybe it was better I had the flu tonight," he said, matter-of-factly. "I didn't get all tensed-up like I usually do for big games. Oh, I had butterflies, but I wasn't all tense like I usually am. Maybe that is good because I stayed within myself. I didn't try to go out there and do something super-human."

The count went 2–0 to Schmidt in the sixth with one out.

"I have been on a pretty good home-run streak lately, so I thought I would try to keep my shoulder in and give it a good swing," he said. "It turned out to be a good guess."

Dallas Green was ecstatic. "The team has been playing great baseball the last week. I am very proud of the guys. They have risen to the occasion. They're all pulling for each other. There is a lot of spirit in the dugout."

"It had been a week since I pitched," said Ruthven, "and I was worried I might be too strong. I kept telling myself it was just another game and tried not to throw the ball 800 miles an hour. I went at them with my fastball and it was successful."

When the Phillies looked out their windows of the Hyatt Regency on Saturday morning, they saw what appeared to be an all-day rain.

"No way we're going to be able to play today," groused Larry Bowa. "I don't like the idea of a double-header on Sunday, either."

The game was scheduled for 2:15 p.m., a time set by the NBC television network.

The Phils, still feeling the excitement of Friday night's momentum, arrived at Olympic Stadium shortly after noon and dressed quickly.

The rain, however, was heavy.

For 3 hours and 10 minutes, they waited.

Owner Ruly Carpenter paced the clubhouse floor and

kept phoning the press box for updates on the University of Delaware-Lehigh football game.

Dallas Green tried to relax.

Some players listened to music, while others battled over card games. Some watched TV. All waited.

Finally, at 5:25 p.m., the game started.

It ended nearly four hours later on the damp, cold turf of Olympic Stadium and the Expos were also-rans for the second straight year.

It was not a baseball game. It was utter lunacy.

And it seemed only fitting, one of the most important victories in the much-maligned franchise's history was something you'd expect to see at a three-ring circus, not in a major-league baseball stadium.

For the second straight day, the arena where Bruce Jenner became famous in 1976 belonged to Michael Jack Schmidt, the gifted third baseman who, critics said, never came through in the clutch.

Schmidt blasted an awesome two-run homer in the 11th inning to propel the Phils to a wacky 6–4 victory over Montreal's dazed Expos.

Schmidt's home run off reliever Stan Bahnsen climaxed one of the most unpredictable comebacks of the season and made Phillies' fans forget about a collection of five errors, numerous base-running blunders and several examples of unbelievably futile batting.

Even after Montreal surged in front in the seventh with two runs, the Phillies refused to call it a day. They eased into a 4–4 tie in the ninth on Bob Boone's clutch, two-out single to center. And after inhuman Tug McGraw chilled the Expos in the ninth and 10th, the decisive rally was started against Bahnsen.

The count went 2–0 to Schmidt and those remaining in the crowd of 50,794 became restless. The next pitch was a high fastball which trailed sparks as it sped to the left-field seats. Thousands of Montrealers headed for the exits.

Such a bizarre, clinching victory should have been expected from a team that had had more domestic problems than the cast of "Dallas."

"I couldn't believe what I was seeing out there today," Green said as champagne dripped from his graying hair during the clubhouse celebration. "As I watched the game unfold, I wasn't sure that was really the Phillies. But when Schmitty hit that ball—boy, did he smoke it!—I began to relax. This team has come through all year and I can't begin to tell you my feelings right now."

"It was almost absurd," said Williams in the morgue that was the Montreal dressing room. "I'm not certain I have ever seen anything like it. I thought we had 'em when we took the 4–3 lead, but it just wasn't to be."

The absurdity of it all can be pointed out by the fact there were six double-plays, two runners thrown out at the plate, two bases-loaded situations and no runs scored, two wild pitches advancing runners, five errors and seven runners on third base who did not score. And the Phillies squandered most of their 17 hits.

Even Steve Carlton, who seldom talks to reporters, commented: "It was ugly, but very, very beautiful."

The much-maligned Boone, battling a 2-for-25 slump came to the plate in the ninth with Bake McBride on second, two out and Woodie Fryman the pitcher. Boon ripped a single to center and the struggle was tied.

In the 11th, Pete Rose singled to right, McBride fouled out and Schmidt sent his tracer to left.

As Schmidt rounded the bases, his teammates came pouring out of the third-base dugout and lined up to form a jumping, hollering, hand-slapping reception committee. Schmidt seemingly jumped up and down all the way home.

"Maybe we have more heart now than we used to have," he said during the celebration. "If we had lost that game today and lost tomorrow, reporters could have had a field day—and justifiably so."

The Phillies were Eastern Division champions again, but the clubhouse victory party had its sobering moments.

"This is very meaningful to me," Schmidt said. "Not very many people thought we could come up here and take two from them in their own park, but we did it. I am deeply satisfied. Today, I made it happen.

"There's all the heart possible in this dressing room right now, but if we don't win the playoffs, people will call us the same old Phillies. The same old Phillies."

The Championship Series
"How's that for team character!"

The smell of champagne lingered in the clubhouse when the newly crowned National League East champions arrived for work the morning after their murky, magnificent triumph over Montreal.

The Sunday game, final date on the 1980 schedule, was now meaningless. All the veterans, with the exception of the durable Pete Rose, would take the day off. So would the drained manager, Dallas Green.

Three previous division championships had been celebrated with much more intensity than the fourth in five years. It had been a long, grueling struggle in 1980, but as Mike Schmidt remarked, it would mean nothing if the Phillies failed to move forward. The restless fans, and the team, wanted more. Much more.

Green, admittedly a bit hung over, relaxed behind his desk in the visiting manager's chamber. He reflected on the weekend in Montreal—and the season.

Instead of dwelling on the freshly minted division title, Green remained true to form. He was not loud, but he was outspoken.

"I'd like nothing better than to win this whole thing (world championship) and step aside," he said. "I would have accomplished what Paul Owens and Ruly Carpenter wanted me to accomplish. There would be nothing left for me as manager. I haven't even talked to Ruly or Paul about this, but that's the way I feel."

Outside Green's chamber, it was business as usual. Players, in various stages of dress and undress, were milling around.

"Take a good look at them," said Green. "There was no big celebration last night. Oh, they had their champagne and did their yelling and shouting, but as soon as they did, they showered and returned to the hotel. There is a determination about them I have never seen before. Winning the division title this time is not enough. They all realize that.

"I really didn't think we'd win the first two games here, but I thought we would win the division. I thought it would come down to the last game on Sunday. But after we won that Friday night game, I thought it might carry over to Saturday— and it did. I can't remember a team that has had a September like we've had. You can talk about backs being against the wall. Well, I think our backs were against the wall many, many times the last month."

Among the players, there seemed to be more interest the morning after in the Western Division race than there was in their own victory.

"Wouldn't it be unbelievable if the Dodgers pull out that thing against Houston?" Pete Rose mused. "Who would have ever thought that race would come down to the final day of the season?"

Before the Phillies boarded their United Air Lines' charter for the triumphant return to Philadelphia, that is exactly what happened.

The Astros arrived in Los Angeles on Friday, October 3, leading the Dodgers by three games in their drive for their first title of any kind in their 19-year history. The Dodgers won the first two games, then sent the Western Division race into a one game playoff with a 4–3 come-from-behind victory.

Thousands of loyal fans began assembling near the Overseas Terminal of Philadelphia International Airport early in the evening to await the Phillies' arrival, scheduled for 8:45 p.m. At the Vet, players' wives also gathered, where Pat Cassidy, director of stadium operations, passed out bottles of champagne and plastic cups. The whole group then boarded buses and went to the airport.

The charter, delayed in Montreal because of mechanical problems, did not touch down until 10:35 p.m., but none of the chilled fans left. They burned pennants of the Los Angeles Dodgers and Houston Astros. They danced to the rhythm of "When the Saints Come Marching In" and when their heroes finally stepped off the airplane, the cheering reached a crescendo.

"It's great to be back here as a winner," said Green after mounting a flood-lit podium. "And it's important this baseball team go on and keep winning. We've proven to you we can win, and we will, I promise you that."

"This has been the most exciting weekend of my career," said Schmidt, from under a huge cowboy hat. "We're going to do our best to keep baseball in Philadelphia for the next two weeks."

"I think we're ready to go all the way," shouted Tug McGraw, who was given the loudest ovation. "There's no way we're going to let it get away this time."

Monday, October 6, was an open date for the Phillies. But there was plenty of unfinished business.

First, Player Personnel Director Paul Owens and Green had to prepare a case for National League President Chub Feeney in an attempt to make rookie phenom Marty Bystrom and left-handed reliever Kevin Saucier eligible for the playoffs and World Series.

Garry Maddox waves the ball he caught for the final out and is hoisted to his teammates' shoulders after the Phillies defeated Houston to win their first National League pennant since 1950.

Second, a light workout was scheduled and then most of the team would watch the telecast of the Houston-Los Angeles playoff.

And, finally, there was the not-so-easy task of putting the distasteful reminders of the 1976–77–78 playoffs on the back burner.

Green and Owens decided they would drop Nino Espinosa and Randy Lerch from the 25-player roster for the post-season tournaments. They had a medical report stating that Espinosa, who had not pitched since going seven innings against St. Louis on September 12, was hurting, that his right shoulder was still sore from chronic bursitis and that he should not pitch.

Lerch was another problem. The left-hander was healthy, but his 4–14 record and 5.16 earned run average had been one of the biggest disappointments of the season. He did not figure to help in October.

Espinosa was the first to meet with Green and Owens behind closed doors.

"He took it professionally," Green told reporters after the session. "Nino's arm was never there this season. He went out there with a lot of professional pride and used his excellent knowledge of how to pitch to achieve some successful results. But his fastball had lost so much velocity that Herm Starrette (pitching coach) should have warmed him up with an infielder's glove. We don't want Nino to jeopardize his career any further. He's only 27 years old with a lot of pitching ahead of him if he can lick this shoulder thing."

Lerch was not as agreeable. He took Green's decision hard and immediately left the team even though no decision would come down from the National League office until the afternoon of the first playoff game. Green invited both Espinosa and Lerch to wear their uniforms and sit on the bench, but only Espinosa accepted.

Meanwhile, in Los Angeles the Astros were avoiding one

of baseball's historic collapses with a 7–1 victory over the Dodgers in the one game playoff for the Western Division title.

In a slow contest, marred by a heated collision at home plate by rival catchers and fans throwing debris from the bleachers, the Astros bounced back from their three straight weekend losses to earn an overnight flight to Philadelphia.

Joe Niekro allowed the Dodgers just six hits and became a 20-game winner for the second season in a row. Art Howe had three hits for the winners, a home run and two singles, and drove in four runs.

The Astros, by winning, avoided being linked in baseball lore to such teams as the 1951 Brooklyn Dodgers, the 1964 Phillies and the 1978 Boston Red Sox—all who lost comfortable leads down the stretch.

In the third inning, a minor confrontation developed between the two teams when Alan Ashby singled and Craig Reynolds drilled a double to center. The throw beat Ashby home and he made a major-league effort to score by crashing into the bulky and well-padded Joe Ferguson. The catcher made a major-league effort to stop him by blocking the plate and Ashby was tagged out. Ferguson did not appreciate Ashby's professionalism and shoved his knee into the Astro's back as they disentangled. The two benches cleared, but there was no further contact.

"After what happened the last three days against the Dodgers, I can't believe we're finally champions," said first baseman Howe, who homered in the third inning. "We have been having trouble scoring runs, but when I looked up there and saw seven, it was a beautiful sight."

While the Astros were spending the night flying to Philadelphia, the Phillies rested. Earlier, Green had announced Steve Carlton would pitch the first playoff game against the Astros' Ken Forsch, 12–13, 3.16.

For the fourth time in five years, the Kansas City Royals

were to meet the New York Yankees to decide the winner of the American League pennant. That best-of-five tournament would open in Kansas City the day after the Phillies tried to get off on the right foot against Houston at Veterans Stadium.

The so-called National League Championship Series had left a sour taste in Philadelphia's mouth.

In 1976, the Pete Rose-powered Cincinnati Reds whipped the Phils in three straight games, 6–3, 6–2 and 7–6.

The first two games that year were at Veterans Stadium and when the show moved to Riverfront, it looked as though the Phils were going to push it to at least a fourth game. They were on top 6–4 in the ninth inning, but back-to-back home runs by George Foster and Johnny Bench off Ron Reed pulled the Reds even. Ken Griffey's slow infield roller produced the winning run.

The Phils felt they had the best team in baseball in 1977. After splitting the first two games with Western Division champ Los Angeles in Dodger Stadium, they returned home convinced they were going to win their first National League pennant since 1950.

"That was the toughest game I ever worked—by far," said homeplate umpire Harry Wendelstedt of the late-afternoon third game.

In the early innings, Dodger pitcher Burt Hooton complained about a 1–2 pitch to Ted Sizemore. The loud Veterans Stadium crowd began to boo Hooton and he eventually lost his composure, walking Sizemore, Larry Christenson, Bake McBride and Larry Bowa to force home three runs. When he finally left the mound, he threw up his hands in disgust. In years to come, Phils' fans would pick up on that incident again and again to rattle opposing pitchers.

But even though the Phils led 5–3 with two out in the ninth inning, this was not going to be their day. In fact, the bitter loss would go down as one of the most costly in the franchise's history.

This was the afternoon Manager Danny Ozark was accused of forgetting Greg Luzinski was still in left field. During most of the season, Ozark had replaced the Bull with Jerry Martin for defense in late innings.

So, with two down, Vic Davalillo beat out a desperation bunt and Manny Mota hit a two-strike double off reliever Gene Garber to left field that bounced off Luzinski's glove at the wall. That scored a run and Mota took third when the Bull's throw hit a seam on the artificial surface and went through second baseman Ted Sizemore.

With the Phils' infield in, Davy Lopes laced a bouncer that caromed off Schmidt's leg, was scooped up by Bowa, who threw a bullet to first base. The television replay was not decisive, but the indication was that Lopes was out. Umpire Bruce Froemming, however, called him safe and the game was tied.

Lopes stole second and scored the winner on Bill Russell's single up the middle.

The following night, the Phils went quietly in a highly-publicized—and criticized—downpour. Tommy John outpitched Steve Carlton, the Dodgers won 4–1, and were on their way to the World Series against New York.

In 1978, the Dodgers won the first two games at the Vet 9–5 and 4–0, leaving the Phillies 0–6 in playoff games in their own playground.

In Dodger Stadium, however, Greg Luzinski, who had already hit safely in 10 straight playoff games, homered to lead a 9–4 triumph that pumped new post-season life into the Phils.

The fourth game was another one of those playoff nightmares. With the score tied at 3–3 in the 10th inning, Tug McGraw walked Ron Cey to lead off the inning, but retired the next two batters. Dusty Baker then hit a liner to short center that Garry Maddox charged, but dropped. Russell followed with another clutch single and the season was over for Philadelphia.

So, after winning the Eastern Division three straight years with outstanding talent, the Phils were unable to make much more than a dent in the best-of-five playoffs.

They needed something, or somebody, to put them over the top.

Enter Peter Edward Rose.

When the Phils signed the celebrated free agent to a four-year, $3.2 million contract in December of 1978, they talked about how he would lead them past the playoff obstacle to a World Series.

That, of course, didn't happen in 1979 even though Rose was superb. He batted .331, collected 208 hits and had the longest hitting streak in the majors, 23 games.

But from the ruins of 1979, the Phils returned to the top of the division and, with Rose aboard, were ready to challenge the Houston Astros.

"Just get me to the playoffs and I'll take over from there," Rose kept teasing his teammates. "I'm ready. I feel great and couldn't be swinging the bat better."

In five previous playoffs, Rose had established a playoff record with 31 hits.

"I didn't worry that much about 1980," Rose white-lied. "People ask me what happened because I only hit .282. They don't take into consideration I batted in more runs this year than last, had more game-winning hits, more doubles, more runs scored and made three less errors. The only thing was I had fewer hits and fewer walks than last year. Heck, my 185 hits this season still was fifth best in the league."

Rose was ready, but were the Phillies?

"We've got a confident, positive attitude," said Mike Schmidt. "We feel we can continue right on. Dallas Green has a strong feeling this club likes to resist authority and he likes to tell the media that. Maybe there's something to it. You don't know what's best for you until you win the World Series—and this team hasn't done that yet.

"The whole team is looking at the playoffs differently this time. Oh, it's the same team except for some young kids. This is the same bunch of guys who have had a great deal of adversity in common. But this team has character. The way we're playing now, the team has proven to me they're ready to play the best teams in baseball."

"As far as I'm concerned, we haven't accomplished a damn thing," said Rose. "The Phillies have been here three times, but it doesn't mean a thing until you go to the World Series. Anybody can win a division. Hell, the California Angels won one last year (1979) and they finished sixth this season. We'll see what everybody in this clubhouse is made of now."

Most of the Phillies were already in uniform when National League President Chub Feeney finally announced his decision on pitchers Marty Bystrom and Kevin Saucier. They would be eligible for the playoffs and World Series; Randy Lerch and Nino Espinosa would be dropped.

The decision was controversial.

How could Espinosa be placed on the injured list when just three weeks before he pitched seven innings, shutting out St. Louis?

And how could Lerch, who had been with the team all season, be dumped that quickly, that coldly?

Lerch, who had been with the Phillies for four full seasons and won 35 games, refused to accept Green's invitation to dress and sit on the bench. Espinosa swallowed hard and remained.

Veterans felt the front-office maneuvering was inhuman, but quietly admitted the Phils' post-season chances were a lot better with Bystrom and Saucier available.

The largest crowd, 65,277, ever to watch a baseball game

in Pennsylvania jammed Veterans Stadium on Tuesday night, October 7, for the first game of the playoffs.

The last Phillies' pitcher to win a post-season game in Philadelphia was Grover Cleveland Alexander and he did that by beating the Boston Red Sox at Baker Bowl in the 1915 World Series.

Now, it was up to 24-game winner Steve Carlton, who had a 2–0 record against the Astros in 1980 and who had beaten them six straight times since May 16, 1978. The Phillies had won nine of the 12 games played between the two teams in 1980, including four of six in the spacious Astrodome. They had beaten Ken Forsch twice.

For the opener, Green elected to go with his veterans. He started Bob Boone (.229), Greg Luzinski (.228) and Garry Maddox (.259).

The manager's hunch on Luzinski was correct.

Fans were getting restless in the sixth inning on the chilly night with the Astros leading 1–0 and Carlton obviously struggling.

But once Pete Rose beat out his second infield single, Luzinski took charge. He sent a 3–2 Forsch fastball screaming to left field, a towering home run that traveled at least 420 feet and gave the Phillies a 2–1 edge.

Greg Gross' pop-fly single that barely cleared the infield in the seventh produced the third run.

And impish Tug McGraw, who had been virtually unhittable since coming off the disabled list on July 17, pitched the final two innings, polishing off the weary Astros who had not gotten to Philadelphia from Los Angeles until about 5 a.m.

For Greg Luzinski, the game-winning blast helped soothe some of the hurt from his second straight disappointing year.

He had been through a hellish summer. It was like being a favorite son whose father suddenly decided he didn't love him anymore.

For most of his eight summers in a Phillies' suit the fans

loved Greg Luzinski. He returned the affection, going so far as to shell out $20,000 a year to assure seats for underprivileged children in the left field section known as the "Bull Ring."

But in 1979, the fans decided they didn't love the big guy anymore. They began to boo him and talk about him and would have been happy had he left town. They quickly forgot all the game-winning home runs and all the contributions Luzinski made during previous Eastern Division championships.

There were people who thought Luzinski did not belong in the opening night line-up against Houston. Dallas Green was not one of them.

"The Bull means an awful lot to Philadelphia Phillies' baseball," he said. "If we are going to win this thing, I felt we needed Luzinski in the line-up."

Luzinski heard the boos when he was introduced. He expected them, but before the game told a friend he felt like he was swinging the bat well and was encouraged.

"I thought all along I could help the team," said Luzinski whose homer was his fifth in playoffs. "The season has been tough on me. I think when you are struggling, you try even harder. That's the way it has been for me lately. I have tried very, very hard and the results have not been there.

"Tonight, I wasn't even thinking about the regular season. I was charged up. I'm not even sure what the pitch was. All I know is it was down and in, but since the count was 3–2, I was just trying to pick the ball up."

"We needed a few innings to get things going," said Pete Rose. "People were trying to do it on their own. I knew Bull's ball was going out. I was happy because it put us ahead 2–1 late in the game. Up to that point, Forsch had been pitching great.

"Now, I hope we don't sit around and wait for home runs. We'd been getting a lot of hits and putting rallies together last week. But if we needed a home run, the guys who hit home runs have been hitting them."

"Carlton was a little wilder than he had been against us in the past," commented Houston Manager Billy Virdon. "But he's always been effective against us and you're never sure you'll get to him.

"Tired? That didn't have much effect on us. I thought we played quite well. We just got beat. I hope we can change that tomorrow."

"Carlton just wasn't Carlton tonight," said Green. "That's not the Lefty we have seen in the past. He didn't have his good slider, so they were sitting on his breaking ball. Lefty busted a few fastballs to get some outs. He pitched better in the later innings than he did earlier."

Houston, a club built on pitching, lost one of the best in the business on July 30 when fireballer J. R. Richard was felled by a major stroke. The Astros no sooner had fallen to the Phillies in the first game of the playoffs than they learned Richard would have to undergo another operation within a few days for the removal of a blood clot in his arm.

"I heard something about it," said Enos Cabell, Richard's closest friend on the team, "but I haven't talked to J. R. since last Sunday, before he went into the hospital. He will be on our minds."

The Phillies blew a golden opportunity to take a 2–0 lead in the playoffs to the Astrodome when they were shocked by Houston 7–4 in 10 innings of the second game. As the crowd of 65,476 poured out of Veterans Stadium that Wednesday night, many fans shook their heads in anger. The Phils had blown another, stranding 14 runners, 10 in the last four innings.

But a controversial decision by third-base coach Lee Elia left a sour taste in the mouths of most fans, not to mention the Phillies.

Start with the bottom of the ninth inning.

With the futile struggle knotted at 3–3, Bake McBride whistled a one-out single to right field off power reliever Frank LaCorte and Mike Schmidt sent him to second with a single to center.

Lonnie Smith, who had remained in the contest after running for Greg Luzinski, fouled off six consecutive pitchers before slicing a semi-liner to right.

McBride was not running on the last 3–2 pitch, but the instant Lonnie's bat hit the ball, he took off for third. Terry Puhl, playing Smith in medium right, was charging.

As Puhl got off his throw to the plate, Elia held McBride up. Just about everyone in the ballpark thought the fleet McBride would score easily, but he had been flashed the red light at third base.

Manny Trillo fanned and Garry Maddox fouled out to snuff the inning.

Houston then scored four in the 10th and held the Phils to just a run to nail down the victory.

"As soon as the ball was hit I took off running because I didn't think Puhl was going to catch it," said McBride, who admitted his first reaction was to try to score. "I got a step from third and Lee told me to stop. So, I stopped and then he said, 'Go!' You know, by the time he says go, it's too late. It's just one of those things."

Elia was signed by the Phillies off the University of Delaware campus, played a little with the Chicago White Sox in 1966 and the Chicago Cubs in 1968. He returned to the Phillies' organization as a minor-league manager in 1975, before Dallas Green hired him as a coach for 1980.

"There was a little delay on Bake's part, but it was no fault of his he didn't score," said the 42-year-old Elia, refusing to make alibis. "My hands went up as if to say stop and at the same time, I said, 'No, come on.' He saw my hands go up and stopped.

"I guess it's putting a lot of pressure on myself, but inside I keep thinking had I urged him on, he would have scored. Unfortunately for the ball club and myself it was a reflex action on my part. For some reason, the fact we only had one out kept sticking in my mind. I wanted that one run badly and thought we could still get it. In retrospect that's probably why I held him. He could have scored had I sent him. I think I'm putting a lot of heat on myself. It took me 22 years to get here."

"When Lonnie hits a ball like that it's really slicing because he was waiting so long on the pitch at 3–2," said McBride. "I just took off running as hard as I could. I don't know if I would have scored or not. I think it would have been a close play. But we had our chances all night."

Singles by Puhl and Jose Cruz, wrapped around an intentional walk to Joe Morgan, set the stage for Dave Bergman's 10th-inning triple that left the Phils looking at a four-run deficit.

The Houston players tried not to crow about their 10th overtime victory in 17 decisions, but they obviously had renewed confidence as they prepared to jet to Texas.

"We had Steve Carlton on the ropes in the first game and couldn't do it," said Puhl, "so we had to win this one. Going to the Astrodome having to win two games is a lot different for the Phillies than having to win just one."

"We were in the same position in Montreal," argued Green. "We had to go up there and win two out of three to take the division. And we didn't do too badly. I don't feel too bad about this."

"I wouldn't say we're in the driver's seat, but it's a little more than even," added Puhl. "We still have to win two, but we'll have fan support on our side now. What makes it more than even is that our pitching is awesome in the Astrodome. The ball doesn't carry well there, so their long ball won't be as effective as here."

Three years before as the Phillies' charter flight was preparing to depart for Los Angeles and the 1977 playoffs, Steve Carlton walked aboard the jet, surveyed the scene and remarked: "What's this, Noah's Ark?"

There were mothers and fathers and children and even dogs filling just about every seat on the large plane. And, oh yes, the Philadelphia Phillies' baseball players.

Carlton took a seat, stuffed cotton in his ears and made the most of the distracting flight to the West Coast.

A month or so before Philadelphia eliminated Montreal to win the division in 1980, Rose chatted informally with Green, telling the manager how important a high level of concentration be developed for the playoffs. Rose encouraged Green to keep everyone except the official, regular-season traveling party off flights during the playoffs.

So, as the Phils flew to Houston for what now was another best-of-three weekend series, there was a lot of grousing because wives were left behind. Several of them, however, flew to Houston at their own expense. There was nothing Green could do about that.

The 1980 playoffs seemingly followed the same pattern of previous post-season tournaments for the haunted Phillies.

The Astros pushed the Phils' backs to the wall with a 1–0, 11-inning victory in the third game on October 10.

Denny Walling's bases-loaded sacrifice fly that scored pinch-runner Rafael Landestoy produced the victory and sent 44,443 Astrodome customers home convinced Houston was virtually in the World Series.

"We hit with them and we pitched with them and having the last at-bat—and luck—was the only reason they won," said Mike Schmidt, who was completely muffled by Houston pitching in the first three games. "They still have to beat Steve Carlton, the best pitcher in the world, and keep us from scoring over another nine innings. If they do that, they deserve to go to the World Series and they're the best team. But I still think we're the best team until they do it."

Joe Morgan ignited the 11th with a leadoff triple off Tug McGraw. Dallas Green, with no other choice, ordered the next two batters intentionally walked and Walling followed with his fly to medium left field. Luzinski fielded it, but the runner beat the off-line throw to the plate.

"I didn't hit it well," said Walling. "I tried to get a base hit, but I hit a fly ball. Morgan got the triple and Landestoy scored the run. All I did was hit the fly ball.

"We're in trouble," Green said, forcing a weak smile. "We only got seven hits. You can't do a helluva lot with that. Naturally, we feel let down right now, but we're going to get ready for tomorrow. We're just not getting any offense right now."

Though Dave Smith got the victory with one inning of relief, it was knuckleballer Joe Niekro who threw the Phils' bats into mothballs all afternoon.

"I can't find the words to tell you what Niekro's done the last month or six weeks," said Houston Manager Billy Virdon. "Joe's been unbeatable. He throws the knuckler and nobody scores any runs off him. Joe's background is he improves as the game goes on. He over-throws at first, but he gets better."

There were smiles in the Houston dressing room, but there was also concern. In the sixth inning, center fielder Cesar Cedeno trying to beat a relay throw which completed a doubleplay, tripped over first base and had to be carried off the field on a stretcher.

Later that day he underwent surgery to repair a compound dislocation and extreme ligament tear of his right ankle. He was out for the playoffs and the World Series.

So, with their backs pinned to the wall, the Phillies sent Steve Carlton against Vern Ruhle on Saturday, October 11, a date that should be etched in marble at the Hall of Fame.

They played with the usual assortment of gloves, bats, pine tar and resin bags, but what each player really needed was a rule book.

The day was long, bizarre—and unbelievably successful for the Phillies. They came back to score three runs in the eighth inning to take the lead, watched Houston tie in the ninth, then went on to win 5–3 with a pair of runs in the 10th.

It was a victory which allowed the giddy Phillies to remain alive in the playoffs just when it appeared the Astros were going to celebrate a National League pennant. It was also a game filled with ridiculous plays, missed opportunities and a colossal controversy.

"There is virtually no element that can happen in a baseball game that hasn't happened here," Howard Cosell blabbed to the ABC-TV audience.

Mike Schmidt slumped onto the stool in front of his locker, took a sigh of relief and blurted: "This was just about to become another chapter in the long saga of bizarre Philadelphia Phillies' playoff games."

Schmidt was wrong.

The difference on October 11 was the fact the Phillies rose from the ashes of defeat. They did it despite two calls by umpires that went against them and they did it just when the Astros were on the verge of letting the corks on their champagne bottles pop.

"Now, there will be champagne in both clubhouses on Sunday," said Schmidt, referring to the fact the best-of-five tournament was even at 2–2. "We get to play tomorrow; that is the important thing."

Had the spunky Astros eliminated the Phillies in front of the frantic 44,952 Houston followers in the Astrodome, it would have been a long winter for the already frustrated Phillies. But to lose a game with so many controversial calls? Forget it.

Aside from the Phillies' eventual playoff victory, the

fourth inning of the fourth game will be remembered and talked about for years to come when hot-stovers rehash the 1980 National League Championship Series.

With two Phils on base and Houston leading 1–0, Garry Maddox hit a soft liner back to Vern Ruhle. The pitcher grabbed the ball—it looked like on one hop—and threw to first baseman Art Howe. Home-plate umpire Doug Harvey, the crew chief, signalled it a trapped ball, but first-base umpire Ed Vargo and third-base umpire Bob Engel said, "No, Ruhle caught it at his shoetops."

Following the putout at first—to complete a doubleplay, the alert Howe ran to second to complete a triple play.

The Phillies screamed. Six umpires huddled for 20 minutes and Harvey conferred with National League President Chub Feeney.

No triple play, just a double-play inasmuch as time had been called before Howe tagged Bake McBride.

Both managers protested the game.

Phils' Player Personnel Director Paul Owens, sitting in a box near the Phils' third-base dugout, was in a rage. He had to be restrained by owner Ruly Carpenter.

Instead of having runners on second and third with one out, the Phils had a runner at second with two out, and Larry Bowa ended that threat by grounding out.

The television replay, provided in the press box, was repeatedly shown from all views. One view was inconclusive, while another seemed to indicate the ball hit the dirt on the mound before it bounced into Ruhle's glove.

Months later, when the Phillies premiered their season highlight film, the sequence left little doubt that Ruhle had trapped the ball.

"The call could have gone either way," said Ruhle after the game. "It was a close call. I reached as far as I could for the ball. It was hard for me to know, but Luis Pujols hollered for me to throw to first, so I did. I got the ball right in the webbing of my glove. If it's in my glove, there's no question I made the play."

"The ball hit the dirt first," said Maddox. "Harvey shouted, 'No catch!' Then, they changed their minds. I'll go to my grave knowing the ball hit the dirt; I couldn't believe the way it was called."

"It was a terrible call," said Dallas Green. "It was neither a triple play nor a double-play. Ruhle clearly trapped the ball. It should have been men on second and third with one out. I asked Harvey if Ruhle caught the ball, why did he go to first instead of third? That makes no sense."

"Garry Maddox is a right-handed batter who usually bends over the plate," said Harvey. "When he made contact, he leaned over and blocked my view. My immediate reaction was the ball was half-speed and it might come up short. Well, I gave the no-catch sign at first. Then, I looked up and saw the charge of people coming towards me. I immediately called time out and conferred with my umpires.

"Ed Vargo said it was a catch. Bob Engel said the same thing. We ruled the runner at second could go back and would not be out."

Harvey added that his no-catch call led to the umpires' final decision.

"I felt my call put the runner on second base in jeopardy," he said. "He went to third base on my call. I felt the runner on first broke immediately and never could have gotten back no matter what my call was. The jeopardy rule has been in the book for years. It gives the umpires the right to correct a mistake that has put a runner in a bad position. That's exactly what happened."

What happened in the remainder of the game was not that weird, but just as mind-boggling.

In the sixth inning, the Astros scored their third run against reliever Dickie Noles, or did they?

No. Gary Woods, the runner on third with one out, left

the bag too soon on a sacrifice fly, an appeal was made and Engel raised his arm. The runner was out, completing an inning-ending double-play.

That was the only crucial call that went in the Phils' favor. In the eighth when they finally cracked the scoring column with three runs, right-field umpire Bruce Froemming made a horrible call.

With Pete Rose on third, Manny Trillo hit a sinking liner to right. The ball hit in front of Jeff Leonard's glove, but Froemming ruled the ball caught. Rose scored on what was a sacrifice fly, but the shocked Schmidt was trapped off first and an easy out.

"I couldn't believe it," said Schmidt. "I was frozen between first and second, watched the ball hit in front of Leonard's glove, then took off for second. To be honest, I thought I might have trouble getting to second in time because he took it on the short hop."

The Astros yelled long and loud, saying Rose should not have been able to score the third run because they completed a double-play. The rule book, however, is clear. As long as Rose scored ahead of the out on Schmidt, the run counted.

The final hero of the 3-hour, 55-minute ordeal was none other than Greg Luzinski.

The Bull, who batted for Bake McBride in the 10th, blasted a game-winning double that brought gang busters Pete Rose crashing into third-string catcher Bruce Bochy with the go-ahead run. Manny Trillo followed with a double that produced the insurance run.

Rose, who was brilliant in the playoffs, inspired the two-run rally when he singled to center with one out. Schmidt flied to left for the second out and as he walked back to the dugout, he yelled at Luzinski, "Pick me up Bull. Pick me up!"

Luzinski drilled a Joe Sambito pitch to left that sliced away from Jose Cruz as Rose steamed around the bases, never stopping.

Shortstop Rafael Landestoy's relay throw short-hopped Bochy and bounced away before Rose gave him a rough, but legal, forearm in the face, seconds before managing to plant a foot on the plate for the winter.

"It was a do-or-die play," said Bochy. "But it took a short hop and I didn't come up with it."

"The catcher was concentrating on a tough throw," said Pete, "and it short-hopped him. It was a tough throw and not many people handle that throw. I hope he's all right. I had no alternative but to do what I did—go over him and tag the plate."

Houston Manager Billy Virdon admitted he was "hurting" about finding a catcher for the Sunday night finale. Alan Ashby was sidelined with a separated rib suffered in his collision with Ferguson. Starter Luis Pujols took a Schmidt foul off his right ankle and had left Saturday's game early for X rays.

Tug McGraw, who pitched the 10th inning to save the verdict for Warren Brusstar, bubbled when it was finally over.

"There has never been a game to compare with this one," he said. "There has never been a game I've ever witnessed that has been more exciting, more controversial, more interesting.

"It was like going through an art museum on a motorcycle. You don't remember any pictures you saw."

So, after all the baseball madness that reached its stretch run on September 26, the Phils' season came down to one game.

On Sunday night, October 12, it would be Nolan Ryan against the Phils' rookie Marty Bystrom.

The score was 8–7 Phillies in 10 innings, the fourth straight overtime game in the wild, dizzy and often dazzling series.

The ball jumped off Enos Cabell's bat and soared into the heavy air of the Astrodome. It seemed to hang there for just a second and all over the Delaware Valley hearts jumped.

There had to be people who were afraid to watch. It came down gently in Garry Lee Maddox' glove and it was over.

Larry Bowa jumped high off the plastic grass. Pete Rose leaped toward the mound. By the time he got there, the whole bench had emptied. Dallas Green was hugging Dick Ruthven and Bobby Wine was grabbing Mike Schmidt and the celebration was on.

But before it got fully under way, somebody shouted something and the whole team raced to center field where Maddox was still clutching the ball, almost frozen. By the time all the players in the baby-blue uniforms arrived Maddox started jogging to the infield, but he didn't have to. The players, all of 'em, hoisted him to their shoulders and gave him a free ride to the dugout and later the clubhouse where corks were popping and champagne was already spilling and squirting around the room.

The Philadelphia Phillies were National League champions!

All the frustrating and waiting, all 30 years of it, seemed to explode at once.

"How's that for team character," Green yelled as he hugged his mentor, Paul Owens, like a baby. "That is the character I have been preaching about ever since spring training. Tonight, there was so much character out on the field, I couldn't believe it. I love it! I love it!"

The Phils again came back from the dead to win the deciding game, a victory that sent Philadelphia into a frenzy as fans battled each other, positioning themselves in line at Veterans Stadium for World Series tickets.

The Phils did it this time by storming from behind with five runs in the eighth inning after the Astros gave Ryan a seemingly insurmountable 5–2 cushion.

Before the five-run explosion, none of the 44,802 fans who jammed the Astrodome ready to raise the pennant would have given the Phils a thread of a chance.

But the Phils, who had been scratching for the top spot ever since they started their September march, refused to pass this one up. Three consecutive hits off Ryan, plus a bases-loaded walk to Pete Rose, got them on their way. And Manny Trillo, voted the Most Valuable Player in the playoffs with a .381 average and brilliant fielding, delivered a clutch triple.

After the Astros wiped out the Phils' 7–5 lead against a fatigued Tug McGraw in the ninth, old folks Del Unser delivered a one-out double to right. He went to third when Trillo cracked a long fly to center.

Up came Garry Maddox. He hit Frank LaCorte's first pitch, lining it to center field for a double. Unser easily scored the eighth run.

Dick Ruthven who had pitched a perfect ninth took the mound for the 10th. Rufus got Danny Heep, batting for La-Corte, to pop out to Bowa. Up came Terry Puhl who had four hits in the game. Puhl lofted an easy fly to Maddox and the only obstacle between the Phillies and a pennant was Enos Cabell.

Easy chance for Maddox, and it was over.

"If you shine, it's because somebody puts a light on you," said Del Unser. "We shined in this series because the Astros put a light on us. They pushed us harder than anyone has ever pushed us."

"Let them say we don't have any heart anymore," said Luzinski. "We proved to the world we don't have a quitter on this team."

"Everybody thought we were a team of destiny," said Terry Puhl in the quiet of the Houston dressing room. "They were wrong. The Phillies were a team of destiny in this series."

"I'm overwhelmed with my own feelings and the feelings I have for all the people who were rooting for us to win this thing," said Maddox. "At first, I didn't think my ball was going to be a hit. I was just trying to make contact, trying to see the ball well. I can't tell you what went through my mind when it dropped in front of the center fielder. It was just about the most important hit I have ever had."

For Maddox, the victory was a happy climax to a season he will never forget. He had battled back from the sunglasses incident and from Green's benching him. He'd fought off the feelings that were eating away at him and in the end his enormous contributions helped the Phils to their most emotional and important victory since that bright, sunny day in Brooklyn when Dick Sisler's home run gave the 1950 Whiz Kids their pennant.

The most interested of all the television viewers were the Kansas City Royals. They had polished off the New York Yankees in three quick American League playoff games and found themselves at a New York airport the night of October 12, not knowing whether they would be flying to Philadelphia or Houston for their first World Series.

When Maddox caught Cabell's fly ball, somebody in the Royals' party yelled: "Let's go to Philadelphia!"

And that's the way it was.

Pete Rose is hugged by Phillies' Manager Dallas Green after the Phils defeated Kansas City 4-1 to win the World Series in six games.

The World Series
"We're World Champions. World Champions!"

". . . take this championship and savor it . . . because you all deserve it."

Mike Schmidt's voice bellowed over the loud speakers at JFK Stadium on the sunny autumn afternoon. The frenzied crowd of nearly a hundred thousand, already on the edge of delirium, drowned out his final, emotional words.

It was a magical moment.

Red and white streamers began floating from the windows of office buildings as early as 9 a.m. By 10, horns were blaring, fireworks were exploding and over 700,000 fans were lined along the parade route.

For the Phillies, all was forgiven. Those many years of frustration and disappointment were forgotten. Philadelphia finally had a baseball world championship and the long-deprived fans made certain they were going to enjoy every precious minute of it.

The night before, on October 21, the Phillies pushed aside Kansas City 4–1 to win their first World Series. Seconds after Tug McGraw struck out Willie Wilson for the final out in the ninth inning, a time bomb exploded throughout the Delaware Valley. Impromptu celebrations lasted all night. The formal heroes' parade followed the next day.

After finally snuffing Houston's determined bid to become National League champion, the Phillies arrived in the 77th World Series mentally drained and physically fatigued.

Only after such a mind-blowing, throat-clutching playoff experience could the best-of-seven tournament for the world championship be called anti-climactic.

In a sense, it was.

From the time Garry Maddox caught Enos Cabell's fly ball to seal their incredible drive to the pennant, life was a blur for the Phillies. Their celebration in Houston seemed more like a jailbreak than a party. They had escaped the prison of the past and now were asked to quickly shift gears and take center stage in baseball's premier showcase.

There was the Monday flight home from Houston, followed by an airport celebration attended by 5,000 wind-chilled fans. A late-afternoon workout, invaded by the ever-probing national media, ended with Dallas Green's startling announcement rookie Bob Walk would pitch the October 14 opener against Kansas City's Dennis Leonard. The Phillies were on an all-time emotional high and at an all-time pitching low.

Before they really knew what hit them, public address announcer Dan Baker was making the introductions, 65,791 Veterans Stadium fans were on their feet roaring their support and 1950 Manager Eddie Sawyer was about to throw out the first ball.

Walk, the gangling, pimple-faced 23-year-older felt his heart pounding against his chest as he finished his warm-up pitches in the right-field bullpen.

He had been chosen to start the Phillies' first World Series game since 1950 because the club's pitching staff was in shambles after the dramatic, fifth-game victory over the Astros.

Steve Carlton had pitched five-plus innings on Saturday and the rest of the starters had worked Sunday night in the clincher. Marty Brystrom went 5⅓ innings, Larry Christenson two-thirds and Dick Ruthven the last two for the victory. McGraw had appeared in all five playoff games.

Walk would become the first rookie to start an opening Series game since the Dodgers' Joe Black faced the Yankees in 1952. Philadelphia hadn't won a World Series game since Grover Cleveland Alexander beat the Red Sox 3–1 on October 8, 1915. The Phillies lost the next four in that one and, of course, four in a row against the Yankees in 1950.

The harsh reality: Dallas Green had little choice but to tap the young right-hander—called Whirlybird by his teammates—who arrived at Veterans Stadium in late May, an emergency call-up from Oklahoma City.

Despite control problems, he was 6-0 with a 3.92 earned run average on July 16 and ended the season with an 11-7 record and 4.56 ERA.

The palms of Walk's hands were damp with sweat when he was informed of his key assignment by pitching coach Herm Starrette.

"I'm a little nervous," confessed Walk, who the year before was pumping gas for $3.75 an hour at a service station in Newhall, California. "I heard something about the possibility of my starting the opening game after we beat Houston, but I didn't get the word definitely until our Monday workout. Herm came up to me and said, 'You know, you're in there tomorrow.' I said, 'OK.' "

"I have no qualms about using Bobby Walk," said Green. "He did the job when we needed him. He had a little slip for a while with his control and poise, but he's OK now."

On the other side of the Veterans Stadium basement, Kansas City Manager Jim Frey scoffed at the suggestion the Royals' layoff after they quickly disposed of the Yankees would stall their momentum.

"It will have no effect," snapped the bespectacled Frey, who the year before was a coach for the Baltimore Orioles.

"All it does is set up my pitching. Larry Gura and Rich Gale will follow Leonard. In terms of psychology, I expect both teams to fight 'til the last out. Both teams will have the same emotion when they walk onto the field."

George Brett, who captivated the American baseball audience with his unsuccessful quest to become the first .400 hitter since Ted Williams batted .406 for Boston in 1941, agreed. "We had a three-week layoff (after the Royals clinched their division title) at the end of the season and it didn't bother us."

Through three innings, the World Series opener seemed like another chapter of the insanity that marked the Phils' pursuit of the pennant.

Walk gave up two-run homers to Amos Otis and Willie Mays Aikens in the second and third innings, respectively, to create a lightning-fast 4–0 deficit.

Instead of telling the young right-hander to take a shower, Green stuck with him. The Phillies rallied for five runs in the third inning against 20-game winner Leonard and Walk was given a reprieve.

"I don't like to say this with him listening, "Green whispered after the 7–6 victory, "but he was one batter from coming out in the third. I thought I'd stick with him and he came through."

Actually, Green was telling a little white-lie. With the designated-hitter rule being used in this Series (Greg Luzinski filled that role for the Phils), he felt it was too early to go to his weary bullpen.

After Aikens' homer, Darrell Porter walked and Otis followed with an infield single. That brought up Clint Hurdle who lined a single to left. Lonnie Smith, a surprise starter in left field, threw out Porter trying to score from second. Walk and the Phillies were out of the inning.

After that, Whirlybird retired nine in a row before Frank

White led off the seventh with a single, but Walk got the next three outs to preserve a 7–4 margin.

In the eighth, however, George Brett doubled and Aikens smoked another two-run homer.

Enter Tug McGraw. Scroogie pitched out of a mini-jam in that inning and put the Royals down in order in the ninth to preserve the victory for Walk.

If the Phillies gave anybody the impression they were content merely to get into the World Series the opening 7–6 victory killed those thoughts.

"We don't like to lose, and we don't plan to lose regardless of what happens," said Green amidst the euphoria of the smashing first-night success. "Winning was something special in front of the home fans. We like giving them what they came to the park for—a victory!"

Bake McBride was ready for a vacation after the Houston classic, but knew his bat needed some work.

"In Houston, even when I was making good contact something was wrong, but I didn't know what it was. I came out here after we got back and hit off the batting tee and let Billy DeMars watch my swing. About the fifth ball I hit he said, 'Bake, you're over-striding.' I cut down on the length of my stride and started to feel better right away when he threw some pitches to me."

Shake 'n Bake's three-run homer off Leonard capped the five-run third inning and helped the Phils to their first victory since 1915 in a World Series.

"Bake's homer really did it for me," said Green. "He's been a clutch guy, an RBI guy, all year. I don't know where we'd be without him. He's given us everything we needed in 1980 and again in the World Series."

"I really don't want to get in the habit of trying for home runs," said McBride. "I just want to put the ball in play. I thought we might be drained after that series in Houston, but this is our second time around and we feel we can get it up."

"Being down 4–0 didn't bother me one bit," said Green. "Not with the Cardiac Kids. Even though we haven't been scoring a lot of runs, I knew the guys would get it going. It was a perfect example of what you can do when you have to do it. I had confidence Bobby would get his act together, too."

After Aikens' first homer made it 4–0, Porter walked and Otis beat out an infield chopper to third. Hurdle then singled to left and Porter, who was on second, never stopped. He stumbled rounding third, but headed for the plate as Lonnie Smith unleashed a bullet. Porter was a dead duck and came in standing up as Boone applied a nonchalant tag.

"That was a big play, a costly play," sighed Frey. "Right now it looks like Porter should not have gone. I thought I saw him stumble a little and I don't know if that slowed him or not.

"I would have preferred him to slide. You hate to see a guy come to the plate and just stop. But if he tries to knock Boone into the seats he could have gotten hurt, too."

"Truthfully, I never expected the ball to get there as quickly as it did," admitted Porter. "I tripped over third base and lost my momentum. I had it in my mind all the time to slide, but I just couldn't get my feet coordinated. If I'd tried to slide, I probably would have broken my ankle."

"I figured Porter would go," said Smith after the game. "The Royals probably knew I didn't have such a good arm or that I make mistakes. Porter didn't have that much to lose by going, but I got off a good throw."

Larry Bowa started the Phils' assault on Leonard with a single to left, stole second and scored when Boone sliced a double down the left-field line to score Manny Trillo. Smith followed with a single to left and, after Lonnie slipped going around first, cutoff man George Brett caught him in a rundown. Boone scored while this was happening.

"Blame 65,000 screaming fans for that," said Frey, absolving Frank White for failing to throw to the plate as Boone raced home. "Normally, you hear your teammates yelling, but you couldn't hear anything tonight."

"I never had control of my breaking pitch," said Leonard. "I had to come in with the fastball and they hit it. I never really got the ball where I wanted it. When I did make good pitches, they just hit them."

The play both managers called the turning point was Leonard hitting Pete Rose with a pitch after Boone scored. Mike Schmidt then walked and McBride did the rest.

"He always does that crap," said Leonard. "He didn't make any attempt to get out of the way of the ball. In fact, he might even have stuck his leg out."

"He sure didn't try to get out of the way," agreed catcher Porter. "But it's a tough call for an umpire."

"I could have gotten away from the ball," Rose told a friend weeks later. "But why? We needed base runners at the time. It was as good as a walk, maybe a hit."

Boone doubled home the Phils' sixth run in the fourth, knocking out Leonard in favor of Renie Martin who grew up in Phillies' country in Dover, Delaware. Martin pitched the next four innings and allowed the Phils' final run in the fifth on Garry Maddox' bases-loaded sacrifice.

"We've been through a very nice kind of hell the last 10 days," Green said. "We've played the types of games that have prepared us for any eventuality. Tonight was a piece of cake compared to some we've played before. It's the first game we've played in some time where if we lost it our backs wouldn't be against the wall.

"I think all the stuff about us being drained by the play-offs, about our pitching staff being exhausted, is overrated. All I needed from Bobby Walk was a good-enough, long-enough outing to give some of my bullpen guys another day of rest. He gave us that and now our pitching staff is all lined up."

The Phillies, obviously fueled by destiny, did it again in

Game 2. They won, that is. And again, they watched the Royals vault ahead 4–3 after six innings at the Vet before finally warming the crowd of 65,775 with a four-spot in the eighth.

It will go down as a 6–4 conquest, but what most everyone in America remembers about this second game of the World Series was the embarrassing and painful affliction that struck George Brett.

Hemorrhoids.

"It is," George said earnestly, "a pain in the ass."

He was speaking after the game and he could have been discoursing on the contest just completed or the state of the Series, as well as his uncomfortable situation.

Brett first noticed the discomfort the day after the Royals finished off the Yankees to win the American League pennant. He was shopping in Billy Martin's Western wear shop with his brothers and teammate Jamie Quirk when the pain started.

"I felt it quite a lot in the first game and it was even worse tonight," said Brett, who had to leave the game in the sixth inning after a perfect night at the plate—two singles and a walk. "I think my inability to move in my normal fashion contributed to two Philadelphia runs in the fifth."

Brett's status for the second bout at the Vet was in question until a decision was made to let him play two hours before Steve Carlton's first pitch.

"George made the decision himself," said the Royals' team physician, Dr. Paul Meyer. "That was our agreement—that he would play until the pain got so bad he couldn't stand it."

"It's the worst pain I've ever felt," said Brett. "I never had so much discomfort. The more you move, the more it hurts. Everybody thought I would be better off in the hospital."

The bewildered Royals jetted out of Philadelphia after the jarring setback and the moment the plane landed in Kansas City, Brett checked into St. Luke's Hospital where Dr. John

Heryer performed surgery. That was October 16, the open day for travel.

Newspapers and the electronic media had a field day with his problem, but he was back in the line-up when the Series resumed on Friday night.

Del Unser, whose pinch-hitting saved the season in Houston, gave the Royals a dose of his magic as the Phils alley-catted their way to victory in the second game.

Unser, whose two doubles sparked the miraculous come-back against the Astros in the fifth game of the playoffs, ripped a double to start the Phils' four-run, eighth-inning rally against the Royals.

In addition to the apprehension about Brett's affliction, the Royals also were numbed by the realization that 26 of the previous 33 clubs who swept the first games of the World Series went on to win the whole thing.

"This isn't just a 15-year itch, it's more like a 30-year itch," the much-traveled, 35-year-old Unser said. "I didn't know about the World Series until I was 5, but I've been fascinated by it ever since. This is a great feeling. This team has the confidence because we've come back so many times before, we expect to now."

The Phils' comeback on another chilly night made a winner of Steve Carlton who struggled and was lucky to escape without a loss.

Walks, a bugaboo of the entire Phils' staff, almost proved Carlton's downfall even though Dallas Green blamed baseballs "slick as ice" for costing Carlton the feel of his deadly slider.

But the stirring rally, a club trademark since the series with Houston, made believers of the sellout crowd and pushed the once-confident Royals into a shell, especially since the fireworks came against their top reliever, Dan Quisenberry.

Bob Boone began the Phils' eighth with a walk and Unser, batting for Lonnie Smith, doubled to the gap in left-center to score the gimpy Boone, still favoring a sore left foot.

"I hit a pretty good sinker," Unser said. "It was the same kind I hit off Kent Tekulve in that last series in Pittsburgh. I was fortunate to hit the ball with the good part of my bat. I could have popped it up very easily. It's tough to pull the ball against a pitcher like Quisenberry."

Unser went to third on Pete Rose's chopper to first and scored when Bake McBride hit a high bouncer over the head of second baseman Frank White to tie the game 4–4.

Mike Schmidt, who had gotten some advice from his father, Jack, doubled against the right-field wall and McBride sped around the bases.

The Phils crammed half their eight hits into the fevered rally and the most important was Schmidt's screamer to right.

Two pitches later Keith Moreland, a designated-hitter selection when Luzinski was sent home with a high fever and the flu, ripped a single to score Schmidt with the run that gave the Phils a 6–4 lead.

Ron Reed nailed down the save with a strong ninth.

"Anytime you see Schmitty going to right like that you know he's staying with the ball," said Rose. "He's getting some big hits now because he's so relaxed and confident."

Jack Schmidt told Mike to stop taking so many first pitches and the advice helped.

"I have a tendency to take a look at the guy's first pitch most of the time to check out his velocity, his breaking ball and how he's trying to set me up," said Mike. "This time I went for the first pitch."

The Royals were trailing 2–1 when Brett limped off in the sixth, but they rallied for three runs in the seventh, two scoring on Amos Otis' bases-loaded double past Schmidt down the left-field line.

After that, Frey called on Quisenberry to protect the 4–2 lead. The side-arm, sinkerball specialist who learned to throw his sinister pitch from the Pirates' Tekulve, had saved 33 games and won 12 others during the regular season. With starter Larry Gura weary, Frey's decision seemed logical.

Quisenberry set the Phils down in the seventh, but as had been their custom they refused to die and charged back in the eighth.

Partly because of the slick baseballs and partly because of some Kansas City strategy, Carlton labored for six innings, putting 12 men on base and getting out of one jam after another with either a strikeout or a Larry Bowa-started double-play.

Carlton fanned eight Royals in the first six innings, including leadoff batter Willie Wilson three times. Bowa, meanwhile, tied a World Series record by starting three double plays.

"I know one thing," chirped Bowa. "Lefty is a tired pitcher, very tired. He's thrown a lot of pitches this year and 159 tonight. But he's carried us. If it weren't for him, Schmidt and Tug, we wouldn't be here."

Carlton, who struck out 10 and walked six, has uncanny ability to concentrate. The Royals tried to break that by jumping in and out of the batter's box and by frequently calling time.

"Billy Connors, Royals' pitching coach, was the pitching coach at Oklahoma City (the Phils' top farm club) before he went to Kansas City," explained Herm Starrette, the Phils' pitching coach "I'm sure between him and their advance scout, Tom Ferrick, they tried to cook something up to disrupt Lefty's concentration. He really didn't have that much trouble concentrating. His big trouble was with the baseballs. It was a cool, kind of damp night and he just couldn't get a good grip on them."

The Phils took their 2–0 lead in the fifth when with one out Moreland beat out an infield chopper to deep short.

Maddox doubled Moreland to third and Trillo brought

Moreland home with a sacrifice fly to the warning track in right. Bowa's single scored Maddox for a 2–0 lead.

"We're going back to Kansas City with our work cut out," said Frey. "It comes down now to a four-out-of-five series for us. We've won four out of five games before. I think it will be different in our own ballpark."

"A 2–0 lead in the World Series is not too shabby," said Green. "I'd much rather be where we are than where they are."

"You've got to wonder what we can do to beat the Phillies," said Wilson. "We had our chances, we got a lot of hits, but nothing seemed to go our way. We're just not playing very good baseball.

"The thing that bothers me the most is for us to have played so well all year, then come the World Series and have it turn out this way. This is a good ball club and I want the Phillies to know that. To even the Series, you've got to have a decent club."

No World Series game had ever been played in Kansas City before and the citizenry, shocked by the Phillies' first two victories, really wondered if the Royals could wipe out that deficit.

George Brett, discharged from the hospital a few hours before the Friday night game, kidded with reporters, saying: "The pain is behind me."

Then, in the first inning at beautiful Royals Stadium, he blasted a bases-empty home run off starter Dick Ruthven to give his teammates a 1–0 lead.

The Phils again tried to work their magic, but it failed them in the third game.

It had worked so many times before. Extra innings and Tug McGraw on the mound.

In this game, it didn't work. Kansas City pulled out a 10-inning, 4–3 victory when Willie Aikens ripped a McGraw pitch past center fielder Garry Maddox. As the sellout crowd of 42,380 went wild, Wilson raced home from second base to nail it down.

"I saw the ball heading for the gap and I know Maddox plays short-center," said Aikens later. "As soon as the ball got up in the air, I knew he didn't have a chance."

The Phillies had many opportunities, but the kayo punch was just not there. Through six innings they stranded 10 runners and when the game finally ended, their left-on-base total was 15.

The Phils never led but at one stage should have been on top by at least five runs.

Mike Schmidt flied out with the bases loaded in the second. Larry Bowa grounded out with runners on second and third and two down in the third, and again in the ninth with runners on first and second. In the fifth, with a runner in scoring position, Manny Trillo grounded out to end the inning. Schmidt flied out to center with runners on first and third in the eighth and ninth.

The 10th, however, was the most excruciating of all for the Phils. With Bob Boone on second, Pete Rose on first and one out in a 3–3 tie, Schmidt hit a screamer that looked like it was going to bounce past Frank White. The second baseman, however, made a brilliant stop to start a double play.

"That was the ball game right there," said Green. "If that ball gets through, it might have rolled to the wall. We certainly had our chances. We got plenty of hits (14) to win most games. We just couldn't come up with the big one."

Had the Phillies made their first appearance in Royals Stadium a successful one, the World Series would have been near its end that night.

Instead, the victory pumped new life in the Royals and convinced them they were still in the chase.

"I feel a lot better than I did in Philadelphia," said Frey. "And I'll feel a lot better than I do right now if we even this thing on Saturday."

The Royals' 10th brimmed with drama—and frustration—for the Phillies who had a chance to escape before Aikens came to the plate.

U. L. Washington had started the inning with a single to left and took second as Wilson walked on four pitches. But catcher Bob Boone faked Washington into an out. On an attempted bunt by White, Boone faked a throw to second and as Washington broke for third, the catcher rifled a throw to Schmidt for an easy out at third.

White eventually fanned, but with Brett batting, Wilson did a strange thing—he took off for second. Boone called for a pitch-out but his one hop throw was a hair late and the runner was safe.

With first base now open, the dangerous Brett was intentionally walked. Aikens came up, hit a 2-1 pitch and it was over.

The two base-running blunders could have been disastrous for the Royals had McGraw been able to retire Aikens.

"In that situation Washington is trying to get a jump," said Frey. "If the pitcher throws a slow curve and the hitter misses it, the catcher has a good shot at the runner on second. A lot of clubs practice that play on defense. The runner is in jeopardy if the hitter doesn't make contact. I don't know if that was the intention of the Phillies, but the only one to blame is the base runner.

"With Brett batting there is no way Wilson had the steal sign. He went on his own and that took the bat out of Brett's hands."

The Phils tied the score at 2–2 in the fifth when Schmidt blasted his first World Series homer, a bases-empty shot to left off starter Gale. Kansas City moved ahead 3–2 in the seventh on Otis' homer, but the Phils pulled even again in the eighth when Bowa scored on Rose's single to center off reliever Renie Martin.

"Nobody said this was going to be easy," offered Green, "and tonight it wasn't."

The fourth game belonged to the Royals' Willie Mays Aikens, and to Dickie Noles—in a not-so-subtle way.

The gloomy looking Aikens blasted two homers in the first game, on his 26th birthday. His 10th-inning hit won the third game and in the fourth, on a delightfully crisp October afternoon, he crashed a two-run homer off Larry Christenson in the first inning and another off Noles in the second.

"Are you sure he's not Willie Mays?" Pete Rose asked.

"I believe we have to start pitching him differently," said Green, in the understatement of the day. "Maybe we're not doing what the book says. But the man is on a roll. Hey, when a guy gets that hot you can throw the book away, baby. He swings the bat and there's a lot to be said for that. He hits fastballs over the fence and curve balls over the fence. And there just isn't any defense against home runs, you know."

Starter Christenson never knew what hit him. The Royals scored four runs on five hits in the first and when he was finally replaced by Noles, he had gotten only one out.

"Quite obviously, he didn't have it today," said Green. "He didn't have that good wrist pop. His fastball wasn't exploding like it usually does for him."

The Phils tried a comeback of sorts, but it never materialized. They were down 5–1 after two innings and when the game finally ended were 5–3 losers and the 77th World Series was tied.

But was it?

It happened in the fourth inning with the Royals on top 5–1. The only mistake gun-fighter Noles had made to this point after taking over for Christenson, was a pitch to Aikens that landed in the outer limits of the Royals' bullpen in right field.

So here was Brett, the .390 hitter, facing Noles with one out in the fourth.

The count went 0-2 and Noles then threw a buzzing fastball under Brett's chin. The great hitter reeled and twisted to the ground.

Brett, emerging from the dirt, gazed out at Noles with a "why-me?" look, and Aikens, in the on-deck circle, blinked.

Frey burst onto the field screaming at plate umpire Don Denkinger, "Let's stop this right now. Let's stop this right now!"

Frey shouted something at Noles, who hollered back. Denkinger intervened and, after words with Frey and Rose, issued a warning—another knockdown would result in ejection. Green, who remained calmly chewing gum at the end of the Phillies dugout, was also warned.

Frey left and Brett fanned.

Dickie Noles insists he wasn't throwing at anybody.

Jim Frey says the Phillies' reliever was trying to decapitate George Brett.

Green isn't sure what happened and Brett doesn't care.

"The last time I was in a fight I was 21 and I got the hell beat out of me," said Frey. "I just went out there because I just wanted to get anything stopped right there.

"I thought it was a knockdown pitch. When a team hits the ball like we did today and with a good hitter like George Brett up with an 0-2 count, well, the situation is there. Noles threw the ball at George's head and I went out there to stop that."

Asked what he said to Noles, Frey answered: "All I said was 'I want it stopped right now.' Noles said he wasn't throwing at George. The pitcher's the only one who knows what's going through his head. I didn't want one of those battles where everybody's throwing at people's heads.

"I don't believe in retaliation and I don't buy that 'high-and-tight' stuff. You can be as much a baseball purist as you want, but if you've seen guys get hit in the head—and I've seen two or three almost killed—you don't want any of that stuff going on."

The Phillies insist Brett wasn't a marked man.

"All I'll say is I wasn't throwing at him," repeated Noles.

"We were pitching George inside," added catcher Bob Boone. "The ball just sailed on Dickie."

"The only guy upset was Jim Frey," said Green. "George Brett didn't get upset and he was the guy getting shot at. All I saw was an 0-2 pitch and the hitter diving. It wasn't a bad one."

Brett shrugged it off.

"Whatever he was doing, it was all right with me," said George, flashing a smile. "It's all part of the game. I believe in an eye-for-an-eye, a tooth-for-a-tooth."

Frey also had words with Rose after walking toward the Kansas City dugout, then circling back toward the field.

"Pete told me to get off the field, that Noles wasn't throwing at anybody," said Frey. "Like I said before, the only guy who knew what was going through Noles' mind was the pitcher himself. Pete Rose didn't know any more than I did."

"I just told him it was a helluva thing for a manager to yell at our pitcher," Rose related. "I can't remember that happening before. Brett was the guy who could have argued if he wanted to, but he didn't say anything. It was really weird."

Reliever Quisenberry, who had unleashed almost as many quips as sinkerballs in the four games he had worked, was asked if he threw hard enough to retaliate in such a situation.

"Sure, with grenades," he said, smiling.

It was easy for Quisenberry to make light of the incident. The Royals, two days before virtually counted out of the Series, had won to square the Octoberfest at 2–2 and Brett had escaped unscathed, if a little shaken.

Asked how the Kansas City pitching staff planned to retaliate the rest of the way, Quisenberry suggested: "We might invest our World Series checks in nuclear arms."

In four games, Aikens had crashed four homers, a triple and driven in eight runs.

"I said when we left Philadelphia we still were in this thing," Aikens reminded reporters after the fourth game. "I honestly never felt we were out of it and now it is a best-of-three Series and we're in the driver's seat."

Mike Schmidt had other thoughts.

"We're right back to square one," he said. "However, it's not a desperate situation by any means. Right now I just want to get out of here with a win on Sunday. If we can do that, it would put them in a position of having to win two in our place. I'm not worried about this team. We've had our backs against the wall most of the year and we've come through."

It should probably be mentioned here that in the dead of a Charlotte, North Carolina winter, Dickie Noles' eyes twinkled when people asked him about the pitch to Brett. He still insisted he didn't throw at the batter. "Why would I do that?" Dickie asked.

Maybe it was just coincidental, but after that celebrated "chin music" Brett would get just three singles and Aikens only one hit. The Royals scored just four more runs.

Life for Tug McGraw has always been in the fast lane. Live today and the hell with tomorrow is the style this blithe spirit follows.

"I'll probably play until I get run over at 6 o'clock one morning by a street cleaner when I'm in some gutter outside a bar, sound asleep with an empty bottle of John Jameson in my hand," the Phillies' ace relief pitcher says. "And that will be the end."

A bitter ending to Tug McGraw's lastest drama momentarily flashed in front of his bloodshot eyes in the fifth game when Kansas City's Hal McRae hit a would-be, game-winning home run to left field in the ninth inning. At the last instant, as McGraw paled, the ball curved foul.

McGraw stood on the mound thumping the fingers of his left hand over his heart.

"And I was cussing him for staying out all night," Dallas Green admitted later.

There was a happy ending to this story. McGraw, who had walked the bases loaded in the ninth, struck out former teammate José Cardenal for the third out to seal the Phillies' dramatic, 4–3 come-from-behind thriller.

Thanks to Frank Edwin McGraw and a two-run rally in the top of the ninth, the Phils moved ahead 3-2 in the Series and returned to Philadelphia for the clincher.

There has never been anything routine about the zany 36-year-old reliever. He put the Royals down one-two-three in the eighth, his second inning of work. That he would do the same thing in the ninth was asking too much. Tug, you see, goes for the spectacular.

He immediately dug himself a hole and sent a murmur of hope through the Royals Stadium mob of 42,369 when he walked Frank White. But a few seconds later he got the world's greatest hitter, George Brett, to look at a third strike. Up came Aikens, hero of the 5–3 fourth-game assault that squared the Series. Aikens, this time, walked.

Now it was up to McRae, one of the most dangerous hitters in Kansas City's batting order. Before forcing Aikens' pinch runner, Onix Concepcion, at second, McRae had hearts throughout the playground fluttering when he cracked his long fly, a shot that would have given the Royals three runs and their third straight victory over the Phillies.

"I'm not sure I can take these tense games much longer," said McGraw. "I thought I would have to be rescued by those cardiac people who have been conventioning here all week."

"*You* can't take them?" McGraw's wife, Phyllis, almost shouted. "What about the people in the stands who are watching you?"

Following McRae to the plate was Amos Otis who had worn out Philadelphia pitching, hitting at a .529 clip in the Series.

Just before Otis stepped in, pitching coach Starrette went to the mound with some advice.

McGraw stared at Herm and after he left, the pitcher they call Scroogie walked Otis on four pitches.

A semi-intentional pass?

"No way," said Tug. "Actually I went out there trying to pitch a one-two-three inning. I began trying to be too careful and then began missing. When Otis was up, I was very careful. I didn't care if I walked him. He had been tough on us in all the games so far and, frankly, I wasn't that concerned about advancing the winning run to second base."

Tug refused to say it, but he had a better chance against Cardenal with the bases loaded than he did against Otis with runners on first and third.

The count went 1-2 to Cardenal. He then fouled off two pitches before McGraw threw a "Cutty Sark fastball" past him and it was over.

"In my mind José is one of the best pinch hitters with runners in scoring position," said McGraw. "But because I know him from when he was with the Cubs and with us, I was fairly comfortable pitching to him. I felt fortunate today. I got him on my Cutty Sark fastball—you know, it sails."

Moments before, Cardenal fouled off a pitch and when he did, his bat slipped out of his hand and landed near the mound. When McGraw handed it back to José, he stuck it in his stomach. The two exchanged bitter glances.

"I didn't say anything to him," said McGraw through a devilish smile. "He said something to me in Spanish that you wouldn't want to hear in church. I know enough Spanish to get the idea of what he was saying. So, when I handed the bat back to him, I kinda stuck it in his stomach."

McGraw, clutching a can of beer in each hand, said he had a guilty feeling when he went to the mound.

"Phyllis and I went out last night. We had some drinks and stayed out later than we should have. Then, when we went to the room she relaxed me. To tell you the truth, I was drained out there today.

"Seriously, this was a very important victory for me. I struck out George Brett twice in three innings and I think that has to be the highlight of my career. He's the best hitter in the game today. But getting Cardenal was the big one I guess."

Aside from McGraw's uncanny relief, another incident in the Phils' important victory almost went unnoticed. To baseball purists, though, it was an intriguing ingredient that undoubtedly tipped the scales in the Phils' favor.

They were just three outs from losing to the Royals 3–2 when Schmidt, who had blasted a two-run homer in the fourth inning off Larry Gura, led off the ninth against Quisenberry.

Just before the Royals took the field, Frey whispered something to third baseman Brett.

"Should I worry about Schmidt dropping a bunt?" Brett asked.

"Don't give it to him," Frey said.

"With a guy like Schmidt up," Brett would say later, "most third basemen want to play 50 feet behind the bag."

So, as Schmidt stepped into the batter's box, Brett took five steps toward the plate, positioning himself even with the bag.

Schmidt ripped a liner to third that bounced off Brett's glove for a single that started the Phils on their way to a two-run rally.

Unser, the pinch-hitting marvel, lined a double to right field to score Schmidt with the tying run. After Moreland advanced Unser to third with an infield out and Maddox grounded out, Trillo blitzed a liner off Quisenberry's glove to bring home what proved to be the winning run.

"I was fearful Schmidt might try to bunt because he had done it before," Frey explained as second-guessers flocked around. "I wanted to play it safe."

"Bunting was low on my list of priorities in that situation," said Schmidt. "All I was trying to do was get a pitch I could drive. I never thought about bunting and didn't even think about where Brett was playing me until it was mentioned."

Normally, with a power hitter such as Schmidt up the third baseman will position himself almost in shallow left field. The object is to guard the foul line and cut off an extra-base hit. Had Brett been playing Schmidt there, Mike would have been an easy out.

In the sixth inning it was evident rookie starter Marty Bystrom had lost some of the pop on his fastball. Otis blasted an 0-1 pitch to left field for a home run that pulled the Royals even. Clint Hurdle then singled to center and Darrell Porter blooped a single to right with the runner stopping at third.

Here, Green brought in Ron Reed. U. L. Washington greeted Reed with a long fly to right that gave Kansas City a 3–2 edge.

Willie Wilson followed with a booming double to right. Bake McBride played the ball perfectly, hit Trillo with the relay and the second baseman threw a bullet to Boone to cut down Porter attempting to score from first base.

"You can't overlook our hits in the ninth inning," said Rose, "but we wouldn't even have been in the game if Manny Trillo hadn't made the perfect throw. If he doesn't make that play, they could have gone on to a big inning and taken us right out of the game."

"Porter trying to score is a judgment call for the third-base coach," said Frey. "Trillo's got a great arm but it's tough to see that play from the dugout or even from the press box. I can't fault the coach. It's not an easy job."

While the national media gave Frey the third-degree, the Phillies quickly dressed and prepared for their flight to Philadelphia.

"Just one victory, one more victory and we're world champions," said Larry Bowa. "Doesn't that sound great?"

Monday, October 20, was another open date in the tournament, 24 hours to allow tension to build for the finale— Steve Carlton vs. Rich Gale.

"I said before the World Series opened we were going to

have to beat Carlton to win this thing," offered Gale, who started the third game but wasn't involved in the decision. "Now, we're at that point. We either beat Carlton or we lose in six."

The Royals, of course, went down in six. Flaming.

The script was perfect. For seven innings, Carlton methodically stymied the Royals, allowing them only three singles. Seven struck out.

Meanwhile, with Mike Schmidt, who would be named Series MVP, leading the way, the Phillies built a 4–0 lead and the 65,838 fans were ready to start the celebration right there.

But it was not over. Two innings remained and nothing had been a cinch for the Phillies this grand and glorious season.

When Carlton let the first two Royals get on base in the eighth, catcher Bob Boone flashed a signal to the bench, indicating Lefty was out of gas.

"Carlton was starting to feather his fastball," Green said. "You notice he used his fastball a lot more tonight. I think Lefty realized from the first start against them they were a little more disciplined than a lot of the National League teams, more disciplined than he would like them to be. And he went with the fastball and stayed with it. The extra day of rest was the key. That was my thinking all the way. It was a gamble to throw a kid out there in Game Five, but it's not much of a gamble when you've got Marty Bystrom to throw out there.

"I knew I had Lefty and Dick Ruthven back-to-back and if they beat us they would beat us with our best. I just figured the extra rest would do Carlton so much good that he'd be a power pitcher again. And he was tonight—a power pitcher."

In came McGraw as Carlton left.

"The eighth inning was fun," McGraw said later. "But my arm was so tired in the ninth all I wanted was for the Royals to please hit the ball at one of our guys.

"I saw the K-9 Corps coming into the field and lining up

behind home plate. I thought, 'That's weird—this doesn't happen on a baseball field.' Then, I thought, 'Don't let that rattle you now.' I see dogs and I'm thinking K-9. The K reminded me of a strikeout. The dogs reminded me of a guy who dogs it on the field. I said, 'There's no way I'm gonna be a dog out here.' My arm was tired, but somehow I reached back and I got the K. I swear to God that's exactly what I was thinking out there."

McGraw went to work with John Wathan on second and Cardenal on first. White fouled to Rose for one out but McGraw walked Wilson, loading the bases. The Royals then reduced the deficit to 4–1 as Washington hit a sacrifice fly to Garry Maddox.

Brett beat out an infield hit to again load the bases and bring up McRae. McGraw fell behind in the count 3-0, McRae fouled off two pitches and then tapped a weak grounder to Trillo.

By now, the Veterans Stadium scene was bizarre. Scores of police, black-helmeted and wielding nightsticks, lined the field. Snarling attack dogs strained at their leashes as they were led to the perimeter, followed by a battalion of riot control police, mounted on horseback.

The celebration was already under way in the stands, but McGraw still had an inning of work to do. Otis was called out on a 3-2 pitch for the first out, but Aikens walked, and Wathan and Cardenal singled to load the bases.

"I was talking to Bobby Wine," Green said, "and he said to me, 'I think Tug's going for the save,' and I said, 'Christ, I think you're right. Maybe I better go talk to him.' So, I went out and talked to him and said, 'Hey, Tug, let's not make this son of a bitch as overly exciting as you're trying here.' "

Frank White was the next batter. It started out as a simple pop foul in front of the Phillies' dugout and ended as a spectacular play fans will remember for years.

The ball dropped into Boone's mitt, then popped out—into Rose's waiting glove.

"That didn't surprise me one bit," said McGraw. "That's typical Pete Rose. He's always there when you need him."

Willie Wilson, who had already struck out 11 times to set a World Series record, was the batter.

The count went 1-2. McGraw reached back and fired.

Wilson swung and missed and at 11:29 on October 21, 1980, the Phillies were world champions.

"I don't know what Dallas Green had in mind," said McGraw, "but if I didn't get Wilson, I was calling him to the mound because I had nothing left. Nothing."

In the quiet Kansas City dressing room, Jim Frey sat behind a desk.

"What was the key for the Phillies?" somebody finally asked, breaking the silence.

"I don't know," said Frey. "I don't know if there is a fair answer to that. Their ability to come back, I guess. Like when we had a two-run lead in the eighth and a one-run lead in the ninth in earlier games. They came back. We saw them do it on television against Houston to win their division. We knew they were capable of doing it. It was a team that just wouldn't die."

Dallas Green

Billy DeMars

Bobby Wine

Dallas Green
"We, Not I!"

Sylvia Taylor had been dating Dallas Green a year or two when she went to watch him play in an Industrial Basketball League game in Wilmington, Delaware.

"By halftime Dallas had fouled out," Sylvia recalled. "As the team went into the dressing room, I could hear what I thought was a mad man yelling and screaming. His voice boomed down the hall. It was Dallas Green.

"I thought, 'Gee, this is a totally different person I am hearing than the one I am going with.' "

Sylvia and Dallas were married on January 31, 1958 and over the years she has backed away from numerous outbursts from her career-minded, baseball husband. They went with the territory.

"But none was like that night at the basketball game," Sylvia said. "That had to be an all-timer."

Until August 10, 1980. The Pittsburgh Address.

The Phillies were embarrassed by the Pirates 7–1 at Three Rivers Stadium in the first game of the Sunday afternoon double-header. After six innings the Pirates were breezing 6–1 and the Phillies had quit. Their sleepy, lackadaisical play convinced many in the traveling party they had called it a season, packed it in for 1980.

Green, the burly rookie manager, couldn't hold back. In 22 years of covering the Phillies, I have never heard anything close to it. Other reporters agree. It was a screeching, screaming, vulgar tirade. I documented it with a sensitive tape recorder while standing outside the locked, "vibrating" clubhouse door.

". . . and this game isn't easy," Green bellowed, his words at times breaking with emotion. "It's bleeping tough and we're bleeping hurting with injuries. But you bleeping guys got your bleeping heads down.

"You gotta stop being so bleeping cool. If you don't get that through your bleeping minds, you're gonna be so bleeping buried it ain't gonna be funny.

"Get the bleep up off your butts and go beat somebody! You're a bleeping good baseball team, but you're not now. You can't look in the bleeping mirror. You keep telling me you can do it, but you bleeping give up. If you don't want to play, get the bleep in that office and tell me, 'I don't bleeping want to play anymore!' Because if you feel that way, I don't want to play you. OK, let's go."

Green, his face still red, was the last out of the sanctuary.

"I'm disappointed and I am sure our guys are disappointed," he bristled. "The worst part of it is we didn't play good baseball and that hurts more than anything else. Sure, you get beat, but you don't quit."

Pittsburgh eased to a 4–1 victory in the nightcap to complete a four-game weekend sweep. And in the eighth inning of that numbing setback, Green and relief pitcher Ron Reed went jaw-to-jaw in the dugout. Teammates and coaches had to restrain them.

With 55 games remaining the Phillies were in third place, six games behind co-leaders Pittsburgh and Montreal—gasping for life.

"The low point?" The scowl on Dallas Green's face could have stopped a 1,000-pound grizzly.

"There have been a lot of low points. I am disappointed and I am sure our guys are disappointed. The worst part of it is we didn't play good baseball. I'm not gonna let them quit on themselves. I haven't quit on them; I'm sure the fans in Philadelphia haven't quit on them, so we're not gonna let them quit. These losses are very frustrating in that this is one of the teams (Pittsburgh) we have to beat if we want to be what we say we want to be and that is a champion."

When asked if his between-games approach was a risky method to wake up the Phillies, Green became pensive.

"Maybe it's not the right way. But I'm doing it the only way I know how. It's the way I've followed through my career in baseball; it's the way I've gotten to where I am in baseball— it's the only way I know. I think the other way was tried very unsuccessfully here in the past (Danny Ozark's mild-mannered approach).

"The results are not always as pleasant because you have a tendency to hurt tender feelings. I have explained I am not a grudge-holder; I don't think I've ever held a grudge against a ball player. I say what I gotta say and forget it. If the players would do the same thing, we'd be in pretty good shape.

"The only way to find out if this will work is the Chicago series. I would hope we have enough character to come back with 55 games left. A lot of things can happen . . . we can make a lot of things happen. We're a very streaky team. If we get on the right streak at the right time, we can turn everything right around."

Nobody really believed Dallas, but in Chicago the Phillies won two out of three then jetted to New York and destroyed the Mets in five games at Shea Stadium. They were on their way. There were occasional steps backward, but the Phils did not stop until the world championship was theirs.

And as the players savor that championship, just about every one of them looks back to that steamy-hot Sunday afternoon in Pittsburgh.

"We started looking in the mirror, just like he said," admitted Bake McBride in January. "That is what lit the fire."

"I've never heard anything like it," said Pete Rose. "He didn't want us to give up on ourselves. From that day on I think it was a different, more-dedicated team. It could have quit, but didn't.

"It came at the perfect time," said Player Personnel Director Paul Owens, Green's mentor. "I had dinner with Dallas the night before. I sensed he was about to blow. I'll tell you one thing. If he hadn't let 'em have it, I was going to do it myself."

Owens' personal revival message was not delivered until Labor Day. It added fuel to the smoldering fire Green ignited August 10.

"When I read about Dallas' explosion in the newspapers the next day, the only time I could remember anything close to it was that basketball game," Sylvia Green said. "But having heard that outburst, I had a pretty good idea what he sounded like."

Out of character?

"Pretty much," said Sylvia, a mother of four and a world cultures' teacher at Christiana High, near Newark, Delaware. "I was all for Dallas taking the job because I thought if anyone could turn the Phillies around, he could. But I wondered if he would be tough enough. Oh, I know he talked about a tight ship and did a lot of yelling, but basically it is important to Dallas that people like him. I knew there would be a conflict, especially with that group of athletes."

Green relaxed in the living room of his rural West Grove, Pennsylvania home and talked about the long-awaited championship. At times the 46-year-old former University of Delaware athlete comes across as a brash, uncomplicated person. On this particular afternoon, he was at peace with the world.

A dog snoozed near his feet and outside, two horses grazed behind a post-and-rail fence. His ordinarily booming voice was muted.

"I guess the only disappointment I have, if I have one at all, is some of the guys still don't understand my methods, my doing what I did," he said, running a hand through his graying hair. "I don't feel they think I contributed that much. That's fine. They had to play the games and they had to win the games, they had to hit and run and throw and field. So they should get the credit, but I hoped more of them would have understood the rationale after it was all over."

As Dallas talked, my mind wandered back over 10 years.

The stands were rickety and uncomfortable and the stifling heat and humidity made the night in Pulaski, Virginia even more unpleasant.

"This is what you have to go through to be a career manager," Dallas Green said later. "You have to pay your dues. I guess you can see why I don't want to make a career out of this."

That was August of 1969 and Green was piloting the Phils' youngsters at Pulaski in the Appalachian League. The players loved the former pitcher, but even then he was strong in his conviction that he didn't want to be a manager. The year before he had handled Huron, South Dakota, in the Northern League, a dreadful assignment.

I remember Paul Owens, then the Phillies' farm director, saying he would not let Dallas settle into a front-office job without some managerial experience.

After the Pulaski tour Green moved inside continuing his close relationship with Owens, the man they call Pope. When Owens became player personnel director, Green took over as farm director and was secure in knowing when the Pope retired, he would succeed him.

But on August 31, 1979, the day Danny Ozark was fired

in Atlanta, Owens coaxed Dallas into putting on the uniform and giving the high-priced fraternity a taste of roughness, to see who gagged on it and who responded.

After all, when Owens fired Frank Lucchesi in 1972 he raised a few starchy baseball eyebrows by announcing he was going to manage the team for the rest of the season. He called it a fact-finding mission.

"My situation was different," said Owens. "When I went down there (to the field), my concern was protecting six or eight young kids we had, as well as evaluating a bad ball club. When Dallas took over, we knew we had talent."

Green could not refuse Owens and owner Ruly Carpenter. He agreed to stay on in 1980 because he thought he was the man for the job and because he felt he owed something to the organization that supported him for 25 years as a pitcher, a minor-league manager and minor-league executive.

"There were guys on this team who turned their noses up when you would mention John Vukovich's name," Green blurted, quickly bringing his visitor back to the present.

"Well, John Vukovich (utility infielder) was a spearhead. To me he's what the guts of our bench was all about. He didn't play much, but he wasn't afraid to get up and scream and yell. He was not afraid to tell the Bull or Bowa or Schmidt or any of the other guys to get off their butts and start doing something."

It was mentioned earlier Green sent shock waves through the troops in spring training when he dumped several veterans, a move that cost Ruly Carpenter a quick million.

"Dammit," snapped Green sarcastically, "we spend close to $3 million a year on player development. How do I justify $3 million to my owner if we don't play the kids we develop? The name of the game is still competition. Just because we have long-term contracts doesn't mean they have to play out those long-term contracts in Philadelphia. Sometimes you add by subtracting."

But Dallas Green did many other things to get the listing ship on an even keel. He criticized the clubhouse card games; he ordered his starters to take infield practice; he told his pitchers to run and he stressed fundamentals.

And he saved the ship on August 10, Black Sunday.

"Oh, a lot of managers have yelled and shouted between games of a double-header," he said, "but when I went at Ron Reed, I wasn't very proud. On the other hand I was anxious to see how the guys would handle it. There was a chance it— or I—really could have hurt the ball club. But we came out of it and I give the guys credit. They put the thing behind and went after the season. I think the bottom line was they *did* look in the mirror."

A few days before Owens mounted the clubhouse pulpit in San Francisco, Green says he felt the players slipping back. His bullying and abrasive style was not clicking.

"Just before September 1, I was afraid they just weren't going to listen to me," he said. "I had to keep reminding them, but I think from September 1 on it fell into place even better than I thought it would. We did start winning some one-run games and that helped. We made a couple of great comebacks and we got juiced. We really did. We got into the thing. I honestly didn't think this team could do that because I felt us slipping back many times.

"I guess what I am trying to say is when I wasn't screaming and yelling, we went back to the old way. In September, though, I had only one half-mad session."

What motivated Green more than anything else and kept him from caving in was his stubbornness. He knew his way was the only way.

"I honestly believed in what I was trying to do," he said. "I felt even though I didn't always do it right, it was still the best thing for this group.

"You know who knew I was right? Most of the team. Some of the players doubted me and talked behind my back about me to the press, but when they looked around the club-house they didn't get much sympathy. And finally, the Bull, Bowa and Maddox agreed and said, 'Hey, maybe we're wrong.'

"And I really think in my heart the blend of kids and veterans is what pulled these guys together, not Dallas Green. I think some of the veterans glanced around the room and there weren't very many guys siding with them anymore. It used to be if Bowa got in a hissing contest with somebody, it was automatically OK. The same with Maddox. Eight or 10 of those guys were bench guys who didn't say anything. But this year the eight or 10 bench guys said, 'Hell with you, I'm going to play.' And they went out and played like hell.

"Guys like Pete Rose and Tug McGraw knew my way was the right way. I think Bob Boone felt that way to some degree. I think deep down Mike Schmidt felt that way. They didn't always show it and they didn't always cooperate, but over the long haul I think it was *they* who got it going. And Steve Carlton. Lefty knew in his heart what I was trying to do was best for the ball club because he had seen it the other way too much."

Green admits he had something few other managers have ever had.

"I had the hammer," he said. "They knew I couldn't and wouldn't be fired. They knew I had the backing from Paul Owens and Ruly Carpenter. Every player knew that.

"They couldn't go running to Paul or Ruly as they had done in the past. Oh, they tried a couple of times, but I got that nipped, to some degree, in the beginning. There weren't as many visits to Ruly Carpenter's office as there had been in the past because I asked Ruly not to allow it. And he went along with me. Sure, there were some, but it wasn't the old 'Chew 'em out down here, pat 'em on the butt up there' thing."

"Dallas Green and I are a lot alike," said shortstop Larry

Bowa, who sneered at the manager's decisions many times. "We'll say things in the heat of anger. But he doesn't hold grudges and tells the guys not to take it personally.

"The difference was his discipline. We didn't have that before. He stood on us for seven days a week, not just two. If we missed batting practice, he let us know about it. If we missed infield, he let us know about it. We needed somebody to come in when we were watching a football game on TV and say, 'You're watching a stupid football game and missing batting practice?' He stayed on us. I didn't think veteran players needed that, but I guess we did."

Rose, who loves to kid Green about the grand-slam home run he once hit off him, remembers him as a battler.

"He was a red-neck on the field," said Pete. "He never gave you an inch. Frankly, I think the biggest upset of the whole season was the fact he wasn't manager of the year. You have to give him credit the way he brought us back from 1979. I mean, he was responsible for Keith Moreland; he brought Marty Bystrom up; he brought Bob Walk up. He restored confidence in the whole team. It took the veterans time to understand what he was really trying to do—a lot of time for some guys and not so much for others."

"I always thought Gil Hodges of the Mets handled pitchers better than anyone I ever saw until Dallas Green came along," said Tug McGraw. "He—and the winter conditioning program I was on—were the big differences in my season."

"Dallas Green won and that is the big factor," said Los Angeles Manager Tommy Lasorda. "There are a lot of little things. A manager has to get the job done the way he thinks he can. Dallas did it his way. He thought it was the best."

To Mike Schmidt, Dallas Green was an excellent manager, except in one area.

"I don't think he was tactful enough," said the MVP. "I think the 'We, Not I' concept was fine, except the manager should be part of the 'we.' I think there were too many times he used the term 'they' when referring to the players. It's supposed to be 'We, Not They,' as far as the manager is concerned and 'We, Not I' as far as the players are concerned."

"Dallas is a little tactless, to say the least," said Sylvia, an intelligent, liberated woman, who once made headlines when she became involved with the National Organization of Women (NOW) and took legal action to make their daughter, Kim, eligible to play with and against boys in Little League baseball. "I jumped all over him for some of the things he said to reporters. There was a game against San Diego where Dick Ruthven threw a bunt away and got hurt. It was true Dick made a mistake, but I thought Dallas came down very hard on him.

"Sometimes he is too honest with the writers. He just wants to shoot from the hip. Sometimes this is good but a lot of times it isn't. Dallas does that a lot. If he is mad at somebody, he won't often say, 'I am mad at you.' By his actions they will know he is mad at them and I think sometimes he has used the press to get his message across to the players. He has to get away from that. It is probably the most offensive thing he does to the ball players. You can't blame them in a way for getting upset.

"His side of it is: the players don't talk to the writers so the press stays in his office for 30 minutes. So, if the players don't want the bad press, they should do more talking."

"Basically, I'm a spontaneous person," countered Dallas. "I say what's on my mind. I am very big on character, whatever that may be. I feel the reason we didn't win the whole thing before 1980 was because we lacked character.

"As far as the Phillies were concerned other teams in the league had caught up to us in terms of natural ability, especially Pittsburgh and Montreal. St. Louis and New York were tougher. So, we had to grind it out. We couldn't let up. How many times early last season did you see us win the first game of a big series, then fall back? How many times did you see us take it to 'em early in a game, then lose in the late innings? That's what changed in the last six weeks. We were grinding out victories. We didn't let them slip away as we had earlier."

"I really don't think Dallas ever doubted his way was the right way," said Sylvia. "I know I never doubted him. He did not come home after an especially tough loss and say he was about to give it up or anything like that. It's very hard with Dallas to determine where he is emotionally; he doesn't wear his emotions on his sleeve. The only difference so obvious to me was how tired he was, especially late in the season. I think the problems weighed on him, but they didn't pull him down."

As a pitcher, Dallas Green had a gifted arm.

He grew up in Newport, Delaware and graduated from Conrad High School in 1952. The Phillies, through scout Jocko Collins, signed him off the University of Delaware campus in the spring of 1955, after his junior year. He had been elected captain of the university basketball team for the next season but turned his back on that honor for a career in baseball.

"Dallas was 6-feet-5 and could throw his fastball 85 to 90 miles an hour," Collins, now a scout for the Milwaukee Brewers, remembered. "He was loose, free, a good athlete and a tough competitor. He had a fastball that just jumped and he was always challenging everyone. If he hadn't hurt his arm, he would have been a great major-league pitcher."

"I think I was as fast as anyone on our staff at one stage in my career," Green said. "I was just getting my act together when the arm went."

Green won 41 games his first four summers in the minors, then won five straight for Buffalo in 1959 at the start of his fifth season.

"I began to feel some stiffness in my arm during the third

game and in the sixth game, it just broke down. I didn't get past the fifth inning. It was cold up there that spring. When the season opened, there was ice on the lake."

Green had the arm examined, even went to Johns Hopkins Hospital in Baltimore where doctors said he had torn muscles. He fought the toothache-like pain and ended the season with a 9-5 record. The following year, after resting the arm all winter, he tried a comeback.

"Buffalo was playing Rochester one night and I drove there to watch Dallas pitch," said Sylvia. "He was bombed. I sat there and cried because I knew how much his arm was hurting. We went through a lot those years."

Green, minus the over-powering fastball, finally made it to the Phillies in 1960 and stayed there until 1964 when Manager Gene Mauch pulled the rug out from under him. That emotional scar still remains.

On Saturday, July 25, 1964, the big guy was sent back to the minors in the middle of a game! He worked two innings, allowing four runs on six hits in a 10–9 loss to St. Louis at old Connie Mack Stadium. When he was finally taken out, Mauch told him he was on his way back to Little Rock.

"We were going for our first pennant in years and years, we had a pretty good lead and it looked like we were going to wrap it up," Green recalled. "It really hurt me, since I was a career Phillies' guy. Here we're going for our first pennant since 1950 and I wasn't going to be a part of it.

"I just felt crushed and, truthfully, in my mind that killed my dad. He had been hanging on with cancer and I think he'd have hung tough had that not happened. But after I was sent back down, he died in August. Just gave up.

"Then I had a decision to make: whether or not to stay in baseball. I rightfully stayed in baseball."

In 1965, Green was sent to the old Washington Senators, ended up at Little Rock again, then spent some time with the New York Mets in 1966 before finishing the year at San Diego.

In 1967, the Phillies, who under owner Bob Carpenter had a reputation for rewarding loyal people, brought him back. He sat around most of the year but got in the then-required five years for his pension.

He ended his major-league career with a 20–22 record and a 4.14 earned run average in 185 games. After that, Owens hired him and it was off to Huron.

"I told Paul then I didn't want to manage," Green said. "I didn't feel it was right. But he was determined I get some experience out in the field, to be alone and know the feelings of a manager dealing with people when no one else is around. He felt that was important to the overall understanding of running a farm system and I have to agree with him now. Again, it's important to point out I was wrong. Paul was right and I was wrong.

"He trained me very well. You know, I hated Lou Kahn (now a Phillies' scout) when I was a manager and I told Paul: 'Don't send him to check on me. I don't want Lou Kahn around my players and I don't want Lou Kahn around me.'

"Know how the Pope handled that? The first day I got to Huron, there's Lou Kahn waiting for me. So, now I'm ticked-off all over again. I called Pope and raised hell. Over the years I grew to respect Lou Kahn as much as anybody in baseball. He has a way of knowing what's right. His judgment of players and players' talents is unequaled in my opinion. I learned to love the guy. Again, I had been wrong."

Green's steel-eyed glares and cutting words are not always appreciated by sensitive souls.

Philadelphia Daily News columnist Stan Hochman who covered the Gene Mauch Phillies wrote about Green's replacement of Ozark.

". . . and then Dallas Green, the Phillies' tall, stark and handsome farm director, took over. Green will swat a complacent fly, kick a lazy dog, whip a loafing horse. Some players wanted to puke, others wanted to fight."

Dallas Green did not arrive with a whip. He came armed with a blowtorch.

"I'm not sure all that's true," Green said when the description was repeated. "I'm really not sure I'm all that tough. I prefer to look at my toughness as more honesty and frankness. There's nothing special about Dallas Green."

Except, that as Sylvia Green pointed out, he shoots from the hip.

"I've always been that way," said Green. "Even before I took over for Danny Ozark, I was involved with this team. Paul Owens and I did a lot of soul-searching, trying to figure out why we were not getting past the playoffs.

"In 1976 I can buy the rationale. It was our first year and Cincinnati had a powerhouse. They steam-rolled us and they out-talented us. We were just kind of blah anyway. Fine. But in 1977 we had the best team in baseball and we should have won. In 1978 we had nearly the best team in baseball and should have won again. We did not. Danny Ozark was very close to being fired at the end of the 1978 season, but I think compassion and Ruly Carpenter's strength in the whole thought process took over and we let him stay. In 1979 we had a lot of injuries and I can't blame Danny for them, but we also had injuries in 1980. Something else was missing."

Had it not been for Green's minor-league background, he knows he would not have been the success he was with the varsity.

"I handled a lot of the players when they were in the minors," he said. "They don't remember it, but I worked with those guys as much as anybody. I didn't have them, but I was still involved with them. I knew who they were. Paul and I patted them on the back and helped them up the minor-league ladder. We knew what kind of kids they were and we knew what kind of talent we had. We knew what they had done to struggle through the minor-league situation. So, I had the background.

"And dealing with 150 kids a year in the system, coddling them and chewing them out—not to mention dealing with their contract problems—had trained me for managing baseball players, period.

"I had no qualms about handling players. I knew there had to be a blend of toughness and yet some compassion. I don't think I'm all that tough; I think that's what a lot of people misunderstand about me. They come to me and expect me to be an ogre, breathing fire, and I'm not that way—at least not all the time. I have compassion and I've tried to show it to the baseball team when I could. But there are times when you can be compassioned to sleep and that's how you end up with the 'Good Guy Syndrome.' There are times when you have to say no in baseball—in an executive or managerial situation. You've got to know when to say no and when to say yes."

As the 1980 season began to unfold, Green said he enjoyed his new-found off-the-field time. He no longer had to drive to the Veterans Stadium office early in the morning. He no longer had to catch a flight to Oklahoma City or some other minor-league outpost.

"The first month and a half, two months, were kind of fun at home," he said, clasping his hands behind his head. "I had three or four hours each day to myself. I could piddle around, maybe cut the grass, fool around with the tractor or work on my garden. But as the season wore on, I started sleeping later and gave all that up.

"You always try to say you can handle pressures and what have you, but I don't think I've gone through any kind of pressures like that last month. And I'm sure the players feel the same way. I mean, there's not a team around that has gone through the kind of pressure we've gone through. Day in and day out. OK, maybe there's been a stretch somewhere along the line in some teams' battles that they've had a week where they've really had to battle like we did. But ours lasted over a month. It was a close race all the way. It seemed like every game was a gut-wrenching, crucial one. We just could not afford to lose."

The most money Green ever earned in the big leagues was $17,000 a season. When he started his apprenticeship as a manager in the minors, he was cut to $10,000. Last year, the Phils paid him $65,000. His World Series share added another $35,000 to his income.

Life has changed abruptly for Sylvia and Dallas Green, and their four children who range in age from 12 to 20. Suddenly, they're all celebrities. They no longer have the privacy they once cherished.

"I wasn't used to it," said Sylvia. "We'd go to University of Delaware football games and people would be breaking their necks to get a look at us. There would be a lot of whispering.

"I sent Dallas to the supermarket one day and it took him four hours to get the groceries. He'd push the cart a foot, sign an autograph, then push it another foot and sign another. He used to be a big help to me with the shopping, but he can't do that anymore.

"Before Christmas, we went to the Christiana Mall (near Newark, Delaware). We stopped at a refreshment stand for Cokes and you might have thought we were being paid by the mall to be there. People lined up 50 deep for autographs. When you're in a hurry, this type of thing is not good. Dallas does not seem to mind it; he handles it well. There are times when I mind it, especially when I am in a hurry. I become impatient."

That, however, is going to be a way of life for the Greens for at least another year. Dallas has agreed to return as manager in 1981 even though he would have preferred to take the Vet elevator back to the ivory tower as Paul Owens' assistant, then take over when the Pope retires.

"You know, Paul Owens and Ruly Carpenter have great powers of persuasion," said Green when he agreed to return.

"But the money ($125,000) is right, three and a half to four times what I can make normally. It's difficult to turn down. And the timing just doesn't seem right for a move. I hate to become a slave to money, but if I can put the kids through college by managing a couple of years, it won't be too bad.

"Beneath all that the Pope and I talked about wanting to stabilize the club for some time. The working relationship we have, me on the field and him upstairs, is good for the perpetuation of this baseball team."

Several of the players were unhappy when they learned George Dallas Green will be back and even more unhappy when he promised not to change his approach.

"It got us over the hump in 1980," he said. "I know there are probably some people who do not believe all that malarkey, but I still think that's the way to win baseball games and I still think it's the way the Phillies have to continue to play baseball."

But no matter what happens in future years, nothing will equal 1980.

"What we did this year was put away some ghosts that were definitely haunting this team," said Green. "The 1980 Phillies—had we not won—would have been remembered as a loser, no question about that. And all those guys would have had that hung around their necks, whether they were or they weren't.

"But they came through. There's not many adjectives you can say other than incredible. What we've gone through mentally was unbelievable. In fact, the whole year was just that—unbelievable."

"It was a dream that just kept unfolding," said Sylvia. "There are so many memories. The celebration the night we won it lasted until daybreak. At 5 o'clock, we found ourselves going into the old Penrose Diner (not too far from Veterans Stadium) for breakfast.

"We walked in and there were a group of policemen.

They had ridden those horses into the stadium to control the crowd and were complaining about how they had not ridden for years and that their rear ends were so sore they could hardly sit down. We laughed and laughed. That's what I remember. And everyone in the diner giving us a standing ovation. It was so sincere.

"It was hard to comprehend. The end was so swift, like a dream. It was like when Dallas and I got married. I wish I could have been in the audience watching!"

Pete Rose
"We learned to win race-horse baseball."

Mike Schmidt won the National League's Most Valuable Player Award. Steve Carlton took the Cy Young Award and Manny Trillo was MVP in the playoffs.

But what about Peter Edward Rose?

All Pete Rose did was catapult the Phillies past Houston into their first World Series since 1950.

When owner Ruly Carpenter signed the celebrated free agent to a four-year, $3.2 million contract in December of 1978, Rose was supposed to be the missing ingredient that would finally get the Phils past the dread playoffs.

This did not happen during the collapse of 1979 even though Pete batted .331, collected 208 hits and put together the longest hitting streak in the majors, 23 games.

But from the charred ruins of that disaster, the Phils returned to first place in the National League East in 1980 and once in the playoffs, the ball caromed to Rose's court.

The night the best-of-five series opened at Veterans Stadium against the Astros, Larry Bowa was dressing in his corner of the spacious clubhouse.

"OK, Pete," the shortstop bellowed. "We're here now, it's time for you to do your thing."

"I will, I will," promised Pete Rose, "but you guys are

The patented Pete Rose head-first slide. Rose slides into third base in one of the Phillies' early season games against Montreal.

going to have to get some hits, too. I'm not going to hit any home runs."

And when the final out of the zany tournament was over, Pete Rose had done his thing. He batted .400 (8-for-20), repeatedly started important rallies when it appeared the Phils were dead, and under a heap of smoking leather, fielded his position brilliantly. In fact, Rose says he was more proud of his work around first base than he was with his hitting. Coming from a guy who makes his millions from hitting, that was quite a switch.

"They were all over me when the playoffs opened," said Rose. "They had read all that stuff when I signed and kept telling me it was my turn. Bowa was especially tough."

Rose was superb in the playoffs, but so were his teammates.

"He was so inspirational," said catcher Keith Moreland. "He never felt we were beaten, no matter how many runs we were behind. I think this rubbed off on all of us during the stretch."

"The difference, I think," Rose said a month after the season ended, "was the team as a whole really learned how to win. It learned how to win what I call race-horse baseball.

"The team matured and I think the reason for that was all the tough series. We had to go to New York and win five in a row, had to go to Montreal and win two out of three, had to go to Houston and win two out of three a week later. Play— and win—that kind of baseball, and you mature. In the past, the Phillies won the Eastern Division on sheer talent and ability. Then, in the playoffs they'd have trouble winning. Against Houston, they all had been there before; they had matured. That was the difference."

And Pete Rose also made a big difference.

He has always performed well in the playoffs. In 1980, he extended his National League Championship Series hitting streak to 14 games. He improved his hits record to 39 and his singles mark to 28.

Pete already held the playoff record for highest batting average, .450 in 1972, hits in a five-game series, 9 in 1972, and total bases in a five-game series, 15 in 1972.

"When you can win 21 of your last 28 road games and finish with a 42–39 record away from the Vet, it shows me what kind of a team this is," said Rose. "It has great intestinal fortitude."

To this astute student of baseball, the abrupt change in the Phillies came after the August 10 debacle in Pittsburgh. That was Black Sunday, the balmy afternoon when the Phils dropped a doubleheader to the Pirates, falling six games out of first place with 55 to play. That also was the day Manager Dallas Green exploded with his never-to-be-forgotten clubhouse tirade between games, then went jaw to jaw with relief pitcher Ron Reed in the dugout during the nightcap.

The next day, in Chicago, the Phils and Cubs were tied 5–5 after 10 innings and because Wrigley Field has no lights, the game was suspended. It was resumed the following afternoon, August 12, and the Phils won 8–5 in 15 innings. Steve Carlton then whipped the Cubs 5–2 in the regular contest.

Chicago won 2–1 on Wednesday, before the Phils stormed into New York and swept the dazed Mets in five straight. Signs all around Shea Stadium read, "The Magic Is Back." When the Phils arrived the Mets were in fourth place, 7½ games back, and had hopes of overtaking third-place Philadelphia.

"Instead, we knocked them out of the race and they never recovered," said Rose, who has always felt that series in New York was more important than most of his teammates think it was. "You know, we not only lost the doubleheader in Pittsburgh but the whole four-game series. I don't know if that gave the guys a relaxed feeling because they thought we were finished, or if they just looked in the mirror after Dallas' shouting and decided to do something about it. You can't expect a lecture like that to take effect in 20 minutes.

"I could see some determination on the flight to Chicago. I just think the guys really thought about what he said and I think that was the thing that started us on our way. We beat the hell out of New York—scored 40 runs on 71 hits in five games. We destroyed 'em. We started a 12-game road trip by losing the first four, then went back to the Vet with a 7–5 record. That wasn't too bad."

Rose batted .261 in the World Series and when the Phils finally eliminated Kansas City, he was rather subdued during the clubhouse celebration.

"I had been there before," he said. "I got a big thrill out of watching the Bowas, the Schmidts, the Luzinskis. I was happy for them and I was tickled to death for Ruly Carpenter and Dallas Green and Paul Owens. I was happier for all of them and for the fans, than I was for myself. I knew what was going through their minds.

"To know I played an important part in it gave me as much satisfaction and joy as I have ever had. I wasn't running around and acting like a maniac, throwing champagne and all that. I let my little boy, Petey, do that because it was his first world championship. I had that wild, exciting feeling in 1975 when the Cincinnati Reds won their first one. I think when we beat Boston in that World Series it was very much like our playoff victory over Houston this year. There was so much pressure. I really don't think there was that much pressure in our World Series against Kansas City. Just like I told our guys. Once you get to the Series, it's a party."

Statistically, 1980 was a sub-par year for Rose. He hit .282 and that was the first time since 1974 (.284) he was not over .300. Even though he led the Phils with 185 hits and topped the National League with 42 doubles, he was below his lifetime standards.

"It was a strange year," said Pete. "Sure, I only hit .282,

but the bottom line is we won the world championship. I think I proved in 1980 that statistics can be misleading. Sometimes you can do less with an average and be more productive with your hitting. I had more runs batted in (64), more runs scored (95), led the league in doubles and had fewer errors (5) than I had in 1979.

"I took a lot of pitches, hit behind the runner and did a lot of things like that. I don't know how many times I did those things and I really don't care how much they hurt my stats because as long as the team won, that's what counts. Hitting second behind Lonnie Smith in a lot of games cost me some hits, and I think the league as a whole was down 20 points. In 1979 the batting champion (Keith Hernandez) hit .344. In 1980 Bill Buckner won the title with a .324 average. See what I mean?"

Baseball historians have called Cincinnati's seven-game victory over Boston in the 1975 Series one of the most exciting ever.

Pete Rose, who was MVP in that classic, agrees.

"It will always be important to me because it was my first world championship. We had lost two World Series before that and one was in seven games. But this one was so rewarding for so many people. The greatest spectacle I have ever seen and the most awesome thing I've ever seen was the parade the day after we beat Kansas City. I don't care whether it's in Philadelphia or in New York or in Los Angeles, I can't imagine it being better anywhere. There were a million people and they all had the same smile on their faces.

"I don't know how many times I have been in restaurants, in clothing stores, in subways, in cabs, on airplanes—you know. People stick their hands out and they shake mine and they look at me and say, 'Thanks.' And I know exactly what they mean. To me, that's more important than hitting .340 or .350."

People also ask Pete Rose about his great catch in the ninth inning of the sixth World Series game.

With one out, the bases loaded and the Phils leading the Royals 4–1, Frank White lofted a pop-up in front of the Philadelphia dugout. Both catcher Bob Boone and Rose raced after the ball. It hit Boone's mitt and bounced out—into Pete's waiting glove.

"Everyone asks me about that play," said Rose, grinning. "Well, you know, when the ball was hit there was a question in my mind whether it was mine or Boonie's. And once I got over there where I'm supposed to be—I can't stand out by the coaching box—I have to realize Boonie's called for it and with 66,000 people screaming, I don't want to try to call him off and then let both of us let it drop, which happens a lot in that situation. So, I just let him go and watched the ball. When it popped out, I happened to be standing close and snapped it up. Really, the reason I reacted so fast was because I didn't know if Tug McGraw, with a runner on third, was covering home plate or not."

Rose turned 39 just as the 1980 season opened and never looked back. He played in all 162 games, one fewer than the year before.

Pete Rose, of course, loves baseball more than anything in the world—except maybe one thing—being Pete Rose. These two loves go hand-in-hand and have fueled the fascinating human being who has been at the top of his profession for over a decade.

"All I've ever tried to do in my career is be consistent," he said. "I've always concentrated on having good years every year, not just one good year, two bad, two good and two more bad. I put a lot of preparation into each season, beginning with spring training. I've been lucky, too. I've been able to stay away from injuries that keep me out for any length of time. You just can't accumulate records and statistics if you don't play. I've averaged over 160 games the last 11 years."

The Sporting News selected Rose its "Player of the Decade" for the 1970s, following previous winners Ted Williams (1940s), Stan Musial (1950s) and Willie Mays (1960s).

"And the only reason I was able to win that award was because of my consistency," said Rose. "That is something my father always preached."

Pete Rose is divorced now. He lives in a modest condominium near his hometown of Cincinnati during the off-season. His 11-year-old son, Petey, visits frequently.

A few weeks after the Phils became world champions, Rose sat in the living room, in front of his giant TV screen, and talked about his remarkable career.

"I keep coming back to consistency," he repeated for the third time. "That, and total dedication to my business, which is baseball, are the keys to my success."

This was a different side of Rose. Away from the spotlight and the clinical analysis of hits, runs, etc., he talked frequently of his dad, Harry Francis Rose, an outstanding semi-pro football player people around Cincinnati called Pete.

Rose obviously worshipped his father, a banker, who died December 8, 1970.

"My father was always pushing me," said Pete. "He was never satisfied with what I achieved. He is the reason I always give 110 percent. He is the reason I run as hard as I can to first base. He would never let me ease up. He once called me aside and said, 'Peter, you always have to give 110 percent. The guy you're playing against, see, may be giving 100 percent. So, if you just give 100 percent, too, no one will win.'

"The entire time I played for Cincinnati my father was in the clubhouse only once. That was a day when he posed for a picture with me for Sports Illustrated. And the only time he would wait for me outside the clubhouse was when he wanted me to meet someone—or chew me out.

"He was a great football player. He had poor eyes because of all the detail work he had to do at the bank, but he was excellent. He played until he was 42. He would have kept playing had my mom not threatened to divorce him."

Pete's mother, now married to Robert Noeth, a close

friend of her first husband, lives near Tampa, Florida. She remains Pete's No. 1 fan and wishes his father were alive to watch
him go after all the records.

"That is what he would be most proud of," she said. "Just
like my son told you. His dad always stressed consistency. I
remember when Peter was a little boy. He would get four hits
and come up to his father, obviously proud. His dad would
only tell him he could have done better. I would be waiting in
the car and want to cry. Each night before Peter went to
sleep, his dad would make him swing a lead bat nearly 100
times, first from the right side and then from the left side.

"Peter was not a good student. His marks were not high
enough for him to graduate with his class at Western Hills
High. They urged him to go to summer school. His father
wouldn't have it. 'No,' he said. 'If you do that, you won't be
able to devote the whole summer to baseball.' So, he made
Peter repeat the whole 12th grade the next fall."

"I used to walk around the streets of Cincinnati and people would come up to me and say, 'You'll never be half the
athlete your father was.' It used to hurt, but it made me determined," said Pete. "Now, they come up to me and say,
'You are your father all over again.' "

"That's absolutely correct," said Laverne Noeth. "He is
just like his father—a carbon copy. We were always strict with
him, but he was a good boy. Now, he's the greatest!"

Pete Rose enjoys adulations as much as most public performers. He is the media's prince and the fans' choice. In Japan a month after the Phillies won the championship he was
in constant demand for appearances, interviews, autograph
sessions, whatever.

When asked about his apparently insatiable appetite for
publicity, baseball's number one goodwill ambassador replies,
"Let's just say I am cooperative." Others suggest his unique
blend of candor and craftiness is nothing more than good business sense. His detractors accuse him of greed, but Pete, fur-

ther described as being intense, talkative, sharp-tongued and ambivalent continues, "I try to get along with people. Even in Cincinnati. I took a lot of heat from the fans for leaving the Reds. It's amazing the number of people who called me a traitor—they called my kids traitors in school. No one knew the situation or the circumstances. Here's a guy who slid ón his belly for 16 years for them and played just as hard as he could for them and all of a sudden they (Reds) decided they didn't want him anymore and he's the villain. But how can one guy, even Pete Rose, take on an organization like the Cincinnati Reds? No way."

After 16 seasons with the Reds, Rose had hit .300 or higher 13 times, won three batting titles, made 13 All-Star teams, compiled nine 200-hit seasons, put together an electrifying 44-game hitting streak and gone well over 3,000 hits for his career.

But the conservative Reds, who were paying him $370,-000 a year, refused to give him $450,000 for two or three years, so following the 1978 season Rose became a free agent. He was chosen by a maximum 13 teams in the re-entry draft on November 3, 1978, then admittedly was shocked at how much some of baseball's richest owners were willing to pay for his services.

"I used to sit and wonder why Dick Wagner didn't like me because I know one thing about Dick Wagner—he likes gamers. He likes people who work hard, and he likes people who play every day," said Rose. "Now, sure, I do some things off the field he didn't like, but he does some things I don't like. One thing you can count on, when I was on the field I produced, and from that standpoint I didn't quite understand. I did anything the Reds ever asked me to do. Go here, promote 'em here, go there, go to the Caribbean—anything the Reds asked me to do, I did. I guess that was just their way of saying thanks. Thanks, but no thanks.

"From what I understand, they did the same thing to Joe Morgan—just forced him out. They didn't give him a contract;

they didn't even re-draft him. At least they re-drafted me. I was the first player they ever drafted.

"Wagner did a lot of things that just don't make sense. He told me one time, and told Reuven Katz, that he wasn't going to negotiate with anybody during the season and turned right around and negotiated with another player's attorney. He said he would never get into the free-agent draft, but picked me. He said he wasn't going to give big contracts in order to keep the salary level down, but gave George Foster a big contract. I'm not saying George didn't deserve it, but if George deserved it in Cincinnati, I did too.

"I guess what disappointed me most about leaving the Reds was the fact I never had an opportunity to talk to the team's owners, Mr. and Mrs. (Louis) Nippert. They are really nice people, down-to-earth people. It didn't make sense to me that people as smart and as rich as they are could let something like that happen without ever saying yes or no . . . or, wait a minute, we'd like to talk. They just gave Dick Wagner all the authority."

In the middle of the summer of '78, Pete told friends how much he wanted to play in Philadelphia, but when the bidding war started it appeared the Phillies would not be able to compete with the likes of Ted Turner in Atlanta, Ewing Kauffman in Kansas City, John Galbreath in Pittsburgh or Gussie Busch in St. Louis.

Just when it appeared the Phils were out of the sweepstakes, some behind-the-scenes wheeling and dealing, a $600,000 commitment from WPHL-TV, and Rose's desire to remain in the National League and break Stan Musial's career hits record (3,630) turned the tide.

The contract the Phils worked out is one of the least complicated ever given a superstar. It paid Pete $910,000 in 1979, $710,000 in 1980 and will pay him $810,000 in 1981 and 1982. His salary is, of course, guaranteed. The only meaningful clause requires him to play a minimum of 140 games in 1982.

Since the historic signing was announced at baseball's

winter meetings in Orlando, Florida, on December 5, 1978, other players have received larger contracts. Nolan Ryan is getting a million a year from Houston, Dave Parker supposedly receives that much from Pittsburgh and the 1980 free agent superstar, Dave Winfield, got an incredible contract from the New York Yankees.

"But if you look closely at mine, it is still probably the best," says Rose. "I do not have to do this or that to earn my money. There are no clauses other than the 140 games in 1982. Those other guys have all kinds of clauses written in their contracts. Their base pay is lower."

In addition to the $810,000 he earns in salary, Pete will pick up another $500,000 from outside sources. He is in constant demand for banquets and appearances and he has a lucrative contract with the Mizuno Corporation in Japan, endorsing its baseball equipment. During his visit to Japan in November of 1980 he shocked American baseball when he agreed to use Mizuno bats as he goes after Musial's record in 1981. He needs just 74 hits to break it.

Relations between Rose and Reds' President Dick Wagner became strained as early as 1977 when Pete signed a two-year pact for $740,000.

In the spring of 1978, Reuven Katz, Rose's highly capable attorney, who incidentally has always been an ardent Reds' fan, approached Wagner and said he thought it would be fitting to work out an agreement that would guarantee Pete Rose would end his career in Cincinnati. On May 21, the Reds would hold Pete Rose Day to honor Pete for becoming the 13th player in the history of baseball to pass 3,000 hits. Katz thought it would be good to announce the new contract on that day. Katz suggested a non-guaranteed contract of about $450,000 a season for two or three years.

"It could last as long as the Reds wanted it to," said Katz. "If in management's opinion he failed to make the team some spring, he could be dropped and not owed any extra money."

Wagner refused to consider the proposal but as the season ended offered Rose $425,000 for two years. Earlier in the year, Rose would have considered it, but after the 44-game hitting streak and with hints of what he might be able to earn flowing in, he turned it down.

There was some casual negotiation after that, but little movement by the Reds, so Rose went the free-agent route. Prior to the re-entry draft he wrote letters to some teams telling them not to draft him because he had no intention of playing for them. After that, Rose and the Reds left for Japan and a 28-game tour.

He returned the day before Thanksgiving, had his final session with the Reds, and on the morning of November 27 started his barnstorming that would take him to the cities of the five finalists: Atlanta, St. Louis, Kansas City, Pittsburgh and Philadelphia.

Atlanta was first.

Flamboyant owner Ted Turner offered Rose a million dollars a year for four years and $100,000 a year for the rest of his life.

"All I want to do is keep you here a couple of years until the Reds get rid of Dick Wagner so you can go back to Cincinnati where you belong," said Turner.

The next day Rose and Katz went to Kansas City in the morning and St. Louis in the afternoon.

Although the Kansas City offer was not the most exotic, it was the one Rose almost chose over Philadelphia's.

"I'll give you a four-year contract with options for the fifth and sixth years," said Kauffman who made his millions by starting Marion Laboratories, a pharmaceutical firm. "I know your dad played football until he was over 40 and I know you have a shot at Ty Cobb's all-time hits (4,191) record. I'd like to see you get it in a Kansas City uniform."

The Kansas City salary was slightly less than the Braves had offered but with performance and attendance clauses would have pushed the total to $1 million a year. In addition, Kauffman offered Rose 25 percent of the receipts from a productive oil well that apparently was gushing dollars right and left.

Rose and Katz visited Cardinals' owner August A. Busch Jr., in a St. Louis hospital where he was to have surgery the next morning. Busch's yearly salary offer was less than that offered by Kansas City and Atlanta, but Pete would also work as a spokesman for Anheuser-Busch. After his career ended, he'd get his own beer distributorship.

The Pirate offer was less than the first three, about $400,000 a season, but John Galbreath, owner of Darby Dan Farm, knew Rose loved racing and tried to reach him that way. He offered to set him up in the horse-breeding business. Pete would receive two brood mares and the stud service of selected Darby Dan Farm stallions.

"It could have been the best offer," said Rose, "but I had to wait too long to see what would happen. If one of those stallions produced one good foal, it could have been real good. The blood lines were excellent. If I had been a millionaire, I would have taken it."

The final visit was to Philadelphia where everybody thought Rose would climax his whirlwind week by signing with the Phillies.

Ruly Carpenter sent cousin Hugh Sharp's private jet to Cincinnati to pick up Katz and Rose, bringing them to Greater Wilmington Airport.

At Carpenter's Montchanin, Delaware home, his wife, Stephanie, served coffee and Katz showed his short video tape depicting how valuable Rose was to baseball from a public relations standpoint. It was the way the negotiating team had opened discussions at each of the previous stops.

Prior to Pete's return from Japan, Carpenter had told Katz the Phillies were willing to pay Rose slightly more than $2 million for three years. When the tape had finished Katz, perhaps the only agent who works on an hourly fee basis, relayed ball park figures of the other offers to Carpenter and the negotiations abruptly ended.

Lunch was served and the men drove to Philadelphia for a press conference to announce that Pete Rose would not be signing with the Phillies—they were out of the bidding.

"It was crazy," Pete remembered. "I felt sick. I wanted to play for the Phillies all along, but their offer was $2 million less than the Kansas City and Atlanta offers. I was willing to take less money to play with them, but not that much less."

Bill Giles, Phillies' executive vice president and son of the late National League president Warren Giles, had been involved in the negotiations from the beginning. Because his job is to promote the team he was as depressed as Rose and Katz. When he drove them back to the airport late that Thursday afternoon he asked Rose, "Would you really take less money to play in Philadelphia?"

"Yes, I really would," said Pete.

Later, Katz told Giles to play around with the figures and see what might happen.

Back at Veterans Stadium, Giles had a brainstorming session with aide Dave Montgomery. The Phillies had just signed a new contract with their TV outlet, WPHL, and in it was a clause stating the team and the station would share the advertising revenue once a certain base figure was passed. That extra money might help pay Rose's salary!

"I think the real hang-up was the fourth year," said Giles. "Other teams were offering that and we were stuck at three. I called executives of the station and they, in turn, called officials of the Providence Journal which owns the station."

The next morning, Friday, December 1, WPHL agreed to guarantee the Phils at least $600,000 extra because the addition of Rose would mean so much added income from advertising.

Giles went to Ruly Carpenter with his proposal and Carpenter, in turn, phoned Reuven Katz. The agent declined to let Rose in on the late developments.

On Sunday morning, December 3, Rose drove to Katz' home to make his long-awaited decision before attending the Cincinnati Bengals' pro football game. Pete was leaning toward Kansas City, but reluctant to leave the National League because of the many records there within his reach. He still wanted to play for the Phillies.

"I wasn't dead set on the National League," he said, "but when the offers got to where they were pretty close on the dollars and cents scale, I got to wondering whether it was worth taking the difference to give up a shot at Musial's record."

"What if I call the Phillies and get $810,000 guaranteed for four years?" Katz asked. He added, "If I call and they agree, you cannot back down. You have to take it."

"Do it," Pete ordered.

It took two hours and several long-distance calls to Delaware, but the deal was finally completed. At the end Rose took the fourth-highest offer but the one that made him the happiest.

The Phillies have been just as happy.

As Rose continued to talk about his contract, something became vividly clear. He is an extraordinary man who often brings a fresh simplicity to the problems facing the modern, professional athlete.

He will be 40 during the 1981 season, but that doesn't bother him.

"I don't fear age," he said. "I only worry about losing my enthusiasm. I'm not worried about my legs going, about my arm going, about my eyes. It would kill me to play on a losing team. It would be impossible at my age, almost insane, to play the way I do for a last-place team.

"I take care of myself. I don't drink, I don't smoke. I love the races because they relax me. People, though, think that is bad. But I would rather spend a night at the races than in a bar."

On finances: "Yes, I know I make more money than the president of the United States, but I don't see it. My advisers handle my money, make my investments. When I was living at home, we were on a $2,300-a-month budget and $700 of that went to the mortgage."

"Sparky Anderson probably said it best," commented Katz. "He said Pete Rose has more street sense than anyone he ever met. I have to agree. People think I merely pull the strings. That is wrong. Pete makes a lot of his own decisions. I merely help."

Early one recent morning Pete was still trying to put in words how he views his lifestyle.

Wide awake, after an eggs-and-bacon breakfast, he comes into full, fiery bloom. He does not merely live life, he charges it.

"Look, I am a baseball player, a sports nut," said the man who can move people and sell tickets perhaps like no other in the game. "Until I can find something that pays me as much money as baseball I am not going to have a lot of side interests. I am not going to worry about something that pays me $50,000 a year at the expense of something that pays as much as I make from baseball.

"Hey, I am a fan! I mean, I know as much about football as I do baseball, and as much about college basketball. I follow all the sports. I love to watch television. I just think sports make the world go 'round."

Rose has had numerous off-the-field problems that would send mere humans running for psychological help. Pete just plays harder.

"My philosophy is if I have problems off the field, why kick that onto the Philadelphia fans? Why should I kick that onto my teammates? Or why should I kick that onto the men who cover the games? It's my problem, not theirs.

"Success eliminates a lot of problems. You understand what I mean? I mean if you're having problems somewhere and hitting .220, you've got a lot of problems, but if you're having a good year, it's easier to have problems."

People who know him well, say Pete Rose is 39 going on 16. There is no better way to describe him and when a visitor mentions it, he flashes a devilish smile.

"When they finish the national anthem and I'm standing at first base, I still get chills—I've even learned the words."

Bake McBride
Mr. Consistency on Gimpy Knees

He would strap makeshift braces around his creaky knees and then force his aching feet into a pair of specially made shoes.

After that, following a few grunts and groans, he would hobble onto the field and play baseball with the precision and expertise of the healthiest man in the sport. Few realized he was hurting.

In 1980 Bake McBride was the Phillies' bionic man.

His knees were a wreck and his feet were killing him, but without Arnold Ray McBride the Phillies would not have buried the disappointments of the past—the ghosts of all those disasters.

McBride batted .309 in 137 regular-season games. He had career highs with 87 RBI and 33 doubles, and was second only to Mike Schmidt in game-winning RBI with 14. Schmidt had 17.

To put it bluntly, Bake McBride had the year of his life. He batted safely in 11 of the Phils' final 12 games, 15-for-46 for a .326 average and six RBI. He had 33 hits in his final 93 at-bats, a .355 clip.

In the best-of-five struggle with Houston for the National League pennant, "Shake 'n Bake" hit only .228, but rebounded quickly in the World Series, batting .304 against Kansas City pitching. He had a homer and drove in five runs, second only to Schmidt's seven.

But in the midst of all the excitement and celebration, Bake McBride became the bad guy.

The night the playoffs opened against Houston Bake told Howard Cosell he might not ever play for Dallas Green again. Then, on the day Mike Schmidt was receiving his World Series Most Valuable Player Award in New York, a Stan Hochman column in the Philadelphia Daily News quoted McBride as saying Schmidt did not deserve the award—that catcher Bob Boone or shortstop Larry Bowa should have gotten it. And, Bake said, he was burning because he was not invited to the Mike Schmidt Golf Classic at Hilton Head Island.

Bake McBride is a quiet, sensitive, often misunderstood man who sometimes parades around the Phillies' clubhouse after a game with a piece of adhesive tape over his lips.

Get the message?

Bake McBride does not like to talk to reporters. He prefers his privacy, the quietness of his locker stall.

McBride was knee-deep in a January snow that had covered his acreage near St. Louis. He said he was having the time of his life celebrating the world championship, but he knew the players in Philadelphia were having an even greater time.

"I try to be a quiet person," said McBride, who turned 32 last February 3. "But it seems like every time I open my mouth what I say goes all over the world.

"The night the playoffs opened Howard Cosell asked me to do an interview with him for ABC-TV. He said, 'Bake, if Dallas Green is the manager of the Phillies next year will you play for him?' Trying to be honest, I said, 'If Dallas Green is the manager next year, I don't know if I will play for him.' I meant that I might be traded and not be back next year. I didn't mean I didn't like him and would refuse to play if he came back. I was misunderstood again. The papers and radio stations picked it up and here we were in the middle of the series with Houston."

Bake McBride says he likes Dallas Green . . . always has.

"But," said the soft-spoken McBride, "there are times when I wish he had better communications with the players. There was an instance last year that really bothered me. In fact, it was the only problem I had with the manager all year.

"The afternoon of a home game against St. Louis on April 25, I had my left knee drained. It hurt like hell. They stuck a big needle in it and took out the fluid. In the game, I was on first when Del Unser or somebody got a hit. I stopped at second instead of going all the way to third because my knee was hurting so much. I couldn't run and we lost the game 3–1.

"First of all, I didn't know if Dallas knew my knee had been drained or not. I was surprised he did not send in a pinch runner after I got my single. But I pick up the newspapers the next day and he's blasting me. He said I loafed.

"I went right into his office and had a good talk with him. He said he didn't know about the knee even though I thought the trainer always submitted a health report to him just before each game. After that, we were great friends. I blame most of that incident on myself because I didn't tell him I had the knee drained thinking all along that he knew."

McBride is not about to say Green's brash approach to managing was the prime reason the Phillies became world champions.

"I can't really say," was McBride's answer to that question. "He ran the club with more discipline than Danny, and he knew from the way a guy was playing whether or not he needed a rest. He stayed on top of things like that. I can't say I had a better relationship with Green than I did with Danny Ozark because Danny treated me like a son.

"The only problem most of the guys had with Dallas centered around communications. If a guy wasn't starting, he wouldn't go to that guy and tell him why he wasn't starting. That's why he and Garry Maddox had their differences. Dallas wouldn't go to Garry and Garry wouldn't go to Dallas. It was a standoff."

Bake says the quotes in Hochman's column about Schmidt were accurate and honest.

"But I was surprised how the story was played up," said Bake. "Three days after we won the world championship, I was already back home. Stan called me and asked me about the World Series MVP. He said, 'Bake, don't you think you should be MVP?' I said, 'Stan, you go on the first two games, yes. But if you go on the entire World Series, no.' Then, he asked me who I thought deserved it. I told him I have nothing against Mike Schmidt and I am happy he won it, but I don't think he deserved it. I felt Larry Bowa, Tug McGraw or Bob Boone should have gotten it. That's all I said, but the next thing I knew friends from Philadelphia were calling. I didn't know what was going on. They acted like I had said something terrible. I was the villain."

But the timing was terrible, Bake. The story was published the day Schmidt received the award.

"I think Mike said himself he might not have deserved it," continued McBride. "He mentioned the names of the same guys I did. Stan Hochman talked to me three days after the Series. After he called, I thought it was over and done with, but the story did not come out until Mike was in New York. Look, I have nothing against Schmitty. We're friends. I told Stan some of the facts. Bowa and Boone each had a great World Series, both on offense and defense. And everybody knows what Tug McGraw did. If anybody else but Bake McBride had said those things, nothing would have been made of it. But when I said it, it went all over the world."

As far as the golf tournament was concerned, McBride said he did receive an invitation.

"That was my mistake," admitted Bake. "After I talked to

Bake McBride tips his hat to the fans moments after his ninth-inning leadoff homer gave the Phillies a 2-1 victory over Montreal and a 1½-game lead in the National League East on September 26.

Hochman I realized Mike had invited me, but I thought it was too late to do anything about it. He invited everybody on the team whether they played golf or not. He put an invitation in everybody's locker."

McBride, a malcontent with the St. Louis Cardinals, arrived in Philadelphia in June of 1977 after a trade, and helped lift the Phils to their second National League East title, batting .339. The next two seasons, plagued with injuries, his average fell to .269 and .280, respectively. The fans felt he did not hustle and did not always give 100 percent. At times, he still does not run out ground balls and this causes boos.

"I enjoy playing in Philadelphia," he said, "but I'm still not sure how much the fans enjoy me. I think they like me now. That night against Montreal, one of my greatest moments in baseball, they gave me a standing ovation. They would not stop until I came out of the dugout and tipped my cap.

"But I don't know how they are going to react in the future. I imagine the first. time I do something wrong, or make an error, I'll probably get booed."

That "night against Montreal" was September 26 when his leadoff home run off the Expos' Dave Palmer in the ninth inning vaulted the Phils to a 2–1 victory.

"I was pretty emotional that night," said McBride, who tries to hide that side of him. "I tried to hold it down, but that was one of the biggest thrills of my career, one of my most important home runs."

McBride went through a contract squabble with the Phils in the spring of 1979, before reaching a four-year agreement estimated at $1.6 million, and wasn't even sure he would be with the club in 1980.

During the winter baseball meetings in Toronto in 1979, he was almost traded to Texas in a deal for relief pitcher Sparky Lyle. The trade was never pulled off. Bake stayed, and had his most rewarding year.

"When I went to spring training in February of 1980, Paul

Owens and I had a nice talk," said McBride. "He told me my name was passed around during the meetings just so he could see what might happen. He said you never can tell what some other team might offer.

"There was really nothing I could do about my situation. I had to sit back and wait. I wanted to remain in Philadelphia. If I hadn't I would not have signed the four-year contract."

McBride was National League rookie of the year in 1974 when he hit .309 for the Cards. He followed that season with .300 and .335 in 1976 before he got in the bad graces of Manager Vernon Rapp.

"When I came to the Phillies I was like a kid opening a toy on Christmas morning," said Bake. "I felt like I was born again. It restored the fun in baseball for me."

In '76 McBride was on his way to a superb year, hitting .335 after 72 games. Then, his season was rudely interrupted by a knee injury which required surgery and ended his year.

The knee healed fine, but McBride went to the Cardinals' camp early in 1977 to test it under stress conditions.

"The Cardinals asked me to come down early," said McBride. "I paid my own expenses."

McBride arrived with a beard and an Afro hair-do.

"Vernon Rapp approached me and right away we went at it," remembered Bake. "He told me I couldn't go out on the field unless I shaved. Hey, I was down there on my own time, and he wanted me to shave. I said, 'No, way.' I said I would cut it off when the rest of the team arrived.

"From then on, he made it hard on me. He was on me all the time about my hair. He didn't seem to care how I played baseball."

Bake was uptight that Rapp was so concerned about his hair and beard, because the manager liked playing Tony Scott, who had a lifetime batting average of .180, in center field.

"Mentally, being in Philadelphia was a big relief for me," said McBride. "Not having to worry about certain things made me want to play ball more, but I still stayed pretty much to myself."

Bake admits he is a recluse of sorts.

As a child, his life was filled with tragedy. His father died and he moved in with his grandmother. She died and he moved in with his aunt and she also died.

"It all happened within 18 months," Bake said. "It hurts too much to be close to people and then one day they're gone. I don't ever want to have a truly close friend in this game. You get traded and then it's pain all over again."

McBride's off-the-field love, in addition to his three children, is afternoon television.

"I watch the soap operas all the time," he said. "I follow them all very closely."

This past season Bake played in pain much of the time, "but it only hurt when we didn't win."

"A lot of people don't realize how many days he went out there and played with pain," said Pete Rose. "But he didn't do anything this year he hasn't always been capable of. His consistency is what impressed me most."

"Several times I considered letting him have a rest," said Green, "but he wanted to keep playing. Once he came into my office and asked if he could play when I had him sitting the game out."

"I have a lot of respect for Bake McBride," said trainer Don Seger. "There are many players in this game who sit out with fewer problems than he had. I think Bake McBride is going to have sore knees right along, whether it be next year or several years from now. He has resigned himself to that fact and has adjusted."

"In the beginning I only had trouble with one knee," said Bake. "Now both of them bother me. And they are painful. This is something I am going to have to learn to deal with for the rest of my career. I don't see any way out of it."

Seger designed a pair of braces for the knees and with

McBride's help a shoe company made special shoes that resemble running shoes, only with heavy leather tops.

"The shoes keep my feet from hurting so much and the braces take some of the pressure off my knees," said Bake. "Still, on hot days on the Astro Turf my feet hurt pretty good."

McBride thinks he slumped to .280 in 1979 because opposing pitchers were feeding him a steady diet of inside pitches, mostly breaking balls.

A minor change in his stance made him less vulnerable to that.

"I moved back from the plate," he said. "I had started crowding the plate the past couple of years because I was trying to hit the ball out of the park. When I finally realized I wasn't going to hit that many home runs I backed off. I still got the inside pitches, but I was able to handle them better.

"All in all, I'm happy," said McBride. "The year was so enjoyable. If everything works out well I will be with the Phillies in 1981 and for years to come.

"I've been working out since early in the winter on a piece of equipment designed to strengthen my knees. Know where I got it? I bought it from Mike Schmidt!"

Herm Starrette

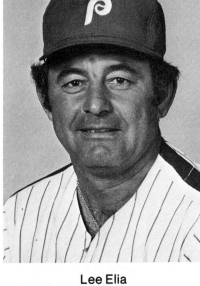

Lee Elia

Mike Ryan

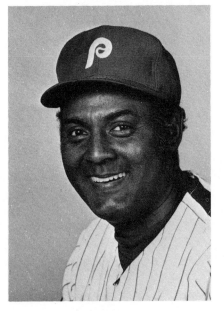

Ruben Amaro

Mike Schmidt
From Captain Cool to MVP

Mike Schmidt was late. As the white Mercedes 450 SL pulled up in front of the large, stately house, 2-year-old Jessica Schmidt started shouting, "Daddy's home! Daddy's home!" and took a flying leap into Mike Schmidt's arms just as he closed the front door.

"Tough catch," Schmidt said, with an impish smile. "I've been working on it. If I don't hold her, she's going to fall on the floor and get hurt."

Catching his daughter when he arrives home from wherever he's been is just about number one in Mike Schmidt's life, but he will never win a Gold Glove for it. He says it's more important than the National League Most Valuable Player Award, the world championship and all the honors that have followed his most productive season for the Phillies.

"It's the best inner-feeling of anything in my life, more than hitting a home run, more than driving a golf ball 260 yards down the middle of a fairway, more than owning a Mercedes, more than looking at a beautiful home. The feeling is second to none."

A tightly knit home life has always been important to Schmidt, and at 31 he looks back on those formative years in Dayton, Ohio believing his close family environment played a

large part in his becoming one of the finest major league baseball players in the game.

Schmidt's wife, Donna, collared Jessica and six-month old
Jonathan, ushering them off to bed.

Mike sorted through some mail while his visitor scanned
the book cases in the warm, walnut-panelled study. The usual
great works bound in gold-leafed leather were present, along
with best sellers from the last four or five years. Squeezed
between two thick volumes dealing with Christianity was an
instructional baseball book by Pete Rose. That arrangement
was obviously not deliberate, but the striking contrast served
as a vivid reminder of the scope of Michael Jack Schmidt's life.

On the other side of the room were shelves filled with
trophies, a reminder that this was not just any other successful
businessman's tastefully decorated den.

To Schmidt, that collection is a quick summary of his
eight-year career with the Phillies—not-so-subtle reminders to
the four seasons (1974–75–76–80) he led the majors in home
runs, to the four consecutive homers he belted in Wrigley
Field on April 17, 1976 to spark one of the most incredible
comebacks in baseball history, and to the five Gold Gloves he
has won as the National League's best defensive third baseman.

The ultimate was the National League's Most Valuable
Player Award, the fitting climax to his greatest season. He was
chosen first on all 24 ballots by a special panel of the Baseball
Writers Association of America. The last player to be so chosen
was Orlando Cepeda of the St. Louis Cardinals, in 1967.

Schmidt also was named MVP in the Phillies' first-ever
World Series triumph, an honor which put to rest a reputation
he had had since the beginning that he could not come
through in the clutch.

Schmidt was brilliant as the Phillies surged to the National League Eastern Division title, then won the best-of-five
playoffs with bizarre come-from-behind victories over Houston

before shocking Kansas City in the World Series. He had 13 home runs in September and hit one each in Philadelphia's last four regular-season games. His blast against Montreal on October 4 in the 11th inning gave the Phils the division title.

Between September 1 and the end of the season, Schmidt hit .304, drove in 27 runs and had a .688 slugging average. With 48, tops in the majors, he wiped out Eddie Mathews' home-run record for a third baseman that had stood since 1957. He also led the league in runs batted in with 121 and in slugging percentage with .624, 107 points higher than runner-up Jack Clark of San Francisco. Schmidt's .286 batting average in 150 games was 31 points above his lifetime standard.

Schmidt has 283 career homers and during the last six seasons nobody in the business has hit more. He has the most explosive bat and probably the least explosive personality of today's super stars. He is quiet, a trait that many feel projects a certain arrogance. His teammates say he is a mystery.

"I've been doing a lot of driving lately," Mike said as he sat down in a comfortable leather chair. "I sit in traffic and I think about the season, about the world championship. This has been a unique experience in my professional life. Even if you're a New York Yankee I don't think it's a common occur-rence—to win a World Series. Well, maybe Babe Ruth at one time didn't have to pinch himself during the off-season when he woke up in the morning, but I still find myself doing that.

"When I have time to gather my thoughts and sort out what this team accomplished in 1980, I feel very, very lucky to have been a part of it. With hopefully five or six years to go in this game, I hope it will happen again, but nothing will be like the first time.

"Personally, I've been very fortunate. I've reaped a lot of individual benefits from the whole thing. I guess maybe I've got to pinch myself a little bit every day. And as long as my normal, everyday thoughts don't engulf all of my thinking, it is very worthwhile."

Schmidt's thinking process has been described as so complicated it has kept his enormous athletic abilities from flowing. During a late-evening conversation, minus the clubhouse distractions and the glare of television lights, his answers to a few questions reveal a great deal about this often misunderstood professional baseball player.

"Sometimes you don't remember, or realize, how much effort you had to put into it," Schmidt said. "It all passes by so quickly. I think in a matter of 15 or 20 seconds I can actually have a flashback of my whole career, vividly realizing what I was shooting for all those years—the right to say I am a world champion.

"And now I'm in the post-world championship period and all of those incidents flash by, another 15 or 20 seconds. There are the accolades, the honors, the parades. And then I focus on the negatives, the negative press, and I come down off my high and wonder why."

There was hurt in Mike Schmidt's eyes as he related an incident. "I was the grand marshal in the Thanksgiving Day parade. People were lining the streets and 999,999 of them were cheering and giving me the high sign and the No. 1 sign and telling me what a great year I had—all the good things any player on our team deserves at this point.

"But there was one guy who said he couldn't wait until he got his tickets behind third base and could start screaming at me because, evidentally, I did not sign an autograph or something for his son. He was screaming at me and telling me how I don't appreciate the fans of Philadelphia, how I don't realize how they made me what I am. I had to yell back at him and tell him how ridiculous he was, and I felt bad I had to do that."

And then there were two stories in the Philadelphia Daily News, the city's largest tabloid, that rained hard on Mike Schmidt's personal parade.

The day Schmidt was in New York to receive the World

Series MVP Award, Stan Hochman devoted a column to an interview with Bake McBride, during which the right fielder suggested Bob Boone or Larry Bowa were more deserving of the World Series MVP honor.

And the day Schmidt's selection as National League MVP was announced, baseball writer Bill Conlin, infuriated the third baseman who had refused to make himself available for an interview prior to the announcement, blasted him. Conlin's last sentence, a takeoff on Tug McGraw's celebrated remark to New York, blared, "Take this award and stick it!"

"It's too bad, but I have focused on some of those negative things," said Schmidt. "I thought Stan Hochman was my friend. I think it was in very poor taste for him to make Bake McBride look so bad. Even if Bake did say those things, why did Stan have to print the story on the day I was getting an important award? The timing was terrible.

"I think because of the McBride story Conlin thought I was sticking it to his newspaper, so he gave me a real tongue-lashing. Frankly, that never entered my mind. I just didn't want reporters calling all hours of the night before the announcement was made. Once things are in print, you cannot bring them back. The reporter can't say, 'I'd like to withdraw that article.' "

Schmidt looked across the room apparently studying an original Jamie Wyeth water color.

"Well, you know, I've taken all the good in stride," he said. "I've thanked the Lord many times for all the good things that have come into my life this year especially. I've also asked the Lord to give me the tolerance, the ability to handle the types of things I have just mentioned. I want to be able to realize that that's all part of being successful, having to look over and around people who apparently resent success or something. I don't know how to put it any other way.

"I guess maybe another way to look at it is that this bit about being world champions is not only new to the players, but also the writers. Some of them won't own up to it, but I think they all probably feel they're world champion writers, too. I felt that all the way through our losing. They all probably thought they were the best when it came to covering baseball, but they should know by now that they have to look in the mirror just like we do after becoming world champions and decide whether or not they gave the Phillies what they deserve. But like I said, I have asked the Lord to give me tolerance."

At each of Mike Schmidt's stops, he gives thanks to God and reminds people he is a re-born Christian. "I go out there every day, I don't play for the fans. I don't play for my owner. I don't play for myself. I do the best I can to glorify God. And the more I achieve as an individual, the better my statistics, that gives me a chance to express the thoughts I have."

Schmidt says he is reluctant to openly discuss his renewed faith, but does.

"I'm not really a fan of talking about my faith through another person's writing," he said as he started sliding deeper into his chair. "It doesn't thrill me to try and explain my faith to the public through another person's eyes. In other words, to have you interpret what I say and write it sort of scares me a little bit. Not because of your style of writing or because I don't trust you, but something like this is a tough subject. Whenever you talk about a person's faith or a person's belief in God or something that abstract, it's tough to trust anyone else to interpret it for you."

Schmidt's religious background in Dayton was typical of many of us. He and his sister were baptized, attended Sunday school and church, then gradually drifted away.

In the mid-1970s Schmidt was shooting baskets one day on the driveway of his, then, home in New Jersey, waiting for close friend and teammate Garry Maddox to pick him up for the ride to Veterans Stadium.

"I had a big, beautiful home, a swimming pool in the

backyard, a Corvette and a Mercedes in the garage. I had a six-year, half-million dollar a year contract with the Phillies. I had not had problems with my knees since those dreadful years in high school. I really had the world by the butt. I bounced the ball once, twice. I just stood there and said to myself, 'Why me? Why all this good for me? Who am I to deserve all this? What would I do if I didn't have all this?'

"All of this to that point, and when I say 'this,' put it in quotes, means all the super-fine material things I owned and were a part of me. They were taking over my life. Those were the things that were making me high. And I just hit a brick wall right at that point in my life. You can only get so high, you can only have so much fun, you can only be so thrilled with material things. All of that crap is temporary. It all dies out. I know if I buy a new car—I know for a fact, that two weeks after I have it, it will be old news. It's then time to move on to something new. I know when I move into a new house, it won't be long before the furnishing is completed and it's old news, too. You know, the fun, all the materialistic desire, all of the excitement of getting it in the beginning and becoming engulfed by it dies out. It fades away."

So, Mike Schmidt took a detailed inventory.

"I was getting my energy from material things. I was married, happily married. I was in love with my wife. We at the time were trying very hard to start a family, but were not able to. Donna was unable to become pregnant, but it was my problem. I was on medication for a long time and it didn't look like we were ever going to have children. I basically lived from that day I was shooting basketballs until around January of 1977 kind of depressed. I had that nagging thought. There was an awareness I wasn't feeling good about such things as unselfishness, humility, friendship, love, giving myself to the community, setting an example for the youth of today."

It was a gradual process.

"Through travel and through baseball, I was introduced

to people who have gone through the same thing. They gave me books to read and I have found a foundation for living. To put it very simply, I acknowledged an entity and gave thanks to that entity—that entity being Jesus Christ—for all the blessings I have in my life. There was, at that point in time, nothing but good happening in my life. I accepted the Lord in January of 1977 and without trying to define and become too personal about the whole thing, I just became a Christian. That's all.

"The only difference in myself and the person who says, 'I believe in God' is I have had an actual experience in my life where I feel I have had a rebirth. I am entitled to my own personal feeling about that and that rebirth, that re-acknowledgement of where the blessings and where the good and where the bad and where everything in my life comes from.

"I remember the time and the place where I got down on my knees and prayed and that was that. That's why I can remember it. I can remember the influential happenings in my life up to that point and if they hadn't happened, I probably would not have come to trust in God. See, becoming reborn or a rebirth, or accepting salvation or accepting the Lord as your savior, those are all one and the same. And the New Testament says unless you have done that, you're not going to heaven. It's very tough to describe this in any more detail."

Just because Schmidt has dedicated himself to the Lord does not make him a perfect person.

"Believe me, I am no angel by any means," he admitted. "I swear on the baseball field, I swear in the dugout, I use the Lord's name in vain. I am a sinner, with a capital S. But what I do understand is that God gave his Son to die for my sins and I know that when I ask for forgiveness of my sins that I'll get it. Not everyone can say that.

"Just one more thing on the personal level. The Lord has perfect timing. He has a way of working this out in everyone's life. Everyone on earth will have a chance to accept Christ as his savior prior to Judgment Day. The Bible explains all this stuff, but the pattern was fairly evident in my life—the way it worked with me. Sure, there are persons who'll argue the reason you are there is because of your ability, but I'll say, 'Well, I got that ability from God when I was born.' God chose me to be this, to have this purpose in life and I'm working my darndest to fullfill it. I've lifted weights, I've run, I've practiced, I've taken batting practice until my hands bled, I've taken ground balls until I was sick of taking them. But I feel this is all channeled toward my fulfilling my purpose in life."

When Schmidt looks back to his younger years, he now sees a pattern, something he was not aware of at the time.

His parents, Lois and Jack Schmidt, gave him everything he wanted. It was a small, affluent family and a close family and there was plenty of love.

At a young age, it became apparent Mike Schmidt was a gifted athlete. Name a sport and he excelled in it. As a sophomore at Fairview High, he was already receiving feelers from the top colleges in the land to play football.

"I had ability and I had motivation," he said. "Everything was perfect. During my sophomore year I tore my left knee, the same kind of injury the 76ers' Doug Collins had. In my junior year, I did the same thing to my right knee. I became a walking roll of adhesive tape and nobody was giving me a second look.

"It was during those pivotal years of my life a direction was determined. I look back now, I look back as a Christian person, and feel that those were all God's protection of his plan for my life. Things happened in such a way that my career was narrowed to baseball. That was the only sport I could play.

"I had always dreamed of being a professional athlete, but I went off to Ohio University with a T-square and a portfolio. I was dead serious about becoming an architect. All I did my freshman year was stay up nights constructing little models of buildings and doing projects for my art courses and to this day I have a great interest in things like that."

Because of the knees, Schmidt says his athletic career was going no place.

Enter Larry Starr.

"Larry's now the Cincinnati Reds' trainer," said Mike. "He gave me some tests and a program to rehabilitate my knees. It was remarkable. Then, some guy got drafted and there was an opening for me on the baseball team. I went on to have a great career in college and got drafted by the Phillies in 1971.

"I was fortunate. I didn't come out of the ghetto and have the pressure to succeed that a lot of kids have nowadays.

"Because my life was so comfortable it was difficult to face up to the disabling injuries I had and continue my quest for success, but for some reason I had an inborn drive that kept me going. It's usually part of a kid who's from a very poor family who sees that pot of gold at the end of the rainbow. I didn't have to scuffle. Not one bit. I was just eaten up with succeeding, but then I hit a crossroad . . . I had all my eggs in that one basket. Everything athletic came so easily. I still find it hard to believe I had the abilities—in sports—that I had at age 7 and 8. Then, I had the injuries and had to readjust. It worked out and, in essence, that's what I did again when I got a new grasp on my life. And that has been the most rewarding."

Each October the third baseman, along with long-time friend Frank Hirt, hosts the Mike Schmidt Golf Classic at Palmetto Dunes on Hilton Head Island, South Carolina. It's a fun event for amateur golfers and major league baseball players. Mike's dad, Jack, always plays and one afternoon following a round in the 1980 event, told a story about his celebrated son.

The elder Schmidt operated a restaurant in Dayton when Mike was in his teens.

"When he was 15, I gave him a summer job as a stockroom clerk and bus boy," Jack remembered. "All he talked about that summer was getting his driver's license. He would turn 16 in September and be eligible for a permit—"

"Let me finish," interrupted Mike. "He told me I could get my license on my birthday, but for every day I begged off from work to do anything else, he was going to hold back the license for a month. He was trying to teach me responsibility, the fact I had a job and I had to be there and couldn't say, 'Forget it, the boss is my dad.' Well, to make a long story short, I didn't get my license until January. He got me for five months!

"But, wouldn't you know it? When I did get the license he also got me a car."

The most disappointing part of 1980 for Mike was the fact his grandmother, Viola Schmidt, was not around to help celebrate the great year. She died of cancer in Dayton at the age of 75 on September 26, the eve of his 31st birthday.

"She had been hanging on for a long time and I think that was because of her interest in my baseball career," said Mike. "I was thinking about her a lot as the season neared its end. She was probably the first person to ever throw me a baseball. She was my most important fan, always a motivating force. She pushed me and encouraged me."

Aside from his off-the-field dedication, Schmidt feels a change in his batting stance made him a more consistent hitter.

"At the All-Star Game break in 1979, I changed my style. I moved away from the plate more. The results were not noticed at first, but the new stance eventually helped me tremendously. I no longer was a dead-pull hitter.

"I think if a power hitter can hit over .270 that means he has been relatively consistent most of the season. And I think I was consistent in 1980. Sure, I had my 0-for-20s and struck out three times in a game, but I was able to cut down on my hitless games, too."

Deep down, Schmidt is most proud of the fact people look at him now as a player who can come through in the clutch.

"There are certain guys who players say, 'He'll get the big hit for you when you need it.' I don't think that label was ever on me, but somebody ought to think about putting it on me now."

On the surface, he projects the image of an emotionless, almost I-couldn't-care-less individual. Teammates have been calling him Captain Cool for years.

"I always want to convey to my teammates and to the opposition I am in control of myself," he said. "I don't want anyone to think I am intimidated by anything that happens on the field, whether it is being done well or poorly. I like to always keep the opposition feeling I'm under control, especially offensively. I feel, in order to succeed as a hitter, you have to have as much poise as you can possibly have while you're hitting the baseball.

"On the other hand, you have to have the least amount of tension that you can have as a hitter. The more tension you have, the more pressure you put on yourself, the more tension you're going to have in your swing and the less you're going to succeed.

"The same thing is true defensively. The more tension and pressure you put on yourself as a fielder, the more likely balls will carom off your body and go too far away to be fielded. But if the ball takes a bad hop and hits a loose, relaxed, limp body, it's more apt to just drop straight down. Sometimes I maybe appear cool on the outside but, you know, and I'm not going to lie to you, there are times when inside I am battling negative thoughts."

In the spring of 1979 Danny Ozark decided Mike Schmidt should be the Phillies' captain. The manager did not conduct a team election or anything close to it. Instead, he talked to a few players, then held a press conference.

Quietly, during Dallas Green's first spring training Schmidt shed the armor.

"I guess you could say I resigned," Schmidt remembers. "I don't know what else you could call it. I went to Dallas and I said, 'Look, why don't we put this captain thing in limbo? You're the manager now. You should be able to decide whether or not you want a captain.'"

Schmidt says he took charge when he thought he had to, "but I don't think my role as captain was ever that visible to the public. I took the line-up card out to home plate for a while in 1978, but I gave that up. It was interferring with my preparation for the game. Once or twice I called team meetings and really aired it out."

Actually, Ozark's reasons for appointing Schmidt were not that valid. Danny thought with added responsibility, Mike would take some of the heat off himself, but it didn't work that way.

Really, the arrival of Pete Rose gave Schmidt the biggest push of his career. At the time, teammates were grumbling about Schmidt's aristocratic ways and fans were accusing him of not caring.

"I called him aside one day in the spring of 1979 and told him he was one of the best I had ever seen," said Rose. "I told him if he wanted to be MVP, he certainly could be."

And the day Mike's selection for that award was announced, he credited Rose.

"I probably would not be standing up here right now if it were not for Pete Rose," he said. "Pete instilled in me a new vitality I think was the turning point for me as far as the athletic part of my baseball career is concerned.

"I am 31 years old and that is an important time for all players. Pete gave me a great new outlook on the game of baseball, a feeling of youth, a feeling that when you go onto the field you should have fun playing the game. Pete and I have a great rapport, second to none in baseball. And I can't think of a better person to have a close rapport with."

"Mike Schmidt is the best player in the National League today. There's no question about that," said Rose. "He honestly doesn't realize how much ability he has. All he has to do is get the most out of those abilities on a daily basis because, believe me, he can play. He can do it all and he's just starting to want to more and more."

Greg Luzinski
". . . produce. That's the bottom line."

Emotion, mostly the unhappy kind, had been swelling inside the Bull for almost a year. With one swing of his bat, he let it out.

April 12, 1980.

Greg Luzinski blasted a towering three-run homer in the first inning to lead the question-mark Phillies to a spirited 6–2 conquest of Montreal in the season opener.

For Luzinski it was home run No. 205, but admittedly one of the most important of his career. It signalled the start of a comeback and helped pay off the debt for all the hard work he put in over the winter and in spring training.

As the Bull circled the bases that cool night, with 48,460 fans screaming their jubilation, it was obvious he was juiced. As he rounded third base he slammed a hand into coach Lee Elia's waiting palm. Then, seconds later, he balled his right fist and threw it above his head.

The last time Luzinski showed so much emotion was when he homered against Pittsburgh in 1978 on the day the Phillies clinched their third straight National League Eastern Division title.

But this home run was propelled by emotion and the paying customers at the 10th Vet opener knew what was happen-

Pete Rose

Bake McBride

Mike Schmidt

Greg Luzinski

ing inside the big man's body. They gave him a standing ovation when he reached the dugout. It lasted for over a minute—until he finally appeared and tipped his cap.

"I was in another world, I don't remember clenching my fist," he bubbled later. "I had a lot of emotion inside of me and it had to come out. I really can't tell you what I was thinking when I ran around the bases. It was just a great, great feeling."

Nearly 25 pounds overweight and injured most of 1979, Luzinski hit only 18 homers and slumped to a .252 average that year. His name was frequently mentioned in trade talks and some people said he was washed up.

But at only 29 the Bull insisted there was plenty of good baseball left in him. He went on a strict diet and lowered his weight from 238 to 215. He got in the best condition of his life and worked on his batting stroke—the quick, powerful stroke that made him one of the most feared hitters in the league.

The 1980 beginning for Luzinski was beautiful. He managed to push aside his feelings for fired Manager Danny Ozark. He swallowed hard and accepted Dallas Green's abrasive style, working as diligently as anyone at spring training in Clearwater. Green, obviously impressed, remarked. "I'm willing to bet my house the Bull has a great, great season."

It started that way. By June 14, Luzinski had 15 homers and had driven in 36 runs with a batting average slightly under .290.

From that point on what appeared to be a great season for the left fielder became another disaster.

On July 5, in St. Louis, Luzinski slid into second base and felt a sharp pain in his right knee, the same one operated on for a ligament injury in 1974.

He tried to work out when the season resumed after the July 8 All-Star Game in Los Angeles, but the knee swelled and he was placed on the disabled list. On July 28 team physician Dr. Phillip J. Marone removed multiple loose cartilaginous bodies and a small portion of actual cartilage during a two-hour operation.

Luzinski did not return until August 24 and did very little until the Phillies reached the stretch run.

After striking out 15 times in his previous 32 at-bats, the Bull came through with two hits in four at-bats against the Expos in the dramatic 6–4, 11-inning victory at Montreal which guaranteed the division title for the gasping Phils.

And in the bizarre playoffs against Houston, Luzinski batted .294 with a clutch homer and four RBI.

Sidelined by the flu and a controversial decision by Green, the Bull was hitless in nine at-bats in the World Series and played in only three of the six games against Kansas City.

What happened to Gregory Michael Luzinski in 1979 and 1980 has even the most critical Phillies' fan wondering.

The gap between him and Green is even more of a mystery. Green was the Bull's first manager and the two had met soon after the 17-year-old kid from Chicago was the Phils' Number One draft pick in June of 1968. At Huron the baby bull and Green, a first-year minor-league manager, got along famously.

But in 1980, they went at each other tooth and nail and as late as this past February it was doubtful the two could continue to coexist in the same clubhouse.

There was some friction before the '80 season but owner Ruly Carpenter, against his better judgment, stepped in. In November of 1979 he called Luzinski and suggested a quiet, private meeting.

"He invited himself over to the house," Luzinski said. "He told me it wasn't urgent but he had some things he wanted to discuss. 'Come on over whenever you want,' I said."

Carpenter drove to Luzinski's New Jersey home a few days before the 1979 winter meetings opened in Toronto.

"I just felt the time had come to put everything on the table, to clear the air," Carpenter remembers.

"A good meeting," Luzinski said. "He told me some things and I told him some things."

When Ruly Carpenter gets in moods like this he can be extremely effective. He thought the problems with one of his friends, a favorite player, had gone too far.

His approach was basically threefold. He told the Bull to get the weight off, to work out during the off-season at Veterans Stadium and to try regular eyeglasses instead of contacts.

Luzinski and Ruly have always had a great relationship. It's not your typical owner-player relationship for they hunt together and have always had great respect for each other.

But when Carpenter watched Luzinski swell to nearly 240 pounds and have a dreadful season in 1979, it nearly tore his heart out. When the fans who had always loved the Bull turned on him, it made matters even worse.

"Ruly was concerned," Luzinski, a man of great pride, said. "In addition to the weight and the glasses, he told me if a deal came up where they could help the team in three or four spots, it would be hard to turn it down. I told him I wouldn't expect him to turn it down."

Carpenter also told the Bull despite what was being reported he was not on the trading block and that Player Personnel Director Paul Owens was not going to Toronto to put him on the block.

"I thought that was great," said Luzinski. "It gave me peace of mind to a degree. Sure I have a certain attachment to Philadelphia, but in this business you have to accept the fact if you're traded, you're traded. There's nothing you can do about it."

Luzinski went on the strict diet, worked out at the Vet and when spring training opened was wearing regular glasses.

"I started spring training at 215 pounds," he said. "In the past I got a lot of static about the weight, but I never felt it bothered me. I got tired of hearing everybody talk about it, so I decided to take the weight off. Frankly, with it off, I felt better than I had in a long, long time. I worked out in spring training then went back to the house and played on the beach with my kids. I never did that before. I was just plain too tired."

In 1979 Luzinski's batting average slipped 33 points below his lifetime standard of .285. His power production also fell off, from 35 homers and 101 runs batted in 1978 to 18 and 81.

He had a nagging thigh injury most of the '79 season and got into some bad habits at the plate. If he had it to do over again, he kept saying after that dreadful summer, he would have gone on the disabled list until he was healthy.

"But I kept wanting to contribute. I played as much as I could," he said. "Then I heard people saying during the off-season I might be through. That really got me thinking about hitting the comeback trail and what I would have to do to regain my old form.

"I have never wanted to get involved with a weight-lifting program because I thought it would build up my chest too much. I explained my reasons and management accepted them. They still wanted me to work on my swing with (coach) Billy DeMars, and do some running. It really helped."

As the Phillies were completing spring training in 1980, Luzinski told a friend: "I'm hoping all those boos will turn to cheers again. Philadelphia has some great fans and before 1979 they always treated me fine. You can talk about injuries and all that, but we let the fans down. I have received a lot of letters of encouragement. That's fine, but I have to produce. That is the bottom line."

Steve Rogers' 2-2 pitch sailed over the plate and Luzinski swung hard that April night as the new season started.

The boos *had* turned to cheers, but they didn't last long. Not even a whole year. He played in just 106 games, hit only .228, with 19 homers and 56 RBI.

Dallas Green was critical.

"No one worked harder than the Bull the first half of the year," the manager told reporters. "But he forgot about his weight and that is what caused the leg injury. Nobody has meant more to Philadelphia Phillies' baseball the last 10 years than Greg Luzinski, but at the end I had no other choice but to play people who were producing."

"The first half was great," agreed Luzinski. "The second half I was hurting and there were other complications. To sum it up, I wasn't worried about myself when we got in the play-offs and World Series because I felt what I did in them would make my season. I think that happened. There weren't many personal goals or anything I could shoot for at that point.

"I have never felt better than I did the first half. The second half was a different story, something I want to forget. A lot of things have been said, a lot of things have been written. I'd prefer not to comment on most of it now."

Although Luzinski can destroy just about anybody who gets in his path, he is basically a quiet, sensitive man. Danny Ozark was a close friend and when he was fired the Bull didn't appreciate the way Green told everybody he was going to find out who wanted to play and who didn't.

That was the beginning of the rift.

Then while the Phillies were losing three games in Atlanta prior to his knee surgery, the Bull stayed at home. He burned inside when he read Green's outspoken comments.

"He runs it (the team) like he was a bleeping Gestapo," said Luzinski. "That alone puts too much pressure on the team. I stayed at home and read the papers and he really disappointed me.

"He preaches the 'We, Not I' philosophy, but Dallas Green shares only when the team wins. That doesn't include him when we lose."

Green's reaction? "He shouldn't read the newspapers!"

"I've read all those quotes about character, about grinding it out," Luzinski told the Daily News' Stan Hochman. "I know some of the players I've talked to have been affected by Green's comments. Anyone who's been around the club can tell who.

"There are some sensitive guys who are getting hurt by all that screaming, getting singled out for one bad pitch, or one bad play.

"A guy like Garry Maddox, let's say. A play the other day when we gave up an extra run and Dallas hollers about him not throwing the ball in. He never mentioned that Lonnie Smith missed the ball in the first place. The thing is, he's got these signs all over the place that say 'We, Not I,' but he sure wouldn't want the players yapping to the press about mistakes he makes. I know what he's thinking, light a fire under somebody. . . . The thing is—and Dallas has said this himself— he's got some shortcomings and one of them is his mouth."

Soon after, Luzinski had surgery and was not around Green much until late August. But even after he was reactivated the two seldom talked.

In fact, Paul Owens played an important role in helping the Bull regain his stroke, the stroke that gave him what little happiness he enjoyed in September and October.

The old black-and-white, silent movies flicked across Owens' office wall.

"Run it back once more," said the Pope. "OK, now put 1977 up next to it. . . . Fine, that's good."

Owens sat in the dark on the afternoon of September 15 watching footage of Luzinski batting—the good years when he could handle a two-strike pitch better than anyone in the business. After Owens studied the film he had Bob Searle, the Phillies' cameraman, run some video tapes of Luzinski's 1980 batting.

Finally, after over an hour Owens detected a small but important difference. When Luzinski was going well there was a little motion to his left knee as he strode into the ball. In 1980, he was merely going straight at the ball.

"I felt he was more then ready to swing the bat the old way," Owens said. "I mentioned it to him on a flight that night to Pittsburgh."

Luzinski's bat began to come to life after the Pope's advice.

"I really appreciated him taking time to look at those films," said the Bull. "You know I have a lot of respect for him and I think that tiny change in my swing was hurting me. My bat was not quick enough the way I was striding."

Owens admitted he had no business getting involved with field matters such as that, but deep down he'll always be a field man, yearning to put on the uniform and actually get involved in the game.

"I didn't want to make a big deal about it," said the Pope. "Billy DeMars is our hitting instructor and has done a good job. It's just that sometimes you need another opinion. I know the Bull as well as anyone, so I thought if I could detect something, it might help him. The best of doctors sometimes asks others for advice."

While most of the Phillies were celebrating their long-awaited World Series victory over Kansas City, Luzinski collared Owens in a quiet corner of the clubhouse. What they said nobody knows for sure. Obviously the Bull was getting something off his chest on that emotional night.

A month before the start of 1981's spring training, he still had not gone face-to-face with Dallas Green. Many comments had been made, some public, some not.

"I think he brought some good things to us and did some good things," said Luzinski. "Really, though, I think it was just time for this team to win. I only wish Danny Ozark could have been around to enjoy it.

"You still have to do it on the field. Dallas might have brought a little more discipline here, but I don't know if you can attribute that to why we won. I think what happened was the team just put it all together.

"As a player I hate to see people think it was all Dallas Green. That takes away from the great years Schmidt and McGraw and Carlton and the rest of the guys had.

"For me to come back from the injury at a time when Lonnie Smith was doing a great job was tough. That put added pressure on me, trying to do maybe more than I could to help the ball club."

Luzinski stopped talking. His mind seemed miles away.

"Ruly Carpenter and I have had another one of our talks and it was good. Have I talked with Dallas? I don't see any reason to get together with him. He has not stopped saying things about me.

"You touched on my feelings about the whole thing when you asked if he should get credit for our winning the world championship after we failed under Danny. I've got an opinion, but I'm going to let it go at that."

Luzinski said his year all came down to "what have you done for me lately?"

"We're world champions and I'll survive," he said matter-of-factly. "That's the bottom line."

Little did Luzinski know then his days with the Phillies were nearly over. On March 25, several days after the Phils obtained Gary Matthews from Atlanta for pitcher Bob Walk, the Bull was sold to the Chicago White Sox for an undisclosed amount of cash.

With that, an era in Phillies' history ended.

Garry Maddox
The Secretary of Defense

The ball floated gently into Garry Maddox' waiting glove. The impact stung his left hand a little, but as he squeezed it shut the pain quickly disappeared.

In fact, a summer of agonizing pain disappeared that October Sunday night in the stuffy Astrodome when Garry Maddox made the final out in the 10th inning against Houston as the Phillies clinched their first National League pennant since 1950.

Maddox loped over to right-center to haul in Enos Cabell's fly ball and for a few seconds did nothing but concentrate on making the catch. He yelled something to right fielder Del Unser and, still clutching the baseball, started toward the infield.

"I was in kind of my own little world at the time," Garry Maddox remembers. "All of a sudden I looked up and the whole team was rushing toward me. They lifted me to their shoulders and were carrying me off the field. I didn't expect that. I didn't know that whoever makes the final out is lifted up like I was. I didn't expect that."

The Phillies did not hoist Garry Maddox to their shoulders because he made the final out. They did it spontaneously because he, above all, symbolized the topsy-turvy season the suddenly crowned league champions had endured.

The great center fielder had struggled at the plate ending the regular season with a .259 average. On three occasions he had been blasted in the press by Manager Dallas Green for losing fly balls in the sun. He had been one of the targets during Player Personnel Director Paul Owens' clubhouse lecture on September 1, and had suffered daily with the reality his name might not be on the starting line-up card.

But when the Phillies needed a miraculous game-saving catch, when they needed a crucial hit down the stretch, Maddox reached back and delivered.

He did it in the deciding game of the bizarre best-of-five playoffs with the Astros, doubling Unser with the winning run in the 10th inning of a stirring 8–7 victory.

He did it the last heart-throbbing week of the season when he came off the bench, stiff and sore, and ripped a clutch two-out single in the 15th inning on September 29 to help rally the seemingly beaten Phillies over the Chicago Cubs, 6–5.

"A lot of things happened so quickly that night in Houston, I never really had a chance to think about how I actually felt," Maddox said several months later. "They all just happened. As I think back now, I can't even say *how* I felt but all the down periods were forgotten. I think after winning you forgive your worst enemy for anything he has done to you. You're so happy that nothing else seems to matter. That's how I probably felt. It was a time when we all kind of forgot about what we had gone through during the season and we became closer. We pulled together even more in the World Series and that's probably why we defeated Kansas City."

Garry Maddox' problems started in spring training. He was entering the option year of his contract and his demands for a new agreement were so high negotiations stalled.

On March 10, Jerry Kapstein, Garry's agent, made a startling announcement: "Negotiations with Philadelphia on a contract for Maddox are at an impasse. The negotiations began in January, 1979 and continued until March 1980. We will not discuss a new contract until after the 1980 re-entry draft."

Owner Ruly Carpenter quickly came back with a rebuttal: "I told Jerry Kapstein we have no alternative but to make a deal for Garry Maddox. There is always the chance we will not be able to trade him. The other owners are no dummies. They know if we are unable to sign him, they might not be able to sign him either."

Meanwhile the sensitive Maddox, who reportedly was asking for $1 million a year, began to worry. How would the fans treat him in Philadelphia? Would he be able to handle the verbal abuse?

"There is no question I want to remain in Philadelphia," Maddox said in March. "I have gotten along well with the press, well with the fans, my teammates and especially the front office. You can imagine what kind of a position I am in and how it bothers me emotionally to have to do this. In the long run, I have to do what I think is best for Garry Maddox."

With negotiations off and the prospect of not having the Gold Glover, Green began to play others in center field. Maddox sat and watched.

Finally, with the secrecy of a Watergate informant, and against the wishes of both Paul Owens and Dallas Green, Ruly Carpenter knocked on Garry Maddox' door the night of March 19. The owner felt there was no way the Phillies could return to the top spot of National League East without Garry Maddox, the team's "Secretary of Defense."

"All I wanted was to talk to him face-to-face," said Carpenter. "I thought if Garry and I reached some kind of an understanding without the agent present, we might be able to re-open the negotiations and make some progress. My dealings with Jerry Kapstein have always been on the highest level and I respect him, but I wanted to have a chat with Maddox and wanted it to be secret.

"I told Garry he was currently the highest-paid ($425,000)

center fielder in baseball and that although he could probably earn more by becoming a free agent, the Phillies would give him a fair contract."

After Carpenter left the Indian Rocks Beach, Florida condominium, Maddox phoned Kapstein. "I asked him to do everything in his power to keep me with the Phillies," Garry said.

Three days later Kapstein announced from his California office negotiations had been re-opened and on April 15, Maddox signed a six-year agreement calling for $675,000 annually. The first four years contained a no-trade clause.

"As I look back, that whole spring ordeal cost me," said Maddox. "I didn't really get a chance to train, to get myself ready for the season the way I usually do. The Phillies were in a situation where they didn't know if I would be with them or not, so they were forced to give the time I normally have to get ready to someone else. It ended up hurting me, but I don't blame anyone for it. It's just a part of baseball you have no control over.

"If Ruly Carpenter had not come to my place that night, I don't know what would have happened. We said things we pretty much knew about one another and he told me how much he would like to have me on the ball club. I told him how much I wanted to be there. He showed good faith, so I called Jerry. Despite what happened this past season, I can't let that dampen the way the organization has treated me ever since I came here."

To understand how difficult 1980 was for Garry Lee Maddox, you have to understand this highly intelligent, complex and extremely sensitive 31-year-old man. And that is not always easy.

Maddox was born in Cincinnati but grew up in Los Angeles. His father, Arthur, supported the family by working for the Chrysler Corporation. Much of their income came from welfare.

"When I think of my children right now," said Garry, his tone somber, "my main concern is I have to teach them good study habits and I've got to teach them how to respect other people's rights. I try to do that to the point where when they reach a certain age and I have no more control over them, I will have had enough of a positive influence that they can handle any kind of a crisis which might come up. That's my main concern.

"When I was growing up, I had to worry about where my next meal was coming from and what kind of toys—if there were to be toys at all—we'd get for Christmas. I had to worry about getting home without getting in a fight. I had a rough childhood.

"There are some things about my family I don't wish to discuss, but I can honestly say that I have put those problems behind me now."

Garry, so sensitive as a child he would run to his room sobbing when Arthur Maddox raised his voice, was bitter. He had a chip on his shoulder and admittedly lacked direction.

"I wasn't a great athlete in high school," said Garry. "I never considered myself a great athlete. I never really did anything. I was never an All-State player, never All-American or anything like that. I played baseball for two years, and played football and basketball one year. I didn't really stick with these sports.

"After my senior year, I was drafted by the San Francisco Giants in the second round and they gave me $1,000 to sign and $500 a month.

"That was 1968. I played at Salt Lake City and Fresno, in rookie leagues, from June until September and after that three buddies and I joined the Army. Professional baseball, to me, was not what life was all about. I didn't appreciate the fact that as a second-round draft choice I only got $1,000 to sign. I saw guys who were drafted in the 10th round who got a lot more money than I did. For whatever reason, I didn't think that was

Garry Maddox grimaces as he slides between Pittsburgh catcher Steve Nicosia's legs with the winning run on a suicide squeeze in the 14th inning against the Pirates on September 9.

right. My parents and I had no experience dealing with scouts. I thought maybe I had been taken advantage of."

The day he received the $1,000, Maddox thought it was a lot of money for signing his name.

"I can tell you exactly my thinking at the time," he said. "Whatever they offered me, I had to take. I didn't know anything about getting an agent and going back and forth with negotiations. I was 19 years old. Put in that same situation with the knowledge I have now, I would say, 'Hey, I was fortunate enough to get a chance to play baseball and be thankful.' But those are the things you learn as you mature. As it worked out, I am even more thankful because after that rookie season I quit and joined the service and ended up going to Vietnam."

Maddox went to Vietnam as a perimeter guard late in 1969 and it was there his life made a drastic turn.

"It was tough," he said, looking across the room. "For Americans, used to the comfort of the United States, it was difficult. I never want to live in any other country. I'm not even keyed up about visiting other countries.

"Vietnam was not as tough on me as it was on some people—a lot of my friends didn't make it back. The guys in the infantry had to go out and beat the bushes for the Viet Cong, not knowing what would happen. There were guys there that can tell you more about the action than I can. Oh, I was shot at a few times in the village at night, but that was the extent of my action. The next morning I would walk through the village, which was on the perimeter, to see if everything was OK.

"I really don't like to talk about my Vietnam experience too much. I had some things happen over there that were pretty rough on me, things that I've just blocked out of my mind completely. But it definitely had an impact on my life. It had to change me."

Garry Lee Maddox says his real life began during his second six months in Vietnam fighting the war nobody cared very much about.

"It happened in a place where things were really rough and people were getting killed around me," he said. "All of a sudden a thought hit me. Where was my life going? What was I doing with it? And I just turned my life over to God at that time. One day I woke up and wanted some answers and I didn't have any. Fortunately, God looked at me at that time and sort of directed me to come to Him, and I turned my life over to Him. And from that standpoint, that was the beginning of my life. I was baptized in January of 1970—over there.

"Before that I could be easily influenced. I just lived from day to day. I was fortunate enough not to get involved in the drug situation. I saw guys get 'Dear John' letters and get involved in all kinds of things. They were over there all alone and could not handle it. I was lucky. That kind of stuff passed me by."

When Maddox returned from Vietnam in the spring of 1970, he still had 14 months of his three years to serve. His father had been having heart problems, but Garry had not been informed while he was in Vietnam.

"When I got back I found I had to help with the support of my family. That gave me grounds to get out of the service early—if I had a job. My dad wrote a letter to the Giants explaining the situation and they invited me to their Instructional League in the fall of 1970. In 1971 I played at Fresno, started the 1972 season with Phoenix and was in the majors after just 11 games.

"I can't take credit for being a great athlete and making it to the big leagues the way I did. It all has to go back to Vietnam when I turned my life over to God. This is something about me that has not been written because it takes so much getting into when you start discussing your faith and things like that. People come up to me after a ball game and they don't want to hear that God did it for me.

"See, I quit baseball and then I joined the service because I didn't want to play anymore and that was it. But from the time I was baptized, everything changed.

"The first time I came to bat in the Instructional League, I could barely see the ball. After the long layoff I was terrible and if that had been the same Garry Maddox who had just graduated from high school, he probably would have quit right away. But I had matured a little bit and turned my life over to God. I stuck with it."

There were many times in 1980 when Maddox wished he could walk away from what was happening.

Considered by many the best center fielder in baseball, the tall, lean Maddox lost two fly balls in the sun in a late August game at San Diego. Then on September 28 against Montreal on the next-to-last weekend of the season he lost a Chris Speier liner in the sun. It rolled to the fence for a triple.

Plus, there were numerous confrontations with Dallas Green with whom he has an admitted, and still existing, philosophical conflict.

"First off, what I'm giving is my opinion and I'm talking about how I feel," said Maddox. "I'm not putting any blame on anyone for anything. I take full responsibility, full blame for the way my season went, for my stats and for any mistakes I made. I always try to face up to mistakes I have made. I face them head-on. I won't try to run from those things."

With that preface, Maddox delved into the problems he had with Dallas Green during what some may call a stormy summer.

"I think Dallas had a lot of problems because he was a new manager," said Maddox in his soft voice. "He had never been in this situation before. Unfortunately, I was one of the guys who had problems. But if I had had the kind of year Mike Schmidt had, there wouldn't have been any negative things going on. If I had played up to my capabilities (.293 lifetime average), I don't think I would have had any trouble. By getting off to a slow start, what with the negotiations and all, I forced him to do some things maybe he wasn't experienced at doing.

"Throughout my career, especially since I came here from the Giants in 1975, I had been in the habit of coming to the ball park knowing I was going to play. I was ready to play. As the 1980 season progressed, I had to come to the park prepared not to play because I didn't know one way or the other ahead of time and he wouldn't tell me. There were times when I could read about my status in the newspapers, but he would not confront me. That's his option, but I've played this game now for eight years in the majors and I've come to expect certain things. I expect if the manager has any gripes with me or is unhappy with anything I'm doing, I expect him to come to me and not go to the press.

"Being a person, a human being with feelings, and having played so long and having been granted this respect, I kind of expected it from him. I had no idea what it was going to be like playing under him, so it was an adjustment."

Green irritated Maddox in September of 1979 when he took over after Danny Ozark was fired. Maddox and Danny were close, and the center fielder probably took the firing harder than anyone on the team.

"Dallas Green arrived and said. 'Now, we're going to see who really wants to play for the Phillies.' That rubbed me the wrong way," continued Maddox. "A lot of people said I took it the wrong way and maybe I wasn't giving him a fair chance, but that's how it affected me. I had spent all summer giving it everything I had, worked as hard as I could up until that time. The team was having a bad season, but we weren't giving up. We had all worked out on our own the winter before. We had put in a lot of time and to have the manager say that, I guess I took it too personally. But that's basically when it all started and it just carried through the season."

On August 31 Maddox lost two routine fly balls in the sun

at spacious San Diego Stadium. He did not have his sunglasses on and this caused Green to come down hard on the center fielder.

"To me, I can play just as well without sunglasses," said Maddox. "Even when I have them on, I have them on for the simple reason baseball says you should have them on. It alleviates people from being able to say, 'Hey, if he had had his sunglasses on, he probably would have caught the ball.' There are balls hit in the sun you can't catch, with sunglasses or without sunglasses. To me the two balls in San Diego were like that. I can say in my mind I don't think I would have been able to catch them with sunglasses. But, so the finger is not pointed at me, I should have had them on. I didn't and I was wrong. It was my fault and the next day that is what I told Dallas.

"OK, there were times when I thought I should have been playing and he thought I should not be playing. I respect his opinion if that's the way it goes. I don't run the team and I should not dictate when I should play.

"After the San Diego incident I went into his office (in San Francisco the next day) and told him I was wrong and he could get the team together and I would apologize to them for what happened. I thought everything was clear. Then Paul Owens calls the team together and singles Larry Bowa and me out for not playing well. I'm not the type of guy who has to go into the manager's office with an excuse every day, and the one time I do go in and apologize I expect it to be accepted and all forgotten. You know if I had done this more than once or something like that, I might have expected what happened."

As it turned out Green benched Maddox for all three games against the Giants and two of the four that followed in Los Angeles.

In the second game at San Francisco, Green planned to play Garry in the middle innings but the outfielder was in the clubhouse, located near right-field at Candlestick Park. An inning later he walked back to the dugout with a cup of coffee in his hand.

"When the press approached me I didn't say anything negative or anything like that," said Maddox. "I said, 'Yes, I would like to be playing but if Dallas chooses not to play me, I respect his decision.'"

But what about the incident where you were not in the dugout when he needed you?

"Well, I went to the clubhouse because it was so cold on the bench. You know how cold it is in San Francisco. I went in first to use the restroom and while I was there I got a cup of coffee, all with permission. I told the coach (Lee Elia) where I was going. Everybody does that. But I guess when Dallas was looking for me, Lee wasn't around. It wasn't until we got to Los Angeles one of my teammates told me how he blew up. I confronted him with that and told him I had permission. I found out Lee also had told Dallas I had permission, so that was smoothed over."

Maddox had his sunglasses on, but not flipped down, late that Sunday afternoon on national television against Montreal when he missed Speier's ball. He insists he could not have caught it had they been down. At that point things between player and manager went from bad to worse.

Green again was critical of him after the game and then benched him along with Bob Boone and Greg Luzinski on Monday and Tuesday nights against Chicago.

About Speier's ball: "It was a line drive," explained Maddox. "There was no time to flip the sunglasses down and, at the same time, use every ounce of speed you have to get to the ball. You can't afford to lose anything by trying to flip the glasses down.

"When the game ended the press came to me and I went over the situation. They then went to Dallas and he made some comments that I could see better in the sun with sun-glasses—something like that. First off, I don't think he was qualified to make comments like that because he's not an out-fielder and he doesn't know what's involved. I think he should have discussed the play with me first. Then if he's got a com-ment, fine. But instead, I talked to the reporters and they went to him. And I don't think even reporters could write it accurately because they don't know actually what's involved. I don't think he was fair to me. Why didn't he get my side first?

"Now, the next day I get benched for this and he hasn't discussed the situation with me. That was completely wrong.

"Also in that Sunday game there was a ball hit behind shortstop. I came in at full-speed, caught the ball, made a run-ning throw and fell. I thought it was a big play, but when I flipped I landed on the finger I had hurt in Pittsburgh on Sep-tember 17. I told the trainer about it then, but I continued to play until I was benched on Monday. I had the finger X-rayed on Tuesday and when I got to the park on Wednesday, I was back in the line-up. I told Bobby Wine I didn't think I could swing the bat and help the team offensively, but could play defense. He told Dallas. This was late in the afternoon. When I went down to the dugout, my name had been scratched out and Del Unser's written in. Without consulting me or finding anything out. . . . I think Dallas thought I was using my fin-ger as an excuse because I had been benched for two games."

Maddox said the same thing happened following the Pitts-burgh series when he originally was injured, but that after tell-ing Green, he still played.

"Given the circumstances, Dallas Green obviously did not want me in the line-up," said Maddox. "The whole thing could have been kept quiet, but when he scratched out my name people knew I was originally in the starting line-up and a lot of questions arose. I think he should have filled out the line-up card a second time and no one would have been the wiser. To be honest, I think he did it his way intentionally. There was plenty of time to do a second card.

"Then, Dallas was in his office giving an interview to a reporter, saying how I was originally in the line-up and that this finger thing came up all of a sudden and he didn't know anything about it. That's when people started to assume it was a mystery injury. From that point on, he didn't try to put me in the line-up until the playoffs."

As the World Series clubhouse celebration began to run out of champagne, Garry Maddox sought Dallas Green out in the players' lounge.

"We had a good conversation," said Maddox. "We shook hands, had our arms around each other and everything like that. I thought we had everything smoothed out.

"But during the winter meetings in Dallas, he told reporters he was going after (Sixto) Lezcano and one of the reasons he gave was 'in case my center fielder goes South again.' He may have felt he needed Lezcano for whatever reason, but I didn't think he had to bring me into it, especially in a negative tone.

"You just have to deal with things like that. I have to build up a shell against what he is going to be doing. I just hope I can continue to keep my enthusiasm about playing baseball. I want to play, but he's the manager and I have to adjust to whatever system he wants."

Maddox thinks Green did a good job handling the pitching staff in 1980 and gives him a lot of credit for being bold enough to blend talented youngsters in with the veterans.

"He also made some good strategic decisions," said Maddox. "I really can't argue about that. I do question his dealings with the press. I think his communications could have been better with the players. It was difficult for some of us to read negative things, quotes attributed to Dallas Green, before he even mentioned the problem to us."

If Garry Maddox comes across as being bitter, that is not the case.

"Our main goal—my main goal—was to win the world championship, especially after I signed the new contract," he said. "I wanted to have good stats. I wanted to be a world champion. We reached that goal, but I didn't contribute as much as I should have. I was fortunate enough to get some key hits and that saved me a little bit. But I wanted to be one of the guys when we won it. I wanted to be one of the guys who got us there and contributed all year.

"It didn't work out for me that way and I had to deal with it. I wanted it so that when everything was written it said Garry Maddox did his part. From that standpoint I am disappointed, but I'm happy we won and I'm thankful for the key hits I got and that I was able to catch the last ball in Houston and get the game-winning hit in that game. That helped a lot."

Garry Lee Maddox is one of the least selfish, one of the most family-devoted, community-minded professional athletes in the Delaware Valley. He spends hundreds of hours each year raising money for the Philadelphia Child Guidance Clinic. This past year alone his celebrity bowling tournament raised over $35,000.

"But it's not the raising of the money that gives me the most satisfaction," he said, his eyes bright. "When you watch those children, when you see how happy they are when you visit them, that's what gives me a great feeling inside."

While many of his teammates spend the off-season hunting and jetting off to exotic vacation spots, Maddox stays home.

"It's difficult on Sondra (his wife) and the two boys when I'm away so much during the season," he said. "I try to spend as much time as I can during the winter with them because to me that's the best way a ball player can spend the off-season. I have to give my family something and being with them is the best thing I can think of."

Lonnie Smith (27) and Pete Rose greet Manny Trillo
after the second baseman delivered a key hit in a
playoff game against Houston. Trillo was the MVP in
the National League Championship Series.

Manny Trillo
". . . is the best second baseman in baseball."

It had been a long day for most of the Phillies, especially
Manny Trillo. The toughest thing was the wait.

After shocking Houston 5–3 in 10 innings in the mind-
boggling fiasco on Saturday afternoon, October 11, the Phillies
had to wait until Sunday night to play the game that would
bring them their first National League pennant in 30 years.

Maria and Manny Trillo watched television in their Sham-
rock Hilton room for a few hours, then went down to the coffee shop for brunch.

Manny sipped coffee and looked out across the huge
swimming pool where several members of the team were passing time away.

"I think I'm going to win the Most Valuable Player Award
(for the playoffs) tonight," Manny told his wife in Spanish. "I
really feel it."

Hours later, as the Phillies were drenching each other
with champagne following their 8–7, 10-inning triumph, Maria
reminded friends of Manny's prediction.

"He's usually not that out-spoken about something as important," she said. "But he was sitting there and told me all of
a sudden he was going to be MVP. I said, 'Why not? After all,

Kansas City's second baseman, Frank White, was MVP in the American League playoffs?' "

Trillo, who batted .292 during the regular season and committed only 11 errors at second base, had a brilliant five-game championship series. He was spectacular afield—no one will ever forget his relay to the plate in the second inning of the deciding game that cut down Luis Pujols.

On offense, Manny hit .381 with four runs batted in. In the five games he lashed out eight hits, including his clutch, two-run triple in the eighth inning of the deciding game when the Phils scored five runs.

The wives, who flew to Houston at their own expense for the Astrodome portion of the playoffs, crashed their husbands' victory party. By the time Maria reached Manny, he was already clutching the sterling silver MVP trophy. In fact, he still had a firm grip on it when the Phillies deplaned at Philadelphia International Airport the following afternoon.

"I'm so happy. I'm so happy," Manny Trillo kept saying in broken English. "I cannot tell you how I feel. That triple made me very, very happy because it meant so much to my team. I just wanted to get a hit in that situation. It was so important. It was very important."

For Dallas Green and Paul Owens, watching Manny Trillo perform as he did in the playoffs, not to mention the season which preceded them, provided them with enormous satisfaction. Especially Dallas Green.

Many times during the championship year, Green thought back to the summer of 1968.

Manny Trillo was 17 and so skinny he had to worry about heavy winds.

When he strapped on catcher's gear, he disappeared. All you could see was a little head sticking out of the armor.

Green took one look at Manny, the catcher, and shook his head. Then he called Paul Owens.

"Pope," Green remembers saying. "This kid is just too

small to be a catcher. I'm going to try him at third base because he has good moves and a great arm."

Green, his major-league pitching career over, was in South Dakota managing Huron in the Northern League. Among the prospects sent him that year by Phillies' Farm Director Owens were Greg Luzinski, a first baseman, and Jesus Manuel Trillo, the skinny catcher from Venezuela.

At Green's suggestion, Trillo shifted to third base and after the 1969 season at Spartanburg was drafted by Oakland during the winter baseball meetings. In October of 1974 he was traded to the Cubs where he was to become one of the best second basemen in the business. On February 23, 1979 the Cubs dealt him back to the Phillies.

"I might not have ever made the major leagues if Dallas Green had not moved me to the infield," said Trillo. "I don't think I would have made it as a catcher."

"I knew he wasn't going to be able to stand the beating that an everyday catcher has to stand," said Green. "With his actions and abilities, I just felt it would be better to move him. He had good running speed and that great arm.

"I played him mostly at third base and a little at shortstop. It was not until he was with the Oakland organization he started playing second."

As an infielder, Trillo was a real prospect but just to back up his memory, Green checked his reports when Manny came back to his original team.

"We liked him, but were unable to protect everyone from the draft," said the manager. "I think we lost him that winter (1969) because a numbers problem developed."

"I was 6-foot-1, 130 pounds," said Trillo, who now weighs 164. "Can you imagine Dave Parker hitting me at home plate then?"

Trillo, who turned 30 on Christmas Day 1980, managed to get in one playoff game when he was with Oakland. He was a pinch runner and scored against the Orioles in 1974. He almost got in the World Series the year before as a pawn in one of Charlie Finley's more controversial moves. In a highly publicized incident Finley unsuccessfully tried to put Trillo on his roster in mid-World Series to replace his least-favorite second baseman, Mike Andrews.

Trillo dreamed of returning to the Phillies, especially during those long, hot summers with the Cubs.

"And I wanted him back, too," said Green. "Everytime he came to Veterans Stadium, it seemed like he killed us. I kept telling the Pope we ought to try and get him back."

"I've known Paul Owens since I was 16," said Trillo. "Philadelphia was always my favorite organization. The only difficult thing for me coming back was adjusting to the artificial surface. At Wrigley Field and in Oakland, I played on real grass.

"I prefer grass because that is what I have played on since I was a little boy in Venezuela. Some guys say that on AstroTurf you always get a true bounce. I don't know. I do think you can make the double-play more easily on AstroTurf."

With the Cubs, it was not unusual for Trillo to start his season as one of the National League's leading hitters, with an average well over .300. Later in the season, he would fall back.

"All those day games in Wrigley Field (the park has no lights) kill you," said Trillo. "It would get so hot. You couldn't help but get tired playing all the time in that heat. I think that is why I wilted. The season is long and when you have to play in that heat so much. There is no chance to get a break."

Phillies' fans love to watch Trillo field a ground ball, cock his gun and then hesitate a few seconds before throwing to first.

"When I played third base, I used to throw the ball in the stands a lot," he explained. "A pitcher once told me that if I gripped the ball like a pitcher before I threw, I would be more accurate. That is why I get hold of the ball the way I do. It doesn't sail."

In the spring of 1979 a Philadelphia attorney flew to Clearwater, intent on representing Trillo in contract negotiations with the Phillies. After several meetings with Mr. and Mrs. Trillo, the lawyer returned to Philadelphia. Maria Trillo took over the negotiations and in July of that year, an agreement through 1983 was reached, calling for an estimated $400,000 per.

Shortly before the contract was signed, the Daily News' Stan Hochman interviewed Maria Trillo. It was an interesting column.

"When Manny Trillo finally signs his new multi-year big-bucks contract with the Phillies," Hochman wrote, "he's going to take his agent out to dinner.

"Then he's going to take his agent home, get in bed with his agent, kiss his agent good-night, maybe lean across his agent to set the alarm for noon.

" 'Manny Trillo likes to sleep,' his agent reported last night."

Manny Trillo's agent, of course, was his wife.

"I know what everybody else is making," Maria Trillo told Hochman. "But that is not important. I only want what is best for Manny. I feel, I'm not sure I should say this but I will, Manny is the best second baseman in baseball, and that's not just because I am his wife.

"My father owned a baseball team in Maracaibo. So, I felt I knew a whole bunch about baseball. Each year my family took a shopping trip to Miami.

"I met Manny on the plane. We talked, we dated, we got married. Manny was in Triple-A then, in the Oakland organization. Always he was up, then down.

"At first, my father was not pleased. In Venezuela, my family is from high, high society. And baseball players, well . . . but now, everything is fine, everyone is happy.

"It was always my dream for Manny to play with the Phillies. He started in their organization. The best way to show how good a player you are is to play with a good team.

"The Phillies, they are always at the top. The Cubs, they were always near the bottom."

Needless to say, Manny Trillo has a good agent and she doesn't even get a fee for handling the negotiations.

"Are you kidding?" Trillo smiled after the World Series. "She gets it all!"

Obviously, coming to the Phillies was the best thing that ever happened to Trillo. Playing in an infield with Larry Bowa, Pete Rose and Mike Schmidt, Trillo has finally gotten the recognition he deserves.

For the most part during 1980, Trillo was happy to play for Dallas Green.

"I really didn't get to know Danny Ozark that well," said Trillo. "He was kind to everyone and I think the players liked him. I knew Dallas before and more or less knew what to expect."

Trillo, however, was more than a little upset when his close friend Nino Espinosa was sidelined with a sore arm and Green told reporters the pitcher should learn to pitch with pain.

"Sometimes, I think he talked too quickly to reporters," said Manny. "I know Nino was very upset. And, I know he had pain in his shoulder. The manager should talk to the player before he talks to the press.

"If we had a problem with Dallas, it was the fact he did not always communicate with the players. I know Bake Mc-Bride had a problem with that, and Garry Maddox had one too. It's just something Dallas should think about in the future."

Trillo thinks the Phils' ability to win close games, especially the last month of the season eventually made the difference.

"Pete Rose talked about this a lot," said Trillo. "What did he call it, race-horse baseball? That's good. This team finally learned that even when it was behind, it had the ability to come back and win games. Just look at the record. We won close games at the end.

"And along the way we really got confidence. I know I had confidence that I could get a hit when it was needed. That is what it takes to be a champion.

"And the Philadelphia Phillies are world champions. I've never been so happy."

Hail the champions. Larry Bowa (left) and Mike Schmidt wave to adoring fans during ticker-tape parade down Broad Street the day after the Phillies won their first World Championship.

Larry Bowa
"The only thing I can't do is hit home runs. . . ."

Willie Wilson struck out and it was over. Larry Bowa stood there for a moment, undecided.

"My first thought was to get down on one knee and thank The Man Upstairs," he said later, his hand gripping a champagne bottle. "Then everything seemed to flash in front of me at once. I thought about the Sundays in the park when my dad hit ground balls to me. I thought about being cut from my high-school team three times. I thought about the writer who said I swung like a Little Leaguer. And I thought about all the terrible stories that had been written about me this year."

That's what went through Larry Bowa's mind in the first few minutes of a world championship he will savor for a lifetime.

This may be unfair, but I think the Phillies' championship means more to the high-strung, highly competitive Larry Bowa than it does any other player on the team. Bowa, you see, had been dreaming about it 24 hours a day since he was old enough to swing a bat. Baseball *is* Larry Bowa's life. Just ask his wife, Sheena, or his father, Paul.

Larry Bowa is the first to tell you much of 1980 was agony for him. At one stage he was hitting only .229 and was struggling in the field. When the Phils dropped a double-header at

Pittsburgh on August 10 to fall six games behind the Pirates and Expos, he said the season was history.

He was, of course, wrong.

Soon after, the Phils, and especially Bowa, turned it around. They surged to their fourth National League East title in five years, shocked Houston in the playoffs and snuffed Kansas City in the World Series. Larry Bowa was brilliant.

When his manager, Dallas Green, openly criticized him he played even harder. When the player personnel director, Paul Owens, singled him out during a clubhouse tongue-lashing he responded with greater determination. And when the Veterans Stadium fans booed him he saluted them, then turned around and helped bring a world championship to their city.

In the World Series Bowa was superb. He set a record at shortstop, starting seven double-plays. At bat he hit safely in every game and led his team with a total of nine hits for a .375 average. In the bizarre playoffs he hit .316, walked three times and scored two runs.

"I can play this game, there's no doubt about it," he bubbled an hour after the final World Series out. "I was horsebleep the first four months. Everybody's entitled to that. There were some reasons. One was those drug stories. And there were a lot of other things, too.

"But when the fans boo, they don't boo me as an individual. They boo No. 10 who's hitting .229. I walk down the street and nobody boos me, but they see this number on the field and they boo.

"The night of the Chicago game in September, I thought the fans were the worst I had ever played before and I said so. But that's 20,000 people, not 2.7 million. That night, they were lousy. I just can't understand why they have to boo when you're in the middle of a pennant race. Think people are trying to make outs? Think people are trying to make errors? Like the Eagles. I remember watching them play the Chicago

Bears. The Eagles played poorly in the first half and the fans booed them.

"Let me tell you something about the sports writers. They all told us we can't win. We weren't supposed to beat Montreal; we weren't supposed to beat Houston. We weren't supposed to beat Kansas City. But look who's world champion!"

As words flowed from Bowa like champagne from the bottles in the clubhouse, his dad sat quietly behind his son at Larry's locker.

Paul Bowa used to play and manage in the St. Louis Cardinals' system and even though he knew his son lacked great ability, he encouraged him to keep trying harder and harder and that someday he would make it to the majors.

"I know I have made my father happy," said Larry. "There were times when I wanted to quit when I was a kid, but he wouldn't let me. Eventually, even though I was cut three times from my high-school team, I began to get my act together. This championship is as much for him as it is for me."

"I helped him a lot," Paul Bowa said later. "But I wasn't the type of father who *made* him play ball. I wanted him to play, but I didn't make him play. When I'd come home from work, he'd be waiting for me. I'd have to pitch him batting practice, hit him ground balls. Just the two of us. I'd have about 25 or 30 balls. He'd hit 'em, then we'd go out and pick them up. Then hit again.

"I wasn't the type of father who made him work. A lot of the guys made their kids get paper routes. I knew he wanted to play ball, so I wanted to give him every opportunity in the world. And he appreciated it."

"Larry had natural baseball instinct. In Little League he used to cut off balls or cut off guys trying to go from first to second if he knew a guy wasn't going to get out of the hole. He had that instinct right away.

"When he went to Sacramento City College, I had a

hunch he was going to make it. He was small and he had disadvantages, but he made it."

"Don't tell me I can't do something," said Larry. "That gets me ticked off. The only thing I can't do is hit home runs. I can steal bases for you, I can field for you, I can hit for you when you want some hits. I ain't a .300 hitter, I'm the first to admit that, but I did hit .300 (.305, 1975). I got close to 2,000 hits (1,696) and they told me I wouldn't even get 200 at-bats in the major leagues. They said I should be playing at Williamsport, Pennsylvania. All the stuff that had been written about our baseball team, how we couldn't win, hit me all at once when Tug struck out Willie Wilson and we were world champions.

"This World Series was very important to me because I might not ever get in another. I wanted to take full advantage of it. Pete Rose told me if we got through the playoffs, the World Series would be fun. That Houston series was tough; if I didn't get an ulcer in that, I never will. I never felt so much pressure in my life as I did down there. It was terrible."

"He really began to show pressure today," his dad interrupted that night. "He barbecued some chicken for lunch and hardly even said a word. The chicken was good, though."

"Today was the worst for me in the World Series," said Larry. "When I got up I didn't want to talk to anyone. My dad kept trying to carry a conversation and I didn't answer him. I didn't want to be around anyone. I was very nervous, but I kept trying to convince myself this was the seventh game, that there was no tomorrow. I wanted to go out onto the field thinking we were even with Kansas City at three games apiece.

"When I get that (World Series) ring on opening day in 1981, I'm going to look down at it everyday. I will think back to this moment and there is going to be a great, great feeling. And it is going to last a long, long time."

The fact Bowa was able to turn his season around as

swiftly and as convincingly as he did was typical of the entire team.

In the sixth inning of an important game with the Dodgers in August, Bowa took a half step to his right to scoop up Steve Yeager's hard, spinning grounder. Easy play for the Gold Glove shortstop. Bowa, however, fumbled the ball and Yeager was safe on the error.

An inning later Jay Johnstone hit a ball towards the hole between second and third. Bowa, who was breaking for second with a runner on first, tried to recover, darted to his right, but could not make the play. The official scorer, who a day later changed Yeager's ball to a hit, also gave Johnstone a hit on this one. Both were tough plays, but Larry Bowa has made them a thousand times.

Two nights before, Bowa was late covering second base for an easy force and Manny Trillo, startled by the shortstop's unexpected absence, unleashed a wild throw to first in a last-ditch attempt to nab the runner.

What had happened to Larry Bowa? The fiery, gutsy shortstop had had a raging love affair with Philadelphia fans for years but as he fell into one defensive lapse after another, they turned on him.

In 1979 Bowa made just six errors, none at Veterans Stadium. When 1980 ended he had 17 after 691 total chances. Most of them came before he got his act together in August.

On the surface, Bowa's problems started in spring training when he complained about his salary. He insisted certain shortstops in the National League who didn't have his credentials were making more than his estimated $325,000. He didn't like that one bit. Later he said he was out of place to rip Ruly Carpenter, and apologized.

Then, on the morning of the All-Star Game in Los Angeles, Larry and Sheena were mentioned in the drug story reported by the Trenton Times.

After that and until the playoffs, Bowa refused to talk to

the press. In the clubhouse, he became withdrawn. He seldom got involved in the normal loud chatter with his teammates and toned down the wisecracks that are a Larry Bowa trademark.

"I think Larry Bowa has an awful lot on his mind," Green said. "I'm not sure it's all baseball. His off-the-field problems have affected his thinking and his play. We'd like to say we can overcome those things and play our game, but some guys can do it and some guys apparently can't."

Other than his bitterness over the drug stories, no one was sure just what was pulling Bowa down most of the year.

"There's a knack to shutting out personal problems and not letting them affect what's happening on the field," added Green. "There's also a knack to shutting out the individual problems we have on the field. You've got to do what you can do best at all times and hope, with time and patience, the other things will come."

Sheena Bowa tried to shed some light on Larry's early 1980 problems.

She is from Clearwater and they met when he was in the minors. They were married in 1970 and when they went to Hawaii for their honeymoon, Sheena spent much of the time poolside alone while Larry was in his room watching the World Series on television.

During the off-season following 1979, Larry was apparently down on his career, worried about his age and his future. Sheena was spending time away from home working on a master's degree.

"We reached a point where I was either going to pack up and leave or he was going to listen to me," Sheena said. "I was screaming because he didn't want me to go to school.

"I'd never considered him a 'baseball player.' I had this image of a 'ballplayer' as one of those macho men who have to live up to that image when in the company of teammates.

Then he goes home to his wife who is ready to wait on him hand and foot.

"Last winter I felt he was trying to be one of them. I wasn't being given any consideration. He felt he had a terrible year in 1979.

"He was so up-tight all the time. I think it was because he is a young man (now 35) and doesn't like the idea of retiring. Baseball is in his blood and he never wants to take the uniform off.

"But instead of turning to me, he turned away from me. We tried to talk about it. I told him there were all kinds of possibilities, like broadcasting. He loves his radio show on WWDB.

"In January I decided he had to do this for himself, so I went home to Florida to give him some time."

"Everything's fine with Sheena and me now," Bowa told me as spring training 1980 started. "We've worked it out."

A day later, he started complaining to reporters about his salary.

"The first four months I had no concentration whatsoever," Bowa said. "No matter what I did, it was wrong. I'd stay back on balls and they would play me. Then, I would charge a ball and I should have stayed back. I was just confused. No excuses. I wasn't playing well and I said that all along. I wasn't worth a damn the first half of the season. I really don't know why, except I wasn't mentally prepared to play offensively or defensively.

"The thing that really bothered me was my defense. In the past I was always able to separate offense and defense. I've had problems at the plate before, but have always made up for it on defense. This time, my defense went to hell."

The marital problem, the salary episode, the strike saga and the drug stories all contributed.

Then, there was Dallas Green.

The background to the stormy relationship between Bowa and Green was cast in 1972.

Dallas had just become minor-league director and had a shortstop in his system named Craig Robinson. Bowa was in his third full season with the Phillies, but Green said he felt Robinson was a better shortstop. Bowa seethed at the remarks and has never forgotten.

"It really wasn't a falling out then," said Bowa, "but he made known his feelings to me. He was one of the guys who wanted Craig Robinson to play shortstop. It was Dallas' opinion. He was the minor-league director and you have to respect his feelings there because I am sure if I were the minor-league director and had a kid I thought could play over the guy in the big leagues, I would push him also.

"It just hurt me that our minor-league director didn't feel the Number One shortstop should be playing. It seems like every year I've had to beat somebody out of the job. I've run four or five out of here and they were all pretty good players. But, I don't hold anything against them. It's just I couldn't believe it would be so cut-and-dried he would think that ball player would be that much better than me. It was just a matter of him being on somebody else's side.

"Like Frank Lucchesi (Bowa's first manager). If it hadn't been for Frank, I probably wouldn't be in the big leagues right now. There is a guy who stuck by me and gave me every opportunity to prove myself in the big leagues. I appreciate what he did for me. He knows how I feel. Again, I look at it this way: Frank liked me as a player the same way Dallas liked Craig Robinson. But it still doesn't alter my feelings that Dallas thought Craig Robinson should be playing over me."

Bowa's feud with Green simmered all last season and is still smoldering.

"Winning the World Series is the ultimate for a professional baseball player," Bowa said. "Ours was maybe tarnished a little by the controversy and the problems we had with Dallas. But the fact remains, we did win and overcame a lot of adversity to do it.

"I think anytime you have a new manager he is going to test you, and the veteran players are going to test him. I would say that the majority of the time we were testing each other to see if Dallas was going to give in, or whether the players were going to give in. It was more like a cat-and-mouse game and then, finally, Dallas gave a little bit and the players gave a little bit and before we knew it, we started to play like we were capable of playing. As we look back it would have been nice to have played the whole year like that, but this team has never done anything easily."

In the beginning Bowa thinks he enrolled in Dallas Green's crash course on building character.

"The very first meeting we had with him, his opening statement was, 'We don't want to get into any shouting matches through the newspapers.' I said to myself, 'Hey, Dallas means what he says.' Then, he got into that 'We, Not I' stuff and it might have been college rah-rah stuff, but it meant something at the time. But when things started going poorly, when guys weren't playing up to their potential, it wasn't 'We,' it was 'I don't know what's wrong with those guys, they don't want to win.' You read some things in the papers about so-and-so not putting out for him. I thought the atmosphere was supposed to be if we had something on our minds, we could just go into his office. If it meant screaming and hollering and maybe somebody being benched, that's the way it was going to be. But it didn't turn out like that at all. I think that was the biggest drawback all year.

"The guys kept reading about their mistakes in the newspapers. Dallas did a helluva job managing with the exception of that part of his strategy, going to certain papers and disclosing the faults of individuals as opposed to calling them in and saying, 'Look, I don't think you are playing the way you are capable of playing. Let's go out and bust a little harder.' I think he would have gotten more out of his athletes that way and I don't think there would have been as much hard feelings during the year."

But to Bowa, Green was needed.

"The difference," he said, "was Dallas' discipline during the whole year. Not just Monday and Tuesday, but Monday, Tuesday, Wednesday, Thursday, Friday, Saturday and Sunday.

"That had a lot to do with the team not quitting. We needed a guy to come in when we were watching a football game and say, 'You're watching a stupid-assed football game and missing batting practice?'

"I don't think it's fair to say the whole team needed discipline, but you would think veteran players knew when to turn off the television set. There were times when some would start the game without having touched a baseball."

Bowa praised Green the night of the World Series celebration.

"I thought he had learned some things," said Larry. "Now, I don't know if he has. That's my judgment. I know he didn't say anything derogatory about me during the off-season, but I can't believe some of the remarks he made about Greg Luzinski and Randy Lerch. Again, he is the manager and if he thinks that is the way to motivate his players, then he is going to continue to do it.

"I just have a feeling if he is going to get a Greg Luzinski or a Randy Lerch—if they are still with us—to perform the way they are supposed to perform, he is going about it the wrong way.

"It upsets me more than anything else to see him take a shot at somebody that has been in this organization from the beginning. I probably get more hurt when I see something written about Greg because I know how much a part of this organization he has been and it seems like people are forgetting. They are forgetting that the three years we won the division title if it had not been for Greg Luzinski we would not have won.

"Or even last year, as bad a year as the Bull had, he got a big hit against Montreal and he got some big hits against Houston. People have a tendency to forget and it makes me mad because of the fact Greg has been here as long as anybody and I think there should be some loyalty there. Sure, he's had a couple of bad years, but the man's not trying to have bad years. The best way to straighten him out, I think, would be to take a positive approach, especially if you are going to have him on your team. If you are going to trade him, trade him. But don't talk about him and then not trade him, because mentally he is not ready to play. I think these little things all affect our team because we all came up together through the system.

"I really think part of Dallas' philosophy was to get everybody to direct all their anger towards him as opposed to one another but unless I am naive or blind, I didn't think there was anger between players on the team. Dallas said the regulars hated the pitchers, the pitchers hated the regulars, the regulars hated the relievers, the relievers hated the starters. I didn't see any of that. Sure there's bickering because we live together from February until October. It's just that in Philadelphia everything is magnified in the press, three or four times larger than it actually was."

Had it not been for Ruly Carpenter, Bowa probably would not have turned his season around.

Green obviously was not getting through to the shortstop.

"I've known Bowa for a long time," said Ruly. "I don't like to interfere with my field men, but I told Dallas I was going to have a talk with Larry."

"Ruly has been more to me than an owner," said Bowa. "He's been a close friend. He has invited me to call him, to talk to him, when things go wrong. He even gave me his home phone number. It has been a dual relationship—I've gone to him and he's come to me. I've been on road trips when we were playing poorly and he'd call me at 8 o'clock in the morning and say, 'What's wrong with you guys? What do you think is the problem?' I would talk about it and say, 'Well, why don't you talk to so-and-so and get him going.' That's been our relationship since I signed. I respect Ruly Carpenter more than anybody I've ever met in baseball.

"So, when he called me up to his office in September, I listened. Things were really going poorly for me at the time; I've never gone through defensive lapses like I was going through. I was getting criticism from all sides—my dad, Dallas Green, Billy DeMars, other players. Ruly said, 'Damn it, the player I'm seeing out there is not Larry Bowa! It doesn't look to me like you're ready to play.' I agreed with him. We then discussed everything. He said if things were really bothering me mentally, I shouldn't be playing. I said, 'No, they weren't that bad. I am just having trouble keeping my total concentration on what I am supposed to be doing.' We talked for two or three hours. Then, we went on a road trip and he called me the first three or four days. Of course, I don't know, maybe it was just the way things turned out, but after that everything started going well for me. Another time he called and said, 'Hey, you look great out there; your attitude seems to be fine.'

"After the World Series, he was the first guy to come to me and tell me how proud he was the way I responded and played. Then, he gave me my biggest boost of the season, 'You know,' he said, 'I don't see any reason why you can't do this for another three or four years for me.' You'll never know how good that made me feel."

Bowa says it was about the same time as his chat with Ruly that Pete Rose made some informal remarks which struck home.

"Luzinski, Schmidt, Boone, Maddox and I were sitting around before a game one day, just rapping," said Bowa. "Pete got serious. He said, 'You guys don't play for Dallas

Green and you don't play for Ruly Carpenter, you play for yourselves. And if you don't have enough pride in what you are doing out there, you'll never win.' I think somebody then said, 'Oh, I can't play for this guy (Green). He's bad.' Then, Pete said, 'You're not playing for him—you're playing for yourself!' It made a lot of sense and I think at that time a lot of guys decided he was right. It was like somebody hit a button."

Earlier, Paul Owens had embarrassed Bowa during a clubhouse lecture in San Francisco when he singled out the shortstop and center fielder Garry Maddox for not playing well.

"I don't think he embarrassed me," argued Bowa. "What he did was make me mad. He is the general manager and if he wants to reprimand players that is his prerogative, but to single me and Garry out as the reasons we weren't winning, I think, was wrong. We were part of the reason, but I don't think it was the total reason. I know why he singled me out; I don't know why he singled Garry out. He jumped on me because regardless of how hard he screams at me I am going to go out there and play hard. I am not going to quit on him and maybe he just wanted to ignite a little flame. I know if you ask him today he feels that more or less turned me around. I don't agree with that, but if the Pope feels that way then it is all right with me."

Bowa seemed to be on a non-stop analysis of the season.

"In the end we realized that no matter how the personalities on the team conflicted with each other, we still had one goal and that was to win the world championship. If we hated five guys on the team or if we hated the manager or hated a coach, we put all that behind. And now we can sit back and say, 'Hey, we're the best!' "

From Boone to Rose. One of the most talked-about plays came in the ninth inning of the sixth game when Frank White's foul pop bounced out of catcher Bob Boone's mitt into Pete Rose's waiting glove. It was the second out of the tense inning.

Bob Boone
"Perfect practice makes perfect. . . ."

The cold, biting wind made the chill factor in South Philadelphia 15 degrees below zero. It was the kind of weather that keeps the U. S. male at home, especially at 5 o'clock in the morning.

But several mornings each week Bob Boone would climb out of his warm bed a few minutes after 4 A.M. and drive to Veterans Stadium so he could torture his body. Then, after meeting sleepy-eyed trainers Don Seger and Jeff Cooper, he would pull on a sweatshirt and jog across Pattison Avenue so he could run up and down the steps of JFK Stadium for an hour.

That is where Bob Boone's 1980 world championship season was born.

It ended with the bright, alert catcher ripping key hit after key hit in the playoffs and World Series. His .412 average led all Phillies in the tournament against Kansas City.

In between, the season was stormy and frustrating for the Stanford grad. He struggled with a woeful .229 average. A Gold Glover in 1979 who made only seven errors, Boone was charged with 17 in 1980. He found himself wondering each day whether or not Manager Dallas Green would see fit to play him.

For Robert Raymond Boone it was all part of the road back.

Boone was injured in a controversial, third-out home-plate collision with the Mets' Joel Youngblood on September 13, 1979. Four days later ligament surgery was performed on his left knee. The cast was removed on November 1 and rehabilitation started immediately.

"I was determined to be ready by the start of spring training last year," he said. "A lot of people didn't think I would be able to do it within a period of five months. Quite frankly, I was amazed too. It is something that really doesn't happen that quickly."

Boone, who had made the All-Star team for the third time, was hitting .286 with nine homers and 58 runs batted in when Youngblood ended his best season in the majors.

The left knee was already hurting when the Mets' outfielder tore into Boone on what turned out to be a game-ending play that gave the Phillies a 2–1 victory. The Mets yelled that Boone didn't hold onto the ball after he tagged Youngblood, but the umpires didn't agree as the catcher, grimacing in pain, tried to get up.

"I was set in a good position and had time," Boone remembered. "When the ball took its second hop, it bounced up on me a little bit and I had to rock back in order to catch it cleanly. So, I was off-balance. I got my knee caught between Youngblood's body and mine. It takes only 30 pounds of pressure to blow out a ligament like that.

"Mine didn't actually tear. It pulled away from the tibia and there was some capsulum damage, but I didn't have the problem of a ligament, which had been spliced back together, having to regenerate. That's what (the Eagles') Bill Bergey went through."

It took Boone an average of eight hours a day to build the knee back up and improve its range of motion. When the cast came off the range was 10 degrees—132 degrees less than normal. In addition, he had lost 2½ inches off his thigh and the muscle tone was gone.

"After working at the stadium I would go to the YMCA and run underwater for 30 minutes," Boone said. "People thought I was crazy but that helped strengthen my knee. It was the toughest injury I have ever had to come back from. I'm sure the fact I was in such good shape when it happened really helped speed my recovery.

"I've worked with Gus Hoefling (strength and flexibility) expert since he came here (in 1977) and I know had it not been for that program, I probably would have missed much of 1980. My leg was exceptionally strong prior to the injury and that helped."

It was not until the third game of the 1976 National League playoffs Boone realized how important strength can be in baseball, a "game of inches."

"I hit a ball up against the fence in Cincinnati and George Foster jumped up and caught it," said Boone. "I didn't hit it really well, but if I had been a hair stronger it would have gone out and I think we would have won the game."

Hoefling arrived soon after that and Boone and Carlton became his most devoted disciples.

"Conditioning has made me feel better and made me a better ball player," Boone says. "From a conditioning standpoint you can work at your skill longer without fatigue when you are in shape. Once you break down as far as fatigue is concerned, you might as well quit. Perfect practice makes perfect—not just practice. Once you're fatigued you are doing it differently and not gaining a thing.

"My skill levels are only average but I think when you have some tools to start with, you can build. That has always been my philosophy."

When Bob started Hoefling's program he could lift only 50 pounds with both legs. Three years later he could lift 270 pounds with both legs.

"Most people can't handle Gus' program because it hurts too much," said Boone. "You reach a certain point where the hurt is pretty good and most people stop there. When you can push past that, it does something for you mentally."

But all of this seemed to fall apart in 1980.

Some say the reason was because Boone is the National League player representative and was deeply involved in Major League Players Association negotiations with owners over a new basic agreement. The strike-threatened days of April and May took their toll and obviously weighed heavily on the psychology major.

"The negotiations didn't bother me that much," he argues. "I really feel my problems traced back to the rehabilitation of my knee; I didn't have time to get in the flow of playing. I felt I was two weeks behind everybody all the time. I couldn't quite get over the hump."

Thirty minutes before every game Boone went through a torturous ordeal just so he could squat behind home plate like a normal catcher.

"After infield practice I'd go into our exercise room and for 10 minutes do nothing but force my legs into a squat," he explained. "It hurt; I mean it really hurt. It wasn't so much the physical trauma as it was the mental thought each day. I'd be walking up the tunnel from the dugout thinking, 'Oh, geez,' I have to do this with my leg again. I've got 150 exercises to do just so I can catch the game?"

Boone just did not have the balance and leverage necessary for accurate throws on that surgically scarred left leg.

"I was concerned and got angry with myself, but I wasn't about to make excuses," he said. "A catcher knows whether he has a shot at throwing out a base-stealer or not. My problem a lot of the time was I'd see the guy had the base stolen and I'd try to be a little faster. That's what puts the ball in the dirt. And before you realize it, you're rushing when you have a shot. I know that happened to me last year because I was so aware of the knee."

Boone was not only nagged by the media, but also his teammates during spring training for information on the negotiations with owners.

"Sure it was on my mind, but if I had had my baseball stuff together, I could have done that and handled them both very easily. I guess it was just a nice, convenient excuse for not doing well. I will say the constant question-and-answer sessions took away from my concentration in spring training. I felt like I was able to shut if off once the games started.

"The problem was that in trying to work and do things and then explain the players' position with the negotiations, I kept getting behind in my preparation for the season. Normally in spring training, I spend some time in the batting cage, then step out and try to concentrate on what I had just done before my next round. Frequently, in that brief time you can mentally get your act together, but that period was taken away from me. I'd come out of the batting cage and start talking about the strike or whatever. I'd be in a running conversation while I was hitting. I really lost my concentration, but like I said, if I had had my baseball stuff together, it wouldn't have bothered me."

Most of the things that pulled Bob Boone down in 1980 he kept inside. It was not until months after the Phillies polished off Kansas City for their first world championship he finally let his feelings out.

"Sure, it was a thrill of a lifetime," said Bob. "Really, though, except for the immediate emotion I experienced after the last game with Kansas City, my feeling was one of total relief from the mental tension that had built up for so long.

"It was tough to enjoy the last three or four weeks of the season because we were in a must-win situation for so long. We had to raise our level of intensity to a point which left us mentally exhausted after every game. I don't think physically it was such a grind, but mentally, I just had had it at the end. I think because of that something was taken away from really savoring the idea of . . . hey, we're world champions!"

That time will come.

"Probably when I am 50 years old!" Boone snorted. "Right now, all I can remember is that we played longer and won two tournaments. The feeling of it being something really special hasn't hit, though it might happen on opening day when we get our World Series rings and are introduced as world champions.

"I think the biggest thing was the feeling we were *not* going to lose. I know in that last game with Houston when we were down 5–2 in the eighth inning I kept thinking there was no *way* we could lose. So many people had bemoaned our position for losing three playoffs that we just couldn't lose another.

"I think the intensity level really came up and was obvious in all the players. And I think that although nobody really said anything, each player felt we just couldn't let another one slip away."

Boone was such a clutch player in the World Series teammate Bake McBride listed him as one of the players who should have gotten the Most Valuable Player Award instead of Mike Schmidt.

Why did he suddenly turn his season around when it counted most?

"I can't explain that," said Boone, with a puzzled look. "For some reason when the situations got tense—most tense—like the ninth inning of the game in Montreal when we won the division—I got big hits. That Saturday in Montreal when my single tied the game (4–4) with two out in the ninth, I have never been that relaxed at the plate in my life. Why that happened to me all of a sudden I don't know. It was a time when I should have been up-tight. For some reason I was relaxed then. Happily that carried over to the playoffs and World Series.

"I just got in a good groove and a light went on in my head: 'Oh, that's what you've been searching for all year.' It's happened to me before and, luckily, it happened at a big, important time."

Although Boone never publicly criticized Manager Dallas Green as some of his teammates did, the relationship at times was strained and Danny Ozark was, again, the biggest reason.

"I think one of the saddest things to me in winning the whole thing was that Danny was not part of it," said Boone, choosing his words carefully. "I really felt Danny got a raw deal in 1979 when he was fired. I felt with all the criticism that was laid on everybody—I just felt that in '79 with all the injuries we had, we had no chance of winning. On top of that, we didn't play very well.

"I just felt Danny got a bum deal and eventually the team did also because we got labeled as a club that didn't want to win. I think that was the farthest thing from the truth. I just think that was a false, unjust, label. When Dallas Green took over I feel he was thinking, 'Ok, I'll show these guys how to win.' I don't think that was a correct assessment of the situation. The team always wanted to win.

"On the other hand, I think Dallas did a good job. Over the course of 162 games, regardless of the talent you have, it still takes that guy (manager) to handle the team by whatever means he believes in. I certainly wouldn't have used the means Dallas did to win, but the fact is you have to look at what happened. He won. And because of that, you have to say he did a good job."

People quickly forget, Boone says, what Danny Ozark did for the Phillies.

"He was maligned, as was the whole team, while he was here. Everybody fails to realize he was one of the winningest managers in baseball over a five-year period. Regardless of what you think about him or the comments you have made, you've got to judge him by his record.

"The same thing is true for Dallas Green. There have been a lot of times in the history of this game when teams have had the talent on paper, but didn't win. It takes a special kind of person to pull it together."

The fact that Boone was frequently benched in favor of rookie Keith Moreland bothered him. But it didn't pull him down.

"My approach to that is I don't worry about anything beyond my control. That's how I handled the Steve Carlton situation and how I handled 1975 when Danny Ozark decided Johnny Oates should be the No. 1 catcher."

When the "designated catcher" thing first cropped up Boone planned to confront Carlton to air out their differences. But like any other breakdown in a relationship, as time passed the gap became too big.

It all began when Carlton bluntly said he did not like the way Boone called, and caught baseball games. Boone refused to alter his style for Carlton, even though the pitcher was a veteran and the catcher was just starting out.

So, the two drifted apart. In 1976, with Tim McCarver back with the Phillies, Carlton demanded that when he pitched McCarver must catch. The marriage thrived until May 7, 1979.

On that night Bob Boone was Carlton's catcher as the Phillies pounded the Padres 11–6 in San Diego Stadium. Following that start, Boone and McCarver alternated behind the plate when Carlton was on the mound. After Timmy retired to the broadcast booth in 1980, it was Boone all the way. Originally Carlton did not like the way Boone set up the target and had disliked the Stanford grad's pitch selection even more.

"Steve said he liked to have the target set where the ball would end up, rather than more in the middle of the plate," Boone related. "Really, I think we have always been good friends. Like I said, I realized a long time ago not to worry about things I have no control over. I've always felt I was definitely qualified to catch Lefty, and felt like I had no problem doing it at all. If there was a hang-up, it was on his part.

"What I saw when Timmy came in and started catching Steve was that Timmy did a great job and Steve physically threw better. Whether it was mental or whatever, the facts remained. So, I just tried to look at the time when I wasn't catching with a positive outlook. First, I had no control over the situation. Second, when Steve was scheduled to pitch I had the opportunity to lift my weights the night before and come to the ball park the next day relaxed, knowing it was my day off. I felt that would make me stronger at the end of the year."

Catching Carlton, though, in 1980 was an experience most catchers only dream about. En route to his third Cy Young Award, Carlton was 14–4 by the All-Star Game. He ended with a 24–9 record, a 2.34 earned run average and led the league with 286 strikeouts.

"I have never had the experience of seeing anybody as consistent as Carlton was this year," said Boone. "I was amazed. From the first day of spring training he had it going. And he went half the season when he was close to being unhittable. After that he had some games when he was not as sharp, but prior to that I've never seen anybody go inning after inning after inning and be as consistent as he was.

"The slider was just awesome. Batters were completely fooled. They just couldn't hit it, it was so nasty."

What was the difference in 1980?

"Obviously, it was the catching," kidded Boone. "Really, I think it was a matter of getting in the groove. Through conditioning he has gotten even stronger. But from the first day in Clearwater, he had his priorities in order. That is the sign of a great player."

Boone gets so wrapped up in his approach to calling a

game, he has difficulty analyzing or remembering the overall result.

"I have trouble putting everything together," Boone said. "As an example, through the playoffs and World Series I can't really tell you all that happened. I know about certain events and I know the scores, but I can't put them together as a game. For me it all runs together because I break games down into sequences of pitch-by-pitch, inning-by-inning. All of a sudden there are three outs and you go to the dugout and think about pitch selection for the next inning. Because of that, I don't see all facets of the game."

Boone, who is considered an excellent field general, admits that after most games, even when he is going well at the plate, he is mentally exhausted.

"But I think catching keeps my interest high," he said. "I love it. I wouldn't want any other position. It's a fun way for me to play the game."

Early in July of 1979 Boone was on a torrid tear. At one stretch he was 18-for-35, a .514 clip and had thrown out 11 of the last 23 batters who tried to steal on his arm.

"I never got in that hitting groove in 1980," he said. "I was lunging at the ball. I was carrying my hands forward and there was no pop. I've battled that all my life, since I was a kid, because I've always been a front-foot hitter.

"To be effective, I've got to wait, let the ball get to me. When you're going bad there are lots of keys to look for. I kept trying to find out what it would take to get me to keep my hands back.

"It's always tough when you're struggling. It's a matter of working out of it. What made it so frustrating for me was I knew exactly what I did wrong every time I made an out. But knowing what's wrong and correcting it are two different things. I never got over the hump until we were in a do-or-die situation."

Boone is a second generation major leaguer. His father,

Ray, was an All-Star third baseman for Cleveland and later Detroit. He never played in a World Series—in 1959 Detroit got close, but Chicago won the pennant. Ray says, "To have your son feeling some of the things I felt about professional baseball is a beautiful thing."

Bob Boone met Susan Roel when she was 15 and he was the super jock at a San Diego high school. They were married when he was a junior at Stanford, a stage in his life when he thought a career in medicine was more logical than one in professional baseball.

Boone struggled so much last season each time he came to plate at Veterans Stadium the boos were loud and plentiful.

"No one likes to hear her husband booed," said Sue, a lovely blonde. "I'm first to admit fans have every right to boo people they feel aren't producing. But if the fans only knew the extent of pain Bob was suffering last year, I don't think they would have been so quick to boo him.

"I like to think the intelligent fans understood and also knew that, defensively, there's not a better catcher around. I've prayed so hard for him. I wanted so much for him to come out of it for his own sake. I just figured that he was being tested for a reason and that when the Lord was ready for Bob to come out of it, he would.

"You know, it's funny—and I don't know how people will take this, but six of the wives were in a taxi going to the final game of the playoffs in Houston. We were all nervous, naturally, so I said, 'How about if we all join hands and say a silent prayer.' We did.

"I prayed for us to win if it was God's will, but if it wasn't, I prayed for them to get through it without getting down. I prayed for Him to give them the strength to accept the outcome, whatever it was, because I knew how badly they all wanted to win.

"Well, that night, even when we were down 5–2, I just knew we would win it, and when Bob got the big hit, I felt fantastic. Even though he had that one and several more in the World Series, I didn't let it affect me too much. Part of not getting too low is not letting myself get too high. There will be days when he goes oh-for-four."

And there will be days when the tough Philadelphia press will come down hard on him.

Boone is intelligent and oozes confidence. To put it in another context, he has his mental act together. To many reporters this comes across as arrogance. I know I've felt that at times.

"I think there's a huge chip on the media's shoulder in Philadelphia," said Boone. "I see it in columns now, months after the World Series. The Eagles lost the Super Bowl to Oakland and somebody wrote 'The Eagles had more class in losing than the Phillies had in winning.' Well, obviously, that particular writer was assessing class with a person's willingness to talk to media. That's what it comes down to.

"What that particular reporter meant was the Philadelphia Eagles talked more to the press after the Super Bowl game than the Phillies talked to the press after they won. I don't assess that attitude as a definition of class. Also, the money issue has always been big with the media here. I don't know whether it's jealousy or what. I've just seen it too many times.

"You (Bodley) wrote a column several years ago and revealed all the Phillies' salaries. That made a lot of us very unhappy. Allen Lewis (former Inquirer baseball writer) ripped us very subtly the other day. I can't think of the exact sentence, but it was something about us being overpaid and not really wanting to win. I just sense this all the time.

"One of the classic examples was the manner in which the Philadelphia-area media—I'm speaking about three or four writers—told the national media during the playoffs and World Series we weren't cooperative. I think this team was as cooperative as any team I've ever been around. We spent hours upon hours talking, explaining each aspect of the games, whatever. Still we got a bad rap. So, I think what finally happened was the players no longer tried to live down a reputation— they tried to live up to it. The feeling you get, I guess, is if I'm going to get ripped for doing this, I might as well be as uncooperative as possible. Take the easy road. That's where the players on this team are coming from."

Of the Phillies, only Steve Carlton refuses to talk to all print media.

"But the reporters keep saying nobody talks on this team," said Boone. "I even got labeled like that in a couple of different articles and nothing could have been further from the truth. I know I went through a stretch of about two weeks without talking to a writer, but it had nothing to do with me not wanting to talk. Heck, I was just going so poorly, nobody wanted to talk to me. That's expected, but don't say I am not cooperative.

"On the other hand, I accept the Philadelphia media. No matter what anybody says, we all read the newspapers. Every day. The real problem from a ball player's point of view is not the long articles. It's the little digs that are thrown into the stories. In my opinion that's not good journalism. I know when I took a course in journalism at Stanford we were taught that you report what happened. If you have comments, they go on the editorial page. I understand that's not entirely true, but there are just so many subtle ways our players are ripped that it is irritating from a personal standpoint.

"I realize that whatever I try to do to change that would not be constructive, so I just go with it. Just say I am thick-skinned."

"The great thing is he never brings any of this home with him," added Sue. "If he's upset about what's going on at the ball park, it's hard to tell when he's at home. He keeps telling me that there are certain things out of his control and not to worry about them. I learned that too, over the years, and the approach works."

"I think the most important lesson I learned from what happened to the Phillies in 1980 was seeing—and realizing—that luck's involved in winning a World Series," said Boone, his psychology background showing. "You know, I don't feel the 1980 team was any more talented than the teams that won the division in the late 1970s. I do think it was a matter of us coming together, getting big hits and all 25 guys participating. Tug McGraw got so hot and there were just a lot of breaks that went our way. I've seen us hit balls right on the nose the same way and they were caught. In 1980 they were big hits. I find that fascinating."

In the fifth game of the World Series with the Phillies leading 5–3, two Royals on base and one out in the ninth inning, Hal McRae hit a long fly ball to left field that had home run written all over it. At the last second it curled foul.

"Had it been fair, the game was over and the Royals were up 3–2 in the Series," said Boone. "I called time and went to the mound. I said, 'Hey, Tug, this is exciting isn't it?' He cracked up. Nothing else was said and he got the third out. That's the way the year went."

The Bench
"Del, get a bat!"

For Del Unser, the season opened on Wednesday night, September 17 in Pittsburgh's Three Rivers Stadium. It was the beginning of an adventure that would not end until the Phillies were world champions.

Montreal was leading National League East by 2½ games over the Phillies. The Pirates were in third place, five back.

The Phils were more concerned about their cross-state nemesis than they were about the pretenders from Canada. The Pirates had always closed with a rush in September, so it was not unusual for the Phils to look over their shoulders at the defending world champions.

The night before Pittsburgh scored early, then held off the Phils 3–2. And when the Bucs scored three times off Steve Carlton in the seventh inning to pull even on the 17th, a Philadelphia victory seemed in jeopardy.

But in the 11th pinch-hitter Del Unser won the game by stroking one of Kent Tekulve's best pitches for a single.

"It was just a little blooper," the much-traveled Unser said, "but it helped my confidence as much as anything. I figured if I could get a big hit coming off the bench with a guy like Tekulve pitching, I must be swinging the bat pretty well."

An understatement.

The world wasn't paying much attention to him in the final, tension-filled week of the season, but it was then that Unser, playing for Maddox, delivered a typical solid effort in center field. He also contributed some big hits.

Against Houston, however, in the fifth and final game of the playoffs he was as incredible, individually, as that series was as a whole.

Pinch-hitting again, Del singled to tie a game the Phillies apparently had lost. Later, when it appeared they were beaten again, he doubled and scored the winning run.

In the World Series against Kansas City he had two doubles and a single in six at-bats for a .500 average. The second game was probably his best. The Royals were on top 4-2 in the eighth inning when Bob Boone led off with a walk. Lonnie Smith was due up but Dallas Green yelled, "Del, get a bat!"

Unser responded with a screaming double to left-center off Tekulve-disciple Dan Quisenberry and Boone rumbled around the bases to score. When the inning finally ended, the Phils were in front 6–4 and en route to a 2–0 lead in the Series.

"I went to the plate thinking about the night in Pittsburgh when I got the hit off Tekulve, another side-armer," said Unser. "I was confident. He threw me a good pitch, one you can just as easily top to shortstop or second base. It's a tough pitch to pull unless you dive out over the plate. I went with it and happened to hit it solidly."

In the fifth game in Kansas City after the Royals squared the Series at 2–2, Unser came up in the ninth inning against gunfighter Quisenberry, rapped a double past first base to score Mike Schmidt with the tying run and eventually scored the game-winner himself on Manny Trillo's infield hit.

"Del Unser is what our bench was all about in 1980," said Green after he had had time to digest the championship. "I'm sure he would have been happier if he had gotten to play more, but no matter what I asked him to do he did it well."

Del Unser

Greg Gross

John Vukovich

George Vukovich

As a pinch-hitter and sometime starter Unser was on stage during the main event. Greg Gross and John Vukovich were also valuable members of Green's veteran reserve corps.

Gross, who struggled much of the season before ending with a .240 average after only 127 at-bats, appeared in four of the playoff games and hit .750. The sure-fielding Vukovich seldom played but contributed mightily in the dugout and clubhouse as a Green lieutenant. He refused to let his teammates give in no matter what the situation.

Delbert Bernard Unser was a man without a team, a nomad whose baseball career had been one long road show.

After stops at Washington (1968–71), Cleveland (1972), Philadelphia (1973–74), New York Mets (1975–76), and Montreal (1976–79), Unser faced the end of his career in the spring of 1979. He had played out his option with Montreal and tossed his hat in the free-agent grab bag. There were few takers.

"I can't promise you anything," Paul Owens told him that March. "You can come on down to spring training, get in shape and maybe we can work something out."

Unser arrived in Clearwater with little hope but the day before the Phillies jetted out of the Florida sunshine for the season opener in St. Louis, Del signed a contract with the team he played for in 1973 and 1974.

When the soft-spoken Unser finally got in his first World Series, somebody asked if it was like scratching a 13-year itch, referring to his previous years in the majors.

"It's more like a 30-year itch," said Unser. "My father (Al) was a major-league catcher so I've always had a great feeling for what it's all about. I'm finally getting the chance to experience the World Series first-hand, though."

Few players have bounced around as much as Unser but he has no regrets.

"The travel has brought me a lot of good friends, both in and out of baseball," he said. "A lot of people—a lot of friends—benefited from the World Series, not just me. Through all the years you meet an awful lot of people and it is nice to know they enjoyed this as much as I did."

Unser's first two seasons in Philadelphia were outstanding but when the Phils got Tug McGraw from the Mets, he was a part of the deal that went the other way.

"Those two years and my first with the Mets were the happiest of my career—at least until the world championship," he said. "I really think it is wonderful the way I was able to come back here.

"I decided to play out my option with Montreal because I didn't think I fit in with their plans. I told the Expos I was going to try to get away from the hassle of playing in Canada and go to a team that could use me in my best capacities—as a reserve outfielder and pinch-hitter. In 1978 the Expos ruined me. I sat on the bench for as many as five weeks at a time. So I decided to go the option route."

Unser admits when he went to spring training with the Phils in 1979 he wasn't even sure he would remain in baseball.

"There was a lot of anxiety involved personally and professionally as to whether or not I had it in me to play out my option," he said. "There's no question if I hadn't done it I would have always second-guessed myself."

Before he surfaced in the playoffs and World Series as Mr. Clutch, Unser had just 110 at-bats.

"Well, in the end I contributed some and when you don't get to play very much that is what you live for. Had it not been for the last few weeks of the season the year could have turned out like that last summer in Montreal. When you get only 110 at-bats it can be very discouraging and if you don't watch it carefully, it can really affect you. But in September we were close enough to be in striking distance and I was lucky enough to get some big hits."

As a pinch-hitter Unser kept thinking back to 1968 when Ted Williams was his rookie manager.

"Ted tried to tell all of us hitters what to expect in certain situations," remembered Unser. "He told us to think along with the pitcher and the catcher—how to study a pitcher and see what he was getting over for strikes—what a pitcher liked to throw to certain types of hitters in certain situations. He helped me a lot.

"And his basic theories of hitting, of getting a good pitch to hit, something that doesn't fool you, is an excellent philosophy. And using a bat that you can handle. These things stayed with me all the years.

"Most hitting instructors have their own theory. A lot of 'em work, but maybe only for certain people. What I've tried to do is take several views from several people and use what worked best for me.

"I was never in a class with Ted Williams as a hitter, but I tried to approach it the same way. As a pinch-hitter you've got to come off the bench swinging. There are going to be times when you go up there and it looks like that pitcher is throwing bullets. There will be other times when it looks like he's throwing beachballs. Either way you've got to swing the bat. You have to make something happen."

When Green benched center fielder Garry Maddox, Unser took over and started the last six games of the regular season—all victories.

"I didn't get a lot of hits, but I think the last week of the season was one of the biggest I've ever had," he said. "I hit the ball pretty well and contributed in center field. If he (Green) wasn't going to play Garry for whatever reason, then it was my job to go out and try to do as well as I could. We had to win every game.

"That was important to me because I still like to play and being able to start those games renewed some of my confidence, especially with management. And because I saw a lot of pitches the last week, I got in a good groove.

"I like to think of myself as a guy who doesn't have an ego so great that I have to play every day to be happy."

To Unser, generally a low-key type, the Phillies jelled in San Francisco on September 1 when Paul Owens blew his top.

"I thought Dallas had used his pitching staff pretty well all year and had done a good job, but Paul Owens gave us that one little spark teams sometimes need.

"When you get your butt chewed like that, it makes you do a little soul searching. It may help you to be a little bit more objective about it and think to yourself, 'Yeah, this guy really *is* trying.' You know most times you just kinda sit there like a bump on a log, but that time I think a lot of the guys took Paul Owens a little more to heart than perhaps they had in the past when somebody else lectured them.

"I think they knew he genuinely cared and that he was more than just a little concerned and that we were a heckuva lot better than the way we had been playing. I'm the first to admit we had been lackadaisical and just going through the motions as individuals rather than team players. I think he hit a few nails on the head and it was like he backed us against the wall to see what we were made of. I think he did it very effectively."

As far as Green was concerned, Unser spent many of his "bench" hours studying the manager's strategy and handling of his players.

"I sat there with some of my buddies and we kinda dissected him," said Unser, smiling. "When you're not in the heat of the actual game, it's different. But as the season progressed we would think a little more deeply as to what moves were and were not made.

"I didn't agree with a lot of his tactics, but overall I thought he did a good job. He didn't let any of the players buffalo him or unduly influence his decisions. There were starting line-ups that surprised a lot of people. You never walked into that clubhouse and took it for granted you weren't playing. I think that kept a lot of guys on their toes.

"I think he rescued a few guys when maybe they didn't want it, and a few that he didn't rescue maybe needed it. As

I said, I think he did a very good job handling the pitching staff, especially Tug McGraw. He didn't bring Tug in every time there was the possibility of a save. Tug could have had a lot more saves if he had, but Dallas used Dickie Noles and Kevin Saucier and Ron Reed. He and Ron didn't see eye-to-eye but they both went out and tried to do their jobs. Dallas brought up some young pitchers that nobody thought could throw in the big leagues and they just pleasantly carried us right through the playoffs and World Series. There were a lot of very positive things he did with the pitching staff.

"The selection of the starting line-up when you have a lot of talent isn't a terribly tough job, but to keep those guys on an aggressive scale, that is a tough job. There were times when people needed to be shaken up and they got it."

Unser never really got involved with the clubhouse bickering over Green's lack of communication with his players.

"I appreciate it when a manager calls me in and, face-to-face, tells me where it's at. Philadelphia, you know, is an interesting city, very similar to New York in that the news coverage and fan interest in what is going on in the clubhouse is intense. As far as Dallas being critical of his players to the press, I think that's his manner. He doesn't care that much what the players think about him. At least that's what he says so that's what you have to go on.

"You know he's going to do it his way because that is his style. And it might be what got the best out of some of our players. I don't think it's a fair statement to say that gets the most out of everyone all the time though. *I* don't agree with it, but I'm not managing.

"He developed a rapport with the press and that's part of being a manager. You have to have that. He talked a lot to the reporters, but there were some things that shouldn't have ever gotten out of the clubhouse, and didn't. Dallas respected that.

"To go back to the other point for a minute—as a player, a professional, you have to say, 'Hey, he's ripping me in the newspaper, what do I do about it?' You might think, 'I'm a public figure but I don't get paid to get ripped in the paper, I get paid to play.' On the other hand, it's probably equally true that if my play is not up to par, the newspaper people will write something anyway. To be honest, my feeling is if the manager is upset with the way I am playing I'm definitely going to hear about it."

Unser, who played out his option again following the world championship before re-signing with the Phillies, thinks he has a home for his next two years in baseball.

"In 1979 I had the feeling I'd found my spot on the team. I hit those pinch home runs (three in a row to set a major-league record) and did the job off the bench. I figure that's my job for at least the next two years, but I don't expect to play very much.

"Sometimes people don't have enough confidence to put the extra men in. Dallas was almost forced to in September and the guys did a good job for him."

Greg Gross was Mr. Sunshine in spring training of 1980.

About the only thing that would have made him happier would have been the chance to play every day.

After declaring his free agency following the 1979 season, he signed a five-year $1.1 million contract with the Phils. He had hit .333 in 111 games after arriving from the Chicago Cubs in the Trillo deal.

"I wouldn't be telling the truth if I didn't say the change in managers was part of my thinking in coming back to the Phillies," Gross said. "Dallas Green impressed me as a man who likes to use his bench more than Danny Ozark did. I thought I would be playing more in 1980 than I did in 1979."

Gross did get in 127 games in '80, but most of the year was a nightmare of sorts.

"It was a mechanical thing," said Gross, who had a .298 lifetime average before his .240 pulled it down. "I was over-striding. It was something very noticeable. Everybody could see it and I could see it when I watched video tapes. But when I went to the plate, I didn't feel myself doing it. I felt comfortable but I obviously wasn't swinging the bat correctly. The over-striding became a bad habit. Complicating the problem was the fact I wasn't playing very much and it is difficult to correct a problem when you're not playing. In August I finally licked the problem and hit pretty well the rest of the season."

The world championship, of course, washed away most of Gross' disappointment. But not all of it.

"It had been a tough year most of the way," he said. "It was frustrating because we all felt we had a better team than we were showing and, personally, I was not contributing. But we all got on-track at the end—everyone was contributing. It was a real good feeling, the high point of the whole year. There was a sense of satisfaction.

"I really thought the season turned around for us when we went into New York in late August and destroyed the Mets in five games. It was just a great offensive series. Then Paul Owens woke us up in San Francisco on Labor Day. I'll never forget the 1-1 game in Candlestick Park (September 2) when Warren Brusstar came in in the ninth inning with runners on first and third, one out and got a double-play ball. Then, in the 11th with the bases loaded and nobody out, he threw three ground balls. We won 2–1 in 13 innings. A big, big game."

Gross did not feel the electricity of the World Series until the fifth game.

"After the Houston series, everything seemed normal until the Sunday game in Kansas City. All of a sudden the thought came to me, 'Wait a minute, we have to win this thing. If we lose the World Series, we haven't accomplished everything we wanted to.'

"And then, after the sixth game it was nice, but I think the parade the next day was when it really sunk in. There were an awful lot of happy people out there. That was a good feeling."

As far as any problems the players had with Green was concerned, Gross felt the clubhouse atmosphere was normal.

"Every other club I have been on has had the same things happening in the locker room," he said. "What happened to us may have gotten more publicity, but players on all the clubs have problems with their manager. When it came down to the bottom line everyone ended up going out and playing hard—and winning. I just think Dallas' personality and the personality of our club caused some of the conflicts. This is just the way it is going to be. Dallas puts all of those things out of his mind when he manages and, hopefully, the players do too.

"There's just no sense worrying or arguing with Dallas. You're making it more difficult because you still have to go out and play. If you're going to worry about every word he says, then that's going to affect your play—and it shouldn't."

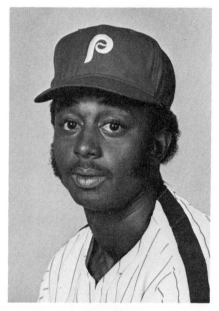

Lonnie Smith

Keith Moreland

Ramon Aviles

Kevin Saucier

The Kids

". . . a lot of spirit and crazy about winning."

After each victory they burst into the clubhouse like silly high-school sophomores. There was laughing and celebration.

In the beginning the crusty old veterans didn't know what to think of the young whippersnappers. Didn't they know when you put on Phillies' pinstripes you're supposed to be cool, unemotional? Don't get high after victories, low after defeats. Face the world the same every day.

In short, keep your cool, man.

The Class of '80 refused to accept that. The rookies, or kids as Dallas Green called them, let their emotions—and talents—flow.

And moments after the Phillies won the World Series just about everyone agreed that had it not been for the breath of fresh air pumped into the clubhouse by this band of eager youngsters, the championship probably would not have come to Philadelphia.

Skeptics said there was no way the Phils could win anything with the bench consisting mostly of rookies, but Green, minor-league director for all those years, had an obligation to give the youngsters a chance. He would soon find out, his critics said, the kids would not be able to cut it. Not in the big leagues.

But they did.

There was catcher Keith Moreland who hit .314 during the regular season, blasted four homers and drove in 29 runs, seven of which were game winners. Against Kansas City in the World Series, he hit .333.

Lonnie Smith, an outfielder with blazing speed, gave the Phillies a new dimension. He batted .339 in 100 games, hit three homers and drove in 21 runs. His 33 stolen bases broke Richie Ashburn's rookie record of 32 set in 1948. In the play-offs Lonnie hit .600 in three games. His average dropped to .263 in the World Series, but after the season he was named National League rookie of the year by The Sporting News.

George Vukovich hit only .224, but several of his 11 pinch hits came in clutch situations.

Aside from those contributions the youngsters gave the team a new spirit. In the beginning this bothered the veterans and split the team down the middle—the experienced players versus the kids. But the youngsters refused to hide in a corner and fall into the attitude of studied nonchalance that had become a Phillies' trademark the last few seasons.

Instead, the rookies continued to yell and, eventually, their enthusiasm for winning began to rub off. In the end, it was the marvelous blend of youth and experience that went a long way towards turning the Phillies into world champions.

"I'm very proud of myself and of that group," said Moreland. "Look, I'm not bold enough to think I should have taken Bob Boone's place. If we were going to win he had to be the catcher. And you had to have Mike Schmidt and Larry Bowa and Pete Rose and Garry Maddox and all the others. But when we were asked to do a job, we tried to produce.

"I think we did the job. We had a lot of spirit and were crazy about winning. From the time I was a little boy I wanted to play on a championship team and it finally happened."

"I guess the biggest thing about the year was the fact Dallas Green gave us a chance," said Smith. "I was in the minors so long I wondered if I would ever make it to the big leagues. It began to bother me."

"It was tough for me coming off the bench," said Vukovich. "I was not used to that role. I tried to stay ready and I feel I contributed some. It was exciting being a part of this."

"The kids had an outstanding year," said Green. "It was a lot of fun watching the clubhouse. At first the veterans did not get involved, but the kids wanted to win so badly enthusiasm rubbed off on the others in the end."

"We had never been through the turmoil of a pennant race," said Moreland. "We got wrapped up in the excitement of being in the big leagues as early as May. We were going out screaming and hollering and it seemed like we were the only guys really doing it. The older guys had been through it many times before. They kept saying it was a 162-game schedule and that by the end we would be exhausted. They were right. When it was finally over I was drained.

"But truthfully I think the other guys got caught up in it in August and by September it was a 25-man thing. Everybody was screaming. It would erupt at any moment. I was proud of the young guys and I think we were a big part of that emotion."

Moreland, during a round of golf one Saturday morning at Wilmington Country Club in August, told friends the Phillies would win everything. They laughed.

"I really felt it," he said later. "I've always had that attitude about any team I have played on. It was instilled in me a long time ago and, sure, it has not always held true. But I have always felt if you think and believe you can win, you will. I set myself that goal when I made the club in April. I kept stating it and just felt like if I said it long enough, I could create some emotion. Then, eventually everyone would create his own emotion and finally it would become *team* emotion."

In the beginning the veterans gave the youngsters a cold shoulder.

"Sure, we got the rookie jabs from the guys who have been around for a long time, but after a while I think they began to realize we weren't putting on an act, that we were for real and we really *wanted* to win. After that, nobody tried to keep us down. I think the more we got excited, the more they felt it inside them."

The key, of course, was that the the rookies came through.

"If we had come in there and fallen flat on our faces, that emotional stuff would have cooled down in a hurry," admitted Moreland. "It's tough, especially when you're a young guy, to try to feel something and be involved in something if you're not competing and playing regularly.

"Had we not produced, we wouldn't have gotten in the games in the first place and then all that emotion would have eventually dried up. It doesn't matter how much I holler, I still have to do it on the field."

The low point for the fiesty Moreland came one day in July when he appeared on Steve Fredericks' WCAU radio show. Moreland boldly announced the National League East race had narrowed to two teams—the Phillies and Montreal Expos.

"People—even my teammates—came down hard on me after that," he said, a guilty look on his face. "Hey, I was saying the 1979 world champions, the Pittsburgh Pirates, were out of it. Dave Parker took shots at me and so did the Pirates' manager, Chuck Tanner. I grew up a lot after that. I learned to keep my mouth shut.

"At the time all three teams were close. We were like a half-game behind Montreal. I truthfully felt with the injuries the Pirates had and the problems with their pitching staff—Bert Blyleven had just quit the team—the season would come down to the Phillies and Expos. I thought Pittsburgh would fold, but a day or so later they got hot.

"A few weeks later they beat us four in a row at their place, we fell six games back and I knew right then I had made a big, big mistake. Not only did I get criticized for my remarks, but I had given the Pirates something to get psyched over. The whole episode really bothered me. After that, I had to watch what I said when reporters came to my locker. My teammates would walk by, look at me and shake their heads. Later I told them I realized I'd made a big mistake."

Moreland, like Boone, was a third baseman when the Phillies signed him in 1975. Two years later they moved him behind the plate during a semester in the Florida Winter Instructional League.

"We had Mike Schmidt at third base and Jim Morrison was looking like a great prospect at third, so they figured the only way I was going to make it was behind the plate," said Moreland. "With 13 games to go in the instructional league, I became a catcher. The first guy I caught was Warren Brusstar who had that nasty sinker. I ran to the screen 13 times in the first three innings."

In 1979, the sturdy Texan gained All-Star honors in the American Association for Oklahoma City. He hit .302 with a career-high 34 doubles, 20 home runs and 109 runs batted in.

"He was the best clutch hitter in the league," said Lee Elia, the Phils' current third-base coach who managed Oklahoma City that year. "He was a pretty good catcher, too."

Moreland got ready for his first full year in the majors by taking over for the injured Boone the final two weeks of '79. He hit .375 in 14 games.

"Those two weeks really helped me. Catching with the big club was more exciting then even I thought it would be because I was in a tough situation. Boone was hurt and he's a great player. But you get a chance to play all of a sudden and you don't know what's going to happen.

"I wanted that chance. It's what I had been waiting five years in the minors for. Baseball is a good life. I get excited about going out there all the time. I just like to take batting practice, sign a few autographs, laugh and party. I have fun playing. I've probably been accused of not being serious enough. I am serious. I'm ready to play. But beforehand, I'm having fun. Life's too short not to have a little fun."

When the red-headed Moreland played baseball at the University of Texas he was considered the best college hitter in the United States. He also played football for Coach Darrell Royal as a defensive back, but when he fractured his left wrist his sophomore year, he gave up football to concentrate on baseball.

"I had some problems hitting early in my professional career," he said, "Mostly because I would get so psyched up to face a particular pitcher. He would get me out one time, then I'd be so keyed up the next time I couldn't do a thing. You can't take out anger and frustration in baseball the way you can in football."

There was a time when Moreland had a temper to go with his hair color. He would slam helmets, kick water fountains and yell at umpires.

"I guess I matured," he said. "I've learned to control my anger. Maybe that's the reason I have had some pretty good years back to back.

"I like to win at anything. Take golf. I used to make a bad shot, then wrap the club around a tree. Sometimes it still happens, but not very often. Even now, though, if I think my body can do something and then find I can't, it tears me apart.

"Maybe 10 years from now if somebody asks me what was the turning point of my career I will say it was the change in my temperament."

And the fact the Phillies gave you a chance in 1980.

"That may be even more important," he said "I know some of the guys had problems with Dallas Green, but I can't say anything bad about him. I've known him since 1975 and he has been in my corner all along. I guess he just likes the way I play baseball—maybe not my statistics, maybe not my ability as much as he just likes the way I go out and play baseball."

Lonnie Smith had a .308 lifetime batting average and 239 stolen bases in the minors but nobody had any faith in him.

Danny Ozark stuck Smith in right field for the 1979 season opener and after Lonnie butchered a couple of fly balls, he was on his way back to Oklahoma City.

"It got to the point where I considered quitting baseball," Smith said. "I had proved everything I could in the minors, so why keep going back?"

Smith did, however, go back in April of 1979 and proceeded to hit .330 with 34 stolen bases. When Green took over as the Phils' manager late in the season, a whole new world opened for Lonnie.

Green gave the 24-year-old Californian a chance and Smith did not let his mentor down.

"I feel like Ronald Reagan," Smith said the day he learned he won rookie award. "This is just a great, great feeling. First the world championship, now this. I feel very honored because the selection was made by opposing players."

Smith, who played all three outfield positions, moved above .300 in his sixth at-bat in April and from then on his lowest average in 1980 was .326 on August 11.

When Greg Luzinski went on the disabled list following the All-Star Game, Smith played left field in 39 of the 45 games Luzinski missed. In those 39 games, as the leadoff batter, Smith had 55 hits, scored 38 runs, stole 19 bases and hit .355. Not so coincidentally the Phils also won 23 of those games.

For years the Phillies had a one-two punch that left opposing pitchers groggy. If Mike Schmidt didn't beat you, Greg Luzinski would.

For much of '80 that once-awesome attack was replaced by the stinging combination of Lonnie Smith and Pete Rose, a pair of singles hitters.

The plot was simple. Smith, the lead off batter, would get on base—with regularity. He'd steal second and before you knew it, Rose would either move him to third or bring him home with a hit.

A typical example was a mid-season game against Cincinnati. In his first three at bats on the scorching afternoon, Smith walked and singled twice. Each time he stole second and each time he scored.

"That is pretty much the way I played in the minors," said Smith. "Having Pete bat behind me really helped. He's such a disciplined hitter; he has such a good eye. He was willing to sacrifice a swing or even give himself up completely if it meant I was going to get in scoring position."

"I had never been in that role before," said Rose, who himself has been a leadoff hitter most of his career. "I had to be more patient and you know I was pretty patient to start with. Lonnie ran on his own, so the coach's signs didn't help. All I did was tell him not to worry if I took two strikes. There are certain pitchers in the league I felt I could take two strikes on because, when I'm swinging the bat well, I'm a better two-strike hitter than I am hitting 2-0."

There were those who felt Ozark, convinced Smith could not cut it in the majors, tried to prove his point in the 1979 opener against the Cardinals in front of 40,526 howling fans.

"I don't really feel Danny tried to embarrass me," said Smith. "It's just that I had no chance to prepare for that start. I didn't have any inkling I was going to be in right field until I got to the park that night. I was nervous and not mentally prepared. I misjudged some balls and fell down once.

"I never felt Danny liked the way I play baseball. So I didn't get much of a chance. With him, I never felt comfortable. He doesn't like to use young players except for pitchers.

I never felt he had enough faith in me to play me. The day I was sent down, in April of '79, I was told some things and to me they were outright lies. Anything Ozark told me after that I didn't believe. He told me I would learn to play right field in Oklahoma City, but from the first day I arrived I was in center. He told me I'd be back up in a month. I didn't get back until September. At that point I almost felt like quitting."

In the beginning Smith was turned off by the Phillies.

"When I first heard Philadelphia was interested in me—I was in high school—they were still a bad team. I didn't really want to sign with them. Montreal showed more interest, so whenever the Phils (scouts) came out to watch me I wouldn't really give it my all.

"Before I got into baseball I wanted to be a policeman. I was going to go to the police academy in Los Angeles. That was the only thing I was really interested in."

Lonnie Smith knows a trade probably would have meant a chance to play everyday with another team.

That all changed with Green at the helm. During the winter, just as 1980's spring training was gearing up, Green refused to let Paul Owens trade Lonnie Smith to Baltimore for infielder Billy Smith.

"I'm a Lonnie Smith man," Green said then, and he kept repeating it all summer. "He is one of the few players in my opinion who, without hitting home runs, can excite and ignite a team. He puts that extra pizzazz into your offense. He breaks up doubleplays as well as anybody I know. He goes from first to third or second to home, as well as anybody I have seen. He has worked hard on his defense and is improving."

"I never really had any doubts about my ability to hit in the majors," said Smith. "I worried a little bit about what it might be like to bat against Nolan Ryan and J. R. Richard and the other good pitchers, but once the season got under way, that was no longer a question mark for me. Now, I feel like I can hit anybody."

The most frustrating thing for Smith was playing well for several games in a row, then having to go back to the bench.

"You go out, get two or three hits then have to sit down," he said, a frown on his face. "At times that was difficult, but I am happy I got to play as much as I did. Next season maybe I'll get to start more, but if I don't, at least I know I'll get to play. I was able to prove my point in 1980."

Smith got on his feet in the major leagues in 1980, but also lost them more times than he would like to remember.

"Falling down when I run is something that has always bothered me," he said. "I keep trying to figure out what causes it. It might be that my feet are too quick for the rest of my body and I slip and lose my balance. It's something I obviously have to work on."

Steve Carlton
Awesome slider . . . awesome record

Steve Carlton sat quietly in the trainer's room sipping Great Western champagne.

Outside, corks were popping. Wine and tears were flowing. The Phillies had just whipped Kansas City to win their first world championship and the whole franchise was exhaling a great sigh of relief.

But the man who was as responsible as anyone for washing away those sorry thoughts of the past sat alone. Despite his calm exterior he was, inside, as excited as his teammates.

Ruly Carpenter spotted Beverly Carlton standing by the door of the mobbed clubhouse and pushed his way toward her.

"Go on in there with Steve," Carpenter ordered as he took her by the arm. "You should be with him."

The attractive Mrs. Carlton, champagne splashing out of a plastic cup, made her way through the unruly crowd and even before she opened the trainer's room door, Steve saw her. The two embraced and tears ran down her face.

"He was so happy and I was so happy for him," Beverly Carlton said a month later. "You'll never know how much winning this meant to him. He would sit up in bed in the middle of the night and almost shout, 'We're world champions!' "

For Steven Norman Carlton 1980 was one of his finest

years. From a pure pitching standpoint nothing will ever equal his 27–10 summer of 1972, but in 1980 he had a 24–9 record, a 2.34 earned run average, led the National League in innings pitched (304) and topped the majors in strikeouts with 286. That performance earned him his third Cy Young Award, making him only the fourth player to win it three times since its inception in 1956. Previous three-time winners were Sandy Koufax (1963–65–66), Tom Seaver (1969–73–75) and Jim Palmer (1973–75–76).

On April 26 the man they call Lefty set a modern National League record with his sixth career one-hitter, a 7–0 victory over St. Louis. Ted Simmons' second-inning single was the only hit he allowed.

On May 5 he was just four outs from his first no-hitter when Atlanta's Bill Nahorodny singled through the middle with two out in the eighth. Carlton gave up two more hits, including Dale Murphy's lead-off homer in the ninth, before winning 7–1.

On July 6 while pitching against St. Louis, the team that traded him to the Phillies for Rick Wise on February 25, 1972, Carlton became the major leagues' all-time left-handed strikeout pitcher when he fanned Tony Scott in the fourth inning. Scott's K nudged Carlton past Mickey Lolich's 2,832 strikeouts. At season's end Steve had 2,969.

In post-season competition he had a 1–0 record in the best-of-five playoffs against Houston, then won both starts in the World Series, including the 4–1 clincher against the Royals in the sixth game.

In spite of these superb statistics it has been over a year since the enigmatic Carlton has granted an interview to print media reporters. He did none in 1980 and only two in 1979.

For this book, however, he discussed the championship season one Saturday morning in February. He had just returned to his suburban St. Louis home after competing in ABC-TV's Super Teams tournament. He agreed, at the outset, that being with his teammates after over three months rekindled all the excitement of the greatest year in Phillies' history.

"When I look back, I think the season was a matter of timing," said Carlton. "Everything came together at the end. We were able to stay close enough to the other teams most of the season, then just about everybody on the club got hot the last month or so. We hadn't really had a hot streak earlier. In the past, I think we went stale in the playoffs."

Carlton, who turned 36 December 22, 1980, feels people are forever comparing anything he does to 1972.

"I'm never going to be able to have a year like 1972 again," he said. "I know that. That was a matter of precision. I made pitches during that year that were unbelievable. I was able to put the ball wherever I wanted to. Sometimes they caught the corner of the plate by a fraction of an inch. This *is* a game of inches.

"I was able to throw breaking balls when I was behind in the count. I threw some nasty sliders."

Yet through June 22 of 1980, Carlton had a 13–2 record and 1.83 ERA and was ahead of his 1972 pace.

"The first four months of the year his slider was almost unhittable," said catcher Bob Boone. "He was just awesome. There is nothing else I can say about him."

Carlton, after completing his 15th full season in the majors, has a 225–169 lifetime record. In addition to his 304 regular-season innings he worked 23 in spring training and 27⅓ in the playoffs and World Series. That's 354⅓ innings, a grueling number even for Steve Carlton's apparently indestructible arm.

"I know Herm Starrette (pitching coach) was keeping a close watch on the number of innings I had pitched," said Carlton, "but I didn't feel I had arm fatigue at the end. I've had it in other years and know what it feels like.

"To tell the truth, I didn't want to come out of the last World Series game. I thought I was still throwing well. At

Most awesome delivery in the majors. News-Journal papers' photographer Fred Comegys uses stop-action to show what National League batters must face when they bat against Cy Young Award winner Steve Carlton.

least that's what I thought. But Jim Kaat used to tell me you sometimes think you're throwing as hard as always, but, in fact, you are not."

Carlton did not allow a hit the first three innings in the sixth game against the Royals on October 21. After seven he had given up just three singles and struck out seven. In the eighth, after John Wathan walked and José Cardenal singled to right, Manager Dallas Green summoned Tug McGraw.

"Dallas decided to make the change so there was nothing I could do," said Carlton, who completed 13 games during the regular season. "But it would have been a nice one to finish."

Boone claims Lefty was in a good groove from the moment he threw his first spring-training pitch and then stayed in it almost the entire year.

"To me, it was really a matter of conditioning," said Carlton. "In the past I have had some arm problems in the spring that delayed my preparation. Normally when you come off a winter program of lifting weights there is some difficulty in getting your arm loose in the spring. I went to Clearwater five days early last year and had no problems from the beginning."

Most of that conditioning can be credited to Gus Hoefling's strength-and-flexibility program which is built around the martial arts and stretching exercises, combining alternate applications of positive and negative tension.

Hoefling, who has been called Steve's guru, doesn't think Carlton worked any harder in 1980 than he did in the previous three years.

"Steve and Roman Gabriel (former Eagles' quarterback) are the hardest-working professional athletes I've ever known," said Hoefling, "and I'd say Steve has surpassed Roman in that aspect. The man just continues to amaze me every time he works out. He has recuperative powers beyond my comprehension. There's no babying, and he puts out more than I ask."

"Gus is the best," said Steve. "He has a program for everyone, every level. One of the most important things for a pitcher is to get ready mentally and physically between starts. I try to peak every fourth or fifth day. Gus has devised a method for pitchers, a type of stretching exercise. With a stick (much like a broom handle), you move and stretch the arm in almost the same motion as when you are pitching. The rehab (rehabilitation) is much quicker than with other methods."

"A pitcher always has some soreness and stiffness between starts," agreed Dick Ruthven, "but with the stick all of that can be worked out quickly. I watched Lefty last season and plan to do even more of it myself in 1981."

In 1980 Carlton's slider was the toughest pitch most National League batters have ever seen. It brought them to their knees as they flailed helplessly at a ball breaking in the dirt.

Again, conditioning.

Carlton's great strength enables him to get a tighter grip on the ball, making it spin tightly like a gyroscope. Because it's thrown so hard, it breaks and drops. The pitch confuses batters because they think it's a fastball—until the last instant.

"The slider has been a very good pitch for me," said Carlton in solemn understatement. "I try to make the pitch look like a strike just before it breaks down in the dirt."

"It's almost impossible to hit," says close friend and former catcher Tim McCarver, now a Phils' broadcaster. "I really am not sure how he throws it. The results speak for themselves. It starts out in the strike zone and the bottom falls out. It's almost like a slider-sinker. Steve's ball has a little less rotation than most sliders."

"Steve Carlton is in a class by himself among lefthanders," said Pittsburgh's Bill Madlock. "The only guy in the league who has ever been close to him was Jerry Koosman when he was having those great years with the Mets. If you don't get to Steve by the fifth inning you might as well put your bats away."

"The slider is the nastiest I have ever seen," said the Cardinals' Ken Reitz. "It breaks down a foot."

The Steve Carlton fans applauded and hitters cussed in 1980 is a much different person than the man who nearly won 30 games for a dreadful team in 1972.

In a sense Steve stepped off the merry-go-round and into the real world one February night in 1973. It was at Tampa International Airport.

The banquets were over, the television appearances had ended and the outside demands on his time were being choked off. Now it was time to get back to baseball, to torture his body, get in shape and go after those 30 victories he had set as his '73 goal.

"You wouldn't believe the winter," Steve said as we drove to Clearwater late that night. "It has been one thing after another. . . . Are there a lot of reporters covering spring training?"

Steve Carlton, Gulliver in a land of Lilliputian performers, had won 27 of the Phils' 59 season victories. With that came his first Cy Young Award and hundreds of lesser honors.

He thought he could handle it. This very private man thought the intrusions into his personal world could be managed the same way he handled a .300 hitter with a full count.

He was wrong. It took Carlton three agonizing summers to recover from the incredible season of 1972.

He was too proud to tell people he had walking pneumonia in 1973 when his record was a dismal 13–20. And there was never a hint his arm was throbbing like a toothache much of the next two summers.

But in 1976 he had a 20–7 record as the Phillies won the National League East title, their first championship of any kind since 1950. He was 23–10 the following season and won the Cy Young Award again.

Carlton has altered his pitching style over the years. He

no longer overpowers the hitters with his fastball as he did when he struck out 19 batters in one game for the Cardinals in 1969. Instead he mixes a hard fastball with the best slider in baseball. Then, on occasion, he throws an outstanding change-up.

"I think Steve has gone the full cycle," said McCarver. "He was an overpowering youngster with a natural curve. I say 'natural' because very few kids are capable of that down-spin and, in fact, most veterans find it difficult to develop.

"In 1972 he showed how overpowering he was. Then he went into a period such as most of us encounter when we slow down and have to make adjustments. When a pitcher makes those adjustments successfully it's often said he has become the complete pitcher. His elbow was bothering him in 1973–74–75, but he seldom admitted it.

"Then, he resumed his stature as a power pitcher, but had 12, 13, 14 years of experience to go with it. So, he was first a power pitcher, then a pitcher, then a power pitcher with experience."

Aside from admittedly being in the best physical condition of his career in 1980, Carlton was also in a great frame of mind. One of the main reasons was that Ozark had been replaced by Green.

Green, a former pitcher, handled Carlton beautifully. In early, one-sided games he took Steve out before the end, knowing anytime he could give Carlton some innings off it would be money in the bank in September.

Green was openly criticized during spring training for not requiring Carlton to run sprints with the other pitchers. The manager answered his critics by pointing out Steve works harder and longer with his own program than just about anyone else on the team.

"The main thing about Carlton's program is that it's as much mental as physical," said Green. "It requires total concentration and a total commitment. His mental preparation for each game is a direct result of this program. And on the physical side, Steve Carlton is one of the strongest men in baseball. I'll tell you one thing, I tried his program and couldn't do it."

"The workouts are tough," added Hoefling. "Every muscle in the body, including the heart, almost reaches momentary failure."

Both Hoefling and Green agree the new manager made a big difference in 1980.

"Steve had a great mental attitude," said Green. "And part of it was his acceptance of me as the manager. It's no secret he had little love for Danny and I'm not sure he loves me, but I know he was happier. I allowed him to conduct his own conditioning without constant questions as to whether he was working. I never had to worry about Gus and Lefty."

"I really don't want to go into the Ozark thing too much," said Carlton. "I do know Dallas was under a lot of pressure when he took over. You know about Danny and me. I always considered Mr. O. my nemesis."

"Well *I* can tell you Steve Carlton was a much happier person when Dallas took over," said shortstop Larry Bowa. "I don't really think Steve had anything personal against Danny Ozark. I think he just thought Danny was an incompetent manager. He respected Dallas more because Dallas actually learned the ropes as a big-league pitcher. Danny had a tendency to go with the hot hand. If Tug McGraw was hot, Danny went with him. Dallas wanted to use everybody and Steve knew that. He knew Dallas knew how to use his pitchers.

"It's like early in the season. We're losing 2–0 to the Mets in the seventh inning. Dallas took Steve out for a pinch hitter. Later, Steve said just one thing to Dallas, 'You did the right thing.' Last year, Steve might have gone crazy. Not in public, of course, but he still might have gone crazy."

"Steve has been transformed into a calm, peaceful person, completely in control," added McCarver. "And, truthfully, there have been times when Lefty was not in complete control. I could tell a real difference between Steve in 1979 and Steve in 1980. A transformation took place."

After Carlton's 27–10, 1.98 ERA summer of '72, he was one of the most agreeable players on the team. He was a good interview and remained that way until a few seasons ago, when he began to withdraw.

When he tried to explain his philosophies on positive thinking a few reporters took cheap shots at him if he failed on the mound. He feels one particular Philadelphia writer had a vendetta against him. Finally Steve cut everyone off except for an occasional radio-TV interview after a game.

"There are a lot of reasons I feel the way I do about the press," he said. "I don't want to go into detail now, but one thing comes to mind that happened two or three years ago. All the so-called heavyweights from the Philadelphia area were around my locker after a game. I talked for 30 minutes about various things. The next day in the papers they ripped the hell out of me. None of the questions I had answered were in their stories. They just ripped me. So, I felt if that's the way it was I had better things to do after games with 30 minutes of time than spend it with them.

"As far as I'm concerned the press is one of the biggest enemies you have in Philadelphia. You have to first worry about the opposition, then all the things that are written in the paper. I have just cut all those distractions off."

Carlton handles failure as well as anyone I know. He has been known to wreck a hotel room with the best of them after an especially excruciating defeat, but when he's pitching he has conditioned himself to handle failure.

"You can't let yourself get on that emotional roller coaster ride over wins and losses," he said. "That's why you have to try to keep an even level of intensity. It becomes harder and harder, rather than easier, with the years.

"There are so many deviations in this game. And there is

always something else going on besides baseball. So often you just have to isolate yourself from everything else to try and keep up with your goals."

Now, Carlton seems to enjoy the lifestyle he has molded for himself. He and Beverly and sons Scott and Steve Jr. have a lavish home with an elaborate wine cellar, Carlton's number one hobby away from the game. He can talk for hours about wine, has some classic bottles in his vast collection and in 1979 toured the famous French vineyards.

In the clubhouse and on airplanes he passes the time reading psychology and Eastern philosophy—Taoism and Buddhism.

"I have been very much involved in a positive approach to life," he said. "It has worked for me. It's a good philosophy. I used to talk about this, but a lot of people (reporters) tore it apart when I was going poorly. I do not think it is necessary to air my personal wars publicly any longer. I would rather keep to myself and everyone will be happier in the long run."

Although because of this policy most reporters consider him rude, Carlton remains one of the most popular players on the team.

"When he had shots at no-hitters," said Green, "you wouldn't believe how much his teammates were pulling for him. They would love to see him get one."

"Gibby (former St. Louis pitcher Bob Gibson) used to tell me no-hitters are flukes," said Carlton. "Maybe I'll get one some day, but that's not a priority. In the game against St. Louis Ted Simmons got the hit early so there was nothing to think about. Against Atlanta, that was different. Bill Nahorodny had not been in the game from the start. He had only pinch-hit in the sixth, I think, so we really didn't have a pattern on him. I struck him out with three sliders the first time, then (in the eighth) tried to waste a pitch. It was a high fastball and he hacked at it. It was not a strike. I think it was a bad choice of pitches in that situation."

Carlton was right because Nahorodny, who grew up in the Phils' system, is a fastball hitter.

"I was very much aware I had a no-hitter going," said Steve. "You always are. You can see it happening. But like Gibby said, those things are flukes."

One of Carlton's biggest adjustments was meshing with a new catcher. Tim McCarver rejoined the Phils in 1975 and became Carlton's regular catcher. In '79, when it became obvious Timmy would retire at the end of the year, Boone began to catch some of Steve's games. The reason Boone had not been catching Carlton in the first place was because the two did not agree on how a game should be called.

"The important thing is communication," said Steve. "Sure, Timmy and I are great friends, and to know the inner workings of the individual is what matters most in handling a game, but you don't have to be great friends to have that type of communication.

"Bob Boone has come a long way in his thinking, but I don't want to get into that. He's made great gains as far as setting up the hitters. I think we work fine together now."

Seeing Steve Carlton become a certain Hall of Fame pitcher and help the Phillies to their first world championship has been the thrill of a lifetime for Steve's dad.

"I remember when I took him to sign up for Little League ball," said Joe Carlton who lives in Miami. "The first year he stood around the batting cage, came back to the car and said he didn't want to play.

"The next year I sat in the car while he went inside the recreation room. He came out a few minutes later and said, 'The coach wants to know what position I play.' I asked him, 'What position *do* you play?' He said, 'First and pitcher,' so I told him to tell the coach that and let him decide. They put Steve at pitcher and he's been there ever since. I'll tell you one thing, he has enjoyed this world championship more than he'll ever let on."

"I really felt once we got to the World Series the pressure was off," said Carlton. "That Houston series was unbelievable. It was even more difficult for the people who were not playing. I sat on the bench and the tension was tremendous. That Sunday we were down 5–2 with Nolan Ryan pitching. It was unbearable. Then, we score five runs off him in one inning. It was draining."

Carlton's first World Series start was in the second game. He struggled most of the night with slick baseballs and the Royals' attempts to break his concentration. He left after eight innings with the Phils trailing 4–2. They scored four runs in the bottom of the inning and Ron Reed saved the victory for him.

"The balls were kinda slick," Carlton remembered. "It was a cold, damp night and I don't think they had been rubbed up enough before the game."

Beverly Carlton says she has never seen Steve as happy as he has been since the team became world champion.

"We've really enjoyed the off-season," Steve agreed. "We took a cruise to the Bahamas last fall and have made two trips to Hawaii. It's been fun."

"He keeps repeating to me, 'We're world champions, we're world champions,'" she said again. "We're not only happy for ourselves and the other players, but also for the Carpenter family. They certainly deserved a world championship."

"It (the world championship) was important for a lot of reasons," said Carlton. "Many things had been said and written about this team in the past. Our winning put most of those to rest."

He paused a moment.

"I *think* they are put to rest."

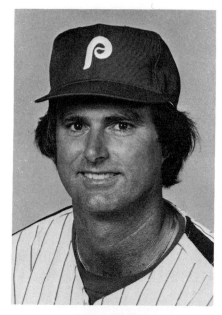

Steve Carlton

Dick Ruthven

Larry Christenson

Nino Espinosa

The Other Pitchers
"... one of the big differencs the second half ..."

A large, impressive-looking book sat on the filing cabinet in Dallas Green's office during the early months of the 1980 season. *How to Avoid Stress Before It Kills You,* the gold lettering stated.

Each day the rookie manager read a few pages, then watched his Phillies. A reporter walked into the Veterans Stadium office one night and suggested maybe Green should read the book *after* the game—rather than before.

During one stage of spring training Green admitted the team's pitching was scary. After a month of the season, it was even worse than the most severe critics thought it would be.

Only Steve Carlton showed consistency.

Dick Ruthven, the number one right-hander on the staff, lost two of his first three starts and had a 9.56 earned run average. Ruthven, who had bone chips removed from his right elbow in September of 1979, was not throwing with his normal velocity.

Larry Christenson, injury-prone ever since he came to the Phils, pulled a groin muscle and missed over a week.

Nino Espinosa and Warren Brusstar, both suffering from sore shoulders, opened the season on the disabled list and were not even being counted on.

Randy Lerch lost his first six decisions and never recovered.

The bullpen, like the starters, was groping for consistency. Dickie Noles, a converted 1979 starter, was trying to determine his actual role. Ron Reed and Tug McGraw were not able to hold late-inning leads with regularity. Lerrin LaGrow, released on July 17, never filled the role the Phils hoped he would. Kevin Saucier provided the only consistency with his adequate middle-inning relief.

Slowly, however, the pitching staff began to jell. Bob Walk arrived from Oklahoma City and reeled off six straight victories. Espinosa and Brusstar came off the disabled list and began to contribute. Ruthven gradually returned to form. Christenson, who missed almost three months after having bone chips removed from his elbow, returned on August 15 and gave the team a lift, ending with a 5–1 record.

Marty Bystrom, of course, came from Oklahoma City with the September 1 call-ups and on September 13, Player Personnel Director Paul Owens obtained reliever Sparky Lyle from the Texas Rangers for cash and a player to be named later (Saucier). By this time McGraw was on his tear. Even so, Lyle gave Scroogie a welcome breather down the stretch, working in 10 games and saving two. His ERA with Philadelphia was 1.93.

"The pitching all seemed to come together," said Green. "That was one of the big differences the second half of the season. We had some healthy arms."

On May 9, 1979, Ruthven blew away the Padres in San Diego. He shut them out 2–0 on just one hit, a seventh-inning double by Dan Briggs.

That night Ruthven had the world, if not the National league batters, in the palm of his hand. The victory gave him a 6–0 record, a 1.64 earned run average.

Little did Rufus know that game would be the highlight of the disastrous 1979 season. On August 21, he was placed on the disabled list for the second time that year and in September his elbow was operated on.

"I had had that kind of surgery before," said Ruthven, "so I felt the experience would help make the recovery faster, but I really didn't get my velocity back until August. I don't think it was so much the surgery as it was the doctor telling me not to do anything afterwards. The only thing he'd let me do was swim. Normally I would have been lifting weights, like I had done all the previous winters of my career.

"But in August and down the stretch I felt the hitters were acting like they did when I was pitching well. I had several games in a row when my control was better than it had been. Boonie (catcher Bob Boone) and I are good friends and I think he felt the same as I did."

Ruthven pitched seven innings but was not the winning pitcher when the Phils shocked Montreal 2–1 on Bake Mc-Bride's ninth-inning homer September 26. The following Friday night in Montreal, Ruthven worked 5⅔ innings as the Phils again edged the Expos 2–1.

"Most rewarding 5⅔ innings I have ever pitched," said Ruthven. "I didn't want to come out of the game when Dallas lifted me. That was an important game. If we had lost it, it would have been damn tough to come back and take two in a row from them in their park."

Ruthven wanted to start the fifth and crucial game of the playoffs against Houston, but Green had other ideas. In the end Rufus was called on to pitch the final two innings of relief and gained the victory in the 8–7, 11-inning classic.

"Dallas told me some conflicting things prior to that game," disclosed Ruthven. "I'm not going to get into his reasoning or my feelings about his reasoning but I really had trouble trying to figure out what was going on.

"I didn't think it was my place to argue with any decision he made. I told him my feelings and he told me I was going to be the first one to relieve in the first five innings. After that

I wouldn't be used because I'd be starting the first game of the World Series.

"I didn't make a big stink of it, but I wanted to start that playoff game. I thought I deserved the chance. Experience-wise, I thought it was a helluva spot to put Marty Bystrom in—but the outcome was fine.

"I was about as sharp as I could be those two innings. Frankly, I was shocked when I was told to warm up that late in the game. If you'll remember, I was up early but Brusstar and then Christenson went in.

"Funny thing, I thought I pitched pretty well in the second game of the playoffs at the Vet, too. I walked Nolan Ryan and he scored on a play that Manny Trillo and Bake McBride made perfectly two times later—once in the playoffs and once in the World Series.

"The ball was hit to right field, Bake fielded it and threw to Manny. For some reason Manny didn't make the relay. He held the ball. Ryan scored, but had Manny thrown, Ryan would have been out by 30 feet. You could hear him huffing and puffing going around the bases.

"I didn't know this, but Garry Maddox told me in Hawaii during Super Teams' competition that after the play was messed up, Bake and Manny went out and practiced it. I said, 'Oh, that's super.' So, even though I was upset at the time, my own experience helped us win a couple other games because those outs were important. I think there were a lot of times during the season where Manny or Bake probably would have said, 'Well, you shouldn't have walked the pitcher.' Or they would have made excuses other than the fact they didn't make the play at the plate."

Ruthven agrees with Steve Carlton the world championship was won by the Phillies because a lot of the players got hot at the same time.

"I also think some people grew up a little bit after Paul Owens scorched us in San Francisco," said Rufus. "I saw players starting to take responsibility that was theirs and do something about it. Neither Dallas' speech in Pittsburgh nor the Pope's lecture had anything to do with me or Lefty (Carlton)— or a certain number of other people. But there are some fragile individuals on this team and I think those clubhouse speeches really helped them.

"And obviously the way Dallas handled certain situations must have helped or else he wouldn't have continued to do some of those things. But I think the talent has always been there. I just think that rather than give Dallas Green's managing that much credit, I think I'd rather agree with Lefty and say we just got hot. Everything fell together. Things like that don't happen on a manager's scale. He's certainly no psychologist, so you can't give him credit on that account. I just think it was time for things to fall together for a team that had a lot of talent.

"I used to think about the Phillies when I was pitching against them in Atlanta. The talent was tremendous and it would have been a shame for them to grow old and split apart without having won it all."

Ruthven insists Green's philosophy was to make the players so mad they took out their frustrations on the opposition.

"I think what he did needed to be done to certain individuals, but I also feel the mistake he made was not being able to separate the people who didn't need that (being made mad) from those who did. He treated everybody the same. And it really bothered some of the guys who had always been self-motivated. They didn't have to have somebody screaming at them to play. I think that hurt some feelings."

Green hurt Ruthven's feelings on June 13 and the right-hander didn't pitch again until June 28.

It was a game against San Diego, won by Ruthven and the Phillies 9–6. During the early innings Ruthven struggled, frequently falling behind in the count. Green made a trip to the mound in an attempt to settle his right-hander.

"He was struggling with his rhythm and control," said Green. "Those 3–1 counts were making .250 hitters into .350 hitters in a hurry."

With two out in the sixth inning, Ruthven fell while fielding Tim Flannery's bunt and had to leave the game with a contusion on his right shoulder.

"Dallas got me so goddamn mad that night I almost broke my shoulder," remembered Ruthven. "He came out to the mound and started screaming at me like I was a rookie or something. I told him I didn't think I needed that, that I knew what I was doing. What he did was get me to try too hard and when Flannery hit the bunt, I tried to make an impossible play and fell on the shoulder. It was just that he couldn't differentiate between the guys who needed to be yelled at and those who didn't.

"I was the subject of his remarks to the press quite a bit, but I just didn't comment on them. Really, I don't think anybody wants to be a third person over something critical.

"If somebody's going to have some kind of criticism to make, he should direct it to you first and then go to the press. When people say Dallas Green went to the press first, they're making a legitimate point. I think it would have been traumatic if that had happened to Dallas when he was a player.

"As manager, Dallas Green needed a .22 and used an atom bomb. Sure, it worked, but it didn't make very many friends."

Ruthven usually is cooperative with reporters, but basically he remains luke-warm with most of us.

"It's a very competitive market," he said. "There are knowledgeable baseball writers and there are some writers who think they are knowledgeable but aren't. They write for major newspapers and it seems they stand in judgment rather than report the games. I think that's the history of Philadelphia sportswriting. I feel like I answer questions when they are asked of me, but I guess the writers don't necessarily think so. I don't think I am rude but I don't read the newspapers. I don't think they are accurate in a lot of cases—from what I hear. And obviously, if you say you don't read the papers they're still in the clubhouse so you end up reading one now and then. But I really try not to get eaten up with it. *My opinion is what I value and what the writer's opinion of a certain game is doesn't bother me because he's only trying to sell newspapers.*"

Despite all the distractions and turmoil, winning the world championship was still the greatest thing—in athletics—that has ever happened to Ruthven.

"Some people said I was blasé about it, but I don't think I was. I might not do somersaults like Tug McGraw, but I thought it was great. From spring training to the end, it was what everybody worked for.

"I thought the way we achieved it was, you know, not logical. It took a sequence of events that were very strange. I can't imagine a more theatrical way of winning. It was a rough two weeks at the end.

"Winning a world championship was one of the goals I had when I started in baseball. I still have a few left. It's just a shame we couldn't have had more fun—as much fun as we had as a team the last month. It seems like this team has trouble having fun as a group."

Larry Christenson was born with one imperfect vertebra way down in his spine.

But contrary to popular belief he was not born on Friday, the 13th and a black cat didn't dash in front of the car en route to the hospital. And, no, his mom wasn't wheeled under a ladder on her way to the delivery room.

Christensen, you see, has checked all these things out because there are times when he wonders why one guy has to be so unlucky.

Heck, the vertebra is enough of a handicap without all the other things.

If ever there was an accident-prone athlete, it's Larry Christenson. He's spent more time in hospitals than Marcus Welby, more time on ice than Eric Heiden.

Since he became a professional pitcher in 1972 he's been out with bad backs, groin and hamstring pulls, broken collarbones, bone spurs, bone chips and other minor ailments.

"Maybe I should have bought the violin after all," Christenson says. "It might have been easier."

When Christenson was in seventh grade a specialist told him to quit sports and take up the violin. With the youngster's vertebra problem, the doc felt Larry would never hold up in athletics.

Christenson found himself under constant pressure in 1980, but that's the way it has been most of his career. After returning from the bone-chip surgery he pulled a groin muscle and again was doubtful. In fact, Green told people L.C. probably would not be available the remainder of '80. But on September 24 the blond right-hander made a start against the Mets.

"Now that was pressure," said Christenson. "I had to worry about my leg breaking down in that start. But it turned out fine. I only gave up four hits over eight innings."

The 26-year-old started just 14 games for the world champions because of all his injuries. He was out most of 1979 because of a fractured collarbone and later a severe groin pull.

Had it not been for his strong showing against the Mets in September, he probably would not have gotten to pitch against Houston in the playoffs and Kansas City in the fourth game of the World Series—a start he would just as soon forget.

Actually, Green had planned to scratch Christenson for post-season play in favor of Bystrom. Larry, however, had other ideas and proved his point against the Mets.

"If I hadn't been a part of the team in the playoffs and against the Royals, it would have been the biggest disappointment of my life," said Christenson, who has had more than a few. "Even though I didn't contribute as much as I would have liked, winning that championship is still the greatest thrill I have ever had."

On August 15, 1979, Nino Espinosa began his warm-up for a start against Cincinnati at Riverfront Stadium.

"It was my 26th birthday," the right-hander remembered. "I threw a couple of pitches and felt a little twinge on top of my right shoulder near the joint. I continued warming up, but it seemed like my arm would not loosen like it usually does. I didn't know what to think."

Espinosa obviously put the pain and stiffness out of his mind. He pitched a complete game, winning 3–2 and allowing the Reds just five hits. The victory left him with a 13–9 record and a 3.60 earned run average.

That start, however, was the beginning of Espinosa's problems—problems that hampered him most of 1980 and kept him out of the playoffs and World Series.

The day after his victory over the Reds, the shoulder stiffened and there was more pain. He lost three of his next four decisions and finally had to call it a season after losing to Montreal 7–4 on September 23.

From then until July 1, 1980, Espinosa lived a nightmare. He returned to his home in the Dominican Republic and rested the arm and shoulder for two months. When he tried to pitch the following December, there was no improvement. When he went to spring training in February, the situation was even worse.

The pain was so excruciating he could hardly lob the ball. When the season opened he was on the disabled list and some people wondered if he would pitch at all in 1980.

Gradually, the pain began to leave, but Nino was left with little or no velocity on his fastball. In June of '80, stories hit area newspapers that quoted Green as saying there comes a time when pitchers with sore arms have to learn to pitch with pain. Brusstar, he said, was in the same category.

One headline blared: "Green to Nino and Bru: Pitch or Quit!"

"I went into Dallas' office with the stories and asked him if he said those things," Espinosa said. "He told me he said sometimes players have to learn to play with pain. He did not say we either had to pitch or quit."

Espinosa and Brusstar both made it back.

Relying on his craftiness as a "pitcher," Espinosa turned in his first complete game since 1979 on August 14, 1980. He defeated his former teammates, the New York Mets 8–1, allowing five hits during the Phillies' important five-game sweep.

Because he feels he was treated so unkindly by reporters when he was struggling to come back, Espinosa seldom grants interviews.

"In a sense, my problem was like J. R. Richard's in Houston," he said. "A lot of people did not think I was hurting, that my arm problem was in my head. Nobody knows when you're hurting except yourself. J. R. Richard almost died. Now, if somebody says he is hurt, people will believe him."

Green, a former pitcher, told Espinosa he (Green) had arm problems. "When all the medical people say you're structurally sound, you have to go out and throw. You have to try to pitch through it."

Espinosa's problem was diagnosed as bursitis. A rehabilitation program was devised by team trainers Don Seger and Jeff Cooper, and by late in June of '80, the arm and shoulder were strong and the pain was gone.

"Dallas wanted me to go to Spartanburg for 20 days," said Espinosa. "I didn't want to go at all, but finally agreed to go for 10. I made three starts and my arm felt fine."

In two previous seasons with the Mets prior to joining the Phils in a deal for Richie Hebner, Espinosa worked 200 and 204 innings, respectively. During his first season with the Phils, he pitched 212 innings.

"I really don't think that is what caused the problem," he said. "We had so many injuries in 1979, I pitched most of the year with three days rest. I had never done that before. Once after I got knocked out of a game in St. Louis I came back two days later and pitched against the Mets. With just three days rest my arm did not have time to come back.

"I had never had any kind of injury before. Just like J. R. Richard. I seldom, if ever, missed a start. Because we were still in the 1979 pennant race in August, I took my turn even though I was hurting. I felt I should not walk out on the team, but I should have rested my arm then. In my last start that year, my arm was hurting so much I did nothing more than push the ball."

Some people insist that's all he did in '80 even though he had a 3–5 record and 3.79 ERA in 12 starts. When Green and Owens decided to get Nino to go on the disabled list for post-season play so Bystrom and Saucier would be eligible, Nino balked at first. Then, he accepted, and was in uniform and in the dugout for each of the games.

"I wanted to be part of the team," he said, still refusing to admit his arm was aching. "Sure, I would have liked to pitch, but the Phillies have been too good to me to turn my back on them."

Earlier, he said: "I don't know why they make such a big deal about my velocity. It would have been different if I had been a power pitcher before I was hurt. True, I struck out 105 batters in 200 innings in 1977, but I was not a power pitcher. I know I used to throw harder than I did last year (1980), but I also know my velocity is coming back.

"I have never gone out and tried to throw the ball down the middle of the plate, to blow people away. I have to pitch in and out—in and out. That's always been my style."

"We think he was still hurting some," said Green. "He showed me something trying to pitch, but there was no way he could help us in the playoffs and World Series."

Lerch took a different approach.

After ending with a 4–14 record and 5.16 ERA, he did not stick around for the happy times after he and Espinosa were dropped for the post-season games.

Minutes after he was told of the team's decision, he left the clubhouse and did not return.

"I was disappointed," he said. "I had been a part of the team, I thought, then I wasn't. I felt they were not fair with me; they never took into consideration the four seasons I gave the Phillies. I had always been devoted to the organization since I signed with them in 1973. I just was not wanted."

It was July 13, 1980 when Brusstar stepped into the bullpen shuttle. The driver turned to him and said: "It must feel good to be back."

"You've got that right," Brusstar said, his piercing eyes staring straight ahead.

The one-time standout reliever had not thrown a pitch in major-league competition since July 24, 1979. He had not pitched effectively since the year before. Nobody in the organization had any reason to think Brusstar would ever pitch again in the majors.

During the off-season prior to 1979, Brusstar injured an ankle playing basketball during Tug McGraw's benefit bicycle caravan in California. When he got to spring training the ankle was still bothering him so he compensated for it. The result was a nagging shoulder injury.

He opened the '79 season on the disabled list, finally was reactivated on June 28, but in 13 appearances had a 7.07 earned run average. He was certainly not the same middle reliever who was so outstanding in 1977 and 1978. He gave up the comeback attempt on July 24 after the Dodgers' Dusty Baker blasted a grand-slam homer.

The injury became a medical mystery. Doctors were unable to find anything clinically wrong, but Brusstar insisted there was pain.

Finally, in April of 1980, he made an appointment with

Dr. David Fitzmorris, a St. Louis chiropractor recommended by Steve Carlton.

"The pain wasn't that bad in the spring," said Bru. "What was bothering me most was the fact I couldn't throw with any velocity."

In St. Louis, Fitzmorris worked on Brusstar twice a day for 17 days. He concentrated on key pressure points in the shoulder and surrounding areas to improve strength and range of motion.

"The first time I saw him he pushed my arm down with two fingers," said Brusstar. "By the time I left, he couldn't put it down at all. He used a technique called Accupressure, using different pressure points down the muscle to get blood flowing properly back into the muscle. It helped quite a lot. Then, I got a program from Gus Hoefling. The rest was just a matter of throwing enough to get all the muscles a pitcher uses back in tune."

Dickie Noles reminds people of a fearless gunslinger in one of those old cowboy flicks. He swaggers into the middle of a saloon brawl, draws his six-shooter and when the smoke settles all the problems are sprawled out on the floor.

The only difference is Noles does not use a six-shooter. He uses his right arm and now people are saying one pitch he threw in the World Series changed the tide in the Phillies' favor.

Who will ever forget it? George Brett certainly won't.

It came in the fourth inning of the fourth game, a duel won by the Royals 5–3.

Noles relieved Christenson in the first inning after L. C. had been bombed for five runs on four hits. Willie Aikens blasted a second-inning homer off Noles, but it was the only run he would allow in 4⅔ innings. In the fourth, he was ahead of Brett 0–2 and his next pitch brushed George back and he fell to the ground. Royals' Manager Jim Frey roared out of the dugout incensed, screaming Noles threw at the superstar.

After the rhubarb, Noles struck Brett out and the Royals

went quietly in the next two Series games, both won by the Phillies.

"Some people think I turned the World Series around with that pitch," said Noles. "Some lady just sent me a newspaper article that said had it not been for that knock-down pitch, the Series would have gone the other way. I don't know.

"When I watched the American League playoffs, I saw Brett hit a homer off the Yankees' Goose Gossage on a pitch out over the plate. So that day I was thinking, 'Boy, there's no way you can pitch this guy away.' Now, with the count 0–2 I made up my mind to come inside on him about hip-high. I wasn't trying to hit him, but he had to get out of the way of it. I wanted him to know I was coming in and my ball rises anyway, but I wasn't trying to hit him.

"Then, Jim Frey came out there and started yelling. The ball started out waist-high and just took off. What else can I say?"

Noles says he has never been excited about relieving, "but I will do anything they ask of me because I am happy being in the big leagues. The year started out for me pretty good in the bullpen, but I didn't like the job. I just don't think I am a reliever; I can win 15 or more games as starter. There's not much I can do, though, when they put me in that situation. When Ron Reed and Tug got in a good groove, there was not much for me to do."

Reed ended with a 7–5 record and 4.05 ERA and nine saves.

"Overall, I was not that happy with last year on a personal basis," he said. "I think there's room for improvement, but winning the World Series was just great. Julie (his wife) and I sat around the fireplace during the winter and all of a sudden we'd start talking about the World Series. You know, I've had 13 years in the big leagues without ever getting there. You work and you work and you work and when you finally get into a World Series, you realize what you've been working for. It was the ultimate. I just can't put my feelings into words.

"Unfortunately, we're paid on individual performance and so naturally when you start recapping a year like I had, there have to be a few bad memories. Not even a world championship can make you forget all of them. I don't think that is being selfish because I think every player on the club probably analyzed his personal performance, you know, what he contributed to the club."

Reed thinks the season turned around after the Pirates swept the Phils four games in Pittsburgh.

"I think when we went into Three Rivers for that crucial four-game series and they blew us away, we had our tails tucked between our legs. We limped out of town much as we had done before. It was pretty quiet on the bus and during the plane trip to Chicago. In Chicago I think everybody was still kinda stunned over the four-game loss in Pittsburgh. But when we got to New York guys were saying, 'Hey, we're not this bad.' I know several of us sat around and just said, 'There is no way we're that bad. It's just impossible.' We went out onto the field and blew away the Mets in five games."

In the second game of the double-header on Sunday, August 10, in Pittsburgh, Reed was called on to relieve. When he was removed, he and Green went face to face in the dugout. Both had to be restrained. Green says it was an important moment for him. Reed agrees.

"I don't know what his reaction was deep inside," said Reed. "I know what he said to me. I think it had a reverse effect. I think that incident brought the team closer together. Not just because I happened to be the one who was the center of attention, but I think from that point on Dallas fully realized the guys on this team would fight for one another. Our confrontation wasn't just because I was mad at him."

Between games of that double-header, of course, Green

delivered his now-famous Pittsburgh Address. Some of the things he said disturbed Reed.

"Several things brought on our confrontation," explained Reed. "I'm sure Dallas would like to forget about it and I'd like to forget about it and let it go at that. But it just wasn't a personal thing. It offends me when I see players ripped or second-guessed who I know are giving 100 percent. I don't think anyone should be—and it doesn't necessarily have to be aimed at me to get me mad. I feel like my teammates will go out and fight for me, and I darn sure would fight for any of those guys on that club at any time. I think the Pittsburgh thing was just spur-of-the-moment where I felt like I was fighting for the club because Dallas had said a few things I didn't like—not just at me, but at some of the other players.

"I think it was just his way of trying to shake up the team and get it turned around because we were obviously getting our butts kicked. And when I came out, I just felt like I wanted him to know this ball club was going to fight and not give up, and try to win the thing (division).

"From then on, we never did really hit it off too well. I don't know whether he was holding a grudge toward me or what. I didn't feel like I was holding a grudge toward him in any way, shape or form. I just had one thing on my mind. I just wanted to do whatever I could for us to win. And I think everybody on the club felt the same way."

"I'm sure Dallas had his reasons for saying some of the things he did to me and to some of the players.

As for his season, Reed said: "Everybody would like to get as much work as he possibly could and know exactly what he is supposed to be doing at all times. With Danny Ozark I knew exactly where I stood 99 times out of a hundred. With Dallas, I never did. One night I'd come in in the second or third inning, and then the next night I'd be finishing up a ball game. I never knew which way to take him. One game really sticks in my mind. It was at Montreal. I came in and the first batter up hit a pop-up to Manny Trillo who dropped the ball. Dallas came to the mound and took me out. It was the eighth or ninth inning. There was no explanation. He just came and got the ball and that was it. Willie Montanez was the next batter up, a left-hander. So, Dallas brought in Sparky Lyle to pitch to Montanez. Danny Ozark never did that to me. I always felt I could get left-handers out just as well as I can right-handers.

"There were a couple of other incidents that I didn't understand, but I told Dallas early in the year, 'Hey, I'm not going to try to manage this club. That's your job and I wouldn't want it. Just a little communication, I think, is what everybody wants.'

"At times he didn't communicate. I never played for a manager before who didn't let me know exactly where I stood. That was the only gripe I had about the year. I could never get myself together because I wasn't really sure what my job was. I'd be in a short relief role for two or three weeks and for one of those weeks I'd be throwing super, then the next week I'd lose it. My inconsistent pitching and the difficulty of not really knowing where I stood with him just added up to a kind of frustrating year for me.

"And as I look back, I know darn well I can pitch better. I'm going to prove it in 1981."

Mike Schmidt promised Tug McGraw while the two were driving to Veterans Stadium for the sixth game of the World Series that he was going to leap on top of the relief pitcher after the final out. He did not let McGraw down as the Phillies started their world championship celebration.

Tug McGraw
". . . Wilson has to be looking for a screwball."

It might happen when he's driving Mark and Cari Lynn to school.

Or during long flights across the country.

Twice it caused him to wake up in the middle of the night in a cold sweat.

Tug McGraw has no control over it. Just when he thinks it's under control, something flicks the switch and his mind flashes back to that last, dramatic pitch of the 1980 World Series.

The bases are drunk with Royals—a walk and two hits have gotten him into that ninth-inning jam. The Phillies are leading 4–1, there are two out and the long-suffering fans are poised for their jailbreak.

The count's 1–2 to Willie Wilson.

"I don't think I've ever been more concerned about being successful and getting out of an inning," McGraw remembers. "I've never been more concerned about my future because my arm was gone. It was numb and I could hardly feel the ball in my hand.

"You know how your arm feels when you bang your crazy bone on a table or something? Your fingers go numb and tingle. When my arm gets tired, that's what happens.

269

"If you keep pitching you can tear the nerve and ruin your arm for life. Then you have real problems.

"I was very close to calling Dallas Green and having him come and get me."

An impish smile came across Tug's face. His brown eyes got brighter as he related one of the greatest moments in Phillies' baseball history.

"But then, I guess I was having too much fun to do that. I just felt if I could muster up enough to get Wilson everything would be OK.

"And I knew if I didn't get Willie, I wouldn't have to call for Dallas anyway. He'd be there.

"So at that point I was trying to regroup. I was trying to remember everything I'd ever learned about pitching. Because in order to get past Wilson, I had to be mechanically perfect, otherwise my arm was going to blow. I also had to remember not to try to throw any harder than I was capable of throwing. 'Stay within yourself,' I kept repeating. 'Throw a strike!'

"And all the time I was standing there trying to get myself wired for that last pitch—it was only a matter of seconds really—I noticed the (police) dogs and horses. Considering the type of pitcher I am, the type of person I am, it happened at the right time. If I hadn't noticed the dogs and horses and policemen, I think I probably would have screwed up the whole thing because I was so tense and so nervous about trying to do everything right, I was almost too up-tight to do anything right.

"And when I saw the horses and dogs it kind of became comical and gave me a chance to put things back in perspective and say, 'Look, this is where you've wanted to be all your life. You're here! So what are you worried about?' And I saw the dogs and I thought, 'Ah, K-9 Corps. This is the ninth inning and I need a K (strikeout).' I can't believe it, but I really did think of that. And then I saw a horse relieving himself and

said to myself, 'There's no way *I'm* going to be horseshit.'
Here I was telling myself jokes and it was kind of humorous.
It just relaxed me enough to come up with the pitch I
needed."

One pitch. Just one pitch.

McGraw shook off catcher Bob Boone several times and
as the 65,839 fans in Veterans Stadium became quiet for a
moment on that cool Tuesday night, he took a deep breath.

"As soon as I let the ball go I knew Wilson was struck
out," said McGraw. "He was expecting a screwball and we
threw him a fastball—a John Jameson fastball. Down the middle, up a little. He acted like he was going to take it for an
instant, then he tried to swing."

Pictures of McGraw joyously leaping off the mound to celebrate the moment were in magazines and newspapers and on
television screens all over the globe the next day. The Phillies
had won their first World Series in 98 seasons and the zany
Frank Edwin McGraw had sealed the championship as he had
done so frequently in crucial games down the stretch.

"The Montreal series (last weekend of regular season) was
the peak of my career," said McGraw in late February. "There
is no way I can pitch any better. I flash back on that all the
time. I see hitters looking at pitches and swinging and missing
pitches that were as perfect as I could throw them—location-
wise, rotation-wise, mechanics-wise. And I'll be thinking about
that great series and then my mind will suddenly flash to the
last pitch. It's a sobering thought, like a cold shower. Willie
Wilson comes up, the bases are loaded and I get nervous all
over again."

Had it not been for the flappable McGraw's magnificent
year, the Phillies would not be world champions. Period.

He came off a reluctant exile to the disabled list on July
17 and proceeded to turn in incredible statistics. In 33 games
he had a 5–1 record over 52⅓ innings, allowed only three
earned runs, recorded 13 saves and had an 0.52 earned run

average. For the entire regular season he was 5–4, had a 1.47 ERA and 20 saves.

He was in all five games in the playoffs against Houston, had two saves and suffered a loss. In the 77th World Series he had a victory, a defeat, two saves and a 1.17 ERA after relieving in four games.

But to the thousands and thousands of Delaware Valley fans, Tugger preserved the world championship by striking out Willie Wilson with the bases loaded and two out in the ninth inning of the sixth game on October 21, 1980.

McGraw tugged on their hearts a little, but he came through.

"I told Boonie when we went out for the ninth inning and before I got in all that trouble, that my arm was getting tired and we ought to be careful about using the screwball too much," said McGraw. "As it turned out, I had to use it. So when Wilson came up, I figured he was definitely going to be looking for the scroogie. Boonie felt the same way. We threw it to him on the first pitch, just to show it to him. As I wound up I said to myself, 'This has to be a good pitch. It has to be the best screwball I have left because it's the only one I am going to throw him. After this, I won't be able to throw it again. Not even once.'

"My fingers were really tingling. So I threw him a real good screwball and my fingers went. They started jumping on me. But it was a strike—a called strike! It was such a good pitch Wilson didn't even swing at it.

"That set the pattern. We had him looking screwball all the way after that. He took that scroogie like a hitter will sometimes, almost saying, 'Throw it again and challenge me.' We came back with a slider on the inside which didn't hurt my hand at all. I didn't even feel anything in my arm because with the slider, you don't extend your elbow nearly as far as you do with other pitches. He fouled it off. I'm ahead 0–2.

"Now Boonie called for another screwball. I had told him

no more screwballs, but he called for it, knowing I'd shake it off. Then he called for a curveball and he knows there's no way I'm going to throw a curve, my fourth-best pitch, in that situation. Knowing I'm going to shake him off, he was just going through the pitches to drive Wilson crazy. I realized right away what Boonie was doing, so I shook off a few more.

"Then we threw what I call the Cutty Sark fastball—it sails a little bit. What we were trying to do was get it up a little bit, not a slider mind you, but something we could really pump. We wanted it up and in, hoping we could get it by him.

"I remember in my wind-up I was rushing. I wound up a little too fast and rushed it. I wanted to get it over with in a hurry because I knew I was going to strike him out with that pitch. I tried to over-throw and my hand tingled. The pitch was high, ball one.

"Now the count's 1–2 and I said to myself, 'If I can still pump the ball that quickly, then we've got to come back with another one because Wilson has to be looking for a screwball.' I remember telling myself to slow my wind-up, bring my leg up a little higher and get my arm up before I started forward. I was really going through the mechanics. And at the same time I was laughing at all the other stuff that was going on around me—the dogs and the cops and the horses. That's the greatest thing that ever happened in American sports, but that's another story.

"And then, just before I was ready to wind up and throw that last pitch, I flashed back to the afternoon driving to the ball park with Mike Schmidt. All through the season we had driven to the park and stopped on the way to get milkshakes or whatever. We're driving along and he says, 'I've got a feeling you're going to be in the game at the end tonight even though Lefty (Steve Carlton) is pitching.'

"He said after the Montreal and Houston games my picture was in all the papers jumping off the mound to celebrate.

'I'm sick and tired of you having your picture splashed across the front pages because you jump up and down all the time,' he said. 'If you're in the game for the final out, I'm going to come across from third, dive across in front of you and my picture's going to be on the front page for a change, jumping up in the air.' So I flashed on that, just before I started my wind-up, because I just had this great feeling this was going to be the pitch. I wound up, threw the ball and as soon as I let go, I knew. I knew that was it. We got him. I started to run towards Boonie, then I remembered Schmitty and I turned and I started hopping toward third base. Schmitty got a late start, but here he came. He dove right across in front of me and that's the picture that was on the front page of every damn newspaper the next day. Schmitty was freaked out."

Those were the highs for the left-handed reliever who turned 36 on August 30.

There were several lows, significant moments to his greatest season in nearly 14 major-league summers.

There was the incident on Monday night, August 25 when he lost his poise and deliberately hit Dodger shortstop Bill Russell. It was not the finest hour for Tug McGraw.

And before that there was the afternoon of August 15 at New York's Shea Stadium when a serious McGraw turned his back on his teammates and decided he really didn't want to remain with the Phillies.

McGraw went to his old ball park early that afternoon, slowly changed his clothes and switched on a radio in his locker. It was playing Elvis Presley music, a tribute to the late rock-and-roll king.

"As the players drifted in and started their card games and put their own songs on, I just lost my privacy," said McGraw. "I lost my seat and it was almost as if I was thrown out of the clubhouse. Their relaxation was more important than mine and I just felt it was kind of selfish on their part."

So McGraw took his radio, left the dressing room and

climbed up into the stands at Shea. He turned his radio up and looked out over the field where he had so many great moments while pitching for the Mets between 1969 and 1974.

"We were coming off difficult times, so maybe I was feeling low to start with," said McGraw. "That was the end of the same trip that started in Pittsburgh when we lost four in a row to the Pirates and Dallas Green exploded.

"But my teammates knew I probably was going to become a free agent at the end of the year and it seemed like all of a sudden the guys didn't seem that close anymore. It was like they were saying, 'Well, he'll probably be gone next year, so what?' Maybe my own insecurities were involved because I have always had those kind of things in my personality.

"At any rate, there was a lot of confusion in everyone's mind as to where we were going and how the season would end. I sat in the stands at Shea and did a lot of reflecting. The Elvis Presley music was loud. I started reflecting on my past adventures with the Mets and thinking about how if this was the way it was going to be around the Phillies' clubhouse, that maybe it would be more fun to come back to where I used to remember having such a great time and having the respect and consideration of the other players.

"Since I'm always goofing around and everything like that, and suddenly wanted to be serious, maybe my teammates didn't take me seriously. It was easy to understand how the situation could have developed without any real need for me to take it so personally.

"Shortly after that—in fact we won all five games from the Mets—the season turned around. Not that it had anything to do with me sitting in the stands that afternoon, but it was an important turning point for everyone."

Interestingly, the out-going McGraw never felt he was really accepted by the Phillies until after he had been with them several seasons.

"At first, it was the adjustment of coming to a new team

(in 1975)," his wife, Phyllis said. "After that, it was just a lot of little things. Nothing ever went very steady for him and throughout his career he's been a pretty consistent ball player. It seemed like there was always something to pull him down."

"When I first joined the Phillies, I felt like an outsider," admitted McGraw, in one of his dead-serious moods. "I didn't feel like I was part of the team. And rightly so. Most of the players had come up through the Phillies' farm system. They were home-grown and I wasn't. Earlier, the team had had some problems with my brother, Hank, when he was in the minor-league system. He had long hair and Lou Kahn wanted him to cut it off.

"After I was here for a short period of time it became obvious the Phillies had a different approach to the game than I had been used to in New York—that of enjoying the entertainment aspects of being a professional athlete and sharing that with the press and the fans. I always had a wide-open relationship with the fans and press. When I came to the Phillies with that attitude, I felt a little bit like the players weren't accepting it and they were a little bit upset with The Tug McGraw Show.

"It took a long time for them to get used to me and for me to get used to them. After having gone through the winning seasons of 1976–77–78 and after the trauma of 1979 when I gave up all those grand-slam homers (tied a major-league record with four), we had pretty much bonded ourselves together. I felt a lot closer to the guys following 1979.

"And then, 1980 was a new beginning for me. I was coming off a bad year and with Dallas taking over as manager we were all excited because the front office had not broken up the team. I think we felt a lot closer. But then with me probably becoming a free agent at the end of the year, some of that went away."

Had it not been for Phyllis McGraw's demanding Tug

give up some of his outside activities and concentrate on baseball, he might not have had his remarkable season.

"I got very upset with him about all the time he was spending on promotions and other activities," she said. "I remember almost shouting at him one night, 'Relax and get your mind on baseball and forget about everything else.' I don't know whether that was the reason or not, but he was a much better pitcher in 1980. He got his act together."

"When I signed my four-year contract in 1976, I figured I was going to be 36 when it expired and there was a pretty good chance it would be my last contract. It was not a far-fetched thought for a guy to be finished at 36. So I kinda had it in my mind that as the last two years of the contract approached I'd begin to involve myself more and more in outside activities. Then I would be able to go through the transition from being an on-the-field player to a post-season career without a lot of problems.

"But for the first time in my career, I began to realize the amount of concentration it requires to be a professional baseball player and to do a good job. I had cheated myself. I had taken from my being 100 percent a baseball player and put my energies in other directions. And all those activities also took away from my family and everything else worthwhile. I was spreading myself too thin and I wasn't able to do a good job at any of it. I wasn't good at trying to be the new things I was trying to be and I wasn't good at trying to be the relief pitcher I had been. And I certainly wasn't as good at being the husband and father I had tried to be. So after talking with Phyllis—and some friends—I decided to work hard after the 1979 season at getting in shape, staying healthy and preparing for 1980. Phyllis pointed out to me both Jim Kaat and Gaylord Perry were winning pitchers and they were in their 40s."

With Phyllis at his side, McGraw decided to go for it.

"She said no matter how successful you're going to be off

the field, you're never going to have the opportunities you're going to have if you play baseball for a few more years.

"We put a lot of things on the back-burner. I cut way back in personal appearances and other off-the-field involvements. I started paying more attention to my family and concentrated on baseball. About the same time I did all that on my own—it really started at the end of 1979—the Phillies decided it was time to do something about the way the team was. They fired Danny Ozark and Dallas came in with some new approaches that were long overdue. The two things happening together, I think, were responsible for my great year. I probably would have had a good year on my own without the change, and if I had not made the personal change I think the Phillies would have had a good year, too, because of the way Dallas used his pitching staff. But I think the two things together, coming at the same time, went hand-in-hand.

"I think Dallas handled the pitching staff as well as anybody could. He used Carlton as the anchor and I feel he used the bullpen very well. Before last year I thought Gil Hodges was the best I'd ever seen at using a pitching staff. Green was just as good."

McGraw was aware of the problems other players had with the manager, "but I had a tendency not to pay much attention to them because they did not involve me. I learned a long time ago from Gil Hodges when he was managing the Mets that aside from your responsibility to get people out, and other than being a member of a team, don't worry about other players unless they come to you for help. So that's what I do. I don't involve myself."

In addition to giving up the grand-slam homers in 1979, McGraw had a 4–3 record, a 5.14 ERA and 16 saves. His failures were not as great as the record indicates, but the grand-slams magnified everything.

"I heard the remarks about the 1979 season all winter long. They called me the 'Slammer,' 'One-Pitch McGraw,' things like that," he said. "Everytime I got the ball in 1980, I made sure I wasn't going to be the one everyone was going to use as an excuse. Ever since I came to the Phillies—whenever we lost playoff games or whatever, when we let a big one slip away—somebody had to make an excuse. It was an umpire's decision. It was the matter of not putting the right guy in for defense. It was the weather. There were injuries. I hate excuses. But somebody came up with every excuse you can think of. And as I saw us getting hot in '80, I was determined *I* was never going to be that excuse."

It was that approach, that determination, that led to McGraw's most embarrassing moment in baseball.

During a tense ninth inning against the Dodgers on August 25, he was ordered to intentionally walk Joe Ferguson.

The Dodger pinch-hitter looked at the first pitch, then leaned across the plate and roped a two-run single to right field that helped Los Angeles to a not-soon-to-be-forgotten 8–4 victory over the Phillies.

Bill Russell was the next batter. McGraw's first pitch was close, the second closer, the third almost hit him and the fourth drilled him on the shoulder. The Dodger shortstop charged the mound and both benches emptied. The brawl lasted five minutes, with Russell and Dodger Manager Tommy Lasorda eventually being ejected.

"That was the first time in my entire professional career I ever lost my temper on the mound because of something I allowed to happen," Tug said. "Trying to intentionally walk a guy and throwing a pitch close enough for him to hit was my fault. I've always felt it unprofessional to intentionally try to throw at a batter for the purpose of hitting him. I still feel that way.

"I was very embarrassed and ashamed I allowed myself to lose my temper like that on the mound. After it was all over and I went home that night I was extremely disappointed in myself. The next day I sent an apology to Bill Russell. I have seen other pitchers do it and never could understand how they let themselves be that way, but now I think I understand it a little better. I will always look back on that as the most embarrassing moment of my career."

McGraw paused a moment. "I don't think I'll ever lose my temper to that degree again. I was too scared of myself, mad at myself and ashamed of myself to let it happen again.

"It all came about because of what I said earlier. I was determined in 1980 not to be the excuse for losses. When I went into the game that night we were still in it, had a chance to win. When I let Ferguson hit a pitch on an intentional walk, we were out of it. That's what burned me up so much. Oh, I'll probably let a guy hit a ball again some time when I'm trying to walk him, but I won't deliberately hit the next batter."

A week later the Phillies were in Los Angeles. The first afternoon in town, McGraw went out and purchased an army combat helmet and infantry jacket. When he appeared prior to the Dodger Stadium game, he was wearing the makeshift uniform. The fans roared. A television announcer got Russell and McGraw to do an interview. Tug with the crazy outfit on, Russell with boxing gloves.

"The only reason I bought the stuff was because I expected a strong reaction from the fans," he said. "I wanted to relax them, make them have some fun. Baseball is supposed to be fun."

And no matter what Tug McGraw does on the field, he tries to have fun.

Off the field he is different. In a sense, when he puts on the uniform and walks onto the diamond, he is nothing more than a showman with athletic ability.

"At home he is different," said Phyllis. "During the last few weeks of the season, especially the World Series, he was like a zombie. His body was at home, but his mind was somewhere else. He gets that way, though. He gets all keyed up and I understand it. When we were first married I'd try to fight it and got my feelings hurt all the time because I thought my husband was ignoring me. I can handle it now.

"Tug is a very serious person. Sometimes I'll make a joke and think it's pretty funny and I go, 'Well, you laugh at Tim McCarver's jokes. Why can't you laugh at mine?' He just doesn't hear me. He's pretending to listen, but he's not.

"Truthfully he was very up-tight and nervous all year because it was the last one on his contract. And, as I said, things hadn't been going that smoothly in the past. Once we got into those close games at the end, it was difficult to be around him. There was so much tension. I started to get gray hairs—I just pulled four of them out today. I never had a single one before. I told Tug, 'Yeah, that's from the end of the season.' All he said was that he didn't have any gray hairs.

"At the end of the season, I even broke out in spots and had to go to the doctor. I asked him what was causing it. He said it was my nerves and I'm really not a nervous person. But the whole thing just got me in knots. It was just too much to handle all of a sudden—too much pressure.

"And then one day we went to New York to appear on 'Good Morning America.' They played the tape of the final World Series game. Tug looked at me and I looked at him and my eyes were filling with tears. The same thing was about to happen to him, too. I just took a big sniffle and controlled myself."

Forget about Tug McGraw's four fastballs—the John Jameson fastball ("I like my Irish whisky straight), the Peggy Lee ("when the hitter swings and misses and says, 'Is that all there is?' "), the Bo Derek ("It has a nice little tail on it.") and the Cutty Sark ("It sails.")

"And there's the Frank Sinatra, too," McGraw reminded. "When I give up a home run—'Fly me to the moon!' "

No, it was not those pitches that carried the Phillies to world championship.

"When you're raising a tomato plant you plant the seed

first," he said. "From the time you plant it it needs a little attention as it grows. Sure, it will mature on its own and produce tomatoes, but if you give it the right kind of attention at the right time it will do much better, produce more. That's what Dallas Green did to our team this year. He gave it attention at the right time, attention that wasn't there before. But as he has said many, many times since we won it, the last month of the season the team didn't need a manager. The plant took care of itself, but it got the proper attention first."

During the JFK Stadium celebration the day following the World Series victory, McGraw was one of the last to speak.

He shocked the throng when he told New York to "take this championship and stick it!"

"Funny thing," Tug said months later. "As each of the players got up to speak they said what I wanted to say. When it was finally my turn, all I could think of was how the New York press had come down so hard on us. They feel if it doesn't happen in New York, it's not important. So I had a message for them.

"There was no way we could have started baseball in the '80s any better than we did. I don't think I have ever been more proud to be a baseball player. It was a very great year."

From Tug McGraw, that was an understatement.

The Rookie Pitchers
Whirlybird and Company

Dallas Green didn't march Bob Walk into his office and say: "Pitch well tonight or you're on your way back to Oklahoma City."

Green didn't say anything. He knew the time had come for the young pitcher to produce and Bob Walk knew it too.

So, on June 25, the 23-year-old right-hander bought some time with the Phillies' varsity with a superb effort against Montreal. He allowed just four hits over eight innings and just one earned run. That run kept him from getting the decision in a 2–1, 10-inning Phillies' victory.

Just to prove it wasn't a fluke Walk followed that with a 5–2 victory over New York that raised his record to 3–0.

"The start against Montreal was really make-or-break," Green remembered. "We just couldn't continue to send him out there."

In Walk's previous start, at San Diego on June 19, he didn't get past the third inning, allowing three runs on four hits. His earned run averaged zoomed to 7.96.

Newspaper headline writers in Philadelphia were having a field day because the young Californian was walking everyone in sight. In his first six starts after being recalled in late May, he issued 15 walks in 26⅓ innings.

Little did Walk realize—or Green for that matter—that on October 14, 1980 the pitcher called Whirlybird would be starting the first game of the World Series.

"I didn't even dream of it," said Walk. "About the only thing I was thinking of then was to pitch well enough to remain in the majors."

Walk was chosen because the Phillies' pitching staff was shot after the grueling drive to the National League pennant.

He became the first rookie to start an opening Series game since the Dodgers' Joe Black faced the Yankees in 1952, quite an honor for a youngster who didn't even make the team in spring training.

Just as unexpected was the fact another rookie, a rookie who didn't arrive until September 1, was called on to start the fifth and deciding game of the playoffs against Houston.

Marty Bystrom, of course, was phenomenal. He methodically throttled the Mets, putting them down 5–0 on five singles in his first start on September 10 at Shea Stadium. With that performance he became the first Phillies' rookie to pitch a shutout since Dave Downs blanked Atlanta and Mike Mc-Queen 3–0 on September 2, 1972.

Without Bystrom and Walk the Phillies probably would not be world champions.

Walk was called up when the pitching staff was struggling. After finally gaining poise—and control, Walk zipped out to a 6–0 record and ended the season with an 11-7 mark and 4.56 ERA.

He did not pitch in the playoffs but gave the Phillies seven gritty innings against the Royals in his World Series start. He also got the victory.

Bystrom, who probably would have made the team in the spring had it not been for an injury, turned in a 5–0 record and a remarkable 1.50 ERA after 36 September innings.

Through some behind-the-scenes maneuvering by Player Personnel Director Paul Owens, Bystrom was made eligible for post-season competition.

Even though he was hampered by a hernia, the 22-year-old Bystrom pitched 5⅓ solid innings in the crucial playoff game and started the fifth game of the World Series. He gave up three hits in five innings and was not involved in the 4–3 victory turned in by Tug McGraw and the Phillies.

Of all the moves Dallas Green made to help bring the Phillies their first world championship, none pleased him more than the emergence of Bystrom and Walk.

"Let's face it," said Green. "With all the injury problems we had with our pitchers, we would not have been able to stay close had it not been for Bob Walk. Marty Bystrom pitched the way we knew he could, but nobody expected him to do the job he did in September. He was just outstanding. Because I was involved in his signing and was a minor-league man all those years, his season had a lot of meaning for me."

Green is the first to tell you his desperate need for a healthy arm forced him to promote Walk from Oklahoma City even though the pitcher had just three years of professional experience.

"The first couple of starts I lost my composure," said Walk, who had a 12–7, 2.24 ERA at Reading of the Eastern League in 1979. "I think I lost my intensity. The hardest thing for a pitcher to deal with mentally when he gets in the big leagues is making himself realize he's on the same level with the other guys. The tendency is to assume they're better, and try to pitch 'up' to them.

"In a sense, I was afraid to let the batters hit the ball. I guess in the back of my mind every hit was going to be a home run. So I tried to make each pitch an exceptional one. When you do that the chances are you're either going to strike the guy out or walk him.

"I realize I'm not going to strike everybody out. After I almost got shipped back to the minors, I tried to make the batters hit the ball. We've got all those Gold Gloves out there, right? So why not let them catch it?"

Pitching coach Herm Starrette knew Walk was a fast

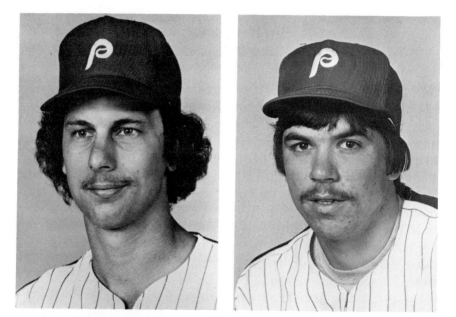

Randy Lerch

Bob Walk

Marty Bystrom

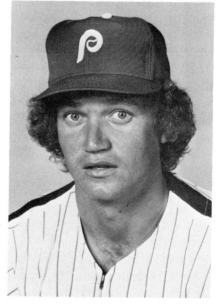

Dickie Noles

worker in the minors, but once Bob arrived in Philadelphia on May 26, his delivery seemed to slow down.

"I began to notice it when he was going poorly," said Starrette. "I think when a pitcher works quickly, it helps everyone on the team."

"When I got to the majors and things went a little rocky," Walk said, "I started to think, 'Oh, God, what do I have to do now?' In the minors, I was not too slow. I never took much time between pitches."

Green, a former pitcher, was first to admit the jump from double-A baseball to the majors, without much triple-A experience, is difficult.

"But Bobby did a fine job," said the manager. "It took him time, but he finally learned major-league pitching isn't as hard as it looks if you just get the ball over the plate. Getting him to work more quickly helped, too, and for most of the year he pitched within himself."

"When the Phillies called me up, the enormity of the whole thing got to me," said Walk. "I had trouble sleeping. I couldn't think of anything but what I would do when I got to the mound. Later, all that stuff went away."

Walk's most rewarding victory from a personal standpoint came on September 5 when he worked seven superb innings to defeat Los Angeles 3–2 at Dodger Stadium.

Just about every Wednesday night a few years before, Walk would fill his orange 1969 Plymouth Roadrunner with friends, put the pedal to the metal and cruise down Van Nuys Boulevard to Los Angeles.

"Most of the time we'd end up at Dodger Stadium," he said. "We used to have a lot of fun. I guess we were lucky we never got thrown in the Van Nuys jail. We were a rowdy group."

Bob Walk would sit high up in the cheap seats in the left-field pavilion and look down on the plush Dodger Stadium grass carpet.

"I never thought much about pitching at Dodger Stadium, but I had a great desire to go down on the field, walk out to the mound and see what it was like," he said. "That was something I thought a lot about."

Once, in 1974, shortly after the gangling Walk graduated from Hart High, he and five other schoolboy athletes made the trip to Dodger Stadium. Beer flowed and they all became tipsy. Bob Walk threw a tennis ball onto the field.

Then Bob Walk was thrown out of the stadium.

"I thought about that the night I pitched the 3–2 victory there," he said. "I finally found out what the Dodger Stadium mound was like. Some of the guys who were with me in 1974, watched me pitch that game. Funny thing, I was the only guy thrown out of the stadium. And it was just a tennis ball."

They call him Whirlybird because he is absent-minded. Once, he went to the mound and forgot his glove. Once or twice he forgot when it was his turn to hit and another time he went to the plate without a bat.

"I've done a few other dumb things," Walk admitted, "but some of it's kind of an act, just to give people something to write about."

The events that led to Marty Bystrom signing with the Phillies resemble a CIA plot.

Green had to fire a scout to get Bystrom signed in December of 1976 out of Miami Dade South Junior College.

Bystrom graduated from Miami Killian High in the spring of '76 and was not drafted by professional baseball. He enrolled at Miami Dade because the junior college has a fall baseball program. That's where Bystrom first attracted the attention of the Phillies.

"This all goes back to what scouting is all about," said Green, who was minor-league director at the time. "There is a very strong Florida scouting clique and it was never more evident than in the Bystrom case."

Scout Gust Poulos was apparently a close friend of the

Miami Dade coach and had hoped to keep Bystrom from being signed until he pitched a couple of seasons for the college and established a better reputation. Then he probably would have gone on to a four-year college, become a high draft pick and everyone would have benefited from the expensive signing.

"We saw him in the fall program and we decided to work him out at our complex in Clearwater," said Green. "Another scout down there, Catfish Smith, followed Miami Dade and helped get him into school.

"Just before the 1977 January draft we looked at Marty several times. Everytime we saw him pitch he was better. Hugh Alexander (Phils' super scout) picked up the fact he had gone through the draft the previous spring and was a free agent. Our scout (Poulos) in charge, however, was sitting on it because he was a part of that scouting clique.

"I called Gust up and said, 'Hey, I want this guy signed.' He said, 'No, you can't sign him.' I said, 'The hell we can't. The rule says we can; I want him signed.' He said, 'Well . . .' and I interrupted. 'You got a good dollar evaluation on him and I want him signed.' He said, 'I don't want to do that, Dallas.' I shot back, 'I don't care what you want to do. You got X amount of dollars on this kid and you go to his house right now and offer it to him! He refused to do it, so I said, 'You're fired! I'll get somebody who will sign him.'

"I sent Hugh Alexander and Catfish over to the house and they signed him. That caused a big stink down there because everybody screamed and yelled, especially his college coach."

Bystrom won 13 games the following summer at Spartanburg and led the league at Peninsula with a 15–7 record and a 2.83 earned run average.

"Paul Owens and I went to the Florida Instructional League to watch him in 1978 and we knew then he could pitch in the majors," said Green. "He had four pitches he could get over the plate and he wasn't afraid to throw them. He had something like an 0.32 earned run average that fall. When we were there he pitched one of the finest games I have ever seen. He threaded the needle, inside and out, used the change-up, backed guys down and then went away with them."

A few days before spring training opened in 1980, Bystrom pulled a hamstring in his right leg working out in Miami. Several days later, he slipped on the concrete in the Phillies' clubhouse and was finished.

"That was disappointing to me," he said. "I had a good chance to make the team in the spring, but with that injury I really didn't start pitching until July. It was depressing, but I was determined to work my way back."

Bystrom might not have even gotten into the rotation in September had it not been for the fact Larry Christenson pulled a groin muscle and missed a start.

Marty came close to reaching the major leagues' consecutive shutout innings record by a rookie pitcher, but his string was snapped at 20 when Chicago's Dave Kingman blasted a two-run homer on September 20 at Wrigley Field. The record of 25 scoreless innings was set by George McQuillan, who, ironically, pitched for the Phillies in 1907.

"Sure I knew about the record. Everybody knew about it," said Bystrom. "I really wasn't worrying about it. I just went out there and tried to win the game (he did 7–3). I tried to jam Kingman with a fastball and he hit it 400 feet. I felt like I pitched the same as I had in my previous two starts, but I didn't get ahead of the batters as I had before."

Bystrom wanted to pitch in the playoffs and World Series, but said he didn't fret about the decision that was so long coming.

"I didn't find out until the day of the first playoff game," he said. "I wasn't really nervous or anything like that. I was just ready to accept it either way. I thought I did deserve a chance to be in the playoffs because I helped the team down the stretch. Sure, it would have been disappointing if I had not been able to be in there.

"Pitching in the World Series was the biggest thrill of my life, but in that fifth game of the playoffs the hernia was bothering me. It wasn't all that serious, but I could feel it. It was like a groin pull and it did take something away from me. I wasn't a hundred percent."

While many of the veterans were quick to question some of Green's methods, Walk and Bystrom had nothing but praise for the manager.

"Dallas gave the young guys a chance," said Bystrom. "Because we were in the minors several years, he knew all of us. A lot of the guys would never have gotten the same shot had Danny Ozark been the manager. With Dallas they got the shot and did the job. There have been quite a few who have been ready for a few years and they showed what they could do. And I think some of this rubbed off on the older players who have been around for awhile."

Finally. Player Personnel Director Paul Owens (left) and Manager Dallas Green hold the World Series trophy moments after Commissioner Bowie Kuhn presented it to them on the night of October 21.

Paul Owens
Above all, he spoke their language.

I t was a blend of gutter talk and high-level brain-storming. Scotch flowed and profanity flowed. As the decibels increased, sharp cutting opinions vibrated up and down the corridors of the San Francisco Airport Hilton.

The Phillies' war room was in session.

Sometime during the early morning hours of September 1 Manager Dallas Green went to sleep and Player Personnel Director Paul Owens stopped cussing, the two lackadaisical losses at San Diego on August 30–31 swept aside in a maelstrom of emotion and anger. All was fine with the Phillies.

Well, almost.

Before the Phillies eased past the Giants 6–4 and climbed into first place the next day, the man they call Pope, prompted by the "soul-searching session" the night before, mounted the clubhouse pulpit and lashed out, as only he can, at the startled athletes. He was loud, profane and threatening. Above all, he spoke their language.

"Strange how the mind works," mused Owens six months later. "We beat Kansas City to win the World Series and as I'm up on that stand in the dressing room to receive the trophy, I looked down at some of the players and I know they were thinking the same thing I was. They remembered the number I did on them Labor Day. How could they forget?"

Dallas Green had delivered his Pittsburgh Address on August 10. Many Phillies trace their incredible surge to the world championship to that memorable day. In a second breath, however, they point to Owens' tirade as the icing on their motivational cake.

"I only talked for six or seven minutes," Owens remembered. "I was about as mad as I've ever been. I've talked to the club at different times in the past, maybe once a year, but I have never been so upset. Dallas Green and all the coaches and even the kids we called up who had just reported that morning were there. 'Maybe they shouldn't be in here,' somebody said, but I shot back, 'The hell with them. They're wearing Phillies' uniforms, so they might as well get used to it. This is a team effort. We're going to need everybody down the stretch.'

"I know I was screaming and my hands were trembling. I said, 'You guys played the first five months for yourselves. You've gone your own different ways. The man (Green) has been trying to get things across to you and now I'm telling you, and I know I'm also speaking for Ruly Carpenter, the man's right and you better stop your goddamn pouting and this and that. I'm damn sick and tired of it. The last month is Ruly Carpenter's and mine. The man's right and I'm telling you he's right.'

"I told them I stuck my neck out after 1979 by not making any moves because I wanted to give them another chance. I told them I felt they had all the ability they needed. After that Pittsburgh fiasco, I watched them battle back and get in the thick of the race again. Then, I felt they were slipping. I put it a little more stronger than that."

If you know Owens, you can picture the fire in his eyes that afternoon, but as he recounted the story they merely twinkled.

"Now that I look back on it, it became funny. I was so

wrought-up I was pacing around the room near the end and I said: 'If any of you guys don't like it and I don't give a goddamn which one of you it is—you're all big, strong son-of-a-bitches and I'm 56 years old. . . .'

"I even remember my room number. I said, 'I'm in 413 and if you don't like this, goddamit, don't be bellyaching and bitching. Come and knock on my damn door!'

"Now, this was the humorous part: I said, 'You may knock me down and you may hurt me, but I'll tell you one thing about me, as soon as Seger (trainer Don Seger) gets some ice on me I'll be back at your door and I'll keep coming back until you son-of-a-bitches realize you got as much ability as you got.'

"I singled out Garry Maddox and Larry Bowa because I thought they were not playing well," he continued. "Maddox lost two balls in the sun during the same game at San Diego. I said, 'Hell, anybody is going to make a mistake and forget his sunglasses, but when you do it twice I'm beginning to wonder what the hell you're trying to prove. You're acknowledged the best center fielder in baseball. You're in the middle of an afternoon with the sun right over the rim (of the stadium) looking at home plate. It just doesn't make sense to me. I know you are intelligent and I know you can make a mistake and no one cares about one mistake, but when you duplicate it in the next inning you are trying to tell me something. I'm goddamn sick and tired of your moods and your pouting around here. All you guys can do your goddamn pouting and mooding somewhere else, but don't bring it into my clubhouse.'

"I got on Bowa's butt pretty good, too. 'Here you are, the shortstop with the greatest fielding record in the history of the game and you're letting the ball play you. You're not being aggressive. You're giving me the impression you're trying to protect your record rather than trying to go out and bust your ass for these guys. It's a damn good thing I'm not one of your teammates because by now, I would have pinched your goddamn head off.'

"I singled those two guys out because I felt they were the keys. They were not playing up to their potential. You know what I mean."

The Pope sat back in a soft chair in his New Jersey home and smiled. "That was pretty much it."

Obviously, he was still pleased with his performance.

"What I really tried to do," he said, "was make sure they knew Dallas Green still had the hammer. And, everybody knows, we had an outstanding September."

"The Pope was a hundred percent correct in everything he said that day," remembered Pete Rose. "He asked anybody who didn't want to play to just plain leave."

"He's the general manager and he has every right to come down here and say what he said," admitted Bowa, who had two singles and drove in two runs in the game immediately following the lecture. "He was right, Garry and I had not been playing well."

Rose feels few general managers could hold such a meeting and get away with it.

"He brought most of these players into the game," said Rose. "He is a former player and a former manager. They respect him. He's not a guy out of Yale or Harvard who hasn't been in a uniform. He's more like a player. He's more like a father to this team than a general manager.

"He takes a beating and a victory more serious than some of them. He hates to see us play poorly, I mean non-aggressive, sloppy baseball. He talks ballplayers' language. We just hadn't been playing very well and he wasn't about to let us stay in the same pattern."

Owens watched the team he built nearly crumble in 1979, but with Green at the helm he was convinced it would return to the top. And to watch it get so close, then appear to let the fight slip away was too much for him to take.

Owens, you see, seldom walks away from anything or anybody, especially challenges. In fact, Owens may be the only player in the history of baseball who had to pay his way into his first professional game.

"Best 75 cents I ever invested," he says of his seldom-talked-about beginning.

That was May of 1951 and the first day of a career that has had stops at just about every phase of the game, including his present position of vice president and director, player personnel for the world champions.

"I often wonder if I would be here today had I not gone to the game that night," he says.

With 37 months of World War II behind him and a freshly minted diploma from St. Bonaventure University, 27-year-old Owens and his wife Marcelle were looking forward to his new job as physical education teacher and coach at the high school in his hometown of Salamanca, New York.

"I helped put myself through college by playing semi-pro baseball," he recalled. "The last year I was at St. Bonaventure, baseball was put back in the athletic program. We won the Little Three championship and the day we clinched the title by beating Niagra, the general manager of the Olean club in the Pony League asked me if I would come for a tryout. I figured, why not? I'd rather play baseball than paint bridges all summer.

"I was supposed to be at Olean, about 15 miles from home, at 4 o'clock. On the way up, there was a tremendous rain storm. When I arrived, the general manager said it would be impossible to work out, but told me to stay for the game. 'Get yourself something to eat and come back. We'll leave you a ticket,' he said. So, I put my equipment back in the car and went to a little diner.

"I was always a modest type, so when I came back I didn't bother to ask for my ticket. I just paid 75 cents and went in. I was talking to some people from my hometown when the general manager came up in the stands. It was 10 minutes before 7 and the game was supposed to start at 7:30. 'Bud

Dowling, our first baseman got hit in the jaw last Saturday and broke it in six places,' the general manager said. 'The manager wants to know if you'll play first base Where's your gear?'

"I zoomed to the car, got my stuff and walked into the clubhouse where they had found a uniform for me. It was now 10 after 7. The manager was explaining all the signs. I shook my head, but didn't hear a word. Out in the dugout, he introduced me to the players and the game started. I ended with a single and a two-run double.

"Now they say they're going to play at Jamestown the next day and want to know if I'll play. The bus has to go through Salamanca and they say they'll pick me up. We win the game 9–5, I go four-for-five and drive in five runs. I've played two professional games and don't even know how much I'm making. The next day, the general manager gives me a contract calling for $175 a month with $1.50-a-day meal money."

Owens led the league with a .407 average and was named rookie of the year and most valuable player.

"We had a banquet after the season and I was sitting next to the Yankees' Gil McDougald, American League rookie of the year," said Owens. "He made some nice remarks about me and when I spoke, I told how I had to pay my way into my first game. A day or two later, I got a check in the mail from the club president—for 75 cents. I have it framed and hanging in my office at Veterans Stadium."

The following year Owens' contract was purchased by the St. Louis Cardinals and he played at Winston-Salem in the Carolina League. In 1953 he went to spring training and from there was assigned to Houston of the Texas League.

"I was teaching school and earning $3,000," he said. "I was offered a job to get a recreational program started in Salamanca. It was to pay $3,000. I didn't want to become a baseball bum, so I didn't report to Houston. Don't forget, because of the war and all, I was much older than most of the players."

In 1955, however, a friend talked him into becoming

player-manager for Olean and Paul Owens has been in professional baseball ever since.

"After 1955 I figured I would give it up, but Gene Martin, the Phillies' farm director, called to say the team was going to have a working agreement with Olean. He wondered if I would be manager. I went to Philadelphia, was offered $4,500 and decided to take it. I kept the recreational job also."

Owens managed four more years, moving to Bakersfield, California for 1958 and 1959.

In 1960 the Phillies coaxed him into becoming a West Coast scout. On May 22, 1965 he was named farm director and on June 3, 1972 succeeded the late John Quinn as general manager.

The Phillies would not be world champions had it not been for the efforts of Paul Francis Owens. He is the most underrated general manager in the majors. It's a crime he has never been chosen executive of the year.

He took a team that had done little since 1950 and molded it into a four-time National League Eastern Division champion and finally, a world champion. During the five-year span of 1976–80, the Phillies won more games (467) than any other National League team.

Check the record and it appears the Pope turned the Phillies around in three or four years.

"Wrong," says Owens. "As far back as my college days I have considered myself a good evaluator of talent and a teacher. I think that is what made me successful with the Phillies.

"It started when they made me a scout on the West Coast. I was a field man and didn't want the job, but Bob Carpenter told me he wanted to completely reorganize the scouting out there. In a sense that was the beginning.

"When I became farm director and took Ruly Carpenter under my wing we instituted a completely new system of player evaluation for our scouts."

Paul Owens is usually one of the most pleasant men you'll

ever meet, but if he flips the switch . . . watch out. That's when you'll see the alley fighter in him. Ask anyone who has attended one of his clubhouse meetings.

When he became farm director it did not take him long to realize there were scouts who were doing very little. He fired them.

"You can't do that. I'll go see Bob Carpenter," one of them shouted.

"Go ahead," said Owens. "You're still finished."

Carpenter supported his new farm director.

Owens will out-work, out-talk, out-manuever just about any mere human. Then, he plays. Hard.

"I have a philosophy," said the Pope. "My parents taught me this. No matter what you're going to do, try to be Number 1 at it. That's what I try to do and what I want my people to do."

One of the most bizarre things Owens has done was to fire Frank Lucchesi as manager on July 10, 1972 and put on the uniform himself—a little more than a month after succeeding the retired Quinn.

"Some people thought it was an ego trip," said Owens. "Bob and Ruly Carpenter wanted me to do it, but didn't push me. I realized I was taking a helluva gamble, but that's life. I was just named to the top job in the organization and could have sat on my butt for two years and done nothing.

"There were serious problems. I felt I knew what we had in the way of talent. Since I always considered myself a good evaluator, I figured if I lived, ate and slept with the players, I would know just what I had. I had confidence I could turn the thing around. I could have buried myself, but I had to do it.

"In a sense, that is what Dallas Green did, although we knew what talent we had when he took over from Danny Ozark."

From the knowledge gained during those 80 games Owens carefully selected the nucleus of the present team and began to build.

Baseball is filled with general managers who have no business being in the job. Teams have been run into the ground because of bad deals. It sounds simple, but to be successful a good general manager must know what is needed and go after it.

"The intriguing part of this job is that it is totally objective oriented," said Owens. "Know what your need is, set a little pattern here and there, and go out and do everything you can to get as close to that goal as possible. I have always felt we have to run our own lives. You can't get in the middle of the stream and back off. That's a mistake too many people in business make.

"If you don't have the courage to live with your own convictions, you don't deserve to be general manager. A lot of baseball men don't have the guts to go out and make decisions, to put their names on the line. I put my name on the line every day I get up."

Owens is first to admit he'll stand up to anyone in the organization if he believes in something.

Take the trade that sent pitcher Tommy Underwood to the Cardinals for outfielder Bake McBride on June 15, 1977.

"Ruly didn't want to make the trade. He liked Underwood," said Owens. "I felt we had to make it. In the end, I said, 'Ruly, the deal's made.' There was a lot of moaning, but later he told me we would not have won the division in 1977 without McBride."

In 1978, Owens traded popular outfielder Jay Johnstone to the New York Yankees for Rawly Eastwick, then turned around and dealt reliever Gene Garber to Atlanta for pitcher Dick Ruthven.

"They say I messed up the bench with that one," said Owens. "Well, without Ruthven, we would not have won the division in 1978. And even though Eastwick didn't work out

for us, there was no way I could let Garber go without having
a reliever to take his place. Besides, Johnstone had done nothing on the bench before the trade. When Davey Johnson became so unhappy, I sent him to Chicago. That's what he
wanted. There's nothing worse than an unhappy ball player.

"I don't really think there has been a really bad deal. Oh,
we have taken chances on players such as Doug Bird and Lerrin LaGrow who didn't work out, but those weren't big deals.
When I traded Ruthven for Jim Kaat, I had nightmares. I was
sure Ruthven would come back to haunt us. Luckily, I was
able to get him back."

Eventually Owens wants to turn his desk over to Green.
Some people thought that would happen after Dallas guided
the Phillies to their first world championship.

"I don't want to hang around when I'm no longer effective," the Pope said. "I believe in surrounding myself with
good, ambitious people—people who can replace me. But before they get the job, they will make me look good."

As recently as 1979, Owens secretly wondered if he would
ever watch his team win a World Series. But when the Phillies
surged to first the division title, then the pennant and the
world championship, Owens' goal was finally reached.

"It was like being the father and watching your kids succeed at something," he said. "Seeing Dallas Green manage the
team and finally getting through to the ballplayers gave me a
wonderful sense of accomplishment.

"I remember his last year with the Phillies. I called him
and said, 'Dallas, I want to bring you into the front office. I
want you to eventually be my assistant'—I was farm director
at the time. But I told him that first I wanted him to go out
and manage for a year or two. I said, 'You've got the background playing-wise and all that, but what I intend to do is
turn most of the player development over to you and I'll break
you into scouting after you get your feet wet. For your own
good you should manage in the minors for a year or two. You

need to be out there working with 25 kids, riding the busses with them and things like that. These are the things you are going to oversee and you'll have a better grasp of the problems if you have to deal directly with them first.' "

Green didn't want to go. He wanted to move immediately behind a desk. Owens stood firm.

"I finally said, 'Well, I'm not forcing you to go manage, but I think it is important to any future success you might have.' Finally, he said, 'OK, I'll do it.' Since then, especially after the 1980 season, he has told me how glad he was I pushed him. I knew how much I had gotten from my managing in the minors and wanted him to have the same background."

If there is a sad footnote to 1980 for Paul Owens, it is the fact some players refuse to give his protegé, Green, full credit for the job he did.

"They ought to be out buying him dinner instead of talking about him," said the Pope. "The point is some of them, and I don't know why this is, keep ripping him even after we won it all. I don't give a damn because he's my friend or your friend, but if he were with any other team I think players would be running through walls for him.

"But here, a few of them—not all of them—had been used to babyish ways and Dallas was so straight-forward he shook some of that out of them. They didn't like it. I honestly feel there will be a different attitude during the 1981 season."

Owens is elated the Phillies are finally world champions, but he says watching the players he has known since they were teenagers celebrate last October gave him the greatest feeling of all.

"Pete Rose and I were talking the other day," Owens said. "Being in a World Series and winning it was not new for him. He said he really didn't get involved with the celebration that much. He got his kicks watching the guys who had never been there before enjoy it. I felt the same way."

"To come out on top this year, with all the in-fighting or whatever you want to call it, made the reward even greater. I'll tell you one thing. I wouldn't trade my World Series ring for a $50,000 bonus.

"And I'll tell you something else, I'd pay to see this team play."

Coming from a man who paid his way into the first professional game he played, that's not surprising.

Ruly Carpenter
". . . we were on the way to something good."

H e's out chopping wood," Stephanie Carpenter said over the phone. "I don't expect him back for hours."

Ruly Carpenter cut and stacked enough firewood that humid August afternoon in 1979 to last through two winters. It was the day his ax fell on Danny Ozark.

You don't have to check the National League standings to see how the Phillies are doing. Just check the wood pile behind the Carpenter home. When it's tall, times are rough; when it's low, the team is winning.

Ruly Carpenter, you see, takes out his frustrations on the trees in the woods behind his Montchanin, Delaware estate. The day Paul Owens was firing Ozark in Atlanta the Phillies' youthful president, a sharp ax over his shoulder, disappeared for six hours.

"A lot of what goes on at the stadium builds up inside him," says Stephanie, his wife of 20 years. "He gets some of it out in the open around the family, but when it gets too much for him you can find him in the woods."

The firing of Danny Ozark as manager on August 31, 1979, was the most difficult thing Robert Ruliph Morgan Carpenter III has sanctioned since he succeeded his father as club president on November 22, 1972.

The Carpenters, almost to a fault, are loyal to their people. In Ruly's eyes Danny Ozark had been a dedicated manager for nearly seven seasons. He had produced three National League Eastern Division champions and the tumble to fourth place in '79 was not entirely his fault.

Key front-office executives, including Owens, hinted Ozark should go as early as October of 1978 when the Phillies failed to get past the Dodgers in the playoffs. Carpenter stood firm.

Then, as storm clouds formed over Veterans Stadium in mid-1979, Ozark's future was frequently discussed in the fourth-level war room. Carpenter still defended his manager.

Several days before August 31, Carpenter, Owens and Dallas Green, the Phils' director of minor leagues, agreed a change was necessary. At the same time, Green startled the group when he volunteered to run the team on an interim basis.

"We had a dreadful homestand, losing eight of nine games to Atlanta, Houston and Cincinnati," said Carpenter. "We were beginning to lose our fans, too. We waited for the team to go to Atlanta before we made the announcement because I didn't want a three-ring media circus. Danny deserved better than that. Had we done it in Philadelphia, that's exactly what it would have been."

Ruly Carpenter says those and other sour times flashed through his mind as the Phillies paraded down Broad Street on October 22, 1980, hailed by nearly a million fans as world champions.

"I can remember when Tug McGraw struck out Willie Wilson (the final out of the World Series). The elation of winning was just tremendous," said Carpenter as he reminisced for several hours in his den. "I was standing next to my father and when the strikeout was complete, I embraced him and then went into the next box and kissed Stephanie. I hurried down to the clubhouse, took off my good shirt and put on an old one, then joined in the celebration.

"But truly, the impact of what we accomplished did not sink in until the next day. The parade was organized in front of 30th Street Station and as it got underway we made a right-hand turn and started toward City Hall. That is when it hit me.

"We rounded the corner and looked down the street and the mass of people was overwhelming. It brought tears to my eyes and when I glanced around at the players the same thing was happening to them—even hardcore guys like Larry Bowa. We went past City Hall and down Broad Street and on to JFK Stadium. People were lining the streets and hanging out of office windows.

"It was the greatest day in my life, more awesome, more emotional than I ever dreamed it would be."

Ruly Carpenter was 10 years old when the Phillies were wiped out in four games by the New York Yankees in the 1950 World Series. His father, Bob, let him skip school to see the home games at Shibe Park, the old playground later re-named Connie Mack Stadium.

"I don't remember too much about that World Series," said Ruly. "It seems so long ago, so I know how our fans felt when we finally made it again. I do remember watching Joe DiMaggio hit a home run, and that the 1950 games were close. That's about all."

Ruly Carpenter's love and respect for his father leaps out at you during an extensive interview. He talks about the agony of the Phillies' repeated failures while he was growing up in Delaware. After becoming an All-State end at Tower Hill School he went on to Yale where his friends and baseball teammates refused to let him forget what a terrible team his father had.

The late Robert R. M. Carpenter Sr. purchased the Phil-

Ruly Carpenter

Paul Owens

R.R.M. Carpenter, Jr.

lies on November 23, 1943 and immediately turned the franchise over to his son, 28 at the time.

The Phillies' second (the first was in 1915) National League pennant came fairly quickly for Bob Carpenter but after that there were very few truly pleasurable moments. So, after 29 years almost to the day, he passed the presidency to Ruly, then only 32.

Ruly was an outstanding athlete in prep school and at Yale. He was tough as nails, but had horrible wheels . . . he couldn't run a lick. That didn't keep him from becoming an outstanding Ivy League pitcher though, and a .350 hitter. In football he was an end—playing both ways for three seasons.

Ruly's closest friend at Tower Hill was Pat Williams, now general manager of the Philadelphia 76ers. When they were both seniors, Bob Carpenter took them to spring training in Clearwater, Florida.

"Our major-league team was awful that year," Ruly remembered, "and I kept needling the old man about it. Pat Williams and I made him a bet that with me pitching, Pat catching and the defense of our choice, we could hold the Phillies to five runs over five innings.

"We ended up winning 5–3 and I struck out some of the major leaguers. What killed me was Joe Lonnett hit a pop fly down the right-field line—it was only 290 feet down that foul line at the old Clearwater park—and the damn wind blew it over the fence for a home run. Then, Pancho Herrera, the first baseman, dropped a fly ball the wind screwed up.

"But Pat and I won the bet and there were a lot of writers around who made a big thing of it. We had a lot of laughs."

For Bob Carpenter, it was a horror show.

"Ruly might have been a pitching prospect had it not been for the fact he injured his arm," his dad said. "He was always a jock. We had a diamond at home and I used to work out with him a lot."

"I learned a little bit about the different levels of talent when I played in the Delaware Semi-Pro League," said Ruly. "I started out playing for (Manager) John Hickman's Parkway team and it was about that time, during my junior year in school, I had my elbow operated on. After that, I played with St. Anthony's and Brooks Armored Car. Brooks had some outstanding teams, with former major leaguers like Ray Narleski, Harry Anderson, Dick Brockell, Bob Davis. Before guys like that joined the club Hickman always won the league, though Brooks had had some great battles with Honest John."

While Ruly was at Yale, the Phillies were horrible. In 1961, they lost 23 consecutive games.

"Sports and baseball had always been my hobby, my love, but I was thinking in terms of a legal career," said Carpenter. "The teasing and the criticism from my classmates and teammates in college convinced me I wanted to do something about the Phillies. It was kind of a challenge.

"I'm not saying just because we won one world championship I'm a genius, but we had to do a lot of hard work to reach that."

After Yale, Ruly served as assistant baseball coach under Tubby Raymond at the University of Delaware, then moved into the Phillies' front office in 1963.

Paul Owens doesn't remember the first time he met the young son of owner Bob Carpenter.

"I think it was in 1963," Owens said, "but I really didn't get to know him until he came to Florida in the spring of 1964."

Ruly Carpenter was on a shakedown cruise designed by his father, who wanted him to learn first-hand what was going on at the team's lowest minor-league level. At Leesburg, Florida Ruly was installed as camp administrator, working under Owens who was camp coordinator.

"He was in charge of all the business operations and I took care of all on-the-field matters," Owens said. "It didn't take him very long to get involved with everything we were doing. He always pictured himself as a tough cookie for a 23-year-older, but we still talk about one night in camp when we decided to release a pitcher from Panama.

"It was almost dark outside and I was in the shower. I heard Ruly knocking on my door, saying something about us not giving the boy a fair shake. Ruly was supposed to be so tough, but the kid had backed him down.

"I said, 'Ruly, everybody gets a fair chance; we don't release these guys unless they're washed out.'

" 'Sure, Pope,' Ruly argued to me, 'but the kid says he still can throw and wasn't treated right. Will you come with me to the park?'

"I'll never forget that night," Owens continued. "I had hardly dried off. I got Dick Teed, a young manager, and we went to the park. We got the kid cranked up and he throws to Teed and Ruly's watching from behind home plate. Finally Ruly says, 'Aw, you guys are right.'

"Now the kid is mad and says he's going to burn down the hotel. The joint was so old and decrepit it would have gone up like a match box and Ruly was so worried he stayed up all night watching the place. The next day we found out the kid had blown his travel money—over a hundred dollars—on clothes. We ended up taking him to the airport in a police car—with handcuffs on!"

Not-so-strangely, Owens looks back to that wacky night in Leesburg as the precise time he realized there was something special about Ruly Carpenter.

"His dedication and intensity were so great, I was certain once he got experience, he would make a fine baseball executive. It was never said, but I figured Bob Carpenter sooner or later would turn the Phillies over to him and wanted him to gain experience in all areas."

That six-week stint at the Magnolia Hotel also saw the birth of a relationship and a philosophy which was to produce the franchise's first world championship.

Owens was a fulltime Phillies' scout in California at the time, a grass-roots baseball man. He had played and managed in the minors, had an uncanny ability to judge talent and would work anybody under the table to accomplish a goal.

Ruly liked this. He already felt it was going to be his responsibility to turn the franchise around and almost immediately began to think of Owens as the team's future general manager.

"Night after night we talked baseball," Ruly remembers. "The Pope felt everything revolved around scouting, player development and the minor leagues. Why at Yale we weren't even NCAA champions but there were guys on my team who were better than most of the hundred or so players we had at Leesburg. We just did not have enough athletes who could run and throw. Paul and I agreed there was something grossly wrong with our scouting."

In May of 1965 Bob Carpenter fired Clay Dennis as farm director. Mostly because of Ruly's recommendations and urging, Paul Owens got the job.

"The day I got that job Bob Carpenter called me into his office," said Owens. "He told me he wanted Ruly to work under me and I was to teach him everything—good, bad and indifferent. He said teach him like any other employee."

"I think we started turning the thing around in 1965," said Ruly. "Most of the good things that happened in 1980 were born in '65 when Paul came in as farm director and I was his assistant. Seventeen of the 25 players who were on our 1980 opening day major-league roster came up through our system. The Yankees, by comparison, this past year had just three players who came up through their organization."

On June 3, 1972, Bob Carpenter fired John Quinn as general manager and Owens moved in. Six months later Ruly became president.

"Ever since Herb Pennock (general manager at the time) died in my father's arms coming out of a New York hotel (January 30, 1948), I think he had been searching for a good field man," said Ruly. "My father and Pennock put the Phillies together, the ones who won the 1950 pennant, much like Paul and I have done now."

Ruly says he begged his dad not to leave in 1972 "because I knew we were on the way to something good and I wanted him to be a part of it."

"Ruly was ready," argued Bob. "He knew all phases of the operation. I just felt the time had come for him to take over. He had worked hard and was ready."

"I think the old man was becoming very disenchanted with the direction the game was going," said Ruly. "There was the continual battling with the Major League Players' Association and we had that six-day strike at the beginning of the 1972 season. When it was finally over he just said he was going to step down. I was very sorry."

It took four years for Ruly Carpenter's Phillies to win their first National League East title. Then, after doing that three seasons in a row they skidded to fourth in 1979 and Danny Ozark was fired.

In like a hurricane came George Dallas Green and the Phillies won the whole thing.

Ruly Carpenter still defends Ozark.

"Hey, he still won three division titles," said Carpenter. "For what the man accomplished, he put up with a lot. Sure he had some great players, but I thought the guy did one helluva job. The record speaks for itself. I don't think he should be embarrassed by his record. And I don't blame him totally for what happened in 1979. I really believe, in many ways, if we hadn't been wiped out by injuries, Danny Ozark might be managing the Phillies today."

But despite the obvious injuries, especially to the pitching staff, Carpenter & Co. still fired Ozark with a month to go of the 1979 season.

Carpenter stumbled over an answer. "Well, with the injuries . . . you know, we started to lose a lot and then other leaks suddenly appeared in the dike that just complicated the problem. The emotions and that kind of thing. I really believe if we had won, if we'd been winning a lot of games, I don't think the other problems would have come up.

"If Danny Ozark had one fault, it was the fact he was just too damn nice. He always accepted the blame for everything and there were a helluva lot of things Danny Ozark never said—never said publicly—that Paul and I were aware of. He was tremendously loyal to his players. There were just times when he should have been a helluva lot tougher on those guys and really chewed their butts out or fined them or done whatever a manager should do. If Danny Ozark ever manages again, I don't think he will be such a nice guy. On the other hand, he was a very tough person to put up with the things he did, the crap he took, and I think 90 percent of that was totally unjustified.

"But on his last home stand in '79, the club looked awful and things started to look desperate, so we made the change."

Why Dallas Green?

"The most accurate thing I can say is Dallas Green just volunteered his services. I mean nobody put a gun to his head. I personally felt it was a good idea. I imagine some day Dallas will want to be a general manager or director of player personnel, and I think it really helped Paul Owens to manage the club when he took over for Frank Lucchesi in 1972. He gained valuable insight into the character of some of his players.

"And I felt, hell, if Dallas wants to do it, it would be good for him and the organization. He went down there and the club certainly responded.

"At the end of the 1979 season, I was fully expecting Dallas to walk away from it. We were trying to figure out who would be a good candidate for the job when he came into my office one day and told Paul and I: 'You know, managing isn't that bad. I'd like to give it a shot next year if it's OK with you guys.' I mean, once again, Dallas kind of volunteered. We didn't put a gun to his head. We were elated at his decision because it certainly took a load off our shoulders.

"I'll tell you the truth, if I'd been manager I'd have retired after a world championship, but Dallas wants to go at it again in 1981. Fine."

Although on the surface it appears Carpenter and Owens are totally united there are times when they fight like cats and dogs. They sit high above the field at Veterans Stadium and watch home games like typical fans.

"We have small bets with each other on certain aspects of the games and second-guess the hell out of both managers," admits Ruly. "It's a constant dialogue back and forth. I remember that Saturday game up in Montreal when we clinched the division. It's the 11th inning, the game's tied 4–4 and Pete Rose gets a single. Mike Schmidt is the batter and Don McCormack is on deck. I turned to Paul and said, 'He's (Manager Dick Williams) going to walk Schmitty and pitch to McCormack. And then I see him (Stan Bahnsen) starting to pitch to Schmidt. And when the count goes two-and-oh, I said, 'Pope, my God, I mean you've got to . . . you've got to call time and go out there and tell him I want two sliders in the dirt.'

"But Bahnsen winds up and throws a fastball, right there in Schmitty's wheelhouse. He hits it out and we'll see you later. It won it for us.

"I said to myself, 'Thank God for Dick Williams' sake he isn't managing in Philadelphia. That Danny Ozark thing when he left Greg Luzinski in left field in the 1977 playoff game against Los Angeles would have been a Sunday School picnic compared to this.'

"But, true to fashion, there was very little written in the Montreal newspapers next day. We were very fortunate because I think most managers in the big leagues would not have pitched to Schmidt in that situation—or let Mike Schmidt beat them.

"The same thing came up in Houston in the fifth game of the playoffs. They had a 1–0 lead and we had men on second and third, two outs and a base open with Bob Boone batting and (pitcher) Marty Bystrom coming up next. With two outs you figure he (Manager Billy Virdon) will walk Boonie and pitch to the pitcher. Well, thank God again. He opted to pitch to Boone and Boonie gets a base hit, two runs score and it's 2–1. So, in the eighth inning it's 5–2 instead of 5–0 and we came back to win the game. Those are just two managerial decisions that helped us—and both of those guys are good managers.

"But I often think if those things happened in Philadelphia, you *know* the wrath of God would have come down on them. It just shows you the difference in the cities as far as the media is concerned."

Ah yes, the media.

No matter what he says, Ruly Carpenter does not understand the newspaper business. He insists he reads only the Wilmington (Delaware) News-Journal papers. He is quick to over-react to certain "negative" stories and when I write one of those, I can usually expect an early morning telephone call.

I suspect his paranoia with the press goes back to his youth when Philadelphia-area reporters were lashing out at his father's teams. He insists that is not true, yet to this day he remains cautious with most reporters and some of his candid remarks about the press obviously have helped create some of the problems between his players and the journalists who cover the team.

"I don't have an innate hatred for the media. That's just not true," he said. "I think you've got to remember you've got unique problems in Philadelphia. Most big-league cities have just one or two major papers. There are four in Philadelphia.

Right away you have a problem because of the intense competition.

"The fans are already emotionally charged because we'd never won a world championship in the 37 years my family owned the team. So, everyone is concerned and interested and over-reacting because of the circumstances. It's just a natural situation, what with the competition of the newspapers plus the emotion and intensity on the part of the fans and the writers. You've got writers in competition, you've got fans craving for everything they can read about a ball club, so the smallest things become controversial, major issues in Philadelphia. These circumstances make it exceedingly difficult for the people who end up being either directly or indirectly the victims of unfair articles."

Carpenter's battle with the media started the same year he became president, the summer Frank Lucchesi was fired.

"It was the horrible battle over the Dave Bristol thing," Ruly said. "Paul Owens was accused of being a two-faced liar and there was even a picture of him in the Inquirer. They did some clever thing showing the two faces of Paul Owens.

"The media had written at that point that Dave Bristol was going to be our next manager. He was going to replace Lucchesi. And I think there are still a few individuals who believe to this day the only reason Dave Bristol wasn't made manager was because it was written that he *would* be the manager and that Phillies' executives just made the decision to try and embarrass the Philadelphia media."

Some insist Dave Bristol was virtually hired.

Well, he was never hired as far as Ruly Carpenter was concerned. "Sure, his name had been mentioned. But let's get this straight. There were two rounds involving Dave Bristol," Carpenter said.

"The first was when Frank Lucchesi was on the verge of losing his job, just before Paul Owens went down on the field and finished out the season. Bruce Keidan, who was covering the team at the time for the Inquirer, wrote the article. It was ridiculous. At the time we were very close to making a deal with the Milwaukee Brewers. Bristol had been fired on May 27 as their manager and obviously had a very good knowledge of the American League. Paul Owens placed a call to Bristol's home in North Carolina to check some information on the player. Keidan somehow found out the call had been made and wrote the story that Paul was talking to Bristol about the managerial job.

"As far as I'm concerned, that's when my problems with the media started. Then, after the season ended, Bristol actually was one of the candidates for the job Ozark ended up getting. Dave figured just because he was interviewed, it meant he had the job. That's strictly his opinion.

"Going back to the first thing, the day we announced Frank Lucchesi's firing I got into a little problem at the press conference. I had an encounter with Mr. Keidan afterwards and he tried to accuse us of some devious practices, that we had embarrassed him by not hiring Dave Bristol. He made innuendos we just did what we did to embarrass the Inquirer and all that crap.

"It all goes back, in my opinion, to the intense competition among the newspapers. Reporters who normally don't want to get involved in the controversial stuff, have to dig in and compete. And there is a helluva lot of pressure from their superiors to emulate the others. It's just a vicious cycle.

"Ninety percent of the guys are good people. I know professional athletes have to expect criticism but I just think there have been some writers who have set the tone for the Philadelphia area. They have exceeded the bounds of what I consider normal journalism."

During Super Bowl week in New Orleans, before the Eagles played the Raiders, the players were fully cooperative with the media and it appeared most Philadelphia-area reporters were pulling for the home team. This was not the case when the Phillies played Kansas City in the World Series. The players were not overly friendly to the media.

"I think that's because over the years there have been so many different incidents between the Phillies and the media. It was a difficult situation when we finally got into the World Series," said Carpenter. "I think there's definitely a gap that's been created between the players and the media. Every year it seems, in spring training, we start out and things seem to be pretty amicable and then something new comes up to destroy that.

"Take a couple of years ago. Greg Luzinski threw some things around the clubhouse one night before a trip to the Dominican Republic. Reporters actually *in* the clubhouse watched it happen and didn't write about the incident. Then, Stan Hochman and Ralph Bernstein get to town several days later and write the story. That's what started things going that spring.

"There always seems to be an incident that comes up. Mind you I think some of my players are wrong in that they shut out all the writing media just because of what one guy writes. I don't expect them to go shake hands with the guy who wrote the story—the bad story—but I don't think you can shut the world out because of what one guy has written. I admit that's a problem we have."

But as owner of the Philadelphia Phillies, Ruly Carpenter could lessen the strain if he ordered his players to cooperate more. That's how Coach Dick Vermeil created such a pleasant atmosphere with the Eagles and the media at the Super Bowl.

"I cannot dictate to my players or order them to talk to reporters," countered Carpenter. "I just can't do that because if I did, I would have problems with the players' association and everything else. But, honestly, I have advised my players as to what I think would be the intelligent approach to take. And the vast majority of them still talk to the press. I mean, this is what made me so mad about the World Series. I thought our guys handled themselves well. The only player who won't talk to anybody is Steve Carlton. Hey, there are players on other teams who won't talk to the media but it's never hyped-up the way our problem has been. Some of our people do have bona fide reasons for not talking to some but I think they are wrong for shutting everyone out. I just think they shouldn't speak to the person who wrote the objectionable story.

"Steve Carlton had that run-in last summer with Tom Boswell of the Washington Post. Steve caught this guy standing in front of his locker and staring into it. Well, I don't know what Boswell was doing, but the fact he was just standing at Steve Carlton's locker at that particular point in time, right after the story on the 'greenies' broke, I don't think it was a very smart thing for Mr. Boswell to do. And then Carlton came in and saw him and they got into a shouting match."

Behind the scenes, Carpenter is much closer to his players and more involved in on-the-field operations than he will admit. He does say, however, he has little interest in the business and promotional end of the operation. "I leave that in the capable hands of Bill Giles."

During spring training of 1980, it appeared negotiations over a new contract for Garry Maddox were stalemated until the end of the season. Carpenter secretly went to Maddox' house, talked with the sensitive center fielder and within a month had signed him.

As the season entered its final two weeks, there was still a huge communications gap between shortstop Larry Bowa and Green. Ruly summoned Bowa to his office one afternoon and most of the problems were eased. The shortstop was outstanding the rest of the year.

"This is where my closeness to a player can help with what we're trying to do," justified Carpenter. "I've known Bowa since 1966 and I've been very close to him. We've been through a lot together. We've had a few shouting matches and conversations in my office since I became president. We also had a few before I became president because we are friends.

"The little guy has become the best fielding shortstop the game has ever known. He's a person who has to be handled in certain ways. I know him probably better than anybody and I'm going to help when I can."

The world championship is still very much on Ruly Carpenter's mind, but he frets about the future of baseball. As we ended our conversation he ticked off a few of his concerns.

"If we had not made the playoffs we would have lost money. Our major-league payroll in 1980 was in excess of $7 million. The free-agent thing scares me. The average salary last year in the majors was $170,000. I just don't know what the future holds." Then he smiled and added, "I'll tell you one thing, I am going to enjoy this championship for as long as I can. It took a long time to earn it."

*   *   *   *   *

(Editor's Note: This book had gone to press when the baseball world was jolted by the sudden announcement that the Phillies' World Championship team was up for sale. The author, on assignment at spring training, wired his update which follows.)

Actually, Ruly Carpenter and his family did not enjoy the championship very long.

It took the Carpenters 37 mostly frustrating years to produce a world championship and fewer than five months after the long-awaited dream came true, they announced their intent to sell the 98-year-old franchise.

Ruly Carpenter made the announcement on March 6, sending shock waves through the baseball world. He waited until the world champions' fourth workout of spring training in Clearwater, Florida to read a one-page statement to the startled players, then conducted a hastily called press conference.

"It was one of the most difficult decisions my family has ever had to make, especially in light of the recent successes the team has had," said the 40-year-old Carpenter. "The primary reason for the decision to sell is it has become very apparent to me some deeply ingrained philosophical differences exist between the Carpenter family and some of the other owners as to how the baseball business should be conducted."

Interpreted, Carpenter was saying he and his family are fed up with the constant bickering between baseball and its players. He then vehemently denied his action was just a ploy to bring the two feuding sides together in light of a possible players' strike that was scheduled for May 29, 1981.

Astronomical salaries, bizarre free-agent signings and the questionable performance of maverick owners soured the Carpenters on the game they say they love so much.

"It's just impossible to continue with our philosophy," said Carpenter. "So rather than continue to beat our heads against the wall, we have decided to sell."

When asked what he thought the franchise would bring, Carpenter quipped, "If he (potential buyer) has to ask how much, he can't afford it."

The price tag was expected to be at least $30 million.

No sooner had the announcement been made than William Y. Giles, Phillies' vice president and son of the late National League president Warren C. Giles, started trying to form a syndicate to purchase the team.

Seldom, if ever, has a team been so successful and then been put up for sale. The Phillies have been second to the Los Angeles Dodgers in season attendance each of the last four years. In 1980 they drew 2,651,650 fans to Veterans Stadium. In addition, during the past five years the Phillies recorded the most victories of any team in the National League, 467.

But Ruly Carpenter has sat on the sidelines for the most part and watched owners such as the Yankees' George Steinbrenner, Atlanta's Ted Turner, San Diego's Ray Kroc and

California's Gene Autry pay millions and millions of dollars for what he considered mediocre talent.

"I guess the straw that broke the camel's back was Ted Turner signing Claudell Washington to a $3.7 million contract," said Carpenter. "I feel like the salaries have basically gotten to ridiculous proportions. When somebody like Claudell Washington gets what he got, the whole scale moves up. That's why Dave Winfield demanded—and got—what he did from the New York Yankees (a 10-year contract in excess of $20 million). The same thing happened last year when the Giants signed Rennie Stennett to that large contract."

Carpenter said he thought there was going to be a players' strike in 1980, but it was avoided by the 11th-hour compromise.

"Because of what happened in the spring, I was very interested in the re-entry draft of 1980," he said. "I hoped the owners had come to their senses, but apparently they had not. Washington and Winfield got those large contracts and we were right back where we started. After that, we made the decision to sell. It is something we had been thinking about for a long time. The announcement was not made before Christmas because I didn't want to ruin everybody's holidays. After that, I decided to wait until spring training."

"It's a sad day for me," said Paul Owens, who was as surprised by the news as anyone. "There has been a lot of jubilation and sadness in six months. I've worked for these people (Carpenters) for 25 years; I feel something has gone out of me. I know how hard it is for Ruly and Bob and Keith. We'll operate as normal; we'll get over this—we'll get another world championship."

Dallas Green, like Owens, was in tears when the announcement was made.

"You know what I think of the Carpenter family," said Green. "Bob has been like a father, Ruly like a brother. They were never in this game for the money; they never took a penny out of the operation. First and foremost, they tried to see that Philadelphia got first-class baseball. As long as Ruly could see light at the end of the tunnel, he was willing to stay in. But the philosophical differences between a baseball fan with money and a non-baseball person with money was too great for him to handle.

"I'll guarantee the Carpenters made this decision alone —Paul and I are as close to them as anybody and we didn't know a thing about it.

"Mr. (Bob) Carpenter darn near raised me. He put me through the University of Delaware on a basketball scholarship, nursed me through my professional baseball career and made sure I stayed in baseball later. This just hurts."

The players also took it hard, especially Bowa and Luzinski.

"It's really a sad day when a guy like Ruly Carpenter has to sell his baseball team," said Bowa. "I don't see this as losing an owner; it's like a death in the family."

"Things are getting out of hand when you run good baseball people out of this game," said Luzinski. "I think Ruly's looking down the road 10 years and feels he doesn't need the aggravation."

"Ruly Carpenter came into my office in late February and said he felt he would have to sell his Philadelphia franchise," said Commissioner Bowie Kuhn. "He told me he was worried about the direction the game was going and was pretty well fed up. There were two heavy hearts in the room that day —mine and Ruly's.

"A lot of people are concerned for the game. The players' association has no such concern."

National League President Chub Feeney, a close friend of both Ruly and Bob Carpenter, was shocked by the news. "The Carpenters have been great for the National League and baseball in general," he said. "I know how Ruly felt about the problems we face. The Carpenters will be sorely missed."

So when Ruly Carpenter said he didn't know what the future holds for him, he obviously knew baseball was not going to be a part of it.

"I've already applied for an assistant football coaching job at the University of Delaware," he said. "Tubby Raymond told me he'd try to work me in."

Ruly Carpenter was joking. Or was he?

Garry Maddox

Manny Trillo

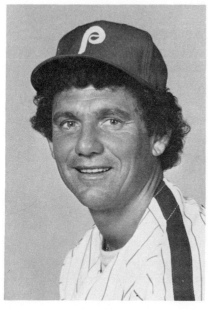

Larry Bowa

Bob Boone

The Media
Not a marriage made in Heaven

We stand outside the bolted red doors, ball-point pens, tablets and tape recorders poised. When the doors finally swing open we burst into the usually quiet sanctuary.

"The vultures are here!" someone will yell from a distant corner and it's business as usual for the horde of reporters who regularly cover the Phillies at Veterans Stadium.

There is probably no major-league team in the country which receives more media attention than the Phillies. And that includes New York and Los Angeles. It's not unusual for reporters from 18 to 20 Philadelphia-area newspapers to cover a typical home game. Add to that half as many radio and television stations.

Because of this extraordinary attention, fired by fierce competition, everything the Phillies do on and off the field is examined, critiqued and magnified.

When I first started covering the Phillies in the late 1950s beat writers were as much a part of the team as the equipment manager and the traveling secretary. In fact, in those days, the ball club paid traveling expenses for many of the reporters who covered for the major dailies.

That, of course, has changed. Now there is a huge gap between the players and the journalists. Some players go so far as to classify the writers as part of the opposition.

In those days there certainly wasn't the interest in the team there is today. The Phils drew 2,651,650 fans last year and 2,775,011 the season before. Newspaper readers demand high-quality coverage of their "heroes" and for the most part they get it.

To many fans the first link with the team is through radio and television. The Phillies have some of the best announcers in the business.

Harry Kalas calls it a love rather than a job.

Rich Ashburn says the game looks much easier from the radio-TV booth "than it did when I was playing it."

Andy Musser says there are two kinds of sportscasters— the ones who are in baseball and those who want to be in baseball.

Chris Wheeler insists he "tells it the way it is" even more than Humble Howard.

And Tim McCarver feels crossing the line from jock to the booth is not as difficult as he thought it would be.

This is the Phillies' broadcast team—a blend of true professionalism, homespun humor and practical knowledge gained from years on the field.

To most fans these men—unlike newspaper reporters— approach the same celebrity status as ball players. Between spring training and the end of the season most of the daily contact between major-league baseball and thousands and thousands of Delaware Valley fans is this radio-TV team.

The sports writers yell that the broadcast booth is nothing more than an extension of the Phillies' public relations department. If you really want to know what's going on, you won't find out from these announcers.

"I disagree with that," says Ashburn, a former two-time National League batting champion who has been in the booth since 1963. "I try to be honest and accurate and so far it has worked out OK. Sometimes you have to tell what is happening and the players do not come out looking very good. If you don't really get involved in editorializing on it and just say what happened and why it happened the players and the front-office understand. Let's face it, the fans in the Philadelphia area are astute. You can't pull the wool over their eyes."

Kalas, one of the best play-by-play men in the business, just completed his 11th season with the Phillies. Prior to that, from 1965 to 1970, he broadcast Houston Astros' games. "Harry the K" as friends call him seldom gets involved with controversy.

"I don't consider myself a journalist," said Kalas. "I tell the fans what happens on the field. I try to build excitement. I dwell on accuracy. I don't think it's my job to delve into what happens off the field. That's not my concern. On the other hand, I get into that stuff—unavoidably—on occasion during pre-game and post-game shows."

Kalas, admittedly, is more emotionally involved with the players than the other broadcasters. The exception might be McCarver who is only a year removed from active playing.

"When you travel with the players from March until the end of the season you cannot help but become close to them," said Kalas. "Hey, I like them. I want to see them win. I root for them, but I do not consider myself a homer or a cheerleader. I try very hard to establish credibility. On the other hand, most of the fans who listen to our broadcasts are interested in the Phillies. They want to hear a certain amount of partiality."

One of Kalas' biggest disappointments was not getting to do the World Series once the Phillies finally got there. NBC-TV held the contract in 1980 to telecast the games and chose its own announcers.

"We knew we were not going to do the games even before the Phillies won the National League pennant," said Kalas. "I think, however, it came as a shock to the fans. When all the letters and phone calls began to come in from unhappy listeners, it was very gratifying. Frankly, I was surprised."

Because of his close relationship with the players, Kalas is considered more critical of the print media than his co-workers in the booth.

"I really disagree with that premise," said Kalas. "When I get upset with stories in the papers I am upset as Harry Kalas the reader, not Harry Kalas the broadcaster. When I pick up newspapers and continually read negative stories it disturbs me. Like the day Mike Schmidt got his MVP award for the World Series in New York. Stan Hochman (Philadelphia Daily News) came out with a story quoting Bake McBride saying Mike didn't deserve to be MVP. Now, I ask you. Even if Bake did say those things, why did the story have to come out the day Schmitty got the award?

"And then Bill Conlin (Philadelphia Daily News) takes an unjust shot at Mike for not granting an interview the day before the National League MVP was to be announced. Was that needed?

"I wondered about all the stories that were written by national writers during the World Series. I don't think our players could have been more cooperative, but they were ripped. Winning the World Series was a very, very positive thing. These things disturb me as a reader."

In addition to his job with the Phillies, Ashburn also writes a twice-weekly column in the Philadelphia Bulletin. It is considered one of the best written by a former player.

"Some call it a conflict of interest, writing about the Phillies for the Bulletin then broadcasting the games," Ashburn said. "I sometimes have to walk a tightrope. Having been with the ballclub for so long and knowing the players as well as I do, there are things you cannot write. So far, I think I have been able to separate the jobs pretty well.

"When the drug thing came up, I had some problems.

The Bulletin asked me to write about it and I covered the hearings in Reading. I wrote what I knew and what I saw. The ballclub wasn't happy about it. I think, however, it understands now. But until then, I was able to do both jobs and do them to my satisfaction.

"I learned when I first started the broadcasting job to tell the fans what's happening on the field. I try to be accurate. If a player misses a sign or does something foolish, I say it. When I write the column, I try to be accurate and honest. I also try to be fair. With that approach, I have had few problems."

Most former players say crossing the line from the clubhouse to the booth is difficult, if not traumatic. One day you are a player, the next day you are the media.

"It took me a long time to realize that," said Ashburn. "When I left the field and went into broadcasting, I still felt like a player and a jock. But I think from day one when I went into the booth the players did not consider me a player anymore. I think a guy who has gone through that and who is a little bit resentful of it is Tim McCarver. He has been very close to the players and all of a sudden finds they are guarded around him. They don't confide in him anymore. I don't think Timmy understands that. I had the same problem."

"Emotionally, there was no problem at all," counters McCarver. "I was enthralled with what I was doing. I was learning a new business. The transition was made easier because of that. I really don't think my relationship with the players changed in any way—and I don't believe anybody thought it would. The thing that dictates any relationship is taste and I tried to use good taste in my observations and objective analysis of the players.

"The most difficult thing was I felt I still could have played another year or two. There was still some baseball left in me. I tried never to look back. I had an opportunity not too many people know about. Joe Torre (Mets' manager and former McCarver teammate at St. Louis) asked me if I would be a player-coach for him. I turned it down because I wanted to stay in the Philadelphia area. Everything worked out well. I got my first year of broadcasting in and still had the opportunity in September to put the uniform back on and be one of the few players who have played in four decades. I thought that was tastefully done and the right thing to do. I like to think I helped the ballclub. From a psychological standpoint I don't think you can have too many players on the club who have experienced the pressures of a stretch run."

McCarver feels he moved into his new position with ease because of the cooperation he received from his co-workers.

"I don't think you can find a group of men who are genuinely as harmonious as we were," he said. "There was no jealousy, professional or otherwise. And the guys have fun. The guys do the games very professionally and they have fun. I caught up on this immediately and it helped me no end."

McCarver, as a recent player turned media member, is probably in a better position to judge his new peers and the problems they have dealing with the Phillies than anyone else.

"Interestingly, I got in trouble with the St. Louis press last year because I said the Philadelphia press is the most objective I have ever run into," related McCarver. "I think it is the fairest and I still stand by that statement. Bob Broeg (longtime St. Louis Post-Dispatch writer) took it as a personal affront. There was nothing personal involved in the thing. I said there's so much more of an opportunity for objectivity in this area because you have so many people watching and they're going to zero in on exactly what the problem is, if any. That also applies to what praise, if any, is to be bestowed on certain players.

"I think while the Philadelphia press is competitive—and with any competitive situation things can be tough—it is the fairest and the most objective. I thought the Boston press when I played with the Red Sox was the toughest. It got too personal at times. And I thought the St. Louis press was too provincial and catered too much to the whims of its readers— instead of being objective."

McCarver feels the collective personality of the Phillies is part of the problem in the team's relations with the media.

"The basic nature of the ball club is one of shyness," he said. "With the exception of Tug McGraw and Pete Rose—and now Sparky Lyle, most of the guys on the club are very quiet individuals. Of course, there is Bowa in his insane way, but you can go right down the list. Because of this personality a lot of things have been misconstrued by the press as being animosity from the players. The same thing happens in reverse. The gap between the press and the players is of real concern.

"From a broadcaster's standpoint you cannot deceive the fans," said Ashburn. "Philadelphia fans are vocal, but they are knowledgeable. They know what's going on and I would be a fool to try to deceive them. I never really have. I think I've only had one player ever come up to me after a game and say, 'You know, I heard you say something bad about me.' That was Billy Grabarkowitz, the second baseman. What I had said was in jest, a tongue-in-cheek thing. Billy had been sent to the Chicago Cubs by us and as you know was not much of a fielder. The Cub manager put him in for defense in that particular game and my remark was that if Billy was put in for defense, the guy who came out must have been a butcher. It did sting him a little bit, but it was just kind of an observation. Sometimes I do get a little carried away, but it's usually tongue-in-cheek."

Phillies' broadcasters have never lacked for a sense of humor.

"It certainly isn't rehearsed," said Kalas. "I think it comes from the fact we are all such good friends. We truly like each other and take liberties on the air."

"The fact we have been together for so long is an important part of it," said Ashburn. "Harry Kalas is probably my best friend. But I think it's a matter of respect, too. I respect his work and know how good he is. And I would like to think that he respects my work also."

As far as the print media is concerned, Ashburn feels certain reporters overreact.

"I don't think there is a better group of writers in terms of ability and baseball knowledge than we have in the Philadelphia area," he said. "I think they have a tendency to overreact to certain situations—to wins and losses. When the Phillies were swept by Pittsburgh in August in that four-game series, the writers who follow the Phillies generally buried the club. I thought that was premature because there was a lot of season left. The writers reacted the other way when the Eagles defeated Dallas in the NFL playoffs. After that, nobody could imagine or accept the fact the Eagles couldn't beat Oakland in the Super Bowl. You know, the writers just made life-and-death situations out of both events. In reality they were not that important at the time."

Chris Wheeler is the Phillies' assistant director of public relations. He was weaned on radio work before joining Larry Shenk in the PR department. Four years ago "Wheels" joined the radio-TV team on a part-time basis. He has become a popular addition but he sometimes surprises me at how objective he can be, especially since his paycheck comes from the Phillies.

"When I started this radio work I figured I would get the most criticism for my lack of objectivity," said Wheeler. "I had no qualms about my ability to do the games; I know baseball. It really hasn't been hard because I have been a Phillies' fan all my life. I grew up in Newtown Square, Pennsylvania. I knew what the people wanted to hear. I knew what Phillies' fans were made of. When I saw the players blow a play, make a mistake or do something stupid, I said it. I guess the thing that worried me most was how the players would react to my comments. When I first started, they did influence me and I don't think I was as objective as I am now. I got to the point where players would come up to me and say what I said on the air was absolutely correct. Maybe a guy like a Larry Bowa would yell at me or something, but that didn't bother me. I had enough guys supportive of me that I didn't worry about the criticism."

"I knew the players would be listening to me and the fact I had never played professional baseball was on my mind. But like I told Larry Bowa one time, at least I made my high school baseball team." (Bowa was cut three times from his.)

Musser appears to take a somewhat different approach from Kalas.

"Before I accepted this job I talked with Harry Kalas and Rich Ashburn," said Musser. "I asked them if there was any pressure from the Phillies as to what not to say. They said they had a virtual free hand.

"I feel a baseball announcer is a reporter first and a showman second. That's the way I attempt to handle the job. On the other hand, I think we are part-salesmen and part-promotion men. Sometimes there are conflicts between these roles but it all seems to work out in the end. When there is a conflict between the various roles I believe the reporter in us comes out. Actually, the world championship season was one that tested us in a lot of ways. The team was going so poorly for a period of time we had a tendency to get critical on the air. All of a sudden the players turned it around and we were quite complimentary at the end.

"The last month of the season the games carried themselves. It was a great contrast from 1979 when we really had to work once the team was out of contention. Thats' the first time I had ever experienced that as a big-league announcer. The Phillies had won the division title my three previous years since taking over for (the retired) Byrum Saam. All we had to do late in 1980 was show up for work and the games broadcast themselves."

The relationship between the print media and the Phillies bothers Musser.

"I see the situation getting worse," he said. "The players and the media are growing more apart. I think basically the reason it is happening is economics. There was always an age difference between these two groups. That kept them from becoming good friends in the past. Now there is almost an animosity. The players are in a different economic situation. I think that is where the problem starts."

While the announcers bask in the spotlight, behind the scenes is Steve Silverman the executive producer. When the games are on television, Silverman works out of a van directing both cameras and audio. For radio he sits in the booth, monitors the program and handles all the details such as commercials, cues, etc.

"All the responsibility, no action," said Silverman. "I just have to answer questions from the bosses next day like: 'What'd Richie say that for?' "

As the radio-TV announcers have more than hinted, the Philadelphia-area sporting press dwells on the third degree and uses a style that is witty, skeptical and hip.

"I've always felt that down through the years the Philadelphia baseball writers hustled more than any writers I have observed in other National League cities," said Stan Hochman, who covered the team for the (Philadelphia) Daily News between 1960 and 1965 before becoming the paper's columnist in 1966. "By that I mean going out to the ball park early, being around the batting cage, being in the clubhouse, going down in the locker room after the game regularly—you know, to find out what really went on, not just on controversial plays, but on key plays.

"I think there is a tradition in the city that even the young guys have picked up on. I don't know whether they read the back issues or somebody talked to them or maybe by coincidence they felt the same way—that there is a rich tradition of guys trying to be on top of things. It goes back before my time, certainly, but I can speak of it during the last 21 years and that's the feel I have for it.

"You start with that kind of framework and it can be good and it can be bad. The 1980 season, I think, was a carry-over from the season before when I think the Phillies' clubhouse had the most hostile, belligerent atmosphere I had ever seen in the 20 years I had been around. It was not just players hiding. Once they came out of hiding, their attitude toward the press was one of distaste. They didn't like us and it was pretty well expressed. Only a handful was cooperative. And that's not a healthy situation. It even turns off writers like Frank Dolson (The Philadelphia Inquirer) who loved the game and loved to talk about it and liked to be around the athletes. *He* even felt uncomfortable.

"A writer like Mark Whicker (The Bulletin) who loves to talk about baseball and the intricacies of it—you know, the small things that don't show up in the boxscores—felt it. Speaking for myself, I certainly felt uncomfortable. I was down to a handful of players who I felt comfortable with. The other guys were either cold or outright belligerent. A guy like Ron Reed, of course, would never say anything to me and indicated how he felt about me. So, you know, it was not a healthy situation."

Hochman, over the years, has analyzed the situation and reached his own conclusions.

"I would trace it generally to long-term contracts. As a grizzled veteran, I can think back to when guys had one-year contracts and towards the end of the year they would be super friendly with the writers because they knew management was going to be tough in negotiations and they wanted the press on their side. They wanted favorable stories written about them. They always made an effort to be nice to the writers and available for interviews.

"That ended when the players started getting five-year, guaranteed, no-cut contracts and they no longer needed the writers to help them sway management in their contract negotiations. Now they have agents handling their long-term contracts. So the basic relationship changed. The player tended to say, 'I don't need them, and if I don't need them, then he's not the kind of guy I want to mingle with anyway.' So, they just turned cool and abrupt and belligerent. Add to that the basic insecurity of players, even those who have long-term contracts and resent anything critical written about them and you have a difficult situation. We suddenly found ourselves with a new breed of players as a result. They had short tempers, long memories and they got into situations where they didn't want to talk to 'that son-of-a-gun' and they would either hide or if they came out, would give nothing but short answers."

Hochman also feels the mood and atmosphere of the Phillies' clubhouse is set by owner Ruly Carpenter.

"He has expressed his outright hostility toward and his distrust for the press," said Hochman. "I think that basically stems from misunderstanding the role of the press. He's not sharp enough to know we owe our allegiance to our readers and our bosses. Even though he might deny it, I think he expects guys to be homers and write favorable things even though he has been in this city for a while and should know by now it's different. He should talk to other owners of other teams in other towns and see what it's like. He just thinks we ought to only emphasize the positive and forget about the negative and so he doesn't understand the role of the press and as a result he resents it. I really don't know where that comes from because his daddy, Bob Carpenter, while we sometimes baffled him, was able to handle it and just accept the role of the press. And God knows, his father got more criticism than Ruly ever got."

Hochman has been criticized for writing a column the day Schmidt received his World Series MVP award that quoted McBride as saying Mike did not deserve the honor.

"My side of it is that it wasn't my primary target that day to write that column," explained Hochman. "I had two other ideas that fell through—two other things I wanted to write. One guy was unavailable and the other gave me a short shrift. I was informed that Bake had been on the radio and said that, indeed, he didn't think Schmitty deserved the MVP of the Series. I called him as much to confirm that as to look ahead to, you know, the award. I asked him about it and he volunteered all that stuff. Of course he said it, but Bake denies it.

"Well, Schmitty went around telling people Bake told him he didn't say all those things. That bothers me as much as anything. I'll admit the timing was not the greatest and there again is a misunderstanding. I don't have to celebrate Schmitty's award. I can enjoy it, you know, because I like Schmitty and I was happy for him, but that doesn't mean I have to celebrate it or that I have to withhold what is an interesting story of a teammate who feels that maybe there were other candidates. What Bake said was interesting reading.

"The only thing that bothers me from a professional standpoint is Schmitty telling people that Bake never said it. That reflects on my honesty, even Schmitty telling me that I should have tape-recorded it—that kind of thing. But for 10 years I have quoted Schmidt accurately and now suddenly he is saying I am not going to quote Bake accurately. That bothers me because I have a lot of pride. As far as the timing was concerned, hell, it was unfortunate, but you don't pick your spots on those stories."

Few sports writers love baseball more than Frank Dolson, the veteran Inquirer columnist. The strained relations between the players and the press bother him also.

"But I think it's different for a beat man than it is for a columnist," he said. "I don't think we have quite the same relationship. Obviously, it has changed because the players have so much more security. I don't honestly think it's just the Phillies. I think there was a time, even 15 years ago, when players were eager to have stuff written about them. They were trying to get new contracts and the stories helped in their negotiations."

Dolson does not think the situation in the clubhouse is as bad as some writers feel it is.

"Some of the guys covering the Phillies are really down on them," he said. "My feeling is on a one-to-one basis as individuals, most of the Phillies are good guys. And I've always felt that. I've known a lot of them very well over a long period of time and in a personal relationship have not seen them change that much. The only time they're bad is when they're together as a group, then the peer pressure is enormous and they all seem to act in a very anti-media way just to be, I guess, one of the gang. They're kinda pressured into it. So, I think they're entirely different, depending on whether you get them as individuals or get them in a group. Even the case—all the crap about Larry Bowa last year when he wouldn't talk to anybody. Once I got him alone, away from the park, he was fine. It was only when he was there with the whole group around him, I guess he felt compelled to live up to whatever he had said initially about not talking to the press."

Like Hochman, Dolson feels the relations would be improved if Ruly Carpenter felt differently toward the press.

"I don't have a negative feeling toward Ruly," said Dolson. "I wish we had more owners like him because he really loves the game and he's part of the game. But having said that I don't have the slightest doubt he's very anti-press. He distrusts the press. And he makes it very obvious. That attitude undoubtedly is passed along to the people who work for him, including the players, some of whom he's very close to."

During and after the World Series several national writers came down hard on the Phillies.

"I guess there were lots of reasons," said Dolson. "I haven't really thought about it much. "For one thing, I think those stories reflected the attitude of some of the people who cover for the Philadelphia papers. That would have to be a major factor because the first thing you do if you're an out-of-towner is check with the guys who regularly cover the home team. And I'm sure the people from other cities who checked to get insight into the Phillies, or who read the Philly papers, got a very large dose of 'these guys are bastards.' They were told they are very hard to deal with, which many of the Philadelphia writers felt. I think some of them have very good reasons to feel that way.

"I'm not taking the players' side now, but I think they brought it on themselves to a very large extent. But the attitude was passed along by the Philadelphia press. I'm sure some of these out-of-town guys, New York guys or whatever, talked to some of the Philly writers and all they heard was it's the worst damned team that's ever come down the pike to work with. So they accepted it. Some of the reasons the Philly press told them were valid. I'm sure they objected to the fact the best pitcher on the Phillies wouldn't talk to the press. And I'm sure there were times when they ran into some of the same stuff in the clubhouse some of our guys ran into."

Dolson is quick to add that he thinks the Philadelphia-area press is near the top as far as expertise is concerned.

"It's certainly very competitive and, in most cases, very knowledgeable. In most cases, it is very critical and particularly in baseball because everybody thinks he's a baseball expert. Some writers aren't. But it's very easy to act expert in baseball, yet some of the stuff I see in the Philadelphia press I object to. Some of the stuff I see all over the country I object to.

"I can see why some athletes get very upset. I can see

why, for example, Mike Schmidt really got ticked off about some of the stuff that went in the paper that I even felt was unfair. I was sorry when it happened. Bill Conlin (Daily News) wrote an unfair story when he could not get ahold of Schmidt the night before the National League MVP was announced. The piece he wrote was petty and vicious, vindictive and ridiculous. I was embarrassed when I read it. I don't think there is any place for that, and yet I think Bill Conlin is the finest baseball writer in the country.

"Hochman's piece about McBride popping off about Schmidt getting the MVP in the World Series and not deserving it came out the day Schmidt got the award. I can see why Schmidt got upset. I am sure the majority of the writers feel the same way. I think Schmitty has gone overboard in being cooperative and available down the years whether he was hitting .190 or was MVP. I just thought he (Hochman) was hitting low to do something to screw up his big moment. On the other hand some of those guys (players) really asked for it, there's no question about it. You've seen all that stuff go on. It's easy to sit down and listen to the players tell you the press is out to get them. Why is the press out to get them? Some of it the players brought on themselves. Look at Larry Bowa popping off about the drug thing when it happened and not talking to anybody, a decision that seems to me to look utterly absurd in light of what's come out since. A number of other things that have gone on there—guys hiding from the press after games and doing all the things they've done has caused some of the problems. Really it's a 50–50 proposition. Both sides have to take some of the responsibility."

Conlin, who took over the Phillies' beat in 1966 when Hochman was promoted, has come down as hard as anyone on the team. By the same token, he is well-respected by most of the players and the front office.

"There's an atmosphere of hostility toward the press which begins at the top," he said. "I don't think Ruly Carpenter is as well disposed toward the media as his father was. Ruly is very conservative. He feels that the press in some cases has been out to get his ballclub. I think he has the same attitude that many conservatives had toward the press when Watergate broke, blaming it for bringing discredit on a man many people considered a great president.

"I think that attitude filters down. Just citing one of my own examples: I don't think a sincere effort was made by the publicity department to impress on Mike Schmidt that the Daily News did not have a newspaper the day after (Thanksgiving) he was named MVP. That effectively, completely killed me on the story. Later, Schmidt told an interviewer that he was not aware I didn't have a paper the day after his formal press conference was scheduled. I would think the publicity department didn't make a real effort to convince him he should talk to me and to other afternoon reporters the night before. That's just one of many instances of communications breakdowns or whatever you want to call it.

"I think probably all ball clubs are tough to cover now."

Conlin agreed with his peers that in the past the players used reporters to help negotiate a contract by writing favorable stories at the end of the season. Now, agents handle that.

"What the agent does is become a professional flak-catcher," Conlin said. "The ball player can go off and play golf or whatever he wants. You know, the agent is a trained professional who's there, who could give a shit whether the general manager calls him an asshole or whatever.

"Our profession is also suffering a great deal of slippage because all we can do is protect the player's image in his eyes. We can't make him any more money; most of them are signed up so all we can do is create ill-will by writing things that reflect negatively on his performance. He feels we became a catalyst which touches off negative fan reaction—as we've heard from athletes on many occasions. He looks favorably on television because television usually gives him a nice gift for giving one tenth of the time that he's required to spend for newspapermen."

When the clubhouse is hostile Conlin says he would just as soon stay out.

"On the other hand, I thought Dallas Green was a breath of fresh air," added Conlin. "I think he said a lot of things that needed to be said. I think Danny Ozark tended to hang himself because he created such a protective shell around his players. He took a lot of undeserved bum raps himself. When a guy would run through a stop sign in the Ozark regime, Danny would make up some excuse for him. Dallas would say, 'Well, the dumb son-of-a-bitch ran through a stop sign.' I think the athletes became painfully aware in time that their sins were not going to be swept under the rug. If they made a mistake they not only were going to hear about it from Dallas, they were going to read about it. And I think that contributed to the sudden attention to details that helped win the thing for them.

"By the same token, Dallas cannot just use us to do his dirty work for him because we're the ones who pick up the flak. It's too convenient later for him to say, 'Well, those guys (writers) blew it out of proportion. I didn't say it in that tone of voice. I was just joking and they thought I was serious.' You know, it gives him too many outs. He's got to be able to stand by his own—by what he says."

They call him "Hard-hitting Ralph Bernstein." He first started covering the Phillies in 1946 and has covered just about all of their home games for the Associated Press since 1967. No one asks tougher questions or works harder on a story.

"I've gone through the revolution," he says. "When I first started, you just covered the game and wrote the story based on your interpretations of what happened on the field. You didn't go to the locker rooms and you didn't talk to the players. You didn't talk to the manager. That wasn't expected of you. It's just the way the job was done.

"Then the revolution came and I think it was because of the advent of television. The newspapers had to find a more in-depth approach to the game because people were able to see the actual play-by-play. You had to give them something different, so that brought on going to the dressing room and talking to the players and manager. We started to probe, we asked players about their philosophies, about why they did certain things. It was a whole new development.

"At first, it worked fairly well. Everyone got along pretty well because the questions generally speaking were of a nature that didn't arouse anybody's emotions. But the longer the thing developed, the writers began to ask questions which sometimes the players considered too personal. They were asked questions at a time when the players were on an emotional high and reaction was somewhat vigorous, to say the least. In many cases this developed into an adversary relationship because the players considered the concept an intrusion of the media. Of course, there are always personality clashes.

"And the writers changed, too. In the old days, the writers were more or less extensions of the public relations department. They rooted for the team and took the defeats almost as hard as the players. Then came the new, young, vigorous, curious type of baseball writer who was objective. If you won, you won. If you lost, you lost. That wasn't his main concern. His concern was to get as much information about the game and the players as he possibly could and present it to his readers. I think this new journalist, this new approach, caused the adversary relationships. They developed to the point where players like the Steve Carltons and the Dave Kingmans cut off relationships with the press completely. And it also made the players wary and very cautious of what they said. The players still think the writers should be rooters.

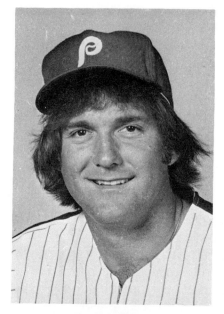

Tug McGraw

Ron Reed

Warren Brusstar

Sparky Lyle

These players have very little understanding of the function of the baseball writer. I think the management or the front office, which should know better, should know the function of the writer and explain it to their players. They just don't bother. Some look the other way and could care less. Some even encourage their players not to cooperate with the press."

Bernstein, too, says the problem with the Phillies starts at the top.

"Ruly Carpenter, to the best of my knowledge, has never cared for the media," said Bernstein. "He felt there were some cheap shots taken at him and his family in the past by certain writers. He may be right. It's like everything else, there is no perfect doctor, there is no perfect lawyer, there is no perfect engineer, there is no perfect architect, there is no perfect journalist. We have guys in our business who sometimes step over the line, the demarcation line of what is printable and what is invasion of privacy. It's a fine line and sometimes it is hard to see it. There have been occasions where that line has been stepped across. I think in the case of Ruly Carpenter that's at the bottom of his feelings for the media. Since he has those feelings, he looks down upon the media when he feels it hurts his ball club. His players know it and I think it's like any business when top management has a certain philosophy about something. It filters to the lowest man on the totem pole and they figure if the boss feels that way, why shouldn't I?

"I've been thrown out of the Phillies' dressing room several times and I don't think on any of those occasions I did anything to deserve being thrown out. Really, though, I have had more confrontations with management types with the Phillies than the players themselves. Some of the players are tough to deal with, others are excellent."

Danny Ozark used to call them Manny, Moe and Jack.

Prior to the 1979 season, three young, extremely talented reporters, arrived on the scene. There was Mark Whicker, replacing Ray Kelly, who retired after covering baseball for over

30 years for the Bulletin. There was Jayson Stark, who took over for the respected Allen Lewis, who retired from the Inquirer. And Gene Collier became the baseball writer for the infant Philadelphia Journal. Each was under 30 and each found the new beat the most difficult thing since Journalism 101.

"This was a job I wanted all my life," said Stark. "I grew up in Philadelphia and when I used to go to the ball park it was exciting for me to look up at the press box with my binoculars and see the writers. I always wanted to be there. I loved the Phillies. Even when I started writing sports, when I started covering the Boston Red Sox for the Providence (Rhode Island) Journal, the Phillies' fan was still inside of me. That was always the one real passion I had. I always felt it might be hard for me to cover them and be objective. Now, after having covered them for two years, they're not the same team. It's just not the same team I used to root for. It hasn't been a very pleasant experience at all.

"I never believed covering a world champion could be that little fun. But, essentially, it was those guys (players) who made it not fun for me. I've read stuff in the paper where Mike Schmidt said he thought most of the writers didn't want them to win. Well, I don't think most of those guys know much about us. They don't know I used to be a Phillies' fan my whole life, that Gene Collier was a Phillies' fan his whole life. Even today his family is just crazy about the Phillies. I think the players think we came in in a sense with the purpose of trying to get them. The whole attitude they bring toward the media, it makes you look upon them differently."

To Stark, the situation developed long before he was hired by the Inquirer.

"Truthfully, I think a lot of it is the product of the individual personalities of the players. I don't think they are bad guys. As a group they are quiet, private people. I respect that. But that particular aspect makes it more difficult for us to do our jobs. Beyond that, there's a certain atmosphere that's developed on this team in which it's cool not to like writers. I think a lot of the guys, if they're swinging one way or the other, get peer pressure and it drives them not to cooperate rather than to cooperate."

The day Stark wrote about Garry Maddox losing a ball in the sun in a crucial game against Montreal on September 28, the center fielder felt the story was the reason Green benched him. The next day, Maddox asked to have a private conversation with Stark.

"Essentially, he did the right thing in trying to talk with me in private," said Jayson. "It's just that I didn't understand his attitude and I really couldn't talk to him about my feelings about it. He felt as though the point of the story was to bury him, he said. To me, I'm being irresponsible if I don't mention the words 'sun' or 'glare' or something in that story. I went back and looked at it and the word glare appeared about eight times. And that wasn't even the lead to the story. That part of the story didn't appear until the jump (continued portion on another page). It just seemed to me I hadn't really written anything tougher than anybody else had written. The whole thing surprised me and surprised me even more when other writers picked up on the closed-door session with Garry. We were in the room a long time and I felt uncomfortable during the whole situation. He was very angry and accusing me of a lot of things that amazed me. I wasn't angry or scared or upset or anything.

"When we finally came out of the room into the main clubhouse, other writers were there and wanted to know what was going on. Guys started asking me questions. So I told them. I didn't think it was any big deal, but the next thing I knew Ralph Bernstein decided to move it on the Associated Press wire and it was all over the country. Now Maddox was more upset over that than the original story. I haven't talked to him since.

"Ray Didinger once described covering the Phillies as sort

of a bad marriage. It's unpleasant for both sides. You don't want to be in there talking to them and they don't want to be talking to you. I think that's the way it is."

"Obviously, covering the Phillies is a problem," said Whicker, now the Bulletin's columnist. "I think it's one that is never going to be solved. As long as Steve Carlton can get away with not talking to the writers, then the rest of them (players) can do just about what they want to. Until that changes the atmosphere in the clubhouse will remain the same. I think it is even something now that goes down to the farm system. For that reason it will not improve as the young players come along.

"It's kinda sad. Pete Rose has the right idea about this whole thing. He figures every time his name is in the news-paper he makes an extra dollar or two. And that's true. Every-time they get something mentioned about them there is a chance somebody will see it and like the profile of the guy we're writing about and end up giving him some kind of an endorsement contract. If I were a player I think I would be selfish enough to be nice to the press. There's a lot of peer pressure involved, too, obviously. I just think it's a bad situa-tion. If the press is so bad in Philadelphia, how come we get along with the Eagles, the Flyers and Sixers?"

Whicker thinks Ruly Carpenter is concerned about the problem. "He even called me in one day in August to talk about the problem. He wanted to know what the problems were. What my thoughts were. He appeared concerned about it and didn't seem to be very sympathetic toward the players. I thought the Phillies did make an effort to be cooperative during the World Series, but they were still bad compared to other teams. So, they got a pretty good licking in the national press although certain guys like Schmidt really turned on the charm when they saw all those national notepads come out."

Whicker agrees some of the uncomplimentary World Se-ries stories may have been written because the reporters knew of the Phillies' media reputation before they even entered the clubhouse.

"Yeah, I think that is probably true," he said. "But they were bad as far as they (national reporters) were concerned, especially compared to the Royals. On the other hand they were better than they had been during the regular season. Look at Schmidt. He was a totally different person when you got a whole bunch of national reporters around. He could see those MVP ballots stacking up, although he probably didn't know the deadline for that was the end of the regular season.

"Personally, I respect Carlton's attitude more than some of the other players. He has a philosophical thing about not talking to us. He never tries to interfere with our jobs. He's consistent. He turns everyone down. I think he turned Barbara Walters (ABC-TV) down. Yet other guys won't talk to certain guys, won't talk on certain days, will talk on other days and are very manipulative about it. I admire Carlton's consistency—and he has an honest basis for doing what he does.

"When the drug thing came out, the players immediately blamed us and we don't have anything to be proud of the way we handled those stories. But that's their favorite ploy. We're to blame for everything; we're probably to blame for the attempted coup in Madrid (February 1981). It's such an ingrained thing."

Gene Collier's problems in 1980 started in spring training with Dallas Green.

"Since we had our first blow-up Dallas and I have gotten along pretty well," said Collier, "but I have not gotten along with the players very well. In spring training the incident was my fault. We were all watching to see if Carlton would run with the other pitchers. The day we all watched Carlton did not run. The next day the pitchers ran in two groups, six or seven apiece. I only saw one group run and concluded the second group did not run because of Carlton. I merely put it in a note, but as it turned out, part of that note ended up in a photo cutline and I got in a lot of trouble for it. I apologized after that, but they never seemed to let me forget.

"Most of my problems were the same the other writers experienced. The players don't seem to be as cooperative as the guys with other teams. And because of this I find myself not doing nearly as good a job when I go into dressing rooms of other teams I cover. Before I covered the Phillies I was much more out-going and more willing to approach athletes. I know I got better stories. Now, when I go say to the Eagles, I find myself a little reluctant to approach the players with a penetrating question because I know it wouldn't get me anywhere with the Phillies. It probably would with most other teams and I know this has hurt me. It's kind of a selfish way to look at it, but that's how I feel."

"Every Phillies' fan in the Delaware Valley would probably trade everything he has to change places with the baseball writers," said Ray Finocchiaro of the Wilmington News-Journal. "It seems to be the greatest job in the world—and probably would be if we didn't have to cover some of the Phillies' players. It would take just a few nights on the beat for that fan-turned-writer to discover a few harsh facts about his heroes—if he could find them in the dressing room after a game.

"And when they did emerge from their off-limits sanctuaries, the snarls, foul language or obvious contempt from these players would turn him off for good.

"They're not all like that, of course. Some cooperate, but others do not. From the positive side there are many plusses, topped by seeing a talented ball club scratch its way to a world championship. It was just a shame the players had to act like spoiled, overpaid brats five months of the year before they got down to the business of the final month."

Bus Saidt covers for the Trenton Times. He works hard, asks tough questions.

"Maybe it's surprising, but I don't feel as intimidated or threatened or I don't feel as strongly about the rigors of the clubhouse as some people do," he said. "I don't like to have the impression given that I have to be walking around with a hat in my hand asking the greats or near-greats to share their feelings with me.

"I don't feel as strong about the situation as say a Ralph Bernstein. I've heard him say, 'I can't face another day.' When I hear that, I kind of smile to myself. To me, my own experience in dealing with the Phillies, or any team for that matter, is that it's a cross-section of personalities. Some of the guys are terrific; some are not. The team is a slice of society as far as I'm concerned. In recent years if I find an antagonistic personality, I just tend to go on my way and seek out another avenue. I resist going home or losing sleep over it."

Saidt subscribes to the theory that the atmosphere in the clubhouse would be better if the owner had more respect for the writers.

"But really," he said, "I think the root of this has to do with professional insecurity. I see it all around the Phillies' clubhouse, no matter how much money the athletes are making."

In August of 1978, Ray W. Kelly of the Camden Courier-Post had his highly publicized battle with Larry Bowa. Kelly, son of the retired Bulletin writer, wrote a critical column about the shortstop after a series in St. Louis. Bowa went at Kelly in the Veterans Stadium clubhouse the next evening and had to be restrained.

"I still have scars from that," said Kelly. "The saddest part is I still like Larry Bowa and that's the deepest scar of all. In all the years I have known him I have written one column that was critical. It became an incident where I can no longer walk into a restaurant with my son without somebody coming up to me and saying, 'Ha, ha, ha, Larry Bowa. Ha, ha, ha!' It's not the kind of notoriety that as a writer, a professional, I want. I want people to comment on my ability not my ability to get hit in the eye. I resent the situation and I'm sure the young players coming up and the players around the league say, 'Oh, yeah, that's the guy Bowa had the run-in with.' I'm sure it hurt me professionally in my dealings with the players. And because of it there was probably more resentment towards some of the other writers.

"I really don't think it was just a matter of Larry Bowa and Ray Kelly. It was a culmination, almost like the speartips of a situation that clashed. There were a number of incidents prior to that and I just got it in my mind that if people were going to treat me the way the players were at the time, I was not going to tolerate it. I was going to respond, which I did in the press. And Larry Bowa was kinda the focal point of a lot of resentment in the clubhouse. In the end, I think we were just the point men. We were pushed out in front psychologically. You know, two groups of kids going at each other and each group pushing two kids in the center and they end up fighting because they have no other choice."

The drastic change in the clubhouse has bothered Kelly more than most. When he was a little boy his dad took him to spring training when he was covering the old Philadelphia A's. The players loved Buzzy Kelly and bought him Cokes in the clubhouse.

"Spring training used to be fun and the whole season used to be fun. That's why I became a writer, but it has changed because the players make so much money. They're in a different strata now," he said. "They're almost like presidents and vice presidents of their own little companies. And presidents of companies don't hang around with sports writers. They think of themselves as being on a different level and I think that is sad."

"It has changed and I don't think the ball players have much respect for the newspaper guys anymore," said the elder Ray Kelly. "I think it's because of radio and television and the money that comes with it. Remember what Stan Hochman said? He was on television (WPVI) doing weekend sports for several years and said more people knew him from that than anything he ever wrote in the Daily News. It's the truth. I wrote for 50 years but a zillion more people know Harry Kalas than Ray Kelly. There's no comparison.

"And I think that is why the players have little time for the newspaper reporters. When I first started, there were very few social differences between writers and players. We used to play cards together, go out to dinner together and all that. They'd get a ride on a fishing boat in spring training and think it was great. Now they own the boat.

"I think the writers in Philadelphia keep everybody, including the players on their toes. It's probably the most competitive area in the country. Certainly much more than New York or even Boston. I think it's that way because there are so many papers and reporters covering the team."

There probably has never been a writer who had a better relationship with the players than Ray Kelly, affectionately nicknamed "The Dean."

"I just think I tried to be straight and honest with them. If I had any success, it was because of that.

"Hell, I had lots of arguments with Gene Mauch and Jim Bunning. But I always felt if I wrote what was true, what could they do? I think the only thing that really ticks them off is if you write things that are not complimentary. I don't think the situation is going to get any better in Philadelphia. I think you just gotta do what you have to do and let it go."

Allen Lewis, who still writes a Sunday baseball column for the Inquirer, first covered the Phillies in 1949 and took over the beat in 1956.

"Covering the team is completely different now," he said. "When I first started the morning newspaper reporters did not go to the clubhouse after games for quotes. Still, there was a good relationship with the players, a friendly one. It was kind of a family. More attention was paid to the game itself then rather than off-the-field activities or personalities.

"It's changed so dramatically. I remember when Jim Bunning was the highest-paid Phillies' player and only making $80,000. The financial gap between players and reporters is one of the biggest reasons for the change in the relationship. The player thought if a good story was written about him, it would help him. Now it doesn't matter. Reporters used to make $300 a week and superstars $30,000 a year. Now, writers make $500 and the superstars $500,000. It's out of sight."

Ray Kelly said television is part of the cause for the change in clubhouse attitudes, but it's no bed of roses for WCAU-TV's Al Meltzer.

"It's the toughest professional team I have ever tried to cover," said Meltzer. "There's no doubt about it. Once they climbed into their shell they climbed in against everybody, including television people. The first sign of a camera crew, they run.

"I think it's a running battle that has gone on for years between the Philadelphia press and the Phillies, and for a while, the Eagles. It's a very tough media town, especially print media. It starts with all the papers and not just the Philly papers. The Camden paper and your paper in Wilmington and the Trenton papers—they're all tough. I don't mean unfair, but tough. You just don't get the Allen Lewises and Ray Kellys anymore, the good guys who have been with the team for years. You have a bunch of new guys on the beat and they're trying to make a name for themselves. So, they're writing negative stories as well as positive stories. I'm not saying it's all negative, but the players read and I think that one thing leads to another and pretty soon everybody who either carries a microphone, a camera or a pencil is a bad guy. We all get lumped together in this thing which bothers me more than anything. If you have a gripe against Hal Bodley, then tell him, but don't tell him you don't want to talk to him because you are upset about about what Bill Conlin wrote.

"The Philadelphia sports press has been tough. I remember traveling with the Sixers in 1967 when they won 68 and lost 13. The writers were rough. Here was a team that was 68–13, but you read all kinds of stuff in the papers, battles between Wilt Chamberlain and Alex Hannum and how unhappy Hal Greer was. At the same time this team was blowing everybody out. Without question, the media in this area from a professional player's view is much tougher than it is in New York or Boston. It's not an easy relationship.

"But winning the world championship was the best thing that ever happened to this city in sports—by far. The frustrations of having never won a championship were eased. Never is a long time. Never won a World Series, hadn't been in one in 30 years. For a franchise that started back in the 1800s, that is a long time. When the Flyers and Sixers won, it was nice, but America does not tune into hockey and basketball. America tunes in to baseball and football. When you get your team in a World Series or Super Bowl, you are recognized. You can win an NBA championship and a Stanley Cup in the same year and it wouldn't mean a damn bit of difference to most of America. You win the World Series or the Super Bowl and you've done it."

Don Tollefson, sports director of WPVI-TV, takes an opposite view on his relations with the Phillies.

"I guess maybe I'm different," he said. "I could never understand why a lot of media guys indicted the team with one broad brush. It always seemed to me that for every problem that arose with the Phillies, for me as a reporter there were seven or eight or even nine incidents where the guys were just as cooperative as most teams. And I think what ended up happening then is that a lot of reporters who didn't make an individual effort to get to know the players on that baseball team would jump on the bandwagon. One guy would be complaining, 'Gee, they are not cooperative, they won't

talk, blah, blah . . .' without making a real effort to individually approach guys on his own and maybe even talk about
non-baseball issues.

"Steve Carlton obviously didn't talk to me or anyone else.
But at least he was consistent. Steve felt he had been burned
in the past, perhaps, and didn't want to risk that again. I don't
agree with his reasoning because he lumps us all together. But
at least I respect his consistency. There were times when this
guy or that guy would not want to go on live or not want to do
this interview in spring training because he was rushing to do
this or that. But guys I would read about as being totally uncooperative would be good to me most of the time."

Tollefson says he thinks he has an advantage because television reporters do not have to get a lot of sound or a lot of
quotes from a player each day.

"No matter how you slice it," he said, "this is a tough
media town because we are so competitive. Print, radio and
television are in a never-ending competitive battle to be ahead
of the next guy. Perhaps we ask too much of the ball players.
We are always bothering them and always calling them at
home and asking them to do just one more thing. Maybe some
of the demands from the media are unreasonable. That's created part of the problem, but I really feel overall when you
keep saying the players are uncooperative, you're making a big
deal out of it. Then it's like adding fuel to the fire and now
players have to choose sides. I just think that at times the
thing is over-blown."

One of the hardest-working sportscasters in Philadelphia
is Howard Eskin of WWDB-FM. In addition to conducting a
very popular two-way talk show, he feeds quotes from players
to the major networks after most games.

"I think I have a different opinion about the atmosphere
in the dressing room than most reporters," he said. "I don't
have that many problems. When I go in there I have to get
sound for the networks from two to three players. Sometimes

I talk to Dallas and sometimes I do not need him depending on the game situation. I've had some problems with people like Ron Reed who refuses to talk to anyone and Steve Carlton who has that policy. Carlton talks to me, but not on tape. I have accepted that. When Larry Bowa was not talking to reporters, he would go on with me. Maybe I was wrong, but I got him.

"My contention is that the problem arose this year when Kenny Bush (clubhouse manager) kept us outside the door for five to 10 minutes. When we went in the room was empty. Some players stayed in the lounge, but at that point I think most of them are already in the showers. When we were able to enter the clubhouse right after the games at the end of the season, I found most of the players available.

"The national reputation the Phillies received after the World Series, I think, was a good part nothing but rumors or stories that were circulated by the Philadelphia media."

Bill Giles, son of the late National League president, is the Phillies' executive vice president. In addition to his Veterans Stadium promotions and other business responsibilities, he is in charge of the team's public relations department. At times he frets over the problems the Philadelphia media allegedly has doing its job.

"I think Philadelphia is probably the most competitive sports newspaper town in the country," he said. "Consequently, there are some headlines and/or articles that are written that stir up some animosity among the athletes, not only the Phillies but other teams in the city as well. The consequence is that the relationship between the media and the players is not what I would like it to be and certainly not what I'm sure a lot of people in this organization would like it to be.

"Whether you put the blame on the players or the media, it is my opinion both should share the blame. I think the system and the fact there are so many papers covering us daily makes the system partly to blame for the unfriendly feeling that seems to persist among the players and the media. I think there have been a lot of instances where inaccurate things have been written—a lot of things misrepresented. I would say that one of the most disappointing things since I started out in baseball is that the media as a whole thinks it has to be controversial and negative in order to sell newspapers. I personally don't think it's necessary, but it appears that a lot of people making the decisions on how to write and how to present a sports page feel that way. I grew up with my dad in baseball and then went to work in Houston where there was a very close family relationship between the writers and the club. Now that has gone completely haywire. It's not only true in Philadelphia, it's true everywhere."

Surprisingly, Giles thinks some negative press is good.

"It sells tickets," he said, chuckling. "It's not good in happy relationships between the athletes and the writers, but it does sell tickets.

"Really, I feel the whole negative national press we received after the World Series stemmed from the regular writers who cover the Phillies. And I also feel that a lot of the writers in Philadelphia do a story to get plaudits or chuckles from their peers. In other words, you can sit in the press box and hear a writer saying, 'Yeah, you really nailed Bowa today.' Or, 'that was really funny what you wrote about Mike Schmidt today.' But on the other hand, I keep telling Larry Shenk and Ruly Carpenter that all this controversial stuff has some plus value."

Late one night in 1963 Larry Shenk was finishing his day's work as a member of the Wilmington News-Journal sports staff. We sat around and talked, and he mentioned how much he would like to have a job in baseball, especially with the Phillies. I knew the position of director of public relations was open and suggested he apply.

I lost a good sports writer because I opened my big mouth

that night and the Phillies got a man who has become one of the best public relations directors in the majors leagues.

Trying to be the middle man between the players and the press is a nightmare at times, but the Baron has held up well.

"During the World Series, I thought our players were very cooperative," said Shenk. "I know the reputation of our players but I think the media blew that out of proportion, probably because of word of mouth.

"I think the Philadelphia media as a whole is good and very interesting. We are in a very large market as far as fans are concerned and we are in a very large market as far as the media is concerned. They go hand-in-hand. I think interest in our ball club is whetted by all the newspaper space we get. Everybody claims New York and Los Angeles are media capitals in this country, but if that is true, I know we are not very far behind in Philadelphia. At home games we have as many as 19 or 20 daily newspapers covering. I don't know what it's like to be in a city where you only have two newspaper covering you.

"Being the middle person is sometimes difficult, but that's part of the job. That's why I am there. Chris Wheeler and I are in the cross-fire. Sometimes I wonder why we we get involved in all these controversies. We seem to get things calmed down and then something else pops up. Everybody talks in generalities like 'the media is no good' and we know that is not true. Then the other side will say 'the players are no good' and we know that is not true either. Sure it's a tough job, but I don't know of anything I would rather be doing."

Paul Owens, the player personnel director, has a great rapport with the press. I think his honesty and openness, at times, have gotten him in trouble, but he remains a true friend of the media.

"I see no reason why we shouldn't cooperate," he said. "The problems you have with the players probably boil down to an old, old story. Everyone likes to have nice things said about him, but doesn't like unkind things said. Hell, if I got upset everytime someone said I made a bad deal, you know what would happen? You just can't be thin-skinned in this business.

"The feeling I get, though, is that about half the writers who cover this team really do not want us to win. I don't know why they feel that way. It's a tough press in Philadelphia, everybody in the country knows that. When the players don't do well, they get criticized and they resent it. But if I make two or three bad deals, I expect to get nailed. It goes with the territory."

The final segment of this chapter devoted to the Philadelphia-area media is a sad one. But let Bill Conlin tell it as he did in the Daily News on Monday, September 22, 1980:

"This is for Harry Hoffman, who was the sports columnist for the Atlantic City Press.

"Let's get the ballgame out of the way quickly. Phillies 7, Cubs 3. Montreal's lead is down to a slender half-game. Dick Ruthven won No. 16 with professional relief from Ron Reed. Greg Luzinski hit a homer. So did Mike Schmidt, who slammed No. 41 in his last 1980 at-bat in Wrigley Field, a park he treats like a telephone booth.

"Harry Hoffman never missed an assignment in a newspaper career which spanned 29 years. He always came to the ballpark early, despite the hour drive from the shore. He hung in there. Once he was robbed at knifepoint in a Connie Mack Stadium phone booth while dictating his game story. 'You'll have to excuse me a second,' he told the Press rewrite man. 'I'm being robbed.' 'OK,' the rewrite man replied, 'but don't forget we're on deadline.'

"I was worried when Harry wasn't in the press box for the national anthem yesterday, but he had mentioned that a guy he used to be friendly with in Atlantic City had given him a call. I thought maybe he was sitting down in the stands with his old friend.

"The worry increased when he didn't show up by the second inning. It was getaway day and I knew he had planned to write a column before the game so he wouldn't get jammed up against his morning-paper deadline after a 7:45 p.m. flight to St. Louis.

"Guys who travel with athletic teams on a regular basis have a recurring nightmare. Nobody wants to have the big one in a hotel room. Nobody wants the indignity of being found by a maid or hotel security guy two days after the team checked out. So we quietly look after each other. I remember Rich Ashburn calling me in San Diego after a wearying flight from Philly. The hotel had failed to deliver the wake-up call I had left before the game and my body was still functioning on Eastern Daylight Time. Whitey told me it was the second inning and I better get started for the park.

"So, with rising misgivings, I asked the hotel operator to ring Harry Hoffman's room. And when she put the call through without comment, the negative vibes were overpowering. When a ballclub checks out, hotels normally pull the folios for everybody. She should have told me that Mr. Hoffman had checked out. His room didn't answer, so I asked for the bell captain and explained my concern. Would he have the room checked and call me back?

"It was the top of third. The game was tied 1–1 and the phone next to me in the press box jangled. It rang just as Greg Luzinski launched a towering two-out homer into the bleachers in left-center.

"The telephone message was brief.

"Life had been too short for Harry Hoffman. He was dead at 56 . . . ."

Harry Hoffman missed what most of us had been waiting a lifetime for—a world championship for the Phillies.

The 1980
World Series Championship ring

Veterans Stadium

PHILADELPHIA

phillies
STATISTICS

Individual and Team
Statistics

From the 1981 Media Guide

The Manager

46—GREEN, George Dallas (Dallas)

Age: 46, turns 47 on Aug. 4 … Born—Newport, Del., 8/4/34 … Home—West Grove, Pa. … B-L, T-R … 6-5, 230 … 1952 Conrad High (Wilmington, Del.) graduate … Attended University of Delaware … signed professionally as a pitcher after junior year … Married Sylvia Taylor (1/31/58); four children: Dana (11/29/61); John (10/8/63); Kim (10/19/64) and Douglas (8/20/68) … Hobbies: small game and deer hunting.

YEAR	CLUB	W-L	ERA	G	GS	CG	IP	H	R	ER	BB	SO
1955	Reidsville	1-1	10.08	7	2	1	17	25	22	19	16	8
	Mattoon	4-3	3.44	11	8	5	55	43	29	21	42	85
1956	Salt Lake	17-12	3.58	33	31	17	239	182	126	95	187	226
1957	Miami	0-1	10.50	2			6	6	8	7	4	5
	Thomasville	12-9	4.02	25	20	8	159	143	84	71	92	147
1958	Miami	7-10	3.74	31	22	5	159	135	73	66	70	103
1959	Buffalo	9-5	2.94	17	15	6	101	94	39	33	28	72
1960	Buffalo	3-4	3.36	11	11	4	75	72	35	28	26	44
1961	Philadelphia	3-6	4.05	23	10	5	109	100	54	49	44	51
1962	Philadelphia	2-4	4.85	42	10	1	128	130	77	69	47	51
1963	Philadelphia	5-6	3.84	37	10	2	129	145	58	55	43	58
1964	Little Rock	7-5	3.23	40	14	4	120	134	53	43	38	68
	Philadelphia	4-1	2.63	7	6	2	48	46	15	14	9	34
1965	Washington	2-1	5.79	25	0	0	42	63	31	27	14	21
	Little Rock	0-0	3.21	6	2	0	14	14	6	5	3	6
1966	New York (N.L.)	12-7	3.66	23	23	12	172	180	81	70	36	119
	San Diego	0-0	5.40	4	0	0	5	6	3	3	2	1
1967	Philadelphia	14-9	3.82	26	26	11	184	200	91	78	28	90
	Philadelphia	0-0	9.00	8	0	0	15	25	16	15	6	12

MANAGERIAL CAREER

	CLUB		Pos.	W-L
1968	Huron, SD	Northern League	5th	26-43
1969	Pulaski, VA	Appalachian	1st	38-28
1979	Phillies	N.L.	4th	19-11
1980	Phillies	N.L.	1st	91-71

The Coaching Staff

12—AMARO, Ruben (Ruben) Coach

Age 45 … Born Monterrey, Nuevo Leon, Mexico, 1/7/36 … Home—Philadelphia, Pa. … B-R, T-R … 5-10, 169 … Married Judith Herman, two children, Ruben (2/12/65) and David (9/3/62).

2—DeMARS, William Lester (Billy) Coach

Age 55, turns 56 on Aug. 26 … Born—Brooklyn, N.Y., 8/26/25 … Home—Wayne, Pa. … B-R, T-R … 5-10, 170 … Married Kate Malick; three children, Janet, Billy and Judy.

3—ELIA, Lee Constantine Coach

Age 43, turns 44 on July 16 … Born—Philadelphia, Pa., July 16, 1937 … Home—Clearwater, Fla. … B-R, T-R … 5-11, 192 … Graduated Olney (Philadelphia) High School … Attended the University of Delaware … Married; Wife's name is Penny.

5—RYAN, Michael James (Mike, Irish) Coach

Age 39, turns 40 on Nov. 25 … Born—Haverhill, Mass., Nov. 25, 1941 … Home—Plaistow, New Hampshire … B-R, T-R … 6-2, 200 … Married Suzanne Graham … Graduated St. James (Haverhill) High (1959) … Signed to his first pro contract by the Boston Red Sox.

4—STARRETTE, Herman Paul (Herm) Coach

Age: 44, turns 45 on Nov. 20 … Born—Statesville, N.C., 11/20/36 … Home—Statesville … B-R, T-R … 6-1, 190 … Married, wife's name Betty Lou; one daughter, Lisa … 1956 Cool Springs High School grad … Attended Lenoir-Rhyne College, Hickory, N.C.

7—WINE, Robert Paul (Wino) Coach

Age 42, turns 43 on Sept. 17 … Born—New York, N.Y., 9/17/38 … Home—Norristown, Pa. … B-R, T-R … 6-1, 190 … Married Fran Majeski; three children, Robbie, Kenny and Beth Lyn … Northport High grad.

The Players

15—AVILES, Ramon Antonio (Ramon) INF
(Pronounced Ah vee less)

Age: 29 . . . Born—Manati, P.R., 1/22/52 . . . Home—Ware Shoals, S.C. . . . B-R, T-R . . . 5-9, 155 . . . Married Betty Jo Richey; one daughter, Amy.

YEAR	CLUB	AVG	G	AB	R	H	2B	3B	HR	RBI	BB	SO	SB
1970	Greenville	.296	94	304	47	90	9	2	0	38	47	34	5
1971	Winston-Salem	.250	33	116	19	29	1	3	0	8	9	20	0
1971	Greenville	.294	89	313	33	92	9	1	0	33	43	26	3
1972	Pawtucket	.183	106	339	29	62	5	1	0	24	45	38	3
1973	Bristol	.224	109	353	39	79	13	1	3	28	62	35	3
1974	Bristol	.247	118	373	48	92	12	3	0	33	42	35	3
1975	Pawtucket	.220	123	287	20	63	6	1	1	22	39	29	1
1976	Rhode Island	.257	134	421	50	108	17	3	2	42	47	21	4
1977	Pawtucket	.218	78	239	32	52	8	1	1	30	29	20	3
	Boston	.000	1	0	0	0	0	0	0	0	0	0	0
1978	Oklahoma City	.270	90	341	41	92	20	2	3	29	28	41	8
1979	Oklahoma City	.250	72	252	37	63	7	1	0	18	28	19	1
	Phillies	.279	27	61	11	17	2	1	0	12	8	8	0
1980	Oklahoma City	.279	11	43	13	12	1	0	1	5	2	8	0
	Phillies	.277	51	101	12	28	6	0	2	9	10	9	0
	M.L. Totals	.216	79	162	19	35	8	0	2	21	18	17	0

LEAGUE CHAMPIONSHIP SERIES RECORD

YEAR	CLUB	AVG	G	AB	R	H	2B	3B	HR	RBI	BB	SO	SB
1980	Phil. vs. Hou.	.000	1	0	1	0	0	0	0	0	0	0	0

8—BOONE, Robert Raymond (Bob) C

Age: 33, turns 34 on Nov. 19 . . . Born—San Diego, Calif., 11/19/47 . . . Home—Medford, N.J. . . . B-R, T-R . . . 6-2, 202 . . . Married Susan Roel; three sons Bret Robert (4/6/69); Aaron John (3/9/73); Matthew Joseph (7/18/79).

YEAR	CLUB	AVG	G	AB	R	H	2B	3B	HR	RBI	BB	SO	SB
1969	Raleigh-Durham	.300	80	300	45	90	13	1	5	46	19	24	0
1970	Reading	.288	20	80	12	23	2	0	3	10	7	9	0
1971	Reading	.265	92	328	41	87	14	4	4	37	28	28	1
1972	Eugene	.308	138	513	77	158	32	1	17	67	45	35	2
	Phillies	.275	16	51	4	14	1	0	2	4	5	7	1
1973	Phillies	.261	145	521	42	136	20	3	10	61	41	36	3
1974	Phillies	.242	146	488	41	118	24	3	3	52	35	29	3
1975	Phillies	.246	97	289	28	71	14	2	2	20	32	14	1
1976	Phillies	.271	121	361	40	98	18	4	4	54	45	44	2
1977	Phillies	.284	132	440	55	125	26	4	11	66	42	54	5
1978	Phillies	.283	132	435	48	123	18	4	12	62	46	37	2
1979	Phillies	.286	119	398	38	114	21	3	9	58	49	33	1
1980	Phillies	.229	141	480	34	110	23	1	9	55	48	41	3
	M.L. Totals	.263	1049	3463	330	912	165	21	61	432	343	295	21

LEAGUE CHAMPIONSHIP SERIES RECORD

YEAR	CLUB	AVG	G	AB	R	H	2B	3B	HR	RBI	BB	SO	SB
1976	Phil. vs. Cinn.	.286	3	7	0	2	0	0	0	0	1	0	0
1977	Phil. vs. L.A.	.400	4	10	1	4	0	0	0	0	0	0	0
1978	Phil. vs. L.A.	.182	3	11	0	2	1	0	0	0	0	1	0
1980	Phil. vs. Hou.	.222	5	18	1	4	0	0	0	2	1	2	0
	L.C.S. Totals	.261	15	46	2	12	0	0	0	3	2	3	0

WORLD SERIES RECORD

YEAR	CLUB	AVG	G	AB	R	H	2B	3B	HR	RBI	BB	SO	SB
1980	Phil. vs. K.C.	.412	6	17	3	7	2	0	0	4	4	0	0

ALL STAR GAME RECORD

YEAR	CLUB	AVG	G	AB	R	H	2B	3B	HR	RBI	BB	SO	SB
1976	N.L., Phil.	.000	1	1	0	0	0	0	0	0	0	0	0
1978	N.L., S.D.	1.000	1	1	1	1	0	0	0	2	0	0	0
1979	N.L., Sea.	.500	1	2	1	1	0	0	0	0	0	0	0
	A.S.G. Totals	.500	0	4	2	2	0	0	0	2	0	0	0

10—BOWA, Lawrence Robert (Larry) SS

Age: 35, turns 36 on Dec. 6 ... Born—Sacramento, Calif., 12/6/45 ... Home—Wynnewood, Pa. ... B-B, T-R ... 5-10, 155 ... Married-Sheena Gibson.

YEAR	CLUB	AVG	G	AB	R	H	2B	3B	HR	RBI	BB	SO	SB
1966	Spartanburg	.312	97	429	70	134	14	2	2	36	18	44	24
	San Diego	.316	5	19	0	6	1	0	0	1	1	3	0
	Bakersfield	.188	7	32	4	6	0	1	0	3		6	2
1967	Reading	.281	22	89	11	25	4	0	0	9	3	17	0
1968	Reading	.242	133	480	47	116	14	2	3	36	24	27	14
1969	Eugene	.287	135	568	80	163	11	6	0	26	24	56	48
1970	Phillies	.250	145	547	50	137	17	6	0	34	21	48	24
1971	Phillies	.249	159	*650	74	162	18	5	1	25	34	61	28
1972	Phillies	.250	152	579	67	145	11	*13	1	31	32	51	17
1973	Phillies	.211	122	446	42	94	11	3	0	23	24	31	10
1974	Phillies	.275	162	669	97	184	19	9	2	36	23	52	39
1975	Phillies	.305	136	583	79	178	18	9	2	38	24	32	24
1976	Phillies	.248	156	624	71	155	15	9	0	49	32	31	30
1977	Phillies	.280	154	624	93	175	19	3	4	41	32	32	32
1978	Phillies	.294	156	654	78	192	31	5	3	43	24	40	27
1979	Phillies	.241	147	539	74	130	17	11	0	31	61	32	20
1980	Phillies	.267	147	540	57	144	16	4	2	39	24	28	21
M.L. Totals		.263	1636	6455	782	1696	190	78	13	398	331	438	272

*League Leader

LEAGUE CHAMPIONSHIP SERIES RECORD

YEAR	CLUB	AVG	G	AB	R	H	2B	3B	HR	RBI	BB	SO	SB
1976	Phil. vs. Cinn.	.125	3	8	1	1	1	0	0	0	3	0	0
1977	Phil. vs. L.A.	.118	4	17	2	2	0	1	0	1	1	2	0
1978	Phil. vs. L.A.	.333	4	18	2	6	1	0	0	0	0	2	0
1980	Phil. vs. Hou.	.316	5	19	2	6	0	0	0	2	3	3	1
L.C.S. Totals		.242	16	62	7	15	1	1	0	2	7	6	1

WORLD SERIES RECORD

YEAR	CLUB	AVG	G	AB	R	H	2B	3B	HR	RBI	BB	SO	SB
1980	Phil. vs. K.C.	.375	6	24	3	9	1	0	0	2	0	0	3

ALL STAR GAME RECORD

YEAR	CLUB	AVG	G	AB	R	H	2B	3B	HR	RBI	BB	SO	SB
1974	N.L., Pitt.	.000	1	2	0	0	0	0	0	0	0	0	0
1975	N.L., Milwk.	.000	1	1	0	0	0	0	0	0	0	0	0
1976	N.L., Phil.	.000	1	1	0	0	0	0	0	0	0	0	0
1978	N.L., S.D.	.667	1	3	1	2	1	0	0	0	0	1	0
1979	N.L., Sea.	.000	1	2	0	0	0	0	0	0	0	0	0
A.S.G. Totals		.250	5	8	1	2	0	0	0	0	0	0	1

A DECADE OF EXCELLENCE
(Bowa's Career Fielding)

Year	PO	A	E	Pct.
1970	202	418	13	.979
1971	272	560	11	.987
1972	212	494	9*	.987
1973	191	361	12	.979
1974	256	462	12	.984
1975	227	403	25	.962
1976	180	492	17	.975
1977	222	518	13	.983
1978	224	502	10	.986
1979	229	448	6	.991*
1980	225	449	17	.975
TOTALS	2440	5107	145	.981**

N.L. Leader in Pct. (1971; 1972; 1976; 1978; 1979)†
*National League Record
**Major League Record
†Ties N.L. Record

40—BRUSSTAR, Warren Scott (Warren) RHP

Age: 29 ... Born—Oakland, Calif., 2/2/52 ... Home—Wynnewood, Pa. ... B-R, T-R ... 6-3, 200 ... Married, Donna Arvanitis.

YEAR	CLUB	W-L	ERA	G	GS	CG	SHO	SV	IP	H	R	ER	BB	SO
1974	Spartanburg	2-4	1.93	22	0	0	0	0	42	39	23	9	24	34
1975	Rocky Mount	†14-8	2.22	25	24	12	2	0	162	117	61	40	94	123
1976	Reading	10-7	2.71	27	27	19	2	0	*199	167	83	60	*90	119
1977	Okla. City	0-1	1.59	2	0	0	0	0	3	3	1	1	5	5
	Phillies	7-2	2.66	46	0	0	0	3	71	64	26	21	24	46
1978	Phillies	6-3	2.33	58	0	0	0	3	89	74	25	23	30	60
1979	Phillies	1-0	7.07	13	0	0	0	1	14	23	12	11	4	3
	Reading	0-0	0.00	1	0	0	0	1	2	0	0	0	0	1

(continued on next page)

Brusstar, *Continued*

Continued

YEAR	CLUB	W-L	ERA	G	GS	CG		IP	H	R	ER	BB	SO
1980	Peninsula**	1-1	4.61	7	0	0	0	14	16	7	7	2	8
	Phillies	2-2	3.69	26	0	0	0	39	42	16	16	13	21
	M.L. Totals	16-7	3.00	143	0	0	4	213	203	79	71	71	130

*League Leader
**On Rehabilitation Assignment
†Tied For League Lead

MAJOR LEAGUE HITTING TOTALS

	AVG	AB	H	HR	RBI
1980	.000	14	0	0	0
Lifetime	.071	14	1	0	0

LEAGUE CHAMPIONSHIP SERIES RECORD

YEAR	CLUB	W-L	ERA	G	GS	CG	IP	H	R	ER	BB	SO
1977	Phil. vs. L.A.	0-0	3.00	2	0	0	2.2	2	1	1	1	2
1978	Phil. vs. L.A.	0-0	0.00	3	0	0	2.2	2	0	0	1	0
1980	Phil. vs. Hou.	1-0	3.00	2	0	0	2.2	1	1	1	1	0
	L.C.S. Totals	1-0	2.25	7	0	0	8	5	2	2	3	2

WORLD SERIES RECORD

YEAR	CLUB	W-L	ERA	G	GS	CG	IP	H	R	ER	BB	SO
1980	Phil. vs. K.C.	0-0	0.00	1	0	0	2.1	0	0	0	1	0

LEAGUE CHAMPIONSHIP SERIES RECORD

YEAR	CLUB	W-L	ERA	G	GS	CG	IP	H	R	ER	BB	SO
1980	Phil. vs. Hou.	0-0	1.80	1	1	0	5.1	7	2	1	2	1

WORLD SERIES RECORD

YEAR	CLUB	W-L	ERA	G	GS	CG	IP	H	R	ER	BB	SO
1980	Phil. vs. K.C.	0-0	5.40	1	1	0	5	10	3	3	1	4

50—BYSTROM, Martin Eugene (Marty) RHP

Age 22, turns 23 on July 26th... Born—Coral Gables, Fla., 7/26/58... Home—Miami, Fla.... B-R, T-R... 6-5, 200... Single.

YEAR	CLUB	W-L	ERA	G	GS	CG	SHO	SV	IP	H	R	ER	BB	SO
1977	Spartanburg	13-11	3.38	†27	27	12	2	0	184	*199	83	69	49	99
1978	Peninsula	†15-7	2.83	26	26	†13	†5	0	*197	170	71	62	46	*159
1979	Okla. City	9-5	4.08	26	26	7	0	0	172	174	102	78	69	108
1980	Okla. City	6-5	3.66	14	14	4	1	0	91	89	49	37	27	68
	Phillies	5-0	1.50	6	6	1	1	0	36	26	6	6	9	21

*League Leader
†Tied For League Lead

STRIKEOUT HIGHS

Phillies Record—RHP: 17, Art Mahaffey, 4/23/61, 2nd game vs Chicago
LHP: 14, Chris Short, 9/13/63, 1st game vs Los Angeles
14, Steve Carlton, 4/25/72 vs San Francisco
14, Steve Carlton, 8/21/77 vs Houston
14, Steve Carlton, 9/9/77 vs St. Louis
14, Steve Carlton, 7/8/79 vs San Francisco
BRUSSTAR—5, 5/13/77 vs San Diego
BYSTROM—6, 9/25/80 vs NY and 9/30/80 vs Chicago
CARLTON—19, 9/9/69 vs NY as a Cardinal
14, four times as a Phillie (see above)... 10 or more strikeouts as a Phillie:
10—seven times, 11—15 times, 12—six times, 13—four times, 14—four times
CHRISTENSON—9, 8/4/78, 1st game Pittsburgh
ESPINOSA—8 as a Met, 1978; as a Phillie, 7, 7/31/79 vs Chicago
LERCH—9, 9/20/79 vs Pittsburgh
McGRAW—10, 9/22/67 vs Houston as a Met; as a Phillie, 6, 9/26/78 vs Mtl., 2nd game.
NOLES—6, four times, last time, 4/19/80 vs Mtl.
REED—13, 9/27/69 vs San Diego as an Atlanta Brave; as a Phillies, 5, three times, last time 7/1/78 vs Chicago
RUTHVEN—10, several times, last time, 4/19/77 vs San Diego.

MOST CY YOUNG AWARDS

STEVE CARLTON, Phillies, 1972, 1977, 1980
Jim Palmer, Baltimore, 1974, 1975, 1976
Sandy Koufax, Los Angeles, 1963, 1965, 1966
Tom Seaver, New York Mets, 1969, 1973, 1975

32—CARLTON, Steven Norman (Steve) LHP

Age 36, turns 37 on Dec. 22 ... Born—Miami, Fla., 12/22/44 ... Home—Chesterfield, Mo. ... B-L, T-L ... 6-5, 219 ... Married Beverly Brooks; two children, Steve (6/2/66) and Scott (10/31/68).

YEAR	CLUB	W-L	ERA	G	GS	CG	SHO	SV	IP	H	R	ER	BB	SO
1964	Rock Hill	10-1	1.03	11	11	5	2	0	79	39	17	9	36	91
	Winnipeg	4-4	3.36	12	12	4	0	0	75	63	40	28	48	79
	Tulsa	1-1	2.63	4	3	0	0	0	24	16	13	7	18	21
1965	Tulsa	0-0	2.52	15	4	0	1	0	25	27	7	7	8	21
1966	St. Louis	9-5	3.59	19	19	2	0	0	128	110	65	51	54	108
	St. Louis	3-3	3.12	9	9	0	1	0	52	56	22	18	18	25
1967	St. Louis	14-9	2.98	30	28	11	2	1	193	173	71	64	62	168
1968	St. Louis	13-11	2.99	34	33	10	5	0	232	214	87	77	61	162
1969	St. Louis	17-11	2.17	31	31	12	2	2	236	185	66	57	93	210
1970	St. Louis	10-19	3.72	34	33	13	2	2	254	239	123	105	109	193
1971	St. Louis	20-9	3.56	37	36	18	4	0	273	275	120	108	98	172
1972	Phillies	*27-10	*1.98	41	*41	*30	8	0	*346	*257	84	76	87	*310
1973	Phillies	*13-20	3.90	40	40	18	3	0	*293	*293	*146	*127	113	223
1974	Phillies	16-13	3.22	39	39	17	1	0	291	249	118	104	*136	*240
1975	Phillies	15-14	3.56	37	37	14	3	0	255	217	116	101	104	192
1976	Phillies	20-7	3.13	35	35	13	2	0	253	224	94	88	72	195
1977	Phillies	*23-10	2.64	36	36	17	2	0	283	229	99	83	89	198
1978	Phillies	16-13	2.84	34	34	12	3	0	247	228	91	78	63	161
1979	Phillies	18-11	3.62	35	35	13	4	0	251	202	112	101	89	213
1980	Phillies	*24-9	2.34	38	†38	13	3	0	*304	243	87	79	90	*286
M.L. Totals		249-169	3.02	525	507	213	45	1	3788	3311	1443	1273	1292	2969
Phillies Totals		172-107	2.99	335	335	147	29	0	2523	2142	947	837	843	2018

*League Leader
†Tied For League Lead

MAJOR LEAGUE HITTING TOTALS

	AVG	AB	H	HR	RBI
1980	.188	101	19	0	6
Lifetime	.207	1287	266	9	106

Last Home Run (Regular Season): 9/5/77 @ Pittsburgh (Kison)
Last Home Run 10/6/78 @ LA (Sutton) LCS Game #3

LEAGUE CHAMPIONSHIP SERIES RECORD

YEAR	CLUB	W-L	ERA	G	GS	CG	IP	H	R	ER	BB	SO
1976	Phil. vs. Cinn.	0-1	6.43	1	1	0	7.	8	5	5	5	6
1977	Phil. vs. L.A.	0-1	6.75	2	2	1	11.2	13	9	8	8	6
1978	Phil. vs. L.A.	1-0	4.00	1	1	1	9.	8	4	4	2	8
1980	Phil. vs. Hou.	1-0	2.25	2	2	0	12	11	3	3	8	6
L.C.S Totals		2-2	4.73	6	6	1	39.2	40	21	21	23	26

WORLD SERIES RECORD

YEAR	CLUB	W-L	ERA	G	GS	CG	IP	H	R	ER	BB	SO
1967	St.L. vs. Bos.	0-1	0.00	1	1	0	6	3	1	0	2	5
1968	St.L. vs. Det.	0-0	6.75	2	0	0	4	7	3	3	1	3
1980	Phil. vs. K.C.	2-0	2.40	2	2	0	15	14	5	4	9	17
W.S. Totals		2-1	2.52	5	3	0	25	24	9	7	12	25

ALL STAR GAME RECORD

YEAR	CLUB	W-L	ERA	IP	H	R	ER	SO	BB
1968	N.L. Hou.	0-0	0.00			0	0		0
1969	N.L. Wash.	1-0	6.00	3	2	2	2		1
1971	N.L. Det.		Did not Pitch						
1972	N.L. Atl.	0-0	0.00	1		0	0		1
1974	N.L. Pitt.		Did not Pitch						
1977	N.L. N.Y.		Did not Pitch						
1979	N.L. Sea.	0-0	27.00	1	2	3	3		
1980	N.L. L.A.		Did not Pitch						
A.S.G Totals		1-0	7.50	6	4	5	5	4	3

CARLTON & ONE-HITTERS

National League Record: 6	American League Record: 12
STEVE CARLTON	Bob Feller

CARLTON's ONE-HITTERS:

June 19, 1968 at Chicago (Glenn Beckert single, 4th inning)
April 25, 1972 at San Francisco (Chris Speier single, 1st batter)
Sept. 27, 1975 vs. New York (Felix Millan single, 6th inning)
June 5, 1979 at Houston (Jeff Leonard single, 7th inning)
July 4, 1979 vs. New York (Elliott Maddox single, 7th inning)
April 26, 1980 vs. St. Louis (Ted Simmons single, 2nd inning)

CARLTON AND ALL-TIME RANKING

VICTORIES

1. Cy Young	511	15. GAYLORD PERRY ... 289
2. Walter Johnson	416	16. Robin Roberts ... 286
3. Grover C. Alexander	373	JIM KAAT ... 272
4. Christy Mathewson	373	FERGUSON JENKINS ... 259
5. Warren Spahn	363	STEVE CARLTON ... 249
6. Pud Galvin	361	TOM SEAVER ... 245
7. Kid Nichols	361	JIM PALMER ... 241
8. Tim Keefe	343	PHIL NIEKRO ... 233
9. John Clarkson	327	DON SUTTON ... 230
10. Charles Radbourn	308	LUIS TIANT ... 225
11. Mickey Welch	307	RICK WISE ... 184
12. Eddie Plank	305	NOLAN RYAN ... 178
13. Lefty Grove	300	JERRY KOOSMAN ... 176
14. Early Wynn	300	VIDA BLUE ... 170

STRIKEOUTS

1. Walter Johnson	3508	13. Bob Feller ... 2581
2. GAYLORD PERRY	3276	14. PHIL NIEKRO ... 2578
3. Bob Gibson	3117	15. Tim Keefe ... 2538
4. NOLAN RYAN	3109	16. Christy Mathewson ... 2511
5. TOM SEAVER	2988	20. JIM KAAT ... 2419
6. STEVE CARLTON	2969	23. LUIS TIANT ... 2354
7. FERGUSON JENKINS	2899	29. BERT BLYLEVEN ... 2250
8. Jim Bunning	2855	30. JERRY KOOSMAN ... 2205
9. Mickey Lolich	2832	35. JIM PALMER ... 2036
10. Cy Young	2819	48. TOMMY JOHN ... 1800
11. DON SUTTON	2652	51. VIDA BLUE ... 1753
12. Warren Spahn	2583	

INNINGS PITCHED

1. Cy Young	7356	14. John Clarkson ... 4536
2. Pud Galvin	5941	15. Charles Radbourn ... 4535
3. Walter Johnson	5924	19. JIM KAAT ... 4365
4. Warren Spahn	5244	26. PHIL NIEKRO ... 4044
5. Grover C. Alexander	5189	27. FERGUSON JENKINS ... 4008
6. Kid Nichols	5089	34. STEVE CARLTON ... 3788
7. Mickey Welch	4802	39. DON SUTTON ... 3728
8. GAYLORD PERRY	4798	42. TOM SEAVER ... 3622
9. Christy Mathewson	4783	47. JIM PALMER ... 3499
10. Tim Keefe	4701	LUIS TIANT ... 3399
11. Robin Roberts	4689	TOMMY JOHN ... 3345
12. Early Wynn	4564	JERRY KOOSMAN ... 3042
13. Anthony Mullone	4540	RICK WISE ... 3025

GAMES STARTED

1. Cy Young	818	13. Christy Mathewson ... 551
2. Pud Galvin	682	14. Mike Welch ... 549
3. Walter Johnson	666	15. Red Ruffing ... 536
4. Warren Spahn	665	16. Jim Bunning ... 519
5. JIM KAAT	622	17. John Clarkson ... 518
6. Early Wynn	612	18. John Powell ... 517
7. Robin Roberts	609	Don Sutton ... 517
8. GAYLORD PERRY	605	20. FERGUSON JENKINS ... 515
9. Grover Alexander	598	21. STEVE CARLTON ... 507
10. Tim Keefe	593	22. Anthony Mullane ... 505
11. Kid Nichols	561	23. PHIL NIEKRO ... 504
12. Eppa Rixey	552	

EARNED RUN AVERAGE

	IP	ER	ERA
1. Walter Johnson	4195	1103	2.37
2. Grover Alexander	4822	1372	2.56
3. TOM SEAVER	3622	1048	2.60
4. JIM PALMER	3539	1067	2.71
5. Whitey Ford	3171	967	2.74
6. Stan Coveleski	3071	982	2.88
7. Juan Marichal	3506	1126	2.89
Wilbur Cooper	3482	1119	2.89
9. Bob Gibson	3885	1258	2.91
10. Carl Mays	3022	979	2.92
11. Don Drysdale	3432	1124	2.95
12. GAYLORD PERRY	4798	1578	2.96
13. Carl Hubbell	3591	1188	2.98
14. STEVE CARLTON	3788	1273	3.02
TOMMY JOHN	3345	1124	3.02

DID YOU KNOW

Steve Carlton of the Phillies and Sandy Koufax of the Dodgers share the modern National League record for most wins by a lefthander in one season, 27. Koufax did it in 1966, Carlton six years later.

MAJOR LEAGUE HITTING TOTALS

	AVG	AB	H	HR	RBI
1980	.368	19	7	1	4
Lifetime	.177	311	55	10	37

LEAGUE CHAMPIONSHIP SERIES RECORD

YEAR	CLUB	W-L	ERA	G	GS	CG	IP	H	R	ER	BB	SO
1976	Phil. vs. Cinn.				Did Not Pitch							
1977	Phil. vs. L.A.	0-0	9.00	1	1	0	3.1	7	3	3	0	2
1978	Phil. vs. L.A.	0-1	13.50	1	1	0	4.1	7	7	6	0	3
1980	Phil. vs. Hou.	0-0	3.86	2	1	0	6.2	5	3	3	5	2
	L.C.S. Totals	0-1	7.71	4	3	0	14.1	19	13	12	5	7

WORLD SERIES RECORD

YEAR	CLUB	W-L	ERA	G	GS	CG	IP	H	R	ER	BB	SO
1980	Phil. vs. K.C.	0-1	108.00	1	1	0	.1	5	4	4	0	0

CARLTON & ALL-TIME N.L. RANKINGS

GAMES WON

1. Grover Alexander (R)	373	
Christy Mathewson (R)	373	
3. Warren Spahn (L)	363	
4. Kid Nichols (R)	360	
5. John Clarkson (R)	327	
6. Pud Galvin (R)	317	
7. Cy Young (R)	289	
8. Charles Radbourn (R)	281	
9. Burleigh Grimes (R)	269	
10. Eppa Rixey (L)	266	
11. Carl Hubbell (L)	253	
12. Bob Gibson (R)	251	
13. STEVE CARLTON (L)	249	

285 OR MORE STRIKEOUTS, SEASON

1. Sandy Koufax, L.A. 1965	382	
2. Sandy Koufax, L.A. 1966	317	
3. J. R. Richard, Hou. 1979	313	
4. STEVE CARLTON 1972	310	
5. Sandy Koufax, L.A. 1963	306	
6. J. R. Richard, Hou. 1978	303	
7. Tom Seaver, N.Y. 1971	289	
8. STEVE CARLTON 1980	286	

CAREER STRIKEOUTS

1. Bob Gibson, St. Louis	3117	
2. Tom Seaver, New York—Cincinnati	2988	
3. STEVE CARLTON	2969	

38—CHRISTENSON, Larry Richard (Larry) RHP

Age: 27, turns 28 on Nov. 10 ... Born—Everett, Wash., 11/10/53 ... Home—Ardmore, Pa. ... B-R, T-R ... 6-4, 213 ... Single.

YEAR	CLUB	W-L	ERA	G	GS	CG	SHO	SV	IP	H	R	ER	BB	SO
1972	Pulaski	4-2	2.57	7	5	2	0	0	35	25	14	10	12	40
1973	Phillies	1-4	6.62	10	9	1	0	0	34	53	25	25	20	11
1974	Eugene	7-6	5.13	16	16	6	1	0	100	109	65	57	54	64
	Toledo	11-9	3.30	27	26	6	1	0	172	131	77	63	82	139
1975	Toledo	1-1	4.30	10	2	0	0	0	23	20	11	11	15	16
	Phillies	2-0	0.00	2	2	0	0	0	12	5	0	0	5	10
1976	Phillies	11-6	3.66	29	26	5	2	1	172	149	73	70	45	88
1977	Phillies	13-8	3.67	32	29	5	1	0	169	199	77	69	42	54
1978	Phillies	19-6	4.07	34	34	9	3	0	219	209	99	69	69	118
1979	Phillies	13-14	3.24	33	33	9	0	0	228	209	90	82	47	131
	Phillies	5-10	4.50	19	17	2	0	0	106	118	56	53	30	53
1980	Phillies	5-1	4.01	14	14	0	0	0	74	62	35	33	27	49
	M.L. Totals	68-50	3.88	181	163	24	6	3	1025	1039	480	442	295	522

35—ESPINOSA, Arnulfo Acevedo (Nino) RHP

Age: 27, turns 28 on Aug. 15 ... Born—Villa Altagracia, D.R., 8/15/53 ... Home—Villa Altagracia, D.R. ... B-R, T-R ... 6-0, 185 ... Married Fidea Bira; Three children: Kathy (10/26/74); and Nadaline (6/8/76) and Anthony Arnulfo (6/13/79).

YEAR	CLUB	W-L	ERA	G	GS	CG	SHO	SV	IP	H	R	ER	BB	SO
1971	Key West	6-12	2.97	41	7	3	0	6	115	116	53	44	32	70
1972	Pompano Bch.	8-6	4.15	40	3	2	0	5	89	115	51	41	12	64
1973	Visalia	10-10	4.19	25	25	7	0	1	174	184	99	81	54	109
1974	Victoria	9-8	3.42	25	18	6	1	1	137	137	66	52	26	63
1975	Tidewater	0-0	5.00	24	4	0	0	0	9	12	5	5	0	2
	N.Y. (N.L.)	8-5	2.61	21	21	8	2	0	141	127	48	41	38	83
1976	Tidewater	0-1	18.00	2	0	0	0	0	3	8	8	6	1	2
	N.Y. (N.L.)	7-3	2.91	14	14	6	1	0	108	106	40	35	34	66
1977	N.Y. (N.L.)	4-4	3.64	12	5	0	0	0	42	41	21	17	13	20
	N.Y. (N.L.)	10-13	3.42	32	29	7	1	0	200	188	82	76	55	105
1978	N.Y. (N.L.)	11-15	4.72	32	32	6	1	0	204	230	117	107	75	76

(continued on next page)

Espinosa, *Continued*

YEAR	CLUB	W-L	ERA	G	GS	CG	SHO	SV	IP	H	R	ER	BB	SO
1979	Phillies	14-12	3.65	33	33	8	3	0	212	211	94	86	65	88
1980	Spartanburg**	1-1	2.65	3	3	1	0	0	17	17	15	5	2	11
	Phillies	3-5	3.79	12	12	1	0	0	76	73	36	32	19	13
M.L. Totals		42-50	3.97	125	112	22	5	0	745	763	361	329	228	316

**On Rehabilitation Assignment

MAJOR LEAGUE HITTING TOTALS

	AVG	AB	R	H	HR	RBI
1980	.115	26	3	3	0	2
M.L. Totals	.169	237		40		17

47—LERCH, Randy Louis (Randy) LHP

Age: 26, turns 27 on Oct. 9 ... Born—Sacramento, Calif., 10/9/54 ... Home—Voorhees, N.J. ... B-L, T-L ... 6-3, 190 ... Married Janet Brown; two children Kristy (3/1/77) and Randy, Jr. (8/15/78).

YEAR	CLUB	W-L	ERA	G	GS	CG	SHO	SV	IP	H	R	ER	BB	SO
1973	Auburn	9-2	2.91	16	13	7	2	1	96	88	41	31	29	75
1974	Rocky Mount	7-6	3.60	21	21	6	1	2	135	143	69	54	50	107
1975	Reading	**16-6	2.69	25	25	14	1	0	177	173	66	53	45	108
	Phillies	0-0	6.43	3	0	0	0	0	7	6	5	5	1	8
1976	Okla. City	13-11	3.34	*29	29	11	2	2	*207	*203	91	77	47	*152
	Phillies	0-0	3.00	1	0	0	0	0	3	3	1	1	0	0
1977	Phillies	10-5	5.06	32	28	3	0	0	169	207	102	95	75	81
1978	Phillies	11-8	3.96	33	33	5	1	0	184	183	89	81	70	96
1979	Phillies	10-13	3.74	37	35	6	1	0	214	228	98	89	60	92
1980	Phillies	4-14	5.16	30	22	2	0	0	150	178	98	86	55	57
M.L. Totals		35-41	4.42	136	113	16	1	1	727	805	393	357	261	334

MAJOR LEAGUE HITTING TOTALS

	AVG	AB	H	HR	RBI
1980	.267	45	12	0	3
Lifetime	.207	232	48	4	22

Last Home Run 5/17/79 @ Chicago (off Donnie Moore)

LEAGUE CHAMPIONSHIP SERIES RECORD

YEAR	CLUB	W-L	ERA	G	GS	CG	IP	H	R	ER	BB	SO
1977	Phil. vs. L.A.	0-0	5.40	1	1	0	5.1	7	3	3	0	0
1978	Phil. vs. L.A.	Did Not Appear										
L.C.S. Totals		0-0	5.40	1	1	0	5.1	7	3	3	0	0

23—GROSS, Gregory Eugene (Greg) OF

Age: 28, turns 29 on Aug. 1 ... Born—York, Pa., 8/1/52 ... Home—Berwyn, Pa. ... B-L, T-L ... 5-11, 175 ... Married Debbie Knight; two children, Megan Nicole (11/14/76); Michael Gregory (10/30/79).

YEAR	CLUB	AVG	G	AB	R	H	2B	3B	HR	RBI	BB	SO	SB
1970	Covington	.351	54	211	40	74	8	3	2	27	17	27	12
1971	Columbus	.291	132	494	57	144	14	4	2	33	39	53	7
1972	Columbus	.302	101	367	55	111	14	2	0	25	54	35	6
	Oklahoma City	.248	28	109	15	27	4	0	0	7	8	7	0
1973	Denver	.330	131	528	98	174	25	6	6	55	86	43	4
	Houston	.231	14	39	5	9	2	1	0	1	4	4	2
1974	Houston	.314	156	589	78	185	21	8	0	36	76	40	12
1975	Houston	.294	132	483	67	142	14	10	0	41	63	37	2
1976	Houston	.286	128	426	52	122	12	3	0	27	64	39	2
1977	Chicago (N.L.)	.322	115	239	43	77	10	4	5	32	33	19	0
1978	Chicago (N.L.)	.265	124	347	34	92	12	7	1	39	33	19	3
1979	Phillies	.333	111	174	21	58	6	3	0	15	29	5	5
1980	Phillies	.240	127	154	19	37	7	2	0	12	24	7	1
M.L. Totals		.295	907	2451	319	722	84	38	6	203	326	170	27

LEAGUE CHAMPIONSHIP SERIES RECORD

YEAR	CLUB	AVG	G	AB	R	H	2B	3B	HR	RBI	BB	SO	SB
1980	Phil. vs. Hou.	.750	4	4	2	3	0	0	0	1	0	0	0

WORLD SERIES RECORD

YEAR	CLUB	AVG	G	AB	R	H	2B	3B	HR	RBI	BB	SO	SB
1980	Phil. vs. K.C.	.000	4	2	0	0	0	0	0	0	0	0	0

19—LUZINSKI, Gregory Michael (Greg, Bull) OF

Age: 30, turns 31 on Nov. 22 . . . Born—Chicago, Ill., 11/22/50 . . . Home—Medford, N.J. . . . B-R, T-R . . . 6-1, 225 . . . Married Jean Allison; two children Kimberly Ann (4/3/70) and Ryan Michael (8/22/73).

YEAR	CLUB	AVG	G	AB	R	H	2B	3B	HR	RBI	BB	SO	SB
1968	Huron	.259	57	212	22	55	5	1	*13	†43	18	64.	3
1969	Raleigh-Durham	.289	129	464	75	134	22	3	*31	*92	58	148	4
1970	Reading	*.325	*141	471	*94	153	25	5	33	*120	85	148	6
	Phillies	.167	8	12	0	2	0	0	0	3		5	1
1971	Eugene	.312	142	548	104	171	30	5	36	114	39	167	1
	Phillies	.300	28	100	13	30	8	0	5	15	12	32	2
1972	Phillies	.281	150	563	66	158	33	5	18	68	42	114	1
1973	Phillies	.285	161	610	76	174	26	4	29	97	51	135	3
1974	Phillies	.272	85	302	29	82	14	1	7	48	33	76	3
1975	Phillies	.300	161	596	85	179	35	3	34	*120	89	151	3
1976	Phillies	.304	149	533	74	162	28	1	21	95	50	107	1
1977	Phillies	.309	149	554	99	171	35	3	39	130	80	*140	3
1978	Phillies	.265	155	540	85	143	32	2	35	101	100	135	8
1979	Phillies	.252	137	452	47	114	23	1	18	81	56	103	3
1980	Phillies	.228	106	368	44	84	19	1	19	56	60	100	3
	M.L. Totals	.281	1289	4630	618	1299	253	21	223	811	572	1098	29

LEAGUE CHAMPIONSHIP SERIES RECORD

YEAR	CLUB	AVG	G	AB	R	H	2B	3B	HR	RBI	BB	SO	SB
1976	Phil. vs. Cinn.	.273	3	11	2	3	2	0	1	3	1	4	0
1977	Phil. vs. L.A.	.286	4	14	2	4	1	0	1	2	3	3	1
1978	Phil. vs. L.A.	.375	4	16	3	6	1	0	2	3	0	2	0
1980	Phil. vs. Hou.	.294	5	17	3	5	2	0	1	4	0	6	0
	L.C.S. Totals	.310	16	58	10	18	5	1	5	12	4	15	1

WORLD SERIES RECORD

YEAR	CLUB	AVG	G	AB	R	H	2B	3B	HR	RBI	BB	SO	SB
1980	Phil. vs. K.C.	.000	3	9	0	0	0	0	0	0	1	5	0

ALL STAR GAME RECORD

YEAR	CLUB	AVG	G	AB	R	H	2B	3B	HR	RBI	BB	SO	SB
1975	N.L. Milwk.	.000	1	1	0	0	0	0	0	0	0	1	0
1976	N.L. Phil.	.000	1	2	0	1	0	0	0	0	0	0	0
1977	N.L. N.Y. (A.L.)	.500	1	2	1	1	0	0	1	2	0	0	0
1978	N.L. S.D.	.500	1	2	1	1	0	0	0	1	1	0	0
	A.S.G. Totals	.286	1	7	1	2	0	0	1	3	1	1	0

39—LYLE, Albert Walter (Sparky) LHP

Age: 36, turns 37 on July 26th . . . Born—Reynoldsville, Pa., 7/22/44 . . . Home—Demarest, N.J. . . . B-L, T-L . . . 6-2, 205 . . . Married, Wife's name Mary; three children, Dane 12, Shane 7, Scott 1.

YEAR	CLUB	W-L	ERA	G	GS	CG	SHO	SV	IP	H	R	ER	BB	SO
1964	Bluefield	3-2	4.36	7	4	1	0	0	23	23	19	16	25	44
	Fox Cities	3-1	2.31	6	6	3	0	0	35	30	14	9	18	51
1965	Winston-Salem	5-5	4.24	37	5	2	0	0	87	84	45	41	55	79
1966	Pittsfield	4-2	3.65	40	1	1	0	0	74	62	35	30	43	72
1967	Toronto	2-2	1.71	16	0	0	0	0	21	13	5	4	14	17
	Boston	1-2	2.30	27	0	0	0	5	43	33	13	11	14	42
1968	Boston	6-1	2.73	49	0	0	0	11	66	67	25	20	14	52
1969	Boston	8-3	2.53	71	0	0	0	17	103	91	33	29	48	93
1970	Boston	1-7	3.90	63	0	0	0	20	67	62	37	29	34	51
1971	Boston	6-4	2.77	50	0	0	0	16	52	41	16	16	23	37
1972	New York (AL)	9-5	1.92	59	0	0	0	*35	108	84	25	23	29	75
1973	New York (AL)	5-9	2.51	51	0	0	0	27	82	66	30	23	18	63
1974	New York (AL)	9-3	1.66	66	0	0	0	15	114	93	30	21	43	89
1975	New York (AL)	5-7	3.13	49	0	0	0	6	89	94	34	31	36	64
1976	New York (AL)	7-8	2.26	64	0	0	0	*23	104	82	33	26	42	61
1977	New York (AL)	13-5	2.17	72	0	0	0	26	137	131	41	33	33	68
1978	New York (AL)	9-3	3.47	59	0	0	0	9	113	116	46	43	33	33
1979	Texas	5-8	3.13	67	0	0	0	13	95	78	37	33	28	48
1980	Texas	3-2	4.67	49	0	0	0	8	81	97	47	42	33	43
	Phillies	0-0	1.93	10	0	0	0	2	14	11	5	3	6	6
	M.L. Totals	87-67	2.72	806	0	0	0	233	1268	1146	452	383	429	825

*League Leader

MAJOR LEAGUE HITTING TOTALS

	AVG	AB	H	HR	R	RBI
1980	.000	0	0	0	0	0
Lifetime	.167	72	12	0	3	3

LEAGUE CHAMPIONSHIP SERIES RECORD

YEAR	CLUB	W-L	ERA	G	GS	CG	IP	H	R	ER	BB	SO
1976	N.Y. (A.L.) vs. K.C.	0-0	0.00	1	0	0	0.1	1	0	0	1	0
1977	N.Y. (A.L.) vs. K.C.	2-0	0.96	4	0	0	9.1	7	1	1	0	3
1978	N.Y. (A.L.) vs. K.C.	0-0	18.00	1	0	0	1.1	3	2	2	0	0
	L.C.S. Totals	2-0	2.25	6	0	0	11.2	10	3	3	1	3

(continued on next page)

(continued on next page)

Lyle, *Continued*

LEAGUE CHAMPIONSHIP SERIES RECORD

YEAR	CLUB	AVG	G	AB	R	H	2B	3B	HR	RBI	BB	SO	SB
1976	Phil. vs. Cinn.	.231	3	13	2	3	1	0	0	1	1	0	0
1977	Phil. vs. L.A.	.429	2	7	1	3	0	0	0	0	0	2	0
1978	Phil. vs. L.A.	.263	4	19	1	5	1	0	0	2	0	2	2
1980	Phil. vs. Hou.	.300	5	20	2	6	2	0	0	3	2	2	2
	L.C.S. Totals	.288	14	59	6	17	3	0	0	8	3	7	2

WORLD SERIES RECORD

YEAR	CLUB	AVG	G	AB	R	H	2B	3B	HR	RBI	BB	SO	SB
1980	Phil. vs. K.C.	.227	6	22	1	5	2	0	1	1	1	3	0

WORLD SERIES RECORD

YEAR	CLUB	W-L	ERA	G	GS	CG	IP	H	R	ER	BB	SO
1967	Boston vs. St.L.			Did Not Play								
1976	N.Y. (A.L.) vs. Cinn.	0-0	0.00	2	0	0	2.2	1	0	0	0	3
1977	N.Y. (A.L.) vs. L.A.	1-0	1.93	2	0	0	4.2	2	1	1	0	2
1978	N.Y. (A.L.) vs. L.A.			Did Not Play								
	W.S. Totals	1-0	1.23	4	0	0	7.1	3	1	1	0	5

ALL STAR GAME RECORD

YEAR	CLUB	W-L	ERA	G	GS	CG	IP	H	R	ER	BB	SO
1973	A.L., K.C.	0-0	0.00	1	0	0	1	1	0	0	0	1
1976	A.L., Phil.			Did Not Play								
1977	A.L., N.Y. (A.L.)	0-0	9.00	1	0	0	2	3	2	2	0	1
	All-Star Totals	0-0	6.00	2	0	0	3	4	2	2	0	2

21—McBRIDE, Arnold Ray (Bake) OF

Age 32 ... Born—Fulton, Mo., 2/3/49 ... Home—Florissant, Mo. ... B-L, T-R ... 6-2, 184 ... Married Celeste Woodley; three children: Tabitha (11/4/69); "Bake Jr," (4/17/75) and Adrienne (2/25/79).

YEAR	CLUB	AVG	G	AB	R	H	2B	3B	HR	RBI	BB	SO	SB
1970	Sarasota	.423	17	71	15	30	2	4	2	13	8	9	5
	Modesto	.294	26	85	17	25	4	5	0	7	8	24	9
1971	Modesto	.303	118	468	85	142	10	8	5	54	64	84	40
1972	Arkansas	.329	67	286	51	94	10	4	12	34	17	57	25
	Tulsa	.315	60	232	41	73	14	5	6	24	26	54	17
1973	Tulsa	.289	58	225	45	65	15	3	6	34	19	25	23
	St. Louis	.302	40	63	8	19	3	0	0	5	4	10	0
1974	St. Louis	.309	150	559	81	173	19	9	5	56	43	57	30
1975	St. Louis	.300	116	413	70	124	19	4	11	56	34	52	26
1976	St. Louis	.335	72	272	40	91	13	4	3	24	18	28	10
1977	StL-Phillies	.316	128	402	76	127	25	5	11	61	32	44	36
	Phillies	.339	85	280	55	95	20	5	11	41	25	25	27
1978	Phillies	.269	122	472	68	127	20	4	10	49	28	68	28
1979	Phillies	.280	151	582	82	163	16	12	12	50	41	77	25
1980	Phillies	.309	137	554	68	171	33	9	9	87	26	58	13
	M.L. Totals	.300	916	3317	493	995	139	50	60	378	226	394	168

31—MADDOX, Garry Lee (Garry) OF

Age: 31, turns 32 on Sept. 1 ... Born—Cincinnati, O., 9/1/49 ... Home—Philadelphia, Pa. ... B-R, T-R ... 6-3, 185 ... Married Sondra Harris; two sons, Garry (10/24/74); Derrick (6/28/76).

YEAR	CLUB	AVG	G	AB	R	H	2B	3B	HR	RBI	BB	SO	SB
1968	Salt Lake City	.252	58	206	34	52	11	2	5	29	17	68	14
	Fresno	.316	5	19	2	6	0	0	0	5	1	5	0
1971	Fresno	.299	120	475	105	142	25	5	30	106	35	102	21
1972	Phoenix	.438	11	48	16	21	3	2	9	22	2	3	2
	San Francisco	.266	125	458	62	122	26	7	12	58	14	97	13
1973	San Francisco	.319	144	587	81	187	30	10	11	76	24	73	24
1974	San Francisco	.284	135	538	74	153	31	8	8	50	29	64	21
1975	SF-Phillies	.272	116	426	54	116	26	6	5	50	42	57	25
1976	Phillies	.330	146	531	75	175	37	6	6	68	42	59	29
1977	Phillies	.292	139	571	85	167	27	10	14	74	24	58	22
1978	Phillies	.288	155	598	62	172	34	6	11	68	39	89	33
1979	Phillies	.281	148	548	70	154	28	6	13	61	17	71	26
1980	Phillies	.259	143	549	59	142	31	3	11	73	18	52	25
	M.L. Totals	.289	1251	4806	622	1388	270	56	91	578	249	620	218

(continued on next page)

McBride, Continued

LEAGUE CHAMPIONSHIP SERIES RECORD

YEAR	CLUB	AVG	G	AB	R	H	2B	3B	HR	RBI	BB	SO	SB
1977	Phil. vs. L.A.	.222	4	18	2	4	0	0	1	2	1	2	0
1978	Phil. vs. L.A.	.222	3	9	2	2	0	0	0	1	0	2	0
1980	Phil. vs. Hou.	.238	5	21	0	5	0	0	0	0	1	5	2
	L.C.S. Totals	.229	12	48	4	11	0	0	2	3	2	9	2

WORLD SERIES RECORD

YEAR	CLUB	AVG	G	AB	R	H	2B	3B	HR	RBI	BB	SO	SB
1980	Phil. vs. K.C.	.304	6	23	3	7	1	0	1	5	2	1	0

ALL STAR GAME RECORD

YEAR	CLUB	AVG	G	AB	R	H	2B	3B	HR	RBI	BB	SO	SB
1976	N.L., Phil					Did Not Play							

17—McCORMACK, Donald Ross (Don) C

Age: 25, turns 26 on Sept. 18th ... Born—Omak, Wash., 9/18/55 ... Home—Omak ... B-R, T-R ... 6-3, 205 ... Married Connie Wilson.

YEAR	CLUB	AVG	G	AB	R	H	2B	3B	HR	RBI	BB	SO	SB
1974	Pulaski	.199	48	161	20	32	5	1	2	17	20	41	1
1975	Batavia	.238	41	143	18	34	10	1	2	23	15	24	1
	Auburn	.111	5	18	3	2	0	0	0	2	3	3	1
1976	Peninsula	.234	94	291	29	68	9	0	6	36	21	52	2
1977	Peninsula	.250	94	316	37	79	13	1	9	37	33	49	1
1978	Reading	.320	78	244	34	78	14	1	7	30	35	37	0
	Oklahoma City	.313	40	147	19	46	7	3	3	31	9	24	2
1979	Oklahoma City	.260	115	384	45	100	18	3	14	55	36	73	4
1980	Oklahoma City	.263	121	411	55	108	16	3	14	64	47	60	2
	Phillies	1.000	2	1	0	1	0	0	0	0	0	0	0

45—McGRAW, Frank Edwin (Tug) LHP

Age: 36, turns 37 on Aug. 30 ... Born—Martinez, Calif., 8/30/44 ... Home—Media, Pa. ... B-R, T-L ... 6-0, 184 ... Married Phyllis Kline; two children, Mark Thomas (5/12/72) and Cari Lynn (9/1/73).

YEAR	CLUB	W-L	ERA	G	GS	CG	SHO	SV	IP	H	R	ER	BB	SO
1964	Cocoa	5-2	1.53	8	5	5	1	0	47	12	11	8	37	52
	Auburn	1-2	1.89	3	3	1	1	0	19	17	12	4	15	14
1965	N.Y. (N.L.)	2-7	3.31	9	9	2	1	0	98	88	47	37	48	57
1966	N.Y. (N.L.)	2-9	5.37	15	12	1	0	0	62	72	38	37	25	34
	Jacksonville	2-2	4.22	11	6	1	1	0	32	34	16	15	9	38
1967	Jacksonville	10-9	*1.99	22	21	14	3	0	167	111	39	37	55	161
	N.Y. (N.L.)	0-3	7.94	4	4	0	0	0	17	13	16	15	13	18
1968	Jacksonville	9-9	3.42	24	23	10	2	0	166	149	70	63	61	132
1969	N.Y. (N.L.)	9-3	2.25	42	4	1	0	12	100	89	31	25	47	92
1970	N.Y. (N.L.)	4-6	3.26	57	1	0	0	10	91	77	40	33	49	81
1971	N.Y. (N.L.)	11-4	1.70	51	1	0	0	8	111	73	21	21	41	109
1972	N.Y. (N.L.)	8-6	1.70	54	0	0	0	27	106	71	26	20	40	92
1973	N.Y. (N.L.)	5-6	3.86	60	2	0	0	25	119	106	53	51	55	81
1974	N.Y. (N.L.)	6-11	4.15	41	4	1	0	3	89	96	43	41	32	54
1975	Phillies	9-6	2.97	56	0	0	0	14	103	84	38	34	36	55
1976	Phillies	7-6	2.51	58	0	0	0	11	97	81	34	27	42	76
1977	Phillies	7-3	2.62	45	0	0	0	9	79	62	25	23	24	58
1978	Phillies	8-7	3.20	55	0	0	0	9	90	82	39	32	23	63
1979	Phillies	4-3	5.14	65	1	0	0	16	84	83	56	48	29	57
1980	Phillies	5-4	1.47	57	0	0	0	20	92	62	16	15	23	75
	M.L. Totals	87-84	3.08	697	38	5	1	164	1338	1139	524	458	527	1002

*League Leader

MAJOR LEAGUE HITTING TOTALS

	AVG	AB	H	HR	RBI
1980	.250	8	2	0	1
Lifetime	.180	205	37	1	17

Home Run: 9/8/71 @ Montreal (Carl Morton)

LEAGUE CHAMPIONSHIP SERIES RECORD

YEAR	CLUB	W-L	ERA	G	GS	CG	IP	H	R	ER	BB	SO
1969	N.Y. (N.L.) vs. Atl.	0-0	0.00	2	0	0	3	1	0	0	1	1
1973	N.Y. (N.L.) vs. Cin.	0-0	0.00	2	0	0	5	4	0	3	3	3
1976	Phil. vs. Cin.	0-0	13.50	2	0	0	2.1	4	3	3	1	5
1977	Phil. vs. L.A.	0-0	0.00	3	0	0	3	2	1	0	5	5
1978	Phil. vs. L.A.	0-1	1.50	3	0	0	5.2	8	4	4	4	5
1980	Phil. vs. Hou.	0-1	4.50	5	0	0	8	8	2	1	4	5
	L.C.S. Totals	0-2	2.67	15	0	0	27	21	9	8	16	22

(continued on next page)

WORLD SERIES RECORD

YEAR	CLUB	W-L	ERA	G	GS	CG	IP	H	R	ER	BB	SO
1973	N.Y. (N.L.) vs. Oak.	1-0	2.57	5	0	0	13.2	8	5	4	9	14
1980	Phil. vs. K.C.	1-1	1.17	4	0	0	8	7	1	1	8	10
	W.S. Totals	2-1	2.05	9	0	0	21.2	15	6	5	17	24

ALL STAR GAME RECORD

YEAR	CLUB	W-L	ERA	IP	H	R	ER	BB	SO
1972	N.L., Atl.	1-0	0.00	2	1	0	0	0	4
1975	N.L., Mil.		Did Not Pitch						

6—MORELAND, Bobby Keith (Keith) C

Age: 26, turns 27 on May 2nd... Born—Dallas, Tx., 5/2/54... Home—Dallas, Tx... B-R, T-R... 6-0, 200... Married Cindy Scott; one daughter, Courtney (11/20/77).

YEAR	CLUB	AVG	G	AB	R	H	2B	3B	HR	RBI	BB	SO	SB
1975	Spartanburg	.276	69	246	28	68	13	1	0	41	21	18	2
	Peninsula	.282	78	294	38	83	12	2	4	47	15	15	2
1976	Reading	.261	61	199	7	52	5	0	0	7	20	14	0
1977	Reading	.327	104	401	61	131	19	1	8	55	42	23	6
	Oklahoma City	.077	7	13	3	1	0	0	0	1	1	1	0
1978	Oklahoma City	.289	130	501	73	145	25	4	16	98	43	32	8
	Phillies	.000	2	2	0	0	0	0	0	0	0	0	0
1979	Oklahoma City	.302	130	494	86	149	†34	3	20	109	64	56	2
	Phillies	.375	14	48	3	18	3	2	0	8	3	5	0
1980	Phillies	.314	62	159	13	50	8	0	4	29	8	14	3
	M.L. Totals	.325	77	209	16	68	11	2	4	37	11	19	3

†Tied for League Lead

LEAGUE CHAMPIONSHIP SERIES RECORD

YEAR	CLUB	AVG	G	AB	R	H	2B	3B	HR	RBI	BB	SO	SB
1980	Phil. vs. Hou.	.000	2	1	0	0	0	0	0	1	0	0	0

WORLD SERIES RECORD

YEAR	CLUB	AVG	G	AB	R	H	2B	3B	HR	RBI	BB	SO	SB
1980	Phil. vs. K.C.	.333	3	12	1	4	0	0	0	1	0	1	0

34—MUNNINGHOFF, Scott Andrew (Scott) RHP

Age: 22, turns 23 on Dec. 5th... Born—Cincinnati, O., 12/5/58... Home—Cincinnati... B-R, T-R... 6-0, 180... Married Colleen Crowley; one daughter, Kelli (4/26/79).

YEAR	CLUB	W-L	ERA	G	GS	CG	SHO	SV	IP	H	R	ER	BB	SO
1977	Auburn	0-5	5.52	6	6	0	0	0	31	29	28	19	35	13
1978	Spartanburg	*17-7	2.30	26	†26	*13	†3	0	180	159	77	46	84	89
1979	Reading	†14-9	3.73	26	*26	15	2	0	188	172	94	78	94	87
	Phillies	0-0	4.50	4	0	0	0	0	6	8	3	3	5	2
1980	Oklahoma City	4-9	5.09	22	14	3	1	4	92	112	63	52	54	30

*League Leader   †Tied For League Lead

MAJOR LEAGUE HITTING TOTALS

	AVG	AB	H	HR	RBI
1980	1.000	1	1	0	0

SPARKY & TUG—ALL-TIME RANKINGS

GAMES PITCHED (Active Pitchers with 525 or More)

1.	Hoyt Wilhelm	1070
2.	Lindy McDaniel	987
3.	Cy Young	906
4.	Don McMahon	874
5.	Roy Face	848
6.	**SPARKY LYLE**	806
7.	Walter Johnson	802
8.	**JIM KAAT**	771
9.	**ROLLIE FINGERS**	767
10.	Darold Knowles	765
11.	Jack Quinn	755
12.	Warren Spahn	750
13.	Ron Perranoski	737
14.	Ron Kline	736
15.	Clay Carroll	731
19.	**TUG McGRAW**	697
24.	**GAYLORD PERRY**	692
35.	PHIL NIEKRO	648
50.	TOM BURGMEIER	607
	DAVE LaROCHE	595
	FERGUSON JENKINS	578
	LUIS TIANT	558
	RON REED	543
	STAN BAHNSEN	534
	DON SUTTON	534
	STEVE CARLTON	525

SAVES (Since 1969)

1.	Rollie Fingers	244	3.	Mike Marshall	178
2.	**SPARKY LYLE**	217**	4.	**TUG McGRAW**	164*

*National League Record
**American League Record

48—NOLES, Dickie Ray   RHP

Age: 24, turns 25 on Nov. 19 . . . Born—Charlotte, N.C., 11/19/56 . . . Home—Charlotte . . . B-R, T-R . . . 6-2, 190 . . . Single.

YEAR	CLUB	W-L	ERA	G	GS	CG	SHO	SV	IP	H	R	ER	BB	SO
1975	Auburn	2-2	3.60	9	9	2	0	0	50	49	30	20	27	31
1976	Spartanburg	4-16	5.91	24	24	7	0	0	137	166	110	90	65	95
1977	Peninsula	10-11	3.66	27	27	10	0	0	199	188	103	81	78	114
1978	Reading	12-8	4.25	27	26	9	1	0	159	177	100	75	72	78
1979	Okla. City	6-4	3.91	12	12	5	0	0	76	69	38	33	28	48
	Phillies	3-4	3.80	14	14	0	0	0	90	80	40	38	38	42
1980	Reading	0-1	4.00	1	1	0	0	0	9	7	5	4	4	2
	Phillies	1-4	3.89	48	3	0	0	6	81	80	42	35	42	57
M.L. Totals		4-8	3.84	62	17	0	0	6	171	160	82	73	80	99

MAJOR LEAGUE HITTING TOTALS

	AVG	AB	H	HR	RBI
1980	.308	13	4	0	2
Lifetime	.163	43	7	0	3

LEAGUE CHAMPIONSHIP SERIES RECORD

YEAR	CLUB	W-L	ERA	G	GS	CG	IP	H	R	ER	BB	SO
1980	Phil. vs. Hou.	0-0	0.00	2	0	0	2.2	1	0	0	3	0

WORLD SERIES RECORD

YEAR	CLUB	W-L	ERA	G	GS	CG	IP	H	R	ER	BB	SO
1980	Phil. vs. K.C.	0-0	1.93	1	0	0	5	5	1	1	2	6

42—REED, Ronald Lee   (Ron)   RHP

Age: 38, turns 39 on Nov. 2 . . . Born—LaPorte, Ind., 11/2/42 . . . Home—Lilburn, Ga. . . . B-R, T-R . . . 6-6, 225 . . . Married Julie Gentry, two children, Jodie (8/17/73) and Ali (7/20/76).

YEAR	CLUB	W-L	ERA	G	GS	CG	SHO	SV	IP	H	R	ER	BB	SO
1965	W. Palm Bch.	3-2	1.47	7	5	4	2	0	43	27	7	7	7	35
1966	Kinston	5-2	1.76	8	6	4	3	0	51	43	16	10	12	39
	Austin	3-1	1.20	4	4	3	0	0	30	19	4	4	7	22
	Richmond	5-2	3.52	14	11	3	1	0	87	74	36	34	26	68
	Atlanta	1-1	2.25	2	2	2	0	0	8	7	2	2	4	6
1967	Atlanta	1-1	3.00	3	3	3	0	0	21	21	8	7	3	11
	Richmond	14-10	2.51	28	27	17	5	0	222	179	68	62	53	172
1968	Atlanta	11-10	3.34	35	28	6	1	1	202	189	87	75	49	111
1969	Atlanta	18-10	3.47	36	33	7	1	0	241	227	103	93	56	160
1970	Shreveport	0-0	2.57	2	2	0	0	0	7	5	2	2	2	6
	Atlanta	7-10	4.40	21	18	6	0	0	135	140	69	66	39	68
1971	Atlanta	13-14	3.73	32	32	8	1	0	222	221	105	92	54	129
1972	Atlanta	11-15	3.93	31	30	9	1	0	213	222	109	93	60	111
1973	Atlanta	4-11	4.42	20	19	2	1	0	116	133	71	57	31	64
1974	Atlanta	10-11	3.39	28	28	6	2	0	186	171	76	70	41	78
1975	Atl.-St. Louis	13-13	3.53	34	34	4	1	0	250	274	118	98	53	139
1976	Phillies	8-7	2.46	59	4	1	0	14	128	88	39	85	82	96
1977	Phillies	7-5	2.76	60	3	0	0	17	124	101	41	38	37	84
1978	Phillies	3-4	2.23	66	0	0	0	17	109	87	32	27	23	85
1979	Phillies	13-8	4.15	61	0	0	0	5	102	110	52	47	32	58
1980	Phillies	7-5	4.05	55	0	0	0	9	91	88	45	41	30	54
M.L. Totals		127-125	3.52	543	234	55	8	61	2152	2079	957	841	544	1254

MAJOR LEAGUE HITTING TOTALS

	AVG	AB	H	HR	RBI
1980	.300	10	3	0	0
Lifetime	.151	595	90	0	34

LEAGUE CHAMPIONSHIP SERIES RECORD

YEAR	CLUB	W-L	ERA	G	GS	CG	IP	H	R	ER	BB	SO
1969	Atl. vs. N.Y. (N.L.)	0-0	18.00	1	0	0	2	5	4	4	3	3
1976	Phil. vs. Cin.	0-0	7.20	2	0	0	4.2	6	4	4	2	2
1977	Phil. vs. L.A.	0-0	1.80	2	0	0	5	3	1	1	0	5
1978	Phil. vs. L.A.	0-0	2.25	2	0	0	4	6	1	1	2	2
1980	Phil. vs. Hous.	0-1	18.00	3	0	0	2	3	4	4	1	1
L.C.S. Totals		0-1	6.50	11	0	0	18	23	13	13	8	13

WORLD SERIES RECORD

YEAR	CLUB	W-L	ERA	G	GS	CG	IP	H	R	ER	BB	SO
1980	Phil. vs. K.C.	0-0	0.00	2	0	0	2	2	0	0	0	2

ALL STAR GAME RECORD

YEAR	CLUB	W-L	ERA	IP	H	R	ER	SO	BB
1968	N.L. Hous.	0-0	0.00	1	0	0	0	1	0

14—ROSE, Peter Edward   (Pete)   INF

Age: 39 turns 40 on April 14... Born—Cincinnati, O., 4/14/41... Home—Cincinnati... B-B, T-R... 5-11, 203... Single.

YEAR	CLUB	AVG	G	AB	R	H	2B	3B	HR	RBI	BB	SO	SB
1960	Geneva	.277	85	321	60	89	8	5	1	43	55	35	18
1961	Tampa	.331	130	484	105	*160	20	*30	2	77	60	33	30
1962	Macon	.330	139	540	*136	178	31	*17	9	71	95	61	15
1963	Cincinnati	.273	157	623	101	170	25	9	6	41	55	72	13
1964	Cincinnati	.269	136	516	64	139	13	2	4	34	36	51	4
1965	Cincinnati	.312	162	*670	117	*209	35	11	11	81	69	76	8
1966	Cincinnati	.313	156	654	97	205	38	5	16	70	37	61	4
1967	Cincinnati	.301	148	585	86	176	32	8	12	76	56	66	11
1968	Cincinnati	*.335	149	626	94	†210	42	6	10	49	56	76	3
1969	Cincinnati	*.348	156	627	†120	218	33	11	16	82	88	65	7
1970	Cincinnati	.316	159	649	120	†205	37	9	15	52	73	64	12
1971	Cincinnati	.304	160	632	86	192	27	4	13	44	68	50	13
1972	Cincinnati	*.307	*154	*645	107	*198	31	11	6	57	73	46	10
1973	Cincinnati	*.338	160	*680	115	*230	36	8	5	64	65	42	10
1974	Cincinnati	.284	*163	652	*110	185	*45	7	3	51	106	54	2
1975	Cincinnati	.317	†162	662	*112	210	*47	4	7	74	89	50	0
1976	Cincinnati	.323	†162	665	*130	*215	42	6	10	63	86	54	9
1977	Cincinnati	.311	†162	655	95	204	38	7	9	64	66	42	16
1978	Cincinnati	.302	159	655	103	198	*51	3	7	52	62	30	13
1979	Phillies	.331	163	628	90	208	40	5	4	59	95	32	20
1980	Phillies	.282	162	655	95	185	*42	1	1	64	66	33	12
	M.L. Totals	.310	2830	11479	1842	3557	654	117	155	1077	1246	964	167

*League Leader
†Tied for League Lead

LEAGUE CHAMPIONSHIP SERIES RECORD

YEAR	CLUB	AVG	G	AB	R	H	2B	3B	HR	RBI	BB	SO	SB
1970	Cinn. vs. Pitt.	.231	3	13	1	3	0	0	0	0	1	0	0
1972	Cinn. vs. Pitt.	.450	5	20	1	9	4	0	0	2	1	2	0
1973	Cinn. vs. N.Y.	.381	5	21	3	8	1	0	2	2	0	2	0
1975	Cinn. vs. Pitt.	.357	3	14	3	5	0	0	1	2	0	2	0
1976	Cinn. vs. Phil.	.429	3	14	3	6	2	1	0	2	1	3	0
1980	Phil. vs. Hou.	.400	5	20	3	8	0	0	0	2	5	3	0
	L.C.S. Totals	.382	24	102	14	39	7	1	3	11	9	9	0

WORLD SERIES RECORD

YEAR	CLUB	AVG	G	AB	R	H	2B	3B	HR	RBI	BB	SO	SB
1970	Cinn. vs. Blt.	.250	5	20	2	5	1	0	0	2	2	2	0
1972	Cinn. vs. Oak.	.214	7	28	3	6	1	0	1	2	4	4	1
1975	Cinn. vs. Boston	.370	7	27	3	10	1	0	0	2	5	1	0
1976	Cinn. vs. N.Y.	.188	4	16	1	3	1	0	0	1	2	2	0
1980	Phil. vs. K.C.	.261	6	23	2	6	1	1	0	8	15	9	1
	W.S. Totals	.263	29	114	11	30	4	1	2	11	11	9	1

ALL-STAR GAME RECORD

YEAR	CLUB	AVG	G	AB	R	H	2B	3B	HR	RBI	BB	SO	SB
1965	N.L.—Minn.—2b	.000	1	2	0	0	0	0	0	0	1	2	0
1967	N.L.—Cal.—2b	.000	1	1	0	0	0	0	0	0	0	0	0
1968	N.L.—Hou.—of	Injured, did not play.											
1969	N.L.—Wash.—of	.000	1	1	0	0	0	0	0	0	1	0	0
1970	N.L.—Cinn.—of	.333	1	3	1	1	0	0	0	0	0	2	0
1971	N.L.—Det.—of	.000	1	3	0	0	0	0	0	0	0	1	0
1972	N.L.—K.C.—of	.000	1	3	1	0	0	0	0	0	0	0	0
1973	N.L.—K.C.—of	.000	1	2	0	0	0	0	0	0	1	1	0
1974	N.L.—Pitt.—of	.000	1	2	0	0	0	0	0	0	0	0	0
1975	N.L.—Milw.—of	.500	1	4	0	2	0	0	0	0	0	1	0
1976	N.L.—Phil.—3b	.667	1	3	1	2	0	0	0	1	0	0	0
1977	N.L.—N.Y	.000	1	2	0	0	0	0	0	0	0	0	0
1978	(A.L.)—ph-3b	.250	1	4	0	1	0	1	0	0	0	0	0
1979	N.L., Seat.—ph-1b	.000	1	2	0	0	0	0	0	0	0	0	0
1980	N.L., L.A.—ph	.000	1	1	0	0	0	0	0	0	0	0	0
	A.S.G. Totals	.214	13	28	3	6	1	0	0	1	3	5	0

ROSE VS. THE NATIONAL LEAGUE

	1980			LIFETIME		
	AB	H	AVE	AB	H	AVE
Milwaukee-Atlanta	46	15	.326	1239	411	.332
Chicago	66	21	.318	1050	326	.310
Cincinnati	49	12	.245	95	24	.253
Houston	42	12	.286	1205	386	.320
Los Angeles	49	15	.306	1206	349	.289
Montreal	79	25	.316	634	194	.306
New York	72	20	.278	1035	321	.310
Philadelphia	—			932	317	.340
Pittsburgh	80	25	.313	1012	292	.289
St. Louis	70	12	.171	1058	319	.302
San Diego	53	16	.302	813	253	.311
San Francisco	49	12	.245	1200	365	.304

ROSE NEARS MUSIAL RECORD

Pete Rose enters the 1981 baseball season needing 74 hits to break Stan Musial's All-Time National League record.

"Stan The Man" collected his 3,630 hits in a brilliant 22-year career, all with the St. Louis Cardinals. Musial's year-by-year breakdown:

YEAR	G	AB	H
1941	12	47	20
1942	140	467	147
1943	157	617	220*
1944	146	568	197
1946	156	624	228*
1947	149	587	183
1948	155	611	230*
1949	157	612	207*
1950	146	555	192
1951	152	578	205
1952	154	578	194*
1953	157	593	200
1954	153	591	195
1955	154	562	179
1956	156	594	184
1957	134	502	176
1958	135	472	159
1959	115	341	87
1960	116	331	91
1961	123	372	107
1962	135	433	143
1963	124	337	86
	3026	10972	3630

*Led League

ROSE & ALL-TIME N.L. RANKINGS

GAMES
1. Aaron.........3076
2. Musial........3026
3. Mays.........2992
4. ROSE.........2830

AT BATS
1. Aaron........11,628
2. ROSE.........11,479

RUNS
1. Aaron.........2107
2. Mays.........2062
3. Musial........1949
4. Ott...........1859
5. ROSE.........1842

HITS
1. Musial........3630
2. Aaron.........3600
3. ROSE.........3557

SINGLES
1. ROSE.........2631

DOUBLES
1. Musial.........725
2. ROSE..........654

TOTAL BASES
1. Aaron.........6581
2. Musial........6134
3. Mays.........6066
4. Ott...........5041
5. ROSE..........4910

ROSE & ALL-TIME RANKINGS

GAMES
1. Aaron.........3298
2. Cobb..........3033
3. Musial........3026
4. Mays.........2992
5. Yastrzemski...2967
6. B. Robinson...2896
7. Kaline........2834
8. ROSE.........2830

AT BATS
1. Aaron........12,364
2. ROSE.........11,479

RUNS
1. Cobb..........2244
2. Aaron.........2174
3. Ruth..........2174
4. Mays.........2062
5. Musial........1949
6. Gehrig........1888
7. Speaker.......1881
8. Ott...........1859
9. ROSE.........1842

HITS
1. Cobb..........4191
2. Aaron.........3771
3. Musial........3630
4. ROSE.........3557

SINGLES
1. Cobb..........3052
2. Collins.......2641
3. ROSE.........2631

DOUBLES
1. Speaker........793
2. Musial.........725
3. Cobb..........724
4. ROSE..........654

TOTAL BASES
1. Aaron.........6856
2. Musial........6134
3. Mays.........6066
4. Cobb..........5863
5. Ruth..........5793
6. F. Robinson...5373
7. Speaker.......5101
8. Yastrzemski...5075
9. Gehrig........5059
10. Ott...........5041
11. Foxx..........4956
12. ROSE.........4910

44—RUTHVEN, Richard David (Dick) RHP

Age: 29, turns 30 on Mar. 27 ... Born—Sacramento, Ca., 3/27/51 ... Home—Glen Mills, Pa. ... B-R, T-R ... 6-3, 190 ... Married Susan Kay Harper, one son, Erik Scot 12/22/79.

YEAR	CLUB	W-L	ERA	G	GS	CG	SHO	SV	IP	H	R	ER	BB	SO
1973	Phillies	6-9	4.22	25	23	3	1	1	128	125	69	60	75	98
1974	Phillies	9-13	4.01	35	35	6	0	0	213	182	106	95	116	153
1975	Toledo	10-12	3.18	23	23	10	0	0	153	148	72	54	69	114
	Phillies	2-2	4.17	11	7	0	0	0	41	37	22	19	22	26
1976	Atlanta	14-17	4.20	36	36	8	4	0	240	255	112	112	90	142
1977	Atlanta	7-13	4.23	25	23	6	2	0	151	158	86	71	62	84
1978	Atl.-Phillies	15-11	3.38	33	33	11	3	0	232	214	95	87	56	120
1979	Phillies	7-5	4.28	20	20	3	1	0	122	121	59	58	37	58
1980	Phillies	17-10	3.55	33	33	6	1	0	223	241	99	88	74	86
M.L. Totals		77-80	3.93	218	210	53	14	1	1350	1333	648	590	532	767

MAJOR LEAGUE HITTING TOTALS

	AVG	AB	H	HR	RBI
1980	.235	68	16	0	8
Lifetime	.197	426	84	1	28

Last Home Run—1977 vs. Houston in Atlanta (Lemongello)

LEAGUE CHAMPIONSHIP SERIES RECORD

YEAR	CLUB	W-L	ERA	G	GS	CG	IP	H	R	ER	BB	SO
1979	Phil. vs. L.A.	0-1	5.40	1	1	0	5	6	3	3	0	4
1980	Phil. vs. Hou.	1-0	2.00	2	1	0	9	3	2	2	5	3
L.C.S. Totals		1-1	3.21	3	2	0	14	9	5	5	5	7

WORLD SERIES RECORD

YEAR	CLUB	W-L	ERA	G	GS	CG	IP	H	R	ER	BB	SO
1980	Phil. vs. K.C.	0-0	3.00	1	1	0	9	9	3	3	0	7

ALL STAR GAME RECORD

YEAR	CLUB	W-L	ERA	G	GS	CG	IP	H	R	ER	SO	BB
1976	N.L., Phil.	Did Not Pitch										

20—SCHMIDT, Michael Jack (Mike) 3B

Age: 31, turns 32 on Sept. 27 ... Born—Dayton, O., 9/27/49 ... Home—Philadelphia, Pa. ... B-R, T-R ... 6-2, 203 ... Married Donna Wightman ... one daughter, Jessica Rae (12/19/78); one son Jonathon Michael (7/14/80).

YEAR	CLUB	AVG	G	AB	R	H	2B	3B	HR	RBI	BB	SO	SB
1971	Reading	.211	74	237	27	50	7	1	8	31	27	66	3
1972	Eugene	.291	131	436	80	127	23	0	26	91	87	145	6
	Phillies	.206	13	34	2	7	0	0	1	3	5	15	0
1973	Phillies	.196	132	367	43	72	11	0	18	52	62	136	8
1974	Phillies	.282	162	568	106	160	28	7	*36	116	106	*138	23
1975	Phillies	.249	158	562	93	140	34	3	*38	95	101	*180	29
1976	Phillies	.262	160	584	112	153	31	4	*38	107	100	*149	14
1977	Phillies	.274	154	544	114	149	27	11	38	101	104	122	15
1978	Phillies	.251	145	513	93	129	27	2	21	78	91	103	16
1979	Phillies	.253	160	541	109	137	25	4	45	114	*120	115	9
1980	Phillies	.286	150	548	104	157	25	8	*48	*121	89	119	12
M.L. Totals		.259	1234	4261	778	1104	208	39	283	787	778	1077	129

LEAGUE CHAMPIONSHIP SERIES RECORD

YEAR	CLUB	AVG	G	AB	R	H	2B	3B	HR	RBI	BB	SO	SB
1976	Phil. vs. Cinn.	.308	3	13	1	4	2	0	0	2	0	1	0
1977	Phil. vs. L.A.	.063	4	16	1	1	0	0	0	2	2	3	0
1978	Phil. vs. L.A.	.200	4	15	1	3	1	0	0	1	1	2	0
1980	Phil. vs. Hou.	.208	5	24	1	5	1	0	0	1	1	6	1
L.C.S. Totals		.191	16	68	5	13	5	0	0	5	5	12	1

WORLD SERIES RECORD

YEAR	CLUB	AVG	G	AB	R	H	2B	3B	HR	RBI	BB	SO	SB
1980	Phil. vs. K.C.	.381	6	21	6	8	1	0	2	7	4	3	0

ALL STAR GAME RECORD

YEAR	CLUB	AVG	G	AB	R	H	2B	3B	HR	RBI	BB	SO	SB
1974	N.L., Pitt.	.000	0	0	0	0	0	0	0	0	0	0	0
1976	N.L., Phil.	.000	1	1	0	0	0	0	0	0	2	0	0
1977	N.L., N.Y. (A.L.)	.000	1	0	0	0	0	0	0	0	0	0	0
1979	N.L., Seattle	.667	1	3	2	2	1	0	1	0	1	0	0
1980	N.L., L.A.	Did Not Play											
A.S.G Totals		.500	4	4	2	2	1	1	1	1	2	0	0

27—SMITH, Lonnie — OF

Age: 25, turns 26 on Dec. 22nd ... Born—Chicago, Ill., 12/22/55 ... Home—Inman, S.C. ... B-R, T-R ... 5-9, 170 ... Married Pearl Jetersmith; one son, Eric (4/16/80).

YEAR	CLUB	AVG	G	AB	R	H	2B	3B	HR	RBI	BB	SO	SB
1974	Auburn	.266	61	210	48	60	10	4	5	27	52	29	12
1975	Spartanburg	.323	131	465	*114	*150	23	4	7	40	96	63	*56
1976	Oklahoma City	.308	134	483	*93	149	24	9	8	54	60	73	26
1977	Oklahoma City	.277	125	477	91	132	14	10	4	41	49	63	45
1978	Oklahoma City	.315	125	480	103	151	20	5	7	43	79	79	*66
	Phillies	.000	17	4	6	0	0	0	0	0	0	3	4
1979	Oklahoma City	.330	110	451	*106	214	26	9	0	44	56	52	34
	Phillies	.167	17	30	4	5	2	4	0	3	1	7	2
1980	Phillies	.339	100	298	69	101	14	4	3	20	26	48	33
M.L. Totals		.319	134	332	79	106	16	4	3	23	31	58	39

*League Leader

LEAGUE CHAMPIONSHIP SERIES RECORD

YEAR	CLUB	AVG	G	AB	R	H	2B	3B	HR	RBI	BB	SO	SB
1980	Phil. vs. Hou.	.600	3	5	2	3	0	0	0	0	0	0	1

WORLD SERIES RECORD

YEAR	CLUB	AVG	G	AB	R	H	2B	3B	HR	RBI	BB	SO	SB
1980	Phil. vs. K.C.	.263	6	19	2	5	1	0	0	1	1	1	0

9—TRILLO, Jesus Manuel (Manny) — INF

Age: 30, turns 31 on Dec. 25 ... Born—Caritito, Ven., 12/25/50 ... Home—Caracas, Ven. ... B-R, T-R ... 6-1, 164 ... Married Maria Elena Rincon Urdaneta; one daughter, Aloha.

YEAR	CLUB	AVG	G	AB	R	H	2B	3B	HR	RBI	BB	SO	SB
1968	Huron	.261	35	92	8	24	2	1	0	4	7	7	0
1969	Spartanburg	.280	83	275	41	77	18	0	1	26	17	32	5
1970	Birmingham	.261	84	241	26	63	10	1	2	19	14	40	5
1971	Birmingham	.280	107	371	37	104	18	1	5	44	28	39	1
1972	Des Moines	.301	133	509	67	153	27	6	9	53	35	75	5
1973	Tucson	.312	135	519	76	162	25	7	8	78	35	70	7
1973	Oakland	.250	17	12	0	3	2	0	0	3	0	4	0

(continued on next page)

SCHMIDT'S HOME RUNS

By Parks

	ATL	CHI	CINN	HOU	LA	MTL	NY	PHIL	PITT	SD	SF	STL	TOT
1972	—	—	—	—	—	—	—	—	—	—	—	—	1
1973	3	2	5	—	—	1*	2	9	3	2	—	1	18
1974	3	3	1	1	2	3*	1	19	3	2	1	3	36
1975	2	7	1	1	1	2*	2	22	2	3	1	—	38
1976	3	1	4	1	1	6*	1	17	2	3	1	2	38
1977	4	4	1	—	2	7	2	13	1	2	—	4	38
1978	1	5	—	—	6	4	1	16	2	2	2	—	21
1979	4	8	2	—	6	1*	4	25	2	2	2	3	45
1980	—	—	—	—	—	3	—	16	—	—	—	2	48
TOTALS	14	30	15	3	14	15	13	139	11	9	4	16	

*Jarry Parc

CAREER TOTAL 283

By Months

	1972	1973	1974	1975	1976	1977	1978	1979	1980	TOT
April	—	1	3	2	11	3	4	4	4	32
May	—	1	5	4	4	4	4	11	12	45
June	1	5	10	8	6	14	3	8	5	60
July	1	1	3	5	7	7	2	13	6	46
August	—	4	9	12	4	4	5	5	8	51
Sept-Oct	1	3	4	7	6	6	5	4	13	49

CAREER TOTAL 283

MAJOR LEAGUE HOME RUN LEADERS

(Last 7 Years)

	'74	'75	'76	'77	'78	'79	'80	TOT.
1. SCHMIDT	36	38	38	38	21	45	48	264
2. JACKSON	29	36	27	32	27	29	41	221
3. KINGMAN	18	36	37	26	28	48	18	211
4. FOSTER	7	23	29	52	40	30	25	206
5. RICE	1	22	25	39	46	39	24	196
6. BENCH	33	28	16	31	23	22	24	177
7. CEY	28	23	30	23	25	18	28	175
8. NETTLES	22	21	32	37	27	20	16	175
9. LUZINSKI	7	34	21	39	35	18	19	173
10. BONDS	21	32	10	37	31	25	5	161

Trillo, *Continued*

YEAR	CLUB	AVG	G	AB	R	H	2B	3B	HR	RBI	BB	SO	SB
1974	Tucson	.253	85	320	31	81	19	1	2	39	27	39	2
1974	Oakland	.152	21	33	3	5	0	0	0	2	2	8	0
1975	Chicago (N.L.)	.248	154	545	55	135	12	2	7	70	45	78	1
1976	Chicago (N.L.)	.239	158	582	42	139	24	3	4	59	53	70	17
1977	Chicago (N.L.)	.280	152	504	51	141	18	5	7	57	50	58	3
1978	Chicago (N.L.)	.261	152	552	53	144	17	5	4	55	50	67	0
1979	Phillies	.260	118	431	40	112	22	1	6	42	20	59	4
1980	Phillies	.292	141	531	68	155	25	9	7	43	32	46	8
	M.L. Totals	.261	913	3190	312	834	120	25	35	331	246	390	33

LEAGUE CHAMPIONSHIP SERIES RECORD

YEAR	CLUB	AVG	G	AB	R	H	2B	3B	HR	RBI	BB	SO	SB
1974	Oak. vs. Blt.	.000	1	0	1	0	0	0	0	0	0	0	0
1980	Phil. vs. Hou.	.381	5	21	1	8	2	1	0	4	0	2	0
	L.C.S. Totals	.381	6	21	2	8	2	1	0	4	0	2	0

WORLD SERIES RECORD

YEAR	CLUB	AVG	G	AB	R	H	2B	3B	HR	RBI	BB	SO	SB
1980	Phil. vs. K.C.	.217	6	23	4	5	2	0	0	2	0	0	0

ALL STAR GAME RECORD

YEAR	CLUB	AVG	G	AB	R	H	2B	3B	HR	RBI	BB	SO	SB
1977	N.L. N.Y. (A.L.)	.000	1	1	0	0	0	0	0	0	0	0	0

25—UNSER, Delbert Bernard   (Del) OF-1B

Age: 36, turns 37 on Dec. 9 . . . Born—Decatur, Ill. 12/9/44 . . . Home—Moraga, Calif. . . . B-L, T-L . . . 5-11, 180 . . . Married Dale Donnelly; two daughters, Corrine (11/3/66), and Angela (12/28/68).

YEAR	CLUB	AVG	G	AB	R	H	2B	3B	HR	RBI	BB	SO	SB
1966	York	.220	39	123	11	27	4	1	3	11	17	32	0
1967	York	.231	138	507	56	117	14	7	6	32	60	93	19
1968	Washington	.230	156	635	66	146	13	8	7	30	46	66	11
1969	Washington	.286	153	581	69	166	19	1	7	57	58	54	8
1970	Washington	.258	119	322	37	83	5	6	5	30	30	29	1
1971	Washington	.255	153	581	63	148	19	9	9	41	69	68	11
1972	Cleveland	.238	132	383	29	91	12	0	1	17	28	46	5
1973	Phillies	.264	136	440	54	127	20	4	11	52	47	55	8
1974	Phillies	.264	142	454	72	120	18	5	11	50	50	62	6
1975	New York (N.L.)	.294	147	531	65	156	18	2	10	53	37	76	4
1976	N.Y. (N.L.) Mtl.	.228	146	496	57	113	19	4	12	61	29	84	7
1977	Montreal	.273	113	289	33	79	14	1	12	40	33	41	2
1978	Montreal	.196	130	179	16	35	5	0	2	15	24	29	2
1979	Phillies	.298	152	141	26	42	8	6	6	29	14	29	2
1980	Phillies	.264	152	110	15	29	6	4	0	10	10	21	0
	N.L. Totals	.266	1005	2640	348	701	108	20	64	300	244	401	31
	A.L. Totals	.253	713	2502	264	634	68	22	23	175	231	263	36
	M.L. Totals	.260	1718	5142	612	1335	176	42	87	475	475	664	67

LEAGUE CHAMPIONSHIP SERIES RECORD

YEAR	CLUB	AVG	G	AB	R	H	2B	3B	HR	RBI	BB	SO	SB
1980	Phil. vs. Hou.	.400	0	5	0	0	0	0	1	0	0	0	0

WORLD SERIES RECORD

YEAR	CLUB	AVG	G	AB	R	H	2B	3B	HR	RBI	BB	SO	SB
1980	Phil. vs. K.C.	.500	0	6	0	3	0	0	0	2	0	0	0

29—VUKOVICH, George Stephen   (George) OF

Age: 24, turns 25 on June 24th . . . Born—Chicago, Ill., 6/24/56 . . . Home—Libertyville, Ill. . . . B-L, T-R . . . 6-0, 198 . . . Married: Carol Murray; one son, Michael (3/20/80).

YEAR	CLUB	AVG	G	AB	R	H	2B	3B	HR	RBI	BB	SO	SB
1977	Auburn	.500	1	2	0	1	0	0	0	0	0	1	0
1978	Peninsula	.311	135	453	94	141	26	10	10	69	86	57	23
1979	Reading	.293	138	501	80	147	14	10	13	88	65	52	16
1980	Phillies	.224	78	58	6	13	1	1	0	8	6	9	0

†Tied For League Lead

LEAGUE CHAMPIONSHIP SERIES RECORD

YEAR	CLUB	AVG	G	AB	R	H	2B	3B	HR	RBI	BB	SO	SB
1980	Phil. vs. Hou.	.000	3	3	0	0	0	0	0	0	0	0	0

18—VUKOVICH, John Christopher (John) INF

Age: 33, turns 34 on July 31st . . . Born—Sacramento, Calif., 7/31/47 . . . Home—Sicklerville, N.J. . . . B-R, T-R . . . 6-1, 190 . . . Married Bonnie Loughran; two children, Nicole (10/4/74) and Vincent (5/6/80) On Oklahoma City roster.

YEAR	CLUB	AVG	G	AB	R	H	2B	3B	HR	RBI	BB	SO	SB
1966	Huron	.257	67	241	30	62	5	2	2	35	21	42	6
1967	Spartanburg	.253	74	261	35	66	12	1	3	40	29	51	4
1968	Spartanburg	.313	37	134	23	42	11	0	4	20	14	16	4
	Tidewater	.280	66	226	23	65	12	0	4	34	14	38	1
1969	Reading	.253	110	372	39	94	9	4	6	45	37	56	9
1970	Eugene	.275	138	520	58	143	21	3	22	96	38	81	7
	Phillies	.125	3	8	1	1	0	0	0	0	1	0	0
1971	Eugene	.308	58	221	31	68	16	0	5	35	15	24	2
	Phillies	.166	74	217	11	36	5	2	0	14	12	34	2
1972	Eugene	.262	139	539	84	141	32	2	13	68	47	98	7
1973	Milwaukee	.125	55	128	10	16	3	0	2	9	9	40	0
1974	Milwaukee	.188	38	80	5	15	1	0	3	11	9	16	2
1975	Cincinnati	.211	31	38	4	8	3	0	0	2	4	5	0
	Indianapolis	.138	49	152	6	21	7	0	0	12	9	20	1
	Toledo	.277	26	97	6	22	5	0	0	10	13	12	1
1976	Reading	.240	47	171	15	41	9	0	5	16	11	27	3
	Phillies	.125	4	8	2	1	1	0	0	2	2	2	0
1977	Reading	.284	80	303	30	86	16	1	8	52	19	29	1
	Phillies	.000	2	2	0	0	0	0	0	0	0	1	0
1978	Oklahoma City	.210	126	429	49	90	16	1	7	47	43	62	2
1979	Oklahoma City	.291	101	382	38	111	20	1	12	66	22	56	2
1980	Phillies	.200	10	15	0	3	1	0	0	1	0	3	0
	Phillies	.161	49	62	4	10	1	1	0	5	2	7	0
M.L. Totals		.161	226	558	37	90	14	6	1	44	29	108	4

MAJOR LEAGUE HITTING TOTALS

	AVG	AB	H	HR	RBI
1980	.140	50	7	0	2

LEAGUE CHAMPIONSHIP SERIES RECORD

YEAR	CLUB	W-L	ERA	G	GS	CG	IP	H	R	ER	BB	SO
1980	Phil. vs. Hou.		Did Not Play									

WORLD SERIES RECORD

YEAR	CLUB	W-L	ERA	G	GS	CG	IP	H	R	ER	BB	SO
1980	Phil. vs. K.C.	1-0	7.71	1	1	0	7	8	6	6	3	3

41—WALK, Robert Vernon (Bob) RHP

Age: 24, turns 25 on Nov. 26th . . . Born—Van Nuys, Calif., 11/26/56 . . . Home—Newhall, Calif. . . . B-R, T-R . . . 6-3, 195 . . . Married Lorrie Shields.

YEAR	CLUB	W-L	ERA	G	GS	CG	SHO	SV	IP	H	R	ER	BB	SO
1977	Peninsula	0-2	4.25	8	8	0	0	0	36	44	31	17	20	23
	Spartanburg	6-9	3.64	15	15	7	1	0	99	90	55	40	46	66
1978	Peninsula	13-8	2.12	26	26	9	0	0	187	147	58	44	64	150
1979	Reading	12-7	*2.24	24	24	11	1	0	185	156	62	46	*77	*135
1980	Oklahoma City	5-1	2.94	8	8	0	0	0	49	39	21	16	17	36
	Phillies	11-7	4.56	27	27	2	0	0	152	163	82	77	71	94

*League Leader

The Medical Staff

COOPER, Jeff Trainer

Born—Wilmington, Del., 12/30/51 . . . Home—Wilmington, Del. . . . Married Alice Denise Bennett.

HOEFLING, Gus Strength and Flexibility Teacher

Born—Merrill, Iowa, 7/11/34 . . . Home—Wynnewood, PA . . . Single, two children, John and Muri.

MARONE, Dr. Phillip J. Team Physician

Born—Philadelphia, Pa., 8/15/30 . . . Home—Philadelphia, Pa. . . . Married Carmela Manfredo, three children, Phillip Jr., Denise and Peter.

SEGER, Don Trainer

Born—Quincy, Ill., 11/4/35 . . . Home—Clementon, N.J. . . . Married Polly Hedrick; two children, Theresa Randolph and Thomas Jonathan.

1980 Season Day-by-Day

CAPS = Home Games

GAME	DATE	DAY	D/N	CLUB	W/L	SCORE	WINNER (Record)	LOSER (Record)	CROWD	NO. OF HOME DATE	HOME TOTAL	TIME	POS.	G.B.	W-L
1	4/11	Fri.	N	MONTREAL	W	6-3	Carlton 1-0	Rogers 0-1	48,460	1	48,460	2:07	1	½	1-0
2	4/12	Sat.	D	MONTREAL	W	6-2	Ruthven 1-0	Lee 0-1	22,065	2	70,525	2:31	1	½	2-0
3	4/13	Sun.	D	MONTREAL	L	5-4 (10)	Sosa 1-0	LaGrow 0-1	28,132	3	98,657	3:02	2	½	2-1
4	4/15	Tues.	N	St. Louis	L	7-2	Vuckovich 2-0	Lerch 0-1	8,166			1:57	2	—	2-2
5	4/16	Wed.	D	St. Louis	W	8-3	Carlton 2-0	BForsch 0-1	10,911			2:03	2	1	3-2
6	4/18	Fri.	D	Montreal	L	7-5	Sanderson 1-0	Ruthven 1-1	41,222			2:45	2	2	3-3
7	4/19	Sat.	D	Montreal	W	13-4	Christenson 1-0	Rogers 1-2	23,088			3:01	—	—	4-3
8	4/20	Sun.	D	Montreal	L	7-6	Sosa 2-0	McGraw 0-1	25,722			2:34	3	1½	4-4
9	4/21	Mon.	N	NEW YORK	L	3-0	Burris 2-1	Carlton 2-1	23,856	4	122,513	2:31	3	2½	4-5
10	4/22	Tues.	N	NEW YORK	W	14-8	Saucier 1-0	Kobel 0-2	21,341	5	143,854	2:42	3	2½	5-5
11	4/23	Wed.	N	NEW YORK	L	3-2	Bomback 1-0	LaGrow 0-2	23,023	6	166,877	2:53	3	2½	5-6
12	4/25	Fri.	N	ST. LOUIS	L	3-1	Vuckovich 3-1	Lerch 0-2	30,516	7	197,393	2:19	T4	2½	5-7
13	4/26	Sat.	N	ST. LOUIS	W	7-0	Carlton 3-1	Fulgham 1-2	25,168	8	222,561	1:46	T3	2½	6-7
14	4/27	Sun.	D	ST. LOUIS	L	10-1	BForsch 1-1	Ruthven 1-2	28,200	9	250,761	2:38	T3	3	6-8
15	4/30	Wed.	N	New York	W	2-0	Bomback 2-0	Lerch 0-3	4,559			1:56	T3	4½	6-9
16	5/1	Thurs.	N	New York	W	2-1	Carlton 4-1	Falcone 1-2	5,928			2:20	4	4½	7-9
17	5/2	Fri.	N	LOS ANGELES	W	9-5	Reed 1-0	Hough 0-1	30,294	10	281,055	2:31	4	3½	8-9
18	5/3	Sat.	N	LOS ANGELES	W	7-3	Christenson 2-0	Hooton 2-2	35,011	11	316,066	2:34	3	2½	9-9
19	5/4	Sun.	D	LOS ANGELES	L	12-10	Beckwith 2-0	Noles 0-1	34,027	12	350,093	3:22	3	3½	9-10
20	5/5	Mon.	N	ATLANTA	W	5-1	Carlton 5-1	Matula 2-2	26,165	13	376,258	2:09	3	3	10-10
21	5/6	Tues.	N	ATLANTA	W	10-5	Ruthven 2-2	Alexander 0-2	25,302	14	401,560	2:43	3	3	11-10
22	5/9	Fri.	N	Cincinnati	L	5-2	Leibrandt 3-2	Lerch 0-4	32,583			2:29	4	4	11-11
23	5/10	Sat.	D	Cincinnati	L	5-3	Seaver 1-1	Carlton 5-2	28,919			1:57	4	5½	11-12
24	5/11	Sun.	D	Cincinnati	W	7-3	Ruthven 3-2	LaCoss 3-3	25,920			2:31	3	4½	12-12
25	5/13	Tues.	N	Atlanta	L	7-3	Alexander 1-2	Lerch 0-5	10,146			2:10	3	4½	12-13
26	5/14	Wed.	N	Atlanta	W	9-1	Carlton 6-2	McWilliams 2-3	4,625			2:43	3	4½	13-13
27	5/16	Fri.	N	Houston	W	3-0	Ruthven 4-2	Richard 4-2	33,610			2:05	2	4	14-13
28	5/17	Sat.	N	Houston	W	4-2	Christenson 3-0	JNiekro 4-3	43,525			2:25	2	3	15-13
29	5/18	Sun.	D	Houston	L	3-0	Ryan 2-3	Lerch 0-6	33,950			2:07	2	3	15-14
30	5/19	Mon.	N	CINCINNATI	W	6-4	Carlton 7-2	Pastore 4-2	25,109	15	426,669	2:08	2	2½	16-14
31	5/20	Tues.	N	CINCINNATI	L	7-6	Moskau 2-0	Ruthven 4-3	25,202	16	451,871	2:33	2	3	16-15
32	5/21	Wed.	N	CINCINNATI	W	9-8	Reed 2-0	Hume 3-4	26,099	17	477,969	2:47	2	3½	17-15
33	5/23	Fri.	N	HOUSTON	W	3-0	Carlton 8-2	Ryan 2-4	27,822	18	505,791	2:11	2	3	18-15
34	5/24	Sat.	D	HOUSTON	W	5-4	Saucier 2-0	Andujar 0-2	28,539	19	534,330	2:28	2	2	19-15
35	5/25	Sun.	D	HOUSTON	W	6-2	Ruthven 5-3	KForsch 5-3	37,349	20	571,679	2:10	2	1	20-15

(continued on next page)

CAPS = Home Games

GAME	DATE	DAY	D/N	CLUB	W/L	SCORE	WINNER (Record)	LOSER (Record)	CROWD	NO. OF HOME DATE	HOME TOTAL	TIME	POS.	G.B.	W-L
36	5/26	Mon.	N	PITTSBURGH	W	7-6	Reed 3-0	Tekulve 5-3	45,394	21	617-073	3:04	1	.004	21-15
37	5/27	Tues.	N	PITTSBURGH	L	3-2 (13)	Romo 3-0	Noles 0-2	35,489	22	652,562	3:26	2	1	21-16
38	5/28	Wed.	N	PITTSBURGH	W	6-3	Lerch 1-6	Robinson 1-1	30,209	23	682,771	2:09	1	.004	22-16
39	5/29	Thurs.	D	PITTSBURGH	L	5-4	Solomon 2-0	Ruthven 5-4	30,630	24	713,401	2:37	2	1	22-17
40	5/30	Fri.	D	Chicago	L	10-7	Reuschel 4-4	Larson 0-1	8,632			2:18	T2	1	22-18
41	5/31	Sat.	D	Chicago	W	7-0	Carlton 9-2	Hernandez 1-4	26,937			2:24	2	1	23-18
42	6/1	Sun.	D	Chicago	L	5-4	Tidrow 2-0	Reed 3-1	20,051			2:40	2	2	23-19
43	6/2	Mon.	N	Pittsburgh	L	9-3	Robinson 2-1	Lerch 1-7	19,990			2:45	3	3	23-20
44	6/3	Tues.	N	Pittsburgh	W	4-3	Jackson 5-1	McGraw 0-2	22,141			2:39	3	4	23-21
45	6/4	Wed.	N	Pittsburgh	W	4-3	Carlton 10-2	Candelaria 2-5	31,075			1:53	3	3	24-21
46	6/6	Fri.	N	CHICAGO	W	6-5	Walk 1-0	Krukow 3-6	30,187	25	743,588	2:31	3	2	25-21
47	6/7	Sat.	N	CHICAGO	W	5-2	Lerch 2-7	Reuschel 5-5	31,153	26	774,741	2:22	2	1	26-21
48	6/8	Sun.	D	CHICAGO	L	2-0	McGlothen 3-2	Ruthven 5-5	40,206	27	814,947	2:19	3	2½	26-22
49	6/9	Mon.	N	SAN FRANCISCO	L	3-1	Ripley 1-0	Noles 0-3	28,702	28	843,649	2:26	3	3	26-23
50	6/10	Tues.	N	SAN FRANCISCO	W	4-3	Saucier 3-0	Knepper 4-8	32,635	29	876,284	2:25	3	3	27-23
51	6/11	Wed.	N	SAN FRANCISCO	W	7-4	Whitson 3-7	Lerch 2-8	37,844	30	914,128	2:34	3	4	27-24
52	6/13	Fri.	N	SAN DIEGO	W	9-6	Ruthven 6-5	Jones 4-6	31,015	31	945,143	2:33	3	4½	28-24
53	6/14	Sat.	N	SAN DIEGO	W	3-1	Carlton 11-2	Mura 0-2	35,231	32	980,374	2:20	3	3½	29-24
54	6/15	Sun.	D	SAN DIEGO	W	8-5	Walk 2-0	Wise 3-4	36,379	33	1,016,753	2:42	3	2½	30-24
55	6/16	Mon.	N	Los Angeles	W	3-2 (12)	Reed 4-1	Sutcliffe 1-4	41,340			2:53	2	1½	31-24
56	6/17	Tues.	N	Los Angeles	W	6-5	Reed 5-1	Castillo 1-3	40,786			2:48	3	1½	32-24
57	6/18	Wed.	N	San Diego	W	5-1	Carlton 12-2	Shirley 5-3	15,621			2:33	2	½	33-24
58	6/19	Thurs.	D	San Diego	L	4-3	Kinney 2-1	Saucier 3-1	16,712			2:53	2	½	33-25
59	6/20	Fri.	N	San Francisco	L	5-1	Ripley 2-1	Larson 0-2	9,490			2:15	2	½	33-26
60	6/21	Sat.	D	San Francisco	L	9-3	Whitson 5-7	Lerch 2-9	11,809			2:25	2	1½	33-27
61	6/22	Sun.	D	San Francisco	W	4-3	Carlton 13-2	Blue 9-4	27,315			2:14	2	1½	34-27
62	6/24	Tues.	N	MONTREAL	L	7-6 (10)	Sosa 5-2	McGraw 0-3	32,157	34	1,048,910	3:32	2	2½	34-28
63	6/25	Wed.	N	MONTREAL	L	2-1 (10)	Reed 6-1	Bahnsen 5-2	31,416	35	1,080,326	2:42	2	1½	35-28
64	6/26	Thurs.	N	MONTREAL	L	1-0	Sanderson 7-4	Lerch 2-10	31,696	36	1,112,022	2:08	2	2½	35-29
65	6/27	Fri.	N	NEW YORK	L	3-2	Pacella 1-0	Carlton 13-3	37,123	37	1,149,145	2:15	2	2½	35-30
66	6/28	Sat.	TWN	NEW YORK	L	2-1 (11)	Allen 4-5	Reed 6-2				2:55			35-31
67				NEW YORK	L	5-4	Hausman 3-2	Saucier 3-2	47,169	38	1,196,314	2:51	3	3	35-32
68	6/29	Sun.	N	NEW YORK	W	5-2	Walk 3-0	Zachry 2-5	41,113	39	1,237,427	2:23	2	3	36-32
69	6/30	Mon.	N	Montreal	W	7-5	Noles 1-3	Gullickson 0-2	36,347			2:39	2	2	37-32
70	7/1	Tues.	N	Montreal	W	5-4 (11)	Lerch 3-10	Fryman 1-3	33,761			2:51	2	1	38-32
71	7/2	Wed.	N	Montreal	L	6-1	Rogers 10-6	Carlton 13-4	23,233			2:25	2	2	38-33
72	7/3	Thurs.	TWN	St. Louis	W	2-1	Ruthven 7-5	BForsch 5-6				1:50			39-33
73				St. Louis	W	8-1	Walk 4-0	Otten 0-3	38,038			2:14		½	40-33
74	7/4	Fri.	D	St. Louis	L	1-0 (10)	Sykes 3-6	Saucier 3-3	15,481			1:56	2	1	40-34
75	7/5	Sat.	N	St. Louis	L	6-1	Kaat 3-5	Lerch 3-11	27,932			1:39	2	1	40-35
76	7/6	Sun.	D	St. Louis	W	8-3	Carlton 14-4	Vuckovich 2-6	17,769			2:06	2	1	41-35

CAPS = Home Games

GAME	DATE	DAY	D/N	CLUB	W/L	SCORE	WINNER (Record)	LOSER (Record)	CROWD	NO. OF HOME DATE	HOME TOTAL	TIME	POS.	G.B.	W-L
77	7/10	Thurs.	N	CHICAGO	W	5-2	Ruthven 8-5	Krukow 6-10	33,130	40	1,270,557	2:38	2	1	42-35
78	7/11	Fri.	N	CHICAGO	W	7-2	Walk 5-0	McGlothen 6-6	50,209	41	1,320,766	2:41	T1	—	43-35
79	7/12	Sat.	N	PITTSBURGH	W	5-4	Saucier 4-3	Tekulve 5-5	53,254	42	1,374,020	2:19	1	½	44-35
80	7/13	Sun.	D	PITTSBURGH	L	7-3	DRobinson 3-4	Espinosa 0-1	48,152	43	1,422,172	2:20	2	½	44-36
81	7/14	Mon.	N	PITTSBURGH	L	13-11	Jackson 7-2	Reed 6-3	44,245	44	1,466,417	3:33	2	1	44-37
82	7/15	Tues.	N	Houston	L	4-2	Sambito 4-1	Ruthven 8-6	24,223			2:08	3	1	44-38
83	7/16	Wed.	N	Houston	W	4-2	Walk 6-0	KForsch 8-9	28,532			2:06	3	1	45-38
84	7/17	Thurs.	N	Houston	W	2-1	Carlton 15-4	JNiekro 10-8	26,403			2:18	3	1	46-38
85	7/18	Fri.	N	Atlanta	W	7-2	Espinosa 1-1	PNiekro 7-12	13,908			2:05	3	1	47-38
86	7/19	Sat.	TWN	Atlanta	L	5-2	Alexander 8-5	Ruthven 8-7				2:08			47-39
87				Atlanta	L	7-2	Boggs 4-5	Larson 0-3	35,524			2:21	2	2	47-40
88	7/20	Sun.	N	Atlanta	L	3-2	McWilliams 7-6	Walk 6-1	9,335			2:23	3	2½	47-41
89	7/21	Mon.	N	Cincinnati	L	5-4	Leibrandt 9-6	Lerch 3-12	27,177			2:33	3	3	47-42
90	7/22	Tues.	N	Cincinnati	L	3-2	Soto 4-4	Carlton 15-5	28,079			2:36	3	4	47-43
91	7/23	Wed.	N	Cincinnati	L	7-3	Berenyi 2-0	Espinosa 1-2	29,614			2:23	3	4	47-44
92	7/25	Fri.	TWN	ATLANTA	W	5-4 (12)	Ruthven 9-7	Camp 3-4				3:03			48-44
93				ATLANTA	L	3-0	Boggs 5-5	Larson 0-4	38,408	45	1,484,825	2:13	3	5	48-45
94	7/26	Sat.	N	ATLANTA	W	6-3	Walk 7-1	PNiekro 8-13	33,112	46	1,537,937	2:03	3	4	49-45
95	7/27	Sun.	D	ATLANTA	W	17-4	Carlton 16-5	Matula 6-9	35,249	47	1,573,186	2:22	2	4	50-45
96	7/28	Mon.	N	HOUSTON	L	3-2	Sambito 6-1	Reed 6-4	30,181	48	1,603,367	2:41	3	5	50-46
97	7/29	Tues.	N	HOUSTON	W	9-6	Saucier 5-3	LaCorte 7-3	30,252	49	1,633,619	3:05	3	4	51-46
98	7/30	Wed.	N	HOUSTON	W	6-4	Ruthven 10-7	Ryan 5-8	31,342	50	1,664,961	2:36	3	3	52-46
99	8/1	Fri.	N	CINCINNATI	W	3-1	Walk 8-1	Leibrandt 9-7	37,409	51	1,702,370	2:33	2	2	53-46
100	8/2	Sat.	N	CINCINNATI	L	2-0	LaCoss 6-9	Carlton 16-6	43,244	52	1,745,614	2:28	3	3	53-47
101	8/3	Sun.	D	CINCINNATI	W	8-4	Espinosa 2-2	Berenyi 2-2	41,328	53	1,786,942	2:28	3	3	54-47
102	8/6	Wed.	N	ST. LOUIS	L	14-0	Sykes 5-8	Walk 8-2	31,629	54	1,818,571	2:16	3	4½	54-48
103	8/7	Thurs.	N	ST. LOUIS	W	3-2	Carlton 17-6	Fulgham 3-4	31,397	55	1,849,968	1:48	3	3½	55-48
104	8/8	Fri.	N	Pittsburgh	L	6-5	Tekulve 8-5	McGraw 0-4	30,354			2:25	3	4	55-49
105	8/9	Sat.	D	Pittsburgh	L	4-1	Candelaria 8-11	Espinosa 2-3	39,984			2:20	3	4½	55-50
106	8/10	Sun.	DH	Pittsburgh	L	7-1	Bibby 14-2	Lerch 3-13				2:32			55-51
107				Pittsburgh	L	4-1	Robinson 4-5	Larson 4-5	37,323			2:20	3	6	55-52
108	8/11	Mon.	D	Chicago	W	8-5 (15)	Brusstar 1-0	Riley 0-2	10,805			4:46	3	6	56-52
109	8/12	Tues.	D	Chicago	W	5-2	Carlton 18-6	Krukow 7-12	20,808			2:03	2	5	57-52
110	8/13	Wed.	D	Chicago	L	2-1	Tidrow 5-3	Ruthven 10-8	13,215			2:15	2	5	57-53
111	8/14	Thurs.	N	New York	W	8-1	Espinosa 3-3	Zachry 6-6	20,149			2:12	2	4½	58-53
112	8/15	Fri.	N	New York	W	8-0	Christenson 4-0	Bomback 9-4	40,436			2:22	3	4½	59-53
113	8/16	Sat.	D	New York	W	11-6	Walk 9-2	Swan 5-9	23,514			2:52	3	4½	60-53
114	8/17	Sun.	DH	New York	W	9-4	Carlton 19-6	Burris 6-7				2:13			61-53
115				New York	W	4-1	Lerch 4-13	Jackson 1-4	25,458			2:13	3	3½	62-53

(continued on next page)

CAPS = Home Games

GAME	DATE	DAY	D/N	CLUB	W/L	SCORE	WINNER (Record)	LOSER (Record)	CROWD	NO. OF HOME DATE	HOME TOTAL	TIME	POS.	G.B.	W-L
116	8/19	Tues.	N	SAN DIEGO	W	7-4	Ruthven 11-8	Shirley 9-9	30,588	56	1,880,556	2:48	3	2½	63-53
117	8/20	Wed.	N	SAN DIEGO	L	7-5	Curtis 5-8	Espinosa 3-4	30,403	57	1,910,959	2:43	3	2½	63-54
118	8/21	Thurs.	D	SAN DIEGO	W	9-8 (17)	Saucier 6-3	Kinney 4-5	36,201	58	1,947,160	5:07	2	1½	64-54
119	8/22	Fri.	N	SAN FRANCISCO	L	4-3 (10)	Holland 5-2	Carlton 19-7	36,073	59	1,983,233	2:41	2	2½	64-55
120	8/23	Sat.	N	SAN FRANCISCO	L	6-2	Ripley 7-6	Christenson 4-1	38,541	60	2,021,774	2:25	2	3½	64-56
121	8/24	Sun.	N	SAN FRANCISCO	W	7-1	Ruthven 12-8	Knepper 9-15	37,325	61	2,059,099	2:12	3	3½	65-56
122	8/25	Mon.	N	LOS ANGELES	L	8-4	Stanhouse 2-2	Noles 1-4	34,267	62	2,093,366	2:39	3	3½	65-57
123	8/26	Tues.	N	LOS ANGELES	L	8-4	Castillo 4-6	Walk 9-3	35,358	63	2,128,724	2:47	3	3½	65-58
124	8/27	Wed.	N	LOS ANGELES	W	4-3	Carlton 20-7	Howe 6-6	39,116	64	2,167,840	2:18	3	2½	66-58
125	8/29	Fri.	N	San Diego	W	3-2	Christenson 5-1	Mura 4-7	10,742			2:35	2	1	67-58
126	8/30	Sat.	TWN	San Diego	W	6-1	Ruthven 13-8	Shirley 9-10	13,209			2:34	2	½	68-58
127				San Diego	L	5-1	Curtis 6-8	Espinosa 3-5				1:52	2	½	68-59
128	8/31	Sun.	D	San Diego	L	10-3	Lucas 5-7	Walk 9-4	7,815			2:30	2	½	68-60
129	9/1	Mon.	D	San Francisco	W	6-4	Carlton 21-7	Minton 3-5	16,952			2:47	1	.001	69-60
130	9/2	Tues.	N	San Francisco	W	2-1	Reed 7-2	Holland 5-3	6,135			3:29	1	.001	70-60
131	9/3	Wed.	N	San Francisco	W	4-3	Ruthven 14-8	Ripley 7-8	5,509			2:30	1	½	71-60
132	9/4	Thurs.	N	Los Angeles	W	3-2	Walk 10-4	Reuss 16-5	41,864			2:19	1	1	72-60
133	9/5	Fri.	N	Los Angeles	L	1-0	Sutton 10-4	Carlton 21-8	41,019			1:54	T1	—	72-61
134	9/6	Sat.	N	Los Angeles	L	7-3	Welch 12-9	Lerch 4-14	45,995			2:32	2	1	72-62
135	9/7	Sun.	D	Los Angeles	L	6-0	Castillo 6-6	Ruthven 14-9	39,083			2:22	2	1	72-63
136	9/8	Mon.	N	PITTSBURGH	W	6-2	McGraw 1-4	Romo 5-5	40,576	65	2,208,416	2:35	2	½	73-63
137	9/9	Tues.	N	PITTSBURGH	W	5-4 (14)	Brusstar 2-0	MLee 0-1	43,333	66	2,251,749	3:24	2	½	74-63
138	9/10	Wed.	N	New York	W	5-0	Bystrom 1-0	Bomback 9-7	6,748			2:31	2	½	75-63
139	9/11	Thurs.	N	New York	W	5-1	Ruthven 15-8	Burris 7-11	6,376			2:38	2	½	76-63
140	9/12	Fri.	TWN	ST. LOUIS	L	7-4	Vuckovich 11-9	Walk 10-5	44,093	67	2,295,842	2:33	2	2	76-64
141				ST. LOUIS	L	5-0	Littlefield 5-3	Reed 7-5				2:40	2	2	76-65
142	9/13	Sat.	N	ST. LOUIS	W	2-1	Carlton 22-8	BForsch 11-9	41,728	68	2,337,570	1:42	2	2	77-65
143	9/14	Sun.	D	ST. LOUIS	W	8-4	Bystrom 2-0	Martinez 5-10	30,137	69	2,367,707	2:14	2	1	78-65
144	9/16	Tues.	N	Pittsburgh	L	3-2	Bibby 17-5	Ruthven 15-9	22,239			2:22	2	2½	78-66
145	9/17	Wed.	N	Pittsburgh	W	5-4	McGraw 2-4	Tekulve 8-10	23,650			2:35	2	1½	79-66
146	9/19	Fri.	D	Chicago	L	4-3	Smith 2-0	Brusstar 2-1	4,352			2:38	2	1½	79-67
147	9/20	Sat.	D	Chicago	W	7-3	Bystrom 3-0	McGlothen 10-13	11,713			2:36	2	1½	80-67
148	9/21	Sun.	D	Chicago	W	7-3	Ruthven 16-10	Lamp 10-12	10,190			2:38	2	½	81-67
149	9/22	Mon.	N	St. Louis	W	3-2 (10)	Carlton 23-8	Seaman 3-2	5,654			2:17	1	½	82-67
150	9/23	Tues.	N	St. Louis	L	6-3	Olmsted 1-0	Walk 10-6	6,915			2:09	2	1½	82-68
151	9/24	Wed.	N	NEW YORK	W	1-0 (10)	McGraw 3-4	Allen 7-9	24,258	70	2,391,965	2:25	2	½	83-68
152	9/25	Thurs.	N	MONTREAL	W	2-1	Bystrom 4-0	Jackson 1-6	20,525	71	2,412,490	2:24	2	½	84-68
153	9/26	Fri.	N	MONTREAL	W	2-1	McGraw 4-4	Palmer 7-6	50,887	72	2,463,377	2:01	2	1½	85-68
154	9/27	Sat.	D	MONTREAL	L	4-3	Sanderson 16-10	Carlton 23-9	53,058	73	2,516,425	2:19	1	½	85-69
155	9/28	Sun.	D	MONTREAL	L	8-3	Rogers 16-11	Walk 10-7	40,305	74	2,556,740	2:42	2	½	85-70
156	9/29	Mon.	N	CHICAGO	W	6-5 (15)	Saucier 7-3	Lamp 10-13	21,127	75	2,577,867	4:27	2	½	86-70
157	9/30	Tues.	N	CHICAGO	W	14-2	Bystrom 5-0	McGlothen 11-14	24,349	76	2,602,216	2:40	2	½	87-70
158	10/1	Wed.	N	CHICAGO	W	5-0	Carlton 24-9	Lamp 10-14	25,658	77	2,627,874	2:13	2	½	88-70
159	10/2	Thurs.	N	CHICAGO	W	4-2	Walk 11-7	Caudill 4-6	23,806	78	2,651,650	2:27	2	½	89-70
160	10/3	Fri.	N	Montreal	W	2-1	Ruthven 17-10	Sanderson 16-11	57,121			2:39	1	1	90-70
161	10/4	Sat.	N	Montreal	W	6-4 (11)	McGraw 5-4	Bahnsen 7-6	50,794			3:51	1	2	91-70
162	10/5	Sun.	D	Montreal	L	8-7 (10)	Lea 7-5	Brusstar 2-2	30,104			3:13	1	1	91-71

1980 Official Stats

Batting

	AVE	G	AB	R	H	2b	3b	HR	RBI	BB-I	SO	SB-CS	E
Aguayo	.277	20	47	7	13	1	2	1	8	2-0	3	1-1	3
Aviles	.277	51	101	12	28	6	0	1	9	10-2	9	0-0	8
Boone	.229	141	480	34	110	23	1	9	55	48-12	41	3-4	17
Bowa	.267	147	540	57	144	16	4	2	39	24-7	28	21-6	17
—LH	.259		425		110					20-7	23		
—RH	.296		115		34					4-0	5		
Dernier	.571	10	7	5	4	1	0	0	1	1-0		3-0	0
Gross	.240	127	154	19	37	7	2	0	12	24-1	7	1-1	0
Isales	.400	3	5	1	2	0	0	0	3	1-0	0	0-0	0
Loviglio	.000	16	5	7	0	0	0	0	0	1-0	0	1-2	1
Luzinski	.228	106	368	44	84	19	1	19	56	60-5	52	1-2	1
Maddox	.259	143	549	59	142	31	3	11	73	18-5	58	25-5	10
McBride	.309	137	554	68	171	33	10	9	87	26-4	58	13-10	
McCarver	1.000	6	1	0	1	0	0	0	2	2-0	0	0-0	
McCormack	.200	2	5	0	1	0	0	0	0	1-0	14	3-1	
Moreland	.314	62	159	13	50	8	1	4	29	8-2	33	0-0	
Rose	.282	162	655	95	185	42	1	1	64	66-5	50	12-8	
—LH	.290		525		163					53-3	30		
—RH	.254		130		22					13-2	19		
Schmidt	.286	150	548	104	157	25	8	48*	121*	89-10	119	12-5	27
Smith	.339	100	298	69	101	14	8	3	20	36-8	46	33-13	4
Trillo	.292	141	531	68	155	25	6	7	43	30-3	48	0-1	11
Unser	.264	96	110	15	29	6	1	0	10	10-1	21	0-0	0
Virgil	.200	1	5		1			0			9	0-0	1
G. Vukovich	.224	78	58	6	13	1	0	0	2	6-0	7	0-0	0
J. Vukovich	.161	49	62	5	10	1	0	0	4	2-1	18	0-1	2
PHILLIES	.270	162	5625	728	1517	272	54	117	674	472-65	708	140-62	136
Opposition	.254	162	5578	639	1419	255	68	87	598	530-83	889	163-78	159

Home 49-32   Road 42-39
Day 25-25   Night 66-46
X-Inn 13-9   DH 2-4-2
vs. LHP 21-17   vs. RHP 70-54
1 run 32-28   ShO 8-12

Pitching

	W-L	ERA	G	GS	CG	SHO	SV	IP	H	R	ER	BB-I	SO	HR
Brusstar	2-2	3.69	26	0	0	0	0	38.2	42	16	16	13-2	21	3
Bystrom	*24-9	1.50	6	5	1	0	0	36*	26	6	6	9-0	21	1
Carlton	24-9	2.34	38	38**	13	3	0	304*	243	87	79	90-12	286*	15
Christenson	5-1	4.01	14	14	0	1	0	73.2	62	35	33	27-3	49	4
Davis	0-0	2.57	2	0	0	0	0	7.0	5	2	2	5-0	5	0
Espinosa	3-5	3.79	12	12	1	0	0	76.1	73	36	32	19-2	13	9
LaGrow	0-0	4.15	5	0	0	0	0	39	46	22	18	7-2	3	1
Larson	0-5	5.16	12	7	0	0	0	45.2	46	30	26	24-6	21	7
Lerch	4-14	5.18	30	22	0	0	0	150	178	98	86	55-5	57	15
Lyle-PHILA	0-0	1.93	10	0	0	0	3	14	11	5	3	6-1	6	0
Lyle-Texas	3-2	4.69	49	0	0	0	0	80.2	97	47	42	28-4	43	9
McGraw	5-4	1.47	57	0	0	0	20	92.1	62	16	15	23-9	75	3
Munninghoff	0-0	4.50	4	0	0	0	0	6	9	3	3	2-0	2	0
Noles	1-4	3.89	48	3	0	0	0	81.1	80	42	35	42-11	57	5
Reed	7-5	4.05	55	0	0	0	9	91.1	88	45	41	30-10	54	4
Ruthven	17-10	3.55	33	33	0	1	0	223.1	241	99	88	74-9	86	9
Saucier	7-3	3.42	40	0	0	0	0	42	50	21	19	20-8	25	2
Walk	11-7	4.56	27	27	0	0	0	151.2	163	82	77	71-2	94	8
PHILLIES	91-71	3.43	162	162	8	8	40	1480	1419	639	564	530-83	889	87
Opposition	71-91	3.96	162	162	25	12	31	1469	1517	728	647	472-65	708	117

COMBINED SHO: Carlton/Noles; Christenson/McGraw (2)
*Indicates League Leader
**Indicates Tied for League Leader

PINCH HITTING ab, h, rbi: Aviles 6-2-0 .333 Boone 4-1-0 .250 Gross 39-10-5 .256 Lerch 1-0-0 .000 Luzinski 1-0-0 .000 Maddox 1-0-0 .000 McBride 3-2-0 .667 Moreland 17-7-6 .412 Rose 1-0-0 .000 Schmidt 1-0-0 .000 Smith 8-2-0 .250 Unser 38-12-6 .316 G. Vukovich 45-11-5 .244 J. Vukovich 4-1-2 .500 TOTALS 174-48-25 .276

GAME WINNING RBI: Boone 6, Bowa 6, Gross 2, Luzinski 8, Maddox 5, McBride 14, Moreland 7, Rose 12, Ruthven, Schmidt 17, Smith, Trillo 5, Unser

DPs 136   Opp DPs 146
April 6-9   June 14-14
May 17-9   July 15-14
August 16-15   October 4-1
September 19-10

HR Home 64-44   HR Road 53-43
Starters 70-51   Relievers 21-20
Artificial Turf 66-53   Grass 25-18
W/L in 8th/9th 13-10   Series: 27-18-10

LOB 1131   Opp LOB 1161

Road Attendance: 76 dates: 1,766,359; average 23,514
Home Attendance: 78 dates: 2,651,650; average 33,996

1980 Highs and Lows

INDIVIDUAL PITCHING

Most strikeouts, game, by Phillies—13, Steve Carlton June 14 vs. San Diego; Steve Carlton, Aug. 22 vs. San Francisco

Most strikeouts, game, by opposition—10, Nolan Ryan May 18 @ Houston, Don Sutton September 5 @ Los Angeles

Most walks, game, by Phillies—6, Randy Lerch May 9 @ Cincinnati; Steve Carlton July 2 vs. Montreal; Dick Ruthven August 19 vs. San Diego

Most walks, game, by opposition—6, Mark Bomback April 30 @ New York

Fewest hits, game, by Phillies—1, Steve Carlton April 26 vs. St. Louis

Fewest hits, game, by opposition—2, Mark Bomback April 30 @ New York, Scott Sanderson June 26 vs. Montreal

Longest winning streak—8 games, Steve Carlton

Longest losing streak—6 games, Randy Lerch

Most consecutive scoreless innings—20, Marty Bystrom

Most innings, game, starter—12, Dick Ruthven July 25 (1st game) vs. Atlanta

Most innings, game, reliever—4, Dickie Noles and Ron Reed

TEAM MISCELLANEOUS

Longest winning streak—6 games (3 times)

Longest losing streak—6 games

Longest game, innings—17, August 21 vs. San Diego

Longest game, time—3:22, May 4 vs. Los Angeles (9 innings)

Shortest game, time—1:39 July 5 @ St. Louis

Largest crowd, home—53,254 July 12 vs. Pittsburgh

Largest crowd, road—57,121 October 3 @ Montreal

INDIVIDUAL BATTING

Most hits, game—5, Lonnie Smith July 14 vs. Pittsburgh, Bake McBride July 29 vs. Houston

Most runs, game—3, Lonnie Smith (4 times); Garry Maddox (2 times); Pete Rose, Mike Schmidt, Bake McBride

Most doubles, game—3, Manny Trillo July 6 @ St. Louis, Pete Rose July 11 vs. Chicago

Most triples, game—2, Bake McBride May 24 vs. Houston, Mike Schmidt July 11 vs. Chicago

Most home runs, game—2, Mike Schmidt (4 times) April 22 vs. New York; May 5 vs. Atlanta; May 31 @ Chicago; July 25 (1st game) vs. Atlanta, Greg Luzinski May 21 vs. Cincinnati

Most RBI's, game—6, Mike Schmidt April 22 vs. New York

Most stolen bases, game—3, Pete Rose (2nd, 3rd, home), 6th inning, May 11 @ Cincinnati; Lonnie Smith July 29 vs. Houston

Longest hitting streak—12 games, Bake McBride (twice); Garry Maddox; Lonnie Smith

Grand Slams—Mike Schmidt April 22 vs. New York (Pacella), Keith Moreland June 30 @ Montreal (Gullickson)

TEAM BATTING

Most runs, inning, by Phillies—7, June 13 vs. San Diego (1st) and June 30 @ Montreal (4th)

Most runs, inning, by opposition—7, August 6 vs. St. Louis (3rd)

Most runs, game, by Phillies—17, July 27 vs. Atlanta

Most runs, game, by opposition—14, August 6 vs. St. Louis

Most hits, game, by Phillies—21, July 27 vs. Atlanta

Most hits, game, by opposition—21, July 14 vs. Pittsburgh

Most home runs, game, by Phillies—4, May 20 vs. Cincinnati

Most home runs, game, by opposition—3, June 17 @ Los Angeles and July 13 vs. Pittsburgh

Most stolen bases, game, by Phillies—4, May 11 @ Cincinnati; July 19 @ Atlanta (2nd game); July 29 vs. Houston

Most stolen bases, game, by opposition—5, April 18 @ Montreal; June 2 @ Pittsburgh; June 24 vs. Montreal; August 30 @ San Diego (2nd game)

The End of the Season

SEPTEMBER 26, 1980
Phillies 2, Expos 1

Montreal	ab	r	h	rbi	Phila'phia	ab	r	h	rbi
White, lf	3	1	1	0	Rose, 1b	4	0	0	0
Scott, 2b	4	0	1	1	McBride, rf	4	1	2	1
Office, rf	4	0	1	0	Schmidt, 3b	3	0	0	0
Dawson, cf	4	0	1	0	Luzinski, lf	2	0	0	0
Carter, c	3	0	0	0	Trillo, 2b	3	0	0	0
Cromartie, 1b	2	0	0	0	Maddox, cf	3	1	1	1
Parrish, 3b	3	0	0	0	Bowa, ss	3	0	1	0
Speier, ss	3	0	0	0	Boone, c	3	0	0	0
Palmer, p	3	0	0	0	Ruthven, p	2	0	1	0
					McGraw, p	1	0	0	0
Totals	29	1	4	1	Totals	28	2	5	2

Montreal..........................0 0 0 0 0 1 0 0 0—1
Philadelphia....................0 1 0 0 0 0 0 0 1—2
None out when winning run scored.

Montreal	IP.	H.	R.	ER.	BB.	SO.
Palmer (L. 7-6)	8°	5	2	2	1	3

Philadelphia	IP.	H.	R.	ER.	BB.	SO.
Ruthven	7	4	1	1	2	2
McGraw (W. 4-4)	2	0	0	0	0	1

°Pitched to one batter in ninth.

Game-winning RBI—McBride.
E—None. DP—Montreal 1, Philadelphia 1. LOB—Montreal 3, Philadelphia 3. 2B—White, Dawson. HR—Maddox (11), McBride (9). SB—Ruthven. Balk—Palmer. T—2:01. A—50,887.

SEPTEMBER 27, 1980
Expos 4, Phillies 3

Montreal	ab	r	h	rbi	Phila'phia	ab	r	h	rbi
White, rf	5	0	2	1	Rose, 1b	4	0	1	0
Scott, 2b	4	0	0	0	McBride, rf	3	0	1	0
Dawson, cf	4	1	2	0	Schmidt, 3b	4	1	1	1
Carter, c	3	2	1	1	Luzinski, lf	4	0	1	0
Cromartie, 1b	2	0	0	0	Loviglio, pr	0	0	0	0
Parrish, 3b	4	0	1	1	Trillo, 2b	4	2	3	1
Speier, ss	4	1	3	1	Maddox, cf	3	0	0	0
Pate, lf	3	0	1	0	Bowa, ss	4	0	0	0
Sanderson, p	2	0	0	0	Boone, c	2	0	0	0
Macha, ph	1	0	0	0	Gross, ph	1	0	0	0
Sosa, p	1	0	0	0	Moreland, c	1	0	1	1
Fryman, p	0	0	0	0	Dernier, pr	0	0	0	0
					Carlton, p	2	0	1	0
					Brusstar, p	0	0	0	0
					G. Vuk'ch, ph	1	0	0	0
					Lyle, p	0	0	0	0
					Unser, ph	0	0	0	0
					L. Smith, ph	1	0	0	0
Totals	33	4	10	4	Totals	34	3	9	3

Montreal..........................0 1 0 1 0 0 1 1 0—4
Philadelphia....................1 1 0 0 0 0 0 0 1—3

SEPTEMBER 28, 1980
Expos 8, Phillies 3

Montreal	IP.	H.	R.	ER.	BB.	SO.
Sand'son (W. 16-10)	6	4	2	2	1	3
Sosa	2⅔	5	1	1	0	1
Fryman (Save 17)	⅓	0	0	0	0	1

Philadelphia	IP.	H.	R.	ER.	BB.	SO.
Carlton (L. 23-9)	7°	8	4	4	1	7
Brusstar	1	1	0	0	1	0
Lyle	1	1	0	0	0	1

°Pitched to one batter in eighth.

Game-winning RBI—White.
E—None. DP—Montreal 1, Philadelphia 2. LOB—Montreal 6, Philadelphia 6. 2B—Dawson 2, Speier, White. HR—Schmidt (44), Carter (27), Trillo (7). SH—Cromartie, Pate, Maddox. T—2:19. A—53,058.

Montreal	ab	r	h	rbi	Phila'phia	ab	r	h	rbi
White, lf	4	1	0	0	Rose, 1b	3	1	0	0
Scott, 2b	4	0	0	0	McBride, rf	3	0	1	1
Office, rf	3	0	0	1	Schmidt, 3b	3	0	1	1
Dawson, cf	5	2	3	0	Luzinski, lf	3	1	0	0
Carter, c	4	2	3	4	Trillo, 2b	4	0	0	0
Cromartie, 1b	5	1	1	0	Maddox, cf	4	0	1	0
Parrish, 3b	4	1	1	0	Bowa, ss	4	0	1	1
Speier, ss	2	1	1	2	Boone, c	4	0	0	0
Rogers, p	3	0	1	1	Walk, p	1	0	0	0
					G. Vuk'ch, ph	1	0	0	0
					Noles, p	0	0	0	0
					Saucier, p	0	0	0	0
					Reed, p	0	0	0	0
					Gross, ph	1	1	1	0
					Lerch, p	0	0	0	0
Totals	34	8	11	8	Totals	31	3	5	3

Montreal..........................0 1 1 0 0 3 2 0 1—8
Philadelphia....................0 1 0 0 0 0 0 2 0—3

Montreal	IP.	H.	R.	ER.	BB.	SO.
Rogers (W. 16-11)	9	5	3	3	3	3

Philadelphia	IP.	H.	R.	ER.	BB.	SO.
Walk (L. 10-7)	5	3	2	2	4	6
Noles	⅓	3	3	3	1	0
Saucier	1⅔	2	2	2	0	1
Reed	1	1	0	0	0	2
Lerch	1	2	1	1	0	0

Game-winning RBI—Office.
E—Bowa. LOB—Montreal 7, Philadelphia 5. 2B—Schmidt, McBride, Carter. 3B—Speier. HR—Carter 2 (29). SB—Scott, White. SH—Scott, Rogers. SF—Office, Schmidt. T—2:42. A—40,305.

Phillies 6, Cubs 5

Chicago	ab	r	h	rbi	Phila'phia	ab	r	h	rbi
DeJesus, ss	7	0	0	0	Lo. Smith, lf	5	1	2	0
Tyson, 2b	3	1	0	0	Rose, 1b	4	1	1	3
Biittner, ph	1	0	0	0	McBride, rf	6	0	1	1
Kelleher, 2b	2	1	0	0	Schmidt, 3b	7	0	1	0
Buckner, 1b	5	1	2	1	Unser, cf	5	0	1	0
T'mpson, 1b	1	0	0	1	Dernier, pr	0	0	0	0
Kingman, lf	3	0	1	0	Maddox, cf	2	1	1	1
Lezcano, cf	4	0	1	1	Moreland, c	7	0	2	0
Tracy, rf	6	0	1	0	Bowa, ss	6	0	0	0
Martin, cf	6	1	3	1	Trillo, 2b	7	2	3	1
Dillard, 3b	6	0	1	1	Christ'son, p	0	1	0	0
O'Berry, c	4	0	0	0	McGraw, p	0	0	0	0
Reuschel, p	2	0	0	0	Gross, ph	0	0	0	0
Tidrow, p	0	0	0	0	Loviglio, pr	0	0	0	0
Vail, ph	1	0	1	0	Reed, p	0	0	0	0
Le. Smith, p	0	0	0	0	Lyle, p	0	0	0	0
Figueroa, ph	1	0	0	0	G. Vuk'ch, ph	1	0	0	0
Sutter, p	0	0	0	0	Brusstar, p	0	0	0	0
Johnson, ph	0	0	0	0	McCarver, ph	1	0	0	0
Caudill, p	0	0	0	0	Noles, p.	0	0	0	0
McG'then, ph	0	0	0	0	Saucier, p	0	0	0	0
Randle, pr	0	1	0	0					
Capilla, p.	0	0	0	0					
Lamp, p	0	0	0	0					
Totals	52	5	10	5	Totals	51	6	12	6

Chicago .... 000 010 200 000 002 — 5
Philadelphia ...... 002 000 100 000 003 — 6
Two out when winning run scored.

Chicago	IP.	H.	R.	ER.	BB.	SO.
Reuschel	6⅓	6	3	1	4	2
Tidrow	⅔	0	0	0	0	0
Le Smith	2	0	0	0	1	0
Sutter	2	1	0	0	1	1
Caudill	3	2	0	0	1	3
Capilla	⅓	0	2	2	2	0
Lamp (L. 10-13)	⅓	3	1	1	1	0

Philadelphia	IP.	H.	R.	ER.	BB.	SO.
Christenson	6⅓	4	3	3	2	4
McGraw	2⅔	3	0	0	0	2
Reed	⅔	0	0	0	1	0
Lyle	2⅓	2	0	0	1	1
Brusstar	2	0	0	0	0	0
Noles	⅓	0	2	0	1	0
Saucier (W. 7-3)	⅔	1	0	0	0	1

Game-winning RBI—Trillo.
E—Dillard, Noles. DP—Chicago 4, Philadelphia 2. LOB—Chicago 9, Philadelphia 12. 2B—Rose, Buckner, Vail, Unser, Lezcano. HR—Martin (23). SB—Trillo, Lonnie Smith. SH—McGraw, O'Berry. SF—Thompson. WP—Capilla. T—4:27. A—21,127.

Phillies 14, Cubs 2

Chicago	ab	r	h	rbi	Phila'phia	ab	r	h	rbi
DeJesus, ss	4	0	1	2	Lo. Smith, lf	5	3	3	0
Tyson, 2b	4	0	0	0	Rose, 1b	2	1	1	0
Buckner, 1b	4	0	1	0	D'nier, pr-cf	1	2	1	1
Kingman, lf	2	0	0	0	McBride, rf	2	2	2	3
Lezcano, cf	1	0	0	0	Isales, rf	1	0	1	2
Tracy, rf-lf	4	0	0	0	Schmidt, 3b	3	0	1	1
Martin, cf-rf	4	0	0	0	J. V'ich, 3b	1	0	0	0
Dillard, 3b	3	2	1	0	Unser, cf-1b	3	1	0	1
O'Berry, c	4	0	1	0	McCarver, 1b	0	0	0	0
McGlothen, p	0	0	0	0	Moreland, c	5	1	1	2
Figueroa, p	0	0	0	0	McCormack, c	0	0	0	0
Riley, p	0	0	0	0	Bowa, ss	3	1	2	1
Le. Smith, p	0	0	0	0	Aviles, ss	2	1	1	0
T'pson, ph	1	0	1	0	Trillo, 2b	3	2	2	0
Capilla, p	0	0	0	0	Noles, p	1	0	0	0
Hayes, ph	1	0	0	0	Bystrom, p	3	0	0	0
					Aguayo, 2b	1	0	0	0
Totals	32	2	5	2	Totals	36	14	15	11

Chicago .... 000 010 100 — 2
Philadelphia .... 401 104 40x — 14

Chicago	IP.	H.	R.	ER.	BB.	SO.
McGlothen (L. 11-14)	4	7	6	6	3	2
Riley	1⅓	2	4	3	2	2
Le Smith	⅔	1	0	0	0	1
Capilla	2	5	4	4	0	0

Philadelphia	IP.	H.	R.	ER.	BB.	SO.
Bystrom (W. 5-0)	7	4	2	2	4	6
Noles	2	1	0	0	0	2

Game-winning RBI—Schmidt.
E—O'Berry, Dillard. LOB—Chicago 7, Philadelphia 6. 2B—Moreland, Aviles. 3B—Isales. SB—Lonnie Smith. SF—Schmidt, McBride, Unser. WP—McClothen, Capilla. PB—O'Berry. T—2:40. A—24,349.

Phillies 5, Cubs 0

Chicago	ab	r	h	rbi	Phila'phia	ab	r	h	rbi
DeJesus, ss	4	0	0	0	Rose, 1b	4	0	0	0
Dillard, 3b	4	0	0	0	McBride, rf	4	0	0	0
Buckner, 1b	4	0	1	0	Schmidt, 3b	4	1	2	1
Martin, rf	4	0	0	0	Luzinski, lf	4	1	1	1
Vail, lf	3	0	1	0	Gross, lf	0	0	0	0
Lezcano, cf	1	0	0	0	Unser, cf	3	1	1	0
Tyson, 2b	3	0	0	0	Trillo, 2b	4	1	1	0
O'Berry, c	2	0	0	0	Bowa, ss	4	1	2	1
Johnson, ph-c	1	0	0	0	Boone, c	4	0	2	1
Lamp, p	2	0	0	0	Carlton, p	3	0	2	1
Tidrow, p	0	0	0	0					
Kingman, ph	1	0	0	0					
Smith, p	0	0	0	0					
Totals	29	0	2	0	Totals	34	5	11	5

Chicago .... 000 000 000 — 0
Philadelphia .... 000 004 01x — 5

Chicago	IP.	H.	R.	ER.	BB.	SO.
Lamp (L. 10-14)	5⅓	8	4	4	1	1
Tidrow	1⅔	1	0	0	0	3
Smith	1	2	1	1	0	1

Philadelphia	IP.	H.	R.	ER.	BB.	SO.
Carlton (W. 24-9)	9	2	0	0	0	10

Game-winning RBI—Schmidt.
E—None. LOB—Chicago 4, Philadelphia 7. 2B—Schmidt, Bowa. 3B—Unser. HR—Schmidt (45), Luzinski (19). SF—Carlton. WP—Lamp. T—2:13. A—25,658.

Phillies 4, Cubs 2

Chicago	ab	r	h	rbi	Phila'phia	ab	r	h	rbi
DeJesus, ss	3	1	1	0	Rose, 1b	4	1	1	0
Dillard, 3b	3	0	0	0	McBride, rf	4	0	1	0
Buckner, 1b	4	0	3	1	Schmidt, 3b	4	2	1	1
Biittner, rf	4	0	1	0	Luzinski, lf	3	0	0	0
Sutter, p	0	0	0	0	Gross, lf	1	0	1	1
Martin, cf-rf	4	1	0	0	Unser, cf	4	1	1	0
Tracy, lf	3	0	1	0	Moreland, c	3	0	1	1
Vail, ph	1	0	1	1	Trillo, 2b	3	0	0	0
Tyson, 2b	2	0	1	0	Bowa, ss	3	0	2	0
Figueroa, ph	1	0	0	0	McGraw, p	1	0	0	0
Kelleher, 2b	0	0	0	0	Walk, p	1	0	0	0
Kingman, ph	1	0	0	0	Aviles, ss	1	0	0	0
O'Berry, c	3	0	0	0					
Johnson, p	1	0	0	0					
Martz, p	2	0	0	0					
T'mpson, ph	1	0	0	0					
Caudill, p	0	0	0	0					
Lezcano, cf	1	0	0	0					
Totals	34	2	8	2	Totals	31	4	8	3

```
Chicago ...................1 0 0  0 0 0  0 0 1–2
Philadelphia .............0 0 0  1 0 0  1 2 x–4
```

Chicago	IP.	H.	R.	ER.	BB.	SO.
Martz	6	4	1	1	0	1
Caudill (L. 4-6)	1⅓	3	2	1	0	0
Sutter	⅔	1	1	0	0	2

Philadelphia	IP.	H.	R.	ER.	BB.	SO.
Walk (W. 11-7)	7⅓	7	1	1	2	7
McGraw (Save 19)	1⅔	1	1	0	0	1

Game-winning RBI—Moreland.
E—Dillard, Tracy, Schmidt. DP—Chicago 1, Philadelphia 2. LOB—Chicago 7, Philadelphia 4. 2B—Unser, Vail. 3B—Tyson, Tracy. HR—Schmidt (46). SB—DeJesus. SH—Walk. WP—Sutter. T—2:27. A—23,806.

Phillies 2, Expos 1

Phila'phia	ab	r	h	rbi	Montreal	ab	r	h	rbi
Rose, 1b	4	1	2	0	White, lf	4	1	1	0
McBride, rf	4	0	1	0	Scott, 2b	2	0	0	0
Schmidt, 3b	2	1	2	2	Office, rf	2	0	1	0
Luzinski, lf	3	0	0	0	Pate, rf	1	0	0	0
Maddox, cf	0	0	0	0	Dawson, cf	2	0	0	1
Unser, cf-lf	4	0	0	0	Carter, c	3	0	0	0
Trillo, 2b	3	0	1	0	Cromartie, 1b	4	0	0	0
Bowa, ss	4	0	1	0	Parrish, 3b	4	0	0	0
Boone, c	3	0	0	0	Speier, ss	2	0	1	0
Ruthven, p	2	0	1	0	LeFlore, pr	0	0	0	0
Lyle, p	0	0	0	0	Manuel, ss	1	0	0	0
Gross, lf	0	0	0	0	Sanderson, p	2	0	0	0
Loviglio, pr	0	0	0	0	Tamargo, ph	1	0	1	0
McGraw, p	0	0	0	0	Raines, pr	0	0	0	0
					Bahnsen, p	0	0	0	0
					Fryman, p	0	0	0	0
Totals	29	2	8	2	Totals	28	1	4	1

```
Philadelphia ................1 0 0  0 0 1  0 0 0–2
Montreal ....................0 0 0  0 0 1  0 0 0–1
```

Philadelphia	IP.	H.	R.	ER.	BB.	SO.
Ruthven (W. 17-10)	5⅔	3	1	1	4	2
Lyle	1⅓	1	0	0	1	0
McGraw (Save 20)	2	0	0	0	0	5

Montreal	IP.	H.	R.	ER.	BB.	SO.
Sanderson (L. 16-11)	7	8	2	2	0	6
Bahnsen	1⅔	0	0	0	3	0
Fryman	⅓	0	0	0	0	0

Game-winning RBI—Schmidt.
E—White. DP—Montreal 1. LOB—Philadelphia 5, Montreal 7. 2B—McBride, White. HR—Schmidt (47). SB—Rose. SH—Office, Maddox. SF—Schmidt, Dawson. WP—Bahnsen. T—2:39. A—57,121.

Phillies 6, Expos 4

Phila'phia	ab	r	h	rbi	Montreal	ab	r	h	rbi
Rose, 1b	5	2	3	1	White, lf	3	1	2	3
McBride, rf	5	2	3	0	Scott, 2b	4	0	3	1
Schmidt, 3b	5	1	3	2	Office, rf	5	0	1	0
Luzinski, lf	4	0	2	2	Dawson, cf	5	0	1	0
Reed, p	0	0	0	0	Carter, c	4	0	0	0
Lyle, p	0	0	0	0	Cromartie, 1b	5	0	0	0
Boone, ph	1	0	1	1	Parrish, 3b	5	0	1	0
Dernier, pr	0	0	0	0	Speier, ss	3	0	0	0
McCorm'k, c	1	0	1	0	LeFlore, pr	0	1	0	0
Unser, cf-lf	4	0	1	0	Manuel, ss	1	0	0	0
Smith, lf	1	0	0	0	Rogers, p	1	1	0	0
Moreland, c	4	0	0	0	Montanez, ph	0	0	0	0
Loviglio, pr	0	0	0	0	Tamargo, ph	0	0	0	0
Brusstar, p	0	0	0	0	Raines, pr	1	0	0	0
Aviles, ph	1	0	0	0	Sosa, p	0	0	0	0
McGraw, p	1	0	0	0	Fryman, p	0	0	0	0
Trillo, 2b	5	0	1	0	Wallace, ph	1	0	0	0
Bowa, ss	4	1	1	0	Bahnsen, p	0	0	0	0
Chris'son, p	2	0	1	0					
Gross, ph-lf	1	0	0	0					
M'dox, ph-cf	2	0	0	0					
Totals	46	6	17	6	Totals	37	4	8	4

```
Philadelphia ............0 0 0  0 1 0  2 0 1  0 2–6
Montreal ..............0 0 2  0 0 0  2 0 0  0 0–4
```

Philadelphia	IP.	H.	R.	ER.	BB.	SO.
Christenson	6	6	2	2	3	3
Reed	⅓	0	1	0	0	1
Lyle	⅔	1	1	1	1	1
Brusstar	1	0	0	0	0	1
McGraw (W. 5-4)	3	1	0	0	0	4

Montreal	IP.	H.	R.	ER.	BB.	SO.
Rogers	7	11	3	3	3	4
Sosa	⅔	2	0	0	0	0
Fryman	1⅓	1	1	1	2	2
Bahnsen (L. 7-6)	2	3	2	2	0	0

Game-winning RBI—Schmidt.
E—Trillo 2, Christenson 2, Parrish, White, Moreland. DP—Philadelphia 3, Montreal 3. LOB—Philadelphia 12, Montreal 6. 2B—Schmidt, Scott. HR—(White (6), Schmidt (48). SB—Dawson, LeFlore, Raines. SH—Scott. SF—White. WP—Rogers. T—3:51. A—50,794.

PHILLIES IN FIRST PLACE

May 1st	June 1st	July 1st
1900	1900	1950
1911	1913	1976
1915	1964	1978
1953	1976	
1964		

August 1st	Sept. 1st
1915	1915
1950	1950
1964	1964
1976	1976
1978	1977
	1978

National League Championship Series

Game #1
OCTOBER 7, 1980
Phillies 3, Astros 1

Houston	ab	r	h	rbi	Phila'phia	ab	r	h	rbi
Lan'stoy, 2b	5	0	0	0	Rose, 1b	4	1	2	0
Cabell, 3b	4	0	1	0	McBride, rf	4	0	1	0
Cruz, lf	3	1	1	0	Schmidt, 3b	3	0	0	0
Cedeno, cf	3	0	1	0	Luzinski, lf	4	1	1	2
Howe, 1b	4	0	0	0	Unser, lf	0	0	0	0
Woods, rf	4	0	2	1	Maddox, cf	3	1	1	0
Pujols, c	3	0	0	0	Bowa, ss	2	0	1	0
Bergman, pr	0	0	0	0	Boone, c	3	0	1	0
Reynolds, ss	2	0	0	0	Carlton, p	2	0	0	0
Puhl, ph	1	0	0	0	Gross, ph	1	0	1	1
Forsch, p	2	0	2	0	McGraw, p	0	0	0	0
Leonard, ph	1	0	0	0					
Totals	32	1	7	1	Totals	30	3	8	3

Houston .... 001 000 000—1
Philadelphia .... 000 002 10x—3

Houston	IP.	H.	R.	ER.	BB.	SO.
Forsch (Loser)	8	8	3	3	1	5

Philadelphia	IP.	H.	R.	ER.	BB.	SO.
Carlton (Winner)	7	7	1	1	3	3
McGraw (Save)	1	0	0	0	1	1

Game-winning RBI—Luzinski.
E—Bowa. DP—Philadelphia 1. LOB—Houston 9, Philadelphia 5. HR—Luzinski. SB—McBride, Maddox. SH—Forsch, Bowa. U—Engel, Tata, Froemming, Harvey, Vargo and Crawford. T—2:35. A—65,277.

How The Runs Scored

Third Inning

ASTROS—Cabell flied to Maddox. Cruz singled off Carlton's glove. Cedeno singled to centerfield, Cruz advanced to second. Howe flied to McBride, runners held. Woods singled to rightfield, Cruz scored, Cedeno advanced to third. Pujols grounded into fielder's choice, Schmidt to Trillo. Woods forced at second. One run, three hits, no errors, two left. **ASTROS 1, PHILLIES 0**

Sixth Inning

PHILLIES—Rose hit infield single to shortstop. McBride struck out. Schmidt flied to Cedeno. Luzinski homered to leftfield, with Rose scoring ahead of him. Trillo struck out. Two runs, two hits, no errors, none left. **PHILLIES 2, ASTROS 1**

Seventh Inning

PHILLIES—Maddox singled to leftfield, Bowa sacrifice bunt, Cabell to Landestoy. Maddox advanced to second. Boone flied to Cruz. Maddox held at second. Gross (batting for Carlton) at bat, Maddox stole second. Gross hit bloop single to leftfield, Maddox scored. Rose grounded out, Howe to Forsch. One run, two hits, no errors, one left. **PHILLIES 3, ASTROS 1**

Game #2
OCTOBER 8, 1980
Astros 7, Phillies 4

Houston	ab	r	h	rbi	Phila'phia	ab	r	h	rbi
Puhl, rf	5	1	3	2	Rose, 1b	4	0	2	0
Cabell, 3b	4	0	0	0	McBride, rf	5	0	1	0
Morgan, 2b	2	1	1	0	Schmidt, 3b	6	1	2	0
L'stoy, pr-2b	0	1	0	0	Luzinski, lf	4	1	2	1
Cruz, lf	4	1	2	2	L. S'th, pr-lf	1	1	1	0
Cedeno, cf	5	1	1	1	Trillo, 2b	3	0	1	0
Howe, 1b	4	0	0	0	Maddox, cf	5	0	2	2
Bergman, 1b	1	0	1	2	Bowa, ss	4	1	2	0
Ashby, c	5	0	0	0	Boone, c	4	0	1	0
Reynolds, ss	3	1	0	0	Ruthven, p	2	0	0	0
Ryan, p	1	1	0	0	Gross, ph	0	0	0	0
Sambito, p	0	0	0	0	McGraw, p	0	0	0	0
D. Smith, p	0	0	0	0	Unser, ph	1	0	0	0
Leonard, ph	1	0	0	0	Reed, p	0	0	0	0
LaCorte, p	1	0	0	0	Saucier, p	0	0	0	0
Andujar, p	0	0	0	0	G. Vuk'ch, ph	1	0	0	0
Totals	36	7	8	7	Totals	40	4	14	3

Houston 001 000 110 4–7
Philadelphia 000 200 010 1–4

Houston	IP.	H.	R.	ER.	BB.	SO.
Ryan	6⅓	8	2	2	1	6
Sambito	⅓	0	0	0	1	1
D. Smith	1⅓	2	1	1	1	2
LaCorte (Winner)	1*	4	1	0	1	1
Andujar (Save)	1	0	0	0	1	0

Philadelphia	IP.	H.	R.	ER.	BB.	SO.
Ruthven	7	3	2	2	5	4
McGraw	1	2	1	1	0	0
Reed (Loser)	1⅓	2	4	4	1	1
Saucier	⅔	1	0	0	1	0

*Pitched to two batters in tenth.
Game-winning RBI—Cruz.
E—Schmidt, McBride, Reynolds. DP—Philadelphia 1. LOB—Houston 8, Philadelphia 14. 2B—Puhl, Morgan, Schmidt, Luzinski. 3B—Bergman. SH—Ryan, Trillo 2, Gross, Cabell. U—Tata, Froemming, Harvey, Vargo, Crawford and Engel. T—3:34. A—65,476.

How the Runs Scored

Third Inning

ASTROS—Ashby grounded out, Trillo to Rose. Reynolds walked. Ryan sacrifice bunt to Rose, unassisted, Reynolds advanced to second. Puhl singled to leftfield, Reynolds scored. Puhl advanced to third on Schmidt's throwing error to second. Schmidt's throw went to McBride in rightfield. Cabell struck out. One run, one hit, one error, one left. **ASTROS 1, PHILLIES 0**

Fourth Inning

PHILLIES—Schmidt doubled to rightfield. Luzinski doubled down the first-base line, Schmidt scored from second. Trillo sacrifice bunt, Howe to Morgan, Luzinski advanced to third. Maddox singled to leftfield, Luzinski scored from third. Bowa flied to Cruz. Boone at bat, Maddox caught stealing, Ashby to Reynolds. Two runs, three hits, no errors, none left. **PHILLIES 2, ASTROS 1**

Seventh Inning

ASTROS—Ashby flied to McBride. Reynolds grounded out, Rose to Ruthven covering first. Ryan walked. Puhl doubled to rightfield, Ryan scored from first. Puhl advanced to third on the throw home. Cabell flied to McBride. One run, one hit, no errors, one left. **PHILLIES 2, ASTROS 2**

Eighth Inning

ASTROS—(Philadelphia pitching change: Tug McGraw replaced Ruthven.) Morgan doubled to rightfield. Cruz singled to centerfield, Morgan scored from second. Cedeno grounded into double play, Bowa to Trillo to Rose. Howe grounded out, Trillo to Rose. One run, two hits, no errors, none left. **ASTROS 3, PHILLIES 2**

PHILLIES—Luzinski singled to leftfield. (Smith running for Luzinski.) Trillo sacrifice bunt, Bergman to Morgan. Smith advanced to second. Maddox singled to centerfield, Smith scored from second. Maddox advanced to second on the throw home. Bowa intentionally walked. Maddox at second. Bowa at first. Boone struck out. Unser flied to Cruz. One run, two hits, no errors, two left. **ASTROS 3, PHILLIES 3**

Tenth Inning

ASTROS—Puhl singled to rightfield. Cabell sacrifice bunt to Rose, unassisted. Puhl advanced to second. Morgan intentionally walked. Cruz singled to rightfield, Puhl scored. Morgan advanced to third, Cruz to second on throwing error by McBride. (Landestoy running for Morgan.) Cedeno grounded into fielder's choice, Bowa to Boone. Landestoy scored from third. Cedeno safe at first on fielder's choice. Cruz held at second. (Philadelphia pitching change: Kevin Saucier replaced Reed.) Bergman tripled to right-center. Cruz and Cedeno scored. Ashby grounded out, Schmidt to Rose. Bergman held at third. Reynolds intentionally walked. LaCorte grounded out, Schmidt to Rose. Four runs, three hits, one error, two left. **ASTROS 7, PHILLIES 3**

PHILLIES—Bowa infield single to first. Boone walked. (G. Vukovitch batting for Saucier.) (Kansas City pitching change: Andujar replaced LaCorte.) Vukovich flied to Cruz. Rose grounded into fielder's choice, Landestoy to Reynolds. Boone forced at second, Bowa scored. Rose advanced to second on throwing error by Reynolds. No RBI. McBride walked. Schmidt flied to Puhl. One run, one hit, one error, two left. **ASTROS 7, PHILLIES 4**

Game #3

OCTOBER 10, 1980

Astros 1, Phillies 0

Phila'phia	ab	r	h	rbi	Houston	ab	r	h	rbi
Rose, 1b	5	0	1	1	Puhl, rf-cf	4	0	2	0
McBride, rf	5	0	1	0	Cabell, 3b	4	0	2	0
Schmidt, 3b	5	0	1	0	Morgan, 2b	4	0	1	0
Luzinski, lf	5	0	0	0	Landestoy, pr	0	1	0	0
Trillo, 2b'	5	0	2	0	Cruz, lf	2	0	1	0
Maddox, cf	4	0	2	0	Cedeno, cf	3	0	0	0
Bowa, ss	3	0	0	0	Bergman, 1b	0	0	0	0
Boone, c	4	0	0	0	Howe, ph	0	0	0	0
Unser, ph	1	0	0	0	W'ling, 1b-rf	3	0	0	1
Moreland, c	0	0	0	0	Pujols, c	3	0	0	0
Christ'son, p	2	0	0	0	Reynolds, ss	3	0	0	0
G. Vuk'ch, ph	1	0	0	0	Niekro, p	3	0	0	0
Noles, p	0	0	0	0	Woods, ph	1	0	0	0
McGraw, p	1	0	0	0	Smith, p	0	0	0	0
Totals	41	0	7	0	Totals	31	1	6	1

Philadelphia	000	000	000	00–0		
Houston	000	000	000	01–1		

One out when winning run scored.

Philadelphia	IP.	H.	R.	ER.	BB.	SO.
Christenson	6	3	0	0	4	2
Noles	1⅓	1	0	0	1	0
McGraw (Loser)	3	2	1	1	3	1
Houston	IP.	H.	R.	ER.	BB.	SO.
Niekro	10	6	0	0	1	2
Smith (Winner)	1	1	0	0	1	2

Game-winning RBI—Walling.
E—Christenson, Bergman. DP—Philadelphia 2. LOB—Philadelphia 11, Houston 10. 2B—Puhl, Maddox, Trillo. 3B—Cruz, Morgan. SB—Schmidt, Maddox SH—Reynolds, Cabell. SF—Walling. HBP—By Niekro (Maddox). PB—Pujols. U—Froemming, Vargo, Harvey, Crawford, Engel and Tata. T—3:22. A—44,443.

How the Run Scored

Eleventh Inning

ASTROS—Morgan tripled to right. (Landestoy running for Morgan.) Cruz intentionally walked. Howe (hitting for Bergman) intentionally walked. Walling flied to Luzinski, Landestoy scored. One run, one hit, no errors, two left. **ASTROS 1, PHILLIES 0**

Game #4

OCTOBER 11, 1980

Phillies 5, Astros 3

Phila'phia	ab	r	h	rbi	Houston	ab	r	h	rbi
L. Smith, lf	4	1	2	0	Puhl, rf-cf	3	0	1	1
Unser, lf-rf	1	0	0	0	Cabell, 3b	4	1	1	0
Rose, 1b	4	2	2	1	Morgan, 2b	3	0	0	0
Schmidt, 3b	5	0	2	1	Woods, rf	2	0	0	0
McBride, rf	4	0	2	0	Walling, ph	1	0	0	0
Luzinski, ph	1	1	1	1	Leonard, rf	1	0	0	0
G. Vuk'ch, lf	1	0	0	0	Howe, ph	3	0	1	1
Trillo, 2b	4	0	2	2	Cruz, lf	3	0	0	0
Maddox, cf	4	0	0	0	Pujols, c	3	1	1	0
Bowa, ss	5	0	1	0	Bochy, c	1	0	0	0
Boone, c	4	0	0	0	Landestoy, ss	3	1	1	1
Carlton, p	2	0	0	0	Ruhle, p	3	0	0	0
Noles, p	0	0	0	0	D. Smith, p	0	0	0	0
Saucier, p	0	0	0	0	Sambito, p	0	0	0	0
Reed, p	0	0	0	0					
Gross, ph	1	1	1	0					
Brusstar, p	1	0	0	0					
McGraw, p	0	0	0	0					
Totals	40	5	13	5	Totals	30	3	5	3

Philadelphia	000	000	030	2–5		
Houston	000	110	001	0–3		

Philadelphia	IP.	H.	R.	ER.	BB.	SO.
Carlton	5⅓	4	2	2	5	3
Noles	1⅓	0	0	0	2	0
Saucier	0*	0	0	0	1	0
Reed	⅓	0	0	0	0	0
Brusstar (Winner)	2	1	1	1	1	0
McGraw (Save)	1	0	0	0	0	1
Houston	IP.	H.	R.	ER.	BB.	SO.
Ruhle	7†	8	3	3	1	3
D. Smith	0‡	1	0	0	0	0
Sambito (Loser)	3	4	2	2	1	5

*Pitched to one batter in seventh.
†Pitched to three batters in eighth.
‡Pitched to one batter in eighth.

Game-winning RBI—Luzinski.
E—Landestoy. DP—Philadelphia 3, Houston 2. LOB—Philadelphia 8, Houston 8. 2B—Howe, Cabell, Luzinski, Trillo. 3B—Pujols. SB—McBride, L. Smith, Landestoy, Woods, Puhl, Bowa. SH—Sambito. SF—Howe, Trillo. U—Harvey, Vargo, Crawford, Engel, Tata and Froemming. T—3:55. A—44,952.

How the Runs Scored

Fourth Inning

ASTROS—Cabell doubled to left. Morgan grounded out to Rose, Cabell advanced to third. Woods walked. Howe flied to Smith, scoring Cabell, Woods out at third. One run, one hit, no errors, none left. **ASTROS 1, PHILLIES 0**

Fifth Inning

ASTROS—Cruz flied to Maddox. Pujols tripled to center. Landestoy singled to left, scoring Pujols. Ruhle struck out. Landestoy stole second. Puhl walked. Cabell flied to Maddox. One run, two hits, no errors, two left. **ASTROS 2, PHILLIES 0**

Eighth Inning

PHILLIES—Gross (hitting for Reed) singled to center. Smith singled to left, Gross advanced to second. Rose singled to right, scoring Gross, Smith to third, Rose to second on throw. (Houston pitching change: Smith replaced Ruhle.) Schmidt is safe on an infield hit, scoring Smith. Rose advances to third. (Houston pitching change: Sambito replaces Smith.) McBride strikes out. Trillo flies to Leonard, scoring Rose. Schmidt is doubled off first. Three runs, four hits, no errors, none left. **PHILLIES 3, ASTROS 2**

Ninth Inning

ASTROS—Landestoy walked. Sambito sacrificed Landestoy to second. Puhl singled to right, scoring Landestoy. Cabell flied to McBride, Puhl is doubled off first. One run, one hit, no errors, one left. **PHILLIES 3, ASTROS 3**

Tenth Inning

PHILLIES—Unser struck out. Rose singled to center. Schmidt flied to Cruz. Luzinski (hitting for McBride) doubled to left, scoring Rose, Luzinski to third. Trillo doubled to center, scoring Luzinski. Maddox intentionally walked. Bowa struck out. Two runs, three hits, no errors, one left. **PHILLIES 5, ASTROS 3**

Game #5
OCTOBER 12, 1980
Phillies 8, Astros 7

Phila'phia	ab	r	h	rbi	Houston	ab	r	h	rbi
Rose, 1b	3	0	1	1	Puhl, cf	6	3	4	0
McBride, rf	3	0	0	0	Cabell, 3b	5	1	1	0
Moreland, ph	1	0	0	1	Morgan, 2b	4	0	0	0
Aviles, pr	0	1	0	0	Lan'stoy, 2b	1	0	1	1
McGraw, p	1	0	0	0	Cruz, lf	3	0	2	2
G. Vuk'ch, ph	1	0	0	0	Walling, rf	5	2	1	1
Ruthven, p	0	0	0	0	LaCorte, p	0	0	0	0
Schmidt, 3b	5	0	0	0	Howe, 1b	4	0	2	1
Luzinski, lf	3	0	1	0	B'man, pr-1b	1	0	0	0
Smith, pr	0	0	0	0	Pujols, c	1	0	0	0
Christ'son, p	0	0	0	0	Ashby, ph-c	3	0	1	1
Reed, p	0	0	0	0	Reynolds, ss	5	1	2	0
Unser, ph-rf	2	2	2	1	Ryan, p	3	0	0	0
Trillo, 2b	5	1	3	2	Sambito, p	0	0	0	0
Maddox, cf	4	1	1	1	Forsch, p	0	0	0	0
Bowa, ss	5	1	2	0	Woods, ph-rf	1	0	0	0
Boone, c	3	1	2	2	Heep, ph	1	0	0	0
Bystrom, p	2	0	0	0					
Brusstar, p	0	0	0	0					
Gross, lf	2	1	1	0					
Totals	39	8	13	8	Totals	43	7	14	6

Philadelphia	020	000	050	1–8			
Houston	100	001	320	0–7			

Philadelphia	IP.	H.	R.	ER.	BB.	SO.
Bystrom	5⅓	7	2	1	2	1
Brusstar	⅔	0	0	0	0	0
Christenson	⅔	2	3	3	1	0
Reed	⅓	1	0	0	0	0
McGraw	1	4	2	2	0	2
Ruthven (Winner)	2	0	0	0	0	0

Houston	IP.	H.	R.	ER.	BB.	SO.
Ryan	7*	8	6	6	2	8
Sambito	⅓	0	0	0	0	0
Forsch	⅔	2	1	1	0	1
LaCorte (Loser)	2	3	1	1	1	1

*Pitched to four batters in eighth.

Game-winning RBI—Maddox.

E—Trillo, Luzinski. DP—Houston 2. LOB—Philadelphia 5, Houston 10. 2B—Cruz, Reynolds, Unser, Maddox. 3B—Howe, Trillo. SB—Puhl. SH—Cabell, Boone. WP—Christenson. U—Vargo, Crawford, Engel, Tata, Froemming and Harvey. T—3:38. A—44,802.

How the Runs Scored

First Inning

ASTROS—Puhl singled to left. Cabell flied to McBride. Puhl stole second. Morgan flied to Maddox, Puhl advanced to third. Cruz doubled to right, Puhl scored. Walling grounded out to Trillo. One run, two hits, no errors, one left. **ASTROS 1, PHILLIES 0**

Second Inning

PHILLIES—Luzinski struck out. Trillo singled to center. Maddox walked, Trillo advanced to second. Bowa grounded out to Ryan, Trillo advanced to third, Maddox to second. Boone singled to center scoring Trillo and Maddox. Bystrom grounded to Reynolds, who forced Boone at second. Two runs, two hits, no errors, one left. **PHILLIES 2, ASTROS 1**

Sixth Inning

ASTROS—Walling reached second on Luzinski's two-base error. Howe grounded out, Schmidt to Rose. Ashby (hitting for Pujols) singled to center. Walling scored. (Philadelphia pitching change: Brusstar replaced Bystrom.) Reynolds flied to Maddox. Ryan flied to McBride. One run, one hit, one error, one left. **PHILLIES 2, ASTROS 2**

Seventh Inning

ASTROS—(Philadelphia pitching change: Christenson replaced Brusstar.) Puhl singled to right. Cabell sacrificed Puhl to second. Morgan grounded to Schmidt, who threw to Rose at first. Cruz intentionally walked. Walling singled to right. Puhl scored, Cruz to third. Cruz scored on wild pitch, Walling to third. (Philadelphia pitching change: Reed replaced Christenson.) Howe tripled to right-center. Walling scored. (Bergman running for Howe.) Ashby flied to Gross. Three runs, three hits, no errors, one left. **ASTROS 5, PHILLIES 2**

Eighth Inning

PHILLIES—Bowa singled to center. Boone singled off Ryan's glove. Gross safe at first on a bunt, bases loaded. Rose walked, Bowa scored, bases loaded. (Houston pitching change: Sambito replaced Ryan.) Moreland (hitting for McBride) grounded to Landestoy, who threw Gross out at second. Boone scored. (Houston pitching change: Forsch replaced Sambito.) (Aviles running for Moreland.) Schmidt struck out. Unser (hitting for Reed) singled to right. Gross scored, Aviles to third. Trillo tripled to left. Aviles and Unser scored. Maddox flied to Puhl. Five runs, five hits, no errors, one left. **PHILLIES 7, ASTROS 5**

ASTROS—(McGraw pitching for Philadelphia.) Reynolds safe on infield hit. Woods (hitting for Forsch) struck out. Puhl singled to right, Reynolds to third. Cabell struck out. Landestoy singled to left. Reynolds scored, Puhl advanced to second. Cruz singled to center. Puhl scored, Landestoy advanced to third. Walling grounded to Bowa, who forced Cruz at second. Two runs, four hits, no errors, two left. **PHILLIES 7, ASTROS 7**

Tenth Inning

PHILLIES—Schmidt struck out. Unser doubled to right. Trillo flied to Puhl, Unser advanced to third. Maddox doubled to center. Unser scored. Bowa lined out to Landestoy. One run, two hits, no errors, one left. **PHILLIES 8, ASTROS 7**

The World Series

Game #1
OCTOBER 14, 1980
Phillies 7, Royals 6

Kansas City	ab	r	h	rbi	Phila'phia	ab	r	h	rbi
Wilson, lf	5	0	0	0	L. Smith, lf	4	0	2	0
McRae, dh	3	1	1	0	Gross, lf	1	0	0	0
G. Brett, 3b	4	1	1	0	Rose, 1b	3	1	0	0
Aikens, 1b	4	2	2	4	Schmidt, 3b	2	2	1	0
Porter, c	2	1	0	0	McBride, rf	4	1	3	3
Otis, cf	4	1	3	2	Luzinski, dh	3	0	0	0
Hurdle, rf	3	0	1	0	Maddox, cf	3	0	0	1
Wathan, rf	1	0	0	0	Trillo, 2b	4	1	1	0
White, 2b	4	0	1	0	Bowa, ss	4	1	1	0
Wash'gtn, ss	4	0	0	0	Boone, c	4	1	3	2
Totals	34	6	9	6	Totals	32	7	11	6

```
Kansas City . . . . . . . . . . . . . . . 022  000  020–6
Philadelphia . . . . . . . . . . . . . . . 005  110  00x–7
```

Houston	IP.	H.	R.	ER.	BB.	SO.
Leonard, L. 0-1	3⅔	6	6	6	1	3
Martin	4	5	1	1	1	1
Quisenberry	½	0	0	0	0	0

Philadelphia	IP.	H.	R.	ER.	BB.	SO.
Walk, (W. 1-0)	7	8	6	6	3	3
McGraw, (S, 1)	2	1	0	0	0	2

Walk pitched to two batters in eighth.

E—Leonard. DP—Philadelphia 1. LOB—Kansas City 4, Philadelphia 6. 2B—Boone 2, G. Brett. HR—Otis 1, Aikens 2, McBride 1. SB—Bowa, White. SF—Maddox. HBP—Leonard (Rose), Martin (Luzinski). WP—Walk. T—3:01. A—65,791.

How the Runs Scored

Second Inning

ROYALS—Porter walked on 3-2 count. Otis hit home run with one on to leftfield on a 2-1 count. Hurdle hit deep fly to Smith in left-center. White flew out to McBride in right. Washington grounded out, Rose to Walk covering at first. Two runs, one hit, no errors, none left. **ROYALS 2, PHILLIES 0**

Third Inning

ROYALS—Wilson grounded out, Trillo to Rose. McRae singled up the middle. Brett struck out swinging on appeal. Aikens hit home run with one on to right-center on 1-2 count. Porter walked on 3-1 count. Otis beat out topped roller to Schmidt for infield single. Porter advanced to second. Hurdle singled to Smith in left, Smith threw out Porter at homeplate. Two runs, four hits, no errors, two left. **ROYALS 4, PHILLIES 0**

PHILLIES—Trillo grounded out, Washington to Aikens at first. Bowa singled through the middle for the Phillies' first hit of the game. Bowa stole second on 1-1 count, Boone at bat. Boone doubled to leftfield corner, driving in Bowa from second. Smith singled to left, Boone stopped at third initially, scored when Smith was caught in rundown between first and second, Smith out, Wilson to Brett to White to Aikens. No RBI. Rose hit by pitch (Leonard). Schmidt walked on 3-1 count, Rose advancing to second. McBride hit home run with two on on 1-1 count. Luzinski struck out swinging. Five runs, four hits, no errors, none left. **PHILLIES 5, ROYALS 4**

Fourth Inning

PHILLIES—Maddox struck out swinging. Trillo beat out infield bouncer to Washington behind second base. Trillo advanced to second base on Leonard's throwing error to first on pick-off attempt. Bowa grounded out, White to Aikens at first, Trillo advancing to third. Boone doubled to right-field corner, driving in Trillo. (Kansas City pitching change: Renie Martin replaced Leonard.) Smith flied out to Hurdle on Martin's first pitch. One run, two hits one error, one left. **PHILLIES 6, ROYALS 4**

Fifth Inning

PHILLIES—Rose grounded out, Washington to Aikens at first. Schmidt walked on 3-1 count. McBride singled to left, Schmidt advancing to second. Luzinski hit by pitch (Martin) on first pitch to load bases. Maddox hit SF to Wilson in left, scoring Schmidt from third, McBride and Luzinski holding at second and first. Trillo popped up to Aikens at first. One run, one hit, no errors, two left. **PHILLIES 7, ROYALS 4**

Eighth Inning

ROYALS—Brett doubled to left-center. Brett advanced to third on wild pitch with Aikens at bat. Aikens hit second homer of game (with one on) to right-center, for third and fourth RBIs of game. Aikens homer came on 2-0 count. (Philadelphia pitching change: Tug McGraw replaced Walk.) Porter flied out to Gross. Otis singled to left. Wathan pinch-hit for Hurdle, grounded into a double play, Washington to White to Aikens. Two runs, three hits, no errors, none left. **PHILLIES 7, ROYALS 6**

Game #2
OCTOBER 15, 1980
Phillies 6, Royals 4

Kansas City	ab	r	h	rbi	Phila'phia	ab	r	h	rbi
Wilson, lf	4	1	1	0	L. Smith, lf	3	0	0	0
Wash'gtn, ss	4	0	1	0	Unser, cf	1	1	1	1
G. Brett, 3b	2	0	2	0	Rose, 1b	4	0	0	0
Chalk, 3b	0	1	0	0	McBride, rf	3	1	1	1
Porter, ph	1	0	0	0	Schmidt, 3b	4	1	2	1
McRae, dh	4	1	3	0	Moreland, dh	4	1	2	1
Otis, cf	5	1	2	2	Maddox, cf	3	1	1	0
Wathan, c	3	0	0	1	Gross, lf	1	0	0	0
Aikens, 1b	3	0	1	0	Trillo, 2b	2	0	1	1
LaCock, 1b	0	0	0	0	Bowa, ss	3	0	1	1
Cardenal, rf	4	0	0	0	Boone, c	1	1	0	0
White, 2b	4	0	1	0					
Totals	34	4	11	3	Totals	29	6	8	6

```
Kansas City . . . . . . . . . . . . . . . 000  001  300–4
Philadelphia . . . . . . . . . . . . . . . 000  020  04x–6
```

Kansas City	IP.	H.	R.	ER.	BB.	SO.
Gura	6	4	2	2	2	2
Quisenberry	2	4	4	4	1	0

Philadelphia	IP.	H.	R.	ER.	BB.	SO.
Carlton, (W. 1-0)	8	10	4	3	6	10
Reed, (S, 1)	1	1	0	0	0	2

E—Trillo. DP—Kansas City 2, Philadelphia 4. LOB—Kansas City 11, Philadelphia 3. 2B—Maddox, Otis, Unser, Schmidt. SB—Wilson, Chalk. S—Washington. SF—Trillo, Wathan. WP—Carlton. T—3:01. A—65,775.

Fifth Inning

PHILLIES—Schmidt grounded out, Brett to Aikens. Moreland singled to deep short. Maddox lined double into leftfield corner, Moreland stopping at third. Trillo flied to Cardenal, scoring Moreland and sending Maddox to third. Bowa lined singled to left, scoring Maddox. Boone walked. Smith flied to Cardenal. Two runs, three hits, no errors, two left. **PHILLIES 2, ROYALS 0**

Sixth Inning

ROYALS—Otis lined single to center. Wathan walked on four pitches. Aikens safe on Trillo's throwing error, Otis scoring and Wathan to third. Cardenal struck out swinging. White grounded into double play, Bowa to Trillo to Rose. One run (unearned), one hit, one error, one left. **PHILLIES 2, ROYALS 1**

Seventh Inning

ROYALS—Wilson walked on four pitches. Washington sacrificed Wilson to second, Carlton to Trillo. Wilson stole third with Chalk batting. Chalk walked. Chalk stole second and Wilson held third with McRae batting. McRae walked. Otis lined double to leftfield corner, scoring Wilson and Chalk and sending McRae to third. Wathan flied to Maddox, scoring McRae and Otis was out on the play going Maddox to Rose to Schmidt. Thre runs, one hit, no errors, none left. **ROYALS 4, PHILLIES 2**

Eighth Inning

PHILLIES—Boone walked on 3-2 pitch. Unser batted for Smith and lined double to left-center, scoring Boone. Rose grounded out to LaCock sending Unser to third. McBride bounced single to right, scoring Unser. Schmidt doubled to right and went to third on throw as McBride scored. Moreland lined single to center, scoring Schmidt. Gross batted for Maddox and grounded into double play, Washington to White to LaCock. Four runs, four hits, no errors, none left. **PHILLIES 6, ROYALS 4**

Game #3
OCTOBER 17, 1980
Royals 4, Phillies 3

Phila'phia	ab	r	h	rbi	Kansas City	ab	r	h	rbi
L. Smith, lf	4	0	2	1	Wilson, lf	4	1	0	0
Gross, lf	0	0	0	0	White, 2b	5	0	0	0
Rose, 1b	4	0	1	1	Brett, 3b	4	1	2	1
Schmidt, 3b	5	1	1	1	Aikens, 1b	5	1	2	1
McBride, rf	5	0	2	0	McRae, dh	4	0	2	1
Moreland, dh	5	0	1	0	Otis, cf	4	1	2	1
Maddox, cf	4	0	1	0	Hurdle, rf	4	0	2	0
Trillo, 2b	5	1	2	0	Concep'cn, pr	0	0	0	0
Bowa, ss	5	1	3	0	Cardenal, rf	0	0	0	0
Boone, c	4	0	1	0	Washg'tn, ss	4	0	1	0
Totals	41	3	14	3	Totals	38	4	11	4

Philadelphia	. . . .	0 1 0	0 1 0	0 1 0	0–3
Kansas City	. . . .	1 0 0	1 0 0	1 0 0	1–4

Philadelphia	IP.	H.	R.	ER.	BB.	SO.
Ruthven	 9	9	3	3	0	7
McGraw (L. 0-1)	. . . . . ⅔	2	1	1	2	1

Kansas City	IP.	H.	R.	ER.	BB.	SO.
Gale	. . . . 4⅓	7	2	2	3	3
Martin	. . . . 3⅓	5	1	1	1	1
Quis'berry (W. 1-1)	. . 2⅓	2	0	0	2	0

Two out when winning run scored.

DP—Philadelphia 1, Kansas City 2. LOB—Philadelphia 15, Kansas City 7. 2B—Trillo, Aikens. 3B—Brett. HR—Brett 1, Schmidt 1, Otis 2. SB—Hurdle, Bowa, Wilson. S—Gross. T—3:19. A—42,380.

How the Runs Scored

First Inning

ROYALS-Wilson grounded out, Trillo to Rose at first base. White grounded out, Schmidt to Rose at first. Brett hit 1-1 pitch into right-field stands, his first World Series home run, third in post-season play in 1980. Aikens grounded out, Trillo to Rose at first. One run, one hit, no errors, none left. **ROYALS 1, PHILLIES 0**

Second Inning

PHILLIES—Maddox grounded out, Brett to Aikens at first. Trillo got infield single on line drive that bounced straight up in the air off either the front of the mound or Gale's foot. Bowa singled to right, Trillo advancing to second. Boone walked, loading bases. Smith lined back to Gale who threw him out at first, Trillo scored from third, 1 RBI, Bowa and Boone advanced. Rose walked, loading the bases again. Schmidt flied out to Otis in left-center. One run, two hits, no errors, three left. **ROYALS 1, PHILLIES 1**

Fourth Inning

ROYALS—Brett popped up to Schmidt in foul territory between third and home. Aikens tripled to leftfield, the ball going to the leftfield wall when Smith dove attempting a shoestring catch. McRae singled to rightfield, driving in Aikens on next pitch. Otis grounded out, Trillo to Rose, advancing McRae to second. Hurdle grounded out, Trillo to Rose at first. One run, two hits, no errors, one left. **ROYALS 2, PHILLIES 1**

Fifth Inning

PHILLIES—Schmidt hit 2-1 pitch over leftfield wall for a home run into left field bullpen. McBride struck out. Moreland singled to left. (Kansas City pitching change: Renie Martin replaced Gale.) Maddox beat out infield single, Washington to White attempting to force Moreland at second. Trillo hit into inning-ending double play, White to Washington at second to Aikens at first. One run, three hits, no errors, one left. **ROYALS 2, PHILLIES 2**

Seventh Inning

ROYALS—McRae grounded out, Schmidt to Rose at first. Otis hit 1-1 pitch for home run over rightfield fence, his second home run of 1980 World Series. Hurdle singled to rightfield. Porter struck out swinging on a 3-2 count, Hurdle stealing second. Washington pop-fouled to Schmidt at the railing. One run, two hits, no errors, one left. **ROYALS 3, PHILLIES 2**

Eighth Inning

PHILLIES—Trillo flied to Wilson in left. Bowa topped roller to left side of mound and beat Martin's throw to Aikens at first for infield single. Boone flied to Otis in center. Bowa stole second with Smith at bat, uncontested (Porter dropped ball as he started to throw). Smith walked on 3-2 count. Rose singled over White's head into rightfield, driving in Bowa, moving Smith over to second. (Kansas City pitching change: Dan Quisenberry replaced Martin.) Schmidt flied to Otis in center (Otis thus set a World Series record with nine-put-outs in the game). One run, two hits, no errors, two left. **ROYALS 3, PHILLIES 3**

Tenth Inning

ROYALS—(Defensive change for Philadelphia: Tug McGraw replaced Ruthven.) Washington singled to left on McGraw's first pitch of the game. Wilson, wanting to sacrifice, walked on four pitches, Washington moving to second. Washington caught stealing at third, Boone to Schmidt, when White, attempting to sacrifice, failed to make contact. White struck out swinging. Wilson stole second, in spite of a pitch-out. Brett walked intentionally. Aikens hit 2-1 pitch into left-center for single, driving in Wilson from second with game-winning run. One run, two hits, no errors, two left. **ROYALS 4, PHILLIES 3**

Game #4
OCTOBER 18, 1980
Royals 5, Phillies 3

Phila'phia	ab	r	h	rbi	Kansas City	ab	r	h	rbi
L. Smith, dh	4	0	0	0	Wilson, lf	4	1	1	0
Rose, 1b	4	1	2	0	White, 2b	5	0	0	0
McBride, rf	3	0	1	0	Brett, 3b	5	1	1	1
Schmidt, 3b	3	0	1	1	Aikens, 1b	3	2	2	3
Unser, lf	4	0	1	0	McRae, dh	4	1	2	0
Maddox, cf	4	0	1	0	Otis, cf	4	0	2	1
Trillo, 2b	4	2	1	0	Hurdle, rf	2	0	1	0
Bowa, ss	4	0	2	1	Porter, c	3	0	0	0
Boone, c	3	0	1	1	Washg'ton, ss	4	0	1	0
Totals	33	3	10	3	Totals	34	5	10	5

```
Philadelphia .................. 010  000  110—3
Kansas City .................. 410  000  00x—5
```

Philadelphia	IP	H.	R.	ER.	BB.	SO.
Chris'son (L. 0-1)	⅓	5	4	4	0	0
Noles	4⅔	5	1	1	2	6
Saucier	⅔	0	0	0	2	0
Brusstar	2⅓	0	0	0	1	0

Kansas City	IP	H.	R.	ER.	BB.	SO.
Leonard (W. 1-1)	7	9	3	2	1	2
Quis'berry (S, 1)	2	1	0	0	0	0

Leonard pitched to one batter in the eighth.

E—White, Christenson, Washington. DP—Kansas City 1. LOB—Philadelphia 6, Kansas City 10. 2B—McRae 2, Otis, Hurdle, McBride, Trillo, Rose. 3B—Brett. HR—Aikens 2 (4). SB—Bowa. SB—Boone, Schmidt. WP—Leonard, Saucier. T—2:37. A—42,363.

How the Runs Scored

First Inning

ROYALS—Wilson hit 2-1 pitch for a single to left. Wilson advanced to third when Christenson's pick-off attempt went pastRose for a two-base error on the throw. White flied to McBride in shallow right, Wilson holding at third. Brett tripled down rightfield line on 1-1 pitch, driving in Wilson from third. Aikens sent 0-1 pitch into the rightfield waterfall for a home run, scoring Brett ahead of him, his third HR of World Series. McRae doubled through the middle when Maddox was slow to field the ball. Otis doubled off rightfield wall (0-1 pitch), driving in McRae from second. (Philadelphia pitching change: Dickie Noles replaced Christenson.) Hurdle walked on four pitches. Porter struck out swinging. Washington was safe at first for infield single when he beat out throw to Rose from Bowa behind second, Otis and Hurdle advancing, bases loaded. Wilson grounded out, Rose to Noles covering first on a very close play. (First inning took 27 minutes.) Four runs, six hits, one error, three left. **ROYALS 4, PHILLIES 0**

Second Inning

PHILLIES—Unser flied to Wilson in left. Maddox singled to right. Trillo forced Maddox at second, White to Washington, advanced to second on throwing error to first by Washington. Bowa singled to left, driving in Trillo from second, advanced to second on throw to plate by Wilson. Boone grounded out, Brett to Aikens. Run unearned. One run, two hits, one error, one left. **ROYALS 4, PHILLIES 1**

ROYALS—White flied to Maddox in center. Brett grounded out, Trillo to Rose at first. Aikens hit 2-1 pitch deep into rightfield bullpen for his second home run of game, fourth of 1980 Series. McRae doubled to rightfield. Otis flied to McBride in right. One run, two hits, no errors, one left. **ROYALS 5, PHILLIES 1**

Seventh Inning

PHILLIES—Maddox popped to Washington. Trillo doubled to right-field wall. Bowa singled to left, Trillo advancing to third. Boone sent sacrifice fly to deep left-center, caught on a fine play by Wilson, driving in Trillo from third, Bowa holding at second. Bowa stole second. Smith grounded out Washington to Aikens. One run, one hit, no errors, one left. **ROYALS 5, PHILLIES 2**

Eighth Inning

PHILLIES—Rose led off inning with a double to the wall in left-center. (Kansas City pitching change: Quisenberry replaced Leonard.) McBride grounded out, White to Aikens, Rose advancing to third. Schmidt hit sacrifice fly to deep right to Hurdle, driving in Rose from third. Unser singled to right. Maddox grounded out, Washington to Aikens. One run, two hits, no errors, one left. **ROYALS 5, PHILLIES 3**

Game #5
OCTOBER 19, 1980
Phillies 4, Royals 3

Phila'phia	ab	r	h	rbi	Kansas City	ab	r	h	rbi
Rose, 1b	4	0	0	0	Wilson, lf	5	0	2	0
McBrice, rf	4	1	0	0	White, 2b	3	0	0	0
Schmidt, 3b	4	2	2	2	Brett, 3b	5	0	1	1
Luzinski, lf	2	0	0	0	Aikens, 1b	3	0	1	0
L. Smith, lf	0	0	0	0	Concep'cn, 1b	0	0	0	0
Unser, lf	1	1	1	1	McRae, dh	5	0	1	0
Moreland, dh	3	0	1	0	Otis, cf	3	1	2	1
Maddox, cf	4	0	0	0	Hurdle, rf	3	1	1	0
Trillo, 2b	4	0	1	1	Cardenal, rf	2	0	0	0
Bowa, ss	4	0	1	0	Porter, c	4	0	2	0
Boone, c	3	0	1	0	Wash'gtn, ss	3	1	2	1
Totals	33	4	7	4	Totals	36	3	12	3

Philadelphia	. . . .	000	200	002–4
Kansas City	. . . .	000	012	000–3

Philadelphia	IP.	H.	R.	ER.	BB.	SO.
Bystrom	5	10	3	3	1	4
Reed	1	1	0	0	0	0
McGraw (W. 1-1)	3	1	0	0	4	5

Bystrom pitched to three batters in sixth.

Kansas City	IP.	H.	R.	ER.	BB.	SO.
Gura	6⅓	4	2	1	1	2
Quis'berry (L, 1-2)	2⅔	3	2	2	0	0

E—Aikens, Brett. DP—Kansas City 2. LOB—Philadelphia 4, Kansas City 13. 2B—Wilson, McRae, Unser. HR—Schmidt (2), Otis (3). SB—Brett. S—White, Moreland. SF—Washington. T—2:51. A—42,369.

Fourth Inning

PHILLIES—Rose grounded out off Gura's glove, White to Aikens. McBride safe at first when Aikens missed tag of bag after taking throw from Gura, who fielded McBride's infield roller between the mound and first. Aikens charged with an error. Schmidt hit 2-2 pitch for a homerun to centerfield, clearing the wall at the 410 sign, scoring McBride ahead of him. (It was Schmidt's second homer of the Series.) Luzinski grounded out, Brett to Aikens. Moreland popped up in the infield to Brett. Two runs, one hit, one error, one left. (One run unearned.) **PHILLIES 2, ROYALS 0**

Fifth Inning

ROYALS—Washington singled to center. Wilson lined toward Schmidt, who could not handle it, Wilson safe at first on infield hit, Washington advancing to second. White sacrificed Washington to third, and Wilson to second, Schmidt to Trillo covering at first (Trillo apparently spiked by White at first). Brett grounded out, Trillo to Rose, Washington scoring from third, Wilson advancing to third. Aikens walked on 3-1 pitch. McRae flied to McBride in foul territory deep in right, McBride bouncing off wall after making the catch. One run, two hits, no errors, two left. **PHILLIES 2, ROYALS 1**

Sixth Inning

ROYALS—Otis homered to leftfield on 0-1 pitch, his third homer of the Series. Hurdle singled to right-center. Porter singled to right, sending Hurdle to third. (Philadelphia pitching change: Ron Reed replaced Bystrom.) Washington drove in Hurdle from third with a sacrifice fly to Luzinski in left. Wilson doubled to wall in right, Porter, trying to score from first was thrown out, McBride to Trillo to Boone. White popped up in foul territory to Schmidt. Two runs, four hits, no errors, one left. **ROYALS 3, PHILLIES 2**

Ninth Inning

PHILLIES—Schmidt singled off Brett's glove. Unser doubled down rightfield line, driving in Schmidt from first. Moreland laid down sacrifice bunt down firstbase line, tagged out by Aikens, Unser advancing to third. Maddox grounded out, Brett to Aikens, Unser holding at third. Trillo lined back to Quisenberry, ball went off Quisenberry, Trillo safe at first, Unser scoring go-ahead run from third. Bowa grounded out, Washington to Aikens. Two runs, three hits, no errors, one left. **PHILLIES 4 ROYALS 3**

Game #6
OCTOBER 21, 1980
Phillies 4, Royals 1

Kansas City	ab	r	h	rbi	Phila'phia	ab	r	h	rbi
Wilson, lf	4	0	0	0	L. Smith, lf	4	2	1	0
Wash'gtn, ss	3	0	1	1	Gross, lf	0	0	0	0
Brett, 3b	4	0	2	0	Rose, 1b	4	0	3	0
McRae, dh	2	0	0	0	Schmidt, 3b	3	0	1	2
Otis, cf	3	0	0	0	McBride, rf	4	0	0	1
Aikens, 1b	2	0	0	0	Luzinski, dh	4	0	0	0
Concpcn, pr	0	0	0	0	Maddox, cf	4	0	2	0
Wathan, c	3	1	2	0	Trillo, 2b	4	0	0	0
Cardenal, rf	4	0	2	0	Bowa, ss	4	1	1	0
White, 2b	4	0	0	0	Boone, c	2	1	1	1
Totals	31	1	7	1	Totals	33	4	9	4

```
Kansas City  ................ 000  000  010—1
Philadelphia ................ 002  011  00x—4
```

Kansas City	IP.	H.	R.	ER.	BB.	SO.
Gale (L. 0-1)	2	4	2	1	1	1
Martin	2⅓	1	1	1	1	0
Splittorff	1⅔	4	1	1	0	0
Pattin	1	0	0	0	0	2
Quis'berry	1	0	0	0	0	0

Philadelphia	IP.	H.	R.	ER.	BB.	SO.
Carlton, (W. 2-0)	7	4	1	1	3	7
McGraw, (S, 2)	2	3	0	0	2	2

Gale pitched to four batters in third. Splittorff pitched to one batter in seventh. Carlton pitched to two batters in eighth.

E—White, Aikens. DP—Kansas City 1, Philadelphia 2. LOB—Kansas City 9, Philadelphia 7. 2B—Maddox, L. Smith, Bowa. SF—Washington. T—3:00. A—65,839.

How the Runs Scored

Third Inning

PHILLIES—Boone walked on four pitches. Smith grounded to White, who threw to Washington covering second, attempting to force Boone. Boone called safe at second by umpire Kunkel, White charged with an error on throw. Rose laid down bunt toward third base, Brett fielded bunt, but Rose beat out throw to first for base hit, Boone advancing to third, Smith to second to load bases. Schmidt singled to right-center, driving in Boone and Smith for first runs of game (Smith fell down rounding third, but was safe when no throw was made to home). (Kansas City pitching change: Martin replaced Gale.) McBride popped up to White in foul territory behind first base, runners holding. Luzinski lined to Brett, runners holding. Maddox flied to Cardenal. Two runs, two hits, one error, two left. (One run unearned.) **PHILLIES 2, ROYALS 0**

Fifth Inning

PHILLIES—Smith doubled to left-center. Rose flied to Otis in deep center, Smith advancing to third. Schmidt walked on 3-2 count. (Kansas City pitching change: Splittorff replaced Martin.) McBride topped roller to left of mound, Washington had no chance at double play, threw to Aikens for out on McBride, Smith scoring from third. Luzinski grounded out, Washington to Aikens. One run, one hit, no errors, one left. **PHILLIES 3, ROYALS 0**

Sixth Inning

PHILLIES—Maddox singled to left. Trillo grounded into double play, Splittorff to Washington to Aikens. Bowa doubled over Wilson's head in left. Boone singled up the middle to drive in Bowa from second. Smith flied to Otis. One run, three hits, no errors, one left. **PHILLIES 4, ROYALS 0**

Eighth Inning

ROYALS—White walked on 3-2 count. Cardenal singled to left, White advanced to second. (Philadelphia pitching change: McGraw replaced Carlton.) White popped to Rose in foul territory. Wilson walked to load the bases on 3-1 count. Washington flied to Maddox in left-center to drive in White from third for SF, Cardenal and Wilson holding at second and first. Brett got infield single when his grounder was fielded behind first by Rose, but he narrowly beat McGraw covering at first. Bases loaded. McRae grounded out, Trillo to Rose. One run, two hits, no errors, three left. **PHILLIES 4, ROYALS 1**

Phillies Statistics

1980 LEAGUE CHAMPIONSHIP SERIES

Player	Avg	G	AB	R	H	TB	2B	3B	HR	RBI	SH	SF	BB	HP	SO	SB	CS
Aviles	---	1	0	1	0	0	0	0	0	0	0	0	0	0	0	0	0
Boone	.222	5	18	1	4	4	0	0	0	2	1	0	1	0	2	0	0
Bowa	.316	5	19	2	6	6	0	0	0	0	1	0	3	0	3	1	0
Gross	.750	4	4	2	3	3	0	0	0	1	1	0	0	0	0	0	0
Luzinski	.294	5	17	3	5	10	2	0	1	4	0	0	2	0	6	0	1
Maddox	.300	5	20	2	6	8	2	0	0	3	0	0	0	0	2	2	0
McBride	.238	5	21	0	5	5	0	0	0	0	0	0	1	1	5	2	0
Moreland	.000	2	1	0	0	0	0	0	0	0	0	0	0	0	0	0	0
Rose	.400	5	20	3	8	8	0	0	0	2	0	0	5	0	3	0	2
Schmidt	.208	5	24	1	5	6	1	0	0	0	0	0	1	0	6	1	0
Smith	.600	3	5	2	3	3	0	0	0	1	0	0	0	0	2	1	0
Trillo	.381	5	21	1	8	12	2	1	0	4	2	0	0	0	2	0	0
Unser	.400	5	5	2	2	3	1	0	0	1	0	1	0	0	0	1	0
G. Vukovich	.000	3	3	0	0	0	0	0	0	0	0	0	0	0	0	0	0
Brusstar	.000	2	1	0	0	0	0	0	0	0	0	0	0	0	1	0	0
Bystrom	.000	1	2	0	0	0	0	0	0	0	0	0	0	0	1	0	0
Carlton	.000	2	4	0	0	0	0	0	0	0	0	0	0	0	1	0	0
Christenson	.000	2	2	0	0	0	0	0	0	0	0	0	0	0	1	0	0
McGraw	.000	5	1	0	0	0	0	0	0	0	0	0	0	0	0	0	0
Noles	---	2	0	0	0	0	0	0	0	0	0	0	0	0	0	0	0
Reed	---	3	0	0	0	0	0	0	0	0	0	0	0	0	0	0	0
Ruthven	.000	2	2	0	0	0	0	0	0	0	0	0	0	0	2	0	0
Saucier	---	2	0	0	0	0	0	0	0	0	0	0	0	0	0	0	0
TOTALS	.290	5	190	20	55	68	8	1	1	19	5	1	13	1	37	7	3

ERRORS: 6   DOUBLE PLAYS: 7   LEFT ON BASE: 43

Pitcher	ERA	G	GS	CG	GF	SV	SHO	W	L	IP	H	R	ER	HR	BB	HB	SO
Brusstar	3.00	2	0	0	0	0	0	1	0	2.2	1	1	1	0	1	0	0
Bystrom	1.80	1	1	0	0	0	0	0	0	5.1	7	2	1	0	2	0	1
Carlton	2.25	2	2	0	0	0	0	0	1	12.1	11	3	3	0	8	0	6
Christenson	3.86	2	1	0	0	0	0	1	0	6.2	5	3	3	0	5	0	2
McGraw	4.50	5	0	0	3	2	0	0	0	8.	8	4	4	0	4	0	5
Noles	0.00	2	0	0	1	0	0	0	1	2.2	1	0	0	0	3	0	0
Reed	18.00	3	0	0	0	0	0	1	0	2.	3	4	4	0	1	0	1
Ruthven	2.00	2	1	0	0	0	0	0	0	9.	7	2	2	0	5	0	4
Saucier	0.00	2	0	0	1	0	0	0	0	2.	1	0	0	0	2	0	0
TOTALS	3.18	5	5	0	5	2	0	3	2	50.2	40	19	18	0	31	0	19

1980 WORLD SERIES

Player	AVG	G	AB	R	H	2B	3B	HR	RBI	GW RBI	BB	SO	SH	SF	HB	SB	CS	E
Boone	.412	6	17	3	7	2	0	0	4	0	4	0	0	1	0	0	0	0
Bowa	.375	6	24	3	9	0	0	0	2	0	0	0	0	0	0	3	0	0
Gross	.000	4	2	0	0	0	0	0	0	0	0	0	1	0	0	0	0	0
Luzinski	.000	3	9	0	0	0	0	0	0	0	1	5	0	0	0	0	0	0
Maddox	.227	6	22	0	5	2	0	0	1	0	1	3	0	0	1	0	0	0
McBride	.304	6	23	3	7	0	0	1	5	1	2	1	0	0	0	0	1	0
Moreland	.333	3	12	1	4	0	0	0	1	0	0	2	0	0	0	0	0	0
Rose	.261	6	23	2	6	1	0	0	1	0	4	3	0	1	0	0	0	0
Schmidt	.381	6	21	6	8	1	0	2	7	2	4	1	0	0	0	0	0	1
Smith	.263	6	19	2	5	1	0	0	1	0	1	0	0	0	1	0	0	0
Trillo	.217	6	23	4	5	2	0	0	4	1	0	1	0	0	0	0	0	0
Unser	.500	3	6	2	3	2	0	0	2	0	0	5	1	0	0	0	0	0
DH Hitters	.174	—	23	1	4	0	0	0	0	0	0	0	0	1	0	0	0	1
PH Hitters	.667	—	3	2	2	0	0	0	2	0	0	0	1	0	1	0	0	0
Others	.000	—	0	0	0	0	0	0	0	0	0	0	0	0	0	0	0	0
TOTALS	.294	6	201	27	59	13	0	3	26	4	15	17	2	4	2	3	3	2

Pitcher	W	L	ERA	G	GS	CG	SHO	SV	IP	H	R	ER	HR	BB	SO	HB	WP
Brusstar	0	0	0.00	1	0	0	0	0	2.1	0	0	0	0	1	0	0	0
Bystrom	0	0	5.40	1	1	0	0	0	5.0	10	3	3	1	1	4	0	0
Carlton	2	0	2.40	2	2	0	0	0	15.0	14	5	4	1	9	17	0	1
Christenson	0	1	108.00	1	1	0	0	0	.1	4	4	4	0	0	0	0	0
McGraw	1	1	1.17	4	0	0	0	2	7.2	7	1	1	1	8	10	0	0
Noles	0	0	1.93	2	1	0	0	0	4.2	5	1	1	0	2	6	0	0
Reed	0	0	0.00	2	0	0	0	0	2.0	2	0	0	0	0	2	0	0
Ruthven	0	0	3.00	1	1	0	0	1	9.0	9	3	3	2	2	7	0	0
Saucier	0	0	0.00	1	0	0	0	0	.2	0	0	0	0	3	3	0	1
Walk	1	0	7.71	1	1	0	0	0	7.0	8	6	6	3	3	3	0	1
TOTALS	4	2	3.68	15	6	0	0	3	53.2	60	23	22	8	26	49	0	3

Detailed Hitting Statistics

1980	BOONE AB	H	HR	RBI	AVE	BOWA AB	H	HR	RBI	AVE	GROSS AB	H	HR	RBI	AVE	LUZINSKI AB	H	HR	RBI	AVE	MADDOX AB	H	HR	RBI	AVE	McBRIDE AB	H	HR	RBI	AVE
	480	110	9	55	.229	540	144	2	39	.267	154	37	2	12	.240	368	84	19	56	.228	549	142	11	73	.259	554	171	9	87	.309
Career	3463	912	61	432	.263	6455	1696	13	390	.263	2451	722	6	203	.295	4630	1299	223	811	.281	4806	1388	91	578	.289	3317	995	60	378	.300
Home	234	57	5	29	.244	271	66	1	26	.244	73	17	0	4	.233	189	55	15	38	.291	279	75	6	42	.269	273	90	4	44	.330
Away	246	53	4	26	.215	269	78	1	13	.290	81	20	2	8	.247	179	29	4	18	.162	270	67	5	31	.248	281	81	5	43	.288
Chi	44	20	2	7	.455	60	16	0	5	.267	8	3	0	2	.375	39	9	2	2	.231	51	12	1	9	.235	74	16	1	11	.216
Mon	55	13	0	4	.236	50	10	0	3	.200	18	4	0	0	.222	53	11	3	8	.208	62	19	2	10	.306	63	23	2	12	.365
NY	57	10	0	2	.175	52	17	0	3	.327	16	4	0	0	.250	42	6	0	6	.143	72	25	2	15	.347	60	15	1	9	.250
Pitt	62	11	0	8	.177	69	16	0	5	.232	20	5	0	1	.250	40	9	0	2	.225	65	21	1	8	.323	60	19	1	6	.317
StL	47	13	1	4	.277	60	14	0	3	.233	20	4	0	0	.200	49	10	0	2	.204	63	13	1	7	.206	42	13	1	7	.310
E. DIV.	265	67	5	30	.253	291	73	0	19	.251	82	20	0	6	.244	223	45	6	25	.202	313	90	9	51	.288	299	86	6	45	.288
Atl	42	7	1	3	.167	46	14	0	4	.304	14	1	0	1	.071	13	2	0	4	.154	40	10	0	5	.250	48	17	0	13	.354
Cinn	34	6	1	6	.176	32	10	1	2	.313	25	8	0	2	.320	22	7	2	6	.318	36	9	0	1	.250	44	16	2	8	.364
Hou	34	4	0	3	.118	37	5	0	1	.135	6	0	0	0	.000	17	7	1	1	.412	44	10	1	6	.227	50	21	0	9	.420
LA	34	9	1	1	.265	43	11	0	1	.256	6	2	0	3	.333	40	13	4	11	.325	31	3	0	3	.097	43	10	0	5	.233
SD	26	10	0	4	.385	48	19	1	6	.396	8	2	0	0	.250	29	5	1	5	.172	48	9	0	3	.188	38	14	1	7	.368
SF	45	7	1	5	.156	43	12	0	6	.279	13	4	0	0	.308	24	7	1	2	.208	37	11	1	2	.297	32	7	0	0	.219
W. DIV.	215	43	4	25	.200	249	71	2	20	.285	72	17	0	6	.236	145	39	13	31	.269	236	52	2	22	.220	255	85	3	42	.316
*1st Half	268	62	5	31	.231	262	64	1	14	.244	79	18	0	8	.228	249	61	15	42	.245	284	78	6	39	.275	266	77	5	47	.289
2nd Half	212	48	4	24	.226	278	80	1	25	.288	75	19	0	4	.253	119	23	4	14	.193	265	64	5	34	.242	288	94	4	40	.326
April	54	16	1	6	.296	56	13	0	3	.232	21	3	0	0	.143	58	15	4	10	.259	62	16	1	11	.258	54	14	0	10	.259
May	95	17	2	10	.179	89	23	1	7	.258	24	3	0	4	.125	93	29	8	18	.312	76	20	1	8	.263	100	33	3	23	.330
June	84	19	0	11	.226	84	24	0	6	.286	18	5	0	2	.278	79	14	3	14	.177	104	27	1	8	.260	81	23	2	10	.284
July	78	17	0	9	.218	95	21	0	6	.221	39	13	0	2	.333	19	3	0	3	.158	105	29	3	20	.276	99	35	0	18	.354
Aug.	80	22	2	14	.275	108	30	1	12	.278	56	7	0	2	.125	25	6	1	3	.240	113	26	3	14	.230	113	31	3	13	.307
Sept.	81	16	0	3	.198	93	27	0	8	.290	21	5	0	1	.238	80	14	2	8	.175	87	24	2	10	.276	102	30	1	13	.294
Oct.	8	3	0	2	.375	15	6	0	1	.400	3	1	0	1	.333	14	3	1	3	.214	2	0	0	0	.000	17	5	0	0	.294
vs. LHP	96	21	0	6	.219	115	34	1	6	.296	21	2	0	0	.095	78	19	5	8	.244	120	31	3	13	.258	87	24	2	16	.276
vs. RHP	384	89	9	49	.232	425	110	1	33	.259	133	35	2	12	.263	290	65	14	48	.224	429	111	8	60	.259	467	147	7	71	.315
Pinch Hitting	4	1	0	0	.250	0	0	0	0	.000	39	10	0	5	.256	1	0	0	0	.000	1	0	0	0	.000	3	2	0	0	.667
Slugging Pct.					.338					.322					.312					.440					.386					.453
Hitting Streak	6					8					3					9					12					12				

Detailed Hitting Statistics

	MORELAND AB	H	HR	RBI	AVE	ROSE AB	H	HR	RBI	AVE	SCHMIDT AB	H	HR	RBI	AVE
1980	159	50	4	29	.314	655	185	1	64	.282	548	157	48	121	.286
Career	209	68	4	37	.325	11479	3557	155	1077	.310	4261	1104	283	787	.259
Home	89	27	1	14	.303	313	89	0	34	.284	282	78	25	64	.277
Away	70	23	3	15	.329	342	96	1	30	.281	266	79	23	57	.297
Chi	28	6	0	3	.214	66	21	0	13	.318	76	28	10	22	.368
Mon	15	5	2	6	.333	79	25	1	6	.316	60	20	6	15	.333
NY	15	4	1	4	.267	72	20	0	6	.278	59	18	6	14	.305
Pitt	15	8	0	1	.533	80	25	0	9	.313	61	11	6	15	.180
Stl	16	4	0	2	.250	70	12	0	5	.171	47	13	2	5	.277
E. DIV	89	27	2	16	.303	367	103	1	39	.281	303	90	29	71	.297
Atl	9	3	0	1	.333	46	15	0	8	.326	47	15	5	14	.319
Cinn	13	4	2	3	.308	49	12	0	4	.245	41	7	3	3	.171
Hou	16	7	0	0	.438	42	12	0	4	.286	28	7	3	8	.250
LA	13	3	0	0	.231	49	15	0	4	.306	38	14	4	3	.368
SD	18	6	0	5	.333	53	16	0	4	.302	46	15	4	7	.326
SF	1	0	0	0	.000	49	12	0	4	.245	45	9	1	7	.200
W. DIV	70	23	2	13	.329	288	82	0	25	.285	245	67	19	50	.273
*1st Half	56	16	3	14	.286	321	96	1	36	.299	270	74	22	61	.274
2nd Half	103	34	1	15	.330	334	89	0	28	.266	278	83	26	60	.299
April	12	3	1	1	.250	62	14	0	2	.237	61	18	4	12	.295
May	27	6	1	8	.222	100	32	1	8	.320	95	29	12	29	.305
June	38	17	2	8	.447	109	30	0	12	.275	86	21	5	15	.244
July	41	14	0	3	.341	114	35	0	18	.307	78	18	6	15	.231
Aug.	27	7	0	5	.259	129	41	0	12	.318	104	34	8	22	.327
Sept	7	1	0	1	.143	122	25	0	11	.205	109	29	9	22	.266
Oct						19	8	0	1	.421	15	8	4	6	.533
vs. LHP	53	14	0	7	.264	130	33	0	19	.254	108	34	10	27	.315
vs. RHP	106	36	4	22	.340	525	152	1	45	.290	440	123	38	94	.280
Pinch Hitting	17	7	0	6	.412	1	0	0	0	.000	1	0	0	0	.000
Slugging Pct					.440					.354					.624
Hitting Streak	7					9					9				

	SMITH AB	H	HR	RBI	AVE	TRILLO AB	H	HR	RBI	AVE	UNSER AB	H	HR	RBI	AVE
1980	298	101	3	20	.339	531	155	7	43	.292	110	29	3	10	.264
Career	332	106	3	23	.319	3190	834	35	331	.261	5142	1335	87	475	.260
Home	159	58	2	11	.365	261	78	4	24	.299	59	16	0	6	.271
Away	139	43	1	9	.309	270	77	3	19	.285	51	13	0	4	.255
Chi	38	18	0	3	.474	73	26	0	4	.356	21	4	0	0	.190
Mon	5	0	0	0	.000	61	19	1	2	.311	16	3	0	0	.188
NY	28	13	1	4	.464	50	15	1	5	.300	7	5	0	1	.714
Pitt	35	10	0	2	.286	70	19	2	6	.271	8	1	0	1	.125
Stl	31	10	0	2	.323	53	14	0	5	.264	10	4	0	3	.400
E. DIV	137	51	1	11	.372	307	93	5	22	.303	62	17	0	6	.274
Atl	35	10	2	2	.286	25	7	0	6	.280	9	2	0	1	.222
Cinn	19	6	0	1	.316	32	10	0	4	.313	11	2	0	1	.182
Hou	20	5	0	0	.250	42	15	0	2	.357	9	2	0	2	.222
LA	21	5	0	1	.238	34	6	0	4	.176	7	3	0	1	.429
SD	30	12	0	2	.400	46	11	1	3	.239	2	1	0	0	.500
SF	36	12	0	2	.333	45	13	1	2	.289	10	2	0	0	.200
W. DIV	161	50	2	9	.311	224	62	2	21	.277	48	12	0	4	.250
*1st Half	86	35	1	4	.407	240	79	1	20	.329	48	13	0	4	.271
2nd Half	212	66	3	16	.311	291	76	6	23	.261	62	16	0	6	.258
April	1	0	0	0	.000	24	10	0	3	.417	5	3	0	2	.600
May	11	5	0	0	.455	66	19	0	6	.288	20	6	0	0	.300
June	39	14	0	3	.359	98	29	0	5	.296	19	2	0	0	.105
July	95	32	2	4	.337	101	34	1	12	.337	19	5	0	0	.263
Aug.	106	36	1	7	.340	115	36	5	13	.313	11	4	0	0	.364
Sept.	44	14	0	5	.318	112	24	1	7	.214	20	4	0	4	.200
Oct.	2	0	0	0	.000	15	3	0	0	.200	16	4	0	1	.250
vs. LHP	94	28	1	4	.298	105	32	1	9	.305	8	3	0	1	.375
vs. RHP	204	73	2	16	.358	426	123	6	34	.289	102	26	0	9	.255
Pinch Hitting	8	2	0	0	.250	0	0	0	0	.000	38	12	0	6	.316
Slugging Pct.					.443					.412					.391
Hitting Streak	12					12					3				

*FIRST HALF: Game # 81—7/14 Pitt @ Vet

Detailed Hitting Statistics

PHILLIES TEAM PITCHING

	AB	H	HR	RBI	AVE
1980	—	—	—	—	—
Career	5625	1517	117	674	.270
Home	2802	774	64	376	.276
Away	2823	743	53	298	.263
Chi	641	195	17	93	.304
Mon	651	179	17	77	.275
NY	628	172	15	81	.274
Pitt	631	160	12	72	.254
StL	599	142	5	53	.000
E. DIV	3150	848	66	376	.269
Atl	429	124	8	65	.289
Cinn	403	105	14	50	.261
Hou	393	105	6	42	.267
LA	401	104	8	50	.259
SD	434	129	8	55	.297
SF	415	102	7	36	.246
W. DIV	2475	669	51	298	.270
*1st Half	2772	747	62	351	.269
2nd Half	2853	770	55	323	.270
April	531	140	10	70	.263
May	883	249	32	137	.282*
June	935	231	15	95	.247
July	1022	292	15	118	.286
Aug.	1070	308	23	127	.288
Sept.	1002	242	17	105	.242
Oct.	183	57	5	22	.311
Pinch Hitting	174	48	0	25	.276

OPPONENTS TEAM PITCHING

	AB	H	HR	RBI	AVE
1980	—	—	—	—	—
Career	5573	1419	87	596	.255
Home	—	—	—	—	—
Away	—	—	—	—	—
Chi	628	148	10	55	.236
Mon	623	160	15	74	.257
NY	607	141	2	40	.232
Pitt	643	184	15	83	.286
StL	621	158	6	72	.254
E. DIV	3122	791	48	324	.253
Atl	399	93	11	41	.233
Cinn	391	111	3	51	.284
Hou	387	88	3	28	.227
LA	424	119	14	59	.281
SD	437	115	2	49	.263
SF	413	102	6	44	.247
W. DIV	2451	628	39	272	.256
*1st Half	2773	717	48	310	.259
2nd Half	2800	702	39	286	.251

*FIRST HALF: Game # 81—7/14 Pitt @ Vet

Detailed Pitching Statistics

BRUSSTAR

	G	W-L	IP	H	ERA	Career W-L
1980	26	2-2	38.2	42	3.69	—
Career	143	16-7	212.2	203	3.00	—
Home	13	1-0	19.2	19	237	8-2*
Road	13	1-2	19.2	23	4.95	—
Chi	3	1-1	5.1	3	3.60	3-1
Mon	3	0-1	3.2	4	6.75	2-1
NY	0	0-0			0.00	3-0
Pitt	3	1-0	5	5	3.60	3-1
StL	3	0-0	3.1	7	6.00	2-0
E. DIV	12	2-2	17.1	19	4.76	13-3
Atl	3	0-0	4	3	0.00	1-0
Cinn	1	0-0	1.1	1	27.00	1-1
Hou	1	0-0	1.1	1	0.00	0-0
LA	5	0-0	6	11	6.00	0-1
SD	2	0-0	4	2	0.00	1-1
SF	2	0-0	4.2	5	0.00	0-1
W. DIV	14	0-0	21.1	23	3.00	3-4
**1st Half	1	0-0	2	3	4.50	—
2nd Half	25	2-2	36.2	39	3.65	—
April	0	0-0	0	0	0.00	—
May	0	0-0	0	0	0.00	—
June	0	0-0	0	0	0.00	—
July	6	0-0	8.2	8	4.00	—
August	8	1-0	14.1	12	2.57	—
Sept.	10	1-1	13	19	3.46	—
Oct.	2	0-1	2.2	3	9.00	—
Winning Streak	2					
Losing Streak	2					
Shutouts—1980:	0		Career:	0		

CARLTON

	G	W-L	IP	H	ERS	Career W-L
1980	38	24-9	304	243	2.34	—
Career	525	249-169	3787	3311	3.03	—
Home	20	11-5	161	122	2.24	100-38*
Road	18	13-4	143	121	2.45	—
Chi	3	1-1	25	14	0.72	30-16
Mon	3	1-2	23.1	23	5.09	19-17
NY	4	2-2	29.2	31	2.40	25-27
Pitt	5	1-0	41	35	3.29	30-21
StL	6	6-0	52	38	1.38	29-8
E. DIV	21	13-4	171	141	2.42	133-89
Atl	3	3-0	22	9	2.45	19-12
Cinn	4	1-3	28	26	3.54	9-17
Hou	2	2-0	18	11	0.50	28-9
LA	2	1-1	15	14	2.40	13-11
SD	2	2-0	16	13	1.13	18-12
SF	4	2-1	34	13	2.38	21-16
W. DIV	17	11-5	133	102	2.23	108-77
**1st Half	21	14-4	163.1	122	2.21	—
2nd Half	17	10-5	140.2	121	2.49	—
April	4	3-1	33.1	22	2.18	—
May	8	6-1	59.2	40	1.65	—
June	6	4-1	47	39	2.11	—
July	6	3-2	45.1	37	3.40	—
August	6	4-2	52.2	50	2.21	—
Sept.	7	3-2	57	53	3.00	—
Oct.	1	1-0	9	2	0.00	—
Winning Streak	8					
Losing Streak	2					
Shutouts—1980:	3		Career:	45		

*Record at Veterans Stadium
**FIRST HALF: Game # 81—7/14 Pitt @ Vet

Detailed Pitching Statistics

CHRISTENSON

	G	W-L	IP	H	ERA	Career W-L
1980	14	5-1	73.2	62	4.01	—
Career	181	68-50	1024	1039	3.88	31-23*
Home	7	1-1	35.2	32	5.25	7-3
Road	7	4-0	38	30	2.84	11-5
Chi	1	0-0	6.1	4	4.50	10-4
Mon	3	1-0	16	16	5.06	6-7
NY	3	1-0	15	9	0.60	3-4
Pitt	0	0-0	0	0	0.00	
StL	0	0-0	0	0	0.00	
E. DIV	7	2-0	37.1	29	3.16	37-23
Atl	0	0-0	0	0	0.00	6-9
Cinn	1	0-0	3	6	18.00	2-6
Hou	1	1-0	5	7	3.60	10-5
LA	2	1-0	8.1	8	5.63	4-1
SD	1	1-0	6.1	4	3.00	4-1
SF	2	0-1	13.2	8	3.21	5-2
W. DIV	7	3-1	36.1	33	5.00	31-27
**1st Half	6	3-0	25.2	28	6.23	—
2nd Half	8	2-1	48	34	2.81	—
April	3	1-0	11	11	6.55	
May	3	2-0	14.2	17	6.00	
June	0	0-0	0	0	0.00	
July	0	0-0	0	0	0.00	
August	3	2-1	18	15	3.50	
Sept.	4	0-0	24	13	2.25	
Oct.	1	0-0	6	6	3.00	
Winning Streak	4					
Losing Streak	1					
Shutouts—1980	0	Career: 6				

ESPINOSA

	G	W-L	IP	H	ERA	Career W-L
1980	12	3-5	76.1	73	3.79	—
Career	125	42-50	7451	763	3.97	—
Home	6	1-2	36	40	4.00	—
Road	6	2-3	40.1	33	3.60	—
Chi	0	0-0	0	0	0.00	5-3
Mon	1	1-0	9	5	1.00	4-7
NY	2	0-2	13	20	6.92	5-1
Pitt	2	0-0	15	6	0.00	5-6
StL	0	0-0	0	0	0.00	3-3
E. DIV	5	1-2	37	31	2.68	22-20
Atl	1	1-0	7	2	2.57	4-5
Cinn	2	1-1	12	11	4.50	4-2
Hou	1	0-0	6.1	6	3.00	3-1
LA	1	0-0	5	6	5.40	2-5
SD	2	0-2	9	17	8.00	3-5
SF	0	0-0	0	0	0.00	1-5
W. DIV	7	2-3	39.1	42	4.85	17-23
**1st Half	2	0-1	15	11	3.60	—
2nd Half	10	2-4	61.1	62	3.84	—
April	0	0-0	0	0	0.00	
May	0	0-0	0	0	0.00	
June	0	0-0	0	0	0.00	
July	5	1-2	34.1	24	3.71	
August	6	2-3	35	45	4.63	
Sept.	1	0-0	7	4	0.00	
Oct.	0	0-0	0	0	0.00	
Winning Streak	1					
Losing Streak	2					
Shutouts—1980	0	Career: 5				

LERCH

	G	W-L	IP	H	ERA	Career W-L
1980	30	4-14	150	178	5.16	—
Career	136	35-41	727	805	4.42	18-14
Home	13	2-3	54.2	67	5.24	5-4
Road	17	2-11	96	111	5.06	2-2
Chi	1	1-0	6.2	5	2.57	5-4
Mon	5	1-1	29.1	30	3.72	2-2
NY	2	1-1	13.2	8	1.29	5-2
Pitt	4	1-2	20	31	6.75	5-6
StL	5	0-3	21.1	25	6.43	5-9
E. DIV	17	4-7	91	99	4.55	22-23
Atl	1	0-1	7	7	2.57	1-2
Cinn	2	0-2	11	17	8.18	2-5
Hou	4	0-1	12	12	9.00	2-2
LA	2	0-1	19.2	24	4.95	4-3
SD	2	0-0	6.1	5	1.50	2-1
SF	2	0-2	8.1	14	10.13	2-5
W. DIV	13	0-7	59	79	6.10	13-18
**1st Half	18	3-11	112.1	128	4.74	—
2nd Half	12	1-3	37.2	50	6.57	—
April	4	0-3	28.1	29	4.50	
May	5	1-3	28.1	38	5.46	
June	6	1-4	38.2	38	3.69	
July	5	1-2	26.1	40	7.27	
August	5	1-1	20	20	4.05	
Sept.	4	0-1	5.1	9	10.80	
Oct.	1	0-0	3	4	9.00	
Winning Streak						
Losing Streak	6					
Shutouts—1980	0	Career: 1				

McGRAW

	G	W-L	IP	H	ERA	Career W-L
1980	57	5-4	92.1	62	1.47	—
Career	716	87-84	1338.1	1139	3.08	42-40
Home	29	3-1	45	30	1.40	—
Road	28	2-3	47.1	32	1.53	—
Chi	6	0-0	9	5	0.00	9-8
Mon	6	1-0	12	9	2.25	11-5
NY	5	1-0	9.1	6	1.00	5-5
Pitt	8	2-2	17.1	15	2.65	5-13
StL	4	0-0	6.1	6	0.00	10-8
E. DIV	29	5-4	54	36	1.50	40-39
Atl	3	0-0	4	3	0.00	4-6
Cinn	5	0-0	8.2	6	1.50	7-10
Hou	5	0-0	8	4	0.00	9-9
LA	7	0-0	7.2	4	0.00	10-5
SD	5	0-0	4	6	6.75	5-3
SF	3	0-0	6	2	3.00	7-7
W. DIV	28	0-0	38.1	25	1.42	42-40
**1st Half	24	0-3	37.2	32	2.70	—
2nd Half	33	5-1	54.2	30	0.52	—
April	4	0-1	6	8	4.50	
May	10	0-0	18.1	12	2.00	
June	10	0-2	15.2	12	2.81	
July	6	0-0	8.2	5	0.00	
August	11	0-1	17.1	14	1.06	
Sept.	13	4-0	18.2	14	0.47	
Oct.	3	1-0	6.2	2	0.00	
Winning Streak	5					
Losing Streak	4					
Shutouts—1980	0	Career: 1				

*Record at Veterans Stadium

***FIRST HALF: Game #81—7/14 Pitt @ Vet

Detailed Pitching Statistics

NOLES

1980	G	W-L	IP	H	ERA	Career W-L
Career	48	1-4	81.1	80	3.89	—
	52	4-8	171.1	160	3.84	2-5*
Home	29	0-3	46	53	4.50	0-0
Road	19	1-1	35.1	27	3.09	2-5*
Chi	8	0-0	12	3	0.00	0-0
Mon	5	1-0	17	24	5.82	1-1
NY	4	0-0	3.1	1	0.00	1-1
Pitt	7	0-1	9	10	4.00	0-2
StL	3	0-0	3	1	9.00	0-0
E. DIV	27	1-1	44.1	39	3.68	2-4
Atl	5	0-0	7.1	11	6.43	0-0
Cinn	2	0-0	2.2	1	3.00	0-0
Hou	3	0-0	5.1	4	1.80	0-0
LA	6	0-2	11	18	6.55	1-2
SD	3	0-0	8	4	0.00	0-0
SF	2	0-1	2.2	3	6.00	1-2
W. DIV	21	0-3	37	41	4.14	2-4
**1st Half	25	1-3	46	46	3.71	—
2nd Half	23	0-1	35.1	34	4.11	—
April	6	0-0	9.2	5	0.00	—
May	10	0-2	13.1	11	3.46	—
June	6	1-1	20.1	27	5.40	—
July	8	0-0	10.2	13	6.55	—
August	9	0-1	17.1	15	2.12	—
Sept.	9	0-0	10	7	5.40	—
Oct.	0	0-0	0	0	0.00	—
Winning Streak	1					
Losing Streak	3					
Shutouts—1980: 0			Career: 0			

REED

1980	G	W-L	IP	H	ERA	Career W-L
Career	55	7-5	91.1	88	4.05	—
	593	127-125	2152	2079	3.52	—
Home	31	4-4	52	43	3.81	—
Road	24	3-1	39.1	45	4.38	—
Chi	9	0-1	15.1	14	2.40	7-16
Mon	7	1-0	10	8	2.70	13-5
NY	5	0-1	10.2	10	3.27	10-8
Pitt	5	1-1	8	7	4.50	12-12
StL	6	0-1	5	13	14.40	6-15
E. DIV	32	2-4	49	52	4.22	48-56
Atl	3	0-0	3	3	0.00	5-2
Cinn	5	1-0	11	8	2.45	16-13
Hou	2	0-1	5	3	1.80	13-10
LA	4	3-0	10	7	3.60	12-13
SD	4	0-0	6	10	9.00	13-8
SF	3	1-0	7	5	5.14	12-15
W. DIV	23	5-1	42	36	3.86	71-61
**1st Half	33	6-3	59.1	54	3.81	—
2nd Half	22	1-2	32	34	4.50	—
April	10	0-0	8.2	6	4.00	—
May	14	3-2	18.1	14	2.50	—
June	7	3-1	26	23	3.81	—
July	9	0-2	11	14	4.91	—
August	9	1-0	15	22	6.60	—
Sept.	5	0-0	12	9	3.00	—
Oct.	1	0-0	.1	0	0.20	—
Winning Streak	3					
Losing Streak	3					
Shutouts—1980: 0			Career: 8			

RUTHVEN

1980	G	W-L	IP	H	ERA	Career W-L
Career	33	17-10	223.1	241	3.55	—
	218	77-80	1350	1333	3.93	—
Home	17	9-4	119	127	3.71	—
Road	16	8-6	104.1	114	3.38	—
Chi	4	2-2	28.2	32	3.10	11-7
Mon	4	2-1	24.1	20	3.38	8-8
NY	3	1-0	18.2	23	3.79	7-3
Pitt	4	0-2	22	34	5.32	5-6
StL	2	1-1	11	12	4.09	7-10
E. DIV	17	6-6	105	121	3.86	38-34
Atl	2	2-1	24	21	3.38	5-2
Cinn	2	1-1	13.1	19	4.85	2-12
Hou	4	3-1	32	29	1.41	7-11
LA	2	0-1	9	13	8.00	2-12
SD	3	3-0	22.2	23	3.91	11-2
SF	3	2-0	17.1	15	2.12	12-4
W. DIV	16	11-4	118.1	120	3.28	39-43
**1st Half	17	8-5	107.2	128	3.92	—
2nd Half	16	9-5	115.2	113	3.18	—
April	4	1-2	15.2	28	9.56	—
May	7	4-2	47.1	53	3.06	—
June	4	1-1	27	32	3.33	—
July	6	4-2	50	47	2.88	—
August	5	3-1	38	36	2.61	—
Sept.	6	3-2	39	42	3.92	—
Oct.	1	1-0	5.2	3	1.50	—
Winning Streak	4					
Losing Streak	2					
Shutouts—1980: 1			Career: 13			

WALK

1980	G	W-L	IP	H	ERA	Career W-L
Career	27	11-7	151.2	163	4.56	—
						7-3*
Home	16	7-3	85.1	101	5.19	—
Road	11	4-4	66.1	62	3.82	—
Chi	6	3-0	38	44	4.03	—
Mon	2	0-1	13	7	1.38	—
NY	2	2-0	15	17	2.40	—
Pitt	2	0-0	9	6	7.00	—
StL	4	1-3	16.2	23	7.41	—
E. DIV	16	6-4	91.2	97	4.30	—
Atl	2	1-1	13.2	18	3.86	—
Cinn	1	1-0	8	10	1.13	—
Hou	1	1-0	9	8	2.00	—
LA	2	1-1	9.1	8	6.00	—
SD	4	1-1	14.2	21	9.00	—
SF	1	0-0	5	6	5.40	—
W. DIV	11	5-3	59.2	66	4.95	—
**1st Half	10	5-0	57.2	58	4.34	—
2nd Half	17	6-7	94	105	4.69	—
April	0	0-0	0	0	0.00	—
May	1	0-0	2.2	2	15.00	—
June	7	3-0	39.1	44	4.62	—
July	5	4-1	38.1	33	2.61	—
August	7	2-3	33.2	49	7.15	—
Sept.	6	1-3	30.1	28	3.90	—
Oct.	1	1-0	7.1	7	1.29	—
Winning Streak	6					
Losing Streak	3					
Shutouts—1980: 0			Career: 0			

*Record at Veterans Stadium
**FIRST HALF: Game # 81—7/14 Pitt @ Vet

1980 STANDINGS

NATIONAL LEAGUE EAST

	W	L	PCT	GB
PHILLIES	91	71	.562	—
Montreal	90	72	.556	1
Pittsburgh	83	79	.512	9
St. Louis	74	88	.457	18
New York	67	95	.414	24
Chicago	64	98	.395	27

NATIONAL LEAGUE WEST

	W	L	PCT	GB
Houston	92	70	.568	—
Los Angeles	92	70	.568	—
Cincinnati	89	73	.549	3
Atlanta	81	80	.503	10½
San Fran.	75	86	.466	16½
San Diego	73	89	.451	19

AMERICAN LEAGUE EAST

	W	L	PCT	GB
New York	103	59	.636	—
Baltimore	100	62	.617	3
Milwaukee	86	76	.531	17
Boston	83	77	.5187	19
Detroit	84	78.	.5185	19
Cleveland	79	81	.494	23
Toronto	67	95	.414	36

AMERICAN LEAGUE WEST

	W	L	PCT	GB
Kansas City	97	65	.599	—
Oakland	83	79	.512	14
Minnesota	77	84	.478	19½
Texas	76	85	.472	20½
Chicago	70	90	.438	26
California	65	95	.406	31
Seattle	59	103	.364	38

RECORD VS. THE NATIONAL LEAGUE

	H	A	TOT		H	A	TOT
Chicago	8-1	5-4	13-5	Atlanta	5-1	2-4	7-5
Montreal	4-5	5-4	9-9	Cincinnati	4-2	1-5	5-7
New York	4-5	8-1	12-6	Houston	5-1	4-2	9-3
Pittsburgh	5-4	2-7	7-11	Los Angeles	3-3	3-3	6-6
St. Louis	4-5	5-4	9-9	San Diego	5-1	3-3	8-4
				San Francisco	2-4	4-2	6-6
TOTALS	25-20	25-20	50-40	TOTALS	24-12	17-19	41-31

Detailed Pitching Statistics

PHILLIES TEAM PITCHING

	G	W-L	IP	H	ERA	Career W-L
1980	162	91-71	1480	1419	3.43	
Career						3.51
Home	81	49-32	765	741	2.98	3.51
Road	81	42-39	715	678	2.66	3.35
Chi	18	13-5	170.2	148	2.63	
Mon	18	9-9	167.1	160	3.93	
NY	18	12-6	164	141	1.98	
Pitt	18	7-11	166.2	184	4.53	
StL	18	9-9	162.1	158	3.72	
E. DIV		50-40				
Atl	12	7-5	107	93	2.78	
Cinn	12	5-7	103	111	4.37	
Hou	12	9-3	107	88	2.10	
LA	12	6-6	108	119	4.58	
SD	12	8-4	113	115	3.74	
SF	12	6-6	111	102	3.57	
W. DIV		41-31				
**1st Half	81	44-37	727.2	717	3.65	
2nd Half	81	47-34	752.1	702	3.22	
April	15	6-9	132.2	135	4.13	
May	26	17-9	233	218	3.32	
June	28	14-14	253	253	3.49	
July	29	15-14	258.1	250	3.63	
August	30	16-14	278.1	289	3.72	
Sept.	29	19-10	324	241	2.44	
Oct.	5	4-1	47.2	33	2.25	
Winning Streak	6					
Losing Streak	6					

OPPONENTS TEAM PITCHING

	G	W-L	IP	H	ERA	Career W-L
1980	162	71-91	1470	1517	3.92	
Career						
Home						
Road						
Chi	18	5-13	166.2	195	4.74	
Mon	18	9-9	166	179	3.90	
NY	18	6-12	161.1	172	4.36	
Pitt	18	11-7	168.2	160	3.57	
StL	18	9-9	162.1	158	3.72	
E. DIV		40-50				
Atl	12	5-7	106.2	124	4.88	
Cinn	12	7-5	104.1	105	4.15	
Hou	12	3-9	104	105	3.55	
LA	12	6-6	108	104	4.08	
SD	12	4-8	111.1	129	4.46	
SF	12	6-6	111	102	2.76	
W. DIV		31-41				
**1st Half	81	37-44	717.2	747	4.14	
2nd Half	81	34-47	752.1	770	3.71	
April	15	9-6	132	140	4.09	
May	26	9-17	227.1	247	5.00	
June	28	14-14	250	231	3.49	
July	29	14-15	261	292	3.83	
August	30	14-16	278.1	308	4.05	
Sept.	29	10-19	274.1	242	3.51	
Oct.	5	1-5	46	57	4.10	

*Record at Veterans Stadium
**FIRST HALF: Game # 81—7/14 Pitt @ Vet

General Club Records

(Since 1900)

Season

Longest Winning Streak	13 Games, 1977
Longest Losing Streak	23 Games, 1961
Longest Game, Innings	21, Chicago 2, Phillies 1; 7/17/18
Longest Game, Innings, At Home	20, Chicago 2, Phillies 1; 8/24/05
	20, Phillies 9; Brooklyn 9 (tie); 4/30/19
Longest Game, Shutout, Ex. In.	20, Phillies 5, Atlanta 4; 5/4/73
	18, Phillies 0, Mets 0 (Tie); 10/2/65, 2nd Game
Most Wins, Vs. One Club	18-3 vs. Brooklyn, 1905
	18-4 vs. Cincinnati, 1950
Most Losses, Vs. One Club	3-19 vs. Brooklyn, 1945
	3-19 vs. Cincinnati, 1943 and 1961
Most Games Won	101 in 1976 and 1977
Most Games Lost	111 in 1941
Highest Percentage, Games Won	.623 in 1976 and 1977
Lowest Percentage, Games Won	.279 in 1941 (43-111)
Most Shutouts Won	24 in 1916
Most Shutouts Lost	23 in 1908, 1909
Most 1-0 Games Won	7 in 1913
Most 1-0 Games Lost	10 in 1967

League

Won-Lost at Veterans Stadium	456-353 ten years
Games Won, League	6719 in 98 years
Games Lost, League	8814 in 98 years

Club Fielding Records

Season

Most Errors	403 in 1904 (155 games)
Fewest Errors	104 in 1978 (162 games)
Most Errorless Games	89 in 1966 (162 games)
Most Consecutive Errorless Games	11 in 1967
Most Double Plays	179 in 1961 (155 games)
	179 in 1973 (162 games)
Fewest Double Plays	117 in 1955 (154 games)
	117 in 1957 (156 games)
Most Consecutive Games, 1 or More DPs	16 (29 DPs) in 1961
Most Passed Balls	27 in 1971 (162 games)
	27 in 1947 (155 games)
Fewest Passed Balls	3 in 1952 (154 games)
	3 in 1956 (154 games)
Most Putouts	4440 in 1980 (162 games)
Fewest Putouts	3887 in 1907 (149 games)
Most Assists	2176 in 1921 (154 games)
Fewest Assists	1437 in 1957 (156 games)
Most Total Chances	6512 in 1980 (162 games)
Fewest Total Chances	5545 in 1955 (154 games)
Highest Percentage	.983 in 1978 (162 games)
	.983 in 1979 (163 games)
Lowest Fielding Percentage	.936 in 1904 (155 games)

Club Hitting Records

CLUB—SEASON (Since 1900)

Most Games............................163 in 1979
Most At Bats..........................5667 in 1930 (156 games)
Most Runs.............................944 in 1930 (156 games)
Fewest Runs...........................394 in 1942 (151 games)
Most Hits.............................1783 in 1930 (156 games)
Fewest Hits...........................1113 in 1907 (149 games)
Most Singles..........................1268 in 1930 (156 games)
Most Doubles..........................345 in 1930 (156 games)
Most Triples..........................82 in 1905 (155 games)
Most Homers...........................186 in 1977 (162 games)
Most Homers, Pinch Hitters............11 in 1958
Most Homers, Bases Filled.........7 in 1925, 1929, 1976
Most Consecutive Games, One Home Run, or more........13
  (16 homers), 1964
Most Consecutive Games, No Home Runs......12 in 1960, 1961
Most Total Bases......................2594 in 1930 (156 games)
Most Stolen Bases.....................200 in 1908 (155 games)
Most Walks............................652 in 1955 (154 games)
Most Strikeouts.......................1130 in 1969 (162 games)
Fewest Strikeouts.....................452 in 1924 (152 games)
Most Hit By Pitcher...................53 in 1962 (161 games)
Most Runs Batted in...................884 in 1930 (156 games)
Highest Batting Average...............315 in 1930 (156 games)
Lowest Batting Average................232 in 1942 (151 games)
Highest Slugging Percentage...........467 in 1929 (154 games)
Lowest Slugging Percentage............305 in 1907 (149 games)
Most Grounded Into Double Play........144 in 1950 (157 games)
Fewest Grounded Into Double Play......91 in 1935 (156 games);
  91 in 1973 (162 games)
Most Left On Base.....................1272 in 1975 (162 games)
Fewest Left On Base...................991 in 1920 (153 games)

CLUB—GAME (Since 1900)

Most Runs....................Phillies 23, Pittsburgh 8; 7/13/00, 8 Inn.
  Chicago 26, Phillies 23; 8/25/22
  Phillies 23, Chicago 22; 5/17/79, 10 Inn.
Most Runs, Opp............St. Louis 28, Phillies 6; 7/6/29, 2d Ga.
Most Runs, Shutout Game......Phillies 18, Pittsburgh 0; 7/11/10
  Phillies 18, Cincinnati 0; 8/10/30, 1st Ga.
Most Runs, Shutout Game. Opp............Chicago 16, Phillies 0;
  5/4/29, 1st Ga.
Most Runs, Inning...........12, Phillies vs. Chicago, 7/21/23,
  1st Ga.; 6th Inning
  11@ SF 7/15/72, 7th Inning
Most Runs, Inning, Opp............14, Chicago; 8/25/22, 2nd Inn.
Most Hits.........26, Phillies vs. Chicago; 8/25/22
Most Hits, Opp............26, Cincinnati; 5/17/79, 10 Inn.
  25, Cincinnati; 8/3/69, 9 Inn.
Most Home Runs............6, Phillies vs. St. Louis; 5/11/23
  6, Phillies vs. Pittsburgh; 8/28/48, 2nd Ga.
  6, Phillies vs. Cincinnati; 6/2/49
  6, Phillies vs. San Francisco, 4/27/65
  6, Phillies @ Chicago; 10/3/72
  6, Phillies @ Chicago; 4/17/76
  6, Phillies @ Chicago; 8/12/77
Most Home Runs, Opp. (Most Recent) 6, Chicago; 5/17/79; 10 Inn.
Most Total Bases, 9 Inn. ......43, Phillies vs. Cincinnati; 5/15/11
Most Total Bases, Extra Inn. Ga. 48, at Chicago; 5/17/79, 10 Inn.
Most Stolen Bases, Since 1946............7, Phillies vs. Pitts.;
  5/29/78, 14 Inn.
  6, Phillies vs. Atlanta; 8/23/77, 9 Inn.

INDIVIDUAL—SEASON

Record	Player (Games Played)	Record	Year
Games	Rose	163	1979
At Bats, LH	Ashburn (154 games)	662	1949
At Bats, RH	Cash (162 games)	699	1975
At Bats, SW	Bowa (162 games)	669	1974
Runs, LH	Klein (156 games)	158	1930
Runs, RH	R. Allen (162 games)	125	1964
Hits, LH	O'Doul (154 games)	254	1929
Hits, RH	Cash (162 games)	213	1975
Singles, LH	O'Doul (154 games)	181	1929
Singles, RH	Ashburn (153 games)	181	1951
Doubles, LH	Cash (162 games)	166	1975
Doubles, RH	Klein (156 games)	59	1930
Triples, LH	E. Allen (154 games)	46	1935
Triples, RH	Flick (138 games)	17	1901
Home Runs, RH	Magee (155 games)	17	1905, 1910
Home Runs, LH	Schmidt (162 games)	48	1980
Home Runs, Rookie, LH	Klein (149 games)	43	1929
Home Runs, Rookie, RH	Montanez, (158 games)	30	1971
Home Runs, Home, LH	R. Allen (162 games)	29	1964
Home Runs, Home	Chuck Klein	29	1932
Home Runs, Road	Schmidt (162 games)	25	1980
Home Runs, Road	Schmidt	29	1979
Home Runs, Month, LH	Williams (May)	15	1923
Home Runs, Month, RH	Schmidt (June)	14	1977
Home Runs, Pinch Hitter, RH	Freese	5	1959
Home Runs, Pinch Hitter, LH	Unser	4	1979
Total Bases, LH	Klein (156 games)	445	1930
Total Bases, RH	R. Allen (162 games)	352	1964
Extra Base Hits, LH	Schmidt (156 games)	107	1930
Extra Base Hits, RH	Schmidt (162 games)	81	1980
Sacrifices	Gleason (155 games)	43	1905
Stolen Bases, LH	Slagle (141 games)	38	1900
Stolen Bases, LH	Bowa (162 games)	39	1974
Stolen Bases, RH	Magee (154 games)	55	1906
Stolen Bases, Rookie	L. Smith (162 games)	33	1980
Walks, LH	Ashburn (153 games)	125	1954
Walks, RH	Schmidt (163 games)	120	1979
Strike Outs, LH	Callison (160 games)	118	1965
Strike Outs, RH	Schmidt (162 games)	180	1975
Fewest Strike Outs, LH	O'Doul (154 games)	19	1929
Fewest Strike Outs, RH	Verban (155 games)	8	1947

Record	Player (Games Played)	Record	Year
Hit By Pitch, LH	Bouchee (154 games)	14	1957
Hit By Pitch, RH	Taylor (162 games)	13	1964
Runs Batted in, LH	Klein (154 games)	170	1930
Runs Batted in, RH	Luzinski (149 games)	130	1977
Average, LH	O'Doul (154 games)	396	1929
Average, RH	Delahanty (139 games)	357	1901
Slugging Percentage, LH	Klein (156 games)	687	1930
Slugging Percentage, RH	R. Allen (141 games)	632	1966
Hitting Streak	Klein (twice)	26	1930
	Montanez	24	1974
Hitting Streak, Rookie	Ashburn	23	1948
	Rapp	23	1921
Grounded Into Double Plays	Ennis (153 games)	25	1950
	Sizemore (152 games)	25	1977
Fewest GI DP	Klein (152 games)	3	1933
	Ashburn (156 games)	3	1953
	Ashburn (153 games)	3	1954

PHILS W/L VS. OPPONENTS AT VET

	1971	1972	1973	1974	1975	1976	1977	1978	1979	1980	TOTAL
Chicago	3-6	3-6	5-4	5-4	5-4	5-4	4-5	8-1	5-4	8-1	48-42
Montreal	6-3	4-3	2-7	4-5	5-4	8-1	5-4	6-4	4-5	9-9	53-45
New York	3-6	1-8	6-3	6-3	6-3	7-2	8-1	6-3	6-3	12-6	61-38
Pittsburgh	3-6	3-6	3-6	8-1	8-1	4-5	7-2	6-3	5-4	7-11	54-45
St. Louis	3-6	4-5	7-2	3-6	5-4	7-2	7-2	6-3	3-6	9-9	54-45
Atlanta	2-4	2-4	2-4	2-4	5-1	2-4	6-0	2-4	1-5	7-5	31-35
Cincinnati	3-3	1-5	1-5	2-4	5-1	4-2	4-2	3-3	2-4	5-7	30-36
Houston	2-4	3-3	2-4	4-2	4-2	5-1	6-0	5-1	3-3	9-3	43-23
Los Angeles	4-2	2-4	1-5	4-2	2-4	2-4	4-2	3-3	6-0	6-6	34-32
San Diego	2-4	2-4	5-1	4-2	5-1	5-1	5-1	4-2	4-2	8-4	44-22
San Francisco	3-3	3-3	4-2	4-2	4-2	4-2	4-2	5-1	4-2	6-6	41-25
Totals	34-47	28-51	38-43	46-35	51-30	53-28	60-21	54-28	43-38	49-32	456-353

Club Pitching Records

INDIVIDUAL—SEASON

Player (Games Played)		Record		Year
Games, RH	Konstanty	74		1950
Games, LH	Knowles	69		1966
Games Started, RH	Alexander	45		1916
Games Started, LH	Carlton	41		1972
Complete Games, RH	Alexander	38		1916
Complete Games, LH	Carlton	30		1972
Games Finished	Konstanty	62		1950
Wins, RH	Alexander	33		1916
Wins, LH	Carlton	27		1972
Losses, RH	Fraser	24		1904
Losses, LH	Rixey	22		1920
Shutouts, RH	Alexander	16		1916
Shutouts, LH	Carlton	8		1972
1-0 Shutouts, Won	Alexander	4		1916
1-0 Shutouts, Lost	McQuillan	5		1908
	Bunning	5		1967
Shutouts, Lost	McQuillan	8		1908
Innings, Pitched, RH	Alexander	399		1916
Innings, Pitched, LH	Carlton	346		1972
Hits, RH	Passeau	348		1937
Hits, LH	Carlton	293		1973
Runs, RH	Benge	175		1930
Runs, LH	Sweetland	164		1930
Earned Runs, RH	Roberts	147		1956
Earned Runs, LH	Sweetland	143		1930
Walks, RH	Moore	164		1911
Walks, LH	Carlton	136		1974
Strike Outs, RH	Bunning	268		1965
Strike Outs, LH	Carlton	310		1972
Hit Batters, RH	Mitchell	19		1903
	Bunning	19		1966
Hit Batters, LH	Lush	16		1906
Wild Pitches, RH	Hamilton	22		1962
Wild Pitches, LH	Short	14		1961
Home Runs, RH	Roberts	46		1956
Home Runs, LH	Carlton	30		1978
Earned Run Average, RH	Alexander	1.22		1915
Earned Run Average, LH	Rixey	1.85		1916
Percentage, RH	Roberts (28-7)	.800		1952
Percentage, LH	Carlton (20-7)	.741		1976
Saves, RH	Konstanty	22		1950
	Selma	22		1970
	McGraw	20		1980
Saves, LH	Carlton	15		1972
Longest Winning Streak	Miller	12		1928
Longest Losing Streak	Mulcahy	12		1940
	Reynolds	12		1972
Balks	Carlton	11		1979

INDIVIDUAL—GAME

No Hitters	(See No Hitters, For—Against in this guide).
One-Hitter (Most Recent)	Carlton vs. St.L.; 4/26/80
One-Hitter, Opp. (Most Recent)	Rogers at Mtl.; 6/23/79
Most Strikeouts, 9 Innings, RHP	17—Mahaffey vs. Chicago; 4/23/61, 2d Ga.
Most Strikeouts, 9 Innings, LHP	14—Short vs. Los Angeles; 9/13/63, 1st Ga.
	14—Carlton vs. S.F.; 4/25/72
	14—Carlton vs. Hou.; 8/21/77
	14—Carlton vs. St. L.; 9/9/77
	14—Carlton vs. S.F.; 7/8/79
Most Strikeouts, 9 Innings, Opp. (since '60)	16—Koufax; 5/26/62
	Koufax; 6/22/59
	Veale; 6/1/65
	Carlton; 9/20/67
	Carlton; 5/21/70
	Gibson; 5/23/70
Most Strikeouts, Extra Inning Game	18—Short (15 Innings) vs. New York; 10/2/65

Phillies All-Time Hitting Records

GAMES

Ashburn	1,794
Taylor	1,669
BOWA	1,636
Ennis	1,630
Delahanty	1,544
W. Jones	1,520
Magee	1,518
Hamner	1,501
F. Williams	1,463
Callison	1,432
Klein	1,405

AT BATS

Ashburn	7,122
BOWA	6,455
Delahanty	6,352
Ennis	6,327
Taylor	5,799
Hamner	5,772
Magee	5,505
W. Jones	5,419
Callison	5,306
Klein	5,238

RUNS

Delahanty	1,365
Ashburn	1,114
Klein	963
S. Thompson	928
R. Thomas	916
Magee	898
Ennis	891
Hamilton	877
F. Williams	825
BOWA	782
SCHMIDT	778
Callison	774
LUZINSKI	618

HOME RUNS

SCHMIDT	283
Ennis	259
Klein	243
LUZINSKI	223
F. Williams	217
R. Allen	204
Callison	185
W. Jones	180
Seminick	123
Cravath	117

TOTAL BASES

Delahanty	3,197
Ennis	3,029
Klein	2,898
Ashburn	2,764
F. Williams	2,539
Magee	2,463
Callison	2,426
LUZINSKI	2,263
SCHMIDT	2,239
W. Jones	2,236
S. Thompson	2,224
Hamner	2,220
BOWA	2,083

RUNS BATTED IN

Delahanty	1,286
Ennis	1,124
Klein	983
S. Thompson	958
Magee	889
LUZINSKI	811
F. Williams	796
SCHMIDT	787
W. Jones	753
Whitney	734
Hamner	705
Cravath	686

HITS

Ashburn	2,217
Delahanty	2,211
Ennis	1,812
Klein	1,705
BOWA	1,696
Magee	1,647
F. Williams	1,553
Hamner	1,518
Taylor	1,511
S. Thompson	1,475
Callison	1,438

DOUBLES

Delahanty	432
Magee	337
Klein	336
Ennis	310
Ashburn	287
Hamner	271
Callison	265
S. Thompson	258
LUZINSKI	253
Luderus	249
Whitney	237
F. Williams	237
SCHMIDT	208
BOWA	192

TRIPLES

Delahanty	151
Magee	127
S. Thompson	103
Ashburn	97
Callison	84
BOWA	78
Cravath	72
Ennis	65
Allen	64
Klein	64
Titus	64
Lajoie	64

EXTRA BASE HITS

Delahanty	667
Klein	643
Ennis	634
Magee	539
Callison	534
SCHMIDT	530
F. Williams	503
LUZINSKI	497
Allen	472
S. Thompson	456
W. Jones	444
Hamner	435

BATTING PCT.

Hamilton	.362
Delahanty	.348
Flick	.345
S. Thompson	.335
Klein	.326
V. Davis	.321
Leach	.312
Ashburn	.311
Whitney	.307
F. Williams	.306

STOLEN BASES

Hamilton	508
Magee	387
BOWA	272
Ashburn	199
R. Thomas	164
MADDOX	159
Paskert	149
Taylor	136
Dooin	132
SCHMIDT	129
Lobert	125
Knabe	122
Titus	120

CAPS = Active Player

Phillies All-Time Pitching Records

GAMES

Roberts	529
Short	459
Farrell	359
Alexander	338
McGRAW	336
CARLTON	335
Baldschun	333
Simmons	325
Konstanty	314
REED	301
P. Collins	291
GARBER	262

COMPLETE GAMES

Roberts	272
Alexander	220
Sparks	150
Orth	149
CARLTON	147
Duggleby	137
Simmons	112
Ring	102
Rixey	100
Short	88

INNINGS PITCHED

Roberts	3,740
CARLTON	2,523
Alexander	2,252
Short	1,939
Simmons	1,691
Duggleby	1,642
Rixey	1,604
Bunning	1,520
Orth	1,505

LOSSES

Roberts	199
Short	127
Simmons	110
CARLTON	107
Rixey	103
Ring	98
Sparks	95
Alexander	91
Benge	85
Bunning	73

WINS

Roberts	234
Alexander	190
CARLTON	172
Short	132
Simmons	115
Orth	101
Sparks	94
Duggleby	91
Bunning	89
Rixey	87

HITS

Roberts	3,661
CARLTON	2,142
Alexander	2,129
Short	1,865
Simmons	1,711
Duggleby	1,687
Orth	1,610
Ring	1,533
Collins	1,518
Rixey	

RUNS

Roberts	1,591
Short	949
CARLTON	947
Simmons	919
Ring	872
Alexander	812
P. Collins	782
Benge	693
Rixey	682
Duggleby	666

EARNED RUNS

Roberts	1,437
Short	845
CARLTON	837
Simmons	789
P. Collins	684
Alexander	603
Ring	599
Benge	569
Rixey	504
Bunning	495

STRIKEOUTS

CARLTON	2,018
Roberts	1,871
Short	1,585
Alexander	1,409
Bunning	1,197
Simmons	1,052
Rixey	690
Sparks	586
Ring	504
Meyer	501

SHUTOUTS

Alexander	61
Roberts	35
CARLTON	29
Short	24
Bunning	23
Sparks	18
Moore	18
Simmons	18
McQuillan	17
Duggleby	16
Rixey	16

WALKS

CARLTON	843
Short	762
Roberts	718
Simmons	718
Ring	630
Alexander	561
Moore	537
P. Collins	496
Rixey	479
Duggleby	390

SAVES

McGRAW	79
Farrell	65
REED	60
Baldschun	59
Konstanty	56
GARBER	52
Roberts	24
Karl	23
Selma	22
J. Meyer	21

CAPS = Active Pitchers

Rules of Interest

PLAYER LIMITS: 40 until opening day, when the number must be reduced to 25 until September 1, when it again becomes 40.

DETERMINING BATTING AVERAGE: Divide the number of at bats into the number of hits.

DETERMINING AN EARNED RUN AVERAGE: Multiply the number of earned runs by nine; take the number and divide it by the number of innings pitched.

DETERMINING SLUGGING PERCENTAGE: Divide the total bases of all hits by the total times at bat (At bats do not include walks, sacrifices, hit by pitcher, or times awarded first base because of interference or obstruction).

DETERMINING FIELDING AVERAGE: Divide the total of putouts and assists by the total of putouts, assists and errors.

DETERMINING PERCENTAGE OF GAMES WON AND LOST: Divide the number of games won by the total games won and lost.

CONSECUTIVE HITTING STREAKS: A consecutive hitting streak shall not be terminated if the plate appearance results in a base on balls, hit batsman, defensive interference or a sacrifice bunt. A sacrifice fly shall terminate the streak.

CONSECUTIVE-GAME HITTING STREAKS: A consecutive-game hitting streak shall not be terminated if all the player's plate appearances (one or more) result in a base on balls, hit batsman, defensive interference or a sacrifice bunt. The streak shall terminate if the player has a sacrifice fly and no hit.

CONSECUTIVE-GAME PLAYING STREAK: A consecutive-game playing streak shall be extended if the player plays one half-inning on defense, or if he completes a time at bat by reaching base or being put out. A pinch-running appearance only shall not extend the streak. If a player is ejected from a game by an umpire before

he can comply with the requirements of this rule, his streak shall continue.

SUSPENDED GAMES: For the purpose of this rule, all performances in the completion of a suspended game shall be considered as occurring on the original date of the game.

TRADING REGULATIONS: Players are available on waivers in reverse order of standings, at the time waivers expire, if more than 30 days after start of the season; otherwise in reverse order of standings at close of preceding season.

INTER-LEAGUE TRADES: Midnight, five days after the World Series—Midnight, night preceding the last scheduled day of the Winter Meetings—No waivers are necessary. Plus Feb. 15 to Mar. 31, 1981.

(continued on next page)

RULE ON RAIN-HALTED GAMES

Two rule changes concerning suspended games and pro-tested contests are in effect.

Rules 4.11 and 4.12 were altered creating suspended games instead of reverting to a prior inning when rain forces the umpires to terminate play under certain circumstances.

If a game is called while an inning is in progress and the visiting team has scored one or more runs to tie the score or take the lead, the game will be considered suspended rather than ended.

The rule on protested games (4.19) now reads: "Even if it is held that the protested decision violated the rules, no replay of the game will be ordered unless, in the opinion of the league president, the violation adversely affected the protesting team's chances of winning the game."

Minor League System

FARM CLUBS

CLUB	CLASS	LEAGUE	MANAGER	GEN. MGR.
Oklahoma City, Ok.	AAA	American Assoc.	Jim Snyder	Ms. Patti Cox
Reading, Pa.	AA	Eastern	Ron Clark	Joe Buzas
Peninsula	A	Carolina	Bill Dancy	Bob Neal
Spartanburg, S.C.	A	S. Atlantic	Tom Harmon	Rick Jacobs
Bend, Ore.	Rookie	Northwest	P. J. Carey	Jack Cain
Helena, Mont.	Rookie	Pioneer	Rollie DeArmas	Ward Goodrich

SCOUTING DEPARTMENT

REGIONAL CROSS-CHECKERS: Gordon Goldsberry, Wilbur Johnson, Randy Waddill.

SPECIAL ASSIGNMENT, MAJOR LEAGUES: Hugh Alexander.

SCOUTING CONSULTANT: Wes Livengood.

HUGH ALEXANDER	BEN MARMO
EDDIE BOCKMAN	GENE MARTIN
KEITH CARPENTER	GARY NICKELS
BRANDY DAVIS	TOM OLIVER
GEORGE FARSON	KEN PARKER
DOUG GASSAWAY	BOB REASONOVER
CHARLES GAULT	SCOTT REID
GORDON GOLDSBERRY	JOE REILLY
BILL HARPER	TONY ROIG
WILBUR H. JOHNSON	ANDY SEMINICK
J. "SPIDER" JORGENSEN	BILL TRACY
LOU KAHN	ELMER VALO
DICK LAWLOR	RANDY WADDILL
TONY LUCADELLO	DON WILLIAMS

Interesting Rules, *continued*

TRADING WITHIN LEAGUE: Midnight, the last day of the season—Midnight, June 15—No waivers necessary. Midnight, June 15—Midnight, the last day of the season—League waivers necessary.

DETERMINING THE MAGIC NUMBER: Determine the number of games yet to be played, add one, then subtract the number of games ahead in the loss column of the standings from the closest opponent.

DOCTORED BAT: If a filled or "doctored" bat is used, the player is to be ejected from the game and suspended three days. Any balls hit by an illegal bat do not count. If the umpire sees the illegal bat before it is used, he issues a warning, but there is no penalty.

DETERMINING A "MAJOR LEAGUE YEAR": 172 days constitute a full year in the major leagues.

GAME WINNING RBI: The RBI which gives a club the lead it never relinquishes.

GOLD GLOVE WINNERS

1963—Bobby Wine, ss
1964—Bobby Shantz, p
       Ruben Amaro, ss
1966—Bill White, 1b
1972—Larry Bowa, ss
1975—Garry Maddox, OF
1976—Garry Maddox, OF
       Mike Schmidt, 3b
       Jim Kaat, p
1977—Garry Maddox, OF
       Mike Schmidt, 3b
       Jim Kaat, p

1978—Garry Maddox, OF
       Mike Schmidt, 3b
       Larry Bowa, ss
       Bob Boone, c
1979—Garry Maddox, OF
       Mike Schmidt, 3b
       Bob Boone, c
       Manny Trillo, 2b
1980—Garry Maddox, OF
       Mike Schmidt, 3b

VET TOTAL ATTENDANCE

Year	Total	No. Dates	Average Per Game
1971	1,511,223	75	20,149
1972	1,343,329	74	18,153
1973	1,475,934	75	19,679
1974	1,808,648	77	23,488
1975	1,909,233	74	25,800
1976	2,480,150	78	31,797
1977	2,700,007	79	34,178
1978	2,583,389	77	33,551
1979	2,775,011	77	36,039
1980	2,651,650	78	33,996
Total:	21,238,574	764	27,780

Average: 2,123,856 per year

VETERANS STADIUM GROUND RULES

Dugouts—Ball has to actually enter dugout area of hit the yellow bars or yellow line to be considered out of play. Ball entering open area above end of dugout inside yellow line is considered OUT OF PLAY.

Foul poles are outside playing area and balls hitting them are to be considered HOME RUN.

Fences—Glass areas have openings at top. If ball sticks in opening it is a GROUND RULE DOUBLE.

In left and right field the stands protrude to a point near the foul lines. If ball lands in fair territory and bounces over the points and lands in the playing area, it is to be considered to be in the stands and ruled a GROUND RULE DOUBLE.

Ball off screen behind home plate is IN PLAY.

Veterans Stadium

Philadelphia Veterans Stadium facts and figures

LOCATION: Broad Street and Pattison Avenue

DIMENSIONS:

Home to LF—330'
Home to CF—408'
Home to RF—330'
Home plate to grandstand—60'
Heights of outfield fence—12'
1st and 3rd base to stands—45'

CAPACITY: 65,454 for baseball

	Seats
Super Boxes & Fourth Level	890
Deluxe Boxes	1,276
Field Boxes	10,361
Terrace Boxes	10,870
Loge Boxes	5,711
Upper Reserved 600 Level	11,367
Upper Reserved 700 Level	9,360
General Admission	15,619

Bob Boone   Ruben Amaro

Warren Brusstar   Dick Ruthven

Manny Trillo   Ramon Aviles

Marty Bystrom

Pete Rose

Larry Bowa   Nino Espinosa

Randy Lerch   George Vukovich

John Vukovich   Mike Ryan

Larry Christenson

Tug McGraw